T0202898

Lecture Notes in Computer Science   10660

Commenced Publication in 1973
Founding and Former Series Editors:
Gerhard Goos, Juris Hartmanis, and Jan van Leeuwen

Advanced Research in Computing and Software Science

Subline of Lecture Notes in Computer Science

More information about this series at http://www.springer.com/series/7409

Nikhil R. Devanur · Pinyan Lu (Eds.)

Web and Internet Economics

13th International Conference, WINE 2017
Bangalore, India, December 17–20, 2017
Proceedings

 Springer

Editors
Nikhil R. Devanur
Microsoft Research
Redmond, WA
USA

Pinyan Lu
Shanghai University of Finance
  and Economics
Shanghai
China

ISSN 0302-9743   ISSN 1611-3349 (electronic)
Lecture Notes in Computer Science
ISBN 978-3-319-71923-8   ISBN 978-3-319-71924-5 (eBook)
https://doi.org/10.1007/978-3-319-71924-5

Library of Congress Control Number: 2017959631

LNCS Sublibrary: SL3 – Information Systems and Applications, incl. Internet/Web, and HCI

Printed on acid-free paper

This Springer imprint is published by Springer Nature
The registered company is Springer International Publishing AG
The registered company address is: Gewerbestrasse 11, 6330 Cham, Switzerland

Preface

This volume contains the papers and extended abstracts presented at WINE 2017, the 13th Conference on Web and Internet Economics, held during December 17–20 at the Indian Institute of Science, in Bangalore. Over the past decade and a half, researchers in theoretical computer science, artificial intelligence, and microeconomics have joined forces to tackle problems at the intersection of computation, game theory, and economics. These problems have gained significant importance in the age of ubiquitous connectivity and computation and with the rise of platforms that involve large and diverse populations. WINE is an annual interdisciplinary forum for the exchange of ideas and results in this area of research, and has a special mission of popularizing it internationally. WINE is held alternatively in North America, Europe, and Asia every three years.

The Program Committee, consisting of 38 top researchers from the field, reviewed 88 submissions and decided to accept 34 papers. Each paper had three reviews, with additional reviews solicited as needed. The review process was conducted entirely electronically via EasyChair. We are grateful to EasyChair for allowing us to handle the submissions and the review process, and to the Program Committee for their insightful reviews and discussions, which made our job easier.

The program also included four invited talks, by Vijay Krishna (Pennsylvania State University), Parag Pathak (MIT), Ariel Procaccia (CMU), and Tim Roughgarden (Stanford), as well as four tutorials by Kira Goldner (University of Washington), Vangelis Markakis (Athens University of Economics and Business), Balu Sivan (Google), and Chaitanya Swamy (Waterloo).

We would like to thank our sponsors, Accenture, Facebook, Microsoft, Sonata, Flipkart, Google, Koinearth and Springer for their financial support. A special thanks to the Indian Institute of Science (IISc), for providing the venue for the conference free of charge! Our gratitude also goes to the general chairs, Y. Narahari and Arunava Sen, and the Organizing Committee chair, Ramasuri Narayanam, without whom it would have been impossible to run the conference. Last but not the least, we thank Ruta Mehta and Siddharth Barman for chairing the tutorial and the poster sessions, respectively.

October 2017

Nikhil R. Devanur
Pinyan Lu

Organization

Program Committee

Lirong Xia   RPI
Yinyu Ye   Stanford University, USA
Yair Zick   National University of Singapore

Additional Reviewers

Abbasi Zadeh, Sepehr
Agrawal, Shipra
Akrida, Eleni
Anshelevich, Elliot
Behnezhad, Soheil
Bei, Xiaohui
Bennabou, Nawal
Berbeglia, Gerardo
Bhardwaj, Onkar
Chakraborty, Mithun
Chan, Hau
Cheng, Yu
Colini-Baldeschi, Riccardo
Dayama, Pankaj
Deligkas, Argyrios
Dey, Palash
Eden, Alon
Feng, Zhe
Filos-Ratsikas, Aris
Fleiner, Tamas
Giannakopoulos, Yiannis
Goldner, Kira
Golrezaei, Negin
He, Simai
Hoefer, Martin
Huang, Weiran
Kang, Ning
Kim, Anthony
Kleer, Pieter
Kominers, Scott
Kulkarni, Janardhan
Li, Bo
Li, Yingkai
Lin, Yuan
Mamageishvili, Akaki
Manurangsi, Pasin

Mao, Jieming
Melissourgos, Themistoklis
Mertzios, George
Monaco, Gianpiero
Niazadeh, Rad
Obraztsova, Svetlana
Oren, Sigal
Panagopoulou, Panagiota
Pountourakis, Emmanouil
Psomas, Christos-Alexandros
Raghavan, Manish
Raptopoulos, Christoforos
Röglin, Heiko
Schrijvers, Okke
Schvartzman, Ariel
Shiragur, Kirankumar
Sikdar, Sujoy
Singer, Yaron
Singh, Shikha
Tang, Zhihao Gavin
Telikepalli, Kavitha
Theodorakopoulos, George
Tsikiridis, Artem
Vaish, Rohit
Waggoner, Bo
Wang, Changjun
Wang, Xiangning
Wang, Zizhuo
Yami, Hadi
Yan, Xiang
Yang, Yuanyuan
Zampetakis, Emmanouil
Zhang, Jialin
Zhang, Shengyu
Zhao, Mingfei

Contents

Short Papers

On Budget-Feasible Mechanism Design for Symmetric Submodular Objectives

Georgios Amanatidis, Georgios Birmpas, and Evangelos Markakis[✉]

Department of Informatics, Athens University of Economics and Business, Athens, Greece
{gamana,gebirbas,markakis}@aueb.gr

Abstract. We study a class of procurement auctions with a budget constraint, where an auctioneer is interested in buying resources from a set of agents. The auctioneer would like to select a subset of the resources so as to maximize his valuation function, without exceeding his budget. As the resources are owned by strategic agents, our overall goal is to design mechanisms that are truthful, budget-feasible, and obtain a good approximation to the optimal value. Previous results on budget-feasible mechanisms have considered mostly monotone valuation functions. In this work, we mainly focus on *symmetric submodular* valuations, a prominent class of non-monotone submodular functions that includes *cut functions*. We begin with a purely algorithmic result, obtaining a $\frac{2e}{e-1}$-approximation for maximizing symmetric submodular functions under a budget constraint. We then proceed to propose truthful, budget feasible mechanisms (both deterministic and randomized), paying particular attention on the Budgeted Max Cut problem. Our results significantly improve the known approximation ratios for these objectives, while establishing polynomial running time for cases where only exponential mechanisms were known. At the heart of our approach lies an appropriate combination of local search algorithms with results for monotone submodular valuations, applied to the derived local optima.

1 Introduction

We study a class of procurement auctions—also referred to as reverse auctions—with budget constraints. In a procurement auction, an auctioneer is interested in buying goods or services from a set of agents. In this setting, selecting an agent comes at a cost and there is a hard budget constraint that should not be violated. The goal of the auctioneer then is to select a budget-feasible subset of the agents so as to maximize his valuation function $v(\cdot)$, where $v(S)$ denotes the value derived when S is the selected subset of agents to get services from.

The purely algorithmic version of the problem results in natural "budgeted" versions of known optimization problems. Since these problems are typically NP-hard, our focus is on approximation algorithms. Most importantly, in the setting considered here, the true cost of each agent is private information and we would like to design mechanisms that elicit truthful reporting by all agents. Hence, our

© Springer International Publishing AG 2017
N. R. Devanur and P. Lu (Eds.): WINE 2017, LNCS 10674, pp. 1–15, 2017.
https://doi.org/10.1007/978-3-319-71924-5_1

ideal goal is to have truthful mechanisms that achieve a good approximation to the optimal value for the auctioneer, and are *budget feasible*, i.e., the sum of the payments to the agents does not exceed the prespecified budget. This framework of budget feasible mechanisms is motivated by recent application scenarios including crowdsourcing platforms, where agents can be viewed as workers providing tasks (e.g., [4,15]), and influence maximization in networks, where agents correspond to influential users (see e.g., [2,30], where the chosen objective is a coverage function).

Budget feasibility makes the problem more challenging, with respect to truthfulness, as it already rules out well known mechanisms such as VCG. We note that the algorithmic versions of such problems often admit constant factor approximation algorithms. However, it is not clear how to appropriately convert them into truthful budget feasible mechanisms. The question is nontrivial even if we allow exponential time algorithms, since computational power does not necessarily make the problem easier (see the discussion in [11]).

The first positive results on this topic were obtained by Singer [29], for the case where $v(\cdot)$ is an additive or a non-decreasing submodular function. Follow-up works provided refinements and further results for richer classes of functions (see the related work section). Most of these works, however, make the assumption that the valuation function is non-decreasing, i.e., $v(S) \leq v(T)$ for $S \subseteq T$, notable exceptions being the works of [5,11]. Although monotonicity makes sense in several scenarios, one can think of examples where it is violated. E.g., [11] studied the unweighted Budgeted Max Cut problem, as an eminent example of a non-monotone submodular objective function. Moreover, when studying models for influence maximization problems in social networks, adding more users to the selected set may some times bring negative influence [6] (some combinations of users may also not be compatible or well fitted together). To further motivate the study of non-monotone submodular objectives, consider the following well-studied sensor placement problem [7,10,21]: assume that we want to monitor some spatial phenomenon (e.g., the temperature of a specific environment), modeled as a Gaussian process. We may place sensing devices on some of the prespecified locations, but each location has an associated cost. A criterion for finding an optimal such placement, suggested by Caselton and Zidek [7] for the unit cost case, is to maximize the *mutual information* between chosen and non chosen locations, i.e., we search for the subset of locations that minimizes the uncertainty about the estimates in the remaining space. Such mutual information objectives are submodular but not monotone. In addition, it is straightforward to modify this problem to model participatory crowdsensing scenarios where users have incentives to lie about the true cost of installing a sensor.

At the moment, the few results known for arbitrary non-monotone submodular functions have very large approximation ratios and often superpolynomial running time. Even worse, in most cases, we do not even know of deterministic mechanisms (see Table 1). In trying to impose more structure so as to have better positive results, there is an interesting observation to make: the examples mentioned so far, i.e., cut functions and mutual information functions, are *symmetric submodular*, a prominent subclass of non-monotone submodular functions, where the value of a set S equals the value of its complement. This subclass has received already considerable attention in operations research, see e.g., [14,27], where more examples are also provided. We therefore find that symmetric submodular functions form a suitable starting point for the study of non-monotone functions.

Contribution: The main focus of this work is on symmetric[1] submodular functions. As suggested in [27], cut functions form a canonical example of this class. Consequently, we use the budgeted Max Cut problem throughout the paper as an illustrative example of how our more general approach could be refined for concrete objectives that have a well-behaved LP formulation.

We begin in Sect. 3 with a purely algorithmic result, obtaining a $\frac{2e}{e-1}$-approximation for symmetric submodular functions under a budget constraint. We believe this result is of independent interest, as it is the best known factor achieved by a deterministic algorithm (there exists already a randomized e-approximation). We then proceed to propose truthful, budget feasible mechanisms in Sects. 4 and 5. Our results significantly improve the known approximation ratios for these problems, establishing at the same time polynomial running time for many cases where only exponential mechanisms were known. As an example, for the budgeted weighted cut problem we obtain the first deterministic polynomial time mechanism with a 27.25-approximation, and for unweighted cut functions we improve the approximation ratio for randomized mechanisms, from 564 down to 10. Analogous improvements are obtained also for arbitrary symmetric submodular functions. Finally, in Sect. 6 we briefly study the class of XOS functions, where we improve the current upper bound by more than a factor of 3. All our contributions in mechanism design are summarized in Table 1. We also stress that our mechanisms for general symmetric submodular functions use the value query model for oracle access to v, which is a much weaker requirement than the demand query model assumed in previous works, e.g., in [11].

Regarding the technical contribution of our work, the core idea of our approach is to exploit a combination of (approximate) local search with mechanisms for non-decreasing submodular functions. The reason local search is convenient for symmetric submodular functions is that it produces two local optima, and we can then prove that the function $v(\cdot)$ is (almost) non-decreasing within each local optimum. This allows us to appropriately adjust mechanisms for non-decreasing submodular functions on the two subsets and then prove that one of the two solutions will attain a good approximation. To the best of our knowledge, this is the first time that this *"robustness under small deviations from monotonicity"* approach is used to exploit known results for monotone objectives.

Related Work: The study of budget feasible mechanisms, as considered here, was initiated by Singer [29]. Later, Chen et al. [9] significantly improved Singer's

---

[1] In some works on mechanism design, symmetric submodular functions have a different meaning and refer to the case where $v(S)$ depends only on $|S|$. Here we have adopted the terminology of earlier literature on submodular optimization, e.g., [14].

results. Several modifications of the deterministic mechanism of [9] have been proposed that run in polynomial time for special cases [2,18,30]. For subadditive functions, Dobzinski et al. [11] suggested a randomized $O(\log^2 n)$-approximation mechanism, and they gave the first constant factor mechanisms for non-monotone submodular objectives, specifically for *cut functions*. The factor for subadditive functions was later improved by Bei et al. [5], who also gave a randomized $O(1)$-approximation mechanism for XOS functions, albeit in exponential time. An improved $O(1)$-approximation mechanism for XOS functions is also suggested in [24]. Finally, there is a line of related work under the *large market* assumption (where no participant can significantly affect the market outcome), which allows for polynomial time mechanisms with improved performance [4,15,19,31].

On maximization of submodular functions subject to knapsack or other type of constraints, there is a vast literature, going back several decades, see, e.g., [26, 33]. More recently, Lee et al. [23] provided the first constant factor randomized algorithm for matroid and knapsack constraints. For knapsack constraints the approximation factor was improved by Gupta et al. [17] and Chekuri et al. [8], followed up by Feldman et al. [13] and Kulik et al. [22] who proposed their own randomized algorithms, achieving an e-approximation.[2]

Table 1. A summary of our results on mechanisms, where $\alpha = (1 + \rho)(2 + \rho + \sqrt{\rho^2 + 4\rho + 1})$ and ρ is an upper bound on the ratio of the optimal fractional solution to the integral one, assuming that we can find the former in polynomial time. The asterisk ($*$) indicates that the corresponding mechanism runs in superpolynomial time.

	Symmetric submod.		Unweighted cut		Weighted cut		XOS
	Rand.	Determ.	Rand.	Determ.	Rand.	Determ.	Rand.
Known	768* [5]	–	564 [11]	5158 [11]	768* [5]	–	768* [5]
This paper	10*	10.90*, α	10	27.25	27.25		244*

2   Notation and Preliminaries

We use $A = [n] = \{1, 2, \ldots, n\}$ to denote a set of n agents. Each agent i is associated with a private cost c_i, denoting the cost for participating in the solution. We consider a procurement auction setting, where the auctioneer is equipped with a valuation function $v : 2^A \to \mathbb{Q}_{\geq 0}$ and a budget $B > 0$. For $S \subseteq A$, $v(S)$ is the value derived by the auctioneer if the set S is selected (for singletons, we will often write $v(i)$ instead of $v(\{i\})$). Therefore, the algorithmic goal in all the problems we study is to select a set S that maximizes $v(S)$ subject to the constraint $\sum_{i \in S} c_i \leq B$. We assume oracle access to v via value queries, i.e., we

---

[2] The algorithm of [22] can be derandomized, but only assuming an oracle for the extension by expectation, of the objective function v.

assume the existence of a polynomial time value oracle that returns $v(S)$ when given as input a set S.

We mostly focus on a natural subclass of submodular valuation functions that includes *cut functions*, namely non-negative symmetric submodular functions. Note that a non-constant v cannot be both symmetric and non-decreasing. Throughout this work we make the natural assumption that $v(\emptyset) = 0$.

Definition 1. *A function v, defined on 2^A for some set A, is* submodular *if $v(S \cup \{i\}) - v(S) \geq v(T \cup \{i\}) - v(T)$ for any $S \subseteq T \subseteq A$, and $i \notin T$. Moreover, it is* non-decreasing *if $v(S) \leq v(T)$ for any $S \subseteq T \subseteq A$, while it is* symmetric *if $v(S) = v(A \setminus S)$ for any $S \subseteq A$.*

We often need to argue about optimal solutions of sub-instances, from an instance we begin with. Given a cost vector $\mathbf{c}$, and a subset $X \subseteq A$, we denote by $\mathbf{c}_X$ the projection of $\mathbf{c}$ on X, and by $\mathbf{c}_{-X}$ the projection of $\mathbf{c}$ on $A \setminus X$. We also let $\mathrm{OPT}(X, v, \mathbf{c}_X, B)$ be the value of an optimal solution to the restriction of this instance on X. Similarly, $\mathrm{OPT}(X, v, \mathbf{c}_X, \infty)$ denotes the value of an optimal solution to the unconstrained version of the problem restricted on X. For the sake of readability, we usually drop the valuation function and the cost vector, and write $\mathrm{OPT}(X, B)$ or $\mathrm{OPT}(X, \infty)$.

Finally, in Sects. 3–5 we make one further assumption: we assume that there is at most one item whose cost exceeds the budget. This is without loss of generality, but the proof is deferred to the full version [3].

Local Optima and Local Search. Given $v : 2^A \to \mathbb{Q}$, a set $S \subseteq A$ is called a $(1+\epsilon)$-*approximate local optimum* of v, if $(1+\epsilon)v(S) \geq v(S \setminus \{i\})$ and $(1+\epsilon)v(S) \geq v(S \cup \{i\})$ for every $i \in A$. When $\epsilon = 0$, S is called an *exact local optimum* of v. Note that if v is symmetric submodular, then S is a $(1 + \epsilon)$-approximate local optimum if and only if $A \setminus S$ is a $(1 + \epsilon)$-approximate local optimum.

Approximate local optima produce good approximations in unconstrained maximization of general submodular functions [12]. However, here they are of interest for a quite different reason that becomes apparent in Lemmata 2 and 3. We can efficiently find approximate local optima using the local search algorithm APPROX-LOCAL-SEARCH of [12].

Lemma 1 (inferred from [12]). *Given a submodular function $v : 2^{[n]} \to \mathbb{Q}_{\geq 0}$ and a value oracle for v, APPROX-LOCAL-SEARCH(A, v, ϵ) outputs $a(1 + \frac{\epsilon}{n^2})$-approximate local optimum using $O\left(\frac{1}{\epsilon}n^3 \log n\right)$ calls to the oracle.*

2.1 Mechanism Design

In the strategic version that we consider here, every agent i only has his true cost c_i as private information. A mechanism $\mathcal{M} = (f, p)$ in our context consists of an outcome rule f and a payment rule p. Given a vector of cost declarations, $\mathbf{b} = (b_i)_{i \in A}$, where b_i denotes the cost reported by agent i, the outcome rule of the mechanism selects the set $f(\mathbf{b})$. At the same time, it computes payments $p(\mathbf{b}) = (p_i(\mathbf{b}))_{i \in A}$ where $p_i(\mathbf{b})$ denotes the payment issued to agent i. Hence, the final utility of agent i is $p_i(\mathbf{b}) - c_i$. The properties we want to enforce in our mechanism design problem are the following.

Definition 2. *A mechanism* $\mathcal{M} = (f, p)$ *is*

1. truthful, *if reporting* c_i *is a dominant strategy for every agent* i.
2. individually rational, *if* $p_i(\mathbf{b}) \geq 0$ *for every* $i \in A$, *and* $p_i(\mathbf{b}) \geq c_i$, *for every* $i \in f(\mathbf{b})$.
3. budget feasible, *if* $\sum_{i \in A} p_i(\mathbf{b}) \leq B$ *for every* $\mathbf{b}$.

For randomized mechanisms, we use the notion of *universal truthfulness*, which means that the mechanism is a probability distribution over deterministic truthful mechanisms.

To design truthful mechanisms, we use the characterization by Myerson [25]. In particular, we say that an outcome rule f is *monotone*, if for every agent $i \in A$, and any vector of cost declarations $\mathbf{b}$, if $i \in f(\mathbf{b})$, then $i \in f(b_i', \mathbf{b}_{-i})$ for $b_i' \leq b_i$. Myerson's lemma implies that monotone algorithms admit truthful payment schemes (often referred to as *threshold payments*). For all of our mechanisms, we assume that the underlying payment scheme is given by Myerson's lemma.

Mechanisms for Non-decreasing Submodular Valuations. In the mechanisms we design for non-monotone submodular functions, we will repeatedly make use of truthful budget feasible mechanisms for non-decreasing submodular functions as subroutines. The best known such mechanisms are due to Chen et al. [9]. Here, we follow the improved analysis of [19] for the approximation ratio of the randomized mechanism RAND-MECH-SM of [9], stated below which makes use of the greedy subroutine GREEDY-SM.

RAND-MECH-SM$(A, v, \mathbf{c}, B)$ [9]

1 Set $A' = \{i \mid c_i \leq B\}$ and $i^* \in \arg\max_{i \in A'} v(i)$
2 with probability $\frac{2}{5}$ **return** i^*
3 with probability $\frac{3}{5}$ **return** GREEDY-SM$(A, v, \mathbf{c}, B/2)$

We also optimize the deterministic mechanism of [9] to obtain MECH-SM.

MECH-SM$(A, v, \mathbf{c}, B)$

1 Set $A' = \{i \mid c_i \leq B\}$ and $i^* \in \arg\max_{i \in A'} v(i)$
2 **if** $(2 + \sqrt{6}) \cdot v(i^*) \geq \text{OPT}(A \setminus \{i^*\}, B)$ **then**
3 $\quad$ **return** i^*
4 **else**
5 $\quad$ **return** GREEDY-SM$(A, v, \mathbf{c}, B/2)$

The subroutine GREEDY-SM used above, is a greedy algorithm that picks agents according to their ratio of marginal value over cost, given that this cost is not too large. For the sake of presentation, we assume the agents are sorted in descending order with respect to this ratio.

GREEDY-SM$(A, v, \mathbf{c}, B/2)$ [9]

---

1 Let $k = 1$ and $S = \emptyset$
2 **while** $k \leq |A|$ **and** $v(S \cup \{k\}) > v(S)$ **and** $c_k \leq \frac{B}{2} \cdot \frac{v(S \cup \{k\}) - v(S)}{v(S \cup \{k\})}$ **do**
3 $\quad\lfloor\quad S = S \cup \{k\}$
4 $\quad\quad\; k = k + 1$
5 **return** S

Theorem 1 (inferred from [9,19]). RAND-MECH-SM *runs in polynomial time, it is universally truthful, individually rational, budget-feasible, and has approximation ratio 5.* MECH-SM *is deterministic, truthful, individually rational, budget-feasible, and has approximation ratio* $3 + \sqrt{6}$.

A discussion on how different results combine into Theorem 1, is deferred to the full version [3].

3   A Simple Algorithm for Symmetric Objectives

This section deals with the algorithmic version of the problem: given a symmetric submodular function v, the goal is to find $S \subseteq A$ that maximizes $v(S)$ subject to the constraint $\sum_{i \in S} c_i \leq B$. The main result is a deterministic $\frac{2e}{e-1}$-approximation algorithm for symmetric submodular functions. For this section only, the costs and the budget are assumed to be integral.

Since our function is not monotone, we cannot directly apply the result of [32], which gives an optimal simple greedy algorithm for non-decreasing submodular maximization subject to a knapsack constraint. Instead, our main idea is to combine appropriately the result of [32] with the local search used for unconstrained symmetric submodular maximization [12]. At a high level, what happens is that local search produces an approximate solution S for the unconstrained problem, and while this does not look related to our goal at first sight, v is "close to being non-decreasing" on both S and $A \setminus S$. This becomes precise in Lemma 2 below, but the point is that running a modification of the algorithm of [32], on both S and $A \setminus S$ will produce at least one good solution.

LS-GREEDY$(A, v, \mathbf{c}, B, \epsilon)$

---

1 $S = $ APPROX-LOCAL-SEARCH$(A, v, \epsilon/4)$
2 $T_1 = $ GREEDY-ENUM-SM$(S, v, \mathbf{c}_S, B)$
3 $T_2 = $ GREEDY-ENUM-SM$(A \setminus S, v, \mathbf{c}_{A\setminus S}, B)$
4 Let T be the best solution among T_1 and T_2
5 **return** T

The first component of our algorithm is the local search algorithm of [12]. By Lemma 1 and the fact that v is symmetric, both S and $A \setminus S$ are $\left(1 + \frac{\epsilon}{4n^2}\right)$-approximate local optima. We can now quantify the crucial observation that v is close to being non-decreasing within S and $A \setminus S$. Actually, we only need this property on the local optimum that contains the best feasible solution.

Lemma 2. *Let S be a $\left(1 + \frac{\epsilon}{4n^2}\right)$-approximate local optimum and consider $X \in$ $\arg\,max_{Z \in \{S, A \setminus S\}}\,\text{OPT}(Z, v, \mathbf{c}_Z, B)$. Then, for every $T \subsetneq X$ and every $i \in X \setminus T$, we have $v(T \cup \{i\}) - v(T) > -\frac{\epsilon}{n}\text{OPT}(X, B)$.*

The second component of LS-GREEDY is an appropriate modification of the greedy algorithm of [32] for non-monotone submodular functions. It first enumerates all solutions of size at most 3. Then, starting from each 3-set, it builds a greedy solution, and it outputs the best among these $\Theta(n^3)$ solutions. Here this idea is adjusted for non-monotone functions.

GREEDY-ENUM-SM$(A, v, \mathbf{c}, B)$

---

1 Let S_1 be the best feasible solution of cardinality at most 3 (by enumerating all such solutions)

2 $S_2 = \emptyset$

3 **for** *every $U \subseteq A$ with $|U| = 3$* **do**

4 $\quad$ $T = U$, $t = 1$, $A^0 = A \setminus U$

5 $\quad$ **while** $A^{t-1} \neq \emptyset$ **do**

6 $\quad\quad$ Find $\theta_t = \max_{i \in A^{t-1}} \dfrac{v(T \cup \{i\}) - v(T)}{c_i}$, and let i_t be an element of A^{t-1} that attains θ_t

7 $\quad\quad$ **if** $\theta_t \geq 0$ *and* $\sum_{i \in T \cup \{i_t\}} c_i \leq B$ **then**

8 $\quad\quad\quad$ $T = T \cup \{i_t\}$

9 $\quad\quad$ $A^t = A^{t-1} \setminus \{i_t\}$

10 $\quad\quad$ $t = t + 1$

11 $\quad$ **if** $v(T) > v(S_2)$ **then**

12 $\quad\quad$ $S_2 = T$

13 Let S be the best solution among S_1 and S_2

14 **return** S

It can be easily seen that at least one of S and $A \setminus S$ contains a feasible solution of value at least $0.5\,\text{OPT}(A, B)$. Then, Lemma 2 guarantees that within this set, v is very close to a non-decreasing submodular function. This is sufficient for GREEDY-ENUM-SM to perform almost as well as if v was non-decreasing.

Theorem 2. *For any $\epsilon > 0$, algorithm LS-GREEDY achieves a $\left(\frac{2e}{e-1} + \epsilon\right)$-approximation.*

Theorem 2 suggests that a straightforward composition of two well known greedy algorithms achieves a good approximation for any symmetric submodular objective. From a mechanism design perspective, however, algorithm LS-GREEDY fails to be monotone and thus it cannot be used directly in the subsequent sections. In the next two sections, we remedy this problem.

4   Mechanisms for Symmetric Objectives: A First Take

Utilizing the algorithmic approach of Sect. 3 to get truthful mechanisms is not straightforward. One of the reasons is that LS-GREEDY is not monotone. We note that the algorithm GREEDY-ENUM-SM without the enumeration part *is* monotone even for general objectives, but, to further complicate things, it is not guaranteed to be budget-feasible or have a good performance anymore. Instead of computing approximate local optima like in Sect. 3, in this section we bypass most issues by computing exact local optima. The highlights of this simplified approach are polynomial mechanisms for unweighted cut functions with greatly improved guarantees. The price we have to pay, however, is that in general, finding exact local optima is not guaranteed to run in polynomial time [28]. We are going to deal further with the issue of running time in Sect. 5.

Below we give a randomized mechanism that reduces the known factor of 768 down to 10, as well as the first deterministic $O(1)$-approximation mechanism for symmetric submodular objectives. In both mechanisms, local search produces a local maximum S for the unbudgeted problem and then the budgeted problem is solved optimally on both S and $A \setminus S$, where v is non-decreasing by Lemma 3. Thus, running the mechanism RAND-MECH-SM or MECH-SM of [9], on $T \in \arg\max_{X \in \{S, A \setminus S\}} \text{OPT}(X, B)$, directly implies a good solution. Since the resulting mechanisms are very similar, we state them together for succinctness.

RAND-MECH-SYMSM$(A, v, \mathbf{c}, B)$ (*resp.* DET-MECH-SYMSM$(A, v, \mathbf{c}, B)$)

---

1 $S = $ APPROX-LOCAL-SEARCH$(A, v, 0)$ //find an exact local optimum
2 **if** OPT$(S, B) \geq$ OPT$(A \setminus S, B)$ **then**
3   **return** RAND-MECH-SM$(S, v, \mathbf{c}_S, B)$ (*resp.* MECH-SM$(S, v, \mathbf{c}_S, B)$)

4 **else**
5   **return** RAND-MECH-SM$(A \setminus S, v, \mathbf{c}_{A \setminus S}, B)$
     (*resp.* MECH-SM$(A \setminus S, v, \mathbf{c}_{A \setminus S}, B)$)

The next simple lemma is crucial for the performance of both mechanisms.

Lemma 3. *Let A be a set and v be a submodular function on 2^A. If S is a local maximum of v, then v is submodular and non-decreasing when restricted on 2^S.*

Since v is symmetric, if S is a local optimum, so is $A \setminus S$. Lemma 3 suggests that we can use RAND-MECH-SM (resp. MECH-SM) on S and $A \setminus S$.

Theorem 3. *The mechanism* RAND-MECH-SYMSM *is universally truthful, individually rational, budget-feasible, and has approximation ratio* 10. *The mechanism* DET-MECH-SYMSM *is deterministic, truthful, individually rational, budget-feasible, and has approximation ratio* $6 + 2\sqrt{6}$.

Clearly, both mechanisms require superpolynomial time in general, unless $P = NP$. Instead of OPT$(\cdot, B)$ we could use the optimal solution of a fractional relaxation of the problem, at the expense of somewhat worse guarantees. This does not completely resolve the problem, but makes local search the sole bottleneck. For certain objectives, however, we can achieve similar guarantees in polynomial time and unweighted cut functions are the most prominent such example.

4.1   Polynomial Time Mechanisms for Unweighted Cut Functions

We begin with the definition of the problem when v is a cut function:

Budgeted Max Weighted Cut. Given a complete graph G with vertex set $V(G) = [n]$, non-negative weights w_{ij} on the edges, non-negative costs c_i on the nodes, and a positive budget B, find $X \subseteq [n]$ so that $v(X) = \sum_{i \in X} \sum_{j \in [n] \setminus X} w_{ij}$ is maximized subject to $\sum_{j \in X} c_j \leq B$.

For convenience, we assume the problem is defined on a complete graph as we can use zero weights to model any graph. In this subsection, we focus on the unweighted version (all weights are equal to either 0 or 1). We call this special case *Budgeted Max Cut*. The weighted version is considered in Subsect. 5.1.

The fact that local search takes polynomial time to find an exact local optimum for the unweighted version [20] does not suffice to make RAND-MECH-SYMSM a polynomial time mechanism, since one still needs to compute OPT(S, B) and OPT$(A \setminus S, B)$. However, a small modification so that RAND-MECH-SM(S, B) and RAND-MECH-SM$(A \setminus S, B)$ are returned with probability $1/2$ each, yields a randomized 10-approximate polynomial time mechanism.

Theorem 4. *There is a randomized, universally truthful, individually rational, budget-feasible mechanism for Budgeted Max Cut that has approximation ratio 10 and runs in polynomial time.*

In order to design deterministic mechanisms that run in polynomial time, we first optimize a mechanism of [2] to obtain MECH-SM-FRAC below, which is applicable for non-decreasing submodular functions. The difference with MECH-SM (Sect. 2), is that now we assume that a fractional relaxation can be solved optimally and that the fractional optimal solution is within a constant of the integral solution. Let $v(\cdot)$ be a non-decreasing submodular function, $A' = \{i \in A \mid c_i \leq B\}$, and consider a relaxation of our problem for which we have an exact algorithm. Moreover, suppose that OPT$_f(A', v, \mathbf{c}_{A'}, B) \leq \rho \cdot$ OPT$(A', v, \mathbf{c}_{A'}, B) = \rho \cdot$ OPT$(A, v, \mathbf{c}, B)$ for any instance, where OPT$_f$ and OPT denote the value of an optimal solution to the relaxed and the original problem respectively.

Theorem 5. MECH-SM-FRAC *is deterministic, truthful, individually rational, budget-feasible, and has approximation ratio $\rho + 2 + \sqrt{\rho^2 + 4\rho + 1}$. Also, it runs in polynomial time as long as the exact algorithm for the relaxed problem runs in polynomial time.*

MECH-SM-FRAC$(A, v, \mathbf{c}, B)$

---

1 Set $A' = \{i \mid c_i \leq B\}$ and $i^* \in \arg\max_{i \in A'} v(i)$

2 **if** $\left(\rho + 1 + \sqrt{\rho^2 + 4\rho + 1} \right) \cdot v(i^*) \geq$ OPT$_f(A \setminus \{i^*\}, v, \mathbf{c}_{-i^*}, B)$ **then**

3 $\quad \lfloor$ **return** i^*

4 **else**

5 $\quad \lfloor$ **return** GREEDY-SM$(A, v, \mathbf{c}, B/2)$

Hence, to obtain a deterministic mechanism for Budgeted Max Cut, we can use an LP-based approach, and run MECH-SM-FRAC on an appropriate local maximum. For this, we first need to compare the value of an optimal solution of a fractional relaxation to the value of an optimal solution of the original problem. Ageev and Sviridenko [1] studied a different Max Cut variant, using the technique of pipage rounding, and we follow a similar approach to obtain the desired bound for our problem as well. We defer the details to the full version of the paper [3], but we should mention here that our analysis is carried out for the weighted version of the problem, as we are going to reuse some results in Subsect. 5.1, which deals with weighted cut functions.

Theorem 6. *There is a LP relaxation for Budgeted Max Weighted Cut, so that* $\text{OPT}_f(I) \leq 4 \cdot \text{OPT}(I)$, *for any instance* I.

Now, we may modify DET-MECH-SYMSM to use OPT_f instead of OPT, and MECH-SM-FRAC instead of MECH-SM. This results in the following deterministic mechanism that runs in polynomial time.

DET-MECH-UCUT$(A, v, \mathbf{c}, B)$

---

1 Set $A' = \{i \mid c_i \leq B\}$ and $i^* \in \arg\max_{i \in A'} v(i)$
2 **if** $26.25 \cdot v(i^*) \geq \text{OPT}_f(A' \setminus \{i^*\}, B)$ **then**
3 $\quad$ **return** i^*
4 **else**
5 $\quad$ $S = $ APPROX-LOCAL-SEARCH$(A, v, 0)$
6 $\quad$ **if** $\text{OPT}_f(S \cap A', B) \geq \text{OPT}_f(A' \setminus S, B)$ **then**
7 $\quad\quad$ **return** MECH-SM-FRAC$(S, v, \mathbf{c}_S, B)$
8 $\quad$ **else**
9 $\quad\quad$ **return** MECH-SM-FRAC$(A \setminus S, v, \mathbf{c}_{A \setminus S}, B)$

Theorem 7. DET-MECH-UCUT *is a deterministic, truthful, individually rational, budget-feasible mechanism for Budgeted Max Cut that has approximation ratio 27.25 and runs in polynomial time.*

5   Mechanisms for Symmetric Objectives Revisited

Can the approach taken for unweighted cut functions be fruitful for other symmetric submodular objectives? In the mechanisms of Subsect. 4.1 the complexity of local search can be a bottleneck even for objectives where an optimal fractional solution can be found fast and it is not far from the optimal integral solution. So, we return to the idea of Sect. 3, where local search runs in polynomial time and produces an approximate local maximum; unfortunately, monotonicity in each side of the partition does not hold any longer.

This means that the approximation guarantees of such mechanisms do not follow in any direct way from existing work. Moreover, budget-feasibility turns out to be an even more delicate issue since it crucially depends on the (approximate) monotonicity of the valuation function. Specifically, when a set X only contains a very poor solution to the original problem, every existing proof of budget feasibility for the restriction of v on X completely breaks down. Since we cannot expect that an approximate local maximum S and its complement $A \setminus S$ both contain a "good enough" solution to the original problem, we need to make sure that GREEDY-SM never runs on the wrong set.

The mechanism DET-MECH-UCUT for the unweighted cut problem seems to take care of this and we are going to build on it, in order to propose mechanisms for arbitrary symmetric submodular functions. To do so we replace the constant 26.25 by $\alpha = (1 + \rho)\left(2 + \rho + \sqrt{\rho^2 + 4\rho + 1}\right) - 1$ and we find an approximate local maximum instead of an exact local maximum. Most importantly, in order to achieve budget-feasibility we use a modification of MECH-SM-FRAC (which we call MECH-SM-FRAC-VAR, described in our full version [3]) that runs GREEDY-SM with a slightly reduced budget. The parameter ϵ' that appears in the description of the mechanism below is determined by the analysis and depends only on the constants ρ and ϵ.

DET-MECH-SYMSM-FRAC$(A, v, \mathbf{c}, B, \epsilon)$

---

1 Set $A' = \{i \mid c_i \leq B\}$ and $i^* \in \arg\max_{i \in A'} v(i)$

2 if $\alpha \cdot v(i^*) \geq \text{OPT}_f(A' \setminus \{i^*\}, B)$ then

3 $\quad$ return i^*

4 else

5 $\quad$ $S = $ APPROX-LOCAL-SEARCH(A, v, ϵ')

6 $\quad$ if $\text{OPT}_f(S \cap A', B) \geq \text{OPT}_f(A' \setminus S, B)$ then

7 $\quad\quad$ return MECH-SM-FRAC-VAR$(S, v, \mathbf{c}_S, B, (1 - (\alpha_1 + 2)\epsilon'))$

8 $\quad$ else

9 $\quad\quad$ return MECH-SM-FRAC-VAR$(A \setminus S, v, \mathbf{c}_{A\setminus S}, B, (1 - (\alpha_1 + 2)\epsilon'))$

Theorem 8 below works for any objective for which we can establish a constant upper bound ρ on the ratio of the fractional and the integral optimal solutions. We view it as the most technically demanding result of this work.

Theorem 8. *For any $\epsilon > 0$, DET-MECH-SYMSM-FRAC is a deterministic, truthful, individually rational, budget-feasible mechanism for symmetric submodular valuations, that has approximation ratio $\alpha + 1 + \epsilon$ and runs in polynomial time.*

5.1 Weighted Cut Functions

Let us return now to the Max Cut problem, and consider the weighted version. An immediate implication of Theorem 8 is that we get a deterministic polynomial-time mechanism for Budgeted Max Weighted Cut with approximation ratio 58.72. This is just the result of substituting $\rho = 4$ in the formula for α.

However, by further exploiting the proof of Theorem 6, we can prove the following improved result that matches the approximation guarantee for unweighted cut functions.

Theorem 9. *There is a deterministic, truthful, individually rational, budget-feasible mechanism for Budgeted Max Weighted Cut that has approximation ratio 27.25, and runs in polynomial time.*

6   An Improved Upper Bound for XOS Objectives

In [5] a randomized, universally truthful and budget-feasible 768-approximation mechanism was introduced for XOS functions. For several of our results the best previously known upper bound follows from this work. In this section we show that one can slightly modify their mechanism to improve its performance.

Definition 3. *A valuation function, defined on 2^A for some set A, is XOS or fractionally subadditive, if there exist non-negative additive functions $\alpha_1, \alpha_2, \ldots, \alpha_r$, for some finite r, such that $v(S) = \max\{\alpha_1(S), \alpha_2(S), \ldots, \alpha_r(S)\}$.*

Note that we define non-decreasing XOS functions. However, there is a relatively straightforward way to extend any result to general XOS functions (as defined in [16]). Like the mechanism of Bei et al., the mechanism of Theorem 10 below is randomized and has superpolynomial running time. In particular, it requires a demand oracle.

Theorem 10. *There is a universally truthful, individually rational, budget-feasible mechanism for XOS objectives that has approximation ratio 244.*

References

1. Ageev, A.A., Sviridenko, M.I.: Approximation algorithms for maximum coverage and max cut with given sizes of parts. In: Cornuéjols, G., Burkard, R.E., Woeginger, G.J. (eds.) IPCO 1999. LNCS, vol. 1610, pp. 17–30. Springer, Heidelberg (1999). https://doi.org/10.1007/3-540-48777-8_2
2. Amanatidis, G., Birmpas, G., Markakis, E.: Coverage, matching, and beyond: new results on budgeted mechanism design. In: Cai, Y., Vetta, A. (eds.) WINE 2016. LNCS, vol. 10123, pp. 414–428. Springer, Heidelberg (2016). https://doi.org/10.1007/978-3-662-54110-4_29
3. Amanatidis, G., Birmpas, G., Markakis, E.: On budget-feasible mechanism design for symmetric submodular objectives. CoRR abs/1704.06901 (2017)
4. Anari, N., Goel, G., Nikzad, A.: Mechanism design for crowdsourcing: an optimal 1-1/e competitive budget-feasible mechanism for large markets. In: 55th IEEE Annual Symposium on Foundations of Computer Science, FOCS 2014, pp. 266–275 (2014)
5. Bei, X., Chen, N., Gravin, N., Lu, P.: Budget feasible mechanism design: from prior-free to Bayesian. In: Proceedings of the 44th Symposium on Theory of Computing Conference, STOC 2012, pp. 449–458 (2012)

6. Borodin, A., Filmus, Y., Oren, J.: Threshold models for competitive influence in social networks. In: Saberi, A. (ed.) WINE 2010. LNCS, vol. 6484, pp. 539–550. Springer, Heidelberg (2010). https://doi.org/10.1007/978-3-642-17572-5_48

7. Caselton, W.F., Zidek, J.V.: Optimal monitoring network designs. Stat. Probab. Lett. **2**(4), 223–227 (1984)

8. Chekuri, C., Vondrák, J., Zenklusen, R.: Submodular function maximization via the multilinear relaxation and contention resolution schemes. SIAM J. Comput. **43**(6), 1831–1879 (2014)

9. Chen, N., Gravin, N., Lu, P.: On the approximability of budget feasible mechanisms. In: Proceedings of the Twenty-Second Annual ACM-SIAM Symposium on Discrete Algorithms, SODA 2011, pp. 685–699 (2011)

10. Cressie, N.A.: Statistics for Spatial Data. Wiley, Hoboken (1993)

11. Dobzinski, S., Papadimitriou, C.H., Singer, Y.: Mechanisms for complement-free procurement. In: Proceedings 12th ACM Conference on Electronic Commerce (EC-2011), pp. 273–282 (2011)

12. Feige, U., Mirrokni, V.S., Vondrák, J.: Maximizing non-monotone submodular functions. SIAM J. Comput. **40**(4), 1133–1153 (2011)

13. Feldman, M., Naor, J., Schwartz, R.: A unified continuous greedy algorithm for submodular maximization. In: IEEE 52nd Annual Symposium on Foundations of Computer Science, FOCS 2011, pp. 570–579. IEEE Computer Society (2011)

14. Fujishige, S.: Canonical decompositions of symmetric submodular systems. Discret. Appl. Math. **5**, 175–190 (1983)

15. Goel, G., Nikzad, A., Singla, A.: Mechanism design for crowdsourcing markets with heterogeneous tasks. In: Proceedings of the Second AAAI Conference on Human Computation and Crowdsourcing, HCOMP 2014 (2014)

16. Gupta, A., Nagarajan, V., Singla, S.: Adaptivity gaps for stochastic probing: submodular and XOS functions. In: Proceedings of the Twenty-Eighth Annual ACM-SIAM Symposium on Discrete Algorithms, SODA 2017, pp. 1688–1702 (2017)

17. Gupta, A., Roth, A., Schoenebeck, G., Talwar, K.: Constrained non-monotone submodular maximization: offline and secretary algorithms. In: Saberi, A. (ed.) WINE 2010. LNCS, vol. 6484, pp. 246–257. Springer, Heidelberg (2010). https://doi.org/10.1007/978-3-642-17572-5_20

18. Horel, T., Ioannidis, S., Muthukrishnan, S.: Budget feasible mechanisms for experimental design. In: Pardo, A., Viola, A. (eds.) LATIN 2014. LNCS, vol. 8392, pp. 719–730. Springer, Heidelberg (2014). https://doi.org/10.1007/978-3-642-54423-1_62

19. Jalaly, P., Tardos, E.: Simple and Efficient Budget Feasible Mechanisms for Monotone Submodular Valuations. arXiv:1703:10681 (2017)

20. Kleinberg, J., Tardos, E.: Algorithm Design. Addison Wesley, Boston (2006)

21. Krause, A., Singh, A.P., Guestrin, C.: Near-optimal sensor placements in Gaussian processes: theory, efficient algorithms and empirical studies. J. Mach. Learn. Res. **9**, 235–284 (2008)

22. Kulik, A., Shachnai, H., Tamir, T.: Approximations for monotone and non-monotone submodular maximization with knapsack constraints. Math. Oper. Res. **38**(4), 729–739 (2013)

23. Lee, J., Mirrokni, V.S., Nagarajan, V., Sviridenko, M.: Maximizing nonmonotone submodular functions under matroid or knapsack constraints. SIAM J. Discret. Math. **23**(4), 2053–2078 (2010)

24. Leonardi, S., Monaco, G., Sankowski, P., Zhang, Q.: Budget Feasible Mechanisms on Matroids. arXiv:1612:03150 (2016)

25. Myerson, R.: Optimal auction design. Math. Oper. Res. **6**(1), 58–73 (1981)
26. Nemhauser, G.L., Wolsey, L.A., Fisher, M.L.: An analysis of approximations for maximizing submodular set functions - I. Math. Program. **14**(1), 265–294 (1978)
27. Queyranne, M.: Minimizing symmetric submodular functions. Math. Program. **82**(1–2), 3–12 (1998)
28. Schäffer, A.A., Yannakakis, M.: Simple local search problems that are hard to solve. SIAM J. Comput. **20**(1), 56–87 (1991)
29. Singer, Y.: Budget feasible mechanisms. In: 51th Annual IEEE Symposium on Foundations of Computer Science, FOCS 2010, pp. 765–774 (2010)
30. Singer, Y.: How to win friends and influence people, truthfully: influence maximization mechanisms for social networks. In: Proceedings of the 5th International Conference on Web Search and Web Data Mining, WSDM 2012, pp. 733–742 (2012)
31. Singla, A., Krause, A.: Incentives for privacy tradeoff in community sensing. In: Proceedings of the First AAAI Conference on Human Computation and Crowdsourcing, HCOMP 2013. AAAI (2013)
32. Sviridenko, M.: A note on maximizing a submodular set function subject to a knapsack constraint. Oper. Res. Lett. **32**(1), 41–43 (2004)
33. Wolsey, L.A.: Maximising real-valued submodular functions: primal and dual heuristics for location problems. Math. Oper. Res. **7**(3), 410–425 (1982)

Don't Be Greedy: Leveraging Community Structure to Find High Quality Seed Sets for Influence Maximization

Rico Angell[1(✉)] and Grant Schoenebeck[2]

[1] University of Massachusetts, Amherst, USA
rangell@cs.umass.edu
[2] University of Michigan, Ann Arbor, USA

Abstract. We consider the problem of maximizing the spread of influence in a social network by choosing a fixed number of initial seeds — a central problem in the study of network cascades. The majority of existing work on this problem, formally referred to as the *influence maximization problem,* is designed for submodular cascades. Despite the empirical evidence that many cascades are non-submodular, little work has been done focusing on non-submodular influence maximization.

We propose a new heuristic for solving the influence maximization problem and show via simulations on real-world and synthetic networks that our algorithm outputs more influential seed sets than the state-of-the-art greedy algorithm in many natural cases, with average improvements of 7% for submodular cascades, and 55% for non-submodular cascades. Our heuristic uses a dynamic programming approach on a hierarchical decomposition of the social network to leverage the relation between the spread of cascades and the community structure of social networks. We present "worst-case" theoretical results proving that in certain settings our algorithm outputs seed sets that are a factor of $\Theta(\sqrt{n})$ more influential than those of the greedy algorithm, where n is the number of nodes in the network.

1 Introduction

A *cascade* is a fundamental social network process in which a number of nodes, or agents, start with some property that they then may spread to neighbors. Network structure has been shown relevant for a wide array of real world cascade processes including the adoption of products [6], farming technology [13], medical practices [12], participation in microfinancing [4], and the spread of information over social networks [26].

The full version is located at https://arxiv.org/abs/1609.06520.

The authors gratefully acknowledge the support of the National Science Foundation under Career Award 1452915 and AifT Award 1535912.

N. R. Devanur and P. Lu (Eds.): WINE 2017, LNCS 10674, pp. 16–29, 2017.
https://doi.org/10.1007/978-3-319-71924-5_2

How to place a limited number of initial seeds, in order to maximize the spread of the resulting cascade, is a natural question known as INFLUENCE-MAXIMIZATION [16,22,23,32,35]. This problem requires as input a network, a cascade process, and the number of initial seeds. For example, which students can most effectively be enrolled in an intervention to decrease student conflict at a school [34]?

To study INFLUENCEMAXIMIZATION, we first need to understand how cascades spread. While many cascade models have been proposed [2,31,42], they can be roughly divided into two categories: *submodular* and *non-submodular*.

In submodular cascade models, such as the Independent Cascade model defined in Sect. 2 [22,23,32], a node's marginal probability of becoming infected after a new neighbor is infected decreases when the number of previously infected neighbors increases [22]. In non-submodular cascade models the marginal probability of being infected may increase as more neighbors are infected. For example, in the Threshold model [20], each node has a threshold for the number of infected neighbors after which it too will become infected. If a node has a threshold of 2, then the first infected neighbor has zero marginal impact, but the second infected neighbor causes this node to become infected with probability 1. Unlike submodular cascades, non-submodular cascades require well-connected regions to spread [7].

For INFLUENCEMAXIMIZATION in submodular cascades, a straightforward greedy algorithm efficiently finds a seed set with influence at least a $(1 - 1/e)$ fraction of the optimal; but for general non-submodular cascades, it is NP-hard even to approximate INFLUENCEMAXIMIZATION to within a $n^{1-\epsilon}$ factor of optimal [22].

Unfortunately, empirical research shows that most cascades are non-submodular [3,27,36], and in this case little is known about INFLUENCEMAXI-MIZATION other than worst-case hardness. INFLUENCEMAXIMIZATION becomes qualitatively different in the non-submodular setting. In the submodular case, one should put as much distance between the k initial adopters as possible, lest they erode each other's effectiveness. However, in the non-submodular case, it may be advantageous to place the initial adopters close together to create synergy and yield more adoptions. Thus, the intuition that it is better to saturate one market first, and then expand implicitly assumes non-submodular influence. However, this synergy renders the problem intractable. Schoenebeck and Tao [37] show that even if the community structure is exactly hierarchical and is given to the algorithm, INFLUENCEMAXIMIZATION remains intractable to approximate in non-submodular settings. This shows that we cannot expect our algorithm to be provably optimal.

However, as we will illustrate, greedy approaches can perform poorly in these settings. Yet, much of the work following Kempe et al. [22], which proposed the greedy algorithm, has attempted to make *greedy approaches* efficient and scalable [8,9,11,30,39,41]. New ideas seem necessary to design effective heuristics for non-submodular INFLUENCEMAXIMIZATION.

We observe that structural problems for networks—such as community detection—are also, in general NP-complete, but many efficient heuristics already exist [10,21]. There are reasons to believe that such problems are not intractable in cases likely to arise in practice [1]. This work asks whether we can design heuristics for INFLUENCEMAXIMIZATION that work well for both submodular and non-submodular cascades, and what new algorithmic techniques might efficiently find hidden synergies necessary to maximize influence.

1.1   Contributions

We provide a new heuristic for solving INFLUENCEMAXIMIZATION designed to work for both submodular and non-submodular cascades. Our algorithm takes as input not only a network, but a hierarchical decomposition of the network. It then uses a dynamic programming technique to search for an influential seed set of nodes. We provide the following results concerning our algorithm[1]:

1. We show theoretically that in certain cases, our algorithm outputs seed sets that are a factor of $\Theta(\sqrt{n})$ more influential than those of the state-of-the-art greedy algorithm, where n is the number of nodes in the network. This stylized example illustrates the intuition behind our algorithm, as well as the poor performance of greedy.
2. We empirically compare our algorithm to the greedy algorithm via simulations on real-world and synthetic networks for a variety of cascade models. Our algorithm appears to do at least as well as greedy and substantially better for non-submodular cascades. Our algorithm achieves average improvements of 7% for submodular cascades and 55% for non-submodular cascades, performing 266% better in one exceptional case.
3. We verify the importance of network structure by showing that the quality of the hierarchical decomposition impacts the quality of our algorithm's output.
4. Finally, we define a generalization of our algorithm to a "message-passing" algorithm. While it provably returns seed sets of at least the quality of our dynamic programming algorithm, it typically only offers marginal improvement in the seed set quality while incurring a greater running time. However, we hope that the versatility the message-passing approach can help with future work than focuses on making more scalable versions of our algorithm. Due to space constraints, the message-passing algorithm can be found in the appendix.

1.2   Related Work

Following the work of Kempe et al. [22], which proposed the greedy algorithm, extensive work has constructed *efficient and scalable* algorithms and heuristics INFLUENCEMAXIMIZATION [8,9,11,30,33,39,41].

---

[1] See the full version for all of these results at https://arxiv.org/abs/1609.06520.

Wang et al. [41] partition the network into communities to inform a greedy-based algorithm in order to increase scalability. The heuristic algorithms presented in [8,9] rely on input parameters from the user that sacrifice accuracy for speed. The authors state that fine tuning the input parameters can make solving INFLUENCEMAXIMIZATION fast and accurate. Borgs et al. [5] provably show fast running times when the influence function is the independent cascade model. Tang et al. [39] extend this work to provide an algorithm that maintains the same theoretical guarantees as the greedy algorithm presented in [22] and is efficient in practice. Lucier et al. [30] show how to parallelize (in a model based on Map Reduce) the subproblem of determining the influence of a particular seed. Additional work has been done to speed up algorithms for solving INFLUENCEMAXIMIZATION by providing techniques to efficiently compute the total influence of a seed set [11,24].

Leskovec et al. [28] consider the analogous problem of effectively placing sensors in a network in order to effectively detect an outbreak in the network. They present the algorithm CELF that uses a greedy approach, but leverages the submodularity of the cascade to reduce the amount of time it takes to evaluate the spread of the cascade. Moreover, CELF is built upon by the work in [17,18], which present modifications to CELF to make an even more cost effective solution to INFLUENCEMAXIMIZATION. Nguyen and Zheng [33] present an algorithm based on belief propagation for INFLUENCEMAXIMIZATION. The algorithm works by systematically removing edges until the resulting graph is a tree, and then running a belief propagation algorithm on the scaled-down network. The article shows that the performance of their algorithm is not substantially worse than that of the greedy algorithm.

In contrast to the aforementioned work, our goal is not to deliver an algorithm that is more efficient and scalable, but rather to present an algorithm that finds higher quality seed sets. Cordasco et al. [14] recently published an algorithm aimed at improving the quality of the seed set discovered, but is limited to deterministic influence patterns where each nodes has a fixed integer threshold. This algorithm greedily maximizes the total influence instead of the total number of infected nodes at the end of the cascade. They show empirically that their algorithm finds higher quality seed sets than the traditional greedy algorithm. On the other hand, our work is focused on the more general and traditional stochastic variant of INFLUENCEMAXIMIZATION. Additionally, with the exception of [33], the prior work is based on a greedy-like approach and suffers from the short-comings of this approach. Our algorithm uses a dynamic programming framework, and is fundamentally different.

Other variations of INFLUENCEMAXIMIZATION have also been considered, e.g. [19,38].

2 Preliminaries

A real function f on sets is ***submodular*** if the marginal gain of from adding an element to a set A is at least as large as the marginal gain from adding the same element to a superset B of A. Formally, f is submodular if for all A, B, u where $A \subseteq B$ we have $f(A \cup \{u\}) - f(A) \geq f(B \cup \{u\}) - f(B)$.

Cascade Model. A cascade model is a triple (G, F, S) where $G = (V, E)$ is an unweighted graph; $F = \{f_v : \{0,1\}^{|\Gamma(v)|} \to [0,1]\}_{v \in V}$ is a collection of **local influence functions**, where $\Gamma(v)$ is the set of v's neighbors, f_v takes in the set of infected neighbors of a node v, and produces a real value which encodes the "influence" of this set on v; and S is the subset of the vertices that are initially infected. The cascade will proceed in rounds. In round 0, the set S is infected and each of the remaining vertices is assigned a threshold value $\theta_v \in [0,1]$ drawn uniformly at random. At each subsequent round, a vertex v becomes infected if and only if $f_v(T) \geq \theta_v$, where T is the set of v's infected neighbors. We will require f_v to be monotone for each v.

We denote the **global influence function** as $\sigma(S)$ which is the *expected* total number of infected vertices due to the influence of the initial seed set S.

It can be shown that if f_v is submodular for each v, then the global influence function σ is submodular too [32]. Thus, we say that a model of cascade is **submodular** if f_v is submodular for each v, and is **non-submodular** otherwise.

The same research that shows the f usually fail to be submodular [3,27,36] shows that this submodularity fails in one particular way: the second adopting neighbor is, on average, more influential than the first; and that after this point, each subsequent adopting neighbor's marginal influence decreases. We call such functions **2-quasi-submodular**. Formally, f is **2-quasi-submodular** if for all A, B, $A \subseteq B$, $|A|, |B| \geq 1$ and $u \notin A, B$, we have $f(A \cup \{u\}) - f(A) \geq f(B \cup \{u\}) - f(B)$; and for $v \neq u$, we have $f(\{u\}) - f(\emptyset) \leq f(\{u, v\}) - f(\{v\})$.

Any nonzero submodular influence function f_v can be turned into a 2-quasi-submodular function by sufficiently decreasing the value of $f_v(\cdot)$ on singleton sets.

For any local influence function f_v, we define the q-**deflated** version f_v^{q-defl} of f_v as follows:

$$f_v^{q-defl}(S) = \begin{cases} q \cdot f_v(S) & |S| = 1 \\ f_v(S) & \text{o.w.} \end{cases}$$

Specific Cascade Models. The two popular cascade models studied in the INFLU-ENCEMAXIMIZATION literature are the Independent Cascade model (ICM) and the Linear Threshold model (LTM). In the **Independent Cascade model**, each newly infected node infects each currently uninfected neighbor in the subsequent round with some fixed probability p. Thus, for all v,

$$f_v^{ICM}(S) = 1 - (1 - p)^{|S|}.$$

In the **Linear Threshold model**, each node has a threshold $\theta_v \in [0,1]$, each of v's neighbors u has influence $b_{u,v}$ on v such that $\sum_{u \in \Gamma(v)} b_{u,v} \leq 1$, and v becomes infected when the sum of the influences of the infected neighbors meets or surpasses v's threshold.

We define the **Deflated Independent Cascade model** (DICM) which takes two parameters: $p, q \in [0, 1]$ to be the q-deflated version of the Independent Cascade model.

In the **S-Cascade model** (SCM) we have that

$$f_d^{SCM}(S) = \frac{\left(\frac{|S|}{2d}\right)^2}{\left(\frac{|S|}{2d}\right)^2 + \left(1 - \frac{|S|}{d}\right)^2}.$$

The fraction $|S|/d$ is the fraction of infected neighbors of a given node. This is a modified version of the Tullock Cost function [40] with power 2.

We note that the Independent Cascade model and the Linear Threshold model are submodular, while the q-Deflated Independent Cascade model (for $q < 1 - p/2$) and S-Cascade are not. Figure 1 illustrates the local influence functions of the various cascade models.

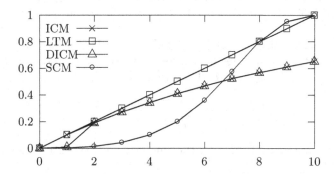

Fig. 1. The local influence functions where the parameters of the ICM and DICM and the influence weights of LTM are all .1; and the vertex's degree in LTM and SCM is 10.

Synthetic Network Model. Most existing synthetic models fail to have meaningful asymmetry between nodes, or significant community structure, or both. Therefore, we design our own synthetic network model. The **directed** (d, ℓ, t)-**hierarchical network model** creates a random network on 2^d nodes as follows: We create an edge-weighted complete binary tree of depth d, each leaf representing a vertex of the graph. The weights are drawn i.i.d from a Binomial$(\ell, 1/2)$ distribution. Each node v issues t random edges, each generated via a random walk — illustrated in Fig. 2. Each random walk starts at v. At each step in the walk, an outgoing edge is chosen proportional to its weight (we disallow exiting the node along the same edge that the walk arrived at the node). The walk terminates when it arrives at a leaf node. If a terminating node is duplicated, we draw again, which keeps the graph simple.

As ℓ grows larger, this approaches the hierarchical Kleinberg model [25]. But for moderately sized ℓ, there is a non-trivial amount of asymmetry introduced into the graph — some subcommunities are more influential than others.

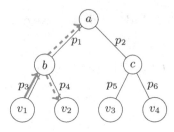

Fig. 2. Illustrative example of a random walk to generate an edge in our synthetic network model.

Hierarchical Decomposition. We define a **hierarchical decomposition** of a graph G to be a rooted full binary tree $T = (V_T, E_T)$ where the leaves of T correspond to the vertices of G. For a tree node $v \in V_T$, define $\boldsymbol{T(v)}$ to be the subset of vertices in G corresponding to the leaves of the subtree rooted at v. Let the **height** of $v \in V_T$ be defined as the length of the path to v's deepest descendent.

We use the recently proposed cost function of Dasgupta [15] to evaluate the quality of a hierarchical decomposition. Let $\mathrm{lca}_T(u, v)$ be the least common ancestor of $u, v \in V$ in the tree T. Then we define

$$Cost(T) = \sum_{\{u,v\} \in E} |T(\mathrm{lca}(u, v))|$$

which sums the number of leaves in the smallest subtree containing each edge.

Influence Maximization. An **InfluenceMaximization Instance** consists of a graph $G = (V, E)$, an influence function σ, and an integer k. Given an Influence-Maximization Instance, the goal is to find a set S of k nodes as to maximize $\sigma(S)$.

The **greedy algorithm** [22] for an INFLUENCEMAXIMIZATION Instance start with a tentative seed set $T = \emptyset$ and for k rounds, simply adds arg $\max_{v \in V} \sigma(T \cup \{v\})$ to T.

3   DPIM: Dynamic Programming Influence Maximization Algorithm

The Dynamic Programming Influence Maximization Algorithm (*DPIM*), formally specified in Algorithm 1, takes as input a graph G, and corresponding hierarchical decomposition T, an integer k, and a global influence function $\sigma(\cdot)$ and outputs a subset of vertices $S \subseteq V$ such that $|S| = k$ and S is a highly influential set of seeds. *DPIM* seeks to maximize the total influence of a fixed-sized seed set S by performing dynamic programming upon T.

For each node $v \in T$, and each $i \in \{0, 1, \ldots, \min(|T(v)|, k)\}$, the algorithm stores $A[v, i]$, a choice of i seeds in $T(v)$ which seeks to maximize the total influence in G. Starting at the leaves of the tree, and moving up level by level until reaching the root, DPIM processes each tree node. For each leaf node $v \in T$, we store $A[v, 0] = \emptyset$ and $A[v, 1] = \{v\}$. For each internal node $v \in T$, which has children v_L and v_R, we set $A[v, i] = A[v_L, j] \cup A[v_R, i - j]$ where $j \in \{0, 1, \ldots, i\}$ is selected as to maximize $\sigma(A[v_L, j] \cup A[v_R, i - j])$. Thus the algorithm optimally splits the seeds between a tree nodes two subtrees given how the algorithm has already determined that each subtree should allocate any particular number seeds.

Algorithm 1. *DPIM*: Dynamic Programming Influence Maximization Algorithm

---

Input: $G = (V, E), T = (V_T, E_T), \sigma(\cdot), k$
Output: $S \subset V$ such that $|S| = k$
Let $A[\cdot, \cdot] = V_T \times [k] \rightarrow 2^V$, such that $A[v_T, j]$ stores a choice of j seeds in $T(v_T)$.
Let $r \in V_T$ be the root of T and h be its height.
for *each height* $i = 0, 1, \ldots, h$ **do**
    for *each node* $v \in V_T$ *with height* i **do**
        if $i = 0$ **then**
            $A[v, 0] = \emptyset$
            $A[v, 1] = \{v\}$
        else
            Let v_L, v_R be the left and right children of v, respectively.
            for *each* $i = 0, 1, \ldots, \min\{|T(v)|, k\}$ **do**
                $j = \underset{j \in \{0,1,\ldots,i\}}{\arg\max}\ \sigma(A[v_L, j] \cup A[v_R, i - j])$
                $A[v, i] = A[v_L, j] \cup A[v_R, i - j]$
            end
        end
    end
end
return $A[r, k]$

The analysis of the running time for *DPIM* is straightforward.

Theorem 1. *Given a graph $G = (V, E)$ with $|V| = n, |E| = m$, fixed positive integers k, r, and a hierarchical decomposition T, DPIM calls the $\sigma(\cdot)$ oracle $O(nk^2)$ times.*

Proof. Observe that, for each node in T, *DPIM* makes $O(k^2)$ queries to $\sigma(\cdot)$. The number of nodes in T is exactly $2n - 1$.

Hence, the number of oracle calls in *DPIM* is $O(nk^2)$.

Note that this is a factor of k more than the greedy algorithm, which requires only $O(nk)$ calls to the oracle. The execution of a single query to $\sigma(\cdot)$ can be approximated by repeatedly, r times, simulating the cascade process and returning the average number of infected vertices. This can be done in time $O(mr)$ because simulating the cascade requires at most simulating the cascade on each edge in G. However, there are often techniques to speed up the oracle access beyond simply running the cascade [5], but they are beyond the scope of this work.

4   Experimental Results About DPIM

In this section, we discuss empirical results of *DPIM*. See the full version for theoretical results and further empirical analysis.

4.1   Experimental Setup

We execute *DPIM* and the greedy algorithm from [22] on a variety of networks and cascades to test the relative quality of solutions.

Cascade Models. We adopt the two common submodular cascade models from the literature: the linear threshold model and the independent cascade model, defined in Sect. 2, and two non-submodular cascades:

(I) *Independent Cascade*(IC): We uniformly assign the probability $p = 1\%$, thus v with ℓ infected neighbors is infected with probability $1 - (0.99)^{\ell}$.

(II) *Linear Threshold* (LT): For each node v, we assign each of $u \in \Gamma(v)$ to have $1/|\Gamma(v)|$ influence on v.

(III) *Deflated Independent Cascade* (DIC): We uniformly assign the probability $p = 1\%$, thus v with $\ell = 1$ infected neighbors is infected with probabilty 0.1% ($q = 0.1$) and with $\ell \geq 2$ infected neighbors is infected with probability $1 - (0.99)^{\ell}$.

(IV) *S-Cascade model* (SCM): The influence on any given node v is

$$\frac{(x/2)^2}{(x/2)^2 + (1-x)^2},$$

where x is the fraction of v's neighbors that are infected.

Both of these algorithms require access to an oracle for $\sigma(\cdot)$, which is also required to evaluate the effectiveness of the algorithms. To implement this oracle, we simulate the cascade 100 times, resampling the randomness for the cascade each time (using pseudorandomness from the standard C++ library) and return the average number of infections.

Networks. We use two real-world networks (from [29]) and two synthetic networks, summarized in Table 1. In the arXiv collaboration network (ca-GrQc), the vertices are authors of e-print scientific articles and edges represent coauthorship relations. The ego-Facebook network is largest such network provided by [29]. This network denotes the facebook friendship ties from a single person's (ego's) set of friends. The ego vertex has been removed. Furthermore, we generate two synthetic networks by first sampling from directed (d, ℓ, t)-hierarchical network model using parameters $(10, 50, 50)$ and $(11, 50, 50)$ (synthetic-1 & synthetic-2, resp.), and then making the graph simple and undirected in the natural way.

Table 1. Networks used to evaluate the effectiveness of our algorithm.

Name	Nodes	Edges
synthetic-1	1,024	51,200
synthetic-2	2,048	102,400
ca-GrQc	5,276	28,827
ego-Facebook	1,034	53,498

Algorithms for Hierarchical Decomposition. Lastly, in order to evaluate our algorithm, we present 4 algorithms for generating a hierarchical decomposition of any network. The algorithms we used in our simulations are implemented as follows:

(I) *Random Pair*: Each node starts in its own partition, and partitions are joined randomly until all of the nodes are contained in one partition.

(II) *Random Edge*: Each node starts in its own partition, and partitions are joined by contracting a random edge between partitions. If no edges remain between the partitions, partitions are merged randomly until all of the nodes are contained in one partition.

(III) *Jaccard Similarity*: Each node starts in its own partition, and pairs of partitions (A, B), for $A, B \subset V$ are joined based on which pair maximizes

$$\frac{|\Gamma(A) \cap \Gamma(B)|}{|\Gamma(A) \cup \Gamma(B)|},$$

where $\Gamma(X \subset V) = \bigcup_{v \in X} \Gamma(v)$.

(IV) *METIS-based*: The whole network starts as one partition; using METIS [21], partitions are recursively divided into two partitions until each partition contains only a single node.

4.2   Algorithm Evaluation

Performance of DPIM. The results of the simulations we ran are shown in Fig. 3. For each execution of *DPIM*, we used the METIS-based hierarchical decomposition algorithm to construct a hierarchical decomposition of the network.

Considering cascades across all four networks with seed set size 20, *DPIM* increases influence on average by 8% for ICM, 6% for LTM, 22% for DICM, and 88% for SCM. Surprisingly, *DPIM* performs marginally better than the greedy algorithm even for submodular cascades. As predicted, when the cascade is non-submodular, *DPIM* outperforms the greedy algorithm by a significant amount. However, gains were more impressive for synthetic-2, ca-GrQc, and ego-Facebook — including an 266% increase in influence for the SCM cascade on the ego-Facebook network — than for synthetic-1, where we see only marginal improvement even when the cascade is non-submodular. Table 2 contains,

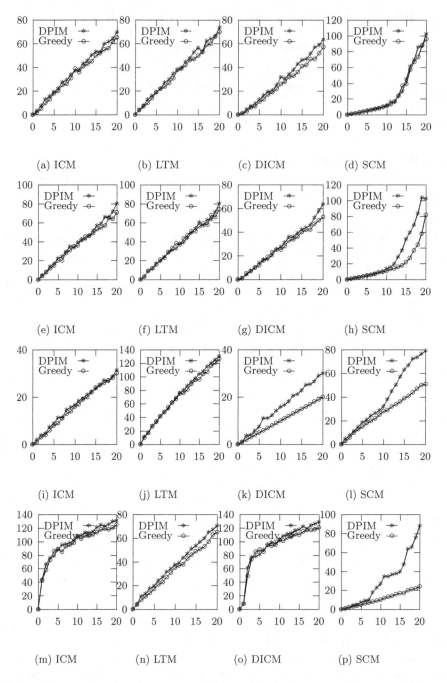

Fig. 3. Comparison of performance: *DPIM* vs. Greedy. The rows from top to bottom correspond to synthetic-1, synthetic-2, ca-GrQc,and ego-Facebook, respectively. For each plot, the x-axis is k and the y-axis is the number of total infections at the end of the cascade.

for $k = 20$, the approximated expected total influence values for each simulation rounded to the nearest integer. Figure 3 includes charts of the improvement for all k.

In the full version of the paper, we present further empirical results and generalize *DPIM* to a message passing algorithm.

Table 2. Expected total influence of the final seed sets of size 20 chosen by both algorithms for each of the simulations (rounded to the nearest integer).

	synthetic-1		synthetic-2		ca-GrQc		ego-Facebook	
	Greedy	*DPIM*	Greedy	*DPIM*	Greedy	*DPIM*	Greedy	*DPIM*
ICM	65	70	71	80	30	31	125	131
LTM	70	74	74	81	126	130	65	70
DICM	57	64	53	64	20	30	121	129
SCM	96	102	82	103	51	79	24	88

5   Future Work

DPIM is typically not as fast as naive greedy, and to be useful in practice, it would greatly help if it were more scalable. We believe that this will prove to be the case. For example, we could stop the recursion before exploring the entire hierarchical decomposition. We might stop dividing if a subtree does not appear to have any additional community structure, and then run a heuristic (such as degree or greedy) to process the rest of the subtree. The intuition here is that dynamic programming works best where the network has strong community structure, so where no structure exists, it may not provide much added benefit. Additionally, the same techniques that have made the greedy algorithm more scalable might be adopted to our dynamic programming framework. Finally, we think that the versatility of when to schedule updates in the "message-passing" algorithm (which generalizes *DPIM*) may be useful in scaling our approach.

Another possible direction of future exploration is to try additional hierarchical decomposition techniques. Interestingly, *DPIM* can be seen as a way to *test* hierarchical decomposition techniques. Decompositions that perform better are intuitively finding a better decomposition.

References

1. Arora, S., Ge, R., Sachdeva, S., Schoenebeck, G.: Finding overlapping communities in social networks: toward a rigorous approach. In: ACM EC 2012 (2012)
2. Arthur, W.B.: Competing technologies, increasing returns, and lock-in by historical events. Econ. J. **99**(394), 116–131 (1989). http://www.jstor.org/stable/2234208
3. Backstrom, L., Huttenlocher, D.P., Kleinberg, J.M., Lan, X.: Group formation in large social networks: membership, growth, and evolution. In: KDD 2006, pp. 44–54 (2006)
4. Banerjee, A., Chandrasekhar, A.G., Duflo, E., Jackson, M.O.: The diffusion of microfinance. Science, 341(6144) (2013)

5. Borgs, C., Brautbar, M., Chayes, J.T., Lucier, B.: Maximizing social influence in nearly optimal time. In: SODA 2014 (2014)
6. Brown, J.J., Reingen, P.H.: Social ties and word-of-mouth referral behavior. J. Consum. Res. **14**, 350–362 (1987)
7. Centola, D.: The spread of behavior in an online social network experiment. Science **329**(5996), 1194–1197 (2010)
8. Chen, W., Wang, Y., Yang, S.: Efficient influence maximization in social networks. In: KDD 2009. ACM (2009)
9. Chen, W., Yuan, Y., Zhang, L.: Scalable influence maximization in social networks under the linear threshold model. In: ICDM 2010, pp. 88–97. IEEE (2010)
10. Clauset, A., Newman, M.E., Moore, C.: Finding community structure in very large networks. Phys. Rev. E **70**(6), 066111 (2004)
11. Cohen, E., Delling, D., Pajor, T., Werneck, R.F.: Sketch-based influence maximization and computation: scaling up with guarantees. In: CIKM 2014, pp. 629–638. ACM (2014)
12. Coleman, J., Katz, E., Menzel, H.: The diffusion of an innovation among physicians. Sociometry **20**, 253–270 (1957)
13. Conley, T.G., Udry, C.R.: Learning about a new technology: pineapple in Ghana. Am. Econ. Rev. **100**(1), 35–69 (2010)
14. Cordasco, G., Gargano, L., Mecchia, M., Rescigno, A.A., Vaccaro, U.: Discovering small target sets in social networks: a fast and effective algorithm. arXiv preprint arXiv:1610.03721 (2016)
15. Dasgupta, S.: A cost function for similarity-based hierarchical clustering. In: STOC 2016, pp. 118–127. ACM, New York, NY, USA (2016). http://doi.acm.org/10.1145/2897518.2897527
16. Domingos, P., Richardson, M.: Mining the network value of customers. In: 7th ACM SIGKDD International Conference on Knowledge Discovery and Data Mining, pp. 57–66 (2001)
17. Goyal, A., Lu, W., Lakshmanan, L.V.: Celf++: optimizing the greedy algorithm for influence maximization in social networks. In: WWW 2011. pp. 47–48. ACM (2011)
18. Goyal, A., Lu, W., Lakshmanan, L.V.: Simpath: an efficient algorithm for influence maximization under the linear threshold model. In: ICDM 2011, pp. 211–220. IEEE (2011)
19. Goyal, S., Kearns, M.: Competitive contagion in networks. In: STOC 2012, pp. 759–774 (2012)
20. Granovetter, M.: Threshold models of collective behavior. Am. J. Sociol. **83**(6), 1420–1443 (1978). http://www.journals.uchicago.edu/doi/abs/10.1086/226707
21. Karypis, G., Kumar, V.: METIS: unstructured graph partitioning and sparse matrix ordering system, Version 4.0. (2009). http://www.cs.umn.edu/~metis
22. Kempe, D., Kleinberg, J.M., Tardos, É.: Maximizing the spread of influence through a social network. In: KDD 2003, pp. 137–146 (2003)
23. Kempe, D., Kleinberg, J., Tardos, É.: Influential nodes in a diffusion model for social networks. In: Caires, L., Italiano, G.F., Monteiro, L., Palamidessi, C., Yung, M. (eds.) ICALP 2005. LNCS, vol. 3580, pp. 1127–1138. Springer, Heidelberg (2005). https://doi.org/10.1007/11523468_91
24. Kimura, M., Saito, K.: Tractable models for information diffusion in social networks. In: Fürnkranz, J., Scheffer, T., Spiliopoulou, M. (eds.) PKDD 2006. LNCS, vol. 4213, pp. 259–271. Springer, Heidelberg (2006). https://doi.org/10.1007/11871637_27

25. Kleinberg, J.: Small-world phenomena and the dynamics of information. In: NIPS 2002, vol. 1, pp. 431–438 (2002)
26. Lerman, K., Ghosh, R.: Information contagion: an empirical study of the spread of news on Digg and Twitter social networks. ICWSM **10**, 90–97 (2010)
27. Leskovec, J., Adamic, L.A., Huberman, B.A.: The dynamics of viral marketing. In: ACM EC 2006, pp. 228–237 (2006)
28. Leskovec, J., Krause, A., Guestrin, C., Faloutsos, C., VanBriesen, J., Glance, N.: Cost-effective outbreak detection in networks. In: KDD 2007, pp. 420–429. ACM (2007)
29. Leskovec, J., Krevl, A.: SNAP datasets: stanford large network dataset collection, June 2014. http://snap.stanford.edu/data
30. Lucier, B., Oren, J., Singer, Y.: Influence at scale: distributed computation of complex contagion in networks. In: KDD 2015, pp. 735–744. ACM (2015)
31. Morris, S.: Contagion. Rev. Econ. Stud. **67**(1), 57–78 (2000). http://restud.oxford journals.org/content/67/1/57.abstract
32. Mossel, E., Roch, S.: Submodularity of influence in social networks: from local to global. SIAM J. Comput. **39**(6), 2176–2188 (2010)
33. Nguyen, H., Zheng, R.: Influence spread in large-scale social networks – a belief propagation approach. In: Flach, P.A., De Bie, T., Cristianini, N. (eds.) ECML PKDD 2012. LNCS, vol. 7524, pp. 515–530. Springer, Heidelberg (2012). https://doi.org/10.1007/978-3-642-33486-3_33
34. Paluck, E.L., Shepherd, H., Aronow, P.M.: Changing climates of conflict: a social network experiment in 56 schools. Proc. Nat. Acad. Sci. **113**(3), 566–571 (2016). http://www.pnas.org/content/113/3/566.abstract
35. Richardson, M., Domingos, P.: Mining knowledge-sharing sites for viral marketing. In: KDD 2012, pp. 61–70 (2002)
36. Romero, D.M., Meeder, B., Kleinberg, J.: Differences in the mechanics of information diffusion across topics : idioms, political hashtags, and complex contagion on twitter. In: WWW 2011. pp. 695–704. ACM (2011). http://dl.acm.org/citation.cfm?id=1963503
37. Schoenebeck, G., Tao, B.: Beyond worst-case (in)approximability of nonsubmodular influence maximization (2017). http://www-personal.umich.edu/bstao/
38. Seeman, L., Singer, Y.: Adaptive seeding in social networks. In: FOCS 2013, pp. 459–468. IEEE (2013)
39. Tang, Y., Xiao, X., Shi, Y.: Influence maximization: near-optimal time complexity meets practical efficiency. In: Proceedings of the 2014 ACM SIGMOD International Conference on Management of Data, pp. 75–86. ACM (2014)
40. Tullock, G.: Towards a theory of the rent-seeking society. In: chap. Efficient Rent Seeking. Texas A&M University Press (1980)
41. Wang, Y., Cong, G., Song, G., Xie, K.: Community-based greedy algorithm for mining top-k influential nodes in mobile social networks. In: Proceedings of the 16th ACM SIGKDD International Conference on Knowledge Discovery and Data Mining, pp. 1039–1048. ACM (2010)
42. Watts, D.J.: A simple model of global cascades on random networks. Proc. Nat. Acad. Sci. **99**(9), 5766–5771 (2002). http://www.pnas.org/content/99/5766.abstract

Information Retention in Heterogeneous Majority Dynamics

Vincenzo Auletta[1], Ioannis Caragiannis[2], Diodato Ferraioli[1(✉)],
Clemente Galdi[3], and Giuseppe Persiano[1]

[1] Università degli Studi di Salerno, Fisciano, Italy
{auletta,dferraioli}@unisa.it, giuper@gmail.com
[2] CTI "Diophantus", University of Patras, Patras, Greece
caragian@ceid.upatras.gr
[3] Università di Napoli "Federico II", Naples, Italy
clemente.galdi@unina.it

Abstract. A dynamics *retains* a specific information about the *starting* state of a networked multi-player system if this information can be computed from the state of the system also after several rounds of the dynamics. Information retention has been studied for the function that returns the majority of the states in systems in which players have states in $\{0,1\}$ and the system evolves according to the majority dynamics: each player repeatedly updates its state to match the local majority among neighbors only. Positive and negative results have been given for probabilistic settings in which the initial states of the players are chosen at random and in worst-case settings in which the initial state is chosen non-deterministically.

In this paper, we study the (lack of) retention of information on the majority state (that is, which states appear in more players) for a generalization of the majority dynamics that we call *heterogeneous* majority dynamics. Here, each player x changes its state from the initial state $\mathbf{b}(x) \in \{0,1\}$ to the opposite state $1 - \mathbf{b}(x)$ only if there is a surplus greater than a_x of neighbors that express that opinion. The non-negative player-dependent parameter a_x is called the *stubbornness* of x. We call *stubborn* the players which never change opinion when they are part of the majority. We give a complete characterization of the graphs that do not retain information about the starting majority; i.e., they admit a starting state for which the heterogeneous majority dynamics takes the system from a majority of 0's to a majority of 1's. We call this phenomenon *"minority becomes Majority"* (or mbM) and our main result shows that it occurs in all graphs provided that at least one player is non-stubborn. In other words, either no player in the majority will ever change its state (because they are all stubborn) or there is a starting configuration in which information regarding the majority is not retained and minority becomes Majority.

Our results are closely related to *discrete preference games*, a game-theoretic model of opinion formation in social networks: an interplay of internal belief (corresponding to the initial state of the player) and of

N. R. Devanur and P. Lu (Eds.): WINE 2017, LNCS 10674, pp. 30–43, 2017.
https://doi.org/10.1007/978-3-319-71924-5_3

social pressure (described by the heterogeneous majority dynamics). Our results show that, because of *local* strategic decisions, the *global* majority can be *subverted*.

1 Introduction

In this paper we study the *information retention* problem with respect to the *asynchronous heterogeneous majority dynamics*. In the *homogeneous majority dynamics* (or, simply, *majority dynamics*) players sit at the vertices of a *social graph*, each player starts with an opinion in $\{0, 1\}$ and repeatedly updates it to match the opinion of the majority of its neighbors. After some number of rounds, an election by majority takes place and we ask whether the *information* regarding the starting majority is *retained* in the election outcome, hence the name of *information retention*. To avoid ties it is assumed that the number of players is odd. The retention of information in majority dynamics has been studied in a probabilistic setting in which the initial opinions are independently conditioned on the majority and biased towards it. Positive and negative results have been given by [18] and, more recently, in [21] both for the *synchronous* model, in which all opinions are updated simultaneously, and the *asynchronous* model, in which at each round a single player updates her opinion. The retention of information in the majority dynamics in a worst-case setting has been first studied by Berger [9] that constructed a series of graphs in which the majority dynamics always results in the adoption of the opinions of the players in a small minority group. Actually, the phenomenon of a *minority becoming Majority* (or, the mbM phenomenon) is not restricted to some families of graphs but instead is a feature of the majority dynamics. Roughly speaking, every graph, except essentially for the complete graph and for the empty graph, admits an initial distribution of opinions which leads the minority opinion to become majority [3] (see also [6] for experimental results about this phenomenon).

Our contribution. In this paper we study the retention of information of majority in the worst-case (or the mbM phenomenon) for the asynchronous *heterogeneous* majority dynamics played on a graph G with vertices $\{1, \ldots, n\}$, each corresponding to a player with a binary state. In the *heterogeneous* majority dynamics, each player x is described by its *stubbornness* a_x that measures the willingness of the player to adopt (and keep) an opinion that differs from its initial opinion. More precisely, we distinguish between the *initial opinion* of a player x, called the *belief* $\mathbf{b}(x)$, and its *current opinion* $\mathbf{s}(x)$. The belief is internal to the player and is never explicitly revealed whereas the opinion is publicly known. A player x with belief $\mathbf{b}(x)$ can make a move from its current opinion $\mathbf{s}(x) = \mathbf{b}(x)$ to its revised opinion $\mathbf{s}(x) = 1 - \mathbf{b}(x)$ only if $d_{1-\mathbf{b}(x)}(x) - d_{\mathbf{b}(x)}(x) > a_x$ where, for $c = 0, 1$, d_c denotes the number of neighbors with opinion c. Similarly, x makes a move from $\mathbf{s}(x) = 1 - \mathbf{b}(x)$ to $\mathbf{s}(x) = \mathbf{b}(x)$ if $d_{1-\mathbf{b}(x)}(x) - d_{\mathbf{b}(x)}(x) \leq a_x$. A set of opinions is in *equilibrium* if no player can make a move.

We say that a pair $(G, (a_1, \ldots, a_n))$ consisting of a graph G (we assume that n is odd so that majority is well-defined) and stubbornness values for the players, is *subvertable* if there exist beliefs $(\mathbf{b}(1),\ldots,\mathbf{b}(n))$ with a majority of 0's and a sequence of moves that goes from the initial *truthful* state, in which $\mathbf{s}(x) = \mathbf{b}(x)$ for each vertex x, to an equilibrium state with a majority of 1's. We call such a belief assignment *subvertable*.

Our main contribution is a characterization of the subvertable pairs and shows that a pair $(G, (a_1,\ldots,a_n))$ is subvertable unless all players are *stubborn*. Roughly speaking, a stubborn player never changes its initial opinion if it happens to be in the starting majority. In order to formalize this definition, let us consider vertex x with $\mathbf{b}(x) = 0$ and $d_0(x)$ neighbors with opinion 0 and $d_1(x)$ neighbors with opinion 1, and suppose that the majority (that is at least $(n+1)/2$ vertices) has belief 0 (and, thus, $d_1(x) \leq (n-1)/2$). Clearly, if its degree $d(x)$ satisfies $d(x) \leq a_x$, then player x cannot make a move from $\mathbf{s}(x) = 0$ to $\mathbf{s}(x) = 1$. If $d(x) \geq n - a_x - 1$ then $d_1(x) - d_0(x) = 2d_1(x) - d(x) \leq n - 1 - d(x) \leq a_x$ and thus vertex x cannot make a move from $\mathbf{s}(x) = 0$ to $\mathbf{s}(x) = 1$. Instead, it is not hard to see that if $d(x) \in [a_x + 1, n - a_x - 2]$, there are values of $d_0(x)$ and $d_1(x)$ such that vertex x can move from $\mathbf{s}(x) = 0$ to $\mathbf{s}(x) = 1$ The same reasoning applies for vertices x with $\mathbf{b}(x) = 1$ in case majority is 1. We have thus the following definition.

Definition 1 (Stubborn vertex). *Vertex x with degree $d(x)$ and stubbornness a_x is stubborn if $a_x \geq \min\{d(x), n - d(x) - 1\}$.*

Clearly, if all vertices are stubborn then majority cannot be subverted as no vertex x in the majority will ever make a move from $\mathbf{s}(x) = \mathbf{b}(x)$ to $\mathbf{s}(x) = 1 - \mathbf{b}(x)$. The main result of this paper shows that:

if there is at least one non-stubborn vertex then there is a subvertable belief assignment.

We find that this sharp phase transition is highly surprising, since it implies that a minority could become majority (for some stubbornness levels) even in very dense graphs (e.g., clique minus a single edge) and in very sparse graphs (e.g., a graph consisting of a single edge plus isolated nodes). Hence, it highlights an interesting lack of robustness of social networks with respect to information retention. This weakness may be relevant to explain some phenomena arising on social media, such as the wide diffusion of misinformation.

To prove this result we design a polynomial-time algorithm that takes as input the social network G and players' stubbornness $a_1,\ldots,a_n$, such that there is at least one non-stubborn vertex, and returns a subvertable belief assignment for this instance. Actually, the algorithm considers the simplest belief assignment from which minority becomes Majority, namely one in which the minority consists of $\frac{n-1}{2}$ vertices. However, we remark that our characterization does not rule out that the subvertable belief assignment can have smaller minorities (even if there are instances on which only very large minorities can become majority, e.g. when there is a single non-stubborn vertex), and our algorithm can be adapted and optimized in order to find these minorities (see, e.g., [6]).

A possible interpretation of our result comes from a game theoretic model of how opinions are formed in societies (see the discussion on discrete preference games below). Within this context, the heterogeneous majority dynamics describes the social pressure on opinions expressed by the players in a social network. Our result shows that social networks are extremely vulnerable to social pressure since there always exists a subvertable majority unless all vertices are stubborn and never change their mind (in which case we do not have much of a social network). This is particularly negative as an external adversary might be able to orchestrate a sequence of steps of the underlying dynamics so as to reach the state in which majority is subverted. In principle, though, this could be very difficult since there could be different sequences of updates that lead to different equilibria with different majorities and the adversary has to be very careful in scheduling the best response moves.

Our characterization instead proves that, as long as we consider subvertable belief assignments with a minority of $\frac{n-1}{2}$ players, a stronger result is possible: there is always one single *swing* player whose best response in the initial state is to change its opinion and this leads to a state in which *any* sequence of moves leads to an equilibrium in which majority has been subverted. In other words, the adversary that wants to subvert the majority only has to influence the swing player and then the system will evolve without any further intervention towards an equilibrium in which majority is subverted. More precisely:

Definition 2. *A vertex u is said to be a* swing *vertex for subvertable belief assignment* **b** *with $\frac{n+1}{2}$ vertices with belief 0 if*

1. $\mathbf{b}(u) = 0$;
2. $d_1(u) - d_0(u) > a_u$, *that is, in the initial state, u can move from $\mathbf{s}(u) = 0$ to $\mathbf{s}(u) = 1$;*
3. *For every x with $\mathbf{b}(x) = 1$, it holds that $d'_x(0) - d'_x(1) \leq a_x$, where $d'_x(c)$ is the number of neighbors y of x with $\mathbf{s}(y) = c$ after u's move from $\mathbf{s}(u) = 0$ to $\mathbf{s}(u) = 1$. That is, after u's move no vertex with belief 1 can make a move from 1 to 0.*

Note that the definition above does not imply that the majority at equilibrium consists of only $\frac{n+1}{2}$ vertices with belief 1 (the initial $\frac{n-1}{2}$ plus the swing vertex). It may be indeed the case that other vertices with belief 0 will make moves from 0 to 1 after the move of the swing vertex u. Still, the third condition above implies that, after u's move, the number of vertices with opinion 1 is a majority and the size of this majority does not decrease.

Our main result then can be improved as follows:

if there exists at least one non-stubborn vertex, then there exists a subvertable belief assignment with a swing vertex.

It is natural to ask whether the characterization can be strengthened to take into account strong initial majorities (i.e., initial majorities of size at least $(1+\delta)\frac{n+1}{2}$ for some $0 < \delta < 1$). That is, to characterize the pairs (consisting of a social network and stubbornness levels) that admit at least a subvertable strong initial majority. We prove that no such characterization can be given by showing that there exists $\delta_{max} \approx 0.85$ such that for all $0 < \delta < \delta_{max}$ it is NP-hard to decide whether a given G and given stubbornness $a_1, \ldots, a_n$ admit a subvertable majority of size at least $(1 + \delta)\frac{n+1}{2}$. That is, unless $P = NP$,

no polynomial-time algorithm exists that characterizes subvertable belief assignments for large initial majorities.

Related work. The majority dynamics and its generalizations are related to a line of research in social sciences that tries to model how opinions are formed and expressed in a social context. A simple classical model has been proposed by Friedkin and Johnsen [16] (see also [14]). Its main assumption is that each individual has a private initial belief and that the opinion she eventually expresses is the result of a repeated averaging between her initial belief and the opinions expressed by other individuals with whom she has social relations. The recent work of Bindel et al. [12] assumes that initial beliefs and opinions belong to $[0, 1]$ and considers the dynamics that repeatedly averages the opinions of the neighbors.

Ferraioli et al. [15] and Chirichetti et al. [13] considered a variant of this model, named *discrete preference games*, in which beliefs and opinions are discrete. These games are directly connected to the work in this paper. For this reason, below we give a more formal description of the games, highlight the conceptual link with the heterogeneous majority dynamics and briefly discuss the significance of our results in this context.

Previous results about these games focused on the rate of convergence of the game under different dynamics [15], and on the price of stability and price of anarchy [13]. Moreover, extensions of the model have been proposed along two main directions: some works assume that connections between nodes evolve over time so that players with similar opinions are more likely to be connected [10,11]; other works consider dynamics that try to capture more complex social relations (e.g., to allies and competitors or among more than two players) [1,4].

The problem of majority retention has been recently investigated even with respect to different dynamics: e.g., in [17], various negative results are proved with respect to a 3-state population protocol introduced in [2]. Similar problems have also been considered in the distributed computing literature, motivated by the need to control and restrict the influence of failures in distributed systems; e.g., see the survey by Peleg [19] and the references therein.

Discrete preference games. A *discrete preference game* consists of a n-vertex undirected graph G (the social network), *coefficients* $\alpha_1, \ldots, \alpha_n \in (0, 1)$ and *beliefs* $\mathbf{b}(1), \ldots, \mathbf{b}(n) \in \{0, 1\}$. Player i's strategy set consists of two possible *opinions* $\mathbf{s}(i) \in \{0, 1\}$ and the cost $c_i(\mathbf{s})$ of player i in state $\mathbf{s} = (\mathbf{s}(1), \ldots, \mathbf{s}(n)) \in \{0, 1\}^n$ is defined as $c_i(\mathbf{s}) = \alpha_i \cdot |\mathbf{s}(i) - \mathbf{b}(i)| + (1 - \alpha_i) \cdot \sum_{j \in N(i)} |\mathbf{s}(i) - \mathbf{s}(j)|$, where $N(i)$ is the set of neighbors of vertex i in G (i.e., friends in the social network). Note that the cost is the convex combination through α_i of two components that depend on whether the opinion coincides with the belief and on the strategies of the neighbors, respectively, and this models players that try to balance social acceptance (which would make the player pick the opinion that is the majority among its neighbors) and faithfulness to her own principles (which would make the player pick opinion equal to belief). Different values of α_i correspond to the different individual behaviors and reflect the heterogeneity of the society.

An *equilibrium* state is defined to be a state $\mathbf{s} = (\mathbf{s}(1), \ldots, \mathbf{s}(n))$ for which there is no player i whose best response is to adopt strategy $1 - \mathbf{s}(i)$. More precisely, $\mathbf{s}$ is an *equilibrium* if for all i $c_i(\mathbf{s}) \leq c_i(1 - \mathbf{s}(i), \mathbf{s}_{-i})$, where we have used the standard game theoretic notation by which $(t, \mathbf{s}_{-i})$ denotes the vector $(\mathbf{s}(1), \ldots, \mathbf{s}(i-1), t, \mathbf{s}(i+1), \ldots, \mathbf{s}(n))$.

It is not difficult to see that the best-response dynamics of a discrete preference game with stubbornness coefficients $\alpha_1, \ldots, \alpha_n \in (0, 1)$ coincides with the heterogeneous majority dynamics with stubbornness $a_1, \ldots, a_n$ where $a_x = \left\lfloor \frac{\alpha_x}{1 - \alpha_x} \right\rfloor$. The fact that the heterogeneous majority dynamics does not retain information about the majority state in the belief of the players translates to the possibility that the social network will express through opinions a majority that differs from the majority of the beliefs. It is thus possible that the *local* behavior of the players affects the *global* behavior of the network and that the social pressure felt by individual members of a social network has effects on the entire network.

2   Definitions and Overview

In this section we introduce the concepts of a bisection and of a good bisection and give an overview of the proof of our main result. Due to page limit most of the proofs are omitted. We refer the reader to the full version [5].

Good bisections yield subvertable belief assignments. A *bisection* $\mathcal{S} = (S, \overline{S})$ of a graph G with an odd number n of vertices is a partition of the vertices of G into two sets S and $\overline{S}$ of cardinality $\frac{n+1}{2}$ and $\frac{n-1}{2}$, respectively. We define the *advantage* $\mathsf{adv}_{\mathcal{S}}(x)$ of a vertex x with respect to bisection $\mathcal{S} = (S, \overline{S})$ as follows:

$$\mathsf{adv}_{\mathcal{S}}(x) = \begin{cases} W(x, S) - W(x, \overline{S}), & \text{if } x \in S; \\ W(x, \overline{S}) - W(x, S), & \text{if } x \in \overline{S}, \end{cases}$$

where $W(x, A)$ denotes the number of neighbors of x in the set A.

We say that a bisection $\mathcal{S} = (S, \overline{S})$ is *good* if

1. for every $x \in S$, $\mathsf{adv}_{\mathcal{S}}(x) \geq -a_x$;
2. there is $u \in S$ with $\mathsf{adv}_{\mathcal{S}}(u) \geq a_u + 1$.

Vertices $u \in S$ with $\mathsf{adv}_{\mathcal{S}}(u) \geq a_u + 1$ are called the *good vertices* of $\mathcal{S}$ and vertices $y \in S$ with $\mathsf{adv}_{\mathcal{S}}(y) < -a_y$ are called the *obstructions* of $\mathcal{S}$. The next lemma proves that if G has a good bisection then one can easily construct a subvertable belief assignment for G.

Lemma 1. *Let $S = (S, \overline{S})$ be a good bisection for graph G and let u be a good vertex of S. Then G admits a subvertable belief assignment $\mathbf{b}$ such that u is a swing vertex for $\mathbf{b}$.*

Minimal bisections. The technical core of our proof is the construction of a good bisection starting from a bisection S of minimal potential Φ. We define the *potential* Φ of a bisection $(S, \overline{S})$ as $\Phi(S, \overline{S}) = W(S, \overline{S}) + \frac{1}{2}\left(\sum_{x \in S} a_x - \sum_{y \in \overline{S}} a_y\right)$. We say that a bisection S has *k-minimal* potential if S minimizes the potential among all the bisections that can be obtained from S by swapping at most k vertices between S and $\overline{S}$. That is, S has *k-minimal* potential if, for all $A \subseteq S$ and for all $B \subseteq \overline{S}$, with $1 \leq |A| = |B| \leq k$, $\Phi(S, \overline{S}) \leq \Phi(S \backslash A \cup B, \overline{S} \backslash B \cup A)$. We will simply write that S has minimal potential whenever S has 1-minimal potential.

The next lemma proves some useful properties of minimal bisections.

Lemma 2. *Let $S = (S, \overline{S})$ be a bisection of minimal potential. Then for all $x \in S$ and $y \in \overline{S}$, $\mathsf{adv}_S(x) + \mathsf{adv}_S(y) + 2W(x, y) \geq a_x - a_y$.*

Swapping vertices. To turn a minimal bisection S into a good bisection $T = (T, \overline{T})$, we need at least one vertex in T with high advantage. One way to increase the advantage of a vertex $u \in S$ is to move vertices that are not adjacent to u away from S and to bring the same number of vertices that are adjacent to u into S. We define the *rank* of a vertex u with respect to bisection S as $\mathsf{rank}_S(u) = \left\lceil \frac{a_u + 1 - \mathsf{adv}_S(u)}{2}\right\rceil$. It is not hard to see that the rank is exactly the number of vertices that need to be moved. Note that a vertex u of $\mathsf{rank}_S(u)$ has advantage $\mathsf{adv}_S(u)$ such that $a_u - 2\mathsf{rank}_S(u) + 1 \leq \mathsf{adv}_S(u) \leq a_u - 2\mathsf{rank}_S(u) + 2$. We next formalize the notion of swapping of vertices and prove that it is always possible to increase the advantage of a non-stubborn vertex x to $a_x + 1$.

Given a bisection $S = (S, \overline{S})$ and a vertex u, a *u-pair* for S is a pair of sets (A_u, B_u) such that:

- if $u \in S$, then $A_u \subseteq S \cap \overline{N}(u)$ and $B_u \subseteq \overline{S} \cap N(u)$ with $|A_u| = |B_u| = \mathsf{rank}_S(u)$;
- if $u \in \overline{S}$, then $A_u \subseteq S \cap N(u)$ and $B_u \subseteq \overline{S} \cap \overline{N}(u)$ with $|A_u| = \mathsf{rank}_S(u)$ and $|B_u| = \mathsf{rank}_S(u) - 1$.

The bisection T *associated* with the u-pair (A_u, B_u) for S is defined as

- if $u \in S$, $T = (S \backslash A_u \cup B_u, \overline{S} \backslash B_u \cup A_u)$;
- if $u \in \overline{S}$, $T = (\overline{S} \backslash B_u \cup A_u, S \backslash A_u \cup B_u)$.

Note that our choice for the size of A_u and B_u implies that in both cases $|T| = \frac{n+1}{2}$ as desired. The next lemma shows that u is a good vertex in the bisection associated with a u-pair.

Lemma 3. *For each bisection S, let u be a vertex of the graph, (A_u, B_u) be a u-pair for S, and T be the bisection associated to (A_u, B_u). Then $\mathsf{adv}_T(u) \geq a_u + 1$.*

The problem now is to understand which vertex we have to choose for making it good. The next lemma says that stubborn vertices cannot be good vertices. But they are sort of neutral: indeed, they cannot be obstructions either.

Lemma 4. *For every bisection* $\mathcal{S} = (S, \overline{S})$ *and every stubborn vertex* $x \in S$ *it holds that* $-a_x \leq \mathsf{adv}_{\mathcal{S}}(x) \leq a_x$.

However, for every bisection $\mathcal{S}$ and every vertex u, a u-pair for $\mathcal{S}$ exists if and only if vertex u is non-stubborn, as showed by the next lemma.

Lemma 5. *For every bisection* $\mathcal{S} = (S, \overline{S})$ *and every vertex* u, *a* u-*pair for* $\mathcal{S}$ *exists if and only if* u *is non-stubborn.*

Hence, if there is a non-stubborn vertex u, there is a u-pair (A_u, B_u) for S, and u is certainly a good vertex for the bisection $\mathcal{T}$ associated to this u-pair. Therefore, if $\mathcal{T}$ is not good then it must be that there is a vertex y that is an obstruction for $\mathcal{T}$. In the last case, we will say that the vertex u, the u-pair (A_u, B_u) and the bisection $\mathcal{T}$ are *obstructed* by y. Most of the proof will be devoted to dealing with these obstructions.

3   Main Theorem

Our main result is the following.

Theorem 1. *Every graph* G *with an odd number of vertices and at least one non-stubborn vertex has a subvertable belief assignment* **b** *and a swing vertex* u *for* **b**. *Moreover,* **b** *and* u *can be computed in polynomial time.*

We prove the theorem by exhibiting a polynomial-time algorithm (see Algorithm 1) that, given a graph G with an odd number of vertices, and at least one of which that is non-stubborn, returns a good bisection $\mathcal{S}$ and a good vertex u for $\mathcal{S}$. The theorem then follows from Lemma 1.

Input: A graph $G = (V, E)$ with $|V|$ odd and at least one non-stubborn vertex
Output: A pair $(\mathcal{S}, u)$ where $\mathcal{S}$ is a good bisection and u is its good vertex
1 $\mathcal{S} = (S, \overline{S})$ is a bisection of G of 3-minimal potential
2 $M =$ non-stubborn vertices of minimum rank in $\mathcal{S}$
3 **if** *there is* $u \in S$ *with* $\mathsf{adv}_{\mathcal{S}}(u) \leq -a_u - 1$ **then**
4   Let $\mathcal{T} = (\overline{S} \cup \{u\}, S \setminus \{u\})$
5   **return** $(\mathcal{T}, u)$
6 **if** *there is* $u \in S$ *with* $\mathsf{adv}_{\mathcal{S}}(u) \geq a_u + 1$ **then**
7   **return** $(\mathcal{S}, u)$
8 **if** *there is* $u \in \overline{S}$ *with* $\mathsf{adv}_{\mathcal{S}}(u) \geq a_u + 1$ **then**
9   Pick $w \in S$ and let $\mathcal{T} = (\overline{S} \cup \{w\}, S \setminus \{w\})$
10   **return** $(\mathcal{T}, u)$
11 **if** *there is* $u \in S \cap M$ *with* $\mathsf{adv}_{\mathcal{S}}(u) < 0$ **then**
12   Let $\mathcal{S}' = (\overline{S} \cup \{u\}, S \setminus \{u\})$
13   Pick u-pair (A_u, B_u) for $\mathcal{S}'$
14   Let $\mathcal{T}$ be the associated bisection
15   **return** $(\mathcal{T}, u)$
16 **if** $M \cap \overline{S} \neq \emptyset$ **then return** $\mathtt{MinRankInNotS}(\mathcal{S})$
17 **else return** $\mathtt{MinRankInS}(\mathcal{S})$

Algorithm 1. Returns a good bisection and a good vertex

First, we note that the algorithm runs in time that is polynomial in the size of the input. Indeed, a bisection of 3-minimal potential at Line 1 can be efficiently computed through a local search algorithm [20], and all remaining steps only involve computationally easy tasks.

Next we prove that the algorithm is correct; that is, it outputs $(\mathcal{T}, u)$ where $\mathcal{T}$ is a good bisection and u is a good vertex for $\mathcal{T}$. Recall that, by Lemma 4, it is sufficient to check that $\mathsf{adv}_\mathcal{T}(u) \geq a_u + 1$ and that non-stubborn vertices $x \in S$ have $\mathsf{adv}_\mathcal{T}(x) \geq -a_x$.

The analysis of the algorithm can be divided in three parts: the warm-up cases, i.e., if Algorithm 1 stops before reaching Line 16; the case there is a non-stubborn vertex $u \in \overline{S}$ of minimum rank; and the case that every non-stubborn vertex u of minimum rank belongs to S. Due to the page limit, we only sketch the proof for the last and most interesting case, i.e. when the algorithm invokes procedure MinRankInS (described in the full version of the paper [5]).

Suppose then that the algorithm invokes procedure MinRankInS. In this case, all non-stubborn vertices of minimum rank belong to S. Moreover, all such vertices have non-negative advantage for otherwise the Algorithm would have stopped at Line 15.

Clearly, if MinRankInS stops at Line 5, Line 18, Line 26, Line 32, Line 39 or Line 49, then the bisection output is good and u is a good vertex for it.

Suppose now that MinRankInS stops at Line 9, Line 30, Line 36, Line 44, Line 47 or at Line 52. Since in all cases the algorithm returns a pair $(\mathcal{T}, v)$ where $\mathcal{T}$ is the bisection associated to a v-pair, then, by Lemma 3, $\mathsf{adv}_\mathcal{T}(v) \geq a_v + 1$. Thus, we only need to prove that $\mathsf{adv}_\mathcal{T}(x) \geq -a_x$ for every non-stubborn $x \in \mathcal{T}$.

3.1 Properties of the Obstructions

Most of the work will be devoted to dealing with obstructions. Therefore, before proceeding, we give some useful properties of the obstructions, whose proof can be found in the full version.

Lemma 6. *Let $u \in \overline{S}$ be a vertex of minimum rank for the bisection S and let y be an obstruction for u. Then $y \in \overline{S}$. Similarly, let $u \in S$ be a vertex of minimum rank for the bisection S and assume there is no vertex of minimum rank in $\overline{S}$. If y is an obstruction for u, then $y \in S$.*

Lemma 7. *Let S be a bisection and let u be a vertex of minimum rank in $\overline{S}$. Let $\mathcal{T}$ be the bisection associated with a u-pair (A_u, B_u) for S. If vertex y is an obstruction for $\mathcal{T}$, then $\mathsf{adv}_S(y) \leq -a_y + 2\mathsf{rank}_S(u) - 3$. Moreover, for every non-stubborn $v \in S$ if $\mathsf{adv}_S(v) + \mathsf{adv}_S(y) + 2W(v, y) \geq a_v - a_y$, then v is adjacent to y, v has minimum rank and $\mathsf{adv}_S(y) \geq -a_y + 2\mathsf{rank}_S(u) - 4$.*

Lemma 8. *Let S be a bisection and suppose that there is no vertex in $\overline{S}$ with minimum rank. Let u be a vertex of minimum rank in S. Let $\mathcal{T}$ be the bisection associated with a u-pair (A_u, B_u) for S. Suppose there is an obstruction y for $\mathcal{T}$ with $\mathsf{adv}_S(y) < 0$ and $\mathsf{rank}_S(y) > \mathsf{rank}_S(u)$. Let $S' = (\overline{S} \cup \{y\}, S \setminus \{y\})$. Then $\mathsf{rank}_{S'}(y) \leq \mathsf{rank}_S(u)$.*

Lemma 9. *Let S be a bisection and let u be a vertex of minimum rank in S. Let T be the bisection associated with a u-pair (A_u, B_u) for S. Suppose there is an obstruction y for T with $\mathsf{adv}_S(y) \geq 0$. Then y has minimum rank $\ell = \left\lceil \frac{a_y+1}{2} \right\rceil$ and $\mathsf{adv}_S(y) = 0$.*

3.2 MinRankInS stops at Line 9

In this case, we have that u is a vertex of S with minimum rank ℓ. Vertex y is an obstruction of bisection T associated with u-pair (A_u, B_u), and $\mathsf{adv}_S(y) < 0$. By Lemma 6, $y \in S$. Observe that $\mathsf{rank}_S(y) > \ell$, for otherwise Algorithm 1 would have stopped at Line 15. From Lemma 8, we obtain that $\mathsf{rank}_{S_0}(y) \leq \ell$. We remind the reader that $S_0 = (\overline{S} \cup \{y\}, S \backslash \{y\})$ and $T_0 = (\overline{S} \cup \{y\} \backslash A_y \cup B_y, S \backslash \{y\} \cup A_y \backslash B_y)$.

For every non-stubborn $x \in T_0 \backslash \{y\}$, $\mathsf{adv}_T(x)$ can be written as: $W(x, \overline{S}) - W(x, S) + 2W(x, y) - 2W(x, A_y) + 2W(x, B_y)$.

If $x \in \overline{S} \backslash A_y$, then

$$\begin{aligned}
\mathsf{adv}_T(x) &= \mathsf{adv}_S(x) + 2W(x, y) - 2W(x, A_y) + 2W(x, B_y) \\
&\geq \mathsf{adv}_S(x) + 2W(x, y) - 2|A_y| \\
&= \mathsf{adv}_S(x) + 2W(x, y) - 2\mathsf{rank}_{S'}(y) \geq \mathsf{adv}_S(x) + 2W(x, y) - 2\ell.
\end{aligned}$$

Since $\mathsf{rank}_S(y) > \ell$, then $\mathsf{adv}_S(y) \leq a_y - 2\ell$. By applying Lemma 2 to $y \in S$ and $x \in \overline{S}$ we obtain that $\mathsf{adv}_S(x) + 2W(x, y) \geq -\mathsf{adv}_S(y) + a_y - a_x \geq -a_x + 2\ell$. Hence $\mathsf{adv}_T(x) \geq -a_x$.

Finally, if $x \in B_y$, then $x \in S$ and, by definition of y-pair, $W(x, y) = 1$. Therefore we have

$$\begin{aligned}
\mathsf{adv}_T(x) &= -\mathsf{adv}_S(x) + 2W(x, y) - 2W(x, A_y) + 2W(x, B_y) \\
&\geq -\mathsf{adv}_S(x) - 2W(x, A_y) + 2 \\
&\geq -\mathsf{adv}_S(x) - 2\mathsf{rank}_{S'}(y) + 2 \geq -\mathsf{adv}_S(x) - 2\ell + 2
\end{aligned}$$

Since ℓ is the minimum rank, it must be the case that $\mathsf{rank}_S(x) \geq \ell$ which implies that $\mathsf{adv}_S(x) \leq a_x + 2 - 2\ell$. Therefore, $\mathsf{adv}_T(x) \geq -a_x$.

3.3 MinRankInS reaches Line 19

We remind the reader that in this case $u \in S$ is a non-stubborn vertex of minimum rank ℓ and y is an obstruction to bisection T associated with u-pair (A_u, B_u) for S. By Lemma 6, $y \in S$. Note also that $\mathsf{adv}_S(y) \geq 0$, for otherwise MinRankInS would have stopped at Line 9. From Lemma 9, it then follows that $\mathsf{adv}_S(y) = 0$ and $\mathsf{rank}_S(y) = \ell = \left\lceil \frac{a_y+1}{2} \right\rceil$. Moreover, given a y-pair (A_y, B_y) of $S_1 = (\overline{S} \cup \{y\}, S \backslash \{y\})$, y_1 is either a vertex of $(\overline{S} \cup \{y\} \backslash A_y) \cap \overline{N}(y)$ with $\mathsf{adv}_S(w) = a_y - a_{y_1}$ or it is an obstruction to bisection T_1 associated with this pair. Note that, by Lemma 6, even in this last case $y_1 \in \overline{S} \cup \{y\} \backslash A_y$.

Properties of y and y_1. We need to state some properties of y and y_1 before proving that the bisections returned by MinRankInS after Line 19 are good.

Lemma 10. $W(y, y_1) = 0$.

Lemma 11. If $\mathsf{adv}_S(y_1) \neq a_y - a_{y_1}$, then a_y is even and $\mathsf{adv}_S(y_1) = a_y - a_{y_1} + 1$.

Lemma 12. If $\mathsf{adv}_S(y_1) \neq a_y - a_{y_1}$, then $\mathsf{adv}_S(w) \geq a_y - a_w + 1 - W(w, y)$ for every $w \in \overline{S}$.

Lemma 13. $\mathsf{rank}_{S_2}(y) = \mathsf{rank}_{S_2}(y_1) = \ell$.

Lemma 14. For every $u \in S_2$ and every $v \in \overline{S}_2 \backslash \{y\}$, we have that if $\mathsf{adv}_S(y_1) = a_y - a_{y_1}$ or $u = y_1$, then $\mathsf{adv}_{S_2}(u) + \mathsf{adv}_{S_2}(v) + 2W(u, v) \geq a_u - a_v$, else $\mathsf{adv}_{S_2}(u) + \mathsf{adv}_{S_2}(v) + 2W(u, v) = a_u - a_v + c + 2W(y, v) + 2W(u, y_1) - 2W(u, y) - 2W(v, y_1)$, for $c \geq \max\{0, 2W(u, v) - 2W(y_1, u) - W(y, v)\}$.

Lemma 15. For every $u \in S \backslash \{y_1\}$ and $v \in \overline{S} \backslash \{y\}$, if $W(u, y) = 1$ and $W(u, y_1) = 0$, then $\mathsf{adv}_{S_2}(u) + \mathsf{adv}_{S_2}(v) + 2W(u, v) \geq a_u - a_v - 1$.

`MinRankInS` **stops at Line 30.** Therefore there is $v \in S_2$, whose rank in S_2 is less than $\mathsf{rank}_{S_2}(y) = \ell$. Note that, since $\mathsf{adv}_{S_2}(v) = \mathsf{adv}_S(v) + 2W(v, y_1) - 2W(v, y)$,

$$
\begin{aligned}
\mathsf{rank}_{S_2}(v) &= \left\lceil \frac{a_v + 1 - \mathsf{adv}_S(v) - 2W(v, y_1) + 2W(v, y)}{2} \right\rceil \\
&= \left\lceil \frac{a_v + 1 - \mathsf{adv}_S(v)}{2} \right\rceil - W(v, y_1) + W(v, y) \\
&= \mathsf{rank}_S(v) - W(v, y_1) + W(v, y).
\end{aligned}
$$

Hence, $\mathsf{rank}_{S_2}(v) < \ell$ if and only if $\mathsf{rank}_S(v) = \ell$ (that is, v has minimum rank in S), $W(v, y_1) = 1$ and $W(v, y) = 0$. From this we obtain that for every vertex v with $\mathsf{rank}_{S_2}(v) < \ell$, it holds that $\mathsf{adv}_S(v) \geq 0$ (since v has minimum rank in S and no vertex of minimum rank in S with negative advantage can exist, otherwise a good bisection was returned at Line 15 of Algorithm 1), and, $\mathsf{adv}_{S_2}(v) \geq 2$. We also observe that every vertex $x \in \overline{S}_2 = \overline{S} \cup \{y\} \backslash \{y_1\}$ has $\mathsf{rank}_{S_2}(x) \geq \ell$. If $x = y$, then this follows from Lemma 13. If $x \neq y$, then it follows since $\mathsf{rank}_S(x) \geq \ell + 1$, and the rank decreases of at most one when two vertices are swapped.

Moreover, if `MinRankInS` stops at Line 30, then the bisection $\mathcal{T}_2$ associated to v-pair (A_v, B_v) for S_2 has an obstruction y_2. By Lemma 6, $y_2 \in S_2 \backslash A_v$. Suppose that $\mathsf{adv}_{S_2}(y_2) \geq 0$, then, from Lemma 9, it follows that $\mathsf{adv}_{S_2}(y_2) = 0$ and has minimum rank, i.e., $\mathsf{rank}_{S_2}(y_2) = \ell - 1$. However, this is a contradiction, since we showed that if $\mathsf{rank}_{S_2}(y_2) = \ell - 1$, then $\mathsf{adv}_{S_2}(y_2) \geq 2$.

It must be then the case that $\mathsf{adv}_{S_2}(y_2) < 0$ and $\mathsf{rank}_{S_2}(y_2) \geq \ell$. Then, by Lemma 8, $\mathsf{rank}_{S_3}(y_2) \leq \ell - 1$, where $S_3 = (\overline{S}_2 \cup \{y_2\}, S_2 \cup \{y_2\})$. It must be also the case that either $\mathsf{rank}_S(y_2) \geq \ell + 1$ or $\mathsf{rank}_S(y_2) = \ell$, $W(y_2, y) = 1$ and $W(y_2, y_1) = 0$. Indeed, $\mathsf{rank}_S(y_2) \geq \ell$, since ℓ is the minimum rank in S. If $\mathsf{rank}_S(y_2) = \ell$, then $\mathsf{adv}_S(y_2) \geq 0$. Thus, if $W(y_2, y) = 0$ and $W(y_2, y_1) = 1$, then $\mathsf{rank}_{S_2}(y_2) = \ell - 1$, a contradiction. If $W(y_2, y) = W(y_2, y_1)$, then $\mathsf{adv}_{S_2}(y_2) = \mathsf{adv}_S(y_2) \geq 0$, still a contradiction.

We now can prove that the bisection $\mathcal{T}_3$ returned at Line 30 is good. Recall that $\mathcal{T}_3$ is associated to y_2-pair (A_{y_2}, B_{y_2}) for $\mathcal{S}_3$, i.e., $\mathcal{T}_3 = (\overline{S}_2 \cup \{y_2\} \backslash A_{y_2} \cup B_{y_2}, S_2 \backslash \{y_2\} \cup A_{y_2} \backslash B_{y_2})$, where $|A_{y_2}| = |B_{y_2}| = \mathsf{rank}_{\mathcal{S}_3}(y_2) \leq \ell - 1$.

We first prove that for every $x \in \overline{S}_2 \cup \{y_2\} \backslash A_{y_2}$, we have that $\mathsf{adv}_{\mathcal{T}_3}(x) \geq -a_x$. If $x \neq y$, we distinguish two cases. If $\mathsf{rank}_{\mathcal{S}}(y_2) \geq \ell+1$, then by applying Lemma 2 to $y_2 \in S$ and $x \in \overline{S}$, we have that $\mathsf{adv}_{\mathcal{S}}(x) + 2W(x, y_2) \geq -\mathsf{adv}_{\mathcal{S}}(y_2) + a_{y_2} - a_x \geq -a_x + 2\ell$, where we used that $\mathsf{rank}_{\mathcal{S}}(y_2) \geq \ell + 1$ and thus $\mathsf{adv}_{\mathcal{S}}(y_2) \leq a_{y_2} - 2\ell$. Then, $\mathsf{adv}_{\mathcal{S}_2}(x) = \mathsf{adv}_{\mathcal{S}}(x) + 2W(x, y) - 2W(x, y_1) \geq -a_x + 2\ell - 2$. If $\mathsf{rank}_{\mathcal{S}}(y_2) < \ell + 1$, then, as stated above, it must be the case that $\mathsf{rank}_{\mathcal{S}}(y) = \ell$, $W(y_2, y) = 1$ and $W(y_2, y_1) = 0$. Then, from Lemma 15, it holds that $\mathsf{adv}_{\mathcal{S}_2}(x) + 2W(x, y_2) \geq -\mathsf{adv}_{\mathcal{S}_2}(y_2) + a_{y_2} - a_x - 1 \geq -a_x + 2\ell - 1$, where we used that $\mathsf{rank}_{\mathcal{S}_2}(y_2) = \mathsf{rank}_{\mathcal{S}}(y_2) + 1 = \ell + 1$ and thus $\mathsf{adv}_{\mathcal{S}}(y_2) \leq a_{y_2} - 2\ell$.

Hence, in both cases, we have $\mathsf{adv}_{\mathcal{T}_3}(x) \geq \mathsf{adv}_{\mathcal{S}_3}(x) - 2W(x, A_{y_2}) \geq \mathsf{adv}_{\mathcal{S}_2}(x) + 2W(x, y_2) - 2(\ell - 1) \geq -a_x + 2\ell - 1 - 2(\ell - 1) \geq -a_x + 1$. If $x = y$, then, by using that $\mathsf{adv}_{\mathcal{S}_2}(y) = -\mathsf{adv}_{\mathcal{S}}(y)$ since $W(y, y_1) = 0$, we have $\mathsf{adv}_{\mathcal{T}_3}(y) \geq \mathsf{adv}_{\mathcal{S}_3}(y) - 2(\ell - 1) = \mathsf{adv}_{\mathcal{S}_2}(y) + 2W(y, y_2) - 2(\ell - 1) = -\mathsf{adv}_{\mathcal{S}}(y) + 2W(y, y_2) - 2(\ell - 1)$. We showed above that $\mathsf{adv}_{\mathcal{S}}(y) = 0$ and $\ell = \left\lceil \frac{a_y + 1}{2} \right\rceil \leq \frac{a_y + 2}{2}$. Hence, $\mathsf{adv}_{\mathcal{T}_3}(y) \geq -a_y + 2W(y, y_2) \geq -a_y$.

Finally, we prove that for all $x \in B_{y_2}$, $\mathsf{adv}_{\mathcal{T}_3}(x) \geq -a_x$. Recall that $B_{y_2} \subseteq S_2 \backslash \{y_2\}$ and $W(x, y_2) = 1$ for all $x \in B_{y_2}$. We have two cases. If $x \neq y_1$, then $\mathsf{adv}_{\mathcal{T}_3}(x) \geq -\mathsf{adv}_{\mathcal{S}_3}(x) - 2(\ell - 1) = -\mathsf{adv}_{\mathcal{S}_2}(x) + 2W(x, y_2) - 2(\ell - 1) = -\mathsf{adv}_{\mathcal{S}}(x) + 2W(x, y) - 2W(x, y_1) - 2(\ell - 2) \geq -a_x + 2\ell - 2 + 2W(x, y) - 2W(x, y_1) + 2 - 2(\ell - 1) \geq -a_x$, where we used that $\mathsf{rank}_{\mathcal{S}}(x) \geq \ell$ and thus $\mathsf{adv}_{\mathcal{S}}(x) \leq a_x - 2\ell + 2$. If $x = y_1$, then $\mathsf{adv}_{\mathcal{T}_3}(y_1) \geq -\mathsf{adv}_{\mathcal{S}_3}(y_1) - 2(\ell - 1) = -\mathsf{adv}_{\mathcal{S}_2}(y_1) + 2W(y_1, y_2) - 2(\ell - 1) = \mathsf{adv}_{\mathcal{S}}(y_1) + 2 - 2(\ell - 1)$, where we used that $\mathsf{adv}_{\mathcal{S}_2}(y_1) = -\mathsf{adv}_{\mathcal{S}}(y_1)$ since $W(y, y_1) = 0$ and $W(y_1, y_2) = 1$ because $y_1 \in B_{y_2}$. Since $\mathsf{adv}_{\mathcal{S}}(y_1) \geq a_y - a_{y_1} \geq 2(\ell - 1) - a_{y_1}$, then $\mathsf{adv}_{\mathcal{T}_3}(y_1) \geq -a_{y_1} + 2 \geq -a_{y_1}$.

MinRankInS stops at Line 36. In this case y and y_1 have minimum rank in $\mathcal{S}_2$ and there is a vertex $w \in S \backslash \{y\} \cup \{y_1\}$ of minimum rank ℓ and negative advantage in $\mathcal{S}_2$. Note that if $\mathsf{rank}_{\mathcal{S}_2}(w) \leq \mathsf{rank}_{\mathcal{S}}(w)$, then $\mathsf{adv}_{\mathcal{S}_2}(w) \geq \mathsf{adv}_{\mathcal{S}}(w)$. Thus, since in $\mathcal{S}$ all vertices of minimum rank have non-negative advantage, it must be the case that $\mathsf{rank}_{\mathcal{S}}(w) = \ell + 1$, and $W(w, y) = 0$ and $W(w, y_1) = 1$. Thus the w-pair defined at Line 35 can be constructed.

Consider now the bisection $\mathcal{S}_4$ defined at Line 34. Observe that $\mathsf{adv}_{\mathcal{S}_4}(w) = -\mathsf{adv}_{\mathcal{S}_2}(w)$ and therefore

$$\mathsf{rank}_{\mathcal{S}_4}(w) = \left\lceil \frac{a_w + 1 - \mathsf{adv}_{\mathcal{S}_4}(w)}{2} \right\rceil = \left\lceil \frac{a_w + 1 + \mathsf{adv}_{\mathcal{S}_4}(w)}{2} \right\rceil - \mathsf{adv}_{\mathcal{S}_4}(w)$$

$$= \left\lceil \frac{a_w + 1 - \mathsf{adv}_{\mathcal{S}_2}(w)}{2} \right\rceil + \mathsf{adv}_{\mathcal{S}_2}(w) = \mathsf{rank}_{\mathcal{S}_2}(w) + \mathsf{adv}_{\mathcal{S}_2}(w),$$

that is at most $\ell - 1$ since w has rank ℓ and negative advantage in $\mathcal{S}_2$.

Now, for every $x \in \overline{S}_2 \backslash A_w$, we have $\mathsf{adv}_{\mathcal{T}_5}(x) \geq \mathsf{adv}_{\mathcal{S}_2}(x) + 2W(x, w) - 2\mathsf{rank}_{\mathcal{S}_4}(w) \geq -\mathsf{adv}_{\mathcal{S}_2}(w) + a_w - a_x - 2(\ell - 1)$, where we used that, by Lemma 14, $\mathsf{adv}_{\mathcal{S}_2}(x) + 2W(x, w) \geq -\mathsf{adv}_{\mathcal{S}_2}(w) + a_w - a_x + 2W(y, x) + 2W(w, y_1) - 2W(w, y) -$

$2W(x, y_1) \geq -\mathsf{adv}_{\mathcal{S}_2}(w) + a_w - a_x$. Since $\mathsf{rank}_{\mathcal{S}_2}(w) = \ell$, then $\mathsf{adv}_{\mathcal{S}_2}(w) \leq a_w - 2\ell + 2$, from which we achieve that $\mathsf{adv}_{\mathcal{T}_5}(x) \geq -a_x$.

Finally, take $x \in B_w \subseteq S_2$. We have $\mathsf{adv}_{\mathcal{T}_5}(x) \geq -\mathsf{adv}_{\mathcal{S}_2}(x) - 2\mathsf{rank}_{\mathcal{S}_4}(w) \geq -\mathsf{adv}_{\mathcal{S}_2}(x) - 2(\ell - 1)$. However, by hypothesis, w has minimum rank among the non-stubborn vertices and thus it must be the case that $\mathsf{rank}_{\mathcal{S}_2}(x) \geq \mathsf{rank}_{\mathcal{S}_2}(w) = \ell$ which implies that $\mathsf{adv}_{\mathcal{S}_2}(x) \leq a_x - 2\ell + 2$. Therefore, $\mathsf{adv}_{\mathcal{T}}(x) \geq -a_x$.

There is still a missing case, for which we refer the reader to the full version.

4   Lower Bound

We next show that deciding if it is possible to subvert the majority when starting from a weaker minority is a computationally hard problem, even if we start with a minority of size very close to $\frac{n-1}{2}$. The main result of this section is given by the following theorem.

Theorem 2. *For every constant $0 < \varepsilon < \frac{133}{155}$, it is NP-hard to decide whether in a graph G with n vertices there exists a subvertable belief assignment with at most $\frac{n-1}{2}(1 - \varepsilon)$ vertices in the initial minority.*

The proof of Theorem 2 uses essentially the same gadgets as a similar proof in [3], but tuned for the current setting.

5   Open Problems

While this work proves information retention for the heterogeneous majority dynamics in unweighted social network when only one player is allowed to update her state at each time step, it would be interesting to understand what happens if one considers weighted graphs or concurrent updates. Preliminary experimental results along this direction have been given in [6]. It would be also interesting to investigate the extent at which the mbM phenomenon occurs if one considers noisy variants of the heterogeneous majority dynamics, see, e.g., [7,8]. Finally, one can be interested in understanding how probable the minority becomes majority phenomenon is, and how is this frequency related to the topological properties of the network.

Acknowledgments. This work was partially supported by a Caratheodory research grant E.114 from the University of Patras and by the "GNCS – INdAM". Part of this work done while G. Persiano was visiting Google, New York.

References

1. Acar, E., Greco, G., Manna, M.: Group reasoning in social environments. In: Proceedings of the 16th Conference on Autonomous Agents and MultiAgent Systems, AAMAS 2017, 8–12 May 2017, São Paulo, Brazil, pp. 1296–1304 (2017)
2. Angluin, D., Aspnes, J., Eisenstat, D.: A simple population protocol for fast robust approximate majority. Distrib. Comput. **21**(2), 87–102 (2008)

3. Auletta, V., Caragiannis, I., Ferraioli, D., Galdi, C., Persiano, G.: Minority becomes majority in social networks. In: Markakis, E., Schäfer, G. (eds.) WINE 2015. LNCS, vol. 9470, pp. 74–88. Springer, Heidelberg (2015). https://doi.org/10.1007/978-3-662-48995-6_6

4. Auletta, V., Caragiannis, I., Ferraioli, D., Galdi, C., Persiano, G.: Generalized discrete preference games. In: Proceedings of the Twenty-Fifth International Joint Conference on Artificial Intelligence, IJCAI 2016, New York, NY, USA, 9–15 July 2016, pp. 53–59 (2016)

5. Auletta, V., Caragiannis, I., Ferraioli, D., Galdi, C., Persiano, G.: Information retention in heterogeneous majority dynamics. arXiv preprint arXiv:1603.02971 (2016)

6. Auletta, V., Caragiannis, I., Ferraioli, D., Galdi, C., Persiano, G.: Robustness in discrete preference games. In: Proceedings of the 2017 International Conference on Autonomous Agents & Multiagent Systems, 8–12 May 2017, Sao Paulo (2017)

7. Auletta, V., Ferraioli, D., Pasquale, F., Penna, P., Persiano, G.: Logit dynamics with concurrent updates for local interaction games. In: Bodlaender, H.L., Italiano, G.F. (eds.) ESA 2013. LNCS, vol. 8125, pp. 73–84. Springer, Heidelberg (2013). https://doi.org/10.1007/978-3-642-40450-4_7

8. Auletta, V., Ferraioli, D., Pasquale, F., Persiano, G.: Mixing time and stationary expected social welfare of logit dynamics. Theor. Comput. Syst. **53**(1), 3–40 (2013)

9. Berger, E.: Dynamic monopolies of constant size. J. Comb. Theor. Ser. B **83**(2), 191–200 (2001)

10. Bhawalkar, K., Gollapudi, S., Munagala, K.: Coevolutionary opinion formation games. In: STOC, pp. 41–50. ACM (2013)

11. Bilò, V., Fanelli, A., Moscardelli, L.: Opinion formation games with dynamic social influences. In: Cai, Y., Vetta, A. (eds.) WINE 2016. LNCS, vol. 10123, pp. 444–458. Springer, Heidelberg (2016). https://doi.org/10.1007/978-3-662-54110-4_31

12. Bindel, D., Kleinberg, J.M., Oren, S.: How bad is forming your own opinion? In: Proceedings of the 52nd Annual IEEE Symposium on Foundations of Computer Science (FOCS), pp. 55–66 (2011)

13. Chierichetti, F., Kleinberg, J.M., Oren, S.: On discrete preferences and coordination. In: Proceedings of the 14th ACM Conference on Electronic Commerce (EC), pp. 233–250 (2013)

14. DeGroot, M.H.: Reaching a consensus. J. Am. Stat. Assoc. **69**(345), 118–121 (1974)

15. Ferraioli, D., Goldberg, P.W., Ventre, C.: Decentralized dynamics for finite opinion games. Theor. Comput. Sci. **648**, 96–115 (2016)

16. Friedkin, N.E., Johnsen, E.C.: Social influence and opinions. J. Math. Sociol. **15**(3–4), 193–205 (1990)

17. Mertzios, G.B., Nikoletseas, S.E., Raptopoulos, C.L., Spirakis, P.G.: Determining majority in networks with local interactions and very small local memory. Distrib. Comput. **30**(1), 1–16 (2017)

18. Mossel, E., Neeman, J., Tamuz, O.: Majority dynamics and aggregation of information in social networks. Auton. Agent. Multi-agent Syst. **28**(3), 408–429 (2014)

19. Peleg, D.: Local majorities, coalitions and monopolies in graphs: a review. Theor. Comput. Sci. **282**, 231–257 (2002)

20. Schäffer, A.A., Yannakakis, M.: Simple local search problems that are hard to solve. SIAM J. Comput. **20**(1), 56–87 (1991)

21. Tamuz, O., Tessler, R.J.: Majority dynamics and the retention of information. Isr. J. Math. **206**(1), 483–507 (2015)

The Strategy of Experts for Repeated Predictions

Amir Ban[✉], Yossi Azar, and Yishay Mansour

Blavatnik School of Computer Science, Tel Aviv University, Tel Aviv, Israel
amirban@me.com, azar@tau.ac.il, mansour.yishay@gmail.com

Abstract. We investigate the behavior of experts who seek to make predictions with maximum impact on an audience. At a known future time, a certain continuous random variable will be realized. A public prediction gradually converges to the outcome, and an expert has access to a more accurate prediction. We study when the expert should reveal his information, when his reward is based on a proper scoring rule (e.g., is proportional to the change in log-likelihood of the outcome).

In Azar et al. (2016), we analyzed the case where the expert may make a single prediction. In this paper, we analyze the case where the expert is allowed to revise previous predictions. This leads to a rather different set of dilemmas for the strategic expert. We find that it is optimal for the expert to always tell the truth, and to make a new prediction whenever he has a new signal. We characterize the expert's expectation for his total reward, and show asymptotic limits.

1 Introduction

Situations where a public is interested in the value of a future continuous variable, and has a time-varying consensus estimate of it, are common. Examples abound: Futures and options markets, the weather or climate, results of sport competitions, election results, new book/movie/album sales (for example, the Hollywood Stock Exchange), or economic indicators (for example, Moody's). We analyze the problem of an expert who makes multiple public predictions in such situations, and in particular, the questions of when to make a first prediction, when to revise a previous prediction, and whether to reveal true beliefs when making a prediction.

Consider, for example, a futures market. A futures market is an exchange where people make contracts to buy specific quantities of a commodity or financial instrument at a specified price with delivery set at a specified time in the future. Traders make money by buying for less than the market's spot price on the delivery date, which we shall henceforth call the *outcome*, or by selling for more. In effect, a futures market is a prediction market for the outcome.

The expert is not a trader himself, but someone who is reputed to have access to a more accurate signal than possessed by regular traders. Often, his reputation and living is based on this. Stock market analysts, investment gurus and various types of journalists fit this description.

© Springer International Publishing AG 2017
N. R. Devanur and P. Lu (Eds.): WINE 2017, LNCS 10674, pp. 44–57, 2017.
https://doi.org/10.1007/978-3-319-71924-5_4

The expert contributes to the market by making a public prediction, and is *post factum* rewarded for it. Such a prediction is a significant market event: Clearly, a market should heed an expert whose prediction already encompasses all current common knowledge and adds to it. We shall below argue that proper scoring rules, and in particular the *logarithmic scoring rule*, are the right incentive for the prediction scenario described. Whether the expert's reward takes the form of actual payment, or less tangibly in a boost to his reputation as an expert, is immaterial to our discussion. We assume that the expert's level of expertise, which we measure by *quality* and describe below, is known to the market.

We investigate the expert's strategy in such a prediction market. The strategy consists of choosing the timing and truthfulness of his predictions. Our treatment is Bayesian, assuming all agents draw all possible inferences from their information. In Azar et al. (2016), we analyzed the case where the expert is allowed a single prediction. In this paper, we study the case of multiple predictions, where an expert is allowed to revise his previous prediction.

1.1 The Market as a Random Walk

The current price in a futures market represents a current consensus on the outcome (assume that interest rates, or inflation rates, have been incorporated into the price). According to the efficient-market hypothesis (EMH), the current price represents all currently available information, and therefore it is impossible to consistently outperform the market. Consistent with the EMH is the random-walk hypothesis, according to which stock market prices (and their derivatives) evolve according to a random walk and thus cannot be predicted. By the random-walk hypothesis, the outcome is the result of a random walk from the current market price. Equivalently, and the point of view we take in this paper, the current price is the result of a random walk, reversed in time, from the outcome (see Fig. 1).

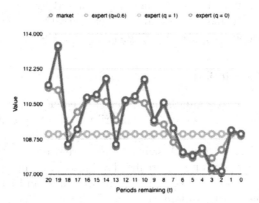

Fig. 1. Time-dependent signals of a market, a typical expert ($q = 0.6$), a know-all expert ($q = 1$), and a know-nothing expert ($q = 0$)

A random walk adds periodical (say, daily) i.i.d. steps to the market price. Assuming prices have been adjusted for known trends, the steps have zero mean. By suitable scaling of the price, the step variance can be normalized to 1. Following a common assumption that the random walk is Gaussian, or lognormal[1], the steps have standard normal distribution (i.e., $N(0, 1)$).

1.2 Expert Quality

The expert's expertise consists of having a more accurate signal of the outcome price x_0 than the market's, and the expert's quality measures by how much. The quality $q \in [0, 1]$ measures what part of the market's uncertainty the expert "knows", so that it does not figure in the expert's own uncertainty. Equivalently, the expert's uncertainty is $1 - q$ of the market's uncertainty. This proportion is statistical: It is the uncertainties' variances, rather than their realizations, that are related by proportion. If the market price is a Gaussian random walk from the outcome with $N(0, 1)$ steps, the expert's prediction is a Gaussian random walk from the outcome with $N(0, 1 - q)$ steps.

The expert's knowledge, i.e., the part of the market's uncertainty that the expert is not uncertain about, has steps of zero mean and q variance. On the assumption that the expert's knowledge steps and uncertainty steps are mutually independent, their sum has the sum mean and sum variance of their parts, i.e., they sum back to the market's uncertainty steps of zero mean and variance $q + (1 - q) = 1$.

Figure 1 illustrates the evolution of a market's signal in the last 20 periods until the outcome (109) becomes known. Also shown are the private signals of 3 experts predicting the same event, with qualities of 0.6, 1 and 0.

An expert with $q = 1$ has no uncertainty at all, and his signal equals the outcome x_0 at all times t. At the other extreme, a (so-called) expert with $q = 0$ has no knowledge beyond common knowledge, and his signal equals the market value x_t at all t.

An expert's quality is common knowledge, shared by all traders as well as himself. Whether its value q represents objective reality, or is a belief, based, e.g., on past performance, makes no difference to our discussion.

1.3 Scoring a Prediction

A scoring rule is a way to evaluate and reward a prediction of a stochastic event, when that prediction is presented as a distribution over possible results. The predictor declares at time $t > 0$ a probability distribution $p \in \Delta(R)$, and at time 0 some $r \in R$ is realized. A *scoring rule* S rewards the predictor $S(p, r)$ when his prediction was p and the realized value is r. In market settings, and many other settings, there exists a current prediction $\bar{p}$ and then the predictor is evaluated on the scoring difference effected $S(p, r) - S(\bar{p}, r)$. Note that the optimization problem of the predictor in a market situation is the same, since

---

[1] Taking logs transforms a lognormal random walk into a Gaussian one.

he has no influence over $S(\bar{p}, r)$, the only difference is that now the predictor might be penalized for making the current prediction less accurate. A *proper* scoring rule is a scoring rule for which reporting the true distribution is optimal according to the predictor's information.

The logarithmic scoring rule, with $S(p, r) = \log p_r$ (where p_r is the value of p at r), scores a prediction by the log-likelihood of the outcome according to the prediction. It is proper, and has strong roots in information theory: In reference to a current prediction $\bar{p}$, it scores $\log p_r / \bar{p}_r$, which, in information theory, is the *self-information*, also called *surprisal*, contained in the outcome. Conditional on p being the correct distribution, the expected score is the Kullback-Leibler divergence between p and $\bar{p}$: $E_{r \sim p}[\log p_r / \bar{p}_r] = D_{KL}(p || \bar{p})$.

In our model expert predictions are scored with the logarithmic scoring rule, which the expert seeks to maximize. This is justified by the following

- The reward is incentive compatible, eliciting truth-telling by the expert. This enables a Bayesian market to adopt predictions verbatim. A reward that is not incentive compatible would greatly complicate the Bayesian interpretation of predictions, possibly even making our problem indeterminate.
- In our model (the essential details of which were already sketched), the entire prediction distribution follows from the prediction mean by common knowledge. Since only proper scoring rules are incentive compatible with predictions phrased as distributions over results, it follows that the reward *must* be by a proper scoring rule.
- The logarithmic scoring rule is favored by its unique information-theory meaning, and other unique attributes (e.g., its locality). It is commonly used in real-world predictions markets, in a mechanism called LMSR (*Logarithmic Market Scoring Rule*) introduced by Hanson (2003). Chen and Pennock (2010) say "LMSR has become the de facto market maker mechanism for prediction markets. It is used by many companies including Inkling Markets, Consensus Point, Yahoo!, and Microsoft".

Proper scoring rules are *myopically* incentive compatible for risk-neutral agents, i.e. they are guaranteed to elicit the truth, but only when future actions are not taken into account (or, when there are no future actions, i.e., at the last prediction). As will be further discussed, when future actions *are* taken into account, incentive compatibility is *not* guaranteed.

1.4   The Expert's Dilemma

Assume that the expert has no obligation to speak at any particular time, or at all. The reward for no prediction is zero, and for each prediction made, the expert is rewarded by the logarithmic scoring rule. The expert may revise his previous prediction by making a new one whenever this is advantageous. The expert faces several dilemmas: When to make the first prediction? and when is it appropriate to revise a previous prediction? Moreover, as proper scoring rules are incentive compatible only with the *last* prediction, is there a strategy more profitable than always telling the truth?

In Azar et al. (2016), we analyzed the single-prediction case, and argued that an expert may pass on making a prediction in the hope of getting a better opportunity later. In the multiple predictions scenario, there is no need to pass, since the opportunity to make a future prediction remains. Conceivably, the expert will want to revise his prediction whenever he gets a fresh signal (we find that this is so), or, he may want to do so only when the new signal significantly changes his prediction (we find otherwise).

Should he always tell the truth? Whenever the expert makes two or more predictions, he may conceivably distort his first prediction, hoping to misdirect a gullibly-Bayesian market, and reaping a net profit by subsequently setting the market right.

1.5   Summary of Results

Our results are satisfyingly tidy: Despite apparent temptation to mislead, it is optimal for the expert to always tell the truth, and therefore it is rational for the market to take his predictions at face value. The optimal prediction schedule for the expert is to make a new one whenever he has a new signal and is allowed to speak. We show that the expected total reward for all predictions is, asymptotically for large t, $\frac{1}{2}q \log t$, proportional to quality (q) and to the log of the number of periods left (t).

To some, these results, and especially the truthfulness result, would seem straightforward. However, this intuition is false, and not supported by the literature (see below in Sect. 1.6, Chen et al. (2010) and Chen and Waggoner (2016)). The following generic example illustrates why.

Example 1. There is a market, who gets public signals, and an expert, who gets private signals. Suppose that at time t the market receives a signal $x_0 + \epsilon$, where x_0 is the outcome, and ϵ is a random variable. At $t - 1$, and (independently) at $t + 1$, the expert receives a signal $x_0 + \epsilon$ with probability $1/2$, and $x_0 - \epsilon$ with probability $1/2$.

The expert makes a prediction at both times. Should he reveal his true information?

Whoever sees two different truthful signals is able to calculate the outcome $x_0 = (x_0 + \epsilon)/2 + (x_0 - \epsilon)/2$ exactly.

For any scoring rule, and any distribution of ϵ, the expert should not tell the truth on his first prediction. This prevents the 50% probability that the market will know x_0 at t, preserving a 75% probability that the expert can announce x_0 on his second prediction.

1.6   Related Literature

Learning from expert opinion and its aggregation has a long history, with DeGroot (1974) and the Bayesian framework of Morris (1977) leading to much subsequent work. While much of this work treats experts as oracles with no motivation of their own, some of it took a look at an expert's concern for his reputation, i.e., the wish to appear well-informed. In Bayarri and DeGroot (1989) the setting was a weighted averaging of several expert opinions, with the weights adjusted by observed accuracy when the outcome is known. Experts wish to maximize their posterior weight. The authors found that incentive compatibility is attainable only by assigning a logarithmic utility to the weight. In Ottaviani and Sørensen (2006) the authors cast the expert's inferred type as the optimization target. Their type, a real number, is a cognate of our quality. The authors argue that truth-telling is generally not possible, as experts are motivated to simulate better quality than they actually have. In our model, expert quality is common knowledge, and so not open to manipulation.

Chen et al. (2010) as well as Chen and Waggoner (2016) studied situations where several agents, each having private information, are given more than one opportunity to make a public prediction. The canonical case is "Alice-Bob-Alice" where Alice speaks before and after Bob's single speaking opportunity, both are awarded by a proper scoring rule for each prediction, and both maximize their total score. The proper scoring rule assures that each will tell the truth on their last prediction, and the open question is whether Alice, when going first, will tell the truth, lie, or keep her silence. Chen et al. (2010) show cases where Alice is motivated to mislead on her first prediction, and make the key observation that truthfulness is optimal if, in a different setup, namely, a single-prediction Alice-Bob game where Alice chooses whether to go first or second, she will always prefer going first. Building on that insight, Chen and Waggoner (2016) show that when the players' information is what they define as "perfect informational substitutes", they will predict truthfully and as early as allowed, while when they are "perfect informational complements", they will predict truthfully and as *late* as allowed, while when players are neither substitutes nor complements, untruthfulness can and will occur.

These works differ from ours in that they model agents having a constant piece of information, which they may choose when to reveal, while we model agents (expert and market) as receiving a time series of signals with new information every time period. In the Discussion we comment on how our results reflect on a possible generalization of the mentioned works to dynamic-information settings.

The Efficient Market Hypothesis was introduced by Fama et al. (1969). The Random Walk Hypothesis is even older, originating in the 19th century, and discussed by, e.g., Samuelson (1965). The Black-Scholes option pricing model Black and Scholes (1973) is based on a Gaussian random walk assumption.

Scoring rules have a very long history, going back to De Finetti (1937), Brier (1950) and Good (1952). Proper scoring rules are often used for incentive-compatible belief elicitation of risk-neutral agents (e.g. Armantier and Treich (2013)).

To keep this paper short, we omitted some proofs. The reader will find a full version, including all proofs, in Ban et al. (2017). The rest of this paper is organized as follows: In Sect. 2 we describe our model. After establishing some preliminary results in Sect. 3, Sect. 4 is devoted to the multiple-prediction problem. In Sect. 5 we summarize and offer concluding remarks.

2 Model

2.1 Market Prediction

A market predicts the outcome of a continuous random variable X_0, whose realized value x_0 will be revealed at time 0. Time is discrete and flows backwards from an initial period T_{max}, i.e., $T_{max}, \ldots, t, \ldots, 1, 0$. At any time $t > 0$ the market observes $X_0 + \mathcal{Z}_t$ where $\mathcal{Z}_t \sim N(0, t)$. We model $\mathcal{Z}_t$ as a random walk with i.i.d. steps $Z_t, \ldots, Z_1$, i.e., $\mathcal{Z}_t = \sum_{\tau=1}^{t} Z_\tau$ and $Z_\tau \sim N(0, 1)$. Let the market prediction (when uninformed by experts) be $X_t := X_0 + \mathcal{Z}_t$ at time t, and let x_t be the realized value. With every passing period t, the value of $Z_t = z_t$ is revealed and becomes common knowledge, and the market's new prediction changes to $x_{t-1} = x_t - z_t$. Note that the variance of $\mathcal{Z}_t$ decreases with time, and at time 0 the market's prediction coincides with the outcome x_0. The random variable X_0 is normally distributed $N(0, \sigma_0^2)$ where we assume $\sigma_0^2 \gg T_{max}$. This assumption means that the outcome is, practically, unconstrained by a prior, and makes posterior computations dependent solely on observed signals, since[2] we have $\mathbb{E}[X_0 | X_t = x_t] = x_t$ and $Var(X_0 | X_t = x_t) = t$.

2.2 Expert Information and Goal

There is an expert, with quality $q \in [0, 1]$, whose quality is common knowledge. The expert's quality consists in "knowing" part of the random steps Z_t of every period, and therefore getting a more accurate signal of X_0. Formally,

- For every t, $Z_t = A_t + B_t$, where $A_t \sim N(0, q)$ and $B_t \sim N(0, 1 - q)$ are mutually independent. (Note that $Z_t \sim N(0, 1)$.)
- The expert's private signal at time t is $Y_t = X_0 + B_1 + \ldots + B_t$ and let y_t be its realized value. (Note that if $q = 0$ then $Y_t = X_t$ and if $q = 1$ then $Y_t = x_0$.)

At every $t > 0$, the expert may choose to make a prediction of the outcome. The market has a varying probability distribution on the outcome, which is affected by its signals and by the expert's predictions. (The market price is the distribution mean). Each prediction is scored by the logarithmic scoring rule as described below. The expert's reward is the total score for all predictions made.

The expert's outcome distribution at t is $N(y_t, (1 - q)t)$.[3] In practice, it is enough for the expert to announce y_t as his entire distribution follows by the model and common knowledge. A prediction's reward is determined at time 0 based on the realized value (x_0) by the logarithmic scoring rule. Namely, if the market distribution prior to the expert prediction is X_{t-} with density f_-,

---

[2] When a normal variable with prior distribution $N(0, \sigma_0^2)$ is sampled with known variance t at value x_t, its Bayesian posterior distribution is normal with mean $\frac{x_t/t}{1/\sigma_0^2 + 1/t}$ and variance $\frac{1}{1/\sigma_0^2 + 1/t}$. Assuming $\sigma_0^2 \gg T_{max} \geq t$, this simplifies to $N(x_t, t)$.

[3] Since the expert is better informed than the market, his prediction depends on his signal alone. This is formally proved in Proposition 1.

and following the expert prediction the posterior market distribution is X_{t+} with density f_+, then the expert reward is $\log(f_+(x_0)/f_-(x_0))$, where x_0 is the realized value.

An expert who refrains from making any prediction is awarded 0. The expert optimization problem is to maximize his expected reward given his private information. *The question before the expert is if and when to make predictions, and whether to make them truthfully.*

3   Preliminaries

3.1   Time and Expectation Notation

Distributions and other variables often use a time subscript, e.g., X_t is market's distribution at t (t periods before delivery date). When a prediction takes place at t, the notation X_{t-}, X_{t+} is used to distinguish between the variable before, and after, respectively, the prediction.

We use the notation $\underset{t}{\mathbb{E}}[Z]$ to denote the expectation of a random variable Z according to the distribution known at t. This is shorthand for $\underset{X_t}{\mathbb{E}}[Z]$ when referring to the market's expectation, or for $\underset{Y_t}{\mathbb{E}}[Z]$ when referring to the expert's expectation. Which of the two is meant will either be clear from the context or explicitly stated. If a prediction was made at t, we use the notation $\underset{t-}{\mathbb{E}}[Z], \underset{t+}{\mathbb{E}}[Z]$ to distinguish between the market's expectation of Z before and after, respectively, the prediction has been made.

3.2   A Criterion for Independence

Here we prove a result about random variables based on model signals that will enable us to determine whether they are stochastically independent.

From the model definitions we have, for every $i \geq j$

$$Cov(X_i, X_j) = j \tag{1}$$
$$Cov(Y_i, X_j) = Cov(X_i, Y_j) = Cov(Y_i, Y_j) = (1-q)j \tag{2}$$

Lemma 1. *Define U to be the random vector $(X_0, X_1, Y_1, \ldots, X_t, Y_t)^T$, and let U_1, U_2 be two random vectors of linear combinations of the U. Then the joint distributions of U_1, U_2 are mutually independent if and only if for every pair $u_1 \in U_1$ and $u_2 \in U_2$ $Cov(u_1, u_2) = 0$.*

Proof. Every linear combination of U is normal, as it is a linear combination of the i.i.d. normal variables $A_i, B_i, i = 1, \ldots t$, and of X_0, which is normal and independent of each of the others. Therefore U has a jointly multivariate normal distribution. Therefore so has random vector $\binom{U_1}{U_2}$. The lemma states a general property of jointly multivariate normal distributions, see Tong (2012) Theorem 3.3.2. □

3.3   Market Effect of a Prediction

Before evaluating, and then optimizing, expert's value for a prediction strategy, we must resolve how a single prediction affects market price, at the time of prediction. For the multiple-prediction problem, we also need to determine the effect *after* the prediction was made. This will be resolved in Sect. 4.1.

Define $\mathcal{Z}_t$ to be the set of all expert and market signals previous to t (X_τ, Y_τ for $\tau > t$).

Assume the expert makes a prediction y_t at time t, implying a distribution of $Y_t \sim N(y_t, (1-q)t)$. Then at time t the market's posterior distribution will be the expert's announced distribution, regardless of the market's signal at this time x_t and all previous signals $\mathcal{Z}_t$.

Proposition 1. *If the expert makes a prediction y_t at time t, the market's posterior distribution is the expert's implied distribution $Y_t \sim N(y_t, (1-q)t)$.*

Proof. Let $\mathcal{Z} = \mathcal{Z}_t \cup \{X_t\}$. Define $\mathcal{Z}' = \mathcal{Z} - Y_t$ to be the set of random variables $Z - Y_t$ with $Z \in \mathcal{Z}$.

By (1), (2) for each $Z \in \mathcal{Z}'$, $Cov(Z, Y_t) = 0$ and $Cov(Z, X_0) = 0$. So, as given Y_t there is a one-to-one correspondence between $\mathcal{Z}$ and $\mathcal{Z}'$, and by Lemma 1

$$\Pr[x_0 | Y_t, \mathcal{Z}] = \Pr[x_0 | Y_t, \mathcal{Z}'] = \frac{\Pr[x_0, Y_t, \mathcal{Z}']}{\Pr[Y_t, \mathcal{Z}']} = \frac{\Pr[x_0, Y_t]\Pr[\mathcal{Z}']}{\Pr[Y_t]\Pr[\mathcal{Z}']} = \Pr[x_0 | Y_t]$$

as claimed.   □

3.4   Prediction Score Expectation

Assume the expert makes a prediction at time t. Let the market prediction prior to the expert prediction be $X_{t-} \sim N(\mu_-, \sigma_-^2)$ with density f_- and let the posterior market prediction be $X_{t+} \sim N(\mu_+, \sigma_+^2)$ with density f_+. Let expert's reward be denoted by W, then

$$W = \log \frac{f_+(x_0)}{f_-(x_0)} = \log \frac{\frac{1}{\sigma_+\sqrt{2\pi}} e^{-\frac{(x_0-\mu_+)^2}{2\sigma_+^2}}}{\frac{1}{\sigma_-\sqrt{2\pi}} e^{-\frac{(x_0-\mu_-)^2}{2\sigma_-^2}}} = \log \frac{\sigma_-}{\sigma_+} + \frac{(x_0-\mu_-)^2}{2\sigma_-^2} - \frac{(x_0-\mu_+)^2}{2\sigma_+^2}$$

$$(3)$$

As the reward depends on x_0, its value is only known at time 0. The expert can calculate his reward expectation when making it (at t), based on his belief about the distribution of x_0.

Consider the case that the expert prediction is truthful.

Proposition 2. *If the market's prediction before an expert prediction is $X_{t-} \sim N(\mu_-, \sigma_-^2)$, and after an expert prediction is $X_{t+} \sim N(\mu_+, \sigma_+^2)$, then if the prediction is truthful the expert's expected reward is positive and equals the Kullback-Leibler divergence $D_{KL}(X_{t+} \| X_{t-})$.*

$$\mathbb{E}_t[W] = D_{KL}(X_{t+} \| X_{t-}) = \frac{(\mu_+ - \mu_-)^2}{2\sigma_-^2} + \frac{1}{2}\left(\frac{\sigma_+^2}{\sigma_-^2} - 1 - \log \frac{\sigma_+^2}{\sigma_-^2}\right) \quad (4)$$

Proof. As the second moment of the normal distribution $N(\mu, \sigma^2)$ is $\mu^2 + \sigma^2$, and since the expert's distribution translates to

$$x_0 - \mu_- \sim N(\mu_+ - \mu_-, \sigma_+^2)$$
$$x_0 - \mu_+ \sim N(0, \sigma_+^2),$$

we get by taking expectations from (3)

$$\mathbb{E}_t[W] = \mathbb{E}_{x_0 \sim N(\mu_+, \sigma_+^2)}[W] = \log \frac{\sigma_-}{\sigma_+} + \frac{(\mu_+ - \mu_-)^2 + \sigma_+^2}{2\sigma_-^2} - \frac{0 + \sigma_+^2}{2\sigma_+^2}$$

$$= \frac{(\mu_+ - \mu_-)^2}{2\sigma_-^2} + \frac{1}{2}\left(\frac{\sigma_+^2}{\sigma_-^2} - 1 - \log \frac{\sigma_+^2}{\sigma_-^2}\right)$$

This is positive, because for every $x < 1$, $\log(1 - x) \leq -x$ □

We use the above result to calculate the expected reward of a *first* prediction.

Proposition 3. *For an expert's first prediction at t, his reward expectation is*

$$\mathbb{E}_t[W] = \frac{(x_t - y_t)^2}{2t} - \frac{1}{2}\left(q + \log(1 - q)\right) \tag{5}$$

Proof. For an expert's first prediction, we have $\mu_- = x_t$, $\sigma_-^2 = t$. By Proposition 1 $\mu_+ = y_t$, and $\sigma_+^2 = (1 - q)t$. Hence, $X_t^- \sim N(x_t, t)$ and $X_t^+ \sim N(y_t, (1 - q)t)$. Substituting these in (4) we derive (5).   □

4 The Optimal Multiple-Prediction Strategy

4.1 Market Effect After a Prediction

When an expert has made a prediction at T, what is the market's posterior distribution at the next periods $T - 1, T - 2, \ldots$, assuming the expert makes no new predictions? This is more complex than at the time of prediction (see Sect. 3.3), and the distribution depends on more than one signal, as stated in the following proposition:

Proposition 4. *At time t, Let $T > t$ be the time of expert's latest prediction y_T. Let $\mathcal{Z} := \mathcal{Z}_T \cup \{y_T, x_T, x_{T-1}, \ldots x_t\}$. Then at t the market's posterior distribution is $N(\mu(x_0|\mathcal{Z}), Var(x_0|\mathcal{Z}))$ with*

$$\mu(x_0|\mathcal{Z}) = \frac{\frac{x_t}{t} + \frac{1}{1-q}\frac{y_T}{T} - \frac{x_T}{T}}{\frac{1}{t} + \frac{q}{1-q}\frac{1}{T}}$$

$$Var(x_0|\mathcal{Z}) = \frac{1}{\frac{1}{t} + \frac{q}{1-q}\frac{1}{T}}$$

Proof. The proof of this proposition is in the full version Ban et al. (2017).

4.2   Truth is Best Policy

Does an expert gain or lose by deviating from the truth, reporting a prediction that is different from his actual belief? When allowed a single prediction, the fact that the logarithmic scoring rule is proper means that the expert's optimal policy is to predict truthfully. If allowed multiple predictions, this is not clear-cut: A false prediction misdirects the market, so that a subsequent true prediction reaps the added benefit of correcting the misdirection. Plausibly, the gain of the latter outweighs the loss of the former.

We shall, however, show

Proposition 5. *If allowed periods when to predict are fixed, it is an equilibrium for the expert to make truthful predictions and for the market to take his predictions as truthful.*

Proof. The proof of this proposition is in the full version Ban et al. (2017).

Therefore, truthfulness is best policy for the expert. Note that if the expert's allowed prediction schedule is not fixed, the result may no longer be true. E.g., if the expert is allowed further predictions only if the discrepancy between his last prediction and the market's prediction exceeded some threshold, the expert may be motivated to distort his prediction so as to be given further prediction opportunities.

4.3   Prediction Reward Expectation

Having seen that there is no profit in lying, we shall from now on assume truthful predictions.

The following lemma will be useful in calculating the expected reward of a *future* prediction, before some of the signals it is based on are known. It shows that current and historic signals affect the reward expectation of the next prediction, but have no effect on the reward expectation of later predictions.

Lemma 2. *Assume that the expert is committed to making two consecutive predictions at T and $t < T$. Let $X_{t-} \sim N(\mu_-, \sigma_-^2)$ and $X_{t+} \sim N(\mu_+, \sigma_+^2)$ be the market's distributions for x_0 before and after, respectively, a prediction μ_+ is made at t.*

Assume that σ_+^2 and σ_-^2 do not depend on any signals, but only on T, t and q. Then, at any time $\tau \geq T$, the expected t-prediction reward is

$$\mathbb{E}_{\tau}[W_t] = \log \frac{\sigma_-}{\sigma_+}$$

Proof. The proof of this lemma is in the full version Ban et al. (2017).

We remark here that it is easy to verify in the proof above, that the lemma also holds *a priori*, before the expert and market have received their first signal. Consequently by Proposition 3 the *a priori* expected benefit of a first prediction is $\frac{1}{2} \log \frac{1}{1-q}$.

Another consequence is the following proposition:

Proposition 6. *Assume that the expert is committed to making two consecutive predictions at T and $t < T$. Then, at or before T, the reward expectation of the latter prediction is*

$$\mathbb{E}[W_t] = -\frac{1}{2} \log\left(1 - q\frac{T-t}{T}\right)$$

Proof. By Proposition 4 $\sigma_-^2 = \frac{1}{\frac{1}{t} + \frac{q}{1-q}\frac{1}{T}}$, while by Proposition 1 $\sigma_+^2 = (1-q)t$.

These depend on t, T and q only, so by Lemma 2, the reward expectation at every $\tau \geq T$ is

$$\mathbb{E}[W_t] = \log\frac{\sigma_-}{\sigma_+} = -\frac{1}{2} \log\left((1-q)t\left[\frac{1}{t} + \frac{q}{1-q}\frac{1}{T}\right]\right) = -\frac{1}{2} \log\left(1 - q\frac{T-t}{T}\right)$$

$\square$

We can now prove the main result: The best strategy is to make predictions whenever allowed, (and truthfully, as already shown in Proposition 5).

Theorem 1. *If allowed periods for prediction are fixed, an expert maximizes his reward by making predictions at every allowed period, speaking the truth at all predictions.*

Proof. The proof of this theorem is in the full version Ban et al. (2017). $\square$

Consequently if the expert is allowed to speak every period, he will. The following proposition gives his reward expectation and its asymptotic behavior for large T.

Theorem 2. *Assume the expert is allowed to make a prediction every period. Mark by $\Xi(T)$ the average reward expectation at period T for an expert using optimal prediction strategy.*

$$\Xi(T) = \frac{1}{2} \sum_{t=1}^{T} \log \frac{t}{t-q} \tag{6}$$

$$= \frac{1}{2} \log \frac{\Gamma(1-q)\Gamma(T+1)}{\Gamma(T+1-q)} \tag{7}$$

For large T, $\Xi(T) = O(\log T)$. More specifically

$$\lim_{T \to \infty} \frac{\Xi(T)}{q \log T + \log \Gamma(1-q)} = \frac{1}{2} \tag{8}$$

Proof. The optimal policy is to predict at every period starting at T. The expected reward (averaged over all random walks) for a first prediction at T is, by Lemma 2, $\frac{1}{2} \log \frac{1}{1-q}$, while for every $t < T$, it is, by Proposition 6, $\frac{1}{2} \log \frac{t+1}{t+1-q}$. (6) follows , and from it (7).

We use the following limit of the Gamma function: For $\alpha \in \mathbb{R}$

$$\lim_{n \to \infty} \frac{\Gamma(n+\alpha)}{\Gamma(n)n^\alpha} = 1$$

(8) follows from this and (7) by substituting $\alpha = -q, n = T+1$. $\square$

5 Discussion

5.1 Conclusions

We analyzed the expert's policy in the prediction scenario described, and found that an expert should make a new, truthful prediction whenever he is allowed to and has an updated signal. For large t, his total reward is on average roughly $\frac{1}{2}q \log t$. This compares to the asymptotic average reward of $q \log \log t$ that Azar et al. (2016) found is achievable by best policy of the expert when restricted to a single prediction.

The ability to revise predictions therefore significantly increases the expert's reward, by a factor $O(\frac{\log t}{\log \log t})$.

5.2 Other Random Walks

In Sect. 1.5 we noted that our main results, and particularly the truthfulness property, does not necessarily apply to any other model. It is an interesting open problem to characterize which models do, in fact, lead to similar results. It needs reminding that our derivations depend on two critical elements of our model: (i) Gaussian random walk, and (ii) variances of all signals and, as a result, of inferred distributions are common knowledge, and consequently independent of signal values. No similar results may apply, for example, in binary prediction markets (where there is a 0/1 outcome), because in the underlying Bernoulli distribution, a prediction p, representing the distribution's mean, also affects the distribution variance $p(1 - p)$.

5.3 Informational Substitutes

Chen and Waggoner (2016) formulate a criterion of "informational substitutes" as leading to being truthful and revealing information at first opportunity, in a world where agents' private information is static. The definition used for "informational substitutes" is that information is more valuable (per the scoring rule in force) earlier than later. While simply stated, working this out for any given case may be involved.

We find the same, in our world where private information is dynamic. In that context, the major part of the proof Theorem 1 was to show that expert and market's signals are informational substitutes.

Our result is therefore consistent with a generalization of Chen and Waggoner (2016) (and Chen et al. (2010)) to dynamic-information contexts. We venture a guess that such a generalization will prove to be valid. As our analysis shows, such a generalization is not straight-forward, but depends, *inter alia*, on the behavior of interdependent martingales.

5.4 Several Experts

This subject is discussed in the full version Ban et al. (2017).

References

Armantier, O., Treich, N.: Eliciting beliefs: proper scoring rules, incentives, stakes and hedging. Eur. Econ. Rev. **62**(2013), 17–40 (2013)

Azar, Y., Ban, A., Mansour, Y.: When should an expert make a prediction? In: Proceedings of the 2016 ACM Conference on Economics and Computation, pp. 125–142. ACM (2016)

Ban, A., Azar, Y., Mansour, Y.: The Strategy of Experts for Repeated Predictions. arXiv preprint arXiv:1710.00537 [cs.GT] (2017)

Bayarri, M.J., DeGroot, M.H.: Optimal reporting of predictions. J. Am. Stat. Assoc. **84**(405), 214–222 (1989)

Black, F., Scholes, M.: The pricing of options and corporate liabilities. J. Polit. Econ. **81**(3), 637 (1973)

Brier, G.W.: Verification of forecasts expressed in terms of probability. Weather Rev. **78**(1950), 1–3 (1950)

Chen, Y., Dimitrov, S., Sami, R., Reeves, D.M., Pennock, D.M., Hanson, R.D., Fortnow, L., Gonen, R.: Gaming prediction markets: equilibrium strategies with a market maker. Algorithmica **58**(4), 930–969 (2010)

Chen, Y., Pennock, D.M.: Designing markets for prediction. AI Mag. **31**(4), 42–52 (2010)

Chen, Y., Waggoner, B.: Informational substitutes. In: 2016 IEEE 57th Annual Symposium on Foundations of Computer Science (FOCS), pp. 239–247. IEEE (2016)

De Finetti, B.: La prévision: ses lois logiques, ses sources subjectives. Ann. Inst. Henri Poincaré **7**, 1–68 (1937)

DeGroot, M.H.: Reaching a consensus. J. Am. Stat. Assoc. **69**(345), 118–121 (1974)

Fama, E.F., Fisher, L., Jensen, M.C., Roll, R.: The adjustment of stock prices to new information. Int. Econ. Rev. **10**, 1–21 (1969)

Good, I.J.: Rational decisions. J. R. Stat. Soc. Ser. B (Methodol.) **14**(1), 107–114 (1952)

Hanson, R.: Combinatorial information market design. Inf. Syst. Frontiers **5**(1), 107–119 (2003)

Morris, P.A.: Combining expert judgments: a Bayesian approach. Manag. Sci. **23**(7), 679–693 (1977)

Ottaviani, M., Sørensen, P.N.: The strategy of professional forecasting. J. Financ. Econ. **81**(2), 441–466 (2006)

Samuelson, P.A.: Proof that properly anticipated prices fluctuate randomly. Ind. Manag. Rev. **6**, 41–49 (1965)

Tong, Y.L.: The Multivariate Normal Distribution. Springer Science & Business Media, Berlin (2012). https://doi.org/10.1007/978-1-4613-9655-0

Shapley Facility Location Games

Omer Ben-Porat[✉] and Moshe Tennenholtz

Technion - Israel Institute of Technology, Haifa, Israel
omerbp@campus.technion.ac.il, moshet@ie.technion.ac.il

Abstract. Facility location games have been a topic of major interest in economics, operations research and computer science, starting from the seminal work by Hotelling. Spatial facility location models have successfully predicted the outcome of competition in a variety of scenarios. In a typical facility location game, users/customers/voters are mapped to a metric space representing their preferences, and each player picks a point (facility) in that space. In most facility location games considered in the literature, users are assumed to act deterministically: given the facilities chosen by the players, users are attracted to their nearest facility. This paper introduces facility location games with probabilistic attraction, dubbed *Shapley facility location games*, due to a surprising connection to the Shapley value. The specific attraction function we adopt in this model is aligned with the recent findings of the behavioral economics literature on choice prediction. Given this model, our first main result is that Shapley facility location games are potential games; hence, they possess pure Nash equilibrium. Moreover, the latter is true for any compact user space, any user distribution over that space, and any number of players. Note that this is in sharp contrast to Hotelling facility location games. In our second main result we show that under the assumption that players can compute an approximate best response, approximate equilibrium profiles can be learned efficiently by the players via dynamics. Our third main result is a bound on the Price of Anarchy of this class of games, as well as showing the bound tight. Ultimately, we show that player payoffs coincide with their Shapley value in a coalition game, where coalition gains are the social welfare of the users.

1 Introduction

In his seminal work [14], Hotelling considers a competition between two ice-cream vendors, who sell ice-cream to sunbathers on the beach, and wish to maximize their payoffs. The vendors sell the same type of product, and charge the same price. Sunbathers are distributed uniformly along the beach and every sunbather walks to his/her nearest ice-cream vendor to buy an ice-cream. As indicated by Hotelling, the vendors will strategically locate their ice-cream carts in the middle of the beach, back to back, as this is the only Nash equilibrium of this game.

Following that seminal work, facility location games have been a topic of major interest in economics, operations research and computer science. Spatial facility location models have successfully predicted the outcome of competition in

© Springer International Publishing AG 2017
N. R. Devanur and P. Lu (Eds.): WINE 2017, LNCS 10674, pp. 58–73, 2017.
https://doi.org/10.1007/978-3-319-71924-5_5

a variety of scenarios. In a typical facility location game, users/customers/voters are mapped to a metric space representing their preferences, and each player picks a point (facility) in that space. Thereupon, each player is awarded one monetary unit for each user attracted to her facility. Even a toy example like the one above supports powerful real-world phenomena.

In most facility location games considered in the literature, users are assumed to act deterministically: given the facilities chosen by the players, users are attracted to their nearest facility. Indeed, such rational behavior of users is justified in many situations. However, far too little attention has been paid to models where users are not deterministic, and are not simply attracted to their nearest facility. Irrational decision making is ubiquitous, as demonstrated by the celebrated work of Kahneman and Tversky [16]. In this context, analyzing probabilistic user attraction introduces new theoretical challenges to overcome, as well as practical implications.

This paper focuses on facility location games with probabilistic attraction. Our proposed attraction function is aligned with the "Satisficing" principle in decision making [30], and the model of selection based on small samples [3,11]. The specific attraction function we adopt can be found in the recent experimental economics benchmark presented in [10], and its usefulness in choice prediction is discussed in [21].

We first formally present the above modeling process to determine the attraction probabilities. Using this attraction, we define the class of facility location games considered in this paper, termed *Shapley facility location games*, due to a surprising connection to the Shapley value [28]. The difference between our model and Hotelling's is analyzed using the toy example above; in particular, we show that when both players choose the middle of the segment, this is no longer an equilibrium profile; indeed, facilities will be selected and located in different locations.

We then show that Shapley facility location games are potential games [19]; hence, they possess pure Nash equilibrium. Moreover, the latter is true for any compact user space, any user distribution over that space, and any number of players. Note that this is in sharp contrast to Hotelling facility location games, where pure Nash equilibrium does not always exist (see, e.g., [9,26,27]).

An interesting question is whether strategic interaction among the players will converge to an approximate Nash equilibrium (see, e.g., [2,7]). The dynamics of Hotelling facility location games refer to intractable problems, and is rarely analyzed. We show that under the assumption that players can compute an approximate best response, approximate equilibrium profiles can be learned efficiently by the players via dynamics in any Shapley facility location game. This result holds for any user space (including an infinite one). We also bound the Price of Anarchy [17,24] of this class of games, and show the bound is tight.

Ultimately, the connection to the Shapley value is provided, as we bind (non-cooperative) facility location games with our selection of probabilistic attraction to cooperative game theory. We show that player payoffs coincide with their Shapley values in a coalition game, where coalition gains are the social welfare of the users.

1.1 Related Work

For a recent survey of Hotelling games the reader is referred to [5]. In the same spirit, Voronoi games (see, e.g., [1,6,12]) look at the game theoretic aspects of facility location with potentially multiple facilities for each player in general (euclidean) spaces.

The above work does not refer to probabilistic selection among facilities, an essential aspect needed in order to deal with realistic commerce and marketing setups. An exception that does adopt some form of probabilistic selection is the model of [13]. We will discuss how [13] can be seen as a special case of our model in Sect. 6.

Probabilistic choice among products [18] is widely explored, and choice prediction [3,11,30] is studied extensively. In this line of work, the authors wish to predict how a subject will make his/her choice among products. In our paper the way users react given a set of products is adopted from that literature, and embedded in the context of facility location games.

A different line of research in the algorithmic game theory literature is the study of facility location in the context of approximate mechanism design [20]. That literature deals with the case where only one entity dictates the place of a facility (or several facilities), while user preferences are their private information and are strategically reported, see e.g. [22,25]. In that context the players are the users, while our work extends facility location games where the players are the facilities' owners.

2   Model

Before we present our model formally, we briefly describe a general facility location game, and elaborate on the component we revisit.

Typically in a facility location game, users are distributed in a space $\mathcal{U}$, where every point $u \in \mathcal{U}$ models a user, be it by his[1] physical location, his preferences towards a product, or his political point of view. The space $\mathcal{U}$ plays one more role: every point in $\mathcal{U}$ is also a potential location for a *facility*, which is a physical location of a store, properties of a product, or political agenda. There are n players, where each player is to locate her facility in $\mathcal{U}$. Namely, a strategy of player i is a location $x_i \in \mathcal{U}$. A strategy profile is a vector describing where each player located her facility, $\boldsymbol{x} = (x_1, \ldots, x_n) \in \mathcal{U}^n$.

Each user $u \in \mathcal{U}$ has a similarity function $\sigma_u : \mathcal{U} :\rightarrow [0,1]$, where $\sigma_u(t)$ quantifies the extent to which $u \in \mathcal{U}$ is satisfied with a facility located in $t \in U$.[2] Given a strategy profile $\boldsymbol{x}$, users are *attracted* to the facilities of the

---

[1] For ease of exposition, third-person singular pronouns are "she" for a player and "he" for a user.

[2] Commonly in facility location models, distances are used to determine the attraction. However, for ease of presentation of the model and the analysis, we employ proximity; clearly, both notions are equivalent.

players according to *some* attraction function, which receives the *similarity vector* $\sigma_u(\boldsymbol{x}) = (\sigma_u(x_1), \ldots, \sigma_u(x_n))$ as input.[3] Players are strategic, namely they locate their facilities with the aim of attracting as many users as possible.

The component we revisit in this paper is the attraction function. Following the behavioral economics literature, users do not just select the facility they are most satisfied with (e.g. are not simple expected utility maximizers [16]). In this work we focus on the analysis of facility location games with a user attraction function that is popular in behavioral science as described in the introduction, thereby incorporating the human aspect in our model. Indeed, it has been shown that this modelling is an extremely effective ingredient in the context of choice prediction [10,21].

Given the locations selected by the players, the process of deciding which facility to select, if any, is modeled as follows: every user samples a satisfaction threshold from the uniform distribution[4], and then chooses a facility with satisfaction level above that threshold, if such a facility exists. If several facilities meet his criterion, he flips an unbiased coin to remain with one facility.

Surprisingly, as we show in Sect. 5, the aforementioned simple and intuitive selection process leads to a standard solution concept in cooperative game theory. More precisely, the probability of u to select facility x_i coincides with the Shapley value of player i in a cooperative game where the value assigned to each coalition is the maximal similarity level of u with the facilities of that coalition. For that reason, we term it the *Shapley attraction function*. A formal definition of the Shapley attraction function is as follows.

Definition 1. *For a strategy profile $\boldsymbol{x}$ and a user u, let $\left(\sigma_u^1(\boldsymbol{x}), \sigma_u^2(\boldsymbol{x}), \ldots \sigma_u^n(\boldsymbol{x})\right)$ denote the result of ordering the similarity vector $\sigma_u(\boldsymbol{x})$ in ascending order, and let $\rho_i = \rho_i(u, \boldsymbol{x})$ be an index such that $\sigma_u(x_i) = \sigma_u^{\rho_i}(\boldsymbol{x})$. Under the Shapley attraction function, u is attracted to each player i with probability*

$$\mu_i(u, \boldsymbol{x}) \triangleq \Pr\left(u \text{ is attracted to } i \text{ under } \boldsymbol{x}\right) = \sum_{j=1}^{\rho_i} \frac{\sigma_u^j(\boldsymbol{x}) - \sigma_u^{j-1}(\boldsymbol{x})}{n - j + 1}, \quad (1)$$

where $\sigma_i^0(\boldsymbol{x}) = 0$.

See Fig. 1 for illustration. We are now ready to formally present the model. A Shapley facility location game is composed of the following:

1. A compact set of users $\mathcal{U}$, and a density function f with mass 1 over $\mathcal{U}$.
2. A similarity function $\sigma : \mathcal{U} \times \mathcal{U} :\rightarrow [0,1]$, such that $\sigma_u(t) \triangleq \sigma(u,t)$ for all $t \in \mathcal{U}$.
3. A set of players, $[n] = \{1, \ldots, n\}$. The strategy set of each player i is a location (facility) in $\mathcal{U}$. The strategy of player i is denoted by $x_i \in \mathcal{U}$, and a strategy profile by $\boldsymbol{x} = (x_1, \ldots, x_n) \in \mathcal{U}^n$.

---

[3] In Hotelling games, for instance, each user u selects a player uniformly from $\{i : \sigma_u(x_i) \geq \max_j \sigma_u(x_j)\}$.

[4] Our results hold for any distribution, as well as in case the distribution is different for each user.

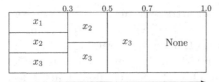

The satisfaction threshold of u

Fig. 1. Consider a user u and a strategy profile $\boldsymbol{x} = (x_1, x_2, x_3)$ such that the similarity vector $\sigma_u(\boldsymbol{x}) = (\sigma_u(x_1), \sigma_u(x_2), \sigma_u(x_3)) = (0.3, 0.5, 0.7)$. Hence, $(\sigma_u^1(\boldsymbol{x}), \sigma_u^2(\boldsymbol{x}), \sigma_u^3(\boldsymbol{x})) = (0.3, 0.5, 0.7)$ as well. User u samples his satisfaction threshold Y (as mentioned, uniformly distributed random variable). If $Y \leq 0.3$, then all the facilities satisfy him, so he chooses one uniformly. If $0.3 < Y \leq 0.5$, only x_2, x_3 satisfy him, and so he flips a coin to choose one of them. If $0.5 < Y \leq 0.7$, the only satisfying facility is x_3, and if $Y > 0.7$ he will not select any facility. It follows that u will select x_1 with probability $\mu_1(u, \boldsymbol{x}) = \frac{\sigma_i^1}{3} = \frac{1}{10}$, x_2 with probability $\mu_2(u, \boldsymbol{x}) = \frac{\sigma_i^1}{3} + \frac{\sigma_i^2 - \sigma_i^1}{2} = \frac{2}{10}$, and x_3 with probability $\mu_3(u, \boldsymbol{x}) = \frac{\sigma_i^1}{3} + \frac{\sigma_i^2 - \sigma_i^1}{2} + \frac{\sigma_i^3 - \sigma_i^2}{1} = \frac{4}{10}$. With probability 0.3 he will select none of the facilities.

4. Users are attracted to player facilities according to the Shapley attraction function. That is, the probability that u will be attracted to facility x_i of player i under $\boldsymbol{x}$ is $\mu_i(u, \boldsymbol{x})$ given in Eq. (1).
5. The payoff of player i under the strategy profile $\boldsymbol{x}$ is the proportion of users attracted to her chosen location, i.e.

$$\pi_i(\boldsymbol{x}) = \int_{\mathcal{U}} f(u)\mu_i(u, \boldsymbol{x})du. \tag{2}$$

Throughout the paper, both $\sigma_u(\cdot)$ and $\sigma(u, \cdot)$ are used interchangeably. We restrict the scope of this work to similarity functions that are Riemann integrable, for instance continuous functions or simple functions (a finite linear combination of indicator functions). In euclidean spaces, natural similarity functions are monotonically non-increasing in the distance. Note, however, that a similarity function need not be monotone.

We say that a strategy profile $\boldsymbol{x} = (x_1, \ldots, x_n) \in \mathcal{U}^n$ is a *pure Nash equilibrium* if for any player $i \in [n]$ and any strategy $x_i' \in \mathcal{U}$ it holds that $\pi_i(x_i, \boldsymbol{x}_{-i}) \geq \pi_i(x_i', \boldsymbol{x}_{-i})$, where $\boldsymbol{x}_{-i}$ denotes the vector $\boldsymbol{x}$ of all strategies, but with the i-th component deleted.

3   An Illustrative Example

In this section we illustrate Shapley facility location games by considering a game instance, thereby demonstrating the elements of the model. We employ the very restricted two-player, uniform distribution on a segment setting considered in [14]. We stress that this section serves as a demonstration only, and our results in the upcoming section apply to the model described above in its full generality.

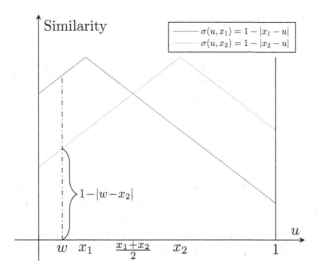

Fig. 2. User similarity with respect to the strategy profile (x_1, x_2). The blue line is the similarity function of x_1 with every user, and the red line is that of x_2. Every user $w \leq \frac{x_1+x_2}{2}$ selects x_1 with probability $\mu_1(w, (x_1, x_2)) = \frac{1-|x_2-w|}{2} + (|x_2-w| - |x_1-w|)$ and x_2 with probability $\mu_2(w, (x_1, x_2)) = \frac{1-|x_2-w|}{2}$. Similarly, every user $v \geq \frac{x_1+x_2}{2}$ selects x_1 with probability $\mu_1(v, (x_1, x_2)) = \frac{1-|x_1-v|}{2}$ and x_2 with probability $\mu_2(v, (x_1, x_2)) = \frac{1-|x_1-v|}{2} + (|x_1-v| - |x_2-v|)$. (Color figure online)

We focxus on a game $\mathcal{G}$ induced by the space of users $\mathcal{U} = [0, 1]$, uniform probability distribution $f(u) = \mathbb{1}_{0 \leq u \leq 1}$, two players, and a symmetric similarity function

$$\forall u, t \in [0, 1] : \sigma(u, t) = 1 - |u - t|.$$

Note that $\sigma(u, t)$ is merely one minus the absolute distance between $u \in [0, 1]$ and a potentially occupied location $t \in [0, 1]$.

Let (x_1, x_2) be a strategy profile such that $x_1 \leq x_2$. Observe that

$$\mu_1(u, (x_1, x_2)) = \begin{cases} \frac{\sigma(u, x_2)}{2} + \sigma(u, x_1) - \sigma(u, x_2) & u < \frac{x_1+x_2}{2} \\ \frac{\sigma(u, x_1)}{2} & u \geq \frac{x_1+x_2}{2} \end{cases}.$$

See Fig. 2 for visualization of the above. The payoff of player 1 is given by

$$\pi_1(x_1, x_2) = \int_0^1 \mu_1(u, (x_1, x_2))\, du = \int_0^{\frac{x_1+x_2}{2}} \left(\sigma(u, x_1) - \frac{\sigma(u, x_2)}{2}\right) du + \int_{\frac{x_1+x_2}{2}}^1 \sigma(u, x_1) du.$$

The construction of player 2's payoff is similar. Using elementary calculations, one can find the pure Nash equilibria of $\mathcal{G}$.

Proposition 1. *The strategy profile $\left(\frac{3}{8}, \frac{5}{8}\right)$ is the unique pure Nash equilibrium of $\mathcal{G}$, up to renaming the players.*

The proof of Proposition 1 is in the appendix. Indeed, in contrast to [14], under equilibrium profile players choose different locations. We leave the complete analysis of this setting (i.e. more players, higher dimensional space) for future work.

4   Analysis

We now examine the properties of Shapley facility location games. We begin with showing that every Shapley facility location game possesses a pure Nash equilibrium. Afterwards, we show that if mild assumptions are satisfied, learning dynamics will efficiently converge to an approximate equilibrium. This is despite of the infinite strategy space of the players. Finally, the price of anarchy is analyzed.

4.1   Pure Nash Equilibrium

In this subsection we show that Shapley facility location games possess pure Nash equilibrium. A non-cooperative game is called a *potential game* [19] if there exists a function $\Phi : \mathcal{U}^n \to \mathbb{R}$ such that for every strategy profile $\boldsymbol{x} = (x_1, \ldots, x_n) \in \mathcal{U}^n$ and every $i \in [n]$, whenever player i switches from x_i to a strategy $x_i' \in \mathcal{U}$, the change in her payoff function equals the change in the potential function, i.e.

$$\Phi(x_i', \boldsymbol{x}_{-i}) - \Phi(x_i, \boldsymbol{x}_{-i}) = \pi_i(x_i', \boldsymbol{x}_{-i}) - \pi_i(x_i, \boldsymbol{x}_{-i}).$$

Theorem 1. *Shapley facility location games are potential games.*

Proof. Fix a player i. Given a strategy profile $\boldsymbol{x}$, define:

$$c_u(y; \boldsymbol{x}) = |\{i \in [n] : y \le \sigma_u(x_i)\}|.$$

The latter represents the number of players that attract the infinitesimal user u under the locations of the players defined by the profile $\boldsymbol{x}$, in case he sampled the satisfaction level y. Consequently, the payoff of player i, formerly defined in Eq. (2), can be reformulated as

$$\pi_i(\boldsymbol{x}) = \int_{\mathcal{U}} f(u) \int_0^{\sigma_u(x_i)} \frac{1}{c_u(y; \boldsymbol{x})} dy\, du. \tag{3}$$

Next, we show that

$$\Phi(\boldsymbol{x}) = \int_{\mathcal{U}} f(u) \int_{y=0}^1 \sum_{i=1}^{c_u(y; \boldsymbol{x})} \frac{1}{i} dy\, du$$

is a potential function of the game. We temporarily focus on a user u. For any strategy profile $\boldsymbol{x}$ and user u, it holds that

$$c_u(y; \boldsymbol{x}) = \begin{cases} c_u(y; \boldsymbol{x}_{-i}) & y > \sigma_u(x_i) \\ c_u(y; \boldsymbol{x}_{-i}) + 1 & y \leq \sigma_u(x_i) \end{cases}.$$

Therefore, we have

$$\int_0^{\sigma_u(x_i)} \frac{dy}{c_u(y; \boldsymbol{x})} + \int_0^1 \sum_{j=1}^{c_u(y;\boldsymbol{x}_{-i})} \frac{1}{j} dy$$

$$= \int_0^{\sigma_u(x_i)} \frac{dy}{c_u(y; \boldsymbol{x}_{-i}) + 1} + \int_0^{\sigma_u(x_i)} \sum_{j=1}^{c_u(y;\boldsymbol{x}_{-i})} \frac{1}{j} dy + \int_{\sigma_u(x_i)}^1 \sum_{j=1}^{c_u(y;\boldsymbol{x}_{-i})} \frac{1}{j} dy$$

$$= \int_0^{\sigma_u(x_i)} \sum_{j=1}^{c_u(y;\boldsymbol{x}_{-i})+1} \frac{1}{j} dy + \int_{\sigma_u(x_i)}^1 \sum_{j=1}^{c_u(y;\boldsymbol{x}_{-i})} \frac{1}{j} dy$$

$$= \int_0^1 \sum_{j=1}^{c_u(y;\boldsymbol{x})} \frac{1}{j} dy. \tag{4}$$

We are now ready for the final argument. Fix two profiles, $(x_i, \boldsymbol{x}_{-i}), (x_i', \boldsymbol{x}_{-i})$. It follows that

$$\pi_i(x_i, \boldsymbol{x}_{-i}) - \pi_i(x_i', \boldsymbol{x}_{-i}) =$$

$$\int_{\mathcal{U}} f(u) \int_0^{\sigma_u(x_i)} \frac{1}{c_u(y; x_i, \boldsymbol{x}_{-i})} dy du - \int_{\mathcal{U}} f(u) \int_0^{\sigma_u(x_i')} \frac{1}{c_u(y; x_i', \boldsymbol{x}_{-i})} dy du =$$

$$\int_{\mathcal{U}} f(u) \int_0^{\sigma_u(x_i)} \frac{1}{c_u(y; x_i, \boldsymbol{x}_{-i}) + 1} dy du - \int_{\mathcal{U}} f(u) \int_0^{\sigma_u(x_i')} \frac{1}{c_u(y; x_i', \boldsymbol{x}_{-i}) + 1} dy du. \tag{5}$$

By adding and removing $\int_{\mathcal{U}} f(u) \int_0^1 \sum_{j=1}^{c_u(y;\boldsymbol{x}_{-i})} \frac{1}{j} dy du$ to Eq. (5), similar to what we showed in Eq. (4), we obtain

$$(5) = \int_{\mathcal{U}} f(u) \int_0^1 \sum_{j=1}^{c_u(y;\boldsymbol{x})} \frac{1}{j} dy du - \int_{\mathcal{U}} f(u) \int_0^1 \sum_{j=1}^{c_u(y;x_i',\boldsymbol{x}_{-i})} \frac{1}{j} dy du$$

$$= \Phi(\boldsymbol{x}) - \Phi(x_i', \boldsymbol{x}_{-i}).$$

□

Since $\mathcal{U}$ is a compact set and the payoff functions are continuous with respect to the strategy space, a direct result from Theorem 1 and [19, Lemma 4.3] is the following.

Corollary 1. *Every Shapley facility location game possesses a pure Nash equilibrium.*

4.2   Convergence to Approximate Equilibrium

In this subsection we examine learning dynamics of Shapley facility location games. The solution concept we are after is (multiplicative) approximate pure Nash equilibrium. In [7], the authors examined convergence of dynamics in symmetric (finite) congestion games. However, in Shapley facility location games the user space may be infinite; hence modifications are needed.

We begin with a few definitions. We say that a strategy profile x is an ϵ-pure Nash equilibrium (ϵ-PNE) for $\epsilon > 0$ if

$$\forall i \in [n], \forall x_i' \in \mathcal{U}: \quad \pi_i(x_i', x_{-i}) \leq (1 + \epsilon)\pi_i(x).$$

Notice that if x is an ϵ-PNE, then any player cannot improve her payoff by a factor of more than $(1 + \epsilon)$ of what she gets under x by unilaterally deviating to another location.

In the upcoming analysis, we assume players can efficiently compute ϵ-best response, if such exists. Indeed, this assumption holds for several plausible scenarios, such as concave payoff functions or discretization of Lipschitz user distribution.

The dynamics we consider are the following:
Best-response dynamics:

– Until reaching ϵ-PNE:
  • Pick an arbitrary player with a $(1 + \epsilon)$ profitable deviation, and move her to her deviating strategy.

It turns out that any such strategic interaction among the players will converge to an ϵ-PNE after efficient number of iterations.

Theorem 2. *Let $\epsilon \in (0, 1)$. In a Shapley facility location game with n players and an initial strategy x_0, after $\mathcal{O}\left(\frac{n \log n}{\epsilon} \log \frac{\Phi_{\max}}{\Phi(x_0)}\right)$ any best-response dynamics converges to ϵ-PNE.*

Before we turn to prove Theorem 2, we prove two supporting lemmas.

Lemma 1. *For every profile x it holds that*

$$\sum_{i=1}^{n} \pi_i(x) \geq \frac{\Phi(x)}{\ln(n) + 1}.$$

Proof. Fix a strategy profile x. Observe that

$$\sum_{i=1}^{n} \pi_i(x) = \sum_{i=1}^{n} \int_{\mathcal{U}} f(u) \int_0^{\sigma_u(x_i)} \frac{1}{c_u(y; x)} dy du$$

$$= \int_{\mathcal{U}} f(u) \sum_{i=1}^{n} \int_0^{\sigma_u(x_i)} \frac{1}{c_u(y; x)} dy du$$

$$= \int_{\mathcal{U}} f(u) \int_{c_u(y;x) \neq 0} 1 dy du.$$

Since $H_n = \sum_{i=1}^{n} \frac{1}{i} < \ln(n) + 1$, we have:

$$\int_{\mathcal{U}} f(u) \int_{c_u(y;x) \neq 0} 1 \, dy \, du \geq \frac{1}{\ln(n) + 1} \int_{\mathcal{U}} f(u) \int_{c_u(y;x) \neq 0} \sum_{i=1}^{n} \frac{1}{i} \, dy \, du$$

$$\geq \frac{1}{\ln(n) + 1} \int_{\mathcal{U}} f(u) \int_{0}^{1} \sum_{i=1}^{c_u(y;x)} \frac{1}{i} \, dy \, du$$

$$= \frac{\Phi(x)}{\ln(n) + 1}.$$

$\square$

Lemma 2. *Denote by i the index of the player chosen by the dynamics, and let x_i' denote her deviation. It follows that:*

$$\forall j \in [n] : \quad \pi_i(x_i', x_{-i}) - \pi_i(x) \geq \frac{\epsilon}{4} \pi_j(x).$$

Proof. In case $\pi_i(x) \geq \frac{\pi_j(x)}{4}$, player i has an ϵ-profitable deviation; hence it holds that

$$\pi_i(x_i', x_{-i}) - \pi_i(x) \geq \epsilon \pi_i(x) \geq \frac{\epsilon}{4} \pi_j(x).$$

Otherwise, $\pi_i(x) < \frac{\pi_j(x)}{4}$. Next, for every u, y such that $y \leq \sigma_u(s_j)$ it holds that

$$c_u(y; s_j, x_{-i}) = 2c_u(y; s_j) + c_u(y; x_{-i,j}) \leq 2c_u(y; s_j) + c_u(y; x_{-i,j}) + c_u(y; x_i)$$

$$= c_u(y; x) + 1 \leq 2c_u(y; x).$$

Thus,

$$\pi_i(s_j, x_{-i}) = \int_{\mathcal{U}} f(u) \int_{0}^{\sigma_u(s_j)} \frac{1}{c_u(y; s_j, x_{-i})} \, dy \, du \geq \int_{\mathcal{U}} f(u) \int_{0}^{\sigma_u(s_j)} \frac{1}{2c_u(y; x)} \, dy \, du$$

$$= \frac{\pi_j(x)}{2}.$$

Hence,

$$\pi_i(x_i', x_{-i}) - \pi_i(x) \geq \pi_i(s_j, x_{-i}) - \pi_i(x) \geq \frac{\pi_j(x)}{2} - \frac{\pi_j(x)}{4} \geq \frac{\epsilon}{4} \pi_j(x).$$

$\square$

We are now ready to prove Theorem 2.

Proof (of Theorem 2). In one iteration of the dynamics it holds that

$$\Phi(x_i', x_{-i}) - \Phi(x) = \pi_i(x_i', x_{-i}) - \pi_i(x)$$

$$\geq \frac{\epsilon}{4} \max_{j} \pi_j(x)$$

$$\geq \frac{\epsilon}{4n} \sum_{j=1}^{n} \pi_j(x)$$

$$\geq \frac{\epsilon}{4n(\ln(n) + 1)} \Phi(x).$$

Let $c = \frac{\epsilon}{4n(\ln(n)+1)} < 1$. Denote by m the number of iterations until convergence. Observe that

$$\Phi_{\max} \geq \Phi(\boldsymbol{x}_m) \geq (1+c)^m \Phi(\boldsymbol{x}_0). \tag{6}$$

If m does not satisfy Eq. (6),

$$\Phi_{\max} < (1+c)^m \Phi(\boldsymbol{x}_0) \leq e^{m \cdot c} \Phi(\boldsymbol{x}_0) \Rightarrow m \geq \frac{4n(\ln(n)+1)}{\epsilon} \ln\left(\frac{\Phi_{\max}}{\Phi(\boldsymbol{x}_0)}\right).$$

Therefore, an ϵ-PNE is obtained after at most $\mathcal{O}\left(\frac{n \log n}{\epsilon} \log \frac{\Phi_{\max}}{\Phi(\boldsymbol{x}_0)}\right)$ iterations of any best response dynamics. $\qquad\square$

4.3 Price of Anarchy

In this subsection we analyze the Price of Anarchy [17,24] of the discussed games, herein denoted PoA. The PoA measures the inefficiency of a game in terms of social welfare, as a result of selfish behavior of the players. Specifically, it is the ratio between an optimal dictatorial scenario and the social welfare of the worst equilibrium. If S is the set of all feasible profiles, and $E \subseteq S$ is the set of pure equilibrium profiles, then:

$$PoA = \frac{\max_{\boldsymbol{x} \in S} V(\boldsymbol{x})}{\min_{\boldsymbol{x} \in E} V(\boldsymbol{x})}.$$

The objective function of interest is the following:

$$V(\boldsymbol{x}) = \int_{\mathcal{U}} f(u) \max_i \sigma_u(x_i) du.$$

Note that V represents the sum of payoffs of the players, as well as the weighted maximum similarity users attain from the facilities under $\boldsymbol{x}$.

Theorem 3. *The PoA of Shapley facility location games is at most* $\frac{2n-1}{n}$.

The proof is in the appendix. After bounding the PoA, our objective is to show that this bound is tight, by presenting a game instance that achieves this bound.

Lemma 3. *There exists a game instance with PoA* $= \frac{2n-1}{n}$.

Proof. Consider an n-player game over $\mathcal{U} = [0,2]^n$. Let e_i denote the i'th vector of the canonical basis of $\mathbb{R}^n$, $\boldsymbol{0}$ be the zero vector in $\mathbb{R}^n$, and let $B_i = \{w \in \mathcal{U} : d(w, e_i) < \epsilon\}$ where $d(\cdot)$ is the euclidean distance and $\epsilon > 0$ is a small constant. Denote by α the volume of each such B_i. Consider the following density function:

$$f(u) = \begin{cases} \frac{1}{\alpha n} & \exists i : u \in B_i \\ 0 & Otherwise \end{cases}.$$

In addition, let the similarity function be

$$\forall u, w \in \mathcal{U} : \sigma_u(w) = \begin{cases} 1 & d(u,w) < \epsilon \text{ and } w \neq \mathbf{0} \\ \frac{n}{2n-1} & w = \mathbf{0} \\ 0 & Otherwise \end{cases}.$$

We now show that the strategy profile $\boldsymbol{x} = (\mathbf{0}, \mathbf{0}, \ldots, \mathbf{0})$ is in equilibrium. Consider player i's payoff under $\boldsymbol{x}$, and a possible unilateral deviation of her to e_i:

$$\pi_i(\boldsymbol{x}) = \frac{n}{2n-1}\frac{1}{n} = \frac{1}{2n-1}, \ \pi_i(e_i, \boldsymbol{x}_{-i}) = \frac{1}{n}\left(\frac{n}{2n-1}\frac{1}{n} + 1 - \frac{n}{2n-1}\right) = \frac{1}{2n-1}.$$

Since strategies outside $\{\mathbf{0}, e_1, \ldots, e_n\}$ are strictly dominated, we obtain $\pi_i(\boldsymbol{x}) \geq \pi_i(w, \boldsymbol{x}_{-i})$ for all $w \in \mathcal{U}$. Observe that $V(\boldsymbol{x}) = \frac{n}{2n-1}$. The optimal social welfare is one, obtained when players select unique locations, e.g. player i selects e_i. Therefore, $PoA = \frac{2n-1}{n}$. □

5 Relation to Shapley Value

Imagine a user being puzzled by the offers of the players. A novel way to decide which facility to select is to consider the players as being collaborative, and divide its share among all players, where each player gets a "fair" part. In this section, we show that the previously defined user reaction function coincides with a core solution concept in cooperative game theory, and can be characterized by a collection of desirable properties.

A cooperative game consists of two elements: a set of players and a *characteristic function*, which assigns a value to every coalition, i.e. every subset of players. The analysis of cooperative games focuses on predicting which coalitions will be formed, and how the payoff of a coalition should be distributed among its members. One core solution concept is the Shapley value [28].

Definition 2 (Shapley value). *Given a cooperative game with a set of players $[n]$ and a characteristic function $v : 2^{[n]} \to \mathbb{R}$ such that $v(\phi) = 0$, the Shapley value is a way to distribute the total gain among the players. According to the Shapley value, the amount that player i gets in a coalition game $(v, [n])$ is:*

$$\phi_i(v) \triangleq \frac{1}{n!} \sum_{R \in \Pi([n])} [v(P_i^R \cup \{i\}) - v(P_i^R)] \tag{7}$$

where $\Pi([n])$ is the set of all permutations of $[n]$ and P_i^R is the set of players which precede i in the permutation R.

The Shapley value is characterized by a collection of desirable properties:

- **Efficiency:** $\sum_{i=1}^n \phi_i(v) = v([n])$, i.e. the total gain is distributed.
- **Null player:** If $\forall \mathcal{C} \subseteq [n]$ it holds that $v(\mathcal{C} \cup \{i\}) = v(\mathcal{C})$, then $\phi_i(v) = 0$.

- **Symmetry:** If i, j are equivalent, namely $v(\mathcal{C} \cup \{i\}) = v(\mathcal{C} \cup \{j\})$ for all $\mathcal{C} \subseteq [n]$, then $\phi_i(v) = \phi_j(v)$.
- **Linearity:** If v, w are two cooperative games and α is a real number, then $\phi_i(\alpha v + w) = \alpha\phi_i(v) + \phi_i(w)$.

For our purposes, we temporarily focus on a specific user u. The characteristic function $v_u(\mathcal{C}; \boldsymbol{x})$ is defined to be the maximum similarity of u to one of the facilities chosen by the members of u under $\boldsymbol{x}$. Formally:

$$v_u(\mathcal{C}; \boldsymbol{x}) = \max_{i \in \mathcal{C}} \sigma_u(x_i).$$

This modeling follows the logic of Hotelling games, where each user is attracted to his nearest facility. Therefore, each user u initiates a cooperative game that consists of the players $[n]$, and $v_u(; \boldsymbol{x})$ as a characteristic function.

Denote the cooperative game defined over all users by V,

$$V(\mathcal{C}; \boldsymbol{x}) = \int_{\mathcal{U}} f(u) v_u(\mathcal{C}; \boldsymbol{x}) du.$$

We now bind the payoff of a player in the facility location model presented above and its Shapley value of the cooperative game V.

Theorem 4. *The payoff of player i under any pure strategy profile $\boldsymbol{x}$ is her Shapley value in the cooperative game $([n], V(; \boldsymbol{x}))$. Namely,*

$$\pi_i(\boldsymbol{x}) = \phi_i\left(V(; \boldsymbol{x})\right).$$

Proof. Due to [8,28], the Shapley value is fully characterized by the properties above. Therefore, if we show that the Shapley attraction function satisfies these properties, the theorem will be proven. Fix a strategy profile $\boldsymbol{x}$ and a user u. We show that $\mu_i(u, \boldsymbol{x})$ is the Shapley value of the cooperative game $v_u(; \boldsymbol{x})$:

- **Efficiency:** Observe that

$$\sum_{i=1}^{n} \mu_i(u, \boldsymbol{x}) = \sum_{i=1}^{n} \sum_{j=1}^{\rho_i} \frac{\sigma_u^j(\boldsymbol{x}) - \sigma_u^{j-1}(\boldsymbol{x})}{n - j + 1} = \sigma_u^n(\boldsymbol{x}) = \max_{i \in [n]} \sigma_u(x_i) = v\left([n]; \boldsymbol{x}\right).$$

- **Null player:** If i is a null player, it follows that $v_u(\mathcal{C}; \boldsymbol{x}) = v_u(\mathcal{C} \cup \{i\}; \boldsymbol{x})$ for every coalition $\mathcal{C}$, and in particular, for $\mathcal{C} = \emptyset$. Therefore $v(\{i\}; \boldsymbol{x}) = v(\emptyset; \boldsymbol{x}) \triangleq 0$, hence $\sigma_u(x_i) = 0$. By definition of μ, it holds that $\mu_i(u, \boldsymbol{x}) = 0$.
- **Symmetry:** $v(\{i\}; \boldsymbol{x}) = v(\{j\}; \boldsymbol{x})$ implies $\sigma_u(x_i) = \sigma_u(x_j)$, thus $\mu_i(u, \boldsymbol{x}) = \mu_j(u, \boldsymbol{x})$.
- **Linearity:** Note that μ is defined for a single user only. Therefore, we hereby extend it: for a distribution f over $\{u_1, u_2\}$, define

$$\mu_i\left((\{u_1, u_2\}, f), \boldsymbol{x}\right) = f(u_1)\mu_i(u_1, \boldsymbol{x}) + f(u_2)\mu_i(u_2, \boldsymbol{x}).$$

Hence, linearity holds as well.

Since μ satisfies Shapley's axioms, $\mu_i(u, \boldsymbol{x}) = \phi_i(v_u(; \boldsymbol{x}))$, and $\mu_i((\mathcal{U}, f), \boldsymbol{x})$ is the Shapley value of player i in the cooperative game $V(; \boldsymbol{x})$. Moreover,

$$\mu_i((\mathcal{U}, f), \boldsymbol{x}) = \int_{\mathcal{U}} f(u) \mu_i(u, \boldsymbol{x}) du = \pi_i(\boldsymbol{x}).$$

Thus the theorem is proved. $\square$

6   Discussion

We introduced Shapley facility location games, a framework incorporating probabilistic user behavior in facility location games. In this framework we considered choice selection among facilities motivated by the behavioral economics literature. Our results show that such probabilistic choice is "fair", and coincides with the Shapley value of a corresponding cooperative game. We proved that Shapley facility location games always possess pure Nash equilibria. We also crystallized the convergence rate in these games, and bounded their price of anarchy.

The reader may wonder whether the model can accommodate an asymmetric attraction function; that is, the case where the extent to which a user is attracted to a player depends not only on her chosen location, but also on her identity. Such asymmetry may result from power or influence a player possesses, which is a very natural assumption. Moreover, asymmetry can take the form of different sets of locations available to each player.

Consider a space $\mathcal{U}$ and a sequence of sets $\mathcal{L}_1, \mathcal{L}_2, \ldots, \mathcal{L}_n$, such that each player i is limited to select a location in $\mathcal{L}_i$. For each player i, we define $\mathcal{S}_i : \mathcal{U} \times \mathcal{L}_i \to [0,1]$ to be the similarity function with respect to player i, where again we require $\mathcal{S}_i$ to be continuous or simple.

All the results obtained are carried on to the asymmetric extension with minor modifications. This is apart from the rate of the convergence to approximate Nash equilibria via best response dynamics, as games are no longer symmetric. In particular, a pure Nash equilibrium is still guaranteed to exist, the PoA bound is still valid, and player payoffs correspond to Shapley values in the cooperative game.

An instance of such an asymmetric game, the *limited attraction model*, was recently discussed in [13,29]. In that model, the attraction of each player i is limited to a ball of size r_i, and users outside her chosen ball will not be attracted to her. Thereupon, each user chooses, with equal probability, a player that attracts him. It can be verified that if $\mathcal{L}_i = \mathcal{U}$ and if the similarity function of player i is

$$\forall u \in \mathcal{U}, l \in \mathcal{L}_i : \mathcal{S}_i(t, l) = \begin{cases} 1 & d(u, l) \leq r_i \\ 0 & Otherwise \end{cases},$$

the model obtained is exactly the model of [13]. In particular, it can be verified that player payoffs in [13] correspond to their Shapley value in the cooperative game introduced in the previous section.

Another interesting question is whether *every* Shapley facility location game possesses a unique pure Nash equilibrium, as it was the case in our illustrative example. Clearly, this is not the case. Taken to the extreme, consider a similarity function which is constant for every user and every location. It follows that every strategy profile is in equilibrium.

It is worth noticing that our work is distinguished from most previous work in facility location games, as our games are not zero-sum. Interestingly, we showed they are potential games [19,23], which allows us to connect to a main branch of research in the interplay between CS and game theory [20].

As for future work, we believe that putting data science tasks in the context of competition may be of interest. Since our model is general, tractable and efficient, it may serve as a benchmark for the study of strategic product selection in data science settings. Such settings include several Internet applications, e.g. where facilities and users are associated with document contents and queries, respectively, and the aim of the players (content authors) is to be the closest in their published content to as many queries as possible [4,15].

Omitted proofs can be found in the full version of this paper available publicly on arXiv http://arxiv.org/abs/1709.10278.

Acknowledgments. This project has received funding from the European Research Council (ERC) under the European Union's Horizon 2020 research and innovation programme (grant agreement no. 740435).

References

1. Ahn, H.K., Cheng, S.W., Cheong, O., Golin, M., Van Oostrum, R.: Competitive facility location: the voronoi game. Theoret. Comput. Sci. **310**(1), 457–467 (2004)
2. Awerbuch, B., Azar, Y., Epstein, A., Mirrokni, V.S., Skopalik, A.: Fast convergence to nearly optimal solutions in potential games. In: Proceedings of the 9th ACM Conference on Electronic Commerce, pp. 264–273. ACM (2008)
3. Barron, G., Erev, I.: Small feedback-based decisions and their limited correspondence to description-based decisions. J. Behav. Decis. Making **16**(3), 215–233 (2003)
4. Ben-Basat, R., Tennenholtz, M., Kurland, O.: The probability ranking principle is not optimal in adversarial retrieval settings. In: Proceedings of the 2015 International Conference on the Theory of Information Retrieval, ICTIR 2015, Northampton, Massachusetts, USA, 27–30 September 2015, pp. 51–60 (2015)
5. Brenner, S.: Location (hotelling) games and applications. In: Wiley Encyclopedia of Operations Research and Management Science (2011)
6. Cheong, O., Har-Peled, S., Linial, N., Matousek, J.: The one-round voronoi game. Discret. Comput. Geom. **31**(1), 125–138 (2004)
7. Chien, S., Sinclair, A.: Convergence to approximate nash equilibria in congestion games. In: Proceedings of the Eighteenth Annual ACM-SIAM Symposium on Discrete Algorithms, pp. 169–178. Society for Industrial and Applied Mathematics (2007)
8. Dubey, P.: On the uniqueness of the shapley value. Int. J. Game Theory **4**(3), 131–139 (1975)
9. Eaton, B.C., Lipsey, R.G.: The principle of minimum differentiation reconsidered: some new developments in the theory of spatial competition. Rev. Econ. Stud. **42**(1), 27–49 (1975)

10. Erev, I., Ert, E., Plonsky, O.: From anomalies to forecasts: a choice prediction competition for decisions under risk and ambiguity. Technical report, Mimeo, pp. 1–56 (2015)
11. Erev, I., Ert, E., Roth, A.E., Haruvy, E., Herzog, S.M., Hau, R., Hertwig, R., Stewart, T., West, R., Lebiere, C.: A choice prediction competition: choices from experience and from description. J. Behav. Decis. Making 23(1), 15–47 (2010)
12. Fekete, S.P., Meijer, H.: The one-round voronoi game replayed. Comput. Geom. 30(2), 81–94 (2005)
13. Feldman, M., Fiat, A., Obraztsova, S.: Variations on the hotelling-downs model. In: Thirtieth AAAI Conference on Artificial Intelligence (2016)
14. Hotelling, H.: Stability in competition. Econ. J. 39(153), 41–57 (1929)
15. Izsak, P., Raiber, F., Kurland, O., Tennenholtz, M.: The search duel: a response to a strong ranker. In: Proceedings of the 37th International ACM SIGIR Conference on Research and Development in Information Retrieval, pp. 919–922. ACM (2014)
16. Kahneman, D., Tversky, A.: Prospect theory: an analysis of decision under risk. Econometrica 47(2), 263–292 (1979)
17. Koutsoupias, E., Papadimitriou, C.: Worst-case equilibria. In: Meinel, C., Tison, S. (eds.) STACS 1999. LNCS, vol. 1563, pp. 404–413. Springer, Heidelberg (1999). https://doi.org/10.1007/3-540-49116-3_38
18. McFadden, D.: Econometric models for probabilistic choice among products. J. Bus. 53(3), S13–S29 (1980). Part 2: Interfaces Between Marketing and Economics
19. Monderer, D., Shapley, L.S.: Potential games. Games Econ. Behav. 14(1), 124–143 (1996)
20. Nisan, N., Roughgarden, T., Tardos, E., Vazirani, V.: Algorithmic Game Theory, vol. 1. Cambridge University Press, Cambridge (2007)
21. Plonsky, O., Erev, I., Hazan, T., Tennenholtz, M.: Psychological forest: Predicting human behavior (2017)
22. Procaccia, A., Tennenholtz, M.: Approximate mechanism design without money. In: EC-09 (2009)
23. Rosenthal, R.W.: A class of games possessing pure-strategy nash equilibria. Int. J. Game Theory 2(1), 65–67 (1973)
24. Roughgarden, T.: Intrinsic robustness of the price of anarchy. In: Proceedings of the Forty-First Annual ACM Symposium on Theory of Computing, pp. 513–522. ACM (2009)
25. Schummer, J., Vohra, R.: Mechanism design without money. In: Nisan, N., Roughgarden, T., Tardos, E., Vazirani, V.V. (eds.) Algorithmic Game Theory, pp. 110–130. Cambridge University Press (2007)
26. Shaked, A.: Non-existence of equilibrium for the two-dimensional three-firms location problem. Rev. Econ. Stud. 42(1), 51–56 (1975)
27. Shaked, A.: Existence and computation of mixed strategy Nash equilibrium for 3-firms location problem. J. Ind. Econ. 31(1/2), 93–96 (1982). Symposium on Spatial Competition and the Theory of Differentiated Markets
28. Shapley, L.S.: A value for n-person games. Techncial report, DTIC Document (1952)
29. Shen, W., Wang, Z.: Hotelling-downs model with limited attraction. In: Proceedings of the 16th Conference on Autonomous Agents and MultiAgent Systems, pp. 660–668. International Foundation for Autonomous Agents and Multiagent Systems (2017)
30. Simon, H.A.: Rational choice and the structure of the environment. Psychol. Rev. 63(2), 129 (1956)

Coordination Mechanisms, Cost-Sharing, and Approximation Algorithms for Scheduling

Ioannis Caragiannis[1(✉)], Vasilis Gkatzelis[2], and Cosimo Vinci[3]

[1] University of Patras, Rion-Patras, Greece
caragian@ceid.upatras.gr
[2] Drexel University, Philadelphia, PA, USA
gkatz@drexel.edu
[3] Gran Sasso Science Institute, L'Aquila, Italy
cosimo.vinci@gssi.it

Abstract. We reveal a connection between coordination mechanisms for unrelated machine scheduling and cost-sharing protocols. Using this connection, we interpret three coordination mechanisms from the recent literature as Shapley-value-based cost-sharing protocols, thus providing a unifying justification regarding why these mechanisms induce potential games. More importantly, this connection provides a template for designing novel coordination mechanisms, as well as approximation algorithms for the underlying optimization problem. The designer need only decide the total cost to be suffered on each machine, and then the Shapley value can be used to induce games guaranteed to possess a potential function; these games can, in turn, be used to design algorithms. To verify the power of this approach, we design a combinatorial algorithm that achieves an approximation guarantee of 1.81 for the problem of minimizing the total weighted completion time for unrelated machines. To the best of our knowledge, this is the best approximation guarantee among combinatorial polynomial-time algorithms for this problem.

1 Introduction

Since the 1950s, the study of scheduling has played a central role in both operations research and computer science. Machine scheduling models have provided a very useful abstraction that has enabled researchers to devise solutions with a wide range of applications. Depending on the context, the "machine" that the schedule is applied to can range from an airport runway serving multiple airplanes, and a classroom used for several courses, to a CPU that needs to process a set of jobs. In all of these examples, the ultimate goal is the efficient utilization of scarce resources. Most of the initial work on machine scheduling focused on designing algorithms that yield efficient schedules, where efficiency is quantified using a measure such as the makespan or the total weighted completion time of the jobs (e.g., see [25]). In the last two decades, motivated by the prevalence of large decentralized environments where the scheduler may have limited information or limited power in enforcing the schedule, many of these machine scheduling problems have been revisited from a game-theoretic point of view.

© Springer International Publishing AG 2017
N. R. Devanur and P. Lu (Eds.): WINE 2017, LNCS 10674, pp. 74–87, 2017.
https://doi.org/10.1007/978-3-319-71924-5_6

In a well-studied example of such a problem, each user controls a job that may require different processing times on each machine. These users are self-interested and they can decide which machine their job is assigned to, aiming to minimize its completion time. Each machine, however, is equipped with a decentralized scheduler, a *coordination mechanism* [12], that decides how the jobs assigned to that machine will be scheduled. Given the strategic nature of the users (which we henceforth call players since they are engaged in a game), these policies affect (and, in a sense, coordinate) their behavior. Unlike scheduling algorithms, which have full control over the outcome and can directly output efficient schedules, coordination mechanisms need to provide the appropriate incentives such that the game induced among the users leads to efficient schedules in equilibrium. Therefore, a highly desired property for a coordination mechanism is to induce potential games: these games guarantee the existence of pure Nash equilibria as well as convergence to them after finite sequences of steps. The *price of anarchy* measure can then be used in order to evaluate how inefficient the equilibria of these games may be, compared to the most efficient schedule.

The design of coordination mechanisms has often borrowed results from the literature on scheduling algorithms. For instance, when the efficiency is measured using the total weighted completion time objective, it is known that the best way to schedule the jobs assigned to each machine is based on the Smith's rule policy [33]. This scheduling policy is therefore a natural first candidate to use when designing a coordination mechanism. But, it turns out that the resulting coordination mechanism may induce games that have no pure Nash equilibria [16]. Furthermore, the price of anarchy of this mechanism is 4 [15], which falls short compared to other mechanisms in this setting. Specifically, Cole et al. [15] propose two alternative coordination mechanisms, ProportionalSharing and Rand (defined in detail later), and they show that their price of anarchy is 2.618 and at most 2.133, respectively. Furthermore, both of these mechanisms induce potential games. As a result, the optimal coordination mechanisms need not be similar to the best scheduling algorithms.

A much more surprising fact is that ideas from coordination mechanisms can actually help in designing new scheduling algorithms! In particular, if one can compute, or at least approximate, an equilibrium of a mechanism with good price of anarchy, then this implies a good approximation algorithm. Using this approach, Cole et al. [15] obtained a $2 + \epsilon$-approximation algorithm for minimizing the total weighted completion time. They first defined a novel coordination mechanism, Approx, which induces potential games, and then designed a local-search algorithm that computes an assignment of jobs to machines by mimicking the best-response dynamics of the players in the game induced by Approx. Once the desired assignment of jobs to machines was reached, the algorithm then used the Smith's rule policy to schedule the jobs within each machine. What is very interesting about this result is that it uses the game-theoretic analysis to design an, otherwise counter-intuitive, algorithm with appealing performance guarantees. Can the ideas behind the design of Approx be generalized to a template that yields even more efficient combinatorial approximation algorithms?

1.1 Related Work

Since the definition of coordination mechanisms [12], a long list of papers has mostly focused on the design of policies in machine scheduling settings, aiming to minimize the makespan (e.g., [2,5,7–9,22,23]) or the total (weighted) completion time (e.g., [1,15,16,20]). Apart from machine scheduling settings, coordination mechanisms have also been proposed for congestion games [14].

A literature that is very closely related to coordination mechanisms aims to design cost-sharing protocols that yield efficient equilibria (e.g., [3,11,13,17–19, 24,27–29]). Two of the most well-known cost-sharing protocols are the *marginal contribution* and the *Shapley value* [31].

The problem of scheduling jobs on unrelated machines aiming to minimize the total weighted completion time has been studied extensively in the machine scheduling literature (for a detailed list of some of the classic results see [25, Chap. 11]). For instances in the specific machine model of *unrelated* machines that we consider in this paper (formally defined in the following section), until very recently, the best approximation guarantee was a factor or 1.5, obtained using a convex quadratic relaxation of the problem [30,32]. This has now been marginally improved by Bansal et al. [6] and Li [26] who showed that an approximation factor better than 1.5 is possible: their algorithms achieve a $(1.5 - c)$–approximation for an insignificantly small, yet positive constant c.

1.2 Our Results

In this paper, we study the interplay between coordination mechanisms and scheduling algorithms in more depth, and we also uncover interesting connections between coordination mechanisms and cost-sharing policies. As our first conceptual contribution, we observe (in Sect. 3) that the three coordination mechanisms ProportionalSharing, Rand, and Approx all follow a common recipe: these mechanisms can be defined as Shapley-value cost-sharing protocols. The Shapley-value is known to induce potential games, hence, the existence of a potential function follows immediately. This suggests a reverse engineering approach in the design of coordination mechanisms: all the designer has to do is to define an appropriate function that maps sets of jobs within each machine to a total cost. Then, the Shapley-value cost-sharing method is used to divide the total cost within each machine to the jobs; the cost charged to each job is then translated into a (weighted) completion time of the particular job.

In the above recipe, there is a feasibility constraint that has to be satisfied for the induced coordination mechanisms to be well-defined: there has to exist a feasible schedule of the jobs such that their completion times yields the desired costs. This is not necessary, however, when designing combinatorial approximation algorithms for the underlying optimization problem. It suffices to define appropriate total cost function and, as in [15], mimic the strategic behavior of (hypothetical) players that experience the Shapley-value share as cost. The last step of using the Smith's rule within each machine to compute the final schedule fixes possible feasibility issues. This template is presented in detail in Sect. 4.

Our main technical contribution is the analysis of a class of combinatorial approximation algorithms that follow the template above. The best among them achieves 1.81-approximate schedules with respect to the total weighted completion time objective. This improves the algorithmic result of Cole et al. [15] and, to the best of our knowledge, is the best worst-case approximation guarantee by a combinatorial polynomial-time algorithm for the problem. Better results are possible for particular input instances. We complement these results by showing (in Sect. 5) that none among the three coordination mechanisms Proportional-Sharing, Rand, and Approx can be used to obtain approximation guarantees better than 2 using this template. Furthermore, we use this last result to obtain a tight lower bound of 4 on the price of anarchy of Approx.

Section 2 is devoted to preliminary definitions and notation. We conclude in Sect. 6. Due to lack of space, all proofs have been omitted; they will appear in the final version of the paper.

2   Preliminaries

We consider machine scheduling instances that consist of a set I of m machines and a set J of n jobs. We denote by p_{ij} the processing time of job j on machine i and by w_j the weight of job j. The *Smith ratio* ρ_{ij} is defined as the ratio p_{ij}/w_j. An *assignment* σ is a function that assigns each job j to a machine σ_j that processes the job. The standard notation (σ_{-j}, i) is used to denote the assignment in which job j is assigned to machine i while the remaining jobs use the same machine they use in σ. We denote by $J_i(\sigma) := \{j \in J : \sigma_j = i\}$ the set of jobs assigned by σ to machine i. In general, we focus on the *unrelated machines* setting, where the processing times p_{ij} can be arbitrary. In the *related machines* setting, each machine i has a speed $s_i > 0$, each job j has a processing requirement p_j, and the processing times are defined as $p_{ij} = p_j/s_i$.

A *coordination mechanism* comprises a set of local scheduling policies, one for each machine. A *scheduling policy* for a machine i determines the schedule of the jobs assigned to machine i by σ. The scheduling policy for machine i is *local* if it does not depend on the set of jobs assigned to other machines. A coordination mechanism $\mathcal{A}$ simply defines the completion time $c_j^{\mathcal{A}}(\sigma)$ of job j on machine σ_j. As scheduling policies are local, $c_j^{\mathcal{A}}$ can be equivalently defined as a function of machine σ_j and the set of jobs $J_{\sigma_j}(\sigma)$ only. The quantity $C^{\mathcal{A}}(\sigma) := \sum_{j \in J} w_j c_j^{\mathcal{A}}(\sigma)$ is the *total weighted completion time* (or *total weighted cost*) of assignment σ. We use the notation $C_i^{\mathcal{A}}(\sigma) := \sum_{j \in J_i(\sigma)} w_j c_j^{\mathcal{A}}(\sigma)$ to refer to the total weighted completion time of the jobs assigned to machine i, i.e., $C^{\mathcal{A}}(\sigma) = \sum_{i \in I} C_i^{\mathcal{A}}(\sigma)$.

For instance, the SmithRule scheduling policy schedules the jobs assigned to machine i in a non-decreasing order of their Smith ratios ρ_{ij}; for resolving ties between pairs of jobs j and k with the same Smith's ratio, a common tie-breaking rule is used in all machines. We use the notation $\rho_{ij} \prec \rho_{ik}$ to denote the fact that either $\rho_{ij} < \rho_{ik}$, or $\rho_{ij} = \rho_{ik}$ but j gets higher priority by the tie-breaking rule. A coordination mechanism can be randomized; in this case, the scheduling policy within each machine is randomized, i.e., a probability distribution over deterministic policies.

Assuming that each job is controlled by a self-interested player who decides the machine on which her job will be assigned, a coordination mechanism naturally defines a strategic game among the players. Each player has any machine as possible strategy and her cost is simply the (expected) weighted completion time of her job as defined by the coordination mechanism. Hence, in an assignment σ, the cost of player j when the coordination mechanism $\mathcal{A}$ is used is simply $w_j c_j^{\mathcal{A}}(\sigma)$. Then, the assignment σ is a *pure Nash equilibrium* if no player has any incentive to deviate from her strategy in σ.

A desirable property from a coordination mechanism is to define *potential games*. This means that there exists a potential function $\Phi^{\mathcal{A}}(\cdot)$ that is defined over assignments with the property that for every pair of assignment σ and σ' that differ only in the strategy of a single player j, it holds $\Phi^{\mathcal{A}}(\sigma) - \Phi^{\mathcal{A}}(\sigma') = w_j c_j^{\mathcal{A}}(\sigma) - w_j c_j^{\mathcal{A}}(\sigma')$. The existence of a potential function implies that a pure Nash equilibrium not only exists but can also be found after a finite sequence of improving deviations (e.g., best-response deviations) by the players.

The total weighted completion time is a natural *social cost* measure that can be used to assess the quality of equilibria. The price of anarchy of a scheduling instance is then defined as the worst-case ratio of $C^{\mathcal{A}}(\sigma)/\text{OPT}$, where σ is a pure Nash equilibrium of the game induced by mechanism $\mathcal{A}$ on instance M and OPT denotes the minimum value of total weighted completion time over all possible assignments and schedules (i.e., including schedules that are not produced by $\mathcal{A}$) of jobs to machines.

Beyond machine scheduling settings, *cost-sharing protocols* define ways in which a total cost is to be shared among a set N of agents who are competing for a collection of resources. Each resource i is characterized by a cost function $C_i : 2^N \rightarrow \mathbb{R}_+$, which quantifies the total cost that this resource would suffer, depending on the subset of the agents that end up using it. For the system to support itself, the agents using a resource need to contribute some amount such that their total contributions cover the total cost that they cause. The decision regarding how the cost f_j that each agent j needs to contributed is defined by a cost-sharing protocol. If the cost-shares that this protocol charges to the agents $S \subseteq N$ using a resource i always add up to exactly the total cost $C_i(S)$, then the cost-sharing protocol is called *budget-balanced*. Under some circumstances, the cost-sharing protocol may also charge the agents more than the total cost that they generated, which is often referred to as *over-charging*.

Two of the best-known cost-sharing protocols are the *marginal contribution* and the *Shapley value* [31]. According to the marginal contribution, the cost-share of each agent $j \in S$ is equal to $C_i(S) - C_i(S \setminus \{j\})$, i.e., equal to the increase in the total cost due to the presence of j. As long as the cost functions, $C_i(\cdot)$ are supermodular, these cost-shares cover the total cost, but they may be overcharging the agents. On the other hand, the Shapley value is budget-balanced and the cost-share of each agent j is equal to the expected value of the following process: order the agents of S uniformly at random, let $S_{<j}$ be the

subset of these agents that lie before j in the ordering, and charge j a cost of $C_i(S_{<j} \cup \{j\}) - C_i(S_{<j})$. In other words, the agents arrive in that random order and each one of them is charged for her marginal contribution with respect to the agents that have arrived up to that point.

We remark that cost-sharing protocols can be naturally defined on machine scheduling instances with each machine corresponding to a resource and with each job corresponding to an agent. This is exactly the analogy we consider in the next section.

3   Coordination Mechanisms as Cost-Sharing Protocols

In this section we revisit coordination mechanisms that led to surprisingly good price of anarchy guarantees through the lens of cost-sharing protocols. In particular, we reveal that these mechanisms can be interpreted as Shapley value cost-sharing protocols of appropriate total cost functions. This connection directly explains why these mechanisms induce potential games, and it sets the stage for a framework that enables the design of novel local-search approximation algorithms, discussed in Sect. 4. In this section we first discuss the coordination mechanisms analyzed in [15], and then we prove how all of these mechanisms can be viewed as cost-sharing protocols.

3.1   Coordination Mechanisms

Arguably the most natural scheduling policy for the problem of minimizing the total weighted completion time is the SmithRule (SR). This is a deterministic policy which schedules the jobs assigned to each machine i without preemption, in non-decreasing order with respect to their smith ratios ρ_{ij}. When the weights of all the jobs are equal, this reduces to the shortest–first policy and, for any given assignment σ, the SmithRule policy is known to minimize the total weighted completion time [33]. Formally, the weighted completion time of each job j under the SmithRule policy is:

$$w_j c_j^{\mathsf{SR}}(\sigma) = \sum_{\substack{k \in J_i(\sigma) \\ \rho_{ik} \prec \rho_{ij}}} w_j p_{ik} + w_j p_{ij}$$

Cole et al. [15] analyzed the game induced by the SmithRule coordination mechanism and showed that its price of anarchy is exactly 4. They also showed that, any mechanism that uses a deterministic policy that orders the jobs without preemption has a price of anarchy of 4.

To achieve a price of anarchy better than 4, Cole et al. [15] analyzed a deterministic but preemptive scheduling policy called ProportionalSharing (PS), and they showed that its price of anarchy is 2.618. According to this policy, all jobs are scheduled in parallel, with each job j receiving a fraction of machine j's processing time that is proportional to its weight, i.e., $w_j / \sum_{k \in J_i} w_k$. The completion times of this scheduling policy are actually equivalent to scheduling the jobs in a nonpreemptive fashion, just as SmithRule would, but then delaying the completion of each job by an appropriate amount. Although these delays increase the social cost of any given assignment, Cole et al. [15] show that this changes the equilibrium structure of the induced game, thus leading to significantly more efficient equilibria. The delay that a job j suffers beyond its SmithRule completion time is equal to the externality that it causes to jobs that SmithRule schedules after them on the same machine, i.e., $\sum_{k:\rho_{ik} \succ \rho_{ij}} w_k p_{ij}$. Formally, the weighted completion time of job j under the ProportionalSharing policy is:

$$w_j c_j^{\mathsf{PS}}(\boldsymbol{\sigma}) = \sum_{\substack{k \in J_i(\boldsymbol{\sigma}) \\ \rho_{ik} \prec \rho_{ij}}} w_j p_{ik} + \sum_{\substack{k \in J_i(\boldsymbol{\sigma}) \\ \rho_{ik} \succ \rho_{ij}}} w_k p_{ij} + w_j p_{ij}$$

Rand (R) is a randomized scheduling policy according to which, given two jobs j and k assigned to the same machine i, the probability that job k is processed before job j is equal to $q_{kj} := \frac{\rho_{ij}}{\rho_{ij} + \rho_{ik}}$. Once the order of the jobs is randomly generated, the jobs are scheduled one after the other, without preemption. Thus:

$$w_j c_j^{\mathsf{R}}(\boldsymbol{\sigma}) = \sum_{k \in J_i(\boldsymbol{\sigma}) \setminus \{j\}} q_{kj} w_j p_{ik} + w_j p_{ij} = \sum_{k \in J_i(\boldsymbol{\sigma}) \setminus \{j\}} \frac{\rho_{ij}}{\rho_{ij} + \rho_{ik}} w_j p_{ik} + w_j p_{ij}$$

Cole et al. [15] showed that this randomized mechanism has a price of anarchy of 2.133.

Finally, Approx (A) is a deterministic scheduling policy that Cole et al. [15] defined not aiming for an improved price of anarchy bound, but rather for the design of an approximation algorithm for the underlying optimization problem. In particular, the completion times defined by this policy are equal to those of the ProportionalSharing policy, but with the addition of delays for each job j on machine i by exactly p_{ij}.

$$w_j c_j^{\mathsf{A}}(\boldsymbol{\sigma}) = \sum_{\substack{k \in J_i(\boldsymbol{\sigma}) \\ \rho_{ik} \prec \rho_{ij}}} w_j p_{ik} + \sum_{\substack{k \in J_i(\boldsymbol{\sigma}) \\ \rho_{ik} \succ \rho_{ij}}} w_k p_{ij} + 2 w_j p_{ij}$$

The price of anarchy of this mechanism is at most 4, and it can be used to define a polynomial time approximation algorithm for the underlying optimization problem with an approximation factor of 2.

3.2   Cost-Sharing Protocols

In the cost-sharing literature, the group of agents using some resource generates a cost on that resource. This cost depends on the nature of the resource at hand, as well as the set of agents using it, and the goal of the cost-sharing protocol is to share this cost among the users of the resource. At first glance, this is unlike the coordination mechanisms defined above, whose scheduling policies define the costs of the agents directly rather than sharing some well-defined cost. However, there is a natural connection between cost-sharing protocols and coordination mechanisms. Given an assignment σ, one can assume that this assignment causes a (social) cost of at least $C_i^{\mathsf{SR}}(\sigma)$ on each machine i, since SmithRule is the policy that minimizes that social cost. Hence, the SmithRule policy can be interpreted as a cost-sharing protocol that decides how this social cost is to be shared among the agents. In fact, this is a budget-balanced cost-sharing protocol since the cost that SmithRule divides among the agents adds up to exactly $C_i^{\mathsf{SR}}(\sigma)$. More generally, using this approach, we can interpret any coordination mechanism $\mathcal{A}$ that induces a social cost $C_i^{\mathcal{A}}(\sigma)$ on machine i as a cost-sharing protocols that decides how this social cost needs to be divided among the jobs using machine i. The following lemmas reveal that, rather surprisingly, ProportionalSharing, Rand, and Approx are all using the exact same cost-sharing protocol to divide their total cost: the Shapley value!

$$f_j(\sigma) = \sum_{S \subseteq J_i(\sigma) \setminus \{j\}} \Pr[S, J_i(\sigma)](C_i(S \cup \{j\}) - C_i(S)),$$

where $\Pr[S, J_i(\sigma)]$ is the probability that the set of jobs that lie before j in the random ordering is exactly the set S.

Lemma 1. ProportionalSharing, Rand, *and* Approx *are all equivalent to the Shapley-value cost-sharing of cost functions* $C^{\mathsf{PS}}(\sigma), C^{\mathsf{R}}(\sigma)$, *and* $2C^{\mathsf{SR}}(\sigma)$ *respectively.*

One important implication of this lemma is that the connection to the Shapley value cost-sharing directly implies that the induced games are potential games, and it also directly implies what the potential function is. Without this observation, Cole et al. [15] had to provide three separate proofs to prove that these games always possess pure Nash equilibria.

More importantly, another implication of this lemma is that it provides a general way of designing coordination mechanisms that are guaranteed to induce potential games: define a cost function $C_i^{\alpha}(\sigma)$ for each machine i, which can depend arbitrarily on the set of jobs assigned to that machine, and then use the Shapley value in order to define the cost-share that each job should suffer. It is important to emphasize that a critical difference between cost-sharing protocols and coordination mechanisms is that the latter are restricted by feasibility constraints implied by the scheduling model. That is, there has to exist some feasible schedule for processing the jobs such that each job's cost is equal to what is dictated by the cost-sharing protocol. For instance, in our model, SmithRule is the only budget-balanced mechanism that is also feasible, since any other feasible way of scheduling the jobs would necessarily lead to a higher social cost. An interesting future research direction would be to understand what constraints on the cost function C_i^{α} can guarantee the feasibility of the Shapley value cost-sharing schedule. However, the main result of this paper shows that, even when the induced mechanisms do not yield feasible schedules, they can be used to design novel approximation algorithms for the underlying optimization problem.

4   Approximation Algorithms via Cost-Sharing

Even if the mechanism designer could control which machine each job is assigned to, the problem of computing a feasible schedule that minimizes the total weighted completion time is known to be APX-hard [21]. The best approximation factor guarantee was only very recently improved beyond 1.5, using elaborate lift-and-round techniques on convex programming relaxations, to reach an approximation factor no less than 1.4999 [6]. The machine scheduling literature has traditionally emphasized the importance of *combinatorial* algorithms which, unlike convex program-based solutions, provide more intuition regarding the structure of the problem at hand. To the best of our knowledge, the combinatorial algorithm providing the best approximation guarantees for this problem, prior to our work, yields a factor of $2 + \epsilon$ for some arbitrarily small constant $\epsilon > 0$ [15].

In light of the connection between coordination mechanisms and cost-sharing identified in the previous section, and using the fact that the Shapley value cost-sharing protocol is guaranteed to induce potential games, we now propose a general framework for designing combinatorial approximation algorithms for this problem, using mechanisms based on the Shapley value. The following steps, explained in more detail later on, provide a high-level description of our framework for designing such algorithms:

1. For each machine i and each subset of jobs J_i define some cost $C_i(J_i)$
2. Using the Shapley value protocol, define the cost $f_j(J_i)$ for each $j \in J_i$
3. In a polynomial number of best-response deviations, reach an assignment σ
4. Assign the jobs according to σ and process them using the SmithRule order

The key ingredient in this framework is that, using the Shapley value to divide the chosen costs, $C_i(J_i)$, is guaranteed to induce a potential game. This implies that any sequence of best response dynamics will eventually lead to an assignment that is a pure Nash equilibrium of this game. This may require an exponential number of such deviations but, as we show, we can guarantee that a polynomial number of deviations suffices for this approach to reach an assignment that is an approximate equilibrium. As a result, if our choice of $C_i(J_i)$ gives rise to high quality (approximate) equilibria, then this framework yields a high quality polynomial time algorithm[1].

The $(2 + \epsilon)$-approximation algorithm proposed by Cole et al. [15] for this problem can be directly presented as an instantiation of this framework. Their algorithm uses Approx to define the costs $C_i(J_i) := C_i^A(J_i)$ in the first step and, unbeknownst to them, this mechanism divides these costs among the jobs according to the Shapley value protocol, as we showed in Lemma 1. Then, they prove that the induced game is, in fact, a potential game, and they use this

---

[1] Note that computing the Shapley value cost-shares can be non-trivial, or even intractable, if the $C_i(J_i)$ is arbitrarily general, but most of the natural choices for this function provide sufficient structure for the shares to be readily computable, as verified in the previous and the following section.

to show that a polynomial number of deviations will lead to an assignment σ whose social cost is essentially no worse than that of any equilibrium of the game induced by Approx. Since the price of anarchy of Approx is at most 4, the assignment σ that this algorithm computes satisfies $C^{\mathsf{A}}(\sigma) \leq (4 + \epsilon)C^{\mathsf{SR}}(\sigma^*)$. But, since $C^{\mathsf{A}}(\sigma) = 2C^{\mathsf{SR}}(\sigma)$, this implies that $C^{\mathsf{SR}}(\sigma) \leq (2 + \epsilon)C^{\mathsf{SR}}(\sigma^*)$, thus verifying the approximation factor. A more natural presentation of the same algorithm would instead use the optimal social cost, $C_i(J_i) := C_i^{\mathsf{SR}}(\sigma)$, in the first step; we refer to the mechanism that shares this optimal cost using the Shapley value as ShapleyValue. Lemma 1 implies that the game induced by ShapleyValue is essentially the same as the one induced by Approx: for every possible assignment σ, the cost of every job j in Approx is exactly twice its cost in ShapleyValue, i.e., $f_j^{\mathsf{A}}(\sigma) = 2f_j^{\mathsf{SR}}(\sigma)$. As a result, the set of equilibrium assignments is exactly the same, and the fact that the price of anarchy of Approx is at most 4 implies that the price of anarchy of ShapleyValue is at most 2. Note that there may not exist feasible schedules that yield completion times compatible with the costs of ShapleyValue, but this is irrelevant since this mechanism is used only as a guide for designing an approximation algorithm.

The obvious open question is whether we can leverage the systematic approach suggested by this framework in order to design improved approximation algorithms. In the following section we show that neither Approx, Rand, or ProportionalSharing can be used to get a better approximation algorithm. However, in the rest of this section, we analyze all the mechanisms that are convex combinations of ShapleyValue and ProportionalSharing and, using our framework, we propose new approximation algorithms, one of which leads to an improved approximation factor of 1.81.

4.1   Approximation Algorithms

Cost Functions. We embark on our search for improved approximation algorithms by considering a class of cost functions that are combinations of the costs implied by ShapleyValue and those implied by ProportionalSharing. We parameterize this class of mechanisms using a value $\beta > 0$, and let $\mathsf{H}(\beta)$ be the mechanism whose social cost on each machine i is

$$C^{\mathsf{H}(\beta)}(\sigma) = 2\beta C^{\mathsf{SR}}(\sigma) - (2\beta - 1)\eta(\sigma),$$

where $\eta(\sigma) = \sum_{i \in I} \sum_{j \in J_i(\sigma)} w_j p_{ij}$ is an abbreviation that we use extensively in the following. It is easy to verify that $C^{\mathsf{H}(\beta)}(\sigma)$ can be expressed as the combination $\kappa C^{\mathsf{SR}}(\sigma) + \lambda C^{\mathsf{PS}}(\sigma)$ for appropriate constants κ and λ. In particular, ProportionalSharing and ShapleyValue are the mechanisms $\mathsf{H}(1)$ and $\mathsf{H}(1/2)$ of the above class. If we share this cost among the set of jobs J_i using machine i, the cost-share of player $j \in J_i$ is

$$f_j^{\mathsf{H}(\beta)}(J_i) = \beta \sum_{\substack{k \in J_i \\ p_{ik} \prec p_{ij}}} w_j p_{ik} + \beta \sum_{\substack{k \in J_i \\ p_{ik} \succ p_{ij}}} w_k p_{ij} + w_j p_{ij}.$$

Since we use the Shapley value for cost-sharing, the induced potential game has the following potential function: $\Phi^{H(\beta)}(\boldsymbol{\sigma}) = \frac{1}{2}C^{H(\beta)}(\boldsymbol{\sigma}) + \frac{1}{2}\eta(\boldsymbol{\sigma})$.

ϵ-approximate ϵ-equilibrium. The algorithms that we propose compute an ϵ-approximate ϵ-equilibrium of the game induced by $H(\beta)$. For the definition of the ϵ-approximate ϵ-equilibrium, we follow the notation of [4]. Given an assignment $\boldsymbol{\sigma}$ and a player j, denote by σ'_j a best-response strategy of j. Hence, σ'_j minimizes $f_j^{H(\beta)}(\boldsymbol{\sigma}_{-j}, \cdot)$ over all strategies of player j. Let $\Delta_j(\boldsymbol{\sigma}) = f_j^{H(\beta)}(\boldsymbol{\sigma}) - f_j^{H(\beta)}(\boldsymbol{\sigma}_{-j}, \cdot)$ denote the maximum decrease in her cost player j can gain when deviating from her strategy in $\boldsymbol{\sigma}$, and $\Delta(\boldsymbol{\sigma}) = \sum_{j \in J} \Delta_j(\boldsymbol{\sigma})$ denote the sum of these quantities over all players. If Q denotes the set of players j who can improve their cost by more than an ϵ fraction, i.e., $\Delta_j(\boldsymbol{\sigma}) > \epsilon f_j^{H(\beta)}(\boldsymbol{\sigma})$, then we say that $\boldsymbol{\sigma}$ is an ϵ-approximate ϵ-equilibrium if the total relative benefit that these players can accrue via unilateral deviations is $\sum_{j \in Q} \Delta_j(\boldsymbol{\sigma}) \leq \epsilon C^{H(\beta)}(\boldsymbol{\sigma})$.

Algorithm $A(\beta, \epsilon)$. Given parameter values for β and ϵ, the $A(\beta, \epsilon)$ algorithm simulates a restricted sequence of best-response play in the game induced by $H(\beta)$ until an ϵ-approximate ϵ-equilibrium assignment $\boldsymbol{\sigma}$ is reached. The restricted sequence begins with an arbitrary assignment and continues while an ϵ-approximate ϵ-equilibrium has not been computed. In each step, among all players who have a deviation that can improve their cost by at least a factor of ϵ, the player who can improve her cost the most is picked to follow a best-response strategy. Once the assignment $\boldsymbol{\sigma}$ is reached, the algorithm terminates by scheduling the jobs within each machine in this final assignment according to SmithRule.

Adapting the results of Awerbuch et al. [4] in our setting (the important condition that allows this adaptation is that $\Phi^{H(\beta)}(\boldsymbol{\sigma}) \leq C^{H(\beta)}(\boldsymbol{\sigma})$), we obtain that the above algorithm is guaranteed to find an ϵ-approximate ϵ-equilibrium after

$$O\left(\frac{n}{\epsilon} \ln \frac{\Phi^{H(\beta)}(\boldsymbol{\sigma}_0)}{\Phi^{H(\beta)}_{\min}}\right) \text{ player moves. Here, } n \text{ is the number of players, } \boldsymbol{\sigma}_0 \text{ denotes}$$

the initial state and $\Phi^{H(\beta)}_{\min}$ is the globally minimum value of the potential function. Crucially, the above running time is polynomial in terms of the number of bits in the representation of the scheduling instance and $1/\epsilon$.

Our main goal in this section is to show that ϵ-approximate ϵ-equilibria of the games induced by $H(\beta)$ (for appropriate values of β) are efficient in terms of their $C^{SR}(\cdot)$ cost. In turn, this will imply good approximation guarantees for algorithm $A(\beta, \epsilon)$. As a result, we propose two algorithms that provide different approximation guarantees: the first one (for $\beta \approx 0.591$) yields a 1.81-approximation for any instance (Theorem 1), and the second (for $\beta = 2/3$) yields an approximation that converges to 1 as $\eta(\boldsymbol{\sigma}^*)/C^{SR}(\boldsymbol{\sigma}^*)$ converges to zero (Theorem 2).

Theorem 1. *Let $\epsilon \in (0, 1/12]$ and $\beta = \frac{9+\sqrt{5}}{19} \approx 0.591$. Algorithm $A(\beta, \epsilon)$ runs in polynomial time and computes an assignment $\boldsymbol{\sigma}$ such that $C^{SR}(\boldsymbol{\sigma}) \leq \left(\frac{5+\sqrt{5}}{4} + 8\epsilon\right) C^{SR}(\boldsymbol{\sigma}^*) \approx (1.809 + 8\epsilon) C^{SR}(\boldsymbol{\sigma}^*)$, where $\boldsymbol{\sigma}^*$ is the assignment that minimizes the total weighted completion time of the scheduling instance on input.*

Finally, Theorem 2 shows that the cost of the solution obtained by $H(2/3)$ approaches optimality as the ratio $\eta(\boldsymbol{\sigma}^*)/C^{SR}(\boldsymbol{\sigma}^*)$ tends to 0.

Theorem 2. *Let $\epsilon \in (0, 1/12]$ and $\beta = 2/3$. Algorithm $A(\beta, \epsilon)$ runs in polynomial time and computes an assignment σ with $C^{SR}(\sigma) \leq (1 + 6\epsilon) \left(C^{SR}(\sigma^*) + \eta(\sigma^*) \right)$, where σ^* is the assignment that minimizes the total weighted completion time of the scheduling instance on input.*

5 Lower Bounds for Approx, Rand, and ProportionalSharing

In this section we show that, even for the special class of related machines, neither one of the coordination mechanisms studied in [15] can be used in order to design an algorithm with an approximation factor better than 2. In particular, we show that each one of these mechanisms possesses an equilibrium assignment σ whose optimal social cost is at least two times $C^{SR}(\sigma^*)$. For the SmithRule policy this was already shown in [15], since its price of anarchy is exactly 4. For the ProportionalSharing policy, [10, Theorem 15] provides an instance showing that its price of anarchy is at least 2.618, i.e., there exists an equilibrium σ such that $C^{PS}(\sigma) \geq 2.618 C^{SR}(\sigma^*)$. Although this inequality is not the desired lower bound, the equilibrium assignment σ in this instance happens to assign a single job on each machine, and hence $C^{SR}(\sigma) = C^{PS}(\sigma) \geq 2.618 C^{SR}(\sigma^*)$, so ProportionalSharing cannot yield an algorithm with an approximation factor better than 2.618.

The main result of this section is a construction verifying that Approx and Rand cannot lead to an improved approximation algorithm either. In particular, we prove that the price of anarchy of ShapleyValue is at least 2, which implies the existence of some assignment σ which is an equilibrium for ShapleyValue and satisfies $C^{SR}(\sigma) \geq 2C^{SR}(\sigma^*)$. But, as we already observed in the previous sections, any equilibrium of ShapleyValue is also an equilibrium of Approx. Furthermore, our lower bound construction uses jobs with $p_{ij} = w_j/s_i$ on each machine i, where s_i is the speed of machine i. Since $\rho_{ij} = \rho_{ik}$ for every machine i and every pair of jobs j and k, we have $f_j^{SR}(\sigma) = f_j^R(\sigma)$, i.e., the game induced by the protocol also coincides with the game induced by Rand on these instances. As a result any equilibrium of ShapleyValue for these instances is also an equilibrium of Rand, and our lower bound construction kills two birds with one stone, verifying the limitations of both Approx and Rand.

It is worth noting that, apart from the implications regarding our inability to design improved approximation algorithms using these policies, this also yields a lower bound of 2 on the price of anarchy of Rand, which improves upon the best previously known lower bound of 5/3 [15].

Theorem 3. *The price of anarchy of ShapleyValue is at least 2, even on related machine instances.*

6 Conclusion

The main contribution of this paper is a framework for the systematic design of coordination mechanisms and approximation algorithms. Leveraging previous work on cost-sharing protocols, this framework produce mechanisms that always possess pure Nash equilibria, and approximation algorithms that terminate in a polynomial number of steps. To verify that this framework can lead to novel results, we provide a combinatorial approximation algorithm for machine scheduling on unrelated machines. Although we focus on the unweighted Shapley value, an even richer family of mechanisms and algorithms can be designed using generalized weighted Shapley value variants [19]. Our results call for a better understanding of the conditions under which the Shapley value cost-shares can be implemented via a (randomized) feasible schedule; using this understanding one could design coordination mechanisms whose price of anarchy bounds outperform the currently best known bound of 2.133 from Rand. Furthermore, our framework could be applied more broady to design mechanisms and algorithms for general resource selection games.

References

1. Abed, F., Correa, J.R., Huang, C.-C.: Optimal coordination mechanisms for multi-job scheduling games. In: Schulz, A.S., Wagner, D. (eds.) ESA 2014. LNCS, vol. 8737, pp. 13–24. Springer, Heidelberg (2014). https://doi.org/10.1007/978-3-662-44777-2_2

2. Abed, F., Huang, C.-C.: Preemptive coordination mechanisms for unrelated machines. In: Epstein, L., Ferragina, P. (eds.) ESA 2012. LNCS, vol. 7501, pp. 12–23. Springer, Heidelberg (2012). https://doi.org/10.1007/978-3-642-33090-2_3

3. Anshelevich, E., Dasgupta, A., Kleinberg, J.M., Tardos, É., Wexler, T., Roughgarden, T.: The price of stability for network design with fair cost allocation. SIAM J. Comput. **38**(4), 1602–1623 (2008)

4. Awerbuch, B., Azar, Y., Epstein, A., Mirrokni, V.S., Skopalik, A.: Fast convergence to nearly optimal solutions in potential games. In: Proceedings of the 9th ACM Conference on Electronic Commerce (EC), pp. 264–273 (2008)

5. Azar, Y., Fleischer, L., Jain, K., Mirrokni, V.S., Svitkina, Z.: Optimal coordination mechanisms for unrelated machine scheduling. Oper. Res. **63**(3), 489–500 (2015)

6. Bansal, N., Srinivasan, A., Svensson, O.: Lift-and-round to improve weighted completion time on unrelated machines. In: Proceedings of the 48th Annual ACM Symposium on Theory of Computing (STOC), pp. 156–167 (2016)

7. Bhattacharya, S., Im, S., Kulkarni, J., Munagala, K.: Coordination mechanisms from (almost) all scheduling policies. In: Proceedings of the 5th Conference on Innovations in Theoretical Computer Science (ITCS), pp. 121–134 (2014)

8. Caragiannis, I.: Efficient coordination mechanisms for unrelated machine scheduling. Algorithmica **66**(3), 512–540 (2013)

9. Caragiannis, I., Fanelli, A.: An almost ideal coordination mechanism for unrelated machine scheduling. In: Gairing, M., Savani, R. (eds.) SAGT 2016. LNCS, vol. 9928, pp. 315–326. Springer, Heidelberg (2016). https://doi.org/10.1007/978-3-662-53354-3_25

10. Caragiannis, I., Flammini, M., Kaklamanis, C., Kanellopoulos, P., Moscardelli, L.: Tight bounds for selfish and greedy load balancing. Algorithmica **61**(3), 606–637 (2011)

11. Chen, H., Roughgarden, T., Valiant, G.: Designing network protocols for good equilibria. SIAM J. Comput. **39**(5), 1799–1832 (2010)

12. Christodoulou, G., Koutsoupias, E., Nanavati, A.: Coordination mechanisms. Theor. Comput. Sci. **410**(36), 3327–3336 (2009)

13. Christodoulou, G., Gkatzelis, V., Sgouritsa, A.: Cost-sharing methods for scheduling games under uncertainty. In: Proceedings of the 18th ACM Conference on Economics and Computation (EC), pp. 441–458 (2017)
14. Christodoulou, G., Mehlhorn, K., Pyrga, E.: Improving the price of anarchy for selfish routing via coordination mechanisms. Algorithmica **69**(3), 619–640 (2014)
15. Cole, R., Correa, J.R., Gkatzelis, V., Mirrokni, V., Olver, N.: Decentralized utilitarian mechanisms for scheduling games. Games Econ. Behav. **92**, 306–326 (2014)
16. Correa, J.R., Queyranne, M.: Efficiency of equilibria in restricted uniform machine scheduling with total weighted completion time as social cost. Naval Res. Logist. (NRL) **59**(5), 384–395 (2012)
17. von Falkenhausen, P., Harks, T.: Optimal cost sharing for resource selection games. Math. Oper. Res. **38**(1), 184–208 (2013)
18. Gkatzelis, V., Kollias, K., Roughgarden, T.: Optimal cost-sharing in general resource selection games. Oper. Res. **64**(6), 1230–1238 (2016)
19. Gopalakrishnan, R., Marden, J.R., Wierman, A.: Potential games are necessary to ensure pure Nash equilibria in cost sharing games. Math. Oper. Res. **39**(4), 1252–1296 (2014)
20. Hoeksma, R., Uetz, M.: The price of anarchy for minsum related machine scheduling. In: Solis-Oba, R., Persiano, G. (eds.) WAOA 2011. LNCS, vol. 7164, pp. 261–273. Springer, Heidelberg (2012). https://doi.org/10.1007/978-3-642-29116-6_22
21. Hoogeveen, H., Schuurman, P., Woeginger, G.J.: Non-approximability results for scheduling problems with minsum criteria. INFORMS J. Comput. **13**(2), 157–168 (2001)
22. Immorlica, N., Li, L.E., Mirrokni, V.S., Schulz, A.S.: Coordination mechanisms for selfish scheduling. Theoret. Comput. Sci. **410**(17), 1589–1598 (2009)
23. Kollias, K.: Nonpreemptive coordination mechanisms for identical machines. Theory Comput. Syst. **53**(3), 424–440 (2013)
24. Kollias, K., Roughgarden, T.: Restoring pure equilibria to weighted congestion games. ACM Trans. Econ. Comput. **3**(4), 21:1–21:24 (2015)
25. Leung, J.Y. (ed.): Handbook of Scheduling - Algorithms, Models, and Performance Analysis. Chapman and Hall/CRC, Boca Raton (2004)
26. Li, S.: Scheduling to minimize total weighted completion time via time-indexed linear programming relaxations. CoRR abs/1707.08039 (2017)
27. Marden, J.R., Wierman, A.: Distributed welfare games. Oper. Res. **61**(1), 155–168 (2013)
28. Mosk-Aoyama, D., Roughgarden, T.: Worst-case efficiency analysis of queueing disciplines. In: Albers, S., Marchetti-Spaccamela, A., Matias, Y., Nikoletseas, S., Thomas, W. (eds.) ICALP 2009. LNCS, vol. 5556, pp. 546–557. Springer, Heidelberg (2009). https://doi.org/10.1007/978-3-642-02930-1_45
29. Moulin, H.: The price of anarchy of serial, average and incremental cost sharing. Econ. Theor. **36**(3), 379–405 (2008)
30. Sethuraman, J., Squillante, M.: Optimal scheduling of multiclass parallel machines. In: Proceedings of the 10th Annual ACM-SIAM Symposium on Discrete Algorithms (SODA), pp. 963–964 (1999)
31. Shapley, L.S.: Additive and Non-additive Set Functions. Princeton University, Princeton (1953)
32. Skutella, M.: Convex quadratic and semidefinite programming relaxations in scheduling. J. ACM **48**(2), 206–242 (2001)
33. Smith, W.: Various optimizers for single stage production. Naval Res. Logist. Quart. **3**(1–2), 59–66 (1956)

A Dynamics for Advertising on Networks

L. Elisa Celis[1(✉)], Mina Dalirrooyfard[2], and Nisheeth K. Vishnoi[1]

[1] École Polytechnique Fédérale de Lausanne (EPFL), Lausanne, Switzerland
elisa.celis@epfl.ch
[2] Massachusetts Institute of Technology (MIT), Cambridge, USA

Abstract. We study the following question facing businesses in the world of online advertising: how should an advertising budget be spent when there are competing products? Broadly, there are two primary modes of advertising: (i) the equivalent of billboards in the real-world and (search or display) ads online that convert a percentage of the population that sees them, and (ii) social campaigns where the goal is to select a set of initial adopters who influence others to buy via their social network. Prior work towards the above question has largely focused on developing models to understand the effect of one mode or the other. We present a stochastic dynamics to model advertising in social networks that allows both and incorporates the three primary forces at work in such advertising campaigns: (1) the type of campaign – which can combine buying ads and seed selection, (2) the topology of the social network, and (3) the relative quality of the competing products. This model allows us to study the evolution of market share of multiple products with different qualities competing for the same set of users, and the effect that different advertising campaigns can have on the market share. We present theoretical results to understand the long-term behavior of the parameters on the market share and complement them with empirical results that give us insights about the, harder to mathematically understand, short-term behavior of the model.

1 Introduction

Online advertising is now a \$1.5 Trillion industry and, on social networks alone, it accounts for over \$23 Billion worldwide [22]. This is currently 13.9% of all digital ad spending, and 70% of marketers will spend more on social media advertisements in the coming year [30]. Comparatively, spending on television advertisements is approximately \$39 Billion [21]. In fact, the market is now so large that outside companies have arisen as consultants in this space; IBM alone spent over \$100 million dollars just to develop their advertising consulting business in 2014 [29].

It is believed that social influence has a powerful effect on customer decisions [1,3,11], and leveraging its power has been an important aspect of many advertising campaigns. In formal studies, this has primarily been addressed by finding the optimal set of *seeds*, i.e., initial adopters who are given the product

© Springer International Publishing AG 2017
N. R. Devanur and P. Lu (Eds.): WINE 2017, LNCS 10674, pp. 88–102, 2017.
https://doi.org/10.1007/978-3-319-71924-5_7

for free, with the goal of maximizing the extent or speed at which the product spreads throughout the social network [14,15]. The success of such campaigns has been heralded; see [25]. More traditional forms of advertising focus on buying ads, either online (keyword or banner ads) or offline (in billboards, magazines or TV). The goal of these ads is to maximize the probability that a user who sees the ad switches to that product. Studies have focused on targeting the right group of people to view the ad, or improving the ad's appeal [13,18].

These two advertising strategies are often related and the social influence can magnify the effect of traditional advertising. Indeed, once a user has a product, they influence their *neighbors* regardless of whether they converted by being seeded, seeing an advertisement, or were themselves influence by another. In order to study these effects quantitatively, one needs a dynamics that can capture the spread and competition of products via social influence when both types of advertisements are at play. Such a model, minimalistically, should capture:

(1) the kind of campaigns (a) via seed selection and (b) via traditional ads,
(2) the mechanism of social influence and competition amongst products, and
(3) the quality (which can take into account the price) of products.

While there is a rich body of prior works where mathematical models have been developed and analyzed for subsets of parameters above, to the best of our knowledge, there is no formal study that incorporates all of the parameters (1)–(3) above; see Sect. 1.2 for a discussion.

1.1   Our Contributions

Our main contributions are a mathematical model to facilitate the study of the effect of parameters (1)–(3) above on the market share, a set of technical results that allow us to understand the long-term behavior of the model, and a set of complementary empirical results that give us insights about the model in the short-term (where it seems difficult to analyze the model rigorously). Our model is inspired by viewing the competition among different products for the same market base as an evolutionary dynamics on a network and realizing that the various advertising parameters such as quality, traditional advertising and the spread of influence can be captured as parameters such as *fitness*, *mutation* and *selection* in this setting; see also [5,17,20,28].

Our Model. Consider the setting in which there are m products and each person uses exactly one product $i \in [m]$ at every time step; i.e., the products compete for the user base.[1] Each time step is a pre-determined time period during which an individual has an opportunity to switch to a different product; depending on the domain, the length of this time period could vary from minutes (e.g., web browsers) to years (e.g., cars). The main quantity we are interested in is the evolution of the *market share*, i.e., the fraction of people using each product.

---

[1] We can think of one products as the "null" choice – i.e., no product is selected.

Quality of a product. We let a_i be a positive number such that, given the option of all products $1, \ldots, m$ and no outside influence, a user selects option i with probability proportional to a_i. Hence, the a_is capture the relative quality (which can take the price into account) of product i compared to other products; we refer to this as the product's *fitness*. The owner of product i can potentially increase a_i by improving their product's quality.

Social network and competition. The influence network is captured by a weighted, directed graph $G = (V, E, w)$ where each user is a node $u \in V$, and a directed edge $uv \in E$ represents the fact that u has influence on v. Let $n = |V|$ denote the number of nodes or users. The weights $w : E \mapsto \mathbb{R}_{\geq 0}$ quantify the amount of influence u has on v. If we let $S_i(t)$ be the set of vertices who are using product i at time t, then the probability that a node v decides to use product i at time $t + 1$ due to social influence is proportional to $\sum_{uv \in E, u \in S_i(t)} w(uv) a_i$. In other words, node v will *select* a product based on which products her neighbors use, the quality of those products, and the amount of influence the neighbors have on her. We expect a node to be more easily influenced by a neighbor using a good product than a bad one – folding the fitness into the influence step captures the competition between products in this way.

Traditional advertising. We allow users to switch products independently of the social influence as in the previous paragraph, e.g., after seeing a billboard ad. We let Q_{ij}^v be the probability that node v using product j spontaneously converts, or *mutates* to product i. For mathematical convenience, we assume that each of these $m \times m$ mutation matrices $Q^v > 0$ and is the same (denoted Q) for each v. Note that Q need not be a symmetric matrix. A company could increase its spending on traditional advertising to increase Q_{ij} for $j \neq i$.

Seed selection. Finally, the owner of a product can select a *seed set* $S \subseteq V$ of people to whom they give the product for free in the beginning of the process, effectively forcing their conversion. The users are under no obligation to continue with this product in future time steps.

The problem. When allocating a budget, a company with product i should then evaluate the tradeoffs between increasing a_i (i.e., improving the product), increasing Q_i. (i.e., increasing ads and hence mutations to itself), or increasing $|S|$ (i.e., getting more initial adopters).

As in prior work, we assume the influence network is fixed, and hence a company cannot modify it to its benefit. We also assume that network can be seeded only at the first time step. These aspects combine to form a stochastic dynamical system that can be viewed as a Markov chain over the state space $\{1, 2, \ldots, m\}^n$. Our Markov chain can be described in several ways without changing the limiting distribution. For instance, one could consider a description where the traditional advertising competes with the social influence; for example, at each time step, with some probability a node spontaneously changes its state from i to j, and with some probability it is influenced by a neighboring node. We discuss possible shortcomings and extensions of our model in Sect. 4.

Theoretical Results. One of the main difficulties that arises in analyzing our model is the fact that the a_is are not all the same. We start by noting that when $Q_{ij} \in (0,1)$ for all i,j and the in-degree of each node in the influence network is at least one, our process forms an ergodic Markov chain (even if the network is not connected) and, thus, has a unique stationary distribution. As a consequence, it is clear that the selection of the seed set S has no effect in the long-term since the process converges to this stationary distribution regardless of the initial state. However, the *network structure may still play a role in determining the shape of the steady state distribution.* Allowing some Q_{ij}s to be zero might give rise to absorbing states in our Markov chain; this would also allow for the possibility of the starting state affecting the steady state. See Sect. 4 for a discussion.

Towards computing this unique steady state, it can be shown that closed form solutions for the steady state do not exist except in the most trivial of cases. Even for a very simple settings of our model (e.g., unweighted, undirected graphs with $Q_{ij} = 0$ for $i \neq j$, a result of [5] can be used to show that computing the steady state exactly is #P hard. This leaves us with two alternatives: (1) derive weaker, but asymptotically good, bounds on the steady state of the stochastic process analytically. Or (2) deploy the Markov Chain Monte Carlo (MCMC) framework to get samples from close to the steady state in order to compute the required statistics – here, it becomes important to prove that the mixing time of the underlying Markov chain is fast.

Deterministic approximation. Towards (1), we study a *deterministic* dynamical system that can be viewed as a mean-field approximation to the stochastic dynamics. Roughly, this process has the same set of parameters, but instead of a single product, it maintains a probability distribution at each node that indicates its preference among the products. The nodes update these probabilities deterministically taking into account the influence of its neighbors and the fitnesses and the matrix Q; see Eq. (1) and Lemma 1. The advantage of working with this deterministic process is that we can precisely characterize its steady state (see Theorem 1). Further, computing this deterministic steady state turns out to be an eigenvector problem for an $m \times m$ matrix. As a simple consequence, for the two-product case, one can even obtain a formula for the steady state in closed form for which it is clear that the steady state will primarily consist of the product with the highest quality.

Concentration. Our theoretical results indicate that, despite the possibility of correlations, the market shares in the steady state of our stochastic dynamics are likely to be *concentrated* around those predicted by the deterministic dynamics (see Theorem 2). The quality of the concentration depends on the number of nodes in the network and the minimum in-degree of the network (the higher these numbers are, the better the concentration). Thus, when the network's size and degree are large, the deterministic process could be taken as a first-order approximation to the stochastic process.

Mixing time. Towards (2), we show that for all graphs with large enough minimum degree (roughly $\log n$ – see Theorem 3), the Markov chain underlying our stochastic dynamics mixes fast. Key to the proof turns out to be the deterministic dynamics mentioned above. We show how the geometry of the unique fixed point of this deterministic dynamics can also allow us to construct a contractive coupling to prove rapid mixing.

To summarize, our model is amenable to a rigorous analysis and, importantly, our theoretical results suggest algorithms with provable bounds to estimate the statistics such as market share from the steady state. Further, the time to convergence to steady state for a particular set of parameters for our model being fast in many cases implies that the advertising strategies are efficient and can have the desired outcome in a reasonable time – after all, a strategy that needs 100 years to attain 99% of the market share is not useful. Extending our results to all networks (removing the minimum degree condition) seems quite challenging.

Empirical Results. While the theoretical results above give an indication of the asymptotic market share, sometimes we may be interested in the short-term value of an advertising campaign.[2] We study this regime in Sect. 3, where we conduct empirical studies in order to understand the effect of the model parameters in the short-term. For each experiment, we isolate a single parameter, either the network, the seed set, the mutation parameters, or the product quality, and strive to evaluate its effect on the market share.

Networks. Despite differences in origin, size and properties of the three real-world networks we consider, we observe that the market share of a product over time converges relatively fast; see Fig. 1(a). While the networks we study have relatively low degree (and hence our theoretical results do not apply), we believe that this fast convergence is because the diameter of the networks, as in most social networks, is small. Proving that small diameter suffices for fast convergence would be an interesting direction for future work. Furthermore, we observe that on all networks, for our simulation parameters, the population convergence to having almost all of its mass on the best product. As we will see in later experiments, the model is extremely sensitive to the gap in quality between the best and second-best product. Perhaps when the qualities are (nearly) the same, the effect of the network in the steady state would be more clear empirically. Despite these similarities, it is clear that the model converges faster on some networks than on others, and an exploration of the short-term market share remains important.

Parameters $S, \mathbf{a}$ and Q. While the choice of which seeds are selected for S affect the market share in the short-term, the improvement is roughly linear in the size of the seed set (see Fig. 1(b)). In contrast, the improvement in market share

---

[2] For example, for products such as cars, time steps may be on the order of years. Hence, we may be interested in a constant number of time steps, which is less than the fastest mixing time we could hope for.

is a sigmoid in a_1 and Q_1. with the inflection point in the range of realistic values (see Fig. 1). Hence, this suggests that there are thresholds for a_1 and Q_1., such that (if our budget allows) we should ensure to cross. The threshold for a_1 is simply the maximum quality of a competing product – intuitively, *having the best product ensures that the steady state is in our favor.* As long as a_1 is larger than the other $a.$, we find that small increases in Q_1. seem to have the largest positive effect in the market share in the short-term. In essence, the Q_1. function as a way to continuously generate seeds (as opposed to selecting them only once with S). This suggests that as long as we have the best product, *in the short-term, increasing Q_1., e.g., by improving or increasing the number of ads, is more important both than selecting seeds and improving product quality.* Overall, our results lead to the following qualitative insights:

- the initial seed set has a minimal effect on the limiting market share,
- a new product must have the highest quality in order to gain significant market share, and
- improving traditional advertisement can be more effective than improving seed set selection.

1.2 Related Work

There is a large literature on optimal advertising strategies in order to maximize the adoption of goods (see [26] for a survey). These works focus on optimizing the ads and product quality; e.g., [13,18]. In parallel, another long line of work on local interaction with regard to social influence and the adoption of products (see [19] for a survey). Such a work often uses stochastic models (known varyingly as diffusion or cascades) and dynamical systems exist (see [7] and [4] respectively). Models for understanding social influence in networks often take the form of some kind of a *threshold rule*, as first proposed by [10,24], and many variations have been studied. Towards this, theoretical and empirical studies have focused on the problems of finding either the optimal size of, or the optimal seeds in, the set S (e.g., [12,14]). For instance, in an important piece of work, [15] proved that the problem of *which* seeds to select, given a size constraint, is NP-hard and also provide greedy approximation algorithms for this problem.

A key contribution of our work is a model which allows us to optimal advertising and in the presence of social influence, thus bridging these two literatures. To the best of our knowledge, very few works have tackled this challenging problem. In two notable exceptions study a monopolist firm (i.e., the a single product) being sold to a network of individuals that can influence each other. Here, the quality of the product can be captured by a level of *effort* [9] or *price* [9] set by the firm, and the product spreads across a (random, infinite) network via a dynamical system which depends on the degree distribution of the vertices. In contrast, our formulation allows us to consider arbitrary and finite networks in which multiple products compete for market share.

Our stochastic model draws from two different models that arose in the study of asexual finite populations; specifically that of [6] and [17] (see also [20] for a general reference on evolutionary models). The first model underlies the study of evolution of viruses and has been used [27] to inform drug design despite their apparent simplicity. There is no explicit network in the first model, although it is equivalent to our model in a complete unweighted graph with self-loops if all $Q_{ij} = q$ for $i \neq j$ and some fixed parameter q. The second model studies network models of evolution and there is recent rigorous work [5], but without mutations which are crucial to our setting. Prior to our work on network models with mutations, the only rigorous studies we are aware of were for the complete graph case; initiated by [6] and followed by [28]. The network structure makes the analysis significantly harder and raise many interesting questions. Our terminology (*fitness*, *mutation*, and *selection*) is emphasized to draw these parallels to the informed reader. The use of deterministic dynamics or mean-field approximations to study stochastic processes has a rich history in the probability literature [2,23,31], however, non-asymptotic results such as our concentration result are rare. Also, the use of such a deterministic dynamics to bound the mixing time of a stochastic process is quite new and, to the best of our knowledge in two different lines of works; see [8,28] and the discussions therein.

2   Theoretical Results

In this section we formally state our theoretical results which concern the behavior of the market share in the long-term. At the expense of slight repetition, we begin by stating the stochastic dynamics formally and introducing the corresponding random variables. Subsequently, we describe the deterministic dynamics that will help us approximate the steady state behavior of our stochastic dynamics for large enough networks. This is followed by a proof of the approximation result. Finally, we present our result on the mixing time of the stochastic process. Due to space constraints, we simply sketch the main ideas; complete proofs appear the full version of this paper.

2.1   Preliminaries and the Stochastic Process

For a vertex v, let $N_{in}[v]$ denote the set of edges coming in to v. Let F be an $m \times m$ diagonal matrix where $F_{ii} = a_i$ and $F_{ij} = 0$ for $i \neq j$. Recall that Q_{ij} denotes the probability of type j mutating to type i. Q is column-stochastic: if 1_m denotes the all 1 vector of dimension m, $1_m^\top Q = 1_m$.

   At each time $t \geq 0$, each node in the graph has a type in $\{1, \ldots, m\}$. We denote the type of vertex $v \in V$ at time t by the random variable $X_v^{(t)}$. In this notation, given $(X_u^{(t)})_{u \in V}$, our stochastic dynamics can be mathematically thought of as the following three steps: (1) Each vertex u replaces the type $X_u^{(t)}$ by $a_{X_u^{(t)}}$ many copies of the same type. (2) Each vertex v looks at the set of vertices which point to it, i.e., $N_{in}[v]$ and *selects* who to copy in the following way. For each $u \in N_{in}[v]$, first it further multiplies each type currently residing at u by a factor of $w(uv)$. Subsequently, it samples a type from the multi-set union of the populations residing at each $u \in N_{in}[v]$ uniformly at random and independently for each v. For a vertex v, call this chosen type $Z_v^{(t+1)}$. (3) $Z_v^{(t+1)}$ independently mutates for each v according to the matrix Q. That is, a type j mutates to a type i with probability Q_{ij}. The resulting type at vertex v is denoted by $X_v^{(t+1)}$. As remarked earlier, there are other ways to describe the model that does not change the stochastic properties; for instance, the order of the second and the third steps are interchangeable or can be combined.

For convenience we work with integral weights and fitnesses, however, note that the matrix F can be scaled by an arbitrary constant without changing either process; similarly, the weights of incoming edges to any node can be scaled by an arbitrary constant. As long as the scaling is by constants, the theorems and their proofs continue to hold as such. For the analysis, by replacing a weighted edge with multiple edges, we may assume without loss of generality that the graph is unweighted. Hence, subsequently, we think of $N_{in}[v]$ as a multi-set and when we talk of its cardinality, it is the cardinality of the multi-set. We let $\delta = \min_v |N_{in}[v]|$.

We start by noting that when $Q > 0$ and $\delta \geq 1$, this stochastic process has a unique stationary distribution which we denote by π. Note, that this π will in general depend on the network structure. Thus, we can study the time to stationarity or the mixing time of the Markov chain. Recall that the *mixing time* $t_{mix}(\varepsilon)$ is defined as the smallest time such that for any starting state, the distribution of the state $X^{(t)}$ at time t is within total variation distance ε of π. For concreteness, we use $t_{mix}(1/4)$. It is well known that $t_{mix}(\varepsilon) \leq t_{mix}(1/4) \log 1/\epsilon$.

2.2   The Deterministic Dynamical System

We now present the deterministic counterpart to our stochastic model and argue how it functions as its first order approximation. Here, at each time $t \geq 0$, each node in the graph has a probability distribution over the set $\{1, \ldots, m\}$. We denote this distribution for a vertex $v \in V$ at time t by the vector $p_v^{(t)} \in \Delta_m$ where $\Delta_m = \{x \in \mathbb{R}^m, x \geq 0, \sum_{i=1}^m x_i = 1\}$. Given $(p_v^{(t)})_{v \in V}$, we now describe how to generate $p_v^{(t+1)}$. In the first step, each vertex v multiplies each coordinate of $p_v^{(t)}$ be the corresponding fitness to obtain $Fp_v^{(t)}$. Note that this is no longer a probability vector. Then, each type present at each vertex, mutates according to the matrix Q resulting in an intermediate population $QFp_v^{(t)}$. Finally, each vertex v looks at the set of vertices which point to it, i.e., $N_{in}[v]$ and updates its distribution over the types to $p_v^{(t+1)}$ by taking the weighted average of the intermediate probability distributions from among $u \in N_{in}[v]$ and subsequently normalizing it to be a probability distribution. Formally,

$$p_v^{(t+1)} = \frac{\sum_{u \in N_{in}[v]} QFp_u^{(t)}}{\sum_{j=1}^m \sum_{u \in N_{in}[v]} QFp_u^{(t)}(j)}. \tag{1}$$

Let $P^{(t)}$ denote the $m \times n$ matrix where the u-th column is the vector $p_u^{(t)}$. Thus, we can think of the deterministic process as implicitly specifying a dynamical system $f : \Delta_m^n \mapsto \Delta_m^n$ defined by the rule $P^{(t+1)} = f(P^{(t)})$. We show that starting from any initial point, the dynamical system converges to a unique limit P which has the property that each column is the same; thus, rather surprisingly, the correlations induced by Eq. (1) disappear with time and the network has no effect in the long-term behavior of this dynamics.

The understanding of this P reduces to understanding the long-term behavior of the dynamics $g : \Delta_m \mapsto \Delta_m$ which maps a point x to $g(x) = \frac{QFx}{\|QFx\|_1}$. Since $QF > 0$, the Perron-Frobenius theorem implies that QF has a unique positive eigenvector $p \in \Delta_m$ with a positive eigenvalue λ_1. Therefore $g(\cdot)$ has a unique fixed point p in the interior of the simplex Δ_m. The Perron-Frobenius theorem also implies that for every $x \in \Delta_m$, $\lim_{t\to\infty}(QF)^t x/\lambda_1^t \to p$. In fact, we show that for all $t > \frac{4\log\frac{1}{c\epsilon}}{\log\frac{\lambda_1}{|\lambda_2|}}$, we have $\|g^t(x) - p\|_\infty < \epsilon$ for any $x \in \Delta_m$, where c is a constant independent of x and $\lambda_1 > |\lambda_2|$ are the top two eigenvalues of QF with largest magnitudes. Using this convergence result, we prove that P, the limit of f, is the matrix $p1_n^\top$.

Theorem 1 (Limit of the deterministic process). *Let f be the dynamical system as defined above. Then, given an $\epsilon > 0$, for all $X \in \Delta_m^n$, $\|f^t(X) - p1_n^\top\|_\infty \le \epsilon$ for $t \ge \frac{4\log\frac{M(m+1)}{c\delta\epsilon}}{\log\frac{\lambda_1}{|\lambda_2|}}$, for some constant c independent of X and the graph. λ_1, λ_2 are as above, $M = \sum_{i=1}^m a_i$ and $\delta = \min_v |N_{\text{in}}[v]|$.*

The difficulty in the proof of this theorem arises from the fact that f is a non-linear dynamical system acting on a matrix. The key observation is that when f is applied on a rank-one matrix, the outcome is a rank-one matrix. Consequently, we can prove the theorem above when the starting point is a rank one matrix. To prove it when the starting point is general rank matrix $\sum_i e_i v_i^\top$, (here e_i is the standard basis vector) we can write it as a sum of rank-one matrices and show that the application of f^t (f t-times) results in, roughly, a matrix of the form $\sum_i (QF)^t e_i v_i B_t^\top$, where A is a fixed positive matrix, while B_t is less nice. However, we can use the fact that $(QF)^t e_i \to p$ for all i, along with the fact that f has a bounded Lipschitz constant to complete the proof of the theorem. The proof of this theorem is deferred to the full version due to space constraints.

2.3 Relationship Between the Stochastic and Deterministic Models

We now present our results relating the deterministic and the stochastic process. We let $X^{(t)} \in \{0,1\}^{m\times n}$ be the matrix where $X_{iv}^{(t)} = 1$ if the state of vertex v is i and 0 otherwise. Thus, with a slight overload of notation (which should be clear from the context), $X_v^{(t)}$ denotes the column vector of $X^{(t)}$ corresponding to the vertex v.

Thus, $(X^{(t)}1_n)e_i$ is the number of vertices of type i. Let $D^{(t)}$ denote the vector $\frac{1}{n} \cdot X^{(t)}1_n$. The starting point is the following easy to verify equality which relates one step of the Markov chain to the deterministic process.

Lemma 1. $E[D^{(t+1)} \mid X^{(t)}] = \frac{1}{n} \cdot f(X^{(t)})1_n.$

Moreover, using Chernoff bounds, we can show that $D^{(t+1)}$ is close to $\frac{1}{n} \cdot f(X^{(t)})1_n$ with high probability. Ideally, we would like to show that if $X \in \{0,1\}^{m \times n}$ is sampled from the stationary distribution π of the stochastic process, then the corresponding counting vector $D = \frac{1}{n}X1_n$ is concentrated around the vector p (as defined in Theorem 1). An obvious approach would be to argue that we can iterate this argument over t steps and take a union bound to ensure that $D^{(t)}$ remains close to the deterministic process with a high probability. However, this approach suffers from a couple of major problems: the first is that it is not clear how to iterate. It would be possible to iterate if we could ensure that $\frac{1}{n} \cdot f(X^{(t)})1_n$ is very close to $g\left(\frac{1}{n}X^{(t)}1_n\right)$. This is for instance true when the underlying graph is a complete graph but does not hold in general. Even assuming that this is true for a moment, the second obstacle is that g is not necessarily a global contraction and in fact might even expand discrepancies, so that the discrepancy between the behavior of the random process and the deterministic prediction can grow exponentially with time. Thus, we can use the union bound only over at most $O(\log n)$ steps. To get around this problem, we use the fact that p is an attracting fixed point of g. Thus, we know that within $O(\log n)$ steps, g reaches a $n^{-\Theta(1)}$-neighborhood of its fixed point, and does not subsequently leave this neighborhood. Using this fact, we can essentially bootstrap the naive union bound argument described in the previous paragraph to show that starting from *any* state, the random process also reaches in $\Theta(\log n)$ steps a distribution that is concentrated on a $n^{-\Theta(1)}$ neighborhood of the fixed point of the deterministic process. Thus, the behavior of the deterministic limit close to its fixed point turns out to be the crucial ingredient in understanding the convergence properties of the stochastic finite population process. The following theorem shows that most of the mass of the stationary distribution of the stochastic process is concentrated around the fixed point of the deterministic process when the underlying network has large minimum degree.

Theorem 2 *(Concentration of the stationary distribution).* *There exist constants $\gamma, \beta > 0$ depending only upon m, Q and F such that if $\sigma \geq (\log n)^{-\gamma}$, and if D is the frequency vector obtained from the stationary distribution π of the stochastic process, then $\Pr\left[\|D - p\|_\infty \leq 2\sigma\right] = 1 - 1/n^\beta$ for all graphs with minimum degree $\delta \geq \Omega((\log n)^{1+\alpha})$ where $\alpha > 0$ is an arbitrarily small constant.*

Note that our empirical results (see Sect. 3) indicate that this should hold for all networks with small diameter and we leave it as a challenging open problem to prove this formally. We omit the proof of this theorem due to space constraints.

2.4 The Mixing Time of the Stochastic Process

We now present our main result on the mixing time of our stochastic dynamics.

Theorem 3 *(Mixing time).* *Let m, Q, F be fixed and let G be a graph on n vertices (for n large enough) such that $\delta = \Omega\left((\log n)^{1+\alpha}\right)$ for any $\alpha > 0$. Then, $t_{\mathrm{mix}}(1/4) = O(\log n)$, where m, Q, F, α are constants.*

Note that the mixing time bound is quite surprising as the size of the state space is 2^n and the mixing time roughly a log of the size of the state space. The proof relies on a multi-phase *coupling* argument. Establishing a coupling between two identical (but correlated) copies of a Markov chain which reduces the expected distance is a generic technique to establish mixing time bounds. At a very high level, we can demonstrate a contractive coupling when the two chains reach close enough to their steady state, which is related to the convergent point of the deterministic dynamical system. To prove that they reach close to their steady state we need to ensure that there is measure concentration in each step of the Markov process, that the number of steps is small, and that is where the minimum degree bound seems to help us. The proof is quite technical and builds on an extends the framework of [28] who proved a similar result for the case of the complete graph. We omit the proof here due to space constraints.

3   Empirical Results: Short-Term Market Share

We now consider an empirical evaluation of the effect of the model parameters on the market share in the short-term. In lieu of a real influence network, we consider three real-world social network datasets for our simulations. We run the stochastic process by considering a network in which all users have the same product, and introduce a single new product to the market (i.e., $m = 2$). We call our new product A, and let it correspond to $i = 1$. We then measure the new product's market share as a function of the various parameters S, $\mathbf{a}$ and Q. Unless specified otherwise, in the simulations we take $a_1 = 1.1$, $a_2 = 1$, and $Q_{ij} = 0.0025$ for $i \neq j$,[3] the seed set S is a single randomly selected node in the graph, and the process is run for $T = 30$ time steps on the Facebook network described below. We average over $k = 50$ simulations; error bars depict the standard error of the mean.

Networks. The networks we use for our simulations were collected by the Stanford Network Analysis Project and are publicly available [16]. We take the largest strongly connected component of each network for our simulations. We use a subset of the Facebook network, an ASTRO-PH collaboration network from the e-print arXiv website in which nodes are authors and there is an edge between two nodes if they are co-authors on at least one paper, and the Enron email network where nodes are email addresses internal to the Enron company and an edge represents the fact that at least one email was exchanged. We purposely select very different types of networks across which influence could propagate, and further compare against the complete graph and the cycle where the number of nodes is the same as for the Facebook graph.

Despite dramatic differences in the origin, size and connectivity of the networks, all networks appear to converge relatively fast to similar steady-states (see Fig. 1(a)). There is no clear relationship between any of the graph properties

---

[3] The choice of parameters is inspired by the parameters we get when a fitting our model to real world datasets; see the full version of the paper.

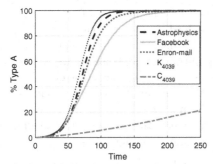

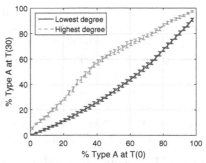

(a) The effect of the network on the convergence to the steady state.

(b) The effect of seed selection on the market share after $T = 30$ time steps.

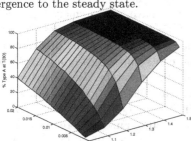

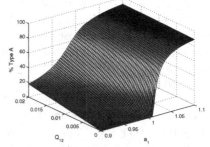

(c) The effect of a_1 and Q_{12} on the market share after $T = 30$ time steps.

(d) The effect of a_1 and Q_{12} on the market share in the limit.

Fig. 1. The effect of the various model parameters on the market share. Unless varied in the given simulation, we take $a_1 = 1.1$, $a_2 = 1$, $Q_{ij} = 0.0025$ for all $i \neq j$, and we use the Facebook network. (Color figure online)

and the observed mixing time, although we hypothesize that the small diameter plays a key role. Indeed, the cycle reaches the steady state at a much slower rate; exploring this further could be an interesting direction for future work. Due to space constraints, in the remainder of this section we only present the simulation results from the Facebook network dataset; the results on the other network topologies are similar and lead to the same qualitative conclusions.

Seed Sets. As observed in Sect. 2, if $Q > 0$, the seed set does not have an effect on the market share in the steady state as the chain is ergodic. However, it could affect the process in the short-term. Hence, we study the effect of the seed set by varying the number of nodes it contains, and which set of nodes are selected. Several empirical studies have shown that a good heuristic for maximizing influence is to select the highest-degree nodes, while poorly performing heuristics include selecting the lowest-degree nodes (see, e.g., [12]). Hence, for a seed set of size k, we compare two possible sets: the set that contains the k highest degree vertices, and the set that contains the k lowest degree vertices, breaking ties arbitrarily.

In Fig. 1(b) we observe that, roughly, increasing the number of seeds in the set only improves the market share linearly; indeed, in order to capture 50% of the market after $T = 30$ time steps, even using high-degree seeds, one would have had to start by seeding 30% of the population. In contrast, as we will see below, there are nonlinear gains observed by increasing either a_1 or Q_{12}. This suggests that, even in the short-term, increasing the number of seeds may not be the best approach. Furthermore, while optimizing the selection of seeds is indeed beneficial, it does not appear to lead to significant gains, simply altering the constant of the linear improvement rather than changing its nature.

Product Fitness and Mutation. We then vary both Q_{12} and a_1 and measure the market share both after $T = 30$ time steps and in the steady state (see Fig. 1). Here, $a_2 = 1$ and $Q_{21} = 0.01$; i.e., our competitors have an extremely aggressive and successful advertising campaign that spontaneously converts nodes. We first observe that Q_{12} has almost no effect on the steady state of the distribution. However, in the short-term, the choice of Q_{12} can result in attaining anything from 0 to the maximal market share within 30 time steps. We observe that $Q_{12} > .001$ suffices to reach close to the steady state distribution, and below this range the transition is a sharp sigmoid; e.g., increasing Q_{12} from 0.0025 to 0.005 when $a_1 = 1.1$ increases the market share by over 30%. Furthermore, we observe that even for very small differences in quality, e.g., $a_1 > 1.05 > 1 = a_2$, which corresponds to users preferring product A approximately 51.2% of the time, product A will capture almost 100% of the market in the limit. However, a_1 needs to be approximately 2.5, which corresponds to being preferred approximately 71.4% of the time, in order to achieve the same market share in the short-term ($T = 30$) when $Q_{12} = 0.001$. Again, the improvement in market share as a function of a_1 is a sigmoid, making the improvement in marketshare superlinear in a_1 when it is less than 50%. These observations suggest that it is likely to be more beneficial to improve the fitness or the advertising as opposed to the seed set in order to improve market share.

4   Conclusion and Future Work

The main conceptual contribution of this paper is to introduce a new model to study the role and interaction of the key forces of interest in online advertising. Technically, we show that our model, not only goes beyond the state-of-the-art in capturing the relevant parameters, but can also be analyzed rigorously for a large class of graphs. Combined with our empirical and numerical results on the short-term behavior of advertising campaigns on the market share, we are led to interesting predictions and take-homes.

An obvious generalization of our model would allow for *node-specific* parameters $\mathbf{a}^v$ and Q_{ij}^v. The different fitnesses/mutations can capture distinct user preferences, or targeted advertising campaigns that only display online ads to certain users. In particular, this may mean that some or all of the Q_{ij}^vs are 0 or tend to 0; this would leads to additional mathematical challenges as the

Markov chain may no longer be ergodic and hence multiple stationary distributions would arise. As with other models that do not incorporate mutations [5], we expect that the initial seed set can have a larger effect in such settings as the process may converge to different steady states.

We expect that the proof techniques that we developed in this paper – in particular the interplay between stochastic and deterministic dynamical systems – might be useful not only to analyze extensions and variations of our model but also in other settings. From a technical standpoint, our theoretical results strongly relied on the minimum degree assumption; an interesting open question is whether we can prove them under the condition that the diameter of the graph is small (as may be the case in many applications).

References

1. Bass, F.M.: A new product growth model for consumer durables. Manag. Sci. **15**(5), 215–227 (1969)
2. Benaïm, M.: Dynamics of stochastic approximation algorithms. In: Azéma, J., Émery, M., Ledoux, M., Yor, M. (eds.) Séminaire de Probabilités XXXIII. LNM, vol. 1709, pp. 1–68. Springer, Heidelberg (1999). https://doi.org/10.1007/BFb0096509
3. Van den Bulte, C., Joshi, Y.V.: New product diffusion with influentials and imitators. Mark. Sci. **26**(3), 400–421 (2007)
4. Chazelle, B.: The dynamics of influence systems. In: 2012 IEEE 53rd Annual Symposium on Foundations of Computer Science (FOCS), pp. 311–320. IEEE (2012)
5. Díaz, J., Goldberg, L.A., Mertzios, G.B., Richerby, D., Serna, M., Spirakis, P.G.: Approximating fixation probabilities in the generalized moran process. Algorithmica **69**(1), 78–91 (2014)
6. Dixit, N., Srivastava, P., Vishnoi, N.K.: A finite population model of molecular evolution: theory and computation. J. Comput. Biol. **19**(10), 1176–1202 (2012)
7. Easley, D., Kleinberg, J.: Networks, Crowds, and Markets. Cambridge University Press, Cambridge (2010)
8. Efthymiou, C., Hayes, T.P., Stefankovic, D., Vigoda, E., Yin, Y.: Convergence of MCMC and loopy BP in the tree uniqueness region for the hard-core model. In: IEEE 57th Annual Symposium on Foundations of Computer Science, FOCS 2016, 9–11 October 2016, Hyatt Regency, New Brunswick, New Jersey, USA, pp. 704–713 (2016). https://doi.org/10.1109/FOCS.2016.80
9. Galeotti, A., Goyal, S.: Influencing the influencers: a theory of strategic diffusion. RAND J. Econ. **40**(3), 509–532 (2009)
10. Granovetter, M.: Threshold models of collective behavior. Am. J. Sociol. **83**(6), 1420–1443 (1978)
11. Herr, P.M., Kardes, F.R., Kim, J.: Effects of word-of-mouth and product-attribute information on persuasion: an accessibility-diagnosticity perspective. J. Consum. Res. **17**(4), 454–462 (1991)
12. Hinz, O., Skiera, B., Barrot, C., Becker, J.U.: Seeding strategies for viral marketing: an empirical comparison. J. Mark. **75**(6), 55–71 (2011)
13. Iyer, G., Soberman, D., Villas-Boas, J.M.: The targeting of advertising. Mark. Sci. **24**(3), 461–476 (2005)

14. Jain, D., Mahajan, V., Muller, E.: An approach for determining optimal product sampling for the diffusion of a new product. J. Prod. Innov. Manag. **12**(2), 124–135 (1995)
15. Kempe, D., Kleinberg, J., Tardos, É.: Maximizing the spread of influence through a social network. In: The 9th ACM SIGKDD International Conference on Knowledge Discovery and Data Mining, pp. 137–146. ACM (2003)
16. Leskovec, J., Krevl, A.: SNAP Datasets, June 2014. http://snap.stanford.edu/data
17. Lieberman, E., Hauert, C., Nowak, M.A.: Evolutionary dynamics on graphs. Nature **433**(7023), 312–316 (2005)
18. Lohtia, R., Donthu, N., Hershberger, E.K.: The impact of content and design elements on banner advertising click-through rates. J. Advertising Res. **43**(04), 410–418 (2003)
19. Marsden, P.V., Friedkin, N.E.: Network studies of social influence. Sociol. Methods Res. **22**(1), 127–151 (1993)
20. Nowak, M.A.: Evolutionary Dynamics. Harvard University Press, Cambridge (2006)
21. Palmeri, C.: Online ad spending to pass tv spots this year, consultant says (2015). http://bloom.bg/1dJ99Zf
22. Palmeri, C.: Social network ad spending to hit $23.68 billion worldwide (2015). http://bit.ly/2fng5yU
23. Pemantle, R.: When are touchpoints limits for generalized pólya urns? Proc. Am. Math. Soc. **113**, 235–243 (1991)
24. Schelling, T.C.: Micromotives and Macrobehavior. WW Norton and Company, New York City (1978)
25. Scott, D.M.: The New Rules of Marketing and PR: How to Use Social Media, Online Video, Mobile Applications, Blogs, News Releases, and Viral Marketing to Reach Buyers Directly. John Wiley and Sons, Hoboken (2013)
26. Shy, O.: The Economics of Network Industries. Cambridge University Press, Cambridge (2001)
27. Tripathi, K., Balagam, R., Vishnoi, N.K., Dixit, N.M.: Stochastic simulations suggest that HIV-1 survives close to its error threshold. PLoS Comput. Biol. **8**(9), e1002684 (2012)
28. Vishnoi, N.K.: The speed of evolution. In: Symposium on Discrete Algorithms (SODA), pp. 1590–1601 (2015)
29. Vranica, S.: IBM pours $100 million into ad consulting (2014). http://on.wsj.com/1dxVhzI
30. Weaver, O.: How to set social advertising goals (2015). http://bit.ly/1yAseR5
31. Wormald, N.C.: Differential equations for random processes and random graphs. Ann. Appl. Probab. **5**(4), 1217–1235 (1995)

Limiting User's Sybil Attack in Resource Sharing

Zhou Chen[1], Yukun Cheng[2], Xiaotie Deng[3], Qi Qi[1], and Xiang Yan[3(✉)]

[1] Department of Industrial Engineering and Logistics Management,
The Hong Kong University of Science and Technology,
Clear Water Bay, Hong Kong
zchenaq@connect.ust.hk, kaylaqi@ust.hk
[2] School of Business, Suzhou University of Science and Technology,
Suzhou 215009, China
ykcheng@amss.ac.cn
[3] Department of Computer Science, Shanghai Jiao Tong University,
Shanghai 200240, China
deng-xt@cs.sjtu.edu.cn, xyansjtu@163.com

Abstract. In this work, we discuss the sybil attack to a sharing economic system where each participant contributes its own resource for all to share. We are interested in the robustness of the market equilibrium mechanism in withstanding such an attack, in terms of the incentive ratio to measure how much one could gain by splitting its identity and reconstructing its communication connections with others. On one hand, weshow that no player can increase more than $\sqrt{2}$ times of their original share from the market equilibrium solution, by characterizing the worst case under which strategic agent can obtain the maximum utility gain after manipulation. On the other hand, such a bound of $\sqrt{2}$ is proved to be tight by constructing a proper instance, for which this bound is reached.

1 Introduction

Resource sharing has now attracted much commercial efforts in many good and service application, such as done in AirBnB, mobike, UBER, etc., to make participants benefit from exchanging each own idle resource with others and to improve the social benefit as well as revenue. A key question in sharing is whether one would be motivated to make their best effort, or in the current setting to share their resources to the maximum availability to the sharing community for others to use. In addition, whether our protocol would prevent the abuse of the system by some to deviate from the expected social behavior by participation agents.

In this paper, we focus on the resource sharing over networks with autonomous participants (or agents), which goes beyond the peer-to-peer (P2P) bandwidth sharing idea [27]. Peers in such networks act as both suppliers and customers of resources and make their resources directly available to their network peers. Their utilities are determined by the total of resources received from

© Springer International Publishing AG 2017
N. R. Devanur and P. Lu (Eds.): WINE 2017, LNCS 10674, pp. 103–119, 2017.
https://doi.org/10.1007/978-3-319-71924-5_8

all others. Such a resource sharing system over P2P network can be modeled as a pure exchange economy, a kind of Arrow-Debreu Market. Therefore, we are interested in the *market equilibrium* as the allocation mechanism to distribute those resources over P2P network.

As a distributed scheme, one of critical issues for the resource sharing problem is how to allocate resource in a fair fashion to maintain agents participation, i.e., ensuring that agents will share their resources fairly, and hence will agree to exchange resource with others. To motivate sharing, [16] pioneered the use of incentive techniques to drive cooperation and to promote voluntary contributions by participating agents. By taking such an approach, Cohen created the BitTorrent protocol, which has been well recognized as an Internet success to change "the entertainment industry and the interchange of information in Web" [5]. From the view of fairness consideration, Wu and Zhang [27], motivated by Bit-Torrent, have pioneered a model of proportional response for the bandwidth sharing problem on peer-to-peer system. Under this model, the resource allocation satisfies the condition that each peer provides each neighbor a portion of its contribution proportional to the percentage it receives from this neighbor among all its neighbors. They showed its economic efficiency by its convergence to a market equilibrium of a pure exchange economy. To obtain the market equilibrium, Wu and Zhang modeled the peer-to-peer system as an undirected graph $G = (V, E)$, where each vertex v represents an agent, with w_v units of divisible underused resources (or weight) to be distributed among its neighbors. And they proposed an elegant network decomposition on such a graph, which is called the *bottleneck decomposition* [27]. Based on this decomposition, they applied the idea of maximum flow to derive a proportional response allocation protocol among all agents whose output just is the allocation of the market equilibrium. This protocol is named as Bottleneck Decomposition Mechanism, or *BD Mechanism* for short [10,11].

However, agents are rational and strategic. The resource allocation from BD Mechanism depends on agents' reported information rather than their true information. So we are interested in the incentives of agents against BD Mechanism: when a system designer proposes BD Mechanism, is it possible for an agent to deviate from it by strategic behavior and improve its utility? Further, if the answer is "yes", does we can characterize the extent to which an agent's utility can be increased by such a strategic play? In recent works, [10,11] proved the incentive compatibility of this protocol against strategic behaviors of misreporting connectivity and the amount of resources agent owns. In this paper, we further explore its resistance to manipulative behavior by considering a kind of strategy that an agent disguises itself by creating several copied false nodes with its resources assigning among them. The motivation for us to discuss this strategic behavior, since it just is the behavior which is called *sybil attack*. In peer-to-peer system, sybil attack is a grave threat and subverts the security of network "by creating a large number of pseudonymous identities, using them to gain a disproportionately large influence" [24]. Compared with collusion, sybil attack strategy is easier to execute on the Internet since getting another identification, such as duplicating IP addresses, is cheap. Further, such a strategy is very difficult to detect since identifying each participant on Internet is virtually impossible. As of 2012, evidence showed that large-scale Sybil attacks could be carried out cheaply and efficiently in extant realistic systems such as BitTorrent Mainline DHT [25,26].

Recently, Chen et al. [6,7] have done a series of work on the sybil attack strategy against BD Mechanism in resource sharing. They first showed BD Mechanism is not robust to such a strategy any more. To characterize how much one can improve its utility at most and formalize such an improvement, they employed the concept of *incentive ratio*. Incentive ratio, which is first introduced by Chen et al. [9], is defined as the factor of the largest possible utility gain that a participant can achieve by behaving strategically, given that all other participants have their strategies unchanged. In the distributed environment, all agents only have limited knowledge due to the decentralization of the system. They need an incredible effort to know the full information of the game and do complicated computation as well. A small incentive ratio provides a safety margin where BD Mechanism will not be breached if no agents will pursue a small improvement in its utility in sacrificing some of its peers. Therefore a smaller incentive ratio implies an agent has less incentive to influence the allocation result from BD Mechanism through strategic considerations. In [6,7], Chen et al. discussed the settings of tree networks and cycle networks and proved that the incentive ratio of BD Mechanism for sybil attack strategy is exactly 2 on trees and is bounded by 2 and 4 on cycles, respectively.

In this paper, we are more concerned about the resource sharing in the context of sharing economy, in which the ideal state is that all of participants are fully connected. Thus our study mainly focuses on the network structure of complete graph and study the agents' incentive against BD Mechanism by sybil attack strategy.

Related Work

The classical economists and algorithmic game theorists have made an extensive study of competitive equilibrium [2], in terms of computation for prices and allocation [20], complexity and approximation [13–15,18,22,28]. Those works have started to have an influence in resource allocation among multiple agents, especially in the important implementations for the Internet enabled economic, management and social activities. How to fairly redistribute and share those resources have become an important issue with more and more online platforms and APPs which facilitate the exchange of commodities and services, such as Uber, Mobike, AirBnB, Opengarden, Swap...

The automated process through information and communication technology for Internet applications has made their successes relied on the voluntary cooperations of participating agents. [16] pioneered the study of such incentive techniques in mechanism design and in performance analysis for such peer-to-peer resource sharing systems. Agent strategic behaviors against market equilibrium mechanism has been analyzed in the Fisher market for linear markets [1] and for constant elasticity of substitution markets [4]. As a special case of Arrow-Debreu market, the proportional response protocol was shown to be equivalent to a market equilibrium solution [27] in the resource sharing system under P2P setting. [10,11] proved that the market equilibrium from the proportional response protocol is incentive compatible to two types of strategic behaviors for each agent: cheating on its connectivity with the rest of network and misreporting its own resource amount. But for the strategy of sybil attack, the proportional response protocol is not truthful any more. In addition, Chen et al. computed the percentage of improvement by this strategy with the aid of incentive ratio. They proved that incentive ratio is exactly 2 if the underlying network is a tree [6] and is bounded by 2 and 4 on cycles [7], respectively. The concept of incentive ratio is first introduced by Chen et al. [9], motivated by the concept of *price of anarchy* [19,23]. Comparing such two kinds of ratios, the former measures the most individual gains one may acquire in deviation from truthful behavior, while the latter models the loss of social efficiency in selfish Nash equilibrium in comparison to social optimality.

The strategy of sybil attack was first discussed by Douceur [12] for the consideration of the security of P2P network. Meanwhile, similar strategic strategies are also discussed in other situations, such as the false-name bidding in Internet auctions. The false-name bidding [30] is a serious fraud, in which false-name bids are submitted by a single agent under multiple fictitious identities. It has been known that the famous VCG mechanism is not incentive compatible against the false-name bidding, as a result of the study on the false-name-proof auction mechanisms design [17,29], and on the efficiency guarantee of the VCG mechanism [3].

Technical Contributions and Main Results

We analyze incentive ratio to quantitatively measure the maximal magnitude of utility gain by sybil attack followed a proportional response mechanism. Our main result in this paper is that the incentive ratios are exactly $\sqrt{2}$ on complete graphs. To obtain the ideal result, we propose a proper example for the lower bound. On the other hand, we characterize all possible bottleneck decompositions before and after manipulation with the help of the structure of complete graphs. And for each different case, we compute the maximal ratio by considering the maximum possible utility improvement, respectively, to reach the upper bound.

There has been several important research results for various utility functions where the most relevant one is the incentive ratio of two matching bound for linear utilities in the Fisher market [8,9], which is not directly applicable to our resource exchange model here but a special case of Arrow-Debreu market. As the incentive ratio for the Arrow-Debreu model is known to be unbounded [21] even in linear exchange economy, it is interesting to show a non-trivial matching bound under the setting discussed here. The practical network sharing economy with a market equilibrium solution still remains to be interesting with a limited rationality in terms of truthful behavior.

2   Preliminary

Our resource sharing system is based on a connected and undirected network $G = (V, E)$. Each vertex $v \in V$ represents an agent with an upload resource amount (weight) $w_v > 0$ for exchanging with its neighbors, where $\Gamma(v) = \{u : (v, u) \in E\}$ is the neighborhood of v. Let x_{vu} be the amount of resource v allocates to neighbor u ($0 \le x_{vu} \le w_v$) and $X = \{x_{uv}\}$ be an allocation. The utility of agent v from allocation X is defined as $U_v(X) = \sum_{u \in \Gamma(v)} x_{uv}$, i.e. all received resource from its neighbors. In the resource sharing environment, one of critical issues is how to design an allocation mechanism to maintain the agents participation, i.e., ensuring that agents will share their resources in a fair fashion. Wu and Zhang [27] pioneered the concept of "proportional response" inspired by the idea of "tit-for-tat" for the consideration of fairness.

Proportional Response. A mechanism is called *proportional response* if an allocation X from this mechanism satisfies $x_{vu} = \frac{x_{uv}}{\sum_{k \in \Gamma(v)} x_{kv}} w_v$, that is the allocation of each agent's resource is proportional to what it receives from its neighbors.

   To achieve a proportional response mechanism, a combinatorial structure, called *bottleneck decomposition* is derived in [27]. For set $S \subseteq V$, define $w(S) = \sum_{v \in S} w_v$ and $\Gamma(S) = \cup_{v \in S} \Gamma(v)$. It is possible that $S \cap \Gamma(S) \ne \emptyset$. Denote $\alpha(S) = \frac{w(\Gamma(S))}{w(S)}$ to be the inclusive expansion ratio of S, or the α-*ratio* of S for short. A set $B \subseteq V$ is called a *bottleneck* of G if $\alpha(B) = \min_{S \subseteq V} \alpha(S)$. A bottleneck with the maximal size is called the *maximal bottleneck*.

Bottleneck Decomposition. Given $G = (V, E; w)$. Start with $V_1 = V, G_1 = G$ and $i = 1$. Find the maximal bottleneck B_i of G_i and let G_{i+1} be the induced subgraph on the vertex set $V_{i+1} = V_i - (B_i \cup C_i)$, where $C_i = \Gamma(B_i) \cap V_i$, the neighbor set of B_i in G_i. Repeat if $G_{i+1} \ne \emptyset$ and set $k = i$ if $G_{i+1} = \emptyset$. Then we call $\mathcal{B} = \{(B_1, C_1), \cdots, (B_k, C_k)\}$ the bottleneck decomposition of G, (B_i, C_i) the i-th bottleneck pair and $\alpha_i = w(C_i)/w(B_i)$ the α-ratio of (B_i, C_i).

B-class and C-class. Given $\mathcal{B} = \{(B_1, C_1), \cdots, (B_k, C_k)\}$. For pair (B_i, C_i) with $\alpha_i < 1$, each vertex in B_i (or C_i) is called a B-class (or C-class) vertex. For the special case $B_k = C_k = V_k$, i.e., $\alpha_k = 1$, all vertices in B_k are categorized as both B-class and C-class.

   Bottleneck decomposition has a lot of beautiful combinatorial properties which are critical for us to obtain the tight incentive ratio of $\sqrt{2}$.

Proposition 2.1 [27]. *Given a graph G, the bottleneck decomposition of G is unique and*

1. $0 < \alpha_1 < \alpha_2 < \cdots < \alpha_k \le 1$;
2. *if $\alpha_i = 1$, then $i = k$ and $B_i = C_i$; otherwise B_i is an independent set and $B_i \cap C_i = \emptyset$;*

BD Mechanism. Given the bottleneck decomposition $\mathcal{B}$, an allocation Wu and Zhang [27] can be determined by distinguishing three cases. Cheng et al. [10,11] named it as BD Mechanism for short.

- For (B_i, C_i) with $\alpha_i < 1$, consider the bipartite graph $\widehat{G} = (B_i, C_i; E_i)$ with $E_i = B_i \times C_i$. Construct a network $N = (V_N, E_N)$ with $V_N = \{s, t\} \cup B_i \cup C_i$ and directed edges (s, u) with capacity w_u for $u \in B_i$, (v, t) with capacity w_v/α_i for $v \in C_i$ and (u, v) with capacity $+\infty$ for $(u, v) \in E_i$. The max-flow min-cut theorem ensures a maximal flow $\{f_{uv}\}$, $u \in B_i$ and $v \in C_i$, such that $\sum_{v \in \Gamma(u) \cap C_i} f_{uv} = w_u$ and $\sum_{u \in \Gamma(v) \cap B_i} f_{uv} = w_v/\alpha_i$. Let the allocation be $x_{uv} = f_{uv}$ and $x_{vu} = \alpha_i f_{uv}$ implying $\sum_{u \in \Gamma(v) \cap B_i} x_{vu} = \sum_{u \in \Gamma(v) \cap B_i} \alpha_i \cdot f_{vu} = w_v$. Figure 1 illustrates it.
- For $\alpha_k = 1$ (i.e., $B_k = C_k$), construct a bipartite graph $\widehat{G} = (B_k, B'_k; E'_k)$ where B'_k is a copy of B_k, there is an edge $(u, v') \in E'_k$ if and only if $(u, v) \in E[B_k]$. Construct a network by the above method, for any edge $(u, v') \in E'_k$, there exists flow $f_{uv'}$ such that $\sum_{v' \in \Gamma(u) \cap B'_k} f_{uv'} = w_u$. Let the allocation be $x_{uv} = f_{uv'}$.
- For any other edge $(u, v) \notin B_i \times C_i$, $i = 1, 2, \cdots, k$, define $x_{uv} = 0$.

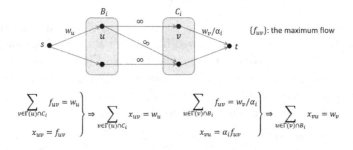

Fig. 1. The illustration of BD Mechanism.

Proposition 2.2 [27]. *BD Mechanism is a proportional response mechanism.*

On the other hand the resource sharing system can be modeled as a pure exchange economy, for which an efficient allocation is the market equilibrium.

Market Equilibrium. In the exchange economy, price vector $p = (p_v)_{v \in V}$ together with an allocation X is called a *market equilibrium* if for any agent $v \in V$ the following holds, 1. $\sum_{u \in \Gamma(v)} x_{vu} = w_v$ (market clearance); 2. $\sum_{u \in \Gamma(v)} p_u \frac{x_{vu}}{w_u} \le p_v$ (budget constraint); 3. $X = (x_{vu})$ maximizes the utility $U_v = \sum_{u \in \Gamma(v)} x_{uv}$ subject to the budget constraint (individual optimality).

BD Mechanism is not only fair as stated above but also efficient, since the proportional response allocation from it also is a market equilibrium. Given a bottleneck decomposition, if a price vector p is well defined as: $p_u = \alpha_i w_u$, if $u \in B_i$; and $p_u = w_u$ otherwise, then

Proposition 2.3 [27]. *(p, X) is a market equilibrium. Furthermore, each agent u's utility is $U_u = w_u \cdot \alpha_i$ if $u \in B_i$; $U_u = \frac{w_u}{\alpha_i}$ if $u \in C_i$.*

Note that $U_u \geq w_u$ if u is in C-class and $U_u \leq w_u$ if u is in B-class, as $\alpha_i \leq 1$ by the first claim in Proposition 2.1. From a system design point of view, although BD Mechanism shall allocate resource among interconnected participants fairly and efficiently, a problem occurs that, an agent may or may not follow BD Mechanism at the execution level. Can agents make strategic moves for gains in their utilities? We call such a problem with incentive compatibility consideration the *resource exchange game*.

In an instance of resource sharing game, the collection $\mathbf{w} = (w_1, \cdots, w_n) \in R^n$ is referred as the *weight profile*. For agent v, let $\mathbf{w}_{-v}$ be the weight profile without v. Since the utility of agent v depends on the underlying network G and $\mathbf{w}$, it is written as $U_v(G; \mathbf{w})$. Now we study a strategic move, called *sybil attack strategy*, that is one agent may create more than one fake identity by splitting itself into several copied nodes, and assign a weight to each node. Thus for a strategic agent v, it shall make multiple decisions as follows:

- how many copied nodes does it split into?
- how to build the connections between the copied nodes and its neighbors?
- how to assign its own weight to each copied node?

In this paper, we model the sybil attack strategy as: the strategic agent v shall split itself into m nodes $v^1, \cdots, v^m$, $1 \leq m \leq d_v$ (d_v is the degree of v), assign an amount w_{v^i} of resource to each node v^i, satisfying $0 \leq w_{v^i} \leq w_v$ and $\sum_{i=1}^{m} w_{v^i} = w_v$, and each neighbor of v in original G is connected to one of copied nodes, not vice versa. Let G' be the resulting network after agent v making above three decisions and agent v's new utility is denoted by $U'_v(G'; w_{v^1}, \cdots, w_{v^m}, \mathbf{w}_{-v})$.

Definition 2.1 (Incentive Ratio). *In a resource exchange game, the incentive ratio of agent v under BD Mechanism for the sybil attack strategy is*

$$\zeta_v = \max_{1 \leq m \leq d_v} \max_{w_{v^i} \in [0, w_v], \sum_{i=1}^{m} w_{v^i} = w_v; \mathbf{w}_{-v}; G'} \frac{U'_v(G'; w_{v^1}, \cdots, w_{v^m}, \mathbf{w}_{-v})}{U_v(G; \mathbf{w}_v)}.$$

The incentive ratio of BD mechanism in resource exchange game is defined to be $\zeta = \max_{v \in V} \zeta_v$.

There is a special case that a strategic agent v splits itself into d_v nodes and each node is connected to one of neighbors. Thus there is one to one correspondence between copied nodes and neighbors. Chen et al. showed the equivalence of the special strategy and the general sybil attack, which simplifies the decision making for strategic agent.

Proposition 2.4 [6,7]. *In a resource sharing game, the incentive ratio of BD mechanism with respect to sybil attack strategy can be achieved by splitting into d_v nodes and making each node be connected to one neighbor, where d_v is the degree of strategic agent v.*

3   Incentive Ratio of BD Mechanism on Complete Graph K_n

In this section, we focus on the resource sharing game in which the underlying network is a complete graph K_n. Before proceeding the details of discussion, let us introduce some necessary notations and propositions.

Lemma 3.1. *For any complete graph K_n, the bottleneck decomposition $\mathcal{B}$ only contains one bottleneck pair $\mathcal{B} = \{(B_1, C_1)\}$ and it shall be*

1. $\alpha_1 = 1$ and $B_1 = C_1 = V$, or
2. $\alpha_1 < 1$, B_1 only has one vertex and C_1 has other $n - 1$ vertices.

Proof. Let us focus on the first pair (B_1, C_1) in $\mathcal{B}$. Of course, there exist two cases: $\alpha_1 = 1$ and $\alpha_1 < 1$. If $\alpha_1 = 1$, then $B_1 = C_1 = V$ and the first claim holds. If $\alpha_1 < 1$, then B_1 must be independent by the first claim in Proposition 2.1. So the structure of complete graph makes B_1 only contain one vertex. Further the neighborhood $\Gamma(B_1) = V - B_1$. Hence C_1 contains other $n - 1$ vertices and $V_2 = V - (B_1 \cup C_1) = \emptyset$ which means there is only one pair (B_1, C_1) in $\mathcal{B}$.   □

Since the complete graph K_n has n vertices, without loss of generality, let the vertex who plays strategically be v, and the others be $u^1, \cdots, u^{n-1}$. In addition, such a strategic vertex v shall split itself into $n - 1$ duplicated nodes by Proposition 2.4. For the sake of convenience, we denote the duplicated node set by $\Lambda(v) = \{v^1, \cdots, v^{n-1}\}$ and the neighborhood of v by $\Gamma(v) = \{u^1, \cdots, u^{n-1}\}$, where each v^j is adjacent to u^j, $j = 1, \cdots, n-1$, in G'. Because of the structure of complete graphs, the induced graph $G'[\Gamma(v)]$ also is a complete graph K_{n-1} and the vertex set of new graph G' after manipulation is $V' = \Gamma(v) \cup \Lambda(v)$.

Similar to the notations of bottleneck decomposition in original K_n, the bottleneck decomposition of G' is denoted by $\mathcal{B}' = \{(B_1', C_1'), \cdots, (B_{k'}', C_{k'}')\}$ and let the α-ratio of each pair (B_i', C_i') be α_i', $i = 1, \cdots, k'$. Likewise, $V_1' = V'$, $V_{i+1}' = V_i' - (B_i' \cup C_i')$ for $i = 1, 2, \cdots, k' - 1$ and $G_i' = G'[V_i']$, $i = 1, 2, \cdots, k'$. The vertex in B_i' or C_i', $i = 1, \cdots, k'$, is called the B'-class or C'-class vertex and $\Gamma'(v)$ is the neighborhood of v in G', $\Gamma'(S) = \cup_{v \in S} \Gamma'(v)$ for any vertex set $S \subseteq V'$. Based on the structure of K_n and G', we characterize the bottleneck decomposition $\mathcal{B}'$ carefully in the following proposition.

Lemma 3.2. *Let $\mathcal{B}'$ be the bottleneck decomposition of G', then it shall be*

1. $\mathcal{B}' = \{(B_1', C_1')\}$, where $B_1' = C_1' = V'$ with $\alpha_1' = 1$, or
2. $\mathcal{B}' = \{(B_1', C_1')\}$, where $B_1' = \{u^j, \Lambda(v) - v^j\}$, $C_1' = \{v^j, \Gamma(v) - u^j\}$, $j \in \{1, \cdots, n-1\}$ (an example in Fig. 3), or
3. $\mathcal{B}' = \{(B_1', C_1'), \cdots, (B_{k'}', C_{k'}')\}$, where for each $i = 1, \cdots, k' - 1$, $B_i' = \{v^{h_1}, \cdots, v^{h_t}\}$, $C_i' = \{u^{h_1}, \cdots, u^{h_t}\}$, $h_1, \cdots, h_t \in \{1, \cdots, n-1\}$; and the last pair $(B_{k'}', C_{k'}')$ shall be
    (a) $B_{k'}' = C_{k'}' = \emptyset$ ($\mathcal{B}'$ actually contains $k' - 1$ pairs), or
    (b) $B_{k'}' = C_{k'}'$ with $\alpha_{k'}' = 1$, or
    (c) $B_{k'}' = \{u^j, \Lambda(v) - \cup_{i=1}^{k'-1} B_i' - v^j\}$, $C_{k'}' = \{v^j, \Gamma(v) - \cup_{i=1}^{k'-1} C_i' - u^j\}$ with $\alpha_{k'}' < 1$.

Proof. To show the correctness of this proposition, we shall discuss two situations depending on $\alpha'_1 = 1$ or $\alpha'_1 < 1$. Of course, if $\alpha'_1 = 1$, then $B'_1 = C'_1 = V$ which induces the first case. Otherwise if $\alpha'_1 < 1$, then B'_1 must be independent by the first claim of Proposition 2.1 and it may contain one vertex u^j from $\Gamma(v)$ or not. For the former that one vertex $u^j \in B'_1$, then $v^j \in C'_1$ and all others in $\Gamma(v)$ except for u^j must belong to C'_1, because the induced subgraph of $\Gamma(v) = \{u^1, \cdots, u^{n-1}\}$ still is a complete graph K_{n-1} in G' as mentioned before. In addition, each $v^h \in \Lambda(v) - v^j$ has a unique neighbor $u^h \in C'_1$, $h \neq j$, and is not adjacent to u^j. So adding all v^h, $h \neq j$, into B'_1 not only keeps the independence property of B'_1, but also makes its α-ratio decrease. Thus we get the second case, that is $B'_1 = \{u^j, \Lambda(v) - v^j\}$ and $C'_1 = \{v^j, \Gamma(v) - u^j\}$.

If B'_1 dose not contain any vertex from $\Gamma(v)$, it must have the form as $B'_1 = \{v^{h_1}, \cdots, v^{h_t}\}$ and $C'_1 = \{u^{h_1}, \cdots, u^{h_t}\}$ with the property of $\frac{w_{u^h}}{w_{v^h}} = \frac{w(C'_1)}{w(B'_1)} = \alpha'_1$. Recalling the process of bottleneck decomposition, $V'_2 = V' - (B'_1 \cup C'_1) = (\Lambda(v) - B'_1) \cup (\Gamma(v) - C'_1)$ and the rest graph G'_2 has the same structure as G'. Now we turn to discuss (B'_2, C'_2) which is the maximal bottleneck in G'_2. If $V'_2 = \emptyset$, then $B'_2 = C'_2 = \emptyset$. It implies case 3-(a). If $V'_2 \neq \emptyset$ and $B'_2 = C'_2 = V'_2$ with $\alpha'_2 = 1$, then case 3-(b) holds. If B'_2 has one vertex $u^j \in \Gamma(v) - C'_1$, then B'_2 and C'_2 has the same structure as case 2. So case 3-(c) is derived. If there is no any u^j in B'_2, then we continue the same analysis until one of above three cases happens.   □

Our main result on the incentive ratio of BD Mechanism for the sybil attack strategy on complete graphs is the following.

Theorem 3.1. *If the network of resource exchange system is a complete graph K_n, then the incentive ratio of BD Mechanism for the sybil attack strategy is exactly $\sqrt{2}$.*

To obtain Theorem 3.1, we try our best to prove the lower bound and upper bound of the incentive ratio on K_n are both equal to $\sqrt{2}$ in the subsequent two subsections.

3.1   Lower Bound of Incentive Ratio on K_n

In this subsection, we will prove the lower bound of $\sqrt{2}$ by proposing an example.

Theorem 3.2. *If the network of resource sharing system is a complete graph, then the incentive ratio of BD Mechanism for the sybil attack strategy is at least $\sqrt{2}$, i.e. $\zeta \geq \sqrt{2}$.*

Proof. Assume network G is a triangle K_3, shown in Fig. 2(a). The weights of all vertices are $w_v = 2\sqrt{2} - 2$, $w_{u^1} = 1$ and $w_{u^2} = 3 - 2\sqrt{2}$. The bottleneck decomposition $\mathcal{B}$ is $\{(B_1, C_1)\}$ with $B_1 = C_1 = \{v, u^1, u^2\}$ and $\alpha_1 = 1$. And the utility of v is $w_v \cdot \alpha_1 = 2\sqrt{2} - 2$.

If vertex v strategically splits itself into v^1 and v^2 and assigns $\sqrt{2} - 1$ units resource to each node, respectively, as shown in Fig. 2-(b). Then the bottleneck

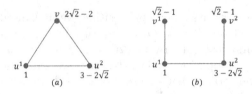

Fig. 2. An example showing the lower bound of incentive ration on complete graphs.

decomposition of new graph shall change to be $\{(B_1', C_1')\}$, where $B_1' = \{u^1, v^2\}$, $C_1' = \{u^2, v^1\}$ with $\alpha_1' = \sqrt{2} - 1$. At this time it is easy to compute $U_{v1}' = (\sqrt{2} - 1)/(\sqrt{2} - 1) = 1$ and $U_{v2}' = (\sqrt{2} - 1) \cdot (\sqrt{2} - 1) = 3 - 2\sqrt{2}$ which imply the total utility of v is $U_v' = 4 - 2\sqrt{2}$ and the incentive ratio of v is at least $\sqrt{2}$. Thus the incentive ratio of BD Mechanism on complete graphs is $\zeta \geq \sqrt{2}$. □

It's worth noting that the above example for lower bound can be generalized to any complete graph K_n with vertex weights $w_v = 2\sqrt{2} - 2$, $w_{u1} = 1$ and $w_{u2} = \cdots = w_{u^{n-1}} = \frac{3 - 2\sqrt{2}}{n-2}$. The bottleneck decomposition of K_n is $\{(B_1, C_1)\}$ with $B_1 = C_1 = \{v, u^1, \cdots, u^{n-1}\}$ and $\alpha_1 = 1$. So $U_v = 2\sqrt{2} - 2$. Now v plays the vertex splitting strategy to replace itself by $n - 1$ duplicated nodes $v^j, j = 1, \cdots, n - 1$, such that each v^j is adjacent to neighbor u^j. Furthermore, v assigns its weight to each node as $w_{v1} = \sqrt{2} - 1$ and $w_{v2} = \cdots = w_{v^{n-1}} = \frac{\sqrt{2} - 1}{n-2}$. Then the bottleneck decomposition changes to be $\{(B_1', C_1')\}$, where $B_1' = \{u^1, v^2, \cdots, v^{n-1}\}$, $C_1' = \{v^1, u^2, \cdots, u^{n-1}\}$ and $\alpha_1' = \sqrt{2} - 1$. So $U_{v1}' = (\sqrt{2} - 1)/(\sqrt{2} - 1) = 1$ and $U_{vj}' = \frac{\sqrt{2} - 1}{n-2} \cdot (\sqrt{2} - 1) = \frac{3 - 2\sqrt{2}}{n-2}, j = 2, \cdots, n - 1$. The total utility of v is $U_v' = U_{v1}' + \sum_{j=2}^{n-1} U_{vj}' = 4 - 2\sqrt{2} = \sqrt{2}U_v$.

3.2 Upper Bound of Incentive Ratio on K_n

The main task of this subsection is to show the upper bound of $\sqrt{2}$. To compute the upper bound of incentive ratio on complete graph K_n, it is necessary to analyze the optimal strategy for the strategic vertex v, by which v can obtain the maximal utility gain.

Theorem 3.3. *If the network of resource sharing system is a complete graph, then the incentive ratio of BD Mechanism for the sybil attack strategy is at most $\sqrt{2}$, i.e. $\zeta \leq \sqrt{2}$.*

Proof. As we know, the strategic vertex v may be a B-class vertex or C-class vertex in G. But if $v \in B_1$ with $\alpha_1 = 1$, it can be viewed as a C-class vertex since $B_1 = C_1 = V$. Thus there are two disjoint cases that $v \in B_1$ with $\alpha_1 < 1$ and $v \in C_1$. From the characterization of bottleneck decomposition $\mathcal{B}$ in Lemma 3.1, we note that if $v \in B_1$ with $\alpha_1 < 1$, then other $n - 1$ vertices are all in C_1 and upload all of their resource to v. In other words, vertex v obtains all possible resource in system, which achieves the maximum. Under this case, such a vertex v has no any incentive to play strategically and its optimal strategy is to keep intact. Hence, the incentive ratio is 1. For the second case that $v \in C_1$, it's obvious that $U_v = w_v/\alpha_1 \geq w_v$. If $\mathcal{B}'$ only contains one bottleneck pair (B_1', C_1') with $\alpha_1' = 1$, then $U_v' = \sum_{j=1}^{n-1} U_{v^j}' = \sum_{j=1}^{n-1} w_{v^j} = w_v \leq U_v$, which implies v's incentive ratio is 1 too. Until now there is only one situation left that $v \in C_1$ and $\mathcal{B}'$ contains at least one bottleneck pair whose α-ratio is less than 1, meaning $\alpha_1' < 1$. Following lemma characterizes the structure of $\mathcal{B}'$ when the strategic agent v plays the optimal strategy.

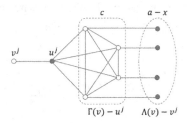

Fig. 3. The bottleneck decomposition $\mathcal{B}'$ when v adopts optimal strategy, where the blue or white vertices represent B'-class or C'-class vertices respectively. (Color figure online)

Lemma 3.3. *Suppose that the network of resource sharing system is a complete graph and the strategic vertex v is in C-class. When v gains the maximal utility by adopting the optimal strategy, the bottleneck decomposition $\mathcal{B}'$ in G' must has the form as $\mathcal{B}' = \{(B_1', C_1')\}$ with $B_1' = \{u^j, \Lambda(v) - v^j\}$ and $C_1' = \{v^j, \Gamma(v) - u^j\}$, $\exists j \in \{1, 2, \cdots, n-1\}$ as shown in Fig. 3.*

Proof. Based on the previous analysis, it is enough to discuss the case that $v \in C_1$ and $\mathcal{B}'$ contains at least one pair whose α-ratio is less than 1, which implies $\alpha_1' < 1$. So the structure of $\mathcal{B}'$ must be case 2 or 3 in Lemma 3.2. If $\mathcal{B}'$ has the structure as case 2, then this lemma holds. Now we turn to discuss case 3 and try to show the impossibility of case 3 when v plays optimally.

If $\mathcal{B}'$ has the structure as case 3-(a) and 3-(b), then each duplicated node v^l, $l = 1, \cdots, n-1$, is in B'-class (for case 3-(b) some v^l may be in $B_{k'}' = C_{k'}'$ with $\alpha_{k'}' = 1$) and $U_{v^l}' \leq w_{v^l}$. Therefore,

$$U_v' = \sum_{l=1}^{n-1} U_{v^l}' \leq \sum_{l=1}^{n-1} w_{v^l} = w_v \leq U_v.$$

The last inequality is from the condition that $v \in C_1$. So v has no incentive to manipulate BD mechanism and its incentive ratio is 1.

If $\mathcal{B}'$ has the structure as case 3-(c), without loss of generality, we assume there are two pairs in $\mathcal{B}'$, which are $B_1' = \{v^h\}$, $C_1' = \{u^h\}$ and $B_2' = \{u^j, \Lambda(v) - \{v^j, v^h\}\}$, $C_2' = \{v^j, \Gamma(v) - \{u^j, u^h\}\}$. Thus, $U_{v^h}' = w_{v^h} \cdot \alpha_1' = w_{u^h}$, $U_{v^j}' = w_{v^j}/\alpha_2'$ and $U_{v^l}' = w_{v^l} \cdot \alpha_2'$, for each $l \neq j, h$. In addition the total utility of v in G' is

$$U_v' = w_{u^h} + \frac{w_{v^j}}{\alpha_2'} + (w_v - w_{v^h} - w_{v^j}) \cdot \alpha_2'.$$

Let us consider a new weight assignment $(\widehat{w}_{v^1}, \widehat{w}_{v^2}, \cdots, \widehat{w}_{v^{n-1}})$ of w_v as

$$\widehat{w}_{v^l} = \begin{cases} w_{v^l} - \delta, & l = h; \\ w_{v^l} + \frac{\alpha_2'}{1+\alpha_2'}\delta, & l = j; \\ w_{v^l} + \frac{1}{(1+\alpha_2')(n-3)}\delta, & l \neq h, j; \end{cases} \qquad (1)$$

where δ is a arbitrarily small and positive number. Obviously, $\sum_{l=1}^{n-1} \widehat{w}_{v^l} = w_v$. Since $\alpha_1' < \alpha_2'$, there must be a small and positive number δ such that the bottleneck decomposition $\mathcal{B}'$ keeps unchanged for the new weight assignment (1). So the new utility of v^h is still $\widehat{U}_{v^h}' = w_{u^h} = U_{v^h}'$ and the fact $\alpha_2' = \frac{w_{v^j} + \sum_{l \neq h,j} w_{u^h}}{w_{u^j} + \sum_{l \neq h,j} w_{v^h}}$ makes

$$\widehat{\alpha}_2' = \frac{w_{v^j} + \sum_{l \neq h,j} w_{u^h} + \frac{\alpha_2'}{1+\alpha_2'}\delta}{w_{u^j} + \sum_{l \neq h,j} w_{v^h} + \frac{1}{1+\alpha_2'}\delta} = \alpha_2'$$

Therefore,

$$\widehat{U}_{v^j}' = \frac{\widehat{w}_{v^j}}{\alpha_2'} = \frac{w_{v^j} + \frac{\alpha_2'}{1+\alpha_2'}\delta}{\alpha_2'} = U_{v^j}' + \frac{1}{1+\alpha_2'}\delta;$$

$$\sum_{l \neq j,h} \widehat{U}_{v^l}' = (w_v - w_{v^h} - w_{v^j} + \frac{1}{1+\alpha_2'}\delta) \cdot \alpha_2' = \sum_{l \neq j,h} U_{v^l}' + \frac{\alpha_2'}{1+\alpha_2'}\delta,$$

which implies $\widehat{U}_v' = U_v' + \delta > U_v'$. Vertex v continues to adjust its weight assignment as (1) by increasing δ until $\widehat{\alpha}_1' = \widehat{\alpha}_2' = \alpha_2'$. At this time, the two bottleneck pairs should be combined together to keep the maximal size and have the form as $B_1' = \{u^j, \Lambda(v) - v^j\}$ and $C_1' = \{v^j, \Gamma(v) - u^j\}$. Furthermore, by the proof of Lemma 3.2, we know once one of $u^j \in \Gamma(v)$ is in B_1' and $\alpha_1' < 1$, then the bottleneck decomposition $\mathcal{B}'$ must have the structure of case 2 in Lemma 3.2. This completes the proof. □

Now we are ready to provide the proof of Theorem 3.3. Here we only discuss the case that $v \in C_1$ in G and $\mathcal{B}'$ contains at least one bottleneck pair whose α-ratio is less than 1. Given any weight profile $\mathbf{w} = (w_v, w_{u^1}, \cdots, w_{u^{n-1}})$. From Lemma 3.3, if vertex v plays the optimal strategy, then the bottleneck decomposition $\mathcal{B}' = \{(B_1', C_1')\}$ has the structure of $B_1' = \{u^j, \Lambda(v) - v^j\}$ and $C_1' = \{v^j, \Gamma(v) - u^j\}$, $j \in \{1, 2, \cdots, n-1\}$. So

$$\alpha_1' = \frac{w_{v^j} + \sum_{l \neq j} w_{u^l}}{w_{u^j} + (w_v - w_{v^j})} \quad \text{and} \quad U_v' = (w_v - w_{v^j}) \cdot \alpha_1' + w_{v^j} \frac{1}{\alpha_1'}.$$

Since the weight profile $\mathbf{w} = (w_v, w_{u^1}, \cdots, w_{u^{n-1}})$ is given in advance, U_v' and α_1' can be viewed as the functions of w_{v^j}. To simplify the notations, we denote $w_v = a$, $w_{u^j} = b$, $\sum_{l \neq j} w_{u^l} = c$ and the decision variable $w_{v^j} = x$, as shown in Fig. 3. Using these notations, the bottleneck decomposition $\mathcal{B} = \{(B_1, C_1)\}$ of

K_n may be: (1) $B_1 = \{u^j\}$ and $C_1 = V - \{u^j\}$ with $\alpha_1 = \frac{a+c}{b}$ when $b > a + c$; or (2) $B_1 = C_1 = V$ with $\alpha_1 = 1$ when $b \leq a + c$. Thus

$$U_v = \begin{cases} a \cdot \frac{1}{\alpha_1} = \frac{ab}{a+c}, & \text{if } b > a + c; \\ a, & \text{if } b \leq a + c. \end{cases} \tag{2}$$

For the strategic vertex v, it tries to maximize the following maximization problem,

$$
\begin{aligned}
\max \quad & U_v'(x)/U_v \\
s.t \quad & \frac{c}{a-x} \geq \frac{c+x}{b+a-x} & (\star) \\
& b + a - x > c + x & (\star\star) \\
& 0 \leq x \leq a & (\star\star\star)
\end{aligned} \tag{3}
$$

Constraint $(\star)$ is from characterization that the bottleneck decomposition $\mathcal{B}'$ shall be $B_1' = \{u^j, \Lambda(v) - v^j\}$ and $C_1' = \{v^j, \Gamma(v) - u^j\}$ under the optimal strategy, and constraint $(\star\star)$ is right since $\alpha_1'(x) = \frac{c+x}{b+a-x} < 1$. Combining constraints $(\star\star)$ and $(\star\star\star)$, the feasible solution $x \leq \min\{a, \frac{a+b-c}{2}\}$. In addition,

$$U_v'(x) = x \cdot \frac{b+a-x}{c+x} + (a-x) \cdot \frac{c+x}{a+b-x} = (a+b+c)\left[\frac{x}{c+x} + \frac{a-x}{a+b-x}\right] - a,$$

and the derivation of $U_v'(x)$ is

$$\frac{dU_v'(x)}{dx} = (a+b+c)\left[\frac{c}{(c+x)^2} - \frac{b}{(a+b-x)^2}\right].$$

It is not hard to see function $U_v'(x)$ has a unique maximum point $x^* = \frac{\sqrt{c}(a+b) - \sqrt{b}c}{\sqrt{b} + \sqrt{c}}$ and $U_v'(x)$ increases when $x \leq x^*$ and decreases when $x \geq x^*$.

Let us consider four intervals where the parameter b is in: $[0, c]$, $[c, a+c]$, $[a+c, \frac{(a+c)^2}{c}]$ and $[\frac{(a+c)^2}{c}, +\infty]$. We can compute that $\frac{a+b-c}{2} \leq x^* < a$ when $b \in [0, c]$; $x^* \leq \frac{a+b-c}{2} \leq a$ when $b \in [c, a+c]$; $x^* \leq a \leq \frac{a+b-c}{2}$ when $b \in [a+c, \frac{(a+c)^2}{c}]$ and $a \leq x^* < \frac{a+b-c}{2}$ when $b \in [\frac{(a+c)^2}{c}, +\infty]$. In the following we shall prove that the ratio $U_v'(x)/U_v$ is no more than $\sqrt{2}$ in each interval.

- $b \in [0, c]$. So $U_v = a$ since $b \leq c \leq a + c$ by (2). On the other hand, we get $x^* \geq \frac{a+b-c}{2}$ and $a \geq \frac{a+b-c}{2}$. Such two inequalities means the feasible solution $x \leq \min\{a, \frac{a+b-c}{2}\} = \frac{a+b-c}{2} \leq x^*$. So the monotonically increasing property of $U_v'(x)$ when $x \leq x^*$ promises

$$U_v'(x) \leq U_v'\left(\frac{a+b-c}{2}\right) = a = U_v.$$

- $b \in [c, a+c]$. On one hand, condition $b \leq a + c$ promises $U_v = a$ by (2) and $a \geq \frac{a+b-c}{2}$. On the other hand, $x^* \leq \frac{a+b-c}{2} = \min\{a, \frac{a+b-c}{2}\}$. Therefore v can get its maximal utility when $x = x^*$, and

$$U_v'(x^*) = x^* \cdot \frac{b+a-x^*}{c+x^*} + (a-x^*) \cdot \frac{c+x^*}{a+b-x^*} = a + (\sqrt{b} - \sqrt{c})^2.$$

Then the ratio

$$\frac{U_v'(x^*)}{U_v} = \frac{a + (\sqrt{b} - \sqrt{c})^2}{a} \leq \frac{a + (\sqrt{a+c} - \sqrt{c})^2}{a} = \frac{2\sqrt{a+c}(\sqrt{a+c} - \sqrt{c})}{a} = \frac{2}{\sqrt{\frac{1}{1+\frac{a}{c}}} + 1},$$

(4)

where the inequality is from condition $b \leq a + c$. Of course, if $U_v'(x)$ achieves its maximum at $x = x^*$, then $x^* = \frac{\sqrt{c}(a+b) - c\sqrt{b}}{\sqrt{b} + \sqrt{c}}$ must satisfy constraint $(\star)$ additionally, i.e., $\frac{c}{a-x^*} \geq \frac{c+x^*}{b+a-x^*}$. So

$$bc \geq x^*(a - x^*) \implies bc \geq \frac{[\sqrt{b}(c+a) - b\sqrt{c}][\sqrt{c}(b+a) - c\sqrt{b}]}{(\sqrt{b} + \sqrt{c})^2}$$

$$\iff bc(b+c) + 2bc\sqrt{bc} \geq [2bc + a(a+b+c)]\sqrt{bc} - 2abc - bc(b+c)$$

$$\iff 2bc(a+b+c) \geq a(a+b+c)\sqrt{bc} \iff 2\sqrt{bc} \geq a$$

Combining the condition $b \leq a + c$, we have $a \leq 2\sqrt{(a+c)c}$, which implies

$$a^2 \leq 4(a+c)c \implies \left(\frac{a}{c}\right)^2 - 4\left(\frac{a}{c}\right) - 4 \leq 0 \implies 0 < \frac{a}{c} \leq 2 + 2\sqrt{2}.$$

(5)

Continue the computation of the upper bound in (4),

$$\frac{U_v'(x^*)}{U_v} \leq \frac{2}{\sqrt{\frac{1}{1+\frac{a}{c}}} + 1} \leq \frac{2}{\sqrt{\frac{1}{1+(2+2\sqrt{2})}} + 1} = \sqrt{2}.$$

- $b \in [a + c, \frac{(a+c)^2}{c}]$. Under this case, we have $U_v = \frac{ab}{a+c}$ by (2), inequalities $a \leq \frac{a+b-c}{2}$ and $x^* \leq a = \min\{a, \frac{a+b-c}{2}\}$. So the utility $U_v'(x)$ must reach the maximum $U_v'(x^*) = a + (\sqrt{b} - \sqrt{c})^2$ at $x = x^*$ and the ratio

$$\frac{U_v'(x^*)}{U_v} = \frac{a + (\sqrt{b} - \sqrt{c})^2}{ab/(a+c)} \leq \frac{a + (\sqrt{a+c} - \sqrt{c})^2}{a} = \frac{2}{\sqrt{\frac{1}{1+\frac{a}{c}}} + 1}.$$

Since the above ratio decreases with b, the inequality is from the condition that $b \geq a + c$. Applying the same analysis for case $b \in [c, a + c]$, we also can get the upper bound of $\sqrt{2}$.

- $b \in [\frac{(a+c)^2}{c}, +\infty]$. Clearly, $U_v = \frac{ab}{a+c}$ and $a \leq \frac{a+b-c}{2}$, $x^* \geq a$. Hence all feasible solutions $x \leq \min\{a, \frac{a+b-c}{2}\} = a \leq x^*$. By the monotonically increasing property of $U_v'(x)$ when $x \leq x^*$, we have

$$U_v'(x) \leq U_v'(a) = \frac{ab}{a+c} = U_v,$$

which implies the incentive ratio of v is no more than 1.

This completes Theorem 3.3. $\qquad\square$

4   Observations and Conclusions

In this paper, we discuss the effect of sybil attack, a possible strategic manipulation of agents, on the resource sharing game over P2P network. Resource sharing can be viewed as a pure exchange economy model, for which pricing and allocation are decided by market equilibrium. As a common strategic behavior in peer-to-peer system, sybil attack is easier to execute and is difficult to detect. This motivates us to study the incentives of agents by taking the sybil attack strategy under the market equilibrium solution and quantitatively measuring the maximal magnitude of agent advantage gained from sybil attack in terms of the incentive ratio.

From the perspective of sharing economy, the ideal state of resource sharing game to consider is where all participants are fully connected. Therefore, it motivates us to focus on the complete graphs. We prove that the incentive ratio of the market equilibrium solution under the sybil attack strategy is exactly $\sqrt{2}$ on complete graphs.

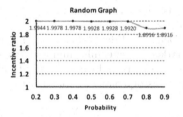

Fig. 4. The numerical experiment results on random graphs.

Through the study of incentive ratio on complete graphs, we may suspect that the density of edges in a graph may decrease the incentive ratio of the resource sharing problem from that of 2 for tree to $\sqrt{2}$ gradually. There then opens up the issue whether the incentive ratio of market equilibrium for resource sharing on random networks decreases as the probability an edge is selected into the network. Therefore, we look into a series of random graphs, in each of which any two vertices are connected by an edge with probability p independent from every other edge. In our numerical experiments, we construct 100 graphs of 10 vertices for each probability $p \in \{0.1, 0.2, \cdots, 0.9\}$, and the weight of each vertex is no more than 100. Then we simulate the sybil attack strategy and compute the maximal incentive ratio among all 100 graphs for each probability p, as shown in Fig. 4. From the results in Fig. 4, we can see that the incentive ratio is no more than 2. Furthermore we have the intuition that, with the increase of p, implying that the underlying network contains more and more edges, the incentive ratio decreases. From the current results that the incentive ratio is 2 on trees and is $\sqrt{2}$ on complete graphs, such an intuition does make sense.

Despite of the randomized results, we are still interested in the incentive ratio in general settings. A key challenge is to find out a proper bound for the incentive ratio of general graphs, which we conjecture to be two.

Acknowledgments. This research was partially supported by the National Nature Science Foundation of China (Nos. 11301475, 11426026, 61632017, 61173011), by a Project 985 grant of Shanghai Jiao Tong University, by the Research Grant Council of Hong Kong (ECS Project Nos. 26200314, GRF Project No. 16213115 and GRF Project No. 16243516), and by Ant Finantial.

References

1. Adsul, B., Babu, C.S., Garg, J., Mehta, R., Sohoni, M.: Nash equilibria in fisher market. In: Kontogiannis, S., Koutsoupias, E., Spirakis, P.G. (eds.) SAGT 2010. LNCS, vol. 6386, pp. 30–41. Springer, Heidelberg (2010). https://doi.org/10.1007/978-3-642-16170-4_4

2. Arrow, K., Debreu, G.: Existence of an equilibrium for a competitive economy. Econometrica **22**(3), 265–290 (1954)

3. Alkalay, C., Vetta, A.: False-name bidding and economic efficiency in combinatorial auctions. In: AAAI, pp. 538–544 (2014)

4. Braanzei, S., Chen, Y., Deng, X., Filos-Ratsikas, A., Kristoffer, S., Frederiksen, S., Zhang, J.: The fisher market game: equilibrium and welfare. In: AAAI (2014)

5. Dalakov, G.: History of computers and computing, internet, internet conquers the world, BitTorrent. http://historycomputer.com/Internet/Conquering/BitTorrent.html

6. Chen, Z., Cheng, Y., Deng, X., Qi, Q., Yan, X.: Agent incentives of strategic behavior in resource exchange. In: Bilò, V., Flammini, M. (eds.) SAGT 2017. LNCS, vol. 10504, pp. 227–239. Springer, Cham (2017). https://doi.org/10.1007/978-3-319-66700-3_18

7. Chen, Z., Cheng, Y., Qi, Q., Yan, X.: Incentive ratios of a proportional sharing mechanism in resource sharing. In: Cao, Y., Chen, J. (eds.) COCOON 2017. LNCS, vol. 10392, pp. 137–149. Springer, Cham (2017). https://doi.org/10.1007/978-3-319-62389-4_12

8. Chen, N., Deng, X., Zhang, H., Zhang, J.: Incentive ratios of fisher markets. In: Czumaj, A., Mehlhorn, K., Pitts, A., Wattenhofer, R. (eds.) ICALP 2012. LNCS, vol. 7392, pp. 464–475. Springer, Heidelberg (2012). https://doi.org/10.1007/978-3-642-31585-5_42

9. Chen, N., Deng, X., Zhang, J.: How profitable are strategic behaviors in a market? In: Demetrescu, C., Halldórsson, M.M. (eds.) ESA 2011. LNCS, vol. 6942, pp. 106–118. Springer, Heidelberg (2011). https://doi.org/10.1007/978-3-642-23719-5_10

10. Cheng, Y., Deng, X., Pi, Y., Yan, X.: Can bandwidth sharing be truthful? In: Hoefer, M. (ed.) SAGT 2015. LNCS, vol. 9347, pp. 190–202. Springer, Heidelberg (2015). https://doi.org/10.1007/978-3-662-48433-3_15

11. Cheng, Y., Deng, X., Qi, Q., Yan, X.: Truthfulness of a proportional sharing mechanism in resource exchange. In: IJCAI, pp. 187–193 (2016)

12. Douceur, J.R.: The Sybil attack. In: Druschel, P., Kaashoek, F., Rowstron, A. (eds.) IPTPS 2002. LNCS, vol. 2429, pp. 251–260. Springer, Heidelberg (2002). https://doi.org/10.1007/3-540-45748-8_24

13. Duan, R., Garg, J., Mehlhorn, K.: An improved combinatorial polynomial algorithm for the linear Arrow-Debreu market. In: SODA (2016)
14. Deng, X., Papadimitriou, C., Safra, S.: On the complexity of equilibria. In: STOC, pp. 67–71 (2002)
15. Devanur, N., Papadimitriou, C., Saberi, A., Vazirani, V.: Market equilibrium via a primal-dual-type algorithm. In: FOCS, pp. 389–389 (2002)
16. Feldman M., Lai, K., Stoica, I.: Robust incentive techniques for peer-to-peer networks. In: EC, pp. 102–111 (2004)
17. Iwasaki, A., Conitzer, V., Omori, Y.: Worst-case efficiency ratio in false-name-proof combinatorial auction mechanisms. In: AMMAS, pp. 633–640 (2010)
18. Jain, K.: A polynomial time algorithm for computing an Arrow-Debreu market equilibrium for linear utilities. SIAM J. Comput. **37**(1), 303–318 (2007)
19. Koutsoupias, E., Papadimitriou, C.: Worst-case equilibria. In: Meinel, C., Tison, S. (eds.) STACS 1999. LNCS, vol. 1563, pp. 404–413. Springer, Heidelberg (1999). https://doi.org/10.1007/3-540-49116-3_38
20. Lange, O.: The computer and the market. Socialism, Capitalism and Economic Growth, pp. 158–161 (1967)
21. Polak, I.: The incentive ratio in exchange economies. In: Chan, T.-H.H., Li, M., Wang, L. (eds.) COCOA 2016. LNCS, vol. 10043, pp. 685–692. Springer, Cham (2016). https://doi.org/10.1007/978-3-319-48749-6_49
22. Papadimitriou, C.: Algorithms, games, and the internet. In: STOC, pp. 749–753 (2001)
23. Roughgarden, T., Tardos, E.: How bad is selfish routing. J. ACM **49**(2), 236–259 (2002)
24. Sybil attack. https://en.wikipedia.org/wiki/Sybil-attack
25. Wang, L., Kangasharju, J.: Real-world sybil attacks in BitTorrent mainline DHT. In: IEEE GLOBECOM (2012)
26. Wang, L., Kangasharju, J.: Measuring large-scale distributed systems: case of BitTorrent mainline DHT. In: IEEE Peer-to-Peer (2013)
27. Wu, F., Zhang, L.: Proportional response dynamics leads to market equilibrium. In: STOC, pp. 354–363 (2007)
28. Ye, Y.: A path to the Arrow-Debreu competitive market equilibrium. Math. Program. **111**(1–2), 315–348 (2008)
29. Yokoo, M.: False-name bids in combinatorial auctions. ACM SIGecom Exch. **7**(1), 1–4 (2007)
30. Yokoo, M., Sakurai, Y., Matsubara, S.: The effect of false-name bids in combinatorial auctions: new fraud in Internet auctions. Games Econ. Behav. **46**, 174–188 (2004)

Mechanism Design with Efficiency and Equality Considerations

Zhou Chen[1], Qi Qi[1], Changjun Wang[2(✉)], and Wenwei Wang[1]

[1] Hong Kong University of Science and Technology, Clear Water Bay, Hong Kong
{zchenaq,kaylaqi,wwangaw}@ust.hk
[2] Beijing University of Technology, Beijing, China
wcj@bjut.edu.cn

Abstract. In this work, we consider the problem of allocating a set of homogenous resources (goods) among multiple strategic players to balance the efficiency and equality from a game-theoretic perspective. For two very general classes of efficiency measures and equality measures, we develop a general truthful mechanism framework which optimally maximizes the resource holder's efficiency while guaranteeing certain equality levels. We fully characterize the optimal allocation rule. Based on the characterizations, we show the optimal allocation and corresponding truthful payments can be computed in polynomial time, which means the truthful mechanism is computationally feasible.

1 Introduction

Efficiency and equality are two essential criteria in resource allocation problems. The trade-off and balance between these two criteria are crucial to many problems and have been studied for a long time in traditional settings [4,16]. Those studies mainly focus on the distribution of public service where a social planner has access to all the relevant information. However, in many real applications, the participants hold their private information, and may act strategically to benefit themselves, which leads to undesirable allocation results. Therefore, mechanism design is needed to prevent untruthfulness in the allocation problems that target dual objectives of efficiency and equality.

In this paper, we study the problem of allocating a set of homogenous resources among multiple strategic players and aim to design a truthful mechanism which could achieve the optimal combination of efficiency and equality. We consider efficiency and equality as two separate criteria and try to find optimal combinations of them. It is a general framework that can fit various scenarios where the social planner has different kinds of efficiency/equality measurements and emphases towards these two objectives.

We define efficiency as the sum of the expected utility gain for the goods holder. It's highly dependent on the players' private values and could cover

This work is partly supported by the Research Grant Council of Hong Kong (GRF Project Nos. 16213115, 16243516 and 16215717), and by the National Natural Science Foundation of China (NSFC Grant No. 11601022).

N. R. Devanur and P. Lu (Eds.): WINE 2017, LNCS 10674, pp. 120–132, 2017.
https://doi.org/10.1007/978-3-319-71924-5_9

many well known criteria, e.g. social welfare, expected revenue. On the other hand, equality should be determined only by the allocation, not related to players' values, since everyone should be treated equally in this criterion. The equality measure we adopt is based on the so called *Generalized Gini index*. It was first proposed by Weymark [25] and has been widely used in many areas [14,22]. Analogous to its original definition, our equality measure is defined as the weighted sum of all players' winning probabilities, and it could include many commonly used equality measures, like Min-probability, Max-difference, Gini-coefficient as special cases.

1.1 Main Results and Our Contributions

- **Truthful Mechanism to Optimally Balance Efficiency and Equality.** For two general classes of efficiency and equality measures, we design a truthful mechanism framework to optimally balance the efficiency and equality. Here 'optimal balancing' means finding Pareto optimal combinations of efficiency and equality.
- **Polynomial-time Feasibility of the Mechanism.** Despite the existence of optimal allocation and corresponding truthful payments for our problem, the computation of them is not trivial.
  - We show that the optimal allocations with respect to any particular bids profile can be obtained through solving a corresponding linear programming(LP), though the equality measure is nonlinear. Then we characterize one of the optimal solutions of the LP: there exists an optimal allocation where all the players can be divided into at most four groups, where the players in the same group have the same allocated winning probability; Of the (at most) four probability values, there are at most two fractional probability values. This nice property is crucial for efficiently computing the truthful payment.
  - The truthful payment of any player in our mechanism is an integration of his winning probability as his bid unilaterally increases from 0 to his current bid. Based on the above mentioned characterization of optimal allocation, we show that any player's winning probability is a piece-wise constant function of his own bid and there are at most $O(N^4)$ different constant pieces, where N is the number of players. Then we propose a polynomial-time algorithm to compute the $O(N^4)$ different winning probability pieces and thus obtain the truthful payment. (Note: When efficiency is the social welfare, the VCG payment can guarantee truthfulness. However, for some case of efficiency, VCG-like payment may be untruthful.)

To the best of our knowledge, our work is the first study on mechanism design with Pareto optimal combination of efficiency and equality, and can be executed in polynomial time.

1.2 Related Work

Our work mainly relates to two streams of research topics: (1) resource allocation problems having concerns of both efficiency and fairness; (2) mechanism design with strategic behaviors.

In the resource allocation literature, there are two approaches of researches to balance efficiency and fairness. The first approach is to use a bicriteria model. Mandell [16] presented a model represented by a bicriteria mathematical programming with efficiency and equality as two separate objectives, then proposed a methodology to obtain the Pareto frontier. Later Golany and Tamir [11] developed a model to analyze tradeoffs among efficiency, effectiveness and equality based on the methodology of Data Envelopment Analysis (DEA). Plenty of follow-up researches considered multiple objectives of efficiency and fairness in various applications [19,20]. However, in their studies, the social planner was assumed to have complete information about each agent's private value of the resource, thus only focused on solving an optimization problem, while we emphase our work on the truthful mechanism design at the same time.

Another approach is to realize a utility-based fairness by designing a single proper objective function such that an allocation maximizing this objective can be considered as a kind of fair result. Atkinson [1] introduced a large family of objectives concerning fairness. Bertsimas et al. [2] defined the price of fairness as the percentage loss of the optimal efficiency under fairness allocation compared to the optimal efficiency under utilitarian allocation, and provided a lower bound on this measure. Bertsimas et al. [3] followed the definitions in [2] and investigated a more general fairness concept (α-fair), and a general bound on the price of fairness was proved. However, they also assumed complete public information while our goal is to provide an incentive compatible mechanism to achieve maximum efficiency with equality guarantee. Besides, their fairness is defined based on utilities while our equality is an opportunity fairness, which is anonymous and only depend on the distributional probabilities.

Another stream of researches that relate to our work is about mechanism design. It is a large topic raised because the principal has no direct access to the agents' private information. In many cases, the principal aims to design an incentive compatible mechanism to encourage agents to act truthfully. The VCG mechanism [5,13,24] and Myerson's optimal auction [18] are two classic truthful mechanisms that maximize the social welfare and auctioneer's revenue, respectively. In recent years, the mechanism design problem with fairness concern has been studied [7,12,17], especially in the area of spectrum allocation. Zivan et al. [26] designed a mechanism for allocating multiple divisible goods that could achieve envy-freeness and Pareto optimality, but failed to prevent agents from strategically bidding untruthfully. Cole et al. [7] proposed a truthful mechanism that yielded an approximation guarantee for proportional fairness, but did not consider efficiency as an objective. In our work, we use a more general concept of efficiency and equality, and take efficiency, equality and truthfulness into consideration.

The rest of this paper is organized as follows. In Sect. 2 we introduce the model and the truthful mechanism framework. In Sect. 3 we characterize the properties of optimal allocations and show how to compute the optimal allocations and truthful payments. Finally, we conclude our work in Sect. 4.

2 The Problem

The goods holder has K (≥ 1) identical indivisible goods that are desired by N ($\gg K$) users. We use $\mathcal{N} = \{1, 2, \ldots, N\}$ to denote the set of users. Each user $i \in \mathcal{N}$ is unit-demand and has a private value $v_i \geq 0$ for the goods, i.e., player i derives value v_i from receiving one of the goods. Meanwhile, the benefit (efficiency increase) that the goods holder receives from i's demand satisfaction may be different from v_i, and we denote it as $f_i(v_i)$. In this work, we assume $f_i(v)$ is a monotone increasing and continuously differentiable function of value v for any player $i \in \mathcal{N}$. This can be seen as high value of consumption for the users would bring about high utility return for the goods holder. For example, users with higher value can pay more. A feasible *allocation* is a vector $\mathbf{q} \in [0, 1]^N$ that indicates each player's probability of obtaining one of the goods and $\sum_{i=1}^{N} q_i = K$ (In this work, we only consider the case where all the goods must be allocated, otherwise the results may not hold). The efficiency of an allocation $\mathbf{q}$ is defined as the expected total utility gain for the goods holder, i.e., $\sum_{i \in \mathcal{N}} f_i(v_i) \cdot q_i$. We use function $\mathbb{E} \colon [0, 1]^N \to [0, 1]$ to denote the equality measure of an allocation, and a larger value of $\mathbb{E}(\mathbf{q})$ means a higher level of equality (or exogenous fairness) of allocation $\mathbf{q}$.

An abstract framework. The social planner prefers the allocation that gives as high efficiency and equality as possible. However, efficiency and equality are usually two conflict objectives, and there is no allocation that could achieve the best efficiency and equality simultaneously. Adopting the constraint approach in multiobjective programming [6,16], we formulate an abstract framework, in which we put one of the criteria into the constraints (requiring it to be no more or no less than some level) and maximize the other one. In our model, we maximize the expected total efficiency, while guaranteeing that the equality measure $\mathbb{E}(\mathbf{q})$ is at least a constant $c \in [0, 1]$, see as the following (1):

$$\max \sum_{i=1}^{N} f_i(v_i) \cdot q_i$$
$$\text{s.t. } \mathbb{E}(\mathbf{q}) \geq c \ ,$$
$$\sum_{i=1}^{N} q_i = K \ , \tag{1}$$
$$0 \leq q_i \leq 1 \ , \ \forall i \ .$$

$$\max \sum_{i=1}^{N} f_i(b_i) \cdot q_i$$

$$\text{s.t. } \mathbb{E}(\mathbf{q}) \geq c \ ,$$

$$\sum_{i=1}^{N} q_i = K \ , \tag{2}$$

$$0 \leq q_i \leq 1 \ , \ \forall i \ .$$

In this way, we could obtain the 'Pareto frontier' compromised of Pareto optimal combinations of efficiency and equality.

Equality. In this work, the equality measure we use is based on the generalized Gini inequality index, which was first presented by Weymark [25]. The generalized Gini inequality index of an allocation $\mathbf{q}$ is defined as

$$1 - \frac{\sum_{i=1}^{N} a_i \tilde{q}_i}{\bar{q}} \tag{3}$$

where $\tilde{\mathbf{q}}$ is a permutation of $\mathbf{q}$ such that $\tilde{q}_1 \geq \tilde{q}_2 \geq \ldots \geq \tilde{q}_N$, and $\bar{q}$ is the average value of $\mathbf{q}$, i.e., $\bar{q} := \frac{\sum_i q_i}{N} = \frac{K}{N}$; And $\{a_i\}$ is a sequence of nonnegative ascending constants satisfying $0 \leq a_1 \leq a_2 \leq \ldots \leq a_N$ and $\sum_{i=1}^{N} a_i = 1$. As the generalized Gini inequality index measures the inequality among an allocation, we use $\frac{\sum_{i=1}^{N} a_i \tilde{q}_i}{\bar{q}}$ as our equality measure, i.e.,

$$\mathbb{E}(\mathbf{q}) := \frac{\sum_{i=1}^{N} a_i \tilde{q}_i}{\bar{q}}. \tag{4}$$

The main idea behind this measure is to assign different weights to different winning probabilities according to their orders in the allocation vector, and a higher winning probability has a relatively lower weight. This is very intuitive as the equality should give more concerns to the players with less opportunities. Furthermore, the increasing of a_i ensures that the equality meets the weak Pigou [21]-Dalton [9] transfer principle, which is equivalent to the principle that the inequality index will decrease if some winning chance is transferred from a higher one to a lower one without changing their orders. Obviously, in our setting, the equality measure reaches its maximum when $q_1 = q_2 = \ldots = q_N = \frac{K}{N}$.

Our equality measure is a large equality evaluation family. By setting different parameters, it could turn into many commonly used and well acceptable equality metrics:

- *Min-probability.* The min-probability is the least winning opportunity among all the players. If we require that each player's winning probability must not be lower than some given constant, we can set $a_1 = \cdots = a_{N-1} = 0$ and $a_N = 1$ in the definition of $\mathbb{E}(\mathbf{q})$, i.e., $\mathbb{E}(\mathbf{q}) := \frac{\tilde{q}_N}{\bar{q}}$. With the condition that $\sum_{i=1}^{N} q_i = K$, the constraint $\mathbb{E}(\mathbf{q}) \geq c$ is equivalent to $\tilde{q}_N \geq \frac{K}{N}c$.

- *Max-difference.* The max-difference measures the largest gap between any two of the players. In many public goods allocation problems, the goods holder has to consider the maximum difference between all the recipients [15]. If we require that the difference between the largest and smallest winning probabilities, i.e., $\tilde{q}_1 - \tilde{q}_N$, is no more than some given constant, we can set $a_1 = 0, a_2 = \cdots = a_{N-1} = \frac{1}{N}$ and $a_N = \frac{2}{N}$, i.e., $\mathbb{E}(\mathbf{q}) := \frac{1}{N\tilde{q}}[\sum_{j=2}^{N-1} \tilde{q}_j + 2\tilde{q}_N]$. Since $\sum_{i=1}^{N} q_i = K$, $\mathbb{E}(\mathbf{q}) = \frac{1}{K}[K + \tilde{q}_N - \tilde{q}_1]$, and the constraint $\mathbb{E}(\mathbf{q}) \geq c$ is equivalent to $\tilde{q}_1 - \tilde{q}_N \leq K(1 - c)$.
- *Gini-coefficient.* In economic theory, Gini-coefficient is often used as a measure of inequality among values of income or wealth [8]. Many literatures also adopt this equality measure in the public resource allocation or location problems [10,11]. The Gini-coefficient among the set of winning probabilities can be expressed as half of the relative mean absolute difference [23], which is a mathematically equivalent definition: $G(\mathbf{q}) = \frac{\sum_{i=1}^{N} \sum_{j=1}^{N} |q_i - q_j|}{2 \sum_i \sum_j q_j} \in [0, 1]$. Because $\sum_{i=1}^{N} q_i = K$ and

$$\sum_{j=1}^{N} \sum_{l=1}^{N} |\tilde{q}_j - \tilde{q}_l| = 2 \sum_{j=1}^{N} \sum_{l=j}^{N} (\tilde{q}_j - \tilde{q}_l) = 2 \left(NK - \sum_j (2j - 1) \cdot \tilde{q}_j \right),$$

$G(\mathbf{q}) = 1 - \frac{1}{NK} \sum_j (2j - 1)\tilde{q}_j$. If we set $a_j = \frac{2j-1}{N^2}$, $j = 1, \ldots, N$, then the generalized Gini index is exactly the Gini-coefficient, and $\mathbb{E}(\mathbf{q}) \geq c$ is equivalent to $\sum_j j\tilde{q}_j \geq \frac{K(Nc+1)}{2}$.

Efficiency. The efficiency measure in our model captures many applications in real life. It is consistent with the reality that $f_i(v)$ is a monotone increasing function of value v and different players could have different efficiency realization functions. Our efficiency concept could cover social welfare, revenue or any long-term or short-term value based objectives as special cases by choosing proper function $f_i(v)$. As illustration, in the following we show three scenarios that are commonly studied in literature or considered in real applications.

- *Social Welfare.* If $f_i(v) = v$ for all $i \in \mathcal{N}$, the sum $\sum_{i=1}^{N} v_i \cdot q_i$ is exactly the expected social welfare of allocation $\mathbf{q}$.
- *Expected Revenue.* Assume the users' values $v_1, \ldots, v_N$ are drawn independently (but not necessarily identically) from some distributions $G_1, \ldots, G_N$, with the probability density functions $g_1, \ldots, g_N$. $\phi_i(v_i) = v_i - \frac{1 - G_i(v_i)}{g_i(v_i)}$ is the virtual value of player i with value v_i. The expected revenue of the optimal mechanism is equal to the expected total virtual value $\sum_i \phi_i(v_i) \cdot q_i$ if the virtual values are monotone increasing, or the expected total ironed virtual values otherwise [18].
- *Long-Term Revenue.* In some cases, the allocation of resource may have long-term positive influence. For example, when a company sells one product to a celebrity, the benefit that the company can derive may also includes his/her influence to other customers. The monotonicity of the function $f_i(v)$ is easy to understand since high consumption value often leads to more positive influence.

2.1   Truthful Mechanism Design

If the goods holder knows every user's value for the goods, then he can solve the programming problem (1) to get an optimal randomized allocation. But users may strategically misreport their true values to be better off. Therefore, to truly solve (1), the goods holder needs a truthful mechanism to drive the users to truthfully report their private values. In the following, we will give a truthful mechanism framework to meet the requirements.

Suppose $\mathbf{b} \in \mathbb{R}_+^N$ is the bid profile that users (or players) report as their values. A *mechanism* $(\mathbf{q}(\mathbf{b}), \mathbf{p}(\mathbf{b}))$ maps a bid profile $\mathbf{b}$ to an allocation $\mathbf{q}(\mathbf{b})$ and a *payment rule* $\mathbf{p}(\mathbf{b})$ for this allocation. Here we only consider such kind of payment rules: A user will pay the price for the goods if and only if he finally gets one after the realization of $\mathbf{q}(\mathbf{b})$. Let vector $\mathbf{p} : \mathbb{R}_+^N \to \mathbb{R}_+^N$ denote the payments that each player needs to pay if she wins one goods. Under our mechanism, the (expected) *utility* of a player $i \in \mathcal{N}$ is $u_i(\mathbf{b}) = u_i(b_i, \mathbf{b}_{-i}) = (v_i - p_i(\mathbf{b}))q_i(\mathbf{b})$, where b_i is player i's bid and $\mathbf{b}_{-i}$ is the vector of other players' bids. A mechanism $(\mathbf{q}(\mathbf{b}), \mathbf{p}(\mathbf{b}))$ is said to be *truthful* if it satisfies the following condition:

Incentive Compatible: For any player, bidding his private true value is a weakly dominant strategy, regardless of what other players' bids are, i.e., $u_i(v_i, \mathbf{b}_{-i}) \geq u_i(b_i, \mathbf{b}_{-i}), \forall i, b_i, \mathbf{b}_{-i}$.

In the following, we will present the allocation and payment rules in our mechanism and show that they compromise a truthful mechanism, and in the meanwhile, have a nice property: ex-post IR.

Since the true values are private information, the actual problem faced by the the goods holder is (2). As we will only concentrate on the optimal allocation, in the following analysis, we use $\mathbf{q}(\mathbf{b})$ to denote one of the optimal solutions to programming (2). Before we propose the general framework for this problem, we first show a property about the optimal allocation $\mathbf{q}(\mathbf{b})$.

Lemma 1. *For every i, $\mathbf{b}_{-i}$, player i's allocated probability $q_i(x, \mathbf{b}_{-i})$ is a monotone non-decreasing function of his bid x.*

Now we focus our attention on the payment rule $\mathbf{p}(\mathbf{b})$. It is natural and meaningful to design a mechanism that every user will finally get a nonnegative utility as long as he truthfully reports his private value. From our previous definition of payments (paying nothing if not allocated the goods finally), that is equivalent to say the mechanism should satisfy the following condition:

Ex-post Individual Rational: For any player, bidding truthfully will always induce a non-negative ex-post utility, no matter what other players' bids are, i.e., $u_i(v_i, \mathbf{b}_{-i}) \geq 0, \forall i, \mathbf{b}_{-i}$.

For any bid profile $\mathbf{b}$, if we choose one of the optimal solutions $\mathbf{q}(\mathbf{b})$ (no matter which one) and use it as the allocation permanently with respect to bids $\mathbf{b}$, we can prove the following payment rule is truthful, as long as every player i's allocation $q_i(x, \mathbf{b}_{-i})$ is monotone non-decreasing in his bid x while fixing $\mathbf{b}_{-i}$:

$$p_i(\mathbf{b}) = \frac{1}{q_i(\mathbf{b})} \int_0^{b_i} x d(q_i(x, \mathbf{b}_{-i})) = b_i - \frac{\int_0^{b_i} q_i(x, \mathbf{b}_{-i}) dx}{q_i(\mathbf{b})}, \quad \forall i \in \mathcal{N}. \quad (5)$$

Theorem 1. *The mechanism* $(\mathbf{q}(\mathbf{b}), \mathbf{p}(\mathbf{b}))$, *where* $\mathbf{q}(\mathbf{b})$ *is the optimal solution of programming (2) and* $\mathbf{p}(\mathbf{b})$ *is defined as (5), is incentive compatible and ex-post individual rational.*

3 Computational Feasibility

In the previous section, we have already proposed a general truthful mechanism framework. To make the mechanism executable in real application, we need to compute the optimal allocation $\mathbf{q}(\mathbf{b})$ and the truthful payments $\mathbf{p}(\mathbf{b})$ as defined in (5) efficiently. This is not an easy task since there is no closed form of the function $q_i(x, \mathbf{b}_{-i})$ with with respect to $x \in [0, b_i]$. As x changes, the allocation may also change correspondingly.

Fortunately, we find that for any bids profile $\mathbf{b}$, there always exists one optimal allocation that has at most four different probability values and at most two different fractional values. And we further show that there are only $O(N^4)$ possible allocations with such structure can be potential optimal allocations. For the optimal allocation, we can traverse all such possible allocations. For the payment, we prove that $q_i(x, \mathbf{b}_{-i})$ is a piecewise function of x and the value can only change at most $O(N^4)$ times, thus the payment can be computed in polynomial time.

In Sect. 3.1, we characterize the structure of one of the optimal solutions $\mathbf{q}(\mathbf{b})$ to programming (2) with respect to any bid profile $\mathbf{b}$. Then in Sect. 3.2, we design a polynomial time algorithm to compute the corresponding truthful payments $\mathbf{p}(\mathbf{b})$.

3.1 Computation of the Optimal Allocation

As we mentioned before, there is no closed form of the function $\mathbf{q}(\mathbf{b})$ about $\mathbf{b}$. Nonetheless, we could still find some nice properties about the $\mathbf{q}(\mathbf{b})$. Surprisingly, if we say players with same winning probability are in the same group, then no matter how large N or K is, there always exists an optimal allocation that divides all the players into at most four groups. If there are exactly four groups, then the players in group 1 can win with probability 1, players in group 2 and 3 could win with probability q' and q'' respectively where $0 < q'' < q' < 1$, and the players in group 4 have no chance to win.

To be convenient for the analysis, we first define some notations. Let (i) denote the player whose efficiency increase to the goods holder, $f_{(i)}(b_{(i)})$, is the i-th highest among the N numbers $\{f_j(b_j) : j \in \mathcal{N}\}$. Then $q_{(i)}(\mathbf{b})$ represents the winning probability of player (i) with respect bids to $\mathbf{b}$. For ease of description, when the bids $\mathbf{b}$ are fixed and there is no misunderstanding, we also simplify $f_{(i)}(b_{(i)})$ as $f_{(i)}$. By the definition of equality measure $\mathbb{E}(\mathbf{q})$, the following claim is natural.

Claim. There must exist an optimal solution $\mathbf{q}$ such that $q_{(1)} \geq q_{(2)} \geq \cdots \geq q_{(N)}$.

According to the above claim, and $\bar{q} = \frac{\sum_i q_i}{N} = \frac{K}{N}$, programming (2) is equivalent to the following linear programming:

$$\max \sum_{j=1}^{N} f_{(j)}(b_{(j)}) \cdot q_{(j)}$$

$$\text{s.t.} \sum_{j=1}^{N} a_j q_{(j)} \geq \frac{K}{N}c, \tag{6}$$

$$\sum_{j=1}^{N} q_{(j)} = K,$$

$$0 \leq q_{(i)} \leq q_{(j)} \leq 1, \ \forall 1 \leq j < i \leq N.$$

The following theorem shows the characterization of one of the optimal solutions.

Theorem 2. *For any bid profile* **b**, *there must exist an optimal solution* $\mathbf{q}(\mathbf{b})$ *to the programming (6) such that excluding values 0 and 1, there are at most two different values in* $\{q_i(\mathbf{b}) : i \in \mathcal{N}\}$.

Based on Theorem 2, we can compute such an optimal solution efficiently by picking up an allocation that generates the maximum expected efficiency from the set of feasible allocations that divides the players into 4 groups (the number of players in a group can be zero or positive), where the winning probabilities of the 4 groups are 1, q', q'', 0, respectively.

In the following, we give a way to compute the optimal allocations with the above characteristics. Although this way may not be the most efficient one, it will be very useful when we compute the truthful payments in the next subsection. In fact, through this way, we can show that there are only at most $O(N^3)$ candidates of all the optimal allocations for all bid profiles. Now we describe all the possible optimal allocations, denoted as *potential* optimal allocations.

Let $n_1(\geq 0)$, $n_2(\geq 0)$ and $n_4(\geq 0)$ denote the number of players in group 1, group 2 and group 4, respectively, where $n_1 + n_2 + n_4 \leq N$, and $u(n_1, n_2, n_4, \mathbf{b}) = \sum_{j=1}^{n_1} f_{(j)} + \sum_{j=n_1+1}^{n_1+n_2} f_{(j)} q' + \sum_{j=n_1+n_2+1}^{N-n_4} f_{(j)} q''$ denote the corresponding expected efficiency under bids profile **b**.

Lemma 2. *Suppose* $\sum_{j=1}^{K} a_j < \frac{K}{N}c$. *We define an allocation in which* n_1 *players' winning probability is* 1, n_2 *players' winning probability is* $q' \in (0, 1)$, $N - n_1 - n_2 - n_4$ *players' winning probability is* $q'' \in (0, q')$ *and* n_4 *players' winning probability is* 0 *as a potential optimal allocation, if* q', q'' *are the solution of the following equations:*

$$\begin{cases} n_1 + n_2 q' + (N - n_1 - n_2 - n_4)q'' = K, \\ \sum_j a_j q_{(j)} = \sum_{j=1}^{n_1} a_j + \sum_{j=n_1}^{n_1+n_2} a_j q' + \sum_{j=n_1+n_2+1}^{N-n_4} a_j q'' = \frac{K}{N}c. \end{cases}$$

Then in the set of potential optimal allocations, there must exist one of the optimal solutions to the programming (6).

By Lemma 2, for a potential optimal allocation, the values of the winning probabilities for group 2 and group 3 players are totally dependent on the number of players in each group, thus we can use the tuple $\mathbf{n} = (n_1, n_2, n_4)$ to represent a potential optimal allocation. Explicitly, if $n_1 + n_2 + n_4 < N$,

$$q'(n_1, n_2, n_4) = \frac{(K - n_1)a'' - \frac{K}{N}c + n_1 a}{(a'' - a')n_2},$$

$$q''(n_1, n_2, n_4) = \frac{\frac{K}{N}c - n_1 a - (K - n_1)a'}{(a'' - a')(N - n_1 - n_2 - n_4)}, \tag{7}$$

$$a' < \frac{\frac{K}{N}c - n_1 a}{K - n_1} < \frac{a_{n_1+1} + \cdots + a_{N-n_4}}{N - n_1 - n_4},$$

where $a = (a_1 + \cdots + a_{n_1})/n_1$, $a' = (a_{n_1+1} + \cdots + a_{n_1+n_2})/n_2$, $a'' = (a_{n_1+n_2+1} + \cdots + a_{N-n_4})/(N - n_1 - n_2 - n_4)$ are the averages of the coefficients of the first three groups. If $n_1 + n_2 + n_4 = N$, we only care about q':

$$q'(n_1, n_2, n_4) = \frac{K - n_1}{n_2}, \tag{8}$$

and in this case, it must hold that $n_1 a + (K - n_1)a' = \frac{K}{N}c$.

We use P to denote the set of potential optimal allocations. For each $\mathbf{n} \in P$, we calculate the corresponding efficiency, and select the optimal one: $\mathbf{n}^* = (n_1^*, n_2^*, n_4^*) = \arg\max_{\mathbf{n} \in P} u(n_1, n_2, n_4, \mathbf{b})$ with respect to bids $\mathbf{b}$. Since there are $O(N^3)$ tuples of (n_1, n_2, n_4), and for each tuple, it takes $O(N)$ time to calculate the efficiency, it requires $O(N^4)$ time to obtain an optimal allocation.

In the following, for any bid profile $\mathbf{b}$, when we mention an optimal solution $\mathbf{q}(\mathbf{b})$ of programming (6), we will always refer to an optimal allocation that is obtained from the above method.

3.2 Computation of the Truthful Payments

In this subsection, we aim to find the truthful payments $\mathbf{p}(\mathbf{b})$ corresponding to the optimal allocation $\mathbf{q}(\mathbf{b})$. To compute the truthful payment $p_k(\mathbf{b})$ for every player k, as shown in formula (5), we are only left with the computation of $\int_0^{b_k} q_k(x, \mathbf{b}_{-k})dx$. As there is no closed form of the function $q_k(x, \mathbf{b}_{-k})$ about variable $x \in [0, b_k]$, we can not compute $\int_0^{b_k} q_k(x, \mathbf{b}_{-k})dx$ directly. In the following, we will show that for any player k, the function $q_k(x, \mathbf{b}_{-k})$ with $x \in [0, b_k]$ is a piecewise constant function with at most $O(N^4)$ pieces, and we can find the constants and pieces in polynomial time.

Given other players' bids $\mathbf{b}_{-k}$, suppose player k's bid is x, then as x increases from 0 to b_k, the order of $f_k(x)$ among all the N utilities $\{f_k(x), f_j(b_j)$ with $j \neq k\}$ can change at most $O(N)$ times. Now we use $[t_{(i+1)}, t_{(i)}]$ to denote each such section that when $x \in [t_{(i+1)}, t_{(i)}]$ then $f_k(x)$ is the i-th highest. We only need to show that for any possible i, $q_k(x, \mathbf{b}_{-k})$ is a piecewise constant function with respect to $x \in [t_{(i+1)}, t_{(i)}]$ and there are at most $O(N^3)$ pieces. Similar to the previous section, we use $\mathbf{n} := (n_1, n_2, n_4)$ to represent a potential optimal allocation in which n_1 players are ensured to obtain an item, n_2 players have winning probability $q'(n_1, n_2, n_4)$, $N - n_1 - n_2 - n_4$ players have winning probability $q''(n_1, n_2, n_4)$ and n_4 players have zero winning probability and P to denote the set of potential optimal allocations.

Lemma 3. *As player k's bid x increases from $t_{(i+1)}$ to $t_{(i)}$, her winning probability in the optimal allocation $\mathbf{q}(x, \mathbf{b}_{-k})$ can change at most $O(N^3)$ times.*

The idea behind Lemma 3 is that $\mathbf{q}(x, \mathbf{b}_{-k})$ is a piecewise constant function with respect to x and after a jump point, the previous optimal allocation will never be optimal again, thus there are no two pieces that have the same optimal allocation. Based on this, we present the Algorithm 1 to compute the truthful payment for any player k, which can be implemented in polynomial time.

Algorithm 1. Computing the truthful payments

Find all the intervals $[t_{(i+1)}, t_{(i)}]$ such that as long as player k's bid is on the interval, the order of all bids is invariant;

for each i **do**

    for each $\mathbf{n} = (n_1, n_2, n_4) \in \mathbb{N}^3$ with $n_1 + n_2 + n_4 \leq N$ **do**

        Compute $q'(n_1, n_2, n_4)$ and $q''(n_1, n_2, n_4)$ by (7),

    end for

    Select all the $\mathbf{n}$ that satisfiy $1 > q'(n_1, n_2, n_4) > q''(n_1, n_2, n_4) > 0$ as the potential optimal allocation set P;

    Select the optimal allocation $\mathbf{n}^* = \arg\max_{\mathbf{n}} u_{\mathbf{n}}(t_{(i+1)}) = \sum_{j=1}^{n_1} f_{(j)} + \sum_{j=n_1+1}^{n_1+n_2} f_{(j)}q' + \sum_{j=n_1+n_2+1}^{N-n_4} f_{(j)}q''$, where $f_{(i+1)} = f_k(t_{(i+1)})$;

    Initialize $z_0 = t_{(i+1)}$;

    repeat

        for each $\mathbf{n} \in P$ with $q_k(\mathbf{n}) > q_k(\mathbf{n}^*)$, where $q_k(\mathbf{n})$ denotes the winning probability of player k under allocation $\mathbf{n}$ **do**

            Solve equation $u_{\mathbf{n}}(z) = u_{\mathbf{n}^*}(z)$ with respect to z, denote the solution as $z_{\mathbf{n}}$;

        end for

        Find the nearest point z at which the efficiency generated by $\mathbf{n}^*$ is surpassed by another allocation $\mathbf{n}'$: $z = z_{\mathbf{n}'} = \arg\min_{\mathbf{n}} z_{\mathbf{n}}$;

        $\mathbf{n}^*$ is optimal on the interval $[z_0, \min\{z, t_{(i)}\}]$, set $\mathbf{n}^* := \mathbf{n}'$, $z_0 := z$;

    until $z > t_{(i)}$

end for

Let S denote the set of all the jump points z and $\Delta q_k(z)$ denote the difference of player k's winning probability at z. The truthful payment is

$$p_k(\mathbf{b}) = \frac{1}{q_k(\mathbf{b})} \sum_{z \in S} z \Delta q_k(z).$$

Theorem 3. *For any bid profile $\mathbf{b}$, Algorithm 1 can compute the optimal allocation $\mathbf{q}(\mathbf{b})$ and the truthful payments $\mathbf{p}(\mathbf{b})$ as defined by formula (5) of Sect. 2.1 in polynomial time.*

4   Conclusion and Future Work

In this paper, we attempt to balance efficiency and equality in the allocation problems in a way that maximizes the efficiency while ensuring the equality level. We prove that there always exists an incentive compatible mechanism, characterize the nice property of an optimal allocation and present an algorithm to compute the optimal allocation and corresponding truthful payments in polynomial time.

In fact, our approach can also be applied to the problem of allocating divisible goods, e.g., emission rights. We consider all the goods as an integrity and define $K = 1$. Let q_i denote the proportion of the whole goods that be allocated to player i, and p_i denote the unit price for player i. When a player obtains q_i of the goods, her has to pay $q_i p_i$ and her utility from the auction is $(v_i - p_i)q_i$. Therefore, all the formulae are the same as those in Sect. 2, and the optimal allocation catches the properties provided in Sect. 3 except for that the players are divided into three groups since generally no single player could get the entire goods.

So far we have a complete framework for the anonymous linear equality measures. One possible future research direction is to study on the nonlinear or more general equality measures, or to adopt other proper fairness criteria, and try to analyze the properties of optimal allocations or design implementable algorithms to compute the optimal allocations and corresponding truthful payments.

References

1. Atkinson, A.B.: On the measurement of inequality. J. Econ. Theor. **2**(3), 244–263 (1970)
2. Bertsimas, D., Farias, V.F., Trichakis, N.: The price of fairness. Oper. Res. **59**(1), 17–31 (2011)
3. Bertsimas, D., Farias, V.F., Trichakis, N.: On the efficiency-fairness trade-off. Manag. Sci. **58**(12), 2234–2250 (2012)
4. Bodily, S.E.: Police sector design incorporating preferences of interest groups for equality and efficiency. Manag. Sci. **24**(12), 1301–1313 (1978)
5. Clarke, E.H.: Multipart pricing of public goods. Public choice **11**(1), 17–33 (1971)
6. Cohon, J.L.: Multiobjective Programming and Planning. Academic Press, Cambridge (1978)
7. Cole, R., Gkatzelis, V., Goel, G.: Mechanism design for fair division: allocating divisible items without payments. In: Proceedings of the fourteenth ACM conference on Electronic commerce, pp. 251–268. ACM (2013)
8. Corrado, G.: On the measure of concentration with special reference to income and wealth. In: Papers Presented at the Cowles Commission Research Conference on Economics and Statistics (Colorado College Publication, 1936) (1936)
9. Dalton, H.: The measurement of the inequality of incomes. The Econ. J. **30**(119), 348–361 (1920)
10. Drezner, T., Drezner, Z., Guyse, J.: Equitable service by a facility: minimizing the gini coefficient. Comput. Oper. Res. **36**(12), 3240–3246 (2009)
11. Golany, B., Tamir, E.: Evaluating efficiency-effectiveness-equality trade-offs: a data envelopment analysis approach. Manag. Sci. **41**(7), 1172–1184 (1995)

12. Gopinathan, A., Li, Z.: Strategyproof auctions for balancing social welfare and fairness in secondary spectrum markets. In: INFOCOM, 2011 Proceedings IEEE, pp. 3020–3028. IEEE (2011)
13. Groves, T.: Incentives in teams. Econom. J. Econom. Soc. **41**, 617–631 (1973)
14. Kakwani, N.: On a class of poverty measures. Econom. J. Econom. Soc. **48**, 437–446 (1980)
15. Kozanidis, G.: Solving the linear multiple choice knapsack problem with two objectives: profit and equity. Comput. Optim. Appl. **43**(2), 261–294 (2009)
16. Mandell, M.B.: Modelling effectiveness-equity trade-offs in public service delivery systems. Manag. Sci. **37**(4), 467–482 (1991)
17. Maya, A., Nisan, N.: Incentive compatible two player cake cutting. In: Goldberg, P.W. (ed.) WINE 2012. LNCS, vol. 7695, pp. 170–183. Springer, Heidelberg (2012). https://doi.org/10.1007/978-3-642-35311-6_13
18. Myerson, R.B.: Optimal auction design. Math. Oper. Res. **6**(1), 58–73 (1981)
19. Ogryczak, W.: Inequality measures and equitable approaches to location problems. Eur. J. Oper. Res. **122**(2), 374–391 (2000)
20. Perugia, A., Moccia, L., Cordeau, J.F., Laporte, G.: Designing a home-to-work bus service in a metropolitan area. Transp. Res. Part B. Methodol. **45**(10), 1710–1726 (2011)
21. Pigou, A.C.: Wealth and welfare. Macmillan and Company Ltd., London (1912)
22. Sauer, P., Zagler, M.: Economic growth and the quantity and distribution of education: a survey. J. Econ. Surv. **26**(5), 933–951 (2012)
23. Sen, A.: On Economic Inequality. Clarendon Paperbacks, Clarendon Press (1973). https://books.google.com.hk/books?id=Kb03KNreUqcC
24. Vickrey, W.: Counterspeculation, auctions, and competitive sealed tenders. J. Finan. **16**(1), 8–37 (1961)
25. Weymark, J.A.: Generalized gini inequality indices. Math. Soc. Sci. **1**(4), 409–430 (1981)
26. Zivan, R., Dudik, M., Okamoto, S., Sycara, K.: Reducing untruthful manipulation in envy-free pareto optimal resource allocation. In: 2010 IEEE/WIC/ACM International Conference on Web Intelligence and Intelligent Agent Technology (WI-IAT), vol. 2, pp. 391–398. IEEE (2010)

The Asymptotic Behavior of the Price of Anarchy

Riccardo Colini-Baldeschi[1], Roberto Cominetti[2], Panayotis Mertikopoulos[3(✉)], and Marco Scarsini[1]

[1] Dipartimento di Economia e Finanza, LUISS, Viale Romania 32, 00197 Roma, Italy
[2] Facultad de Ingeniería y Ciencias, Universidad Adolfo Ibáñez, Santiago, Chile
[3] Univ. Grenoble Alpes, CNRS, Inria, LIG, 38000 Grenoble, France
panayotis.mertikopoulos@imag.fr

Abstract. This paper examines the behavior of the price of anarchy as a function of the traffic inflow in nonatomic congestion games with multiple origin-destination (O/D) pairs. Empirical studies in real-world networks show that the price of anarchy is close to 1 in both light and heavy traffic, thus raising the question: can these observations be justified theoretically? We first show that this is not always the case: the price of anarchy may remain bounded away from 1 for all values of the traffic inflow, even in simple three-link networks with a single O/D pair and smooth, convex costs. On the other hand, for a large class of cost functions (including all polynomials), the price of anarchy *does* converge to 1 in both heavy and light traffic conditions, and irrespective of the network topology and the number of O/D pairs in the network.

1 Introduction

Almost every commuter in a major metropolitan area has experienced the frustration of being stuck in traffic. At best, this might mean being late for dinner; at worst, it means more accidents and altercations, not to mention the vastly increased damage to the environment caused by huge numbers of idling engines. To name but an infamous example, China's G110 traffic jam in August 2010 brought to a standstill thousands of vehicles for 100 km between Hebei and Inner Mongolia. Not caused by weather or a natural disaster, this massive 10-day tie-up was instead laid at the feet of a bevy of trucks swarming on the shortest route to Beijing, thus clogging the G110 highway to a halt (while ironically carrying supplies for construction work to ease congestion). This, therefore, raises the question: how much better would things have been if all traffic had been routed by a social planner who could calculate (and enforce) the optimum traffic assignment?

In game-theoretic terms, this question boils down to the inefficiency of Nash equilibria. The most widely used quantitative measure of this inefficiency is the so-called *price of anarchy* (PoA): introduced by Koutsoupias and Papadimitriou (1999) and so dubbed by Papadimitriou (2001), the PoA is the ratio between the

© Springer International Publishing AG 2017
N. R. Devanur and P. Lu (Eds.): WINE 2017, LNCS 10674, pp. 133–145, 2017.
https://doi.org/10.1007/978-3-319-71924-5_10

social cost of the least efficient Nash equilibria and the minimum achievable cost. By virtue of this simple definition, deriving worst-case PoA bounds has given rise to a vigorous literature at the interface of computer science, economics and operations research, with many surprising results.

In the context of network congestion, Pigou (1920) was probably the first to note the inefficiency of selfish routing, and his elementary two-road example with a PoA of 4/3 is one of the two prototypical examples thereof. The other is due to Braess (1968), and consists of a four-edge network where the addition of a zero-cost segment makes things just as bad as in the Pigou case. These two examples were the starting point for Roughgarden and Tardos (2002) who showed that the price of anarchy in (nonatomic) routing games with affine costs may not exceed 4/3. On the other hand, if the network's cost functions are polynomials of degree at most d, the price of anarchy may become as high as $\Theta(d/\log d)$, implying that selfish routing can be arbitrarily bad in networks with polynomial costs (Roughgarden 2003).

At the same time however, these worst-case instances are usually realized in networks with delicately tuned traffic loads and costs; if a network operates beyond this regime, it is not clear whether the price of anarchy is still high. Indeed, using both analytical and numerical methods, a recent study by O'Hare et al. (2016) suggests that the PoA is usually close to 1 for very high and very low traffic, and it fluctuates in the intermediate regime. In a similar setting, Monnot et al. (2017) recently used a huge dataset on commuting students in Singapore to estimate the so-called "empirical" PoA (a majorant of the ordinary price of anarchy); their observations yield a value between 1.11 and 1.22, suggesting that the actual value of the price of anarchy is even lower.

All this leads to the following natural questions:

1. Under what conditions does the PoA converge to 1 in light or heavy traffic?
2. Do these conditions depend on the network topology, its costs, or both?
3. Can general results be obtained only for networks with a single origin-destination pair or do they extend to networks with multiple such pairs?

1.1   Our Results

Our first result is a cautionary tale: we show that the price of anarchy may oscillate between two bounds strictly greater than 1 for all values of the traffic inflow, even in simple parallel-link networks with a single origin-destination (O/D) pair (cf. Fig. 1). The cost functions in our example are convex and differentiable, so neither convexity nor smoothness seems to play a major role in the efficiency of selfish routing. Moreover, our construction only involves a three-link network, so such phenomena may arise in any network containing such a three-link component.

Heuristically, the reason for this behavior is that the network's cost functions exhibit higher-order oscillations which persist at any scale, for both high and low traffic. Thus, to account for such pathologies, we take a two-pronged approach:

- In the *low congestion* limit, we focus on cost functions that are *real analytic*, i.e., they are equal to their power series expansion near 0. Under this regularity assumption, we show that the PoA converges to 1, no matter the network topology or the number of O/D pairs in the network.
- At the other end of the spectrum, to tackle the *high congestion* limit, we introduce the concept of a *benchmark function*. This is a regularly varying function $c(x)$ that classifies edges into *fast, slow* or *tight*, depending on the growth rate of the cost along each edge;[1] paths are then classified as fast, slow or tight, based on their slowest edge.[2] We then establish the following general result: *if the "most costly" O/D pair in the network admits a tight path, the network's PoA converges to 1 under heavy traffic.*

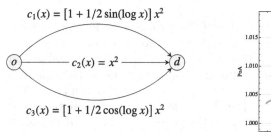

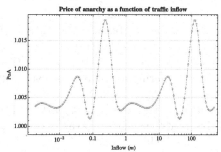

Fig. 1. A network where selfish routing remains inefficient for both light and heavy traffic.

Among other classes of functions, polynomials satisfy all of the above requirements, leading to the following general principle:

In networks with polynomial cost functions,
the price of anarchy becomes 1 under both light and heavy traffic.

In other words, a benevolent social planner with full control of traffic assignment would not do any better than selfish agents in light or heavy traffic. Only if the traffic falls in an intermediate regime can there be a substantial gap between optimum and equilibrium states.

1.2   Related Work

Much of the literature on congestion games is devoted to the study of bounds for the price of anarchy under different conditions. Roughgarden and Tardos

---

[1] Regular variation means here that $\lim_{t \to \infty} c(tx)/c(t) \in (0, \infty)$ for all $x > 0$ (cf. Sect. 4.2).

[2] As an example, if all the network's cost functions are polynomials of degree d, all edges, paths and O/D pairs are tight with respect to the benchmark function $c(x) = x^d$.

(2002) proved a bound of 4/3 in the case of affine costs, independently of the network topology. This bound is sharp in that, for every $M > 0$, there exists a network with traffic inflow M and affine costs such that the PoA equal to 4/3. Importantly, our analysis shows that the order of the quantifiers *cannot be exchanged:* in any network as above, the PoA gets arbitrarily close to 1 if the traffic inflow is sufficiently large.

Worst-case PoA bounds have been obtained for larger classes of cost functions. For polynomial costs with degree at most d, Roughgarden (2003) showed that the worst possible instance grows as $\Theta(d/\log d)$. Dumrauf and Gairing (2006) provided sharper bounds for monomials of maximum degree d and minimum degree q, while Roughgarden and Tardos (2004) provided a unifying result for costs that are differentiable with $xc(x)$ convex, while Correa et al. (2004; 2008) considered less regular classes of cost functions. For a survey, the reader is referred to Roughgarden (2007).

The difference between the mean value of the price of anarchy and its worst value has been studied in the context of cognitive radio networks by Law et al. (2012). Youn et al. (2008) studied the difference between optimal and actual system performance in real transportation networks, focusing in particular on Boston's road network. They observed that the price of anarchy depends crucially on the total traffic inflow: it starts at 1, it then grows with some oscillations, and ultimately returns to 1 as the flow increases. González Vayá et al. (2015) studied optimal scheduling for the electricity demand of a fleet of plug-in electric vehicles: without using the term, they showed that the PoA goes to 1 as the number of vehicles grows. Cole and Tao (2016) showed that in large Walrasian auctions and in large Fisher markets the price of anarchy goes to one as the market size increases. Finally, Feldman et al. (2016) took a different asymptotic approach and considered atomic games where the number of players grows to infinity. Applying the notion of (λ, μ)-smoothness to the resulting sequence of atomic games, they showed that the price of anarchy converges to the corresponding nonatomic limit.

From an analytic standpoint, the closest antecedent to our paper is the recent work of Colini-Baldeschi et al. (2016) who studied the heavy-traffic limit of the price of anarchy in paralell-link networks with a single O/D pair. The analysis of Colini-Baldeschi et al. (2016) identified that regular variation plays an important part in heavy traffic; however, it offered no insights into the light traffic regime or the heavy-traffic limit of the PoA in non-parallel networks with more than one O/D pair. Our paper provides an in-depth answer to these questions: we show that (a) the light-traffic analogue of regular variation is real analyticity; (b) the topology of the network doesn't matter; and (c) the advent of several O/D pairs doesn't matter as long as they admit a common benchmark (which is always the case if the network's costs are polynomial).

Finally, on the empirical side, our work should be compared to that of Monnot et al. (2017) who performed an empirical study of the price of anarchy based on data from thousands of commuting students in Singapore. Focusing on the network's *empirical* price of anarchy (a PoA majorant), they showed that routing choices are near-optimal and the price of anarchy is much lower than traditional worst-case bounds would suggest. Interestingly, the study of Monnot et al. (2017) also suggests that the Singapore road network is often lightly congested: as such, their results can be seen as a practical validation of the light traffic results presented here (and, conversely, our results provide a theoretical justification for their empirical observations).

2 Model and Preliminaries

2.1 Network Model

Following Beckmann et al. (1956) and Roughgarden and Tardos (2002), the basic component of our model is a finite directed multi-graph $\mathcal{G} \equiv \mathcal{G}(\mathcal{V}, \mathcal{E})$ with vertex set $\mathcal{V}$ and edge set $\mathcal{E}$. We further assume there is a finite set of *origin-destination*(O/D) pairs $i \in \mathcal{I}$, each with an individual *traffic demand* $m^i \geq 0$ which has to be routed from an origin $o^i \in \mathcal{V}$ to a destination $d^i \in \mathcal{V}$ via $\mathcal{G}$.

To route this traffic, the i-th O/D pair employs a set $\mathcal{P}^i$ of (simple) paths joining o^i to d^i, each path $p \in \mathcal{P}^i$ comprising a sequence of edges that meet head-to-tail in the usual way.[3] For bookkeeping reasons, we also make the standing assumption that (a) $M \equiv \sum_i m^i > 0$ (so there is a positive amount of traffic in the network); and (b) the sets $\mathcal{P}^i$ are disjoint (which holds in particular when all pairs (o^i, d^i) are different). Then, writing $\mathcal{P} \equiv \bigcup_{i \in \mathcal{I}} \mathcal{P}^i$ for the union of all such paths, the set of feasible *routing flows* $f = (f_p)_{p \in \mathcal{P}}$ in the network is defined as

$$\mathcal{F} = \left\{ f \in \mathbb{R}_+^{\mathcal{P}} : \sum_{p \in \mathcal{P}^i} f_p = m^i \text{ for all } i \in \mathcal{I} \right\}. \tag{2.1}$$

In turn, a routing flow $f \in \mathcal{F}$ induces a *load* on each edge $e \in \mathcal{E}$ as $x_e = \sum_{p \ni e} f_p$, and we write $x = (x_e)_{e \in \mathcal{E}}$ for the corresponding *load profile* on the network.

Given all this, the delay (or latency) experienced by an infinitesimal traffic element in order to traverse edge e is determined by a nondecreasing, nonzero continuous *cost function* $c_e \colon [0, \infty) \to [0, \infty)$. Specifically, if $x = (x_e)_{e \in \mathcal{E}}$ is the load profile induced by a feasible routing flow $f = (f_p)_{p \in \mathcal{P}}$, then the incurred delay on edge $e \in \mathcal{E}$ is $c_e(x_e)$. Hence, with a slight abuse of notation, the associated cost of path $p \in \mathcal{P}$ is given by

$$c_p(f) \equiv \sum_{e \in p} c_e(x_e). \tag{2.2}$$

Putting together all of the above, the tuple $\Gamma = (\mathcal{G}, \mathcal{I}, \{m^i\}_{i \in \mathcal{I}}, \{\mathcal{P}^i\}_{i \in \mathcal{I}}, \{c_e\}_{e \in \mathcal{E}})$ will be referred to as a *(nonatomic) routing game*.[4]

---

[3] To be clear, we do not assume here that $\mathcal{P}^i$ is the set of *all* paths joining o^i to d^i, but only some subset thereof. This distinction is important for packet-switched networks where only paths with a low hop count are used.

[4] For simplicity, when there is a single O/D pair, we will drop $\mathcal{I}$ and the index i altogether.

2.2 Equilibrium, Optimality, and the Price of Anarchy

In this setting, the notion of Nash equilibrium is captured by *Wardrop's first principle*: at equilibrium, the delays along all utilized paths are equal and no higher than those that would be experienced by an infinitesimal traffic element going through an unused route (Wardrop 1952). Formally, a routing flow f^* is said to be a *Wardrop equilibrium* (WE) of Γ if, for all $i \in \mathcal{I}$, we have

$$c_p(f^*) \leq c_{p'}(f^*) \quad \text{for all } p, p' \in \mathcal{P}^i \text{ such that } f_p^* > 0. \tag{2.3}$$

By the work of Beckmann et al. (1956), it is well-known that Wardrop equilibrium can be characterized equivalently as solutions of the (convex) minimization problem:

$$\text{minimize} \quad \sum_{e \in \mathcal{E}} C_e(x_e),$$

$$\text{subject to} \quad x_e = \sum_{p \ni e} f_p, \ f \in \mathcal{F}, \tag{WE}$$

where $C_e(x_e) = \int_0^{x_e} c_e(w) \, dw$ denotes the primitive of c_e. On the other hand, a *socially optimum* (SO) flow is defined as a solution to the total cost minimization problem:

$$\text{minimize} \quad L(f) = \sum_{p \in \mathcal{P}} f_p c_p(f),$$

$$\text{subject to} \quad f \in \mathcal{F}. \tag{SO}$$

To quantify the gap between solutions to (WE) and (SO), we write

$$\text{Eq}(\Gamma) = L(f^*) \quad \text{and} \quad \text{Opt}(\Gamma) = \min_{f \in \mathcal{F}} L(f), \tag{2.4}$$

where f^* is a Wardrop equilibrium of Γ. As Beckmann et al. (1956) showed, $L(f^*)$ has the same value for all equilibria f^*. The game's *price of anarchy* (PoA) is then defined as

$$\text{PoA}(\Gamma) = \frac{\text{Eq}(\Gamma)}{\text{Opt}(\Gamma)}. \tag{2.5}$$

Obviously, $\text{PoA}(\Gamma) \geq 1$ with equality if and only if Wardrop equilibria are also socially efficient. Our main objective in what follows will be to study the asymptotics of this ratio when $M \to 0$ or $M \to \infty$.

3 A Network Where Selfish Routing is Always Inefficient

We begin by constructing a three-link network where the price of anarchy oscillates between two values strictly greater than 1, no matter the traffic inflow M. To that end, let Γ_M be a nonatomic routing game consisting of a single O/D pair with traffic inflow M. This traffic is to be routed over the three-link parallel graph of Fig. 1 with cost functions

$$c_1(x_1) = x_1^d \left[1 + \tfrac{1}{2}\sin(\log x_1)\right], \tag{3.1a}$$

$$c_2(x_2) = x_2^d, \tag{3.1b}$$

$$c_3(x_3) = x_3^d \left[1 + \tfrac{1}{2}\cos(\log x_3)\right], \tag{3.1c}$$

where d is an integer. It is easy to see that the cost functions (3.1) are convex and differentiable on $[0, \infty)$ for all $d \geq 2$. Furthermore, the functions $x_e c_e(x_e)$ are *strictly* convex, so the problem (SO) admits a unique optimum traffic distribution. Hence, the only way for the game's price of anarchy to be equal to 1 is if the game's (also unique) Wardrop equilibrium coincides with the network's socially optimum flow.

For a given value of the total inflow $M = x_1 + x_2 + x_3$, the load profile $x = (x_1, x_2, x_3)$ is a Wardrop equilibrium if and only if $c_1(x_1) = c_2(x_2) = c_3(x_3)$,[5] i.e., if the normalized profile $z = x/M$ satisfies

$$z_1^d \left[1 + \tfrac{1}{2}\sin(\log M z_1)\right] = z_2^d = z_3^d \left[1 + \tfrac{1}{2}\cos(\log M z_3)\right]. \tag{3.2}$$

Likewise, after differentiating and rearranging, the corresponding conditions for the network's socially optimum flow are

$$z_1^d \left[1 + \tfrac{1}{2}\sin(\log M z_1) + \tfrac{1}{2(d+1)}\cos(\log M z_1)\right]$$
$$= z_2^d = z_3^d \left[1 + \tfrac{1}{2}\cos(\log M z_3) - \tfrac{1}{2(d+1)}\sin(\log M z_3)\right]. \tag{3.3}$$

A simple algebraic argument shows that Eqs. 3.2 and 3.3 never admit a common solution; since Eqs. 3.2 and 3.3 are periodic in $\log M$, it also follows that the game's price of anarchy oscillates periodically at a logarithmic scale. Thus, focusing on the period $1 \leq M \leq e^{2\pi}$, we conclude that

$$\inf_{M \geq 0} \mathrm{PoA}(\Gamma_M) = \min_{1 \leq M \leq e^{2\pi}} \mathrm{PoA}(\Gamma_M) > 1, \tag{3.4}$$

i.e., Wardrop equilibrium in the network of Fig. 1 *remain strictly inefficient no matter the value of* M.

4 Networks with a Single O/D Pair

The example of the previous section shows that the price of anarchy may be bounded away from 1 for all values of the traffic inflow, even in a three-link parallel network with a *single* O/D pair. That being said, the behavior of the cost model (3.1) at both ends of the congestion spectrum is fairly irregular, so the question remains: *is selfish routing bad under light/heavy traffic for more "reasonable" classes of cost functions?*

---

[5] Since an unused edge always has a cost of zero, all paths are used at equilibrium.

4.1   The Light Traffic Limit

A key observation regarding the counterexample (3.1) is that the "topologist's trig" terms $\sin(\log x)$ and $\cos(\log x)$ are highly pathological: their oscillations become dense near 0, so the corresponding cost functions do not admit derivatives of all orders at 0. To exclude such singularities, we will instead focus on functions that are smooth enough to admit a faithful Taylor expansion at 0:

Definition 1. *A function $g\colon \mathbb{R} \to \mathbb{R}$ is called* (real) analytic *at x_0 if there exists an open neighborhood U of x_0 and real numbers g_k, $k = 0, 1, \ldots$, such that*

$$g(x) = \sum_{k=0}^{\infty} g_k\,(x - x_0)^k \quad \text{for all } x \in U. \tag{4.1}$$

All polynomials are analytic, as are exponential, trigonometric, and most special functions (like the gamma function). Remarkably, under this mild regularity requirement, we have the following general result for lightly congested networks with a single O/D pair:

Theorem 1. *Let Γ_M be a nonatomic routing game with a single O/D pair and traffic inflow M. If the network's cost functions are analytic, we have*

$$\lim_{M \to 0^+} \mathrm{PoA}(\Gamma_M) = 1. \tag{4.2}$$

Despite appearances, Theorem 1 is fairly surprising. Indeed, at first sight, one would expect that when $M \to 0$, traffic is so light that it doesn't really matter how it is routed. This is indeed the case if, for instance, all paths in the network exhibit a positive cost for $M = 0$. However, if the cost of an empty path is zero, this is no longer the case: the optimum and equilibrium assignments could be fairly different (even for low traffic), so there is no *a priori* reason that the price of anarchy should converge to 1 as $M \to 0$ (the example of Sect. 3 clearly illustrates this phenomenon). Theorem 1 shows that all that is needed for this to occur is for the network's cost functions to be faithfully represented by their Taylor series. When this regularity condition is met, optimum and equilibrium costs no longer fluctuate but, instead, they converge to the same value.

4.2   The Heavy Traffic Limit

In the heavy traffic limit, Taylor expansions are no longer meaningful so we require a different criterion to rule out pathological oscillations. We do so by means of the notion of regular variation:

Definition 2. *A function $g\colon [0, \infty) \to (0, \infty)$ is said to be* regularly varying *if*

$$\lim_{t \to \infty} \frac{g(tx)}{g(t)} \quad \text{is finite and nonzero for all } x \geq 0. \tag{4.3}$$

In words, regular variation means that $g(x)$ grows at the same rate when viewed at different scales. Standard examples of regularly varying functions include all affine, polynomial and (poly) logarithmic functions. The concept itself dates back to Karamata (1933) and has been used extensively in probability and large deviations theory (see e.g. de Haan and Ferreira, 2006; Jessen and Mikosch, 2006; Resnick, 2007); for a comprehensive survey, the reader is referred to Bingham et al. (1989).

With all this at hand, we will discard growth irregularities (such as those observed in Sect. 3) by positing that each cost function $c_e(x)$ can be compared asymptotically to some regularly varying function $c(x)$. Specifically, given an ensemble of cost functions $\mathcal{C} = \{c_e\}_{e \in \mathcal{E}}$, we say that a regularly varying function $c \colon [0, \infty) \to (0, \infty)$ is a *benchmark* for $\mathcal{C}$ if the (possibly infinite) limit

$$\alpha_e = \lim_{x \to \infty} \frac{c_e(x)}{c(x)} \tag{4.4}$$

exists for all $e \in \mathcal{E}$.

When it exists, this limit will be called the *index* of edge e, and e will be called *fast*, *slow*, or *tight* (relative to c) if α_e is respectively 0, ∞, or in-between. Since bottlenecks in a path are caused by the slowest edges, we also define the *index of a path* $p \in \mathcal{P}$ as

$$\alpha_p = \max_{e \in p} \alpha_e, \tag{4.5}$$

and we say that p is *fast*, *slow*, or *tight* based on whether α_p is 0, ∞, or in-between. Finally, we say that the network is *tight* if the *index of the network*

$$\alpha = \min_{p \in \mathcal{P}} \alpha_p \tag{4.6}$$

is finite and positive $(0 < \alpha < \infty)$.

In words, a path is fast (resp. tight/slow) if its slowest edge is fast (resp. tight/slow), and the network is tight if its fastest path is tight. In particular, tightness guarantees that the network admits a path whose cost grows asymptotically as a multiple of some regularly varying benchmark function $c(x)$. The importance of this growth requirement is illustrated by the counterexample of Sect. 3: if we slightly relax the tightness concept by asking that the network admits a path whose cost grows as $\Theta(c(x))$, the price of anarchy may be bounded away from 1 for all values of M. Instead, under tightness, we have:

Theorem 2. *Let Γ_M be a nonatomic routing game with a single O/D pair and traffic inflow M. If the network is tight, then*

$$\lim_{M \to \infty} \mathrm{PoA}(\Gamma_M) = 1. \tag{4.7}$$

In other words, if the fastest path in the network is tight, selfish routing becomes efficient in the high congestion limit.

As an immediate corollary, we then have:

Corollary 1. *In networks with polynomial costs and a single O/D pair, we have* $\mathrm{PoA}(\Gamma_M) \to 1$ *as* $M \to \infty$.

Proof. Let d_e be the degree of c_e, set $d_p = \max_{e \in p} d_e$, and let $d = \min_{p \in \mathcal{P}} d_p$. The network is clearly tight with respect to $c(x) = x^d$, so Theorem 2 applies. ∎

Combining Theorem 1 and Corollary 1, we conclude that selfish routing becomes efficient under both light and heavy traffic in networks with polynomial costs. Beyond the polynomial case, Theorems 1 and 2 show that analyticity and regular variation can be seen as different sides of the same coin: they both ensure asymptotic regularity and they both exclude pathological oscillations (at zero and infinity respectively). As such, our results for light and heavy traffic are chiefly set apart by the notion of tightness (which only applies for heavy traffic). The reason for this qualitative difference is that costs might diverge to infinity at very different rates when the traffic inflow grows large; by contrast, all costs are finite when there is no traffic, so the notion of tightness is redundant then.

5 Networks with Multiple O/D Pairs

We now extend our analysis to networks with multiple O/D pairs. In this case, the total traffic inflow in the network is given by $M = \sum_{i \in \mathcal{I}} m^i$ and we write

$$\lambda^i = \frac{m^i}{M} \tag{5.1}$$

for the fraction of the traffic generated by the i-th O/D pair. In what follows, we will be assuming that the relative traffic inflow λ^i of every O/D pair $i \in \mathcal{I}$ is a fixed positive constant. At the cost of heavier notation, our analysis also extends to variable $\lambda^i \equiv \lambda^i(M)$ but, due to space constraints, we focus on this setting for clarity and concision.

5.1 The Light Traffic Limit

As in the previous section, we begin with the low congestion regime. Here, our main result is essentially the same as in networks with a single O/D pair:

Theorem 3. *Let* Γ_M *be a nonatomic routing game with total traffic inflow* M. *If the network's cost functions are analytic, we have*

$$\lim_{M \to 0^+} \mathrm{PoA}(\Gamma_M) = 1. \tag{5.2}$$

In words, the advent of several O/D pairs does not change the asymptotic behavior of the price of anarchy at the light traffic limit: Theorem 3 is a direct extension of Theorem 1 (which it implies).

5.2   The Heavy Traffic Limit

In the high congestion regime, tightness plays a crucial role, but its definition must be re-examined in the presence of multiple O/D pairs. In particular, the cost of routing for different O/D pairs might grow at completely different rates as $M \to \infty$, so the definition of the network's index must take this into account. To make this precise, we define the *index of a pair* $i \in \mathcal{I}$ as

$$\alpha^i = \min_{p \in \mathcal{P}^i} \alpha_p, \tag{5.3}$$

reflecting the fact that the traffic of a given O/D pair will tend to be routed along the pair's fastest available path. The network's index is then defined as

$$\alpha = \max_{i \in \mathcal{I}} \alpha^i, \tag{5.4}$$

and, as before, we say that the network is *tight* if $0 < \alpha < \infty$. With all this at hand, our main result for highly congested networks is as follows:

Theorem 4. *Let Γ_M be a nonatomic routing game with total inflow M. If the network is tight, then*

$$\lim_{M \to \infty} \mathrm{PoA}(\Gamma_M) = 1. \tag{5.5}$$

In words, if the "most costly" O/D pair in the network admits a tight path, selfish routing becomes efficient in the high congestion limit.

Note that Theorem 2 follows directly from Theorem 4 because the definitions (4.6) and (5.4) coincide if $\mathcal{I}$ is a singleton. However, in contrast to the light traffic regime (where the presence of multiple O/D pairs does not change the result), there is more going on in the high congestion limit. Specifically, when there are multiple O/D pairs in the network, Theorem 4 posits that every O/D pair must have a path which is not slow, and at least one of the O/D pairs must be tight (i.e., its index must be finite and positive). This is a considerably lighter requirement than asking that *every* O/D pair be tight, so the conditions under which the price of anarchy converges to 1 are very lax in this regard.

We close this section with an immediate corollary of Theorem 4

Corollary 2. *In networks with polynomial costs, $\lim_{M \to \infty} \mathrm{PoA}(\Gamma_M) = 1$.*

Proof. Let d_e be the degree of c_e, set $d_p = \max_{e \in p} d_e$, $d^i = \min_{p \in \mathcal{P}^i} d_p$ and $d = \max_{p \in \mathcal{P}} d_p$. Then, simply verify that the network is tight with respect to the benchmark function $c(x) = x^d$. ∎

Thus, by Theorem 3 and Corollary 2, we conclude that:

In networks with polynomial cost functions,
the price of anarchy becomes 1 under both light and heavy traffic.

6 Discussion

Our goal in this paper was to assess when selfish routing becomes efficient by examining the behavior of the price of anarchy at each end of the congestion spectrum. Under fairly mild assumptions (that always include networks with polynomial costs), we found that the price of anarchy goes to 1 in both cases, independently of the network's topology and the number of O/D pairs in the network. What we find intriguing about this result is that it suggests that self-ishness is not the real cause of increased delays under heavy traffic: from a social planner's point of view, sophisticated tolling/rerouting schemes that target the optimum traffic assignment will not yield considerable gains over a "laissez-faire" approach where each traffic element takes the fastest available path.

Acknowledgments. R. Colini-Baldeschi and M. Scarsini are members of GNAMPA-INdAM. R. Cominetti and P. Mertikopoulos gratefully acknowledge the support and hospitality of LUISS during a visit in which this research was initiated. R. Cominetti's research is also supported by FONDECYT 1130564 and Núcleo Milenio ICM/FIC RC130003 *"Información y Coordinación en Redes"*. P. Mertikopoulos was partially supported by the French National Research Agency (ANR) project ORACLESS (ANR–16– CE33–0004– 01) and the ECOS/CONICYT Grant C15E03. He gratefully acknowl-edges the support and hospitality of FONDECYT 1130564 and Núcleo Milenio *"Infor-mación y Coordinación en Redes"*. The authors also gratefully acknowledge financial support from the PGMO grant HEAVY.NET.

References

Beckmann, M.J., McGuire, C., Winsten, C.B.: Studies in the Economics of Transporta-tion. Yale University Press, New Haven, CT (1956)

Bingham, N.H., Goldie, C.M., Teugels, J.L.: Regular Variation. Encyclopedia of Math-ematics and its Applications, vol. 27. Cambridge University Press, Cambridge (1989)

Braess, D.: Über ein Paradoxon aus der Verkehrsplanung. Unternehmensforschung **12**, 258–268 (1968)

Cole, R. and Tao, Y.: Large market games with near optimal efficiency. In: Proceedings of the 2016 ACM Conference on Economics and Computation, pp. 791–808. ACM (2016)

Colini-Baldeschi, R., Cominetti, R., Scarsini, M.: On the price of anarchy of highly congested nonatomic network games. In: Gairing, M., Savani, R. (eds.) SAGT 2016. LNCS, vol. 9928, pp. 117–128. Springer, Heidelberg (2016). https://doi.org/10.1007/978-3-662-53354-3_10

Correa, J.R., Schulz, A.S., Stier-Moses, N.E.: Selfish routing in capacitated networks. Math. Oper. Res. **29**(4), 961–976 (2004)

Correa, J.R., Schulz, A.S., Stier-Moses, N.E.: A geometric approach to the price of anarchy in nonatomic congestion games. Games Econ. Behav. **64**(2), 457–469 (2008)

de Haan, L., Ferreira, A.: Extreme Value Theory: An Introduction. Operations Research and Financial Engineering. Springer, New York (2006). https://doi.org/10.1007/0-387-34471-3

Dumrauf, D., Gairing, M.: Price of anarchy for polynomial wardrop games. In: Spirakis, P., Mavronicolas, M., Kontogiannis, S. (eds.) WINE 2006. LNCS, vol. 4286, pp. 319–330. Springer, Heidelberg (2006). https://doi.org/10.1007/11944874_29

Feldman, M., Immorlica, N., Lucier, B., Roughgarden, T., and Syrgkanis, V.: The price of anarchy in large games. In: Proceedings of the 48th Annual ACM Symposium on the Theory of Computing, STOC 2016 (2016)

González Vayá, M., Grammatico, S., Andersson, G., and Lygeros, J.: On the price of being selfish in large populations of plug-in electric vehicles. In: Proceedings of the 53rd IEEE Annual Conference on Decision and Control, CDC 2015, pp. 6542–6547. IEEE (2015)

Jessen, A.H., Mikosch, T.: Regularly varying functions. Publ. Inst. Math. (Beograd) (N.S.) **80**(94), 171–192 (2006)

Karamata, J.: Sur un mode de croissance régulière. Théorèmes fondamentaux. Bull. Soc. Math. France **61**, 55–62 (1933)

Koutsoupias, E., Papadimitriou, C.: Worst-case equilibria. In: Meinel, C., Tison, S. (eds.) STACS 1999. LNCS, vol. 1563, pp. 404–413. Springer, Heidelberg (1999). https://doi.org/10.1007/3-540-49116-3_38

Law, L.M., Huang, J., Liu, M.: Price of anarchy for congestion games in cognitive radio networks. IEEE Trans. Wireless Commun. **11**(10), 3778–3787 (2012)

Monnot, B., Benita, F., and Piliouras, G.: How bad is selfish routing in practice? Technical report (2017). arXiv:1703.01599v2

O'Hare, S.J., Connors, R.D., Watling, D.P.: Mechanisms that govern how the price of anarchy varies with travel demand. Transp. Res. Part B. Methodol. **84**, 55–80 (2016)

Papadimitriou, C.H.: Algorithms, games, and the internet. In: Proceedings of the 33rd Annual ACM Symposium on the Theory of Computing, STOC 2001 (2001)

Pigou, A.C.: The Economics of Welfare, 1st edn. Macmillan and Co., London (1920)

Resnick, S.I.: Heavy-Tail Phenomena. Operations Research and Financial Engineering. Springer, New York (2007). https://doi.org/10.1007/978-0-387-45024-7. Probabilistic and statistical modeling

Roughgarden, T.: The price of anarchy is independent of the network topology. J. Comput. System Sci. **67**(2), 341–364 (2003)

Roughgarden, T.: Routing games. In: Algorithmic Game Theory, pp. 461–486. Cambridge Univ. Press, Cambridge (2007)

Roughgarden, T., Tardos, É.: How bad is selfish routing? J. ACM **49**(2), 236–259 (2002)

Roughgarden, T., Tardos, É.: Bounding the inefficiency of equilibria in nonatomic congestion games. Games Econ Behav. **47**(2), 389–403 (2004)

Wardrop, J.G.: Some theoretical aspects of road traffic research. Proc. Inst. Civil Eng. Part II **1**, 325–378 (1952)

Youn, H., Gastner, M.T., Jeong, H.: Price of anarchy in transportation networks: efficiency and optimality control. Phys. Rev. Lett. **101**(12), 128701 (2008)

Fixed Price Approximability of the Optimal Gain from Trade

Riccardo Colini-Baldeschi[1]([⊠]), Paul Goldberg[2], Bart de Keijzer[3],
Stefano Leonardi[4], and Stefano Turchetta[5]

[1] LUISS Rome, Rome, Italy
rcolini@luiss.it
[2] University of Oxford, Oxford, England
paul.goldberg@cs.ox.ac.uk
[3] Centrum Wiskunde & Informatica (CWI), Amsterdam, Netherlands
keijzer@cwi.nl
[4] Sapienza University of Rome, Rome, Italy
leonardi@diag.uniroma1.it
[5] KPMG Italy, Rome, Italy
stefano.turchetta@gmail.com

Abstract. *Bilateral trade* is a fundamental economic scenario comprising a strategically acting buyer and seller (holding an item), each holding valuations for the item, drawn from publicly known distributions. It was recently shown that the only mechanisms that are simultaneously dominant strategy incentive compatible, strongly budget balanced, and ex-post individually rational, are *fixed price* mechanisms, i.e., mechanisms that are parametrised by a price p, and trade occurs if and only if the valuation of the buyer is at least p and the valuation of the seller is at most p. The *gain from trade (GFT)* is the increase in welfare that results from applying a mechanism. We study the GFT achievable by fixed price mechanisms. We explore this question for both the bilateral trade setting and a *double auction* setting where there are multiple i.i.d. unit demand buyers and sellers. We first identify a fixed price mechanism that achieves a GFT of at least $2/r$ times the optimum, where r is the probability that the seller's valuation does not exceed that of the buyer's valuation. This extends a previous result by McAfee. Subsequently, we improve this approximation factor in an asymptotic sense, by showing that a more sophisticated rule for setting the fixed price results in a GFT within a factor $O(\log(1/r))$ of the optimum. This is asymptotically the best approximation factor possible. For the double auction setting, we present a fixed price mechanism that achieves for all $\epsilon > 0$ a gain from trade of at least $(1-\epsilon)$ times the optimum with probability $1-2/e^{\#T\epsilon^2/2}$, where $\#T$ is the expected number of trades of the mechanism. This can be interpreted as a "large market" result: Full efficiency is achieved in the limit, as the market gets thicker.

© Springer International Publishing AG 2017
N. R. Devanur and P. Lu (Eds.): WINE 2017, LNCS 10674, pp. 146–160, 2017.
https://doi.org/10.1007/978-3-319-71924-5_11

1   Introduction

Bilateral trade is a fundamental economic scenario comprising a buyer and a seller. The seller holds one item, and can possibly trade this item with the buyer for some price. The buyer and the seller each have a (non-negative real-valued) valuation for the item that is up for trade. The buyer's valuation is only known by the buyer and the seller's valuation is only known by the seller. The buyer and seller both want to maximise their utility, which is assumed to be *quasi-linear*, i.e., of the form $x \cdot v - p$, where x is a 0/1-variable that is set to 1 if and only if the agent holds the item, v is the agent's value for the item, and p is the price paid/received by the agent. In the buyer's case p is non-negative and represents how much the buyer has to pay. In the seller's case, the price p is non-positive because the seller receives money to transfer her item.

The main problem studied for this bilateral trade setting is one in mechanism design: which mechanism maximises the *social welfare* (i.e., total utility of both players)? A direct revelation mechanism for this setting solicits the valuations of the buyer and the seller. Subsequently it determines whether the buyer and the seller should trade and which prices they have to pay or receive. We would like any mechanism to satisfy the following properties:

- Dominant strategy incentive compatibility (DSIC): It should be a dominant strategy for the buyer and seller to submit their true valuations to the mechanism.
- Ex-post individual rationality (ex-post IR): Neither agent should end up with a negative utility if the agent's true valuation is submitted to the mechanism.
- Strong budget balance (SBB): The price paid by the buyer is equal to the price received by the seller, i.e., the mechanism does not extract money from the market, nor does it inject money into the market.

While the valuations of the buyer and seller are known by the buyer and seller only, it is assumed that there is still distributional public knowledge about their valuations. More precisely, it is assumed that there are two publicly known distributions from which the buyer and seller independently draw their valuations. The mechanism may use this knowledge in order to determine the outcome.

Ideally, we would want the mechanism to have the seller trade with the buyer whenever the buyer's valuation exceeds the seller's valuation. The expected total utility that would result from trading as such is referred to as the *optimal* social welfare. Unfortunately the optimal social welfare is not achievable, as shown by Myerson and Satterthwaite [16]: No bilateral trade mechanism is simultaneously DSIC, IR, *weakly* budged balanced, and social-welfare optimizing. Weak budget balance (WBB) is less restrictive than strong budget balance, as WBB only requires that no money be injected into the market, while the mechanism is allowed to extract money from the market.

For the classic bilateral trade setting, it was recently shown [5] that the only direct revelation mechanisms that are simultaneously incentive compatible, strongly budget balanced, and ex-post individually rational, are *fixed price* mechanisms, i.e., mechanisms that are parametrised by a price p, and trade occurs if and only if the valuation of the buyer is at least p and the valuation of the seller is at most p.

An alternative—and more challenging to approximate—objective to the social welfare is the *gain from trade*, which measures the expected increase in total utility that is achievable by applying the mechanism, with respect to the initial allocation. For example, if a seller holds an item that she values \$4 and a buyer values the same item \$10, whenever a fix price mechanism sets a price $4 \leq p \leq 10$, the buyer and the seller trade producing a gain from trade of \$6. Whenever the price p is set lower than \$4 or greater than \$10 no trade occur, and the gain from trade is 0.

McAfee [15] has shown that if the median of the distribution of the seller's valuation is less than the median of the distribution of the buyer's valuation, then there is a fixed price mechanism for which the expected gain from trade is at least half of the optimal gain from trade. In fact, it was shown for this special case that by setting the fixed price anywhere in between the two medians, half of the optimal gain from trade is guaranteed. We extend this result by showing that the optimal gain from trade is at least $2/r$ times the gain from trade achievable by a fixed price mechanism, where r is the probability that the seller's valuation does not exceed the buyer's valuation (which is the condition under which a gain from trade is possible in the first place).

Subsequently, we improve this approximation factor in an asymptotic sense, by showing that a more sophisticated rule for setting the fixed price results in an expected gain from trade within a factor $O(\log(1/r))$ of the optimal gain from trade. This is asymptotically the best approximation factor possible, which is shown by an appropriate example of a bilateral trade setting for which every fixed price achieves an expected gain from trade of $\Omega(\log(1/r))$ times the optimum.

It follows from our results that our mechanisms cannot approximate the gain from trade if r is small. Indeed, we prove a general negative result showing that the ratio between the gain from trade of a DSIC mechanism and the optimal gain from trade can be arbitrarily small as the support of the distribution grows. A similar result was proved independently in [2].

We finally extend our study to the *double auction* setting, where there are multiple buyers and sellers, each seller holding one item and each buyer having a demand for obtaining at most one item. The valuations of the n buyers are independently drawn from a common probability distribution, and the same holds for the m sellers, although the probability distribution of the sellers may be distinct from that of the buyers.

1.1   Our Results

The first results presented in this paper concern the bilateral trade problem. It is known that if a mechanism has to satisfy IR, DSIC, and SBB, then it must be a fixed price mechanism [5], i.e., the mechanism fixes a price p and posts it to the buyer and the seller. We want to understand p has to be chosen.

McAfee's result of [15] states that in case the seller's median is less than the buyer's median, then setting the price in between the medians of the buyer and the seller results in a 2-approximation to the optimal gain from trade. Our first result is a strict generalization of [15] where the approximation to the optimal gain from trade is given as a function of the probability that a trade is efficient, in other words: the probability that the valuation drawn from the buyer is greater than the valuation drawn from the seller. This parameter is referred to as $r = \mathbf{Pr}_{v \sim f, w \sim g}[v \geq w]$, where f is the buyer's distribution and g is the seller's distribution.

In particular, we show that setting the price p such that $\mathbf{Pr}_{v \sim f}[v \geq p] = \mathbf{Pr}_{w \sim g}[w \leq p]$ results in a $r/2$-approximation to the optimal gain from trade.

Then, we show how that it is possible to improve the approximation factor of $2/r$ considerably in an asymptotic sense: We prove that by using a more complex rule for determining the fixed price p, the optimal gain from trade is at most a factor of $O(\log(1/r))$ times the gain from trade when trading at price p. When r is small, this results in a big improvement when compared to the approximation factor that we established in the previous section. Our mechanism works by showing that we can decompose "roughly" the entire probability space into at most $\log(1/r)+1$ such events, so that choosing the best fixed price corresponding to each of these events results in a gain from trade that is an $O(\log(1/r))$-approximation to the optimal gain from trade. Finally, we want to consider the double auction setting. In this setting, we extend the definition of a fixed price mechanism in a natural way: the mechanism computes a single price p, buyers with a valuation greater than p and sellers with a valuation lower than p will be allowed to trade. If the sets of allowed buyers and allowed sellers have different cardinalities, agents will be removed from the biggest set uniformly at random so that the cardinality of the two sets will be equal. The fixed price mechanism that we propose for the double auction setting achieves a gain from trade that is a $1-\epsilon$ approximation to the optimal gain from trade with probability $(1 - 1/e^{\epsilon^2 \#T/2})$ where $\#T$ is the expected number of trades of the mechanism. This implies that if the double auction instance is such that a relatively small expected number of trades can happen at this price, then a reasonably good approximation factor is achieved by our mechanism (see Sect. 5 for a detailed discussion). One may also interpret our result as a "large market" result: the approximation factor approaches 1 as we let the number of buyers and sellers in the market grow proportionally, since in that case the number of trades grows arbitrarily large. This is, to the best of our knowledge, the first fixed price mechanism that is DSIC, SBB, and ex-post IR, and achieves a near-optimal gain from trade under mild conditions on the size of the market.

1.2   Related Literature

The impossibility result of [16] proved that no two-sided mechanism can be simultaneously BIC, IR, WBB, and optimise the social welfare even in the simple bilateral trade setting. Thus, many subsequent works studied how it is possible to relax some of the constraints to achieve positive results in the context of maximise the social welfare or the gain from trade.

In [3], a BIC mechanism is devised that approximates the expected gain from trade in bilateral trade up to a factor of $1/e$ when the buyer's distribution function satisfies a property known as the monotone hazard rate condition. The mechanism of [3] is not DSIC since it achieves this approximation factor from a Bayes-Nash equilibrium by using the valuation of the seller in the price offered to the buyer. It is also shown in the same work that no BIC mechanism can achieve an approximation bound better than $2/e$. Mechanisms that are DSIC/BIC, IR, and SBB have been given for bilateral trade in [1]. In addition to this, the authors proposed a WBB mechanism for a general class of markets known as combinatorial exchange markets.

Mechanisms for double auctions with near-optimal gain from trade have been previously proposed for the prior-free setting. McAfee [14] has shown a WBB, DSIC, IR mechanism which achieves a $1 - 1/k$-approximation to the optimal gain from trade if the number of trades under the optimum allocation is k. This rate of convergence requires the prior distributions of traders to be bounded above zero, over an interval $[0, 1]$, but the mechanism is not a function of the priors. More recently, Segal-Halevi et al. [20] devised a SBB mechanism with the same performance guarantee. The mechanisms of [14,20] are direct revelation mechanisms where the price depends crucially on the reported valuations. In contrast, the goal in our present paper is to find out how much gain from trade can be generated by means of setting a single fixed price, independent of the valuations of the players, at which all agents trade. Such mechanisms have the advantage that they are conceptually simpler and have a pricing scheme that is extremely easy to understand. They also can be implemented as sequential posted price mechanisms.

In [19], the authors present a mechanism that combines random sampling and random serial dictatorship techniques which is IR, SBB and DSIC, and asymptotically approaches the optimum gain from trade. Recently, [4] provides an IR, SBB, and BIC mechanism that achieves a constant approximation to the best gain from trade achievable among the IR, WBB, and BIC mechanisms, which is an alternative (more permissive) benchmark. Two recent papers by Feldman and Gonen [9,10] study a multi-unit variant of double auctions for online advertising purposes. They design IR, WBB, and DSIC mechanisms that well-approximate the gain from trade under certain technical conditions, as a function of the number of trades under the optimum allocation.

Deng et al. [7] study revenue maximisation in a setting of multiple buyers and sellers with uncorrelated priors and a single type of item being traded. The same objective was studied by [8] yet in the *prior-free* model. Gerstgrasser et al. [11] also study the objective of maximising expected revenue, in a setting where there is a small number of buyers and seller, who have a prior distribution whose support size represents the complexity of instances of the problem. In [11], this distribution is otherwise unrestricted, and in particular may be correlated. Giannakopoulos et al. [12] study a similar double auction setting to the one studied here in Sect. 5: there are multiple buyers and sellers and one kind of item, with unit supply and demand. Buyers have a common prior distribution on their valuations, as do sellers. [12] study market intermediation from the perspective of welfare maximisation, and revenue maximisation. Colini-Baldeschi et al. [6] also study market intermediation, in the context of buyers and seller of a collection of heterogenous items, aiming to maximise welfare and achieve a strong notion of budget balance.

In the context of social welfare in the economics literature, [13] showed that duplicating the number of agents by τ results in a market where the optimal IR, IC, WBB mechanism's expected social welfare approximation factor approaches 1 at a rate of $O(\log \tau / \tau^2)$. The papers [17,18] investigated a family of non-IC double auctions, and study the inefficiency and the extent to which agents misreport their valuations in these double auctions.

2   Preliminaries

As a general convention, we use $[a]$ to denote the set $\{1, \ldots, a\}$. We will use $1(X)$ to denote the indicator function that maps to 1 if and only if event/fact X holds.

Double Auction Setting. In a double auction setting there are n buyers and m sellers. Initially, each seller $j \in [m]$ holds one item and has a valuation w_j for it. The sellers are not interested in possess more than one item. Each buyer $i \in [n]$ is interested in obtaining no more than one item and has a valuation v_i for it. Moreover, they are indifferent among the different items.

The valuations of the buyers and the sellers are private knowledge, but they are independently drawn from publicly known distributions f and g, where f is the probability distribution for the valuation of a buyer and g is the probability distribution for the valuation of a seller. We treat f and g as probability density functions. All the buyers share the same distribution f and all the sellers share the same mass probability distribution g, but f and g may be distinct. Moreover, let G be the corresponding cumulative distribution functions of g and let $\bar{F}$ be the corresponding complementary cumulative distribution function (or survival function) of f.

Given a double auction setting (n, m, f, g), our goal is to redistribute the items from the sellers to the buyers. An *allocation* for a double auction setting (n, m, f, g) is a pair of vectors $(\boldsymbol{X}, \boldsymbol{Y}) = ((X_1, \ldots, X_n), (Y_1, \ldots, Y_m))$ such that all the elements $X_1, \ldots, X_n, Y_1, \ldots, Y_m \in \{0, 1\}$, and $\sum_{i \in [n]} X_i + \sum_{j \in [m]} Y_j = m$. The set $\mathcal{A}$ represents the set of all allocations for the double auction setting.

The redistribution of the items from sellers to buyers is done by running a *mechanism* $\mathbb{M}$. A mechanism receives input from the agents, and outputs an allocation $(\boldsymbol{X}, \boldsymbol{Y})$ and a price p. The allocation $(\boldsymbol{X}, \boldsymbol{Y})$ and the price p represents the *outcome* of the mechanism $\mathbb{M}$. Thus, an outcome is a tuple $(\boldsymbol{X}, \boldsymbol{Y}, p)$. The price p represents how much a buyer has to pay to obtain an item and how much a seller has to receive to sell her item.[1]

---

[1] More generally, we may define the notion of a mechanism such that more complex pricing schemes are possible, but our definition suffices for the mechanisms that we will define later in this paper.

Agents are assumed to be utility maximisers. The *utility* is defined as the valuation for the items that they possess with respect to the allocation vector, minus the payment charged by the mechanism. Specifically, the utility of a buyer i will be $u_i^B(\boldsymbol{X}, \boldsymbol{Y}, p) = (v_i - p) \cdot X_i$. Similarly, the utility of a seller j will be $u_j^S(\boldsymbol{X}, \boldsymbol{Y}, p) = w_j Y_j + p \cdot (1 - Y_j)$.

Furthermore, agents are assumed to be fully rational, so that they will strategically interact with the mechanism to achieve their goal of maximising utility. Our goal is to design a mechanism that is DSIC, IR, SBB (as defined in the introduction) such that the the *gain from trade* is high. For an outcome $(\boldsymbol{X}, \boldsymbol{Y}, p)$, the gain from trade GFT$(\boldsymbol{X}, \boldsymbol{Y}, p)$ is defined as the increase in total utility as a result of running the mechanism. It can be expressed as follows.

$$\mathrm{GFT}(\boldsymbol{X}, \boldsymbol{Y}, p) = \sum_{i=1}^{n} v_i X_i + \sum_{j=1}^{m} w_j (Y_j - 1)$$

For a double auction setting (n, m, f, g), the *expected optimal gain from trade* is defined as

$$\mathrm{OPT}_{n,m,f,g} = \mathbf{E}_{v \sim f^n, w \sim g^m} \left[\max \left\{ \sum_{i=1}^{n} v_i X_i + \sum_{i=1}^{m} w_j (Y_j - 1) \,\middle|\, (\boldsymbol{X}, \boldsymbol{Y}) \in \mathcal{A} \right\} \right].$$

We will sometimes omit the subscript, as in those cases the instance being discussed will be clear from context.

We say that a mechanism $\mathbb{M}$ α-*approximates the optimal gain from trade* for some $\alpha > 1$ if and only if OPT $\le \alpha \mathbf{E}[\mathrm{GFT}(\boldsymbol{X}, \boldsymbol{Y}, p)]$, where $(\boldsymbol{X}, \boldsymbol{Y}, p)$ is the random allocation that the mechanism generates, when valuations v and w are drawn from f^n and g^m respectively. Our goal is to find a DSIC, ex-post IR, and SBB mechanism that α-approximates the optimal gain from trade for a low α.

Bilateral Trade Setting. The bilateral trade setting is a special case of the double auction setting where there is only one unit-demand buyer and one unit-supply seller. Thus, we can represent a bilateral trade setting as a pair of valuation distribution function, one for the buyer f and one for the seller g, i.e., (f, g). It is known that if a mechanism has to satisfy IR, DSIC, and SBB, then it must be a fixed price mechanism [5], i.e., the mechanism fixes a price p a priori, and trade happens if and only if both the buyer's valuation is at least p and the seller's valuation is at most p.

For a bilateral trade instance, the gain from trade of a fixed price mechanism with fixed price p will be denoted by GFT$_{f,g}(p)$. That is,

$$\mathrm{GFT}_{f,g}(p) = \mathbf{E}_{v \sim f, w \sim g}[\max\{0, v - w\} \mathbf{1}(w \le p \le v)].$$

Moreover, note that for the bilateral trade setting we can express OPT$_{f,g}$ as $\mathbf{E}_{v \sim f, w \sim g}[\max\{0, v - w\}]$.

For the bilateral trade setting, the goal of this paper is to study how to set the price p such that the gain from trade achieved by the fixed price mechanism with price p is as close as possible to the optimal gain from trade. We will design fixed price mechanisms where the ratio between $\text{OPT}_{f,g}$ and $\text{GFT}_{f,g}(p)$ is a function of the probability that the buyer has a value greater than the seller, i.e., the provability that a trade is efficient. This probability will be represented by the parameter r. Thus, $r = \mathbf{Pr}_{v \sim f, w \sim g}[v \geq w]$.

Due to space constraints, proofs of the theorems and lemmas have been omitted, and will be provided in a full version of this paper.

3 An $O(1/r)$-Approximation Mechanism for Bilateral Trade

In the bilateral trade setting there is only one unit-demand buyer and one unit-supply seller. It can be proven that if a mechanism has to satisfy IR, DSIC, and SBB, then it must be a fixed price mechanism [5], i.e., the mechanism fixes a price p and posts it to the buyer and the seller. Trade happens if and only if both the buyer's valuation is at least p and the seller's valuation is at most p.

We will show in this section that there exists a fixed price mechanism that achieves an expected gain from trade that is at least $r/2$ times the expected optimal gain from trade. In the fixed price mechanism that we propose for this, the fixed price p is set such that $\mathbf{Pr}_{v \sim f}[v \leq p] = \mathbf{Pr}_{w \sim g}[w \leq p]$. The main theorem that we prove is thus as follows.

Theorem 1. *Let (f, g) be a bilateral trade instance, let $p \in \mathbb{R}_{\geq 0}$ be any fixed price, and let q be the minimum of $\mathbf{Pr}_{v \sim f}[v \geq p]$ and $\mathbf{Pr}_{w \sim g}[w \leq p]$. Then,*

$$\frac{1}{q} GFT_{f,g}(p) \geq OPT_{f,g}. \tag{1}$$

Moreover, if p is chosen such that q is maximised (i.e., p is such that $\mathbf{Pr}_{w \sim g}[w \leq p] = \mathbf{Pr}_{v \sim f}[v \geq p]$), it holds that

$$\frac{2}{r} GFT_{f,g}(p) \geq OPT_{f,g}. \tag{2}$$

Note that this theorem strictly generalises McAfee's result of [15], which states that in case the seller's median is less than the buyer's median, then setting the price in between the medians of the buyer and the seller results in a 2-approximation to the optimal gain from trade: If we take p to be any price in between the median of the seller and the buyer, then q is at least $1/2$, and (1) then states that the gain from trade at fixed price p is at least half the optimal gain from trade.

4 Improving the Asymptotic Dependence on r

In this section, we show how it is possible to improve the approximation factor implementing a more involved rule to determine the fixed price p. When the trading price p will be set with the new rule the approximation factor will improve from $2/r$ to $O(\log(1/r))$. Notice that when r is small, this is a big improvement with respect to the approximation shown in the previous section. All logarithms used in this section are to base 2.

Let us first give a high level description of how we determine the fixed price of the mechanism. Let us consider any two points z and z' such that $\mathbf{Pr}[v \geq z] = 2\mathbf{Pr}[v \geq z']$. Let E be the event that the buyer's valuation exceeds z, and that the sellers valuation lies in between z and z'. Let $\overline{F}_E$ be the complementary cumulative distribution function of the buyer conditioned on E and let G_E be the cumulative distribution function of the seller conditioned on E. We now see that on the interval $[z, z']$, the function $\overline{F}_E$ decreases from 1 to 1/2 and the function G_E increases from 0 to 1. Thus, the functions cross each other in $[z, z']$ at a value of at least 1/2, which means that the median of the buyer exceeds the median of the seller when conditioning on E. Using Theorem 1, we thus obtain that when conditioning on E there exists a fixed price that achieves a 2-approximation to the optimal gain from trade.

Our mechanism works by showing that we can decompose "roughly" the entire probability space into at most $\log(1/r)+1$ such events, so that choosing the best fixed price corresponding to each of these events results into an $O(\log(1/r))$ approximation to the optimal gain from trade. More precisely, we show that there are two sets of roughly $\log(1/r) + 1$ such events, and we prove that in case one of these sets does not cover a fraction of the probability space that accounts for at least 1/2 of the optimal gain from trade, then the other set of events does. To determine the desired fixed price, we can thus

1. first determine which of the two event sets "covers" a large part of the optimal gain from trade,
2. and subsequently select the best fixed price among the $\log(1/r) + 1$ prices corresponding to the event set.

The two event sets have the following properties: one of them excludes the part of the probability space where the buyer's complementary CDF is below the threshold $r/2$. The other one switches the roles of the seller and buyer, and excludes the part of the probability space where the seller's CDF is below a the threshold $r/2$. From this property of the event sets (i.e., having these particular thresholds on the tails of the two distributions), we are able to show that one of the event sets covers a large part of the optimal gain from trade. We now proceed by making these ideas precise.

We first describe how we determine the price, which we denote by p^*, for a given instance (f, g). In contrast with the last section, we assume (for convenience of exposition) without loss of generality that f and g are continuous distributions without point masses, where we treat f and g as probability density functions, and we let F and G be the corresponding cumulative distribution functions. We write $\overline{F}$ to denote the buyer's complementary cumulative distribution function $1 - F$. Let r be the probability $\mathbf{Pr}_{v \sim f, w \sim g}[v \geq w]$ of a trade being possible (as before). Let x be the value such that $F(x) = r/2$ and let y be the value such that $\overline{G}(y) = r/2$. We distinguish between two cases.

- If $\mathbf{E}_{v \sim f, w \sim g}[(v - w)\mathbf{1}(w \leq v \wedge w > y)] \geq \mathrm{OPT}_{f,g}/2$, then let p^* be the price that achieves the maximum gain from trade among the prices $p_1, \ldots, p_{\lceil \log(2/r) \rceil}$, where for $i \in [[\lceil \log(2/r) \rceil]]$, price p_i is such that

$$\mathbf{Pr}_{w \sim g}[w \leq p_i \mid \overline{F}^{-1}(1/2^{i-1}) \leq w \leq \overline{F}^{-1}(1/2^i)]$$
$$= \mathbf{Pr}_{v \sim f}[v > p_i \mid \overline{F}^{-1}(1/2^{i-1}) \leq v].$$

- Otherwise, let p^* be the price that achieves the maximum gain from trade among the prices $p'_1, \ldots, p'_{\lceil \log(2/r) \rceil}$, where for $i \in [[\lceil \log(2/r) \rceil]]$, price p'_i is such that

$$\mathbf{Pr}_{v \sim f}[v > p_i \mid G^{-1}(1/2^i) \leq v \leq G^{-1}(1/2^{i-1})]$$
$$= \mathbf{Pr}_{w \sim g}[w \leq p_i \mid G^{-1}(1/2^i) \leq w],$$

where we define $G^{-1}(1) = \infty$ if there exists no point $t \in \mathbb{R}_{\geq 0}$ such that $G(t) = 1$.

This completes the definition of the fixed price p^*.

First we can show that if the first of the two cases does not apply (i.e., if the inequality $\mathbf{E}_{v \sim f, w \sim g}[(v - w)\mathbf{1}(w \leq v \wedge w > y)] \leq \mathrm{OPT}_{f,g}/2$ does not hold), then the symmetric inequality $\mathbf{E}_{v \sim f, w \sim g}[(v - w)\mathbf{1}(w \leq v \wedge w < x)] \leq \mathrm{OPT}_{f,g}/2$ holds for the second case.

Lemma 1. *If $\mathbf{E}_{v \sim f, w \sim g}[(v - w)\mathbf{1}(w \leq v \wedge w > y)] > OPT_{f,g}/2$, then $\mathbf{E}_{w \sim f, v \sim g}$ $[(v - w)\mathbf{1}(w \leq v \wedge v < x)] \leq OPT_{f,g}/2$.*

Using the above lemma, it is possible to prove the intended approximation factor for price p^*.

Theorem 2. *Let (f, g) be any bilateral trade instance, and let p^* be the price for (f, g), as defined above. It holds that*

$$OPT_{f,g} \leq 4 \log \left(\left\lceil \frac{2}{r} \right\rceil \right) GFT_{f,g}(p^*).$$

Note that the approximation bound of $2/r$ that we established in the first section is better than the approximation bound of $4\lceil \log(2/r) \rceil$ when r is roughly greater than 0.05. At $r = 0.05$, the approximation factor $4\lceil \log(2/r) \rceil$ already takes a value around 20. Hence, the result of this section is intended to provide theoretical insight into how the approximability of the gain from trade depends on r asymptotically. An (asymptotically) matching lower bound is given in the appendix of [2], which shows that $\Theta(\log(1/r))$ is asymptotically the best possible factor by which the optimal gain from trade that can always be approximated.

5   A Fixed Price Double Auction

We now turn to the double auction setting. Recall that in this setting there are $n \geq 1$ buyers and $m \geq 1$ sellers. The sellers each hold one item, and neither the buyers or the sellers are interested in holding more than one item. As before, we refer to f for the probability distribution function from which the buyers' valuations are independently drawn, and to g for the probability distribution from which the sellers' valuations are independently drawn. We denote the (random) valuation of buyer $i \in [n]$ by v_i and the (random) valuation of seller $j \in [m]$ by w_j. See Sect. 2 for the definition.

In order to present the definition of a *fixed price mechanism* for the double auction setting, let us first introduce the concept of *feasible pair*.

Definition 1. *Let (n, m, f, g) be an instance of a double auction setting, let $(v, w) \in \mathbb{R}^n \times \mathbb{R}^m$ be a valuation profile for the buyers and sellers, and let $p \in \mathbb{R}_{\geq 0}$. We call $(i, j) \in [n] \times [m]$ a feasible pair with respect to profile (v, w) and fixed price p iff $v_i \geq p \geq w_j$.*

Now, we can define a fixed price mechanism as follows.

Definition 2. *We define a fixed price mechanism $\mathbb{M}$ for a double auction setting (n, m, f, g) as a direct revelation mechanism for which there is a price p such that the mechanism selects a uniform random maximal subset of feasible pairs with respect to reported profile (v, w) and p, and makes these pairs trade with each other. Moreover, for every selected trading pair (i, j), the mechanism makes buyer i pay an amount of p to seller j. We refer to p as the price of $\mathbb{M}$.*

This is perhaps the most natural generalization of the notion of a fixed price mechanism that one may think of. Please note that in a fixed price mechanism with price p, given a reported valuation profile (v, w), the number of pairs that trade is always the minimum of $|\{v_i : v_i \geq p\}|$ and $|\{w_i : w_i \leq p\}|$.

It is easy to show that fixed price mechanisms clearly satisfy the three basic properties that we want:

Theorem 3. *For every double auction setting, every fixed price mechanism is ex-post IR, SBB, and DSIC.*

Fixed price mechanisms have some additional advantanges.

- First, a fixed price mechanism is entirely symmetric: Each seller has the same expected utility, and each buyer has the same expected utility. The mechanism treats buyers with the same valuation entirely symetrically and does not break ties in favour of one over the other. This symmetricity is desirable from the point of view of fairness.
- Secondly, the mechanism does not require the agents to fully reveal their entire valuation, since it can be implemented as a *two-sided sequential posted price mechanism* [5]. Under such an implementation, the mechanisms goes over the buyers and sellers one by one. It proposes a take-it-or-leave-it price (equal to p, in this case) to each buyer and seller, which the buyers and sellers can choose to accept or reject. As soon as an accepting (buyer, seller)-pair is found, the mechanism lets this pair trade at price p. Taking a uniform random order of buyers and sellers will result in a random subset of feasible

pairs who trade at price p, i.e., it will result in an implementation of the fixed price mechanism with price p. Under such an implementation, each buyer and seller has to reveal only one bit of information, which indicates whether her valuation is above or below p.

We aim to design a simple fixed price mechanism for which the gain from trade is a good approximation to the optimal gain from trade. The mechanism we use is as follows.

Definition 3. *Given an instance (n, m, f, g) of a double auction setting, let $\overline{p}$ be the price such that $n\overline{F}(\overline{p}) = mG(\overline{p})$. We refer to the fixed price mechanism with price $\overline{p}$ as the* balanced fixed price double auction. *For ease of presentation, we refer to $\overline{F}(\overline{p})$ as $\overline{q}^B$ and we refer to $G(\overline{p})$ as $\overline{q}^S$. We denote by $GFT(\overline{p})$ the expected gain from trade achieved by the balanced fixed price double auction, and we denote by $\#T$ the expected number of trades that the balanced fixed price double auction generates.*

Observe that the balanced fixed price double auction is a generalization of the mechanism of Theorem 1 that achieves for the bilateral trade setting a $2/r$-approximation of the optimal gain from trade. We note that the value $\#T$ is by definition equal to $n\overline{q}^B = m\overline{q}^S$.

The main result we prove in this section is as follows.

Theorem 4. *For all $\epsilon \in [0, 1]$, with probability at least $1 - 2/e^{\#T\epsilon^2/2}$, the balanced fixed price double auction achieves a gain from trade that is at least $(1-\epsilon)$ times the expected optimal gain from trade.*

Note that $\#T$, the expected number of trades of the balanced fixed price double auction, needs to exceed $2\ln(2)/\epsilon^2$ by any constant for the above theorem to yield a constant approximation guarantee. The value $\#T$ can be regarded as a property of the instance (n, m, f, g) on which the mechanism is run, and is equal to the value where the functions $n\overline{F}$ and mG cross each other. The requirement on $\#T$ is reasonably mild: For example, the above theorem says that when $\#T$ is at least 10, the balanced fixed price double auction yields an expected gain from trade that is a (<4)-approximation to the optimal gain from trade, by taking $\epsilon \approx 0.61$ (since $(1 - 2/e^{0.61^2 \cdot 5}) \cdot (1 - 0.61) > 0.25$). The theorem provides a constant approximation ratio for all instances where $\#T > 2\ln(2) \approx 1.38$, but grows unbounded as $\#T$ approaches $2\ln 2$ from above.

There is an interesting interpretation of this theorem in terms of large markets: Observe that increasing the number of buyers or sellers in the market also increases $\#T$. In particular, by increasing both the number of buyers and the number of sellers simultaneously, $\#T$ grows unboundedly. From our theorem we may therefore infer that the balanced fixed price double auction approximation approximates the gain from trade by a factor that goes to 1 as the market grows.

To prove the desired approximation property of the balanced fixed price double auction, we note that due to symmetry, we may assume that under the optimum allocation every buyer has the same a priori probability of trading with a seller, and every seller has the same a priori probability of trading with a buyer. This motivates the following definition.

Definition 4. *For a double auction setting* (n, m, f, g) *we define the values* q^S *as the probability that any buyer receives an item under the optimum allocation, and we define* q^S *as the probability that any seller loses her item under the optimum allocation. We define the prices* p^B *and* p^S *as the prices closest to* $\bar{p}$ *such that* $\overline{F}(p^B) = q^B$ *and* $G(p^S) = q^S$. *That is:* p^B *is such that a buyers' probability of her valuation exceeding* p^B *is equal to the probability of obtaining an item under the optimum allocation, and if there multiple such prices then* p^B *is defined as the unique one closest to* $\bar{p}$. *Likewise,* p^S *is such that a sellers' probability of her valuation being at most* p^S *is equal to the probability of losing her item under the optimum allocation. Lastly, we let OPT denote the expected gain from trade achieved by the optimum allocation.*

The values $\mathrm{GFT}(\bar{p})$, OPT, $\#T$, $\bar{p}$, $\bar{q}^B$, $\bar{q}^S$, p, q^B, and q^S all depend (like r) on the instance (n, m, f, g). We will leave this dependence implicit.

Theorem 4 can be proved by means of the following sequence of lemmas.

Lemma 2. *For every instance* (n, m, f, g) *of a double auction setting, the following property of the optimal allocation is satisfied.*

$$nq^B = mq^S.$$

The following lemma states that our price $\bar{p}$ always lies in between p^B and p^S.

Lemma 3. *For every instance* (n, m, f, g) *of a double auction setting,* $p^B \geq \bar{p} \geq p^S$ *or* $p^S \geq \bar{p} \geq p^B$.

The following lemma provides a useful bound on OPT.

Lemma 4. *For every instance* (n, m, f, g) *of a double auction setting, it holds that*

$$OPT \leq nq^B \mathbf{E}[v_1 \mid v_1 \geq p^B] - mq^S \mathbf{E}[w_1 \mid w_1 \leq p^S].$$

We then use the following technical lemma to bound OPT further.

Lemma 5. *For every instance* (n, m, f, g) *of a double auction setting, it holds that*

$$nq^B \mathbf{E}[v_1 \mid v_1 \geq p^B] - mq^S \mathbf{E}[w_1 \mid w_1 \leq p^S]$$
$$\leq n\bar{q}^B \mathbf{E}[v_1 \mid v_1 \geq \bar{p}] - m\bar{q}^S \mathbf{E}[w_1 \mid w_1 \leq \bar{p}].$$

Using the above lemmas, Theorem 4 can be proved by showing an appropriate bound on the gain from trade of the balanced fixed price double auction, along with applying a Chernoff bound.

Acknowledgements. We thank Tim Roughgarden for helpful discussions at the early stages of this work.

References

1. Blumrosen, L., Dobzinski, S.: Reallocation mechanisms. In: Proceedings of the 15th ACM Conference on Economics and Computation (EC), p. 617. ACM (2014)
2. Blumrosen, L., Dobzinski, S.: (Almost) Efficient Mechanisms for Bilateral Trading. ArXiv/CoRR, abs/1604.04876 (2016)
3. Blumrosen, L., Mizrahi, Y.: Approximating gains-from-trade in bilateral trading. In: Cai, Y., Vetta, A. (eds.) WINE 2016. LNCS, vol. 10123, pp. 400–413. Springer, Heidelberg (2016). https://doi.org/10.1007/978-3-662-54110-4_28
4. Brustle, J., Cai, Y., Wu, F., Zhao, M.: Approximating gains from trade in two-sided markets via simple mechanisms. In: Proceedings of the 2017 ACM Conference on Economics and Computation (EC), pp. 589–590 (2017)
5. Colini-Baldeschi, R., de Keijzer, B., Leonardi, S., Turchetta, S.: Approximately efficient double auctions with strong budget balance. In: Proceedings of the 27th ACM-SIAM Symposium on Discrete Algorithms (SODA), pp. 1424–1443. SIAM (2016)
6. Colini-Baldeschi, R., Goldberg, P.W., de Keijzer, B., Leonardi, S., Turchetta, S., Roughgarden, T.: Approximately efficient two-sided combinatorial auctions. In: Proceedings of the 18th ACM Conference on Economics and Computation (EC), pp. 591–608. ACM (2017)
7. Deng, X., Goldberg, P.W., Tang, B., Zhang, J.: Revenue maximization in a Bayesian double auction market. Theor. Comput. Sci. **539**, 1–12 (2014)
8. Deshmukh, K., Goldberg, A.V., Hartline, J.D., Karlin, A.R.: Truthful and competitive double auctions. In: Möhring, R., Raman, R. (eds.) ESA 2002. LNCS, vol. 2461, pp. 361–373. Springer, Heidelberg (2002). https://doi.org/10.1007/3-540-45749-6_34
9. Feldman, M., Gonen, R.: Markets with strategic multi-minded mediators. ArXiv/CoRR, abs/1603.08717 (2016)
10. Feldman, M., Gonen, R.: Online truthful mechanisms for multi-sided markets. CoRR, abs/1604.04859 (2016)
11. Gerstgrasser, M., Goldberg, P.W., Koutsoupias, E.: Revenue maximization for market intermediation with correlated priors. In: Gairing, M., Savani, R. (eds.) SAGT 2016. LNCS, vol. 9928, pp. 273–285. Springer, Heidelberg (2016). https://doi.org/10.1007/978-3-662-53354-3_22
12. Giannakopoulos, Y., Koutsoupias, E., Lazos, P.: Online Market Intermediation. ArXiv/CoRR, abs/1703.09279 (2017)
13. Gresik, T.A., Satterthwaite, M.A.: The rate at which a simple market converges to efficiency as the number of traders increases: an asymptotic result for optimal trading mechanisms. J. Econ. Theory **48**(1), 304–332 (1989)
14. McAfee, P.R.: A dominant strategy double auction. J. Econ. Theory **56**(2), 434–450 (1992)
15. McAfee, R.P.: The gains from trade under fixed price mechanisms. Appl. Econ. Res. Bull. **1**, 1–10 (2008)
16. Myerson, R.B., Satterthwaite, M.A.: Efficient mechanisms for bilateral trading. J. Econ. Theory **29**(2), 265–281 (1983)
17. Rustichini, A., Satterthwaite, M.A., Williams, S.R.: Convergence to efficiency in a simple market with incomplete information. Econometrica **62**(5), 1041–1063 (1994)
18. Satterthwaite, M.A., Williams, S.R.: The optimality of a simple market mechanism. Econometrica **70**(5), 1841–1863 (2002)

19. Segal-Halevi, E., Hassidim, A., Aumann, Y.: A random-sampling double-auction mechanism. ArXiv/CoRR, abs/1604.06210 (2016)
20. Segal-Halevi, E., Hassidim, A., Aumann, Y.: SBBA: a strongly-budget-balanced double-auction mechanism. In: Gairing, M., Savani, R. (eds.) SAGT 2016. LNCS, vol. 9928, pp. 260–272. Springer, Heidelberg (2016). https://doi.org/10.1007/978-3-662-53354-3_21

On Strong Equilibria and Improvement Dynamics in Network Creation Games

Tomasz Janus[1] and Bart de Keijzer[2(✉)]

[1] Faculty of Mathematics, Informatics and Mechanics, Institute of Informatics,
University of Warsaw, Warsaw, Poland
t.janus@mimuw.edu.pl
[2] Networks and Optimization Group, Centrum Wiskunde and Informatica (CWI),
Amsterdam, The Netherlands
keijzer@cwi.nl

Abstract. We study strong equilibria in network creation games. These form a classical and well-studied class of games where a set of players form a network by buying edges to their neighbors at a cost of a fixed parameter α. The cost of a player is defined to be the cost of the bought edges plus the sum of distances to all the players in the resulting graph. We identify and characterize various structural properties of strong equilibria, which lead to a characterization of the set of strong equilibria for all α in the range $(0, 2)$. For $\alpha > 2$, Andelman et al. [4] prove that a star graph in which every leaf buys one edge to the center node is a strong equilibrium, and conjecture that in fact *any* star is a strong equilibrium. We resolve this conjecture in the affirmative. Additionally, we show that when α is large enough ($\geq 2n$) there exist non-star trees that are strong equilibria. For the strong price of anarchy, we provide precise expressions when α is in the range $(0, 2)$, and we prove a lower bound of $3/2$ when $\alpha \geq 2$. Lastly, we aim to characterize under which conditions (coalitional) improvement dynamics may converge to a strong equilibrium. To this end, we study the (coalitional) finite improvement property and (coalitional) weak acyclicity property. We prove various conditions under which these properties do and do not hold. Some of these results also hold for the class of pure Nash equilibria.

1 Introduction

The Internet is a large-scale network that has emerged mostly from the spontaneous, distributed interaction of selfish agents. Understanding the process of creating of such networks is an interesting scientific problem. Insights into this process may help to understand and predict how networks emerge, change, and evolve. This holds in particular for social networks.

The field of game theory has developed a large number of tools and models to analyze the interaction of many independent agents. The Internet and many other networks can be argued to have formed through interaction between many strategic agents. It is therefore natural to use game theory to study the process of

© Springer International Publishing AG 2017
N. R. Devanur and P. Lu (Eds.): WINE 2017, LNCS 10674, pp. 161–176, 2017.
https://doi.org/10.1007/978-3-319-71924-5_12

network formation. Indeed, this has been the subject of study in many research papers, e.g. [1,2,6,14–16,22], to mention only a few of them.

We focus here on the classical network creation model of [15], which is probably the class of network formation game that is most prominently studied by algorithmic game theorists. This model stands out due to its simplicity and elegance: It is simply defined as a game on n players, where each player may choose an arbitrary set of edges that connects herself to a subset of other players, so that a graph forms where the vertices are the players. Buying any edge costs a fixed amount $\alpha \in \mathbb{R}$, which is the same for every player. Now, the cost of a player is defined as the total cost of set of edges she bought, plus the sum of distances to all the other players in the graph. A network creation game is therefore determined by two parameters: α and n.

Another reason for why these network creation games are an ineresting topic of study, are the surprisingly challenging questions that emerge from this simple class of games. For example, it is (as of writing) unknown whether the *price of anarchy* of these network creation games is bounded by a constant, where the term price of anarchy is defined as the factor by which the total cost of a pure Nash equilibrium is away from the minimum possible total cost [20,21].

In the present work, we study *strong equilibria*, which are a refinement of the pure Nash equilibrium solution concept. Strong equilibria are defined as pure Nash equilibria that are resilient against strategy changes that are made collectively by arbitrary *sets* of players, in addition to strategy changes that are made by *individual* players (see [5]). Generally, such an equilibrium may not exist, since this is already the case for pure Nash equilibria. On the other hand, in case they do exist, then strong equilibria are extremely robust, and they are likely to describe the final outcome of a game in case they are, in a realistic sense, "easy to attain" for the players. Fortunately, as [4] points out, in network creation games, strong equilibria are guaranteed to exist except in a very limited number of cases. The combination of the facts that strong equilibria are robust, and are almost always guaranteed to exist, calls for a detailed study of these equilibria in network creation games, which is what we do in the present work.

We provide in this paper a complete characterization of the set of all strong equilibria for $\alpha \in (0,2)$. Moreover, for $\alpha > 2$ we prove in the affirmative the conjecture of [4] that any strategy profile that forms a star graph (i.e., a tree of depth 1) is a strong equilibrium. We also show that for large enough α (namely, for $\alpha \geq 2n$), there exist strong equilibria that result in trees that are not stars.

The price of anarchy restricted to strong equilibria is called the *strong price of anarchy*. This notion was introduced in [4], where also the strong price of anarchy of network creation games was studied first. The authors prove there that the strong price of anarchy is at most 2. We contribute to the understanding of the strong price of anarchy by providing a sequence of examples of strong equilibria where the strong price of anarchy converges to 3/2, thereby providing the first non-trivial lower bound (to the best of our knowledge).

Regarding the reachability and the likelihood for the players to actually attain a strong equilibrium, we study the question whether they can be reached by *response dynamics*, i.e., the process where we start from any strategy profile, and we repeatedly let a player or a set of players make a change of strategies that is beneficial for each player in the set, i.e., decreases their cost. In particular, we are interested in whether network creation games posess the *coalitional finite improvement property* (that is: whether such response dynamics are guaranteed to result in a strong equilibrium), and the *coalitional weak acyclicity property* (that is: whether there exists a sequence of coalitional strategy changes that ends in a strong equilibrium when starting from any strategy profile). We prove various conditions under which these properties are satisfied. Roughly, we show that coalitional weak acyclicity holds when $\alpha \in (0, 1]$ or when starting from a strategy profile that forms a tree (for $\alpha \in (0, n/2]$), but that the coalitional finite improvement property is unfortunately not satisfied for any α. Some of these results hold for pure Nash equilibria as well.

1.1   Our Contributions

A key publication that is strongly related to our work is [4], where the authors study the existence of strong equilibria in network creation games. The authors prove that the strong price of anarchy of network creation games does not exceed 2 and provide insights into the structure and existence of strong equilibria. This is to the best of our knowledge the only paper studying strong equilibria in network creation games. Let us therefore summarize how the present paper complements and contributes to the results in [4]: First, we provide additional results on the strong equilibrium structure, such that together with the results from [4] we obtain a characterization of strong equilibria for $\alpha \in (0, 2)$. Furthermore, in [4] it was conjectured that all strategy profiles that form a star (and such that no edge is bought by two players at the same time) are strong equilibria. We answer this conjecture positively. Because [4] does not provide examples of strong equilibria that are not stars (for $\alpha > 2$), this may suggest the conjecture that *all* strong equilibria form a star for $\alpha > 2$. We show however that the latter is not true: We provide a family of examples of strong equilibria which form trees of diameter four (hence, not stars). More interestingly, the latter sequence of examples has a price of anarchy that converges to $3/2$, thereby providing (again, to the best of our knowledge) the first non-trivial lower bound on the strong price of anarchy. Related to this set of results, we want to mention the following interesting open questions for future research: (i) What is the exact strong price of anarchy of the class of network creation games? Our work shows that it must lie in the interval $[3/2, 2]$. (ii) Does there exist a non-star strong equilibrium for $\alpha \in (2, 2n)$? (iii) Do there exist strong equilibria that form trees of arbitrarily high diameter, and do there exist strong equilibria that are not trees?

A second theme of our paper is to investigate under which circumstances the coalitional finite improvement and coalitional weak acyclicity properties are satisfied, as satisfying those properties contribute to the credibility of strong equilibria as a realistic solution concept. We show to this end that coalitional weak acyclicity always holds for $\alpha \in (0, 1]$ and holds for $\alpha \in (1, n/2)$ in case the starting strategy profile is a tree. We prove on the negative side that for all α

there exists a number of players n such that the coalitional finite improvement property does not hold. The only special case for which we manage to establish existence of the coalitional finite improvement property is for $n = 3$ and $\alpha > 1$. With regard to convergence of response dynamics to strong equilibria, an interesting question that we leave open is whether the coalitional weak acyclicity property holds for $\alpha > n/2$, and for $\alpha \in (1, n/2)$ when starting at non-tree strategy profiles. We will see throughout that some of our results on these properties also hold for the set of pure Nash equilibria.

An overview of results is summarized in the tables below. Table 1 provides an overview for our characterization and structure theorems for strong equilibria, Table 2 shows our bounds on the strong price of anarchy, and Table 3 shows our results on the finite improvement and weak acyclicity properties of network creation games. Due to space constraints, the proofs of many of our results have been omitted and will be published in a full version of the paper.

Table 1. Overview of strong equilibria characterization results and structural results.

	$\alpha \in (0,1)$	$\alpha = 1$	$\alpha \in (1,2)$	$\alpha \geq 2$
Strong equilibria	Characterized (in [4])	Characterized (Theorem 1)	Characterized (Proposition 1)	Every star is a strong equilibrium (Theorem 2), existence of non-star strong equilibria (Theorem 3)

Table 2. Overview of bounds on the strong price of anarchy.

	$\alpha \in (0,1)$	$\alpha = 1$	$\alpha \in (1,2)$	$\alpha \geq 2$
Strong price of anarchy	1 (Trivial)	10/9 if $n \leq 4$ and $(3n+2)/3n$ if $n \geq 5$ (Theorem 4)	$(2\alpha+8)/(3\alpha+6)$ if $n = 3$, and $(4\alpha+16)/(6\alpha+12)$ if $n = 4$ (Proposition 3)	At least 3/2 (Theorem 5) and at most 2 [4]

Table 3. Summary of results on the c-FIP and c-weak acyclicity of network creation games.

	$\alpha \in (0,1)$	$\alpha = 1$	$\alpha \in (1,2)$	$\alpha = 2$	$\alpha > 2$
c-FIP	Negative (Lemma 6)	Negative (Lemma 6)	Negative (Lemma 6)	Negative (Lemma 6)	Negative (in [9])
			Positive for $n = 3$ (Lemma 4)		
c-weak acyclicity	Positive (Corollary of Lemma 8)	Positive (Proposition 9)	Positive with respect to trees for $\alpha \in (1, n/2)$ (Lemma 11)		

2   Related Literature

We discussed already extensively the works [4,15]. The latter is the article in which network creation games were first defined. Moreover, [15] conjectured that there exists an $A \in \mathbb{R}_{\geq 0}$ such that all non-transient equilibria (where *transience* stands for a particular notion of instability) are trees for $\alpha \geq A$.

This conjecture was subsequently disproved by [1], where the authors construct non-tree equilibria for abitrarily high α. These equilbiria are *strict* (i.e., for no player there is a deviation that keeps her cost unchanged) and therefore non-transient, and their construction uses finite affine planes. In this paper, the authors moreover show that the price of anarchy is constant for $\alpha \leq \sqrt{n}$ and for $\alpha \geq 12n \log n$, as for the second case they prove that any pure equilibrium is a tree. In [27], the latter bound was improved, as it was shown there that for $\alpha \geq 273n$ all pure equilibria are trees. Later on, in [24], this was further improved by showing that it even holds for $\alpha \geq 65n$. Very recently, in [3], further progress has been made in this direction by showing that every pure Nash equilibrium is a tree already when $\alpha > 17n$, and that the price of anarchy is bounded by a constant for $\alpha > 9n$. In [12], some constant bounds on the price of anarchy were improved, and it was shown that for $\alpha \leq n^{1-\epsilon}$ the price of anarchy is constant, for all $\epsilon \geq 0$. It remains an open question whether the price of anarchy is constant for all $\alpha \in \mathbb{R}_{\geq 0}$. In particular, the best known bound on the price of anarchy for $\alpha \in [n^{1-\epsilon}, 9n]$ is $2^{O(\sqrt{\log n})}$, shown in [12]. For all other choices of α the price of anarchy is known to be constant. The master's thesis [25] provides some simplified proofs for some of the above facts, and proves that if an equilibrium graph has bounded degree, then the price of anarchy is bounded by a constant. It also studies some related computational questions.

Many other variants of network creation games have been considered as well. A version where disconnected players incur a finite cost rather than an infinite one was studied in [9]. In [1], a version is introduced where the distance cost of a player i to another player j is weighted by some number w_{ij}. A special case of this weighted model was proposed in [26]. The paper [12] introduces a version of the game where the distance cost of a player is defined the *maximum* distance from i to any other player (instead of the sum of distances), and studies the price of anarchy for these games. Further results on those games can be found in [27]. Another natural variant of a cost sharing game is one where both endpoints of an edge can contribute to its creation, as proposed in [26], or must share its creation cost equally as proposed in [11] and further investigated in [12]. In [6], a version of the game is studied where the edges are directed, and the distance of a player i to another player j is the minimum length of a directed path from i to j. The literature on these games and generalizations thereof (see e.g., [8,13,14]) concerns existence of equilibria and the properties of response dynamics. See [7,16–18] for another undirected network creation model and properties of pure equilibria in those models. Further, in the very recent paper [10], a variant of network creation games is studied where the cost of buying an edge to a player is proportional to the number of neighbors of that player.

In [2], the authors analyze the outcomes of the game under the assumption that the players consider deviations by swapping adjacent edges. Better response dynamics under this assumption have been studied in [22]. A modified version of this model is introduced in [26], where players can only swap their *own* edges. The authors prove some structural results on the pure equilibria that can then arise. Furthermore, in [23] the deviation space is enriched by allowing the players to *add* edges, and various price of anarchy type bounds are established under this assumption. In [19], the dynamics of play in various versions of network creation games are further investigated.

3   Preliminaries

A *network creation game* Γ is a game played by $n \geq 3$ players where the strategy set of $\mathcal{S}_i$ of a player $i \in [n] = \{1, \ldots, n\}$ is given by $\mathcal{S}_i = \{s : s \subseteq [n] \setminus \{i\}\}$. That is, each player chooses a subset of other players. Let $\mathcal{S} = \times_{i \in [n]} \mathcal{S}_i$ be the strategy profiles of Γ and for a subset $K \subseteq [n]$ of players let $\mathcal{S}_K = \times_{i \in K} \mathcal{S}_i$. Given a strategy profile $s \in \mathcal{S}$, we define $G(s)$ as the undirected graph with vertex set $[n]$ and edge set $\{\{i, j\} : j \in s_i \lor i \in s_j\}$. For a graph G on vertex set $[n]$, we denote by $d_G(i, j)$ the length of the shortest path from i to j in G (and we define the distance between two disconnected vertices as infinity).

The cost of player i under s is given by $c_i(s) = c_i^b(s_i) + c_i^d(s)$, where $c_i^b(s_i) = \alpha |s_i|$ is referred to as the *building cost*, $\alpha \in \mathbb{R}_{\geq 0}$ is a player-independent constant, and $c_i^d(s) = \sum_{j=1}^n d_{G(s)}(i, j)$ is referred to as the *distance cost*. The interpretation given to this game is that the players buy edges to other players and that creates a network. Buying a single edge costs α. The shortest distance $d_{G(s)}(i, j)$ to each other player j is furthermore added to the cost of a player i. We denote a network creation game by the pair (n, α)

For a strategy profile $s \in \mathcal{S}$ let $d(s) = \sum_i c_i^d(s)$. The social cost of strategy profile s, denoted $C(s)$, is defined as the sum of all individual costs: $C(s) = \sum_{i \in [n]} c_i(s) = \alpha \sum_i |s_i| + d(s)$.

We study the *strong equilibria* of this game. A *strong equilibrium* of an n-player cost minimization game Γ with strategy profile set $\mathcal{S} = \times_{i=1}^n \mathcal{S}_i$ is an $s \in \mathcal{S}$ such that for all $K \subseteq [n]$ and for all $s'_K \in \mathcal{S}_K$ there exists a player $i \in K$ such that, $c_i(s) \leq c_i(s'_K, s_{-K})$, where c_i is the cost function of player i and (s'_K, s_{-K}) denotes the vector obtained from s by replacing the $|K|$ elements at index set K with the elements s'_K. (A *pure Nash equilibrium* is a strategy profile that satisfies the latter condition only for singleton K.) Strong equilibria are guaranteed to exist in almost all network creation games, as we will explain later.

We are interested in determining the *strong price of anarchy* [4]. The *strong price of anarchy* of a network creation game Γ is the ratio $\mathrm{PoA}(\Gamma) = \max\{C(s)/C(s^*) : s \in \mathrm{SE}\}$, where s^* is a *social optimum*, i.e., a strategy profile that minimizes the social cost. Furthermore SE is the set of strong equilibria of the game.

A strategy profile s is called *rational* if there is no player pair $i, j \in [n]$ such that $j \in s_i$ and $i \in s_j$. It is clear that all pure Nash equilibria (and thus all strong equilibria) of any network creation game are rational, as are all the social optima. When s is a rational strategy profile, the social cost can be written as $C(s) = \alpha|E(G(s))| + d(s)$, where $E(G(s))$ denotes the edge set of the graph $G(s)$.

We write $\deg_{G(s)}(i)$ to denote the degree of player i in graph $G(s)$, and we denote by $\mathrm{diam}(G(s))$ the diameter of $G(s)$. We define the *free-riding* function $f : \mathcal{S} \times [n] \to \mathbb{N}$ by the formula $f(s, i) = \deg_{G(s)}(i) - |s_i|$. For any strategy profile $s \in \mathcal{S}$ we have the following lower bound for the cost of player i,

$$c_i(s) \geq 2n - 2 - \deg_{G(s)}(i) + |s_i|\alpha = 2n - 2 - f(s, i) + |s_i|(\alpha - 1). \quad (1)$$

Moreover, we see that in case s is rational,

$$\sum_{i \in [n]} |s_i| = |E| = \sum_{i \in [n]} f(s, i). \quad (2)$$

Graph theory notions. We define an *n-star* to be a tree of n vertices with diameter 2, i.e., it is a tree where one vertex is connected to all other vertices. It is straightforward to verify that (1) is tight when $G(s)$ is an n-star, and (more generally) when $G(s)$ has diameter at most 2. We denote by K_n the complete undirected graph on vertex set $[n]$. We denote by C_n the undirected cycle on vertex set $[n]$. We denote by P_n the undirected path on vertex set $[n]$. Lastly, we define a *centroid* vertex of a tree $T = (V, E)$ as a vertex $v \in V$ that minimizes $\max\{|V_i| : (V_i, E_i) \in \mathcal{C}_{T-v}\}$, where $\mathcal{C}_{T-v}$ denotes the set of connected components of the subgraph of T induced by $V \setminus \{v\}$.

Coalitional improvement dynamics. A sequence of strategy profiles $(s^1, s^2, \ldots)$ is called a *path* if for every $k > 1$ there exists a player $i \in [n]$ such that $s^k = (s'_i, s^{k-1}_{-i})$. We call a path an *improvement path* if it is maximal and for all $k > 1$ holds $c_i(s^k) < c_i(s^{k-1})$ where i is the player who deviated from s^{k-1}. We say that it is an *improvement cycle* if additionally there exists a constant T such that $s^{k+T} = s^k$ for all $k \geq 1$. A sequence of strategies $(s^1, s^2, \ldots)$ is called a *best response improvement path* if for all $k > 1$ and all i such that $s^k_i \neq s^{k-1}_i$ we have $c_i(s^k) < c_i(s^{k-1})$ and there is no $s'_i \in \mathcal{S}_i$ such that $c_i(s'_i, s^k_{-i}) < c_i(s^k)$ (that is: s^k_i is a *best response* to s^{k-1}_{-i}). A sequence of strategies $(s^1, s^2, \ldots)$ is called a *coalitional improvement path* if for all $k > 1$ and all i such that $s^k_i \neq s^{k-1}_i$ we have $c_i(s^k) < c_i(s^{k-1})$.

A game has the *(coalitional) finite improvement property ((c-)FIP)* if every (coalitional) improvement path is finite. A game has *finite best response property (FBRP)* if every best response improvement path is finite. We call a game *(c-) weakly acyclic* if for every $s \in \mathcal{S}$ there exists a finite (coalitional) improvement path starting from s. Lastly, we call a network creation game *(c-)weakly acyclic with respect to a class of graphs $\mathcal{G}$* if for every $s \in \mathcal{S}$ such that $G(s) \in \mathcal{G}$, there exists a (coalitional) finite improvement path starting from s.

4   Structural Properties of Strong Equilibria

We provide in this section various results that imply a full characterization of strong equilibria for $\alpha \in (0, 2)$, and we resolve a conjecture of [4] by showing that any rational strategy $s \in \mathcal{S}$ such that $G(s)$ is a star is a strong equilibrium for all $\alpha \geq 2$. Moreover, we give a family of examples of strategy profiles that form trees of diameter 4 (hence do not form stars) and are strong equilibria when $\alpha \geq 2n$. First, for $\alpha \in (0, 1)$ the strong equilibrium set is straighforward to derive, as has been pointed out in [4]: in this case a strategy profile is a strong equilibrium if and only if it is rational and forms the complete graph. It is easy to see that this characterization also holds for the set of Nash equilibria.

For $\alpha = 1$, the situation is more complex. First, we can show that the following lemma holds for all $\alpha < 2$.

Lemma 1. *Fix $\alpha < 2$ and suppose that $s \in \mathcal{S}$ is a strong equilibrium. For each sequence of players $(i_0, i_1, \ldots, i_k = i_0)$ such that $k \geq 3$ in $G(s)$ there exists an $t \in \{0, \ldots, k-1\}$ such that $(i_t, i_{t+1}) \in E(G(s))$. In other words, the complement of $G(s)$ is a forest.*

Therefore, if $\alpha < 2$ and $s \in \mathcal{S}$ is a strong equilibrium, then there is no independent set of size 3 in $G(s)$. Also, if $\alpha < 2$ and $|V| \geq 4$, then a strategy profile $s \in \mathcal{S}$, such that $G(s)$ is a star is not a strong equilibrium. Since when $\alpha \in [1, 2)$, a rational strategy profile that forms a star is a Nash equilibrium, this implies that the pure Nash equilibria and strong equilibria do not coincide.

In order to characterize the strong equilibria for $\alpha = 1$, we first provide a characterization of the pure Nash equilibria.

Lemma 2. *For $\alpha = 1$, a strategy profile $s \in \mathcal{S}$ is a Nash equilibrium if and only if s is rational and $G(s)$ has diameter at most 2.*

The following theorem then characterizes the set of strong equilibria for $\alpha = 1$.

Theorem 1. *For $\alpha = 1$, a strategy profile $s \in \mathcal{S}$ is a strong equilibrium if and only if s is rational, $G(s)$ has diameter at most 2, and the complement of $G(s)$ is a forest.*

For $\alpha \in (1, 2)$, it was shown in [4] that strong equilibria do not exist for $n \geq 5$. It can be shown that for $n = 3$ the set of strong equilibria are the rational strategy profiles that form the 3-star. (Hence, all pure Nash equilibria are strong equilibria in this case). For $n = 4$ we observe that the only strong equilibria are those that form the cycle on 4 vertices such that every player buys exactly one edge. Thus, the following proposition completes our characterization of strong equilibria for $\alpha \in (1, 2)$.

Proposition 1. *Let $\alpha \in (1, 2)$ and let $s \in \mathcal{S}$. Then: (i) If $n = 3$, strategy profile s is a strong equilibrium if and only if s is rational and $G(s)$ is a 3-star. (ii) If $n = 4$, strategy profile s is a strong equilibrium if and only if s is rational, $|s_i| = 1$ for all i, and $G(s)$ is a cycle. (iii) If $n \geq 5$, s is not a strong equilibrium.*

Next, we prove the following conjecture of [4].

Theorem 2. *Let $\alpha \geq 2$ and $s \in \mathcal{S}$. If s is rational and $G(s)$ is a star, then s is a strong equilibrium.*

The proof of this theorem relies on two lemmas. The first lemma provide bounds on the free-riding function of player sets who manage to deviate profitably, while the second lemma bounds the change in the free-riding function for players who do not deviate.

Lemma 3. *Let $\alpha \geq 2$ let $s \in \mathcal{S}$ be a rational strategy profile such that $G(s)$ is a star. Let $K \subseteq [n]$ be a set of players and let $s' = (s'_K, s_{-K})$ be a profitable deviation for K, i.e., for all $i \in K$, it holds that $c_i(s'_K, s_{-K}) < c_i(s)$. Then for every $i \in K$ such that $\deg_{G(s)}(i) = 1$ it holds that $f(s', i) > f(s, i)$ and $f(s', i) - f(s, i) \geq |s'_i| - |s_i| + 1$.*

Lemma 4. *Let $\alpha \geq 2$ and let $s \in \mathcal{S}$ be a rational strategy profile such that $G(s)$ is a star. Let $K \subseteq [n]$ be a player set and $s' = (s'_K, s_{-K})$ be a strategy profile that decreases the costs of all members of K. Then $\sum_{j \in [n] \setminus K} f(s', j) - f(s, j) > -|K|$. Moreover, if K contains a vertex i such that $\deg_{G(s)}(i) > 1$ then $\sum_{j \in [n] \setminus K} f(s', j) - f(s, j) \geq 0$.*

Proof of Theorem 2. Let $s \in \mathcal{S}$ be a strategy profile that is rational such that $G(s)$ is a star. It is easy to see that s is a Nash equilibrium (see also [15]). Suppose that $K \in [n]$ and $s' \in \mathcal{S}_K$ are such that strategy profile $s' = (s'_K, s_{-K})$ decreases the costs of all players in K. Let $k = |K|$, we have two cases to consider.

If $\deg_{G(s)}(i) = 1$ for all $i \in K$, then $\sum_{i \in K}(f(s', i) - f(s, i)) \geq k + \sum_{i \in K}(|s'_i| - |s_i|) = k + \sum_{i \in [n]}(|s'_i| - |s_i|) = k + \sum_{i \in [n]}(f(s', i) - f(s, i))$, where the inequality follows from Lemma 3 and the last equality follows from (2). Hence $\sum_{i \in [n] \setminus K} f(s', i) - f(s, i) \leq -k$, which is the contradiction with Lemma 4.

If K contains the center vertex i (i.e., the vertex for which $\deg_{G(s)}(i) > 1$), then $\sum_{j \in K \setminus \{i\}}(f(s', j) - f(s, j)) \geq (k - 1) + \sum_{j \in K \setminus \{i\}}(|s'_j| - |s_j|) = (k - 1) + \sum_{j \in [n]}(|s'_j| - |s_j|) - (|s'_i| - |s_i|) = (k-1) + \sum_{j \in [n]}(f(s', j) - f(s, j)) - (|s'_i| - |s_i|)$, where again the inequality follows from Lemma 3 and the last equality follows from (2).

Since i is a central vertex, we have $c_i^d(s') \geq c_i^d(s)$. Moreover, $i \in K$, hence $c_i(s') < c_i(s)$. This implies that $c_i^b(s') < c_i^b(s)$ or equivalently $|s'_i| < |s_i|$. So $\sum_{j \in K \setminus \{i\}}(f(s', j) - f(s, j)) \geq k + \sum_{j \in [n]}(f(s', j) - f(s, j))$. Thus: $-k \geq \sum_{j \in [n] \setminus K}(f(s', j) - f(s, j)) + (f(s', i) - f(s, i)) \geq f(s', i) - f(s, i)$, where the last inequality follows from Lemma 4. On the other hand we have $f(s', i) - f(s, i) \geq -(k - 1)$, since the change from s to s' could have removed at most $k - 1$ edges going to player i, which is a contradiction. $\square$

Next, for $\alpha > 2$, we present a family of strong equilibria none of which forms a star. The graphs resulting from these strong equilibria are trees of diameter 4.

Example 1. Our examples are paramatrized by two values $A \in \mathbb{N}$, $A \geq 4$ and $k \in \mathbb{N}$. Let $\alpha \geq 2n$, and let $n = Ak + 2$. In the following strategy profile s the only players who buy edges are $1, \ldots, A-1$ and n, i.e., for all $i \in [n]$, $A \leq i < n$, it holds that $s_i = \varnothing$. We denote player n by R. The total number of edges bought by players $\{1, \ldots, A-1, R\}$ is $n - 1 = Ak + 1$ such that $G(s)$ is a tree. $L_1 = \{A, A+1, \ldots, (A-1)k\}$ and $L_2 = \{(A-1)k+1, \ldots, n-1\}$ denote the remaining $k+1$ players who do not buy edges. The strategy sets are defined as follows: Player R buys edges to L_2. Each player in $[A-1]$ buys an edge to $k-1$ players of L_1 in such a way that the degree in $G(s)$ equals 1 for every player in L_1. Moreover, each player in $[A-1]$ buys an edge to R. Thus, each player in $\{1, \ldots, A-1\}$ buys k edges, R buys $k+1$ edges, and all the remaining players (i.e., in L_1 and L_2) buy no edges and are leaves in $G(s)$. Figure 1 depicts this strategy profile.

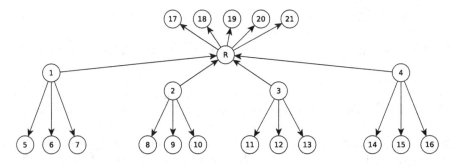

Fig. 1. Depiction of the graph $G(s)$ formed by the strong equilibrium s. The graph $G(s)$ is a is a tree of diameter 4. Strategy profile s is a strong equilibrium for $\alpha \geq 2n$ and $n = A \cdot k + 2$ where $A \in \mathbb{N}$, $A \geq 4$ is the number of players that buy edges and $k \in \mathbb{N}$. One player (called R) buys $k+1$ edges to leaves. The remaining $A-1$ players (that buy edges) each buy $k-1$ edges to leaves and one edge to R. In the depicted instance of the example we have: $A = 5$, $k = 4$, $L_1 = \{5, 6, \ldots, 16\}$, $L_2 = \{17, 18, \ldots, 21\}$ and the set of players buying edges is $\{1, \ldots, 4\} \cup \{R\}$.

Despite that s is relatively easy to define, establishing that s is a strong equilibrium is challenging.

Theorem 3. *If $\alpha \geq 2n$, strategy profile s forms a (non-star) tree and is a strong equilibrium.*

Proof. In s, there are four different types of node: The root R, the players $1 \ldots, A-1$, the leaves L_1, and the leaves L_2. The distance costs for each of these types are as follows.

$$c_i^d(s) = \begin{cases} 2n - A - k - 2 & \text{if } i = R & \text{(3a)} \\ 3n - A - 3k - 2 & \text{if } i \in [A - 1] & \text{(3b)} \\ 3n - A - k - 4 & \text{if } i \in L_2 & \text{(3c)} \\ 4n - A - 3k - 4 & \text{if } i \in L_1 & \text{(3d)} \end{cases}$$

Proposition 2. *Let $s \in S$. For all $i \in [n]$, $c_i^d(s) \geq= 2n - 2 - deg_{G(s)}(i)$.*

To show that s is a strong equilibrium, suppose for contradiction that $K \subseteq [n]$ and $s_K' \in S_K$ are such that in $s' = (s_K', s_{-K})$ it holds that $c_i(s') < c_i(s)$ for all $i \in K$. Under this assumption, using $(3a - 3d)$, we show that no player in K buys more edges under s' than it does under s.

Lemma 5. *For all $i \in K$, it holds that $|s_i'| \leq |s_i|$.*

The proofs of this lemma and the following lemma are omitted. Since $G(s)$ is a tree, it has the minimum number of edges among all connected graphs. Combining this with the lemma above yields that every player buys in s' *exactly* as many edges as in s.

Corollary 1. *Graph $G(s')$ is a tree, and for all $i \in [n]$, it holds that $|s_i'| = |s_i|$.*

Lemma 6. *Player R is not in K.*

Denote by $L_K = \{j \in L_1 \mid \exists i \in K : j \in s_i\}$ the leaves in L_1 that are directly connected to a player in K in $G(s)$. Let C_R be the players in the connected component of $G(\varnothing, s_{-K})$ containing R. Let $i \in \arg_{i'} \max\{d_{G(s')}(i', C_R) : i' \in K\}$ be a player in K that has the highest distance to C_R among all players in K.

Lemma 7. *The distance $d_{G(s')}(i, C_R)$ of i to C_R in $G(s')$ is as least 2.*

In s, the distance from i to C_R is 1. As C_R contains at least $k + 2$ vertices, by deviating from s to s' the distance increase of player i to C_R is at least $k + 1$. We complete the proof of Theorem 3 by showing that by deviating from s to s', the distance decrease of player i to the players of $[n] \setminus C_R$ does not exceed $k + 1$. This is sufficient, as it implies that $c_i(s') \geq c_i(s)$ which contradicts that $i \in K$. To see this, observe that in $G(s)$ player i has in his neighborhood at most one player in K. If in $G(s')$ there are two or more players in K in i's neighborhood, then one of them is further away from C_R than i (contradicting the definition of i), or there is a cycle in $G(s')$ (contradicting Corollary 1). Let us separately compute the distance improvement to nodes in L_K and to nodes in K:

- In $G(s)$, the distance from i to all $|K| - 1$ players in K is 2. In $G(s')$ the distance from i to at most one player in K is 1, while at least $K - 2$ player are at distance 2 from i. Therefore, the total decrease in distance from i to players in K is at most 1.

- In $G(s)$, there are $k-1$ players of L_K at distance 1 from i, and the remaining $|L_K| - k + 1$ players of L_K are at distance 3 from i. In $G(s')$ there are at most k players at distance 1 from i, there are at most $k-1$ players at distance 2 from i (since the unique player i' of K that is directly connected to i (and buys the edge (i', i)) has at most $k-1$ connections to L_K). Hence at least $|L_K| - 2k + 1$ players of L_K are at distance 3 from i. Therefore, the total decrease in distance from i to players in L_K is at most $(k-1) + (3|L_K| - 3k + 3) - k - (2k - 2) - (3|L_K| - 6k + 3) = k + 1$.

It follows that by deviating from s to s', the maximum possible distance improvement for i to players in $[n] \setminus C_R$ is $k + 2$, while the distance to at least $k + 2$ vertices of C_R increases by 1. As $|s_i'| = |s_i|$ by Corollary 1, the building cost of i is not affected by the deviation, so the deviation is not profitable for i; a contradiction. $\qquad\square$

5   Bounds on the Strong Price of Anarchy

In this section we analyze the strong price of anarchy of network creation games. First, for $\alpha < 2$, we provide exact expressions on the strong price of anarchy using the various insights of Sect. 4. Subsequently, for higher values of α, we provide a sequence of examples that converges to a price of anarchy of $3/2$. This shows that the strong price of anarchy of the complete class of network creation games must lie in the interval $[3/2, 2]$, due to the upper bound of 2 established in [4]. It is trivial that for $\alpha \in (0, 1)$, the strong price of anarchy is 1. This holds because any rational strategy profile that forms the complete graph minimizes the social cost. The picture turns out to be relatively complex for $\alpha = 1$.

Theorem 4. *For $\alpha = 1$, the strong price of anarchy is $10/9$ if $n \in \{3, 4\}$, and the strong price of anarchy is $(3n + 2)/3n$ if $n \geq 5$.*

Proof. By Theorem 1, for $\alpha = 1$ a strategy profile s is a strong equilibrium always if and only if it is rational and forms a graph of diameter at most 2 that is the complement of a forest. This means that vertices connected by an edge are distance 1 apart, and vertices not connected by an edge are distance 2 apart. A forest F has at most $n - 1$ edges, so we obtain the following bound on the social cost of a strong equilibrium: $\alpha(n(n-1)/2 - |F|) + 2(2|F| + n(n-1)/2 - |F|) = 3n(n-1)/2 + |F| \leq 3n(n-1)/2 + (n-1)$. This bound is achieved for $n \geq 5$ by taking for F any Hamiltonian path. Thus for $\alpha = 1$ and $n \geq 5$, given that the social optimum forms a complete graph, we obtain that the strong price of anarchy is $(3n(n-1)/2 + (n-1))/(3n(n-1)/2) = (3n(n-1) + 2(n-1))(3n(n-1)) = 3n + 2/3n$. For $n = 4$, the maximum size forest (such that the complement of it has diameter 2) has only 2 edges, and for $n = 3$ it has only 1 edge. Therefore, the strong price of anarchy for $\alpha = 1$ and $n \in \{3, 4\}$ equals $10/9$. $\qquad\square$

For $\alpha \in (1, 2)$, there exists no strong equilibrium if $n \geq 5$ (see [4]). Therefore, it remains to derive the strong equilibria for $\alpha \in (1, 2)$ and $n \in \{3, 4\}$.

Proposition 3. *For $\alpha \in (1,2)$ the strong price of anarchy is $(2\alpha + 8)/(3\alpha + 6)$ if $n = 3$, and the strong price of anarchy is $(4\alpha + 16)/(6\alpha + 12)$ if $n = 4$.*

For $\alpha > 2$ it seems very challenging to prove precise bounds on the strong price of anarchy. However, it is known that for $\alpha \geq 2$ the strong price of anarchy is at most 2 [4]. We now complement this bound by showing that for Example 1 (given in Sect. 4), the strong price of anarchy is at least $3/2$.

Theorem 5. *The price of anarchy of network creation games is at least 3/2.*

Proof. Let $x \geq 4$ and consider the strong equilibrium s given in Example 1, for $\alpha = 2n$ and $k = A = x$. The players in L_1 each have a distance cost of $4n - 4 - A - 3k = 4x^2 + 4 - x - 3x$. Since $|L_1| = (A-1)(k-1) = x^2 - 2x + 1$ the total distance cost of s is at least $4x^4 - 12x^3 + 16x^2 - 12x + 4$. Moreover, $G(s)$ is a tree, so the total building cost of s equals $(n-1)\alpha = (Ak+1)2(Ak+2) = 2x^4 + 6x^2 + 4$. Therefore, the social cost of s satisfies $C(s) \geq 6x^4 - 12x^3 + 22x^2 - 12x + 4$.

For $\alpha \geq 2$, the social optimum forms an n-star. Thus, the optimal social cost is $(n-1)\alpha + 2(n-1)^2 = 2n(n-1) + 2(n-1)^2 \leq 4n(n-1) = 4x^4 + 12x^2 + 8$. Combining these two bounds and taking x to infinity, we obtain that the strong price of anarchy is at least $\lim_{x \to \infty}(6x^4 - 12x^3 + 22x^2 - 12x + 4)/(4x^4 + 12x^2 + 8) = 3/2$. $\square$

6 Convergence of Coalitional Improvement Dynamics

In this section we study the c-FIP and coalitional weak acyclicity of network creation games. On the positive side, c-weak acyclicity holds for $\alpha \in (0,2)^1$ and for all $\alpha \leq n/2$ in case the starting strategy profile forms a tree. On the other hand, our negative results encompass that the c-FIP is not satisfied for any $\alpha.^2$ First, running best response dynamics on a network creation game ends up in a pure Nash equilibrium.

Lemma 8. *For $\alpha < 1$, every network creation game has the FBRP.*

From Lemma 8 and the fact that Nash equilibria and strong equilibria coincide for $\alpha < 1$ (as we also pointed out in Sect. 4), we obtain as a corollary that for $\alpha < 1$, every network creation game is c-weakly acyclic. For $\alpha = 1$ we can also show weak acyclicity and c-weak acyclicity.

Lemma 9. *For $\alpha = 1$, every network creation game is weakly acyclic and c-weakly acyclic.*

We may also prove that for $\alpha \in (1,2)$ and $n \in \{3,4\}$, network creation games are c-weakly acyclic. (Recall that for $\alpha \in (1,2)$ and $n \geq 5$, strong equilibria do not exist.)

---

[1] Except for $\alpha \in (1,2)$ and $n \geq 5$, in which case we know that strong equilibria do not exist.

[2] An exception to this is that we can prove that the coalitional finite improvement property is satisfied for the very special case that $\alpha > 1$ and $n = 3$.

Proposition 4. *For $\alpha > 1$ and $n = 3$ network creation games have the c-FIP. For $\alpha \in (1,2)$ and $n = 4$, network creation games are c-weakly acyclic.*

For $\alpha \leq n/2$ we can show that c-weak acyclicity is satisfied as long as our starting strategy profile forms a tree. This result relies on the following lemma about centroid vertices of trees.

Lemma 10. *Let $T = (V, E)$ be a tree, and let $v \in V$ be a centroid vertex of T. It holds that $\max\{|V_i| : (V_i, E_i) \in \mathcal{C}_{T-v}\} \leq (1/2)|V|$.*

Lemma 11. *For $\alpha \in (1, n/2)$, let $s \in \mathcal{S}$ be such that $G(s)$ is a tree. Then there exists an improvement path resulting in a strong equilibrium. Hence, every network creation game is weakly acyclic and c-weakly acyclic with respect to trees.*

Proof. Let $s \in \mathcal{S}$ and suppose $G(s)$ is a tree. Let $v \in [n]$ be a centroid vertex of $G(s)$. Consider the following sequence of deviations. If there is a player i such that $d_{G(s)}(i, v) \geq 2$, then $s_i' = s_i \cup \{v\}$ and $s' = (s_i', s_{-i})$. Repeat this step with $s = s'$ until $d_{G(s)}(i, v) = 1$ for all $i \in V \setminus \{v\}$. Observe that since v is a centroid vertex of $G(s)$, by Lemma 10, player i decreases the distance to at least $n/2$ players by at least 1 by buying an edge to v. This exceeds the cost of α, hence this deviation is profitable. Otherwise, if there is no player i such that $d_{G(s)}(i, v) \geq 2$, and $G(s)$ is not a star, then there are players $i, j \in [n]$ such that $i \neq v$, $j \neq v$ and $j \in s_i$, then let $s_i' = s_i \setminus \{j\}$. Repeat this step until $G(s)$ is a star. Observe that player i is better off by the strategy change. She saves $\alpha > 1$ in her building cost and her distance cost increases by only 1, since for each player not in i's neighborhood there is a shortest path through v. Hence the only loss is the distance increase between i and j. If s is rational after this sequence of deviations, then we have reached a strong equilibrium by Theorem 2. Otherwise there are i, j such that $i \in s_j$ and $j \in s_i$. We set $s_i' = s_i \setminus \{j\}$ and repeat this step until we reach a rational s. $\square$

However, we may show that in general, network creation games do not have the c-FIP, regardless of the choice of α.

Theorem 6. *For every α there exists a number of players n such that network creation game (n, α) does not have the c-FIP.*

This above theorem is proved by providing examples for $\alpha < 1, \alpha = 1, \alpha \in (1, 2)$, and $\alpha = 2$ separately. For $\alpha > 2$, the example in Theorem 1 of [9] implies that network creation games are not potential games. Hence they do not possess the FIP and the c-FIP for this range of α.

Acknowledgments. The first author was partially supported by the NCN grant 2014/13/B/ST6/01807 and the second author by the NWO grant 612.001.352. We thank Krzysztof R. Apt for many useful suggestions concerning the results and organization of this paper. We thank Mateusz Skomra for many helpful discussions and feedback.

References

1. Albers, S., Eilts, S., Even-Dar, E., Mansour, Y., Roditty, L.: On Nash equilibria for a network creation game. In: Proceedings of the 17th Symposium on Discrete Algorithms (SODA), pages 89–98. SIAM (2006)
2. Alon, N., Demaine, E.D., Hajiaghayi, M.T., Leighton, T.: Basic network creation games. SIAM J. Discrete Math. **27**(2), 656–668 (2013)
3. Álvarez, A., Messegué, A.: Selfish network creation with non-uniform edge cost (2017). arXiv: 1706.09132
4. Andelman, N., Feldman, M., Mansour, Y.: Strong price of anarchy. Games Econ. Behav. **65**(2), 289–317 (2009)
5. Aumann, R.J.: Acceptable points in general cooperative N-person games. In: Luce, R.D., Tucker, A.W. (eds) Contribution to the Theory of Games, vol. IV (Annals of Mathematical Study 40), pp. 287–324. Princeton University Press (1959)
6. Bala, V., Goyal, S.: A noncooperative model of network formation. Econometrica **68**(5), 1181–1229 (2000)
7. Bala, V., Goyal, S.: A strategic analysis of network reliability. Rev. Econ. Des. **5**(3), 205–228 (2000)
8. Billand, P., Bravard, C., Sarangi, S.: Existence of Nash networks in one-way flow models. Econ. Theor. **37**(3), 491–507 (2008)
9. Brandes, U., Hoefer, M., Nick, B.: Network creation games with disconnected equilibria. In: Papadimitriou, C., Zhang, S. (eds.) WINE 2008. LNCS, vol. 5385, pp. 394–401. Springer, Heidelberg (2008). https://doi.org/10.1007/978-3-540-92185-1_45
10. Chauhan, A., Lenzner, P., Melnichenko, A., Molitor, L.: Selfish network creation with non-uniform edge cost (2017). arXiv:1706.10200
11. Corbo, J., Parkes, D.C.: The price of selfish behavior in bilateral network formation. In: Proceedings of the 24th Symposium on Principles of Distributed Computing (PODC), pp. 99–107. ACM (2005)
12. Demaine, E.D., Hajiaghayi, M., Mahini, H., Zadimoghaddam, M.: The price of anarchy in network creation games. ACM Trans. Algorithms **8**(2), 13:1–13:3 (2012)
13. Derks, J., Kuipers, J., Tennekes, M., Thuijsman, F.: Local dynamics in network formation. Technical report, Maastricht University (2008)
14. Derks, J., Kuipers, J., Tennekes, M., Thuijsman, F.: Existence of Nash networks in the one-way flow model of network formation. Model. Comput. Optim. **6**, 9 (2009)
15. Fabrikant, A., Luthra, A., Maneva, E., Papadimitriou, C.H., Shenker, S.: On a network creation game. In: Proceedings of the 22nd Symposium on Principles of Distributed Computing (PODC), pp. 347–351. ACM (2003)
16. Galeotti, A.: One-way flow networks: the role of heterogeneity. Econ. Theor. **29**(1), 163–179 (2006)
17. Haller, H., Kamphorst, J., Sarangi, S.: (non-)existence and scope of Nash networks. Econ. Theor. **31**(3), 597–604 (2007)
18. Haller, H., Sarangi, S.: Nash networks with heterogeneous links. Math. Soc.Sci. **50**(2), 181–201 (2005)
19. Kawald, B., Lenzner, P.: On dynamics in selfish network creation. In: Proceedings of the 25th Symposium on Parallelism in Algorithms and Architectures (SPAA), pp. 83–92. ACM (2013)
20. Koutsoupias, E., Papadimitriou, C.: Worst-case equilibria. In: Meinel, C., Tison, S. (eds.) STACS 1999. LNCS, vol. 1563, pp. 404–413. Springer, Heidelberg (1999). https://doi.org/10.1007/3-540-49116-3_38

21. Koutsoupias, E., Papadimitriou, C.H.: Worst-case equilibria. Comput. Sci. Rev. **3**(2), 65–69 (2009)
22. Lenzner, P.: On dynamics in basic network creation games. In: Persiano, G. (ed.) SAGT 2011. LNCS, vol. 6982, pp. 254–265. Springer, Heidelberg (2011). https://doi.org/10.1007/978-3-642-24829-0_23
23. Lenzner, P.: Greedy selfish network creation. In: Goldberg, P.W. (ed.) WINE 2012. LNCS, vol. 7695, pp. 142–155. Springer, Heidelberg (2012). https://doi.org/10.1007/978-3-642-35311-6_11
24. Mamageishvili, A., Mihalák, M., Müller, D.: Tree Nash equilibria in the network creation game. Internet Math. **11**(4–5), 472–486 (2015)
25. Messegué, B.: The price of anarchy in network creation. Master's thesis, Universitat Politècnica de Catalunya (2014)
26. Mihalák, M., Schlegel, J.C.: Asymmetric swap-equilibrium: a unifying equilibrium concept for network creation games. In: Rovan, B., Sassone, V., Widmayer, P. (eds.) MFCS 2012. LNCS, vol. 7464, pp. 693–704. Springer, Heidelberg (2012). https://doi.org/10.1007/978-3-642-32589-2_60
27. Mihalák, M., Schlegel, J.C.: The price of anarchy in network creation games is (mostly) constant. Theor. Comput. Syst. (TOCS) **53**(1), 53–72 (2013)

Sequential Deliberation for Social Choice

Brandon Fain[1]([✉]), Ashish Goel[2], Kamesh Munagala[1],
and Sukolsak Sakshuwong[2]

[1] Computer Science Department, Duke University, Durham, NC, USA
{btfain,kamesh}@cs.duke.edu
[2] Management Science and Engineering Department,
Stanford University, Stanford, CA, USA
{ashishg,sukolsak}@stanford.edu

Abstract. Social choice is a normative study of designing protocols for collective decision making. However, in instances where the underlying decision space is too large or complex for ordinal voting, standard voting methods may be impractical. How then can we design a protocol - preferably decentralized, simple, scalable, and not requiring any special knowledge of the decision space - to reach consensus? We propose sequential deliberation as a natural solution to this problem. In this iterative method, successive pairs of agents bargain over the decision space using the previous decision as a disagreement alternative. We show that sequential deliberation finds a 1.208-approximation to the optimal social cost when the space of preferences define a median graph, coming very close to this value with only a small constant number of agents sampled from the population. We also give lower bounds on simpler classes of mechanisms to justify our design choices. We further show that sequential deliberation is ex-post Pareto efficient and has truthful reporting as an equilibrium of the induced extensive form game. Finally, we prove that for general metric spaces, the first and second moment of the distribution of social cost of the outcomes produced by sequential deliberation are also bounded by constants.

1 Introduction

Suppose a university administrator plans to spend millions of dollars to update her campus, and she wants to elicit the input of students, staff, and faculty. In a typical social choice setting, she could first elicit the bliss points of the students, say "new gym," "new library," and "new student center." However, voting on these options need not find the social optimum, because it is not clear

B. Fain—Supported by NSF grants CCF-1637397 and IIS-1447554.

A. Goel—Supported by the Army Research Office Grant No. 116388, the Office of Naval Research Grant No. 11904718, by NSF grant CCF-1637418, and by the Stanford Cyber Initiative.

K. Munagala—Supported by NSF grants CCF-1408784, CCF-1637397, and IIS-1447554.

N. R. Devanur and P. Lu (Eds.): WINE 2017, LNCS 10674, pp. 177–190, 2017.
https://doi.org/10.1007/978-3-319-71924-5_13

that the social optimum is even on the ballot. In such a setting, *deliberation* between individuals would find entirely new alternatives, for example "replace gym equipment plus remodeling campus dining plus money for scholarship." This leads to finding a social optimum over a wider space of semi-structured outcomes that the system/mechanism designer was not originally aware of, and the participants had not initially articulated.

We therefore start with the following premise: The mechanism designer may not be able to enumerate the outcomes in the decision space or know their structure, and this decision space may be too big for most ordinal voting schemes. (For instance, ordinal voting is difficult to implement in complex combinatorial spaces [25] or in continuous spaces [15].) However, we assume that agents can still reason about their preferences and small groups of agents can negotiate over this space and collaboratively propose outcomes that appeal to all of them. Our goal is to design protocols based on such a primitive by which small group negotiation can lead to an aggregation of societal preferences without a need to formally articulate the entire decision space and without every agent having to report ordinal rankings over this space.

The need for small groups is motivated by a practical consideration as well as a theoretical one. On the practical side, there is no online platform, to the best of our knowledge, that has a successful history of large scale deliberation and decision making on complex issues; in fact, large online forums typically degenerate into vitriol and name calling when there is substantive disagreement among the participants. Thus, if we are to develop practical tools for decision making at scale, a sequence of small group deliberations appears to be the most plausible path. On the theoretical side, we understand the connections between sequential protocols for deliberation and axiomatic theories of bargaining for small groups, e.g. for pairs [8,34], but not for large groups, and we seek to bridge this gap.

Summary of Contributions. Our main contributions are two-fold:

- A simple and practical sequential protocol that only requires agents to negotiate in pairs and propose outcomes that appeal to both agents.
- A canonical analytic model in which we can precisely state properties of this protocol in terms of approximation of the social optimum, Pareto-efficiency, and incentive-compatibility, as well as compare it with simpler protocols.

1.1   Background: Bargaining Theory

Before proceeding further, we review bargaining, the classical framework for two-player negotiation in Economics. Two-person bargaining, as framed in [29], is a game wherein there is a disagreement outcome and two agents must cooperate to reach a decision; failure to cooperate results in the adoption of the disagreement outcome. Nash postulated four axioms that the bargaining solution ought to satisfy assuming a convex space of alternatives: Pareto optimality (agents find an outcome that cannot be simultaneously improved for both of them), symmetry between agents, invariance with respect to affine transformations of utility (scalar multiplication or additive translation of any agent's utility should not change the outcome), and independence of irrelevant alternatives (informally that the presence of a feasible outcome that agents do not select does not influence their decision). Nash proved that the solution maximizing the Nash product (that we describe later) is the unique solution satisfying these axioms. To provide some explanation of how two agents might find such a solution, [34] shows that Nash's solution is the subgame perfect equilibrium of a simple repeated game on the two agents, where the agents take turns making offers, and at each round, there is an exogenous probability of the process terminating with no agreement.

The two-person bargaining model is therefore clean and easy to reason about. As a consequence, it has been extensively studied. In fact, there are other models and solutions to two-person bargaining, each with a slightly different axiomatization [21,22,28], as well as several experimental studies [7,30,33]. In a social choice setting, there are typically many more than two agents, each agent having their own complex preferences. Though bargaining can be generalized to n agents with similar axiomatization and solution structure, such a generalization is considered impractical. This is because in reality it is difficult to get a large number of individuals to negotiate coherently; complexities come with the formation of coalitions and power structures [19,24]. Any model for simultaneous bargaining, even with three players [6], needs to take these messy aspects into account.

1.2 A Practical Compromise: Sequential Pairwise Deliberation

In this paper, we take a middle path, avoiding both the complexity of explicitly specifying preferences in a large decision space that any individual agent may not even fully know (fully centralized voting), and that of simultaneous n-person bargaining (a fully decentralized cooperative game). We term this approach *sequential deliberation*. We use 2-person bargaining as a basic primitive, and view deliberation as a sequence of pairwise interactions that refine good alternatives into better ones as time goes by.

More formally, there is a decision space S of feasible alternatives (these may be projects, sets of projects, or continuous allocations) and a set $\mathcal{N}$ of agents. We assume each agent has a hidden cardinal utility for each alternative. We encapsulate deliberation as a sequential process. The framework that we analyze in the rest of the paper is captured in Fig. 1.

Our framework is simple with low cognitive overhead, and is easy to implement and reason about. Though we don't analyze other variants in this paper, we note that the framework is flexible. For instance, the bargaining step can be replaced with any function $\mathcal{B}(u, v, a)$ that corresponds to an interaction between u and v using a as the disagreement outcome; we assume that this function maximizes the Nash product, that is, it corresponds to the Nash bargaining solution. Similarly, the last step of social choice could be implemented by a central planner based on the distribution of outcomes produced.

1. In each round $t = 1, 2, \ldots, T$:
   (a) A pair of agents u^t and v^t are chosen independently and uniformly at random with replacement.
   (b) These agents are presented with a disagreement alternative a^t, and perform bargaining, which is encoded as a function $\mathcal{B}(u, v, a)$ as described below.
   (c) Agents u_t and v_t are asked to output a consensus alternative; if they fail to reach a consensus then the alternative a^t is output.
   (d) Let o^t denote the alternative that is output in round t. We set $a^{t+1} = o^t$, where we assume a^1 is the bliss point of an arbitrary agent.
2. The final social choice is a^T. Note that this is equivalent to drawing an outcome at random from the distribution generated by repeating this protocol several times.

Fig. 1. A framework for sequential pairwise deliberation.

1.3   Analytical Model: Median Graphs and Nash Bargaining

The framework in Fig. 1 is well-defined and practical irrespective of an analytical model. However, we provide a simple analytical model for specifying the preferences of the agents in which we can precisely quantify the behavior of this framework as justification.

Median Graphs. We assume that the set $\mathcal{S}$ of alternatives are vertices of a *median graph*. A median graph has the property that for each triplet of vertices u, v, w, there is a unique point that is common to the three sets of shortest paths (since there may be multiple pairwise shortest paths), those between u, v, between v, w, and between u, w. This point is the unique *median* of u, v, w. We assume each agent u has a bliss point $p_u \in \mathcal{S}$, and his disutility for an alternative $a \in \mathcal{S}$ is simply $d(p_u, a)$, where $d(\cdot)$ is the shortest path distance function on the median graph. (Note that this disutility can have an agent-dependent scale factor.) Several natural graphs are median graphs, including trees, points on the line, hypercubes, and grid graphs in arbitrary dimensions [23]. As we discuss in Sect. 1.5, because of their analytic tractability and special properties, median graphs have been extensively studied as structured models for spatial preferences in voting theory. Some of our results generalize to metric spaces beyond median graphs; see Sect. 5.

Nash Bargaining. The model for two-person bargaining is simply the classical *Nash bargaining* solution described before. Given a disagreement alternative a, agents u and v choose that alternative $o \in \mathcal{S}$ that maximizes:

$$\text{Nash product} = (d(p_u, a) - d(p_u, o)) \times (d(p_v, a) - d(p_v, o))$$

subject to individual rationality, that is, $d(p_v, o) \leq d(p_v, a)$ and $d(p_u, o) \leq d(p_u, a)$. The Nash product maximizer need not be unique; in the case of ties we postulate that agents select the outcome that is closest to the disagreement outcome. As mentioned before, the Nash product is a widely studied axiomatic notion of pairwise interactions, and is therefore a natural solution concept in our framework.

Social Cost and Distortion. The *social cost* of an alternative $a \in S$ is given by $SC(a) = \sum_{u \in \mathcal{N}} d(p_u, a)$. Let $a^* \in S$ be the minimizer of social cost, *i.e.*, the *generalized median*. We measure the Distortion of outcome a as

$$\text{Distortion}(a) = \frac{SC(a)}{SC(a^*)} \tag{1}$$

where we use the expected social cost if a is the outcome of a randomized algorithm. Note that our model is fairly general in that the bliss points of the agents in $\mathcal{N}$ form an arbitrary subset of S. Assuming that disutility is some metric over the space follows recent literature [2,3,9,10,17], and our tightest results are for median graphs specifically.

1.4 Our Results

Before presenting our results, we re-emphasize that while we present analytical results for sequential deliberation in specific decision spaces, the framework in Fig. 1 is well defined regardless of the underlying decision space and the mediator's understanding of the space. At a high level, this flexibility and generality in practice are its key advantages.

Bounding Distortion. Our main result is in Sect. 3, and shows that for sequential Nash bargaining on a median graph, the expected Distortion of outcome a^T has an upper bound approaching 1.208 as $T \to \infty$. Surprisingly, we show that in $T = \log_2 \frac{1}{\epsilon} + 2.575$ steps, the expected Distortion is at most $1.208 + \epsilon$, independent of the number of agents, the size of the median space, and the initial disagreement point a^1. For instance, the Distortion falls below 1.22 in at most 9 steps of deliberation, which only requires a random sample of at most 20 agents from the population to implement.

In Sect. 3.2, we ask: *How good is our numerical bound?* We present a sequence of lower bounds for social choice mechanisms that are allowed to use increasingly richer information about the space of alternatives on the median graph. This also leads us to make qualitative statements about our deliberation scheme.

- We show that any social choice mechanism that is restricted to choosing the bliss point of some agent cannot have Distortion better than 2. More generally, it was recently shown [18] that even eliciting the top k alternatives for each agent does not improve the bound of 2 for median graphs unless $k = \Omega(|S|)$.
- Next consider mechanisms that choose, for some triplet (u, v, w) of agents with bliss points p_u, p_v, p_w, the median outcome $m_{uvw} = \mathcal{B}(u, v, p_w)$. We show this has Distortion at least 1.316, which means that sequential deliberation is superior to one-shot deliberation that outputs o^1 where a^1 is the bliss point of some agent.

- Finally, for every pair of agents (u, v), consider the set of alternatives on a shortest path between p_u and p_v. This encodes all deliberation schemes where $\mathcal{B}$ finds a Pareto-efficient alternative for some 2 agents at each step. We show that any such mechanisms has Distortion ratio at least $9/8 = 1.125$. This space of mechanisms captures sequential deliberation, and shows that sequential deliberation is close to best possible within this space.

Properties of Sequential Deliberation. We next show that sequential deliberation has several natural desiderata on median graphs in Sect. 4. In particular:

- Under mild assumptions, the limiting distribution over outcomes of sequential deliberation is *unique*.
- For every $T \geq 1$, the outcome o^T of sequential deliberation is *ex-post Pareto-efficient*, meaning that there is no other alternative that has at most that social cost for all agents and strictly better cost for one agent. This is not a priori obvious, since the outcome at any one round only uses inputs from two agents.
- Interpreted as a mechanism, truthful play is a *sub-game perfect Nash equilibrium* of sequential deliberation. This interpretation is made precise in Sect. 4, but at a high level, we seek to address the following concern: In a sequential setting, would any agent have incentive to misrepresent their preferences so that they gain an advantage?

Beyond Median Graphs. In Sect. 5, we consider general metric spaces. We show that the Distortion of sequential deliberation is always at most a factor of 3. More surprisingly, we show that sequential deliberation has constant distortion even for the second moment of the distribution of social cost of the outcomes, *i.e.*, the latter is at most a constant factor worse than the optimum squared social cost. The practical implication is that one can look at the distribution of outcomes produced by deliberation and know that the standard deviation in social cost is comparable to its expected value.[1]

1.5   Related Work

While the real world complexities of the model are beyond the analytic confines of this work, deliberation as an important component of collective decision making and democracy is studied in political science. For examples (by no means exhaustive), see [14,37]. There is ongoing related work on Distortion of voting for simple analytical models like points in $\mathbb{R}$ [13], and in general metric spaces [2,3,9,10,17]. This work focuses on optimally aggregating ordinal preferences, say the top k preferences of a voter [18]. In contrast, our scheme elicits alternatives as the outcome of bargaining rounds that require agents to reason

---

[1] See also recent work by [38] that considers minimizing the variance of randomized truthful mechanisms.

about cardinal preferences. We essentially show that for median graphs, unless k is very large, such deliberation has provably lower distortion than social choice schemes that elicit purely ordinal rankings.

Median graphs and their ordinal generalization, median spaces, have been extensively studied in social choice. The special cases of trees and grids have been studied as structured models for voter preferences [5,36]. For general median spaces, the Condorcet winner (an alternative that pairwise beats any other alternative in terms of voter preferences) is related to the generalized median [4,35,39] – if the former exists, it coincides with the latter. Nehring and Puppe [31] show that any single-peaked domain which admits a non-dictatorial and neutral strategy-proof social choice function is a median space. Clearwater et al. [11] also showed that any set of voters and alternatives on a median graph will have a Condorcet winner. In a sense, these are the largest class of structured preferences where ordinal voting over the entire space of alternatives leads to a "clear winner" (importantly, we assume this is impractical).

Our paper is inspired by the *triadic consensus* results of Goel and Lee [16], where the authors also focus on small group interactions to make a collective decision. The authors show that the Distortion of their protocol approaches 1 on median graphs. However, the protocol crucially assumes individuals know the positions of other individuals, and requires the space of alternatives to coincide with the space of individuals. We make neither of these assumptions – in our case, the space of alternatives can be much larger than the number of agents, and individuals interact with others only via bargaining. This makes our protocol more practical, but restricts our Distortion to be bounded away from 1.

The notion of *democratic equilibrium* [15,20] considers social choice mechanisms in continuous spaces where individual agents with complex utility functions perform update steps inspired by gradient descent. However, these schemes do not involve deliberation between agents and have little formal analysis of convergence. Several works have considered *iterative voting* where the current alternative is put to vote against one proposed by different random agent chosen each step [1,26,32], or other related schemes [27]. In contrast with our work, these protocols are not deliberative and require voting among several agents each step; furthermore, the analysis focuses on convergence to an equilibrium instead of welfare or efficiency guarantees.

2   Median Graphs and Nash Bargaining

In this section we will use the notation $\mathcal{N}$ for a set of agents, $\mathcal{S}$ for the space of feasible alternatives, and $\mathcal{H}$ for a distribution over $\mathcal{S}$. Most of our results are for the analytic model given earlier wherein the set $\mathcal{S}$ of alternatives are vertices of a *median graph*. All proofs are given in the full version of the paper [12].

Definition 1. *A median graph $G(\mathcal{S}, E)$ is an unweighted and undirected graph with the following property: For each triplet of vertices $u, v, w \in \mathcal{S} \times \mathcal{S} \times \mathcal{S}$, there is a unique point that is common to the shortest paths (which need not be unique* *between a given pair) between u, v, between v, w, and between u, w. This point is the unique median of u, v, w.*

In the framework of Fig. 1, we assume that at every step, two agents perform Nash bargaining with a disagreement alternative. The first results characterize Nash bargaining on a median graph. In particular, we show that Nash bargaining at each step will select the median of bliss points of the two agents and the disagreement alternative. After that, we show that we can analyze the Distortion of sequential deliberation on a median graph by looking at the embedding of that graph onto the hypercube.

Lemma 1. *For any median graph $G = (\mathcal{S}, E)$, any two agents u, v with bliss points $p_u, p_v \in \mathcal{S}$, and any disagreement outcome $a \in \mathcal{S}$, let M be the median. Then M maximizes the Nash product of u and v given a, and is the maximizer closest to a.*

Hypercube Embeddings. For any median graph $G = (\mathcal{S}, E)$, there is an isometric embedding $\phi\colon G \to Q$ of G into a hypercube Q [23]. This embedding maps vertices $\mathcal{S}$ into a subset of vertices of Q so that all pairwise distances between vertices in $\mathcal{S}$ are preserved by the embedding. A simple example of this embedding for a tree is shown in Fig. 2. We use this embedding to show the following result, in order to simplify subsequent analysis.

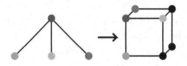

Fig. 2. The hypercube embedding of a 4-vertex star graph

Lemma 2. *Let $G(\mathcal{S}, E)$ be a median graph, and let ϕ be its isometric embedding into hypercube $Q(V, E')$. For any three points $t, u, v \in \mathcal{S}$, let M_G be the median of vertices t, u, v and let M_Q be the median of vertices $\phi(t), \phi(u), \phi(v) \in V$. Then $\phi(M_G) = M_Q$.*

3   The Efficiency of Sequential Deliberation

In this section, we show that the Distortion of sequential deliberation is at most 1.208. We then show that this bound is significant, meaning that mechanisms from simpler classes are necessarily constrained to have higher Distortion values. All proofs are given in the full version of the paper [12].

3.1 Upper Bounding Distortion

Recall the framework for sequential deliberation in Fig. 1 and the definition of Distortion in Eq. (1). We first map the problem into a problem on hypercubes using Lemma 2.

Corollary 1. *Let $G = (\mathcal{S}, E)$ be a median graph, let $\phi\colon G \to Q$ be an isometric embedding of G onto a hypercube $Q(V, E')$, and let $\mathcal{N}$ be a set of agents such that each agent u has a bliss point $p_u \in \mathcal{S}$. Then the Distortion of sequential deliberation on G is at most the Distortion of sequential deliberation on $\phi(G)$ where each agent's bliss point is $\phi(p_u)$.*

Our main result in this section shows that as $t \to \infty$, the Distortion of sequential deliberation approaches 1.208, with the convergence rate being exponentially fast in t and independent of the number of agents $|\mathcal{N}|$, the size of the median space $|\mathcal{S}|$, and the initial disagreement point a^1. In particular, the Distortion is at most 1.22 in at most 9 steps of deliberation, which is indeed a very small number of steps.

Theorem 1. *Sequential deliberation among a set $\mathcal{N}$ of agents, where the decision space $\mathcal{S}$ is a median graph, yields $\mathbb{E}[Distortion(a^t)] \leq 1.208 + \frac{6}{2^t}$.*

3.2 Lower Bounds on Distortion

We will now show that the Distortion bounds of sequential deliberation are significant, meaning that mechanisms from simpler classes are constrained to have higher Distortion values. We present a sequence of lower bounds for social choice mechanisms that use increasingly rich information about the space of alternatives on a median graph $G = (\mathcal{S}, E)$ with a set of agents $\mathcal{N}$ with bliss points $V_\mathcal{N} \subseteq \mathcal{S}$. We first consider mechanisms that are constrained to choose outcomes in $V_\mathcal{N}$. For instance, this captures the Random Dictatorship algorithm that chooses the bliss point of a random agent. It shows that the compromise alternatives found by deliberation do play a role in reducing Distortion.

Lemma 3. *Any mechanism constrained to choose outcomes in $V_\mathcal{N}$ has Distortion at least 2.*

We next consider mechanisms that are restricted to choosing the median of the bliss points of some three agents in $\mathcal{N}$. This captures sequential deliberation run for $T = 1$ steps, as well as mechanisms that generalize dictatorship to an oligarchy composed of at most 3 agents. This shows that iteratively refining the bargaining outcome has better Distortion than performing only one iteration.

Lemma 4. *Any mechanism constrained to choose outcomes in $V_\mathcal{N}$ or a median of three points in $V_\mathcal{N}$ must have Distortion at least 1.316.*

We finally consider a class of mechanisms that includes sequential deliberation as a special case. We show that any mechanism in this class cannot have Distortion arbitrarily close to 1. This also shows that sequential deliberation is close to best possible in this class.

Lemma 5. *Any mechanism constrained to choose outcomes on shortest paths between pairs of outcomes in $V_\mathcal{N}$ must have Distortion at least $9/8 = 1.125$.*

The significance of the lower bound in Lemma 5 should be emphasized: though there is always a Condorcet winner in median graphs, it need not be any agent's bliss point, nor does it need to be Pareto optimal for any pair of agents. The somewhat surprising implication is that any local mechanism (in the sense that the mechanism chooses locally Pareto optimal points) is constrained away from finding the Condorcet winner.

4 Properties of Sequential Deliberation

In this section, we study some natural desirable properties for our mechanism: uniqueness of the stationary distribution of the Markov chain, ex-post Pareto-efficiency of the final outcome, and subgame perfect Nash equilibrium. All proofs are given in the full version of the paper [12].

Uniqueness of the Stationary Distribution. We first show that the Markov chain corresponding to sequential deliberation converges to a unique stationary distribution on the actual median graph, rather than just showing that the marginals and thus the expected distances converge.

Theorem 2. *The Markov chain defined in Theorem 1 has a unique stationary distribution.*

Pareto-Efficiency. The outcome of sequential deliberation is ex-post Pareto-efficient on a median graph. In other words, in any realization of the random process, suppose the final outcome is o; then there is no other alternative a such that $d(a,v) \le d(o,v)$ for every $v \in \mathcal{N}$, with at least one inequality being strict. This is a weak notion of efficiency, but it is not trivial to show; while it is easy to see that a one shot bargaining mechanism using only bliss points is Pareto efficient by virtue of the Pareto efficiency of bargaining, sequential deliberation defines a potentially complicated Markov chain for which many of the outcomes need not be bliss points themselves.

Theorem 3. *Sequential deliberation among a set $\mathcal{N}$ of agents, where the decision space $\mathcal{S}$ is a median graph and the initial disagreement point a^1 is the bliss point of some agent, yields an ex-post Pareto Efficient alternative.*

Truthfulness of Extensive Forms. Finally, we show that sequential deliberation has truth-telling as a sub-game perfect Nash equilibrium in its induced extensive form game. Towards this end, we formalize a given round of bargaining as a 2-person non-cooperative game between two players who can choose as a strategy to report any point v on a median graph; the resulting outcome is the median of the two strategy points chosen by the players and the disagreement alternative presented. The payoffs to the players are just the utilities already defined; i.e., the player wishes to minimize the distance from their true bliss point to the outcome point. Call this game the non-cooperative bargaining game (NCBG).

The extensive form game tree defined by non-cooperative bargaining consists of $2T$ alternating levels: Nature draws two agents at random, then the two agents play NCBG and the outcome becomes the disagreement alternative for the next NCBG. The leaves of the tree are a set of points in the median graph; agents want to minimize their expected distance to the final outcome.

Theorem 4. *Sequential NCBG on a median graph has a sub-game perfect Nash equilibrium where every agent truthfully reports their bliss point at all rounds of bargaining.*

5   General Metric Spaces

We now work in the very general setting that the set S of alternatives are points in a finite metric space equipped with a distance function $d(\cdot)$ that is a metric. As before, we assume each agent $u \in \mathcal{N}$ has a bliss point $p_u \in S$. An agent's disutility for an alternative $a \in S$ is simply $d(p_u, a)$. We first present results for the Distortion, and subsequently define the second moment, or Squared-Distortion. For both measures, we show that the upper bound for sequential deliberation is at most a constant regardless of the metric space. All proofs are given in the full version of the paper [12].

Theorem 5. *The Distortion of sequential deliberation is at most 3 when the space of alternatives and bliss points lies in some metric, and this bound is tight.*

The bound of 3 above is quite pessimistic. The metric space employed in the lower bound is contrived in the following sense: Every pair of agents has some unique (to that pair) alternative they very slightly prefer to the social optimum. For structured spaces, we expect the bound to be much better. We have already shown this for median spaces. In the full version of this paper [12], we provide more evidence in this direction by considering a structured space motivated by budgeting applications that is not a median graph. For this space, we show that sequential deliberation has Distortion at most $4/3$.

5.1   Second Moment of Social Cost

We now show that for any metric space, sequential deliberation has a crucial advantage in terms of the distribution of outcomes it produces. For this, we consider the second moment, or the expected squared social cost. Recall that the *social cost* of an alternative $a \in S$ is given by $SC(a) = \sum_{u \in \mathcal{N}} d(p_u, a)$. Let $a^* \in S$ be the minimizer of social cost, *i.e.*, the *generalized median*. Then define:

$$\text{Squared-Distortion} = \frac{\mathbb{E}[(SC(a))^2]}{(SC(a^*))^2}$$

where the expectation is over the set of outcomes a produced by Sequential Deliberation.[2] We show that sequential deliberation has Squared-Distortion upper bounded by a constant. This means the standard deviation in social cost of the distribution of outcomes is comparable to the optimal social cost. This has a practical implication: A policy designer can run sequential deliberation for a few steps, and be sure that the probability of observing an outcome that has γ times the optimal social cost is at most $O(1/\gamma^2)$. In contrast, Random Dictatorship (choosing an agent uniformly at random and using her bliss point as the solution) has unbounded Squared-Distortion, which means its standard deviation in social cost cannot be bounded. In other words, deliberation between agents eliminates the outlier agent, and concentrates probability mass on central outcomes.

Theorem 6. *The Squared-Distortion of sequential deliberation for $T \geq 1$ is at most 41 when the space of alternatives and bliss points lies in some metric. Furthermore, the Squared-Distortion of random dictatorship is unbounded.*

6 Open Questions

Our work is the first step to developing a theory around practical deliberation schemes. We suggest several future directions. First, we do not have a general characterization of the Distortion of sequential deliberation for metric spaces. We have shown that for general metric spaces there is a small but pessimistic bound on the Distortion of 3, but that for specific metric spaces the Distortion may be much lower. We do not have a complete characterization of what separates these good and bad regimes.

More broadly, an interesting question is extending our work to take opinion dynamics into account, *i.e.*, proving stronger guarantees if we assume that when two agents deliberate, each agent's opinion moves slightly towards the other agent's opinion and the outside alternative. Furthermore, though we have shown that all agents deliberating at the same time does not improve on dictatorship, it is not clear how to extend our results to more than two agents negotiating at the same time. This runs into the challenges in understanding and modeling multiplayer bargaining [6,19,24].

Finally, it would be interesting to conduct experiments to measure the efficacy of our framework on complex, real world social choice scenarios. There are several practical hurdles that need to be overcome before such a system can be feasibly deployed. In a related sense, it would be interesting to develop an axiomatic theory for deliberation, much like that for bargaining [29], and show that sequential deliberation arises naturally from a set of axioms.

---

[2] The motivation for considering Squared-Distortion instead of the standard deviation is that the latter might prefer a more deterministic mechanism with a worse social cost, a problem that the Squared-Distortion avoids.

References

1. Airiau, S., Endriss, U.: Iterated majority voting. In: Rossi, F., Tsoukias, A. (eds.) ADT 2009. LNCS, vol. 5783, pp. 38–49. Springer, Heidelberg (2009). https://doi.org/10.1007/978-3-642-04428-1_4

2. Anshelevich, E., Bhardwaj, O., Postl, J.: Approximating optimal social choice under metric preferences. In: AAAI, vol. 15, pp. 777–783 (2015)

3. Anshelevich, E., Postl, J.: Randomized social choice functions under metric preferences. In: 25th International Joint Conference on Artificial Intelligence (2016)

4. Bandelt, H.J., Barthelemy, J.P.: Medians in median graphs. Discret. Appl. Math. **8**(2), 131–142 (1984)

5. Barbera, S., Gul, F., Stacchetti, E.: Generalized median voter schemes and committees. J. Econ. Theor. **61**(2), 262–289 (1993)

6. Bennett, E., Houba, H.: Odd man out: bargaining among three players. Working Papers 662, UCLA Department of Economics, May 1992. http://www.econ.ucla.edu/workingpapers/wp662.pdf

7. Binmore, K., Shaked, A., Sutton, J.: Testing noncooperative bargaining theory: a preliminary study. Am. Econ. Rev. **75**(5), 1178–1180 (1985)

8. Binmore, K., Rubinstein, A., Wolinsky, A.: The nash bargaining solution in economic modelling. Rand J. Econ. **17**(2), 176–188 (1986)

9. Boutilier, C., Caragiannis, I., Haber, S., Lu, T., Procaccia, A.D., Sheffet, O.: Optimal social choice functions: a utilitarian view. Artif. Intell. **227**, 190–213 (2015)

10. Cheng, Y., Dughmi, S., Kempe, D.: Of the people: voting is more effective with representative candidates. In: EC (2017)

11. Clearwater, A., Puppe, C., Slinko, A.: Generalizing the single-crossing property on lines and trees to intermediate preferences on median graphs. In: Proceedings of the 24th International Conference on Artificial Intelligence, IJCAI 2015, pp. 32–38 (2015)

12. Fain, B., Goel, A., Munagala, K., Shaksuwong, S.: Sequential deliberation for social choice (2017). https://arxiv.org/abs/1710.00771

13. Feldman, M., Fiat, A., Golomb, I.: On voting and facility location. In: Proceedings of the 2016 ACM Conference on Economics and Computation, EC 2016, pp. 269–286. ACM, New York (2016)

14. Fishkin, J., Luskin, R.: Experimenting with a democratic ideal: deliberative polling and public opinion. Acta Polit. **40**(3), 284–298 (2005)

15. Garg, N., Kamble, V., Goel, A., Marn, D., Munagala, K.: Collaborative optimization for collective decision-making in continuous spaces. In: Proceedings of the World Wide Web (WWW) Conference (2017)

16. Goel, A., Lee, J.: Towards large-scale deliberative decision-making: small groups and the importance of triads. In: ACM EC (2016)

17. Goel, A., Krishnaswamy, A.K., Munagala, K.: Metric distortion of social choice rules. In: EC (2017)

18. Gross, S., Anshelevich, E., Xia, L.: Vote until two of you agree: mechanisms with small distortion and sample complexity. In: Proceedings of the Thirty-First AAAI Conference on Artificial Intelligence, 4–9 February 2017, San Francisco, California, USA, pp. 544–550 (2017)

19. Harsanyi, J.C.: A simplified bargaining model for the n-person cooperative game. Int. Econ. Rev. **4**(2), 194–220 (1963)

20. Hylland, A., Zenkhauser, R.: A mechanism for selecting public goods when preferences must be elicited. Working Paper (1980)

21. Kalai, E.: Proportional solutions to bargaining situations: interpersonal utility comparisons. Econometrica **45**(7), 1623–1630 (1977)
22. Kalai, E., Smorodinsky, M.: Other solutions to nash's bargaining problem. Econometrica **43**(3), 513–518 (1975)
23. Knuth, D.E.: The Art of Computer Programming: Combinatorial Algorithms, Part 1, 1st edn. Addison-Wesley Professional, Boston (2011)
24. Krishna, V., Serrano, R.: Multilateral bargaining. Rev. Econ. Stud. **63**(1), 61–80 (1996)
25. Lang, J., Xia, L.: Voting in combinatorial domains. In: Brandt, F., Conitzer, V., Endriss, U., Lang, J., Procaccia, A.D. (eds.) Handbook of Computational Social Choice. Cambridge University Press, Cambridge (2016)
26. Lev, O., Rosenschein, J.S.: Convergence of iterative voting. In: Proceedings of the 11th International Conference on Autonomous Agents and Multiagent Systems, vol. 2, pp. 611–618. International Foundation for Autonomous Agents and Multiagent Systems (2012)
27. Meir, R., Polukarov, M., Rosenschein, J.S., Jennings, N.R.: Convergence to equilibria in plurality voting. In: Proceedings of the 24th Conference on Artificial Intelligence (AAAI 2010), pp. 823–828 (2010)
28. Myerson, R.B.: Two-person bargaining problems and comparable utility. Econometrica **45**(7), 1631–1637 (1977)
29. Nash, J.F.: The bargaining problem. Econometrica **18**(2), 155–162 (1950). http://www.jstor.org/stable/1907266
30. Neelin, J., Sonnenschein, H., Spiegel, M.: An experimental test of Rubinstein's theory of bargaining. Working Papers 587, Princeton University, Department of Economics, Industrial Relations Section, May 1986
31. Nehring, K., Puppe, C.: The structure of strategy-proof social choice. Part I: general characterization and possibility results on median spaces. J. Econ. Theor. **135**(1), 269–305 (2007)
32. Rabinovich, Z., Obraztsova, S., Lev, O., Markakis, E., Rosenschein, J.S.: Analysis of equilibria in iterative voting schemes. In: AAAI, vol. 15, pp. 1007–1013. Citeseer (2015)
33. Roth, A.E.: Bargaining phenomena and bargaining theory. In: Roth, A.E. (ed.) Laboratory Experiments in Economics: Six Points of View, pp. 14–41. Cambridge University Press, Cambridge (1987)
34. Rubinstein, A.: Perfect equilibrium in a bargaining model. Econometrica **50**(1), 97–109 (1982). http://www.jstor.org/stable/1912531
35. Saban, D., Stier-Moses, N.: The competitive facility location problem in a duopoly: connections to the 1-median problem. In: Goldberg, P.W. (ed.) WINE 2012. LNCS, vol. 7695, pp. 539–545. Springer, Heidelberg (2012). https://doi.org/10.1007/978-3-642-35311-6_44
36. Schummer, J., Vohra, R.V.: Strategy-proof location on a network. J. Econ. Theor. **104**(2), 405–428 (2002)
37. Thompson, D.F.: Deliberative democratic theory and empirical political science. Annu. Rev. Polit. Sci. **11**(1), 497–520 (2008)
38. Wajc, D., Procaccia, A., Zhang, H.: Approximation-variance tradeoffs in mechanism design, January 2017
39. Wendell, R.E., McKelvey, R.D.: New perspectives in competitive location theory. Eur. J. Oper. Res. **6**(2), 174–182 (1981)

Computing Approximate Pure Nash Equilibria in Shapley Value Weighted Congestion Games

Matthias Feldotto[1]($\boxtimes$), Martin Gairing[2], Grammateia Kotsialou[3], and Alexander Skopalik[1]

[1] Paderborn University, Paderborn, Germany
{feldi,skopalik}@mail.upb.de
[2] University of Liverpool, Liverpool, UK
m.gairing@liverpool.ac.uk
[3] King's College London, London, UK
grammateia.kotsialou@kcl.ac.uk

Abstract. We study the computation of approximate pure Nash equilibria in Shapley value (SV) weighted congestion games, introduced in [19]. This class of games considers weighted congestion games in which Shapley values are used as an alternative (to proportional shares) for distributing the total cost of each resource among its users. We focus on the interesting subclass of such games with polynomial resource cost functions and present an algorithm that computes approximate pure Nash equilibria with a polynomial number of strategy updates. Since computing a single strategy update is hard, we apply sampling techniques which allow us to achieve polynomial running time. The algorithm builds on the algorithmic ideas of [7], however, to the best of our knowledge, this is the first algorithmic result on computation of approximate equilibria using other than proportional shares as player costs in this setting. We present a novel relation that approximates the Shapley value of a player by her proportional share and vice versa. As side results, we upper bound the approximate price of anarchy of such games and significantly improve the best known factor for computing approximate pure Nash equilibria in weighted congestion games of [7].

Keywords: Approximate pure Nash equilibria · Computation
Shapley cost-sharing · Weighted congestion games
Approximate Price of Anarchy

1 Introduction

In many applications the state of a system depends on the behavior of individual participants that act selfishly in order to minimize their own private cost. Non-cooperative game theory uses the concept of Nash equilibria as a tool for the

This work was partially supported by the German Research Foundation (DFG) within the Collaborative Research Centre "On-The-Fly Computing" (SFB 901) and by EPSRC grant EP/L011018/1.
The full version of this paper is available at http://arxiv.org/abs/1710.01634.

N. R. Devanur and P. Lu (Eds.): WINE 2017, LNCS 10674, pp. 191–204, 2017.
https://doi.org/10.1007/978-3-319-71924-5_14

theoretical analysis of such systems. A Nash equilibrium is a state in which no participant has an incentive to deviate to another strategy. While mixed Nash equilibria, i.e., Nash equilibria in randomized strategies, are guaranteed to exist under mild assumptions on the players' strategy spaces and the private cost functions they are often hard to interpret. As a consequence, attention is often restricted to pure Nash equilibria, i.e., Nash equilibria in deterministic strategies.

Rosenthal [26] introduced a class of games, called *congestion games* that models a variety of strategic interactions and is guaranteed to have pure Nash equilibria. In a congestion game, we are given a finite set of players N and a finite set of resources E. A strategy of each player i is to choose a subset of the resources out of a set $\mathcal{P}_i$ of subsets of resources allowable to her. In each strategy profile, each player pays for all used resources where the cost of a resource $e \in E$ is a function c_e of the number of players using it. Rosenthal used an elegant potential function argument to show that iterative improvement steps by the players converge to a pure Nash equilibrium and hence its existence is guaranteed.

Note that in congestion games each player using a resource has the same influence on the cost of this resource. To alleviate this limitation, [10,24] studied a natural generalization called *weighted congestion games* in which each player i has a weight w_i and the *joint cost* of the resource is $f_e \cdot c_e(f_e)$, where f_e is the total weight of players using e. The joint cost of resource e has to be covered by the set of players S_e using it, i.e., $\sum_{i \in S_e} \chi_{ie} = f_e \cdot c_e(f_e)$, where χ_{ie} is the cost share of player i on resource e. The *cost sharing method* of the game defines how exactly the joint cost of a resource is divided into individual cost shares χ_{ie}. For weighted congestion games, the most widely studied cost sharing method is *proportional sharing* (PS), where the cost share of a player is proportional to her weight, i.e., $\chi_{ie} = w_i \cdot c_e(f_e)$. Unfortunately, weighted congestion games with proportional sharing in general do not admit a *pure* Nash equilibrium (see [16] for a characterization).

Kollias and Roughgarden [19] proposed to use the *Shapley value* (SV) for sharing the cost of a resource in weighted congestion games. In the *Shapley cost-sharing* method, the cost share of a player on a resource is the average marginal cost increase caused by her over all permutations of the players. Using the Shapley value restores the existence of a potential function and therefore the existence of pure Nash equilibria to such games [19].

Potential functions immediately give rise to a simple and natural search procedure to find an equilibrium by performing iterative improvement steps starting from an arbitrary state. Unfortunately, this process may take exponentially many steps, even in the simple case of unweighted congestion games[1] and linear cost functions [1]. Moreover, computing a pure Nash equilibrium in these games is intractable as the problem is PLS-complete [9], even for affine linear cost functions [1]. This result directly carries over to our game class with Shapley cost-sharing. Given these intractability results, it is natural to ask for

---

[1] Note that in the unweighted case, proportional sharing and Shapley cost sharing coincide.

approximation which is formally captured by the concept of an ρ-approximate pure Nash equilibrium. This is a state from which no player can improve her cost by a factor of $\rho \geq 1$. Recently, Caragiannis et al. [6] provided an algorithm to compute ρ-approximate Nash equilibria for unweighted congestion games under proportional sharing. They also generalised their technique to weighted congestion games [7].

1.1   Our Contributions

We present an algorithm to compute ρ-approximate Nash equilibria in weighted congestion games under Shapley cost sharing. In games with polynomial cost functions of degree at most d, our algorithm achieves an approximation factor asymptotically close to $\left(\frac{d}{\ln 2}\right)^d \cdot poly(d)$. Similar to [7] our algorithm computes a sequence of improvement steps of polynomial length that yields a ρ-approximate Nash equilibrium. Hence, our algorithm performs only a polynomial number of strategy updates. We show that our algorithm can also be used to compute ρ-approximate pure Nash equilibria for weighted congestion games with proportional sharing which improves the approximation factor of $d^{2 \cdot d + o(d)}$ in [7] to $\left(\frac{d}{\ln 2}\right)^d \cdot poly(d)$.

We note that our method does not immediately yield an algorithm with polynomial running time since computing the Shapley cost share of a player and hence an improvement step is computationally hard. However, we show that there is a polynomial-time randomized approximation scheme that can be used instead. This results in a randomized polynomial time algorithm that computes a strategy profile that is an approximate pure Nash equilibrium with high probability.

In the course of the analysis we exhibit an interesting relation between the Shapley cost share of a player and her proportional share. In the case of polynomial cost functions with constant degree, each of them can be approximated by the other within a constant factor. This insight leads to an alternative proof to [15] for the existence of approximate pure Nash equilibria in weighted congestion games with proportional cost sharing.

Finally, we derive bounds on the approximate Price of Anarchy which may be of independent interest as they allow to bound the inefficiency of approximately stable states.

1.2   Further Related Work

Congestion games have been introduced by Rosenthal [26] who proved the existence of pure Nash equilibria by an exact potential function. Games admitting a potential function are called potential games and each potential game is isomorphic to a congestion game [25]. Weighted congestion games were introduced by Milchtaich [24] and studied by Fotakis et al. [10]. Based on the Shapley value [17], the class of weighted congestion games using Shapley values (instead of proportional shares) was introduced by [19] and it was shown that such games

are potential games. [14] extends this result by proving that a weighted generali-
sation of Shapley values is the only method that guarantee pure Nash equilibria.
In contrast, proportional sharing does not guarantee existence of equilibria in
general [16]. Further research focuses on the quality of equilibria, measured by
the Price of Anarchy (PoA) [20]. For proportional sharing, Aland et al. [3] show
tight bounds on the PoA. Gkatzelis et al. [13] show that, among all cost-sharing
methods that guarantee existence of pure Nash equilibria, Shapley values min-
imise the worst PoA. Furthermore, tight bounds on PoA for general cost-sharing
methods were given [11]. For the extended model with non-anonymous costs
by using set functions it was also shown that Shapley cost-sharing is the best
method and tight results are given [18,27].

Computing a pure Nash equilibrium for congestion games was shown to be
PLS-complete [9] even for games with linear cost function [1] or games with only
three players [2]. Chien and Sinclair [8] study the convergence towards $(1 + \epsilon)$-
approximate pure Nash equilibria in symmetric congestion games in polynomial
time under a mild assumption on the cost functions. In contrast, Skopalik and
Vöcking show that this result cannot be generalized to asymmetric games and
that computing a ρ-approximate pure Nash equilibrium is PLS-hard in general [28]. Caragiannis et al. [6] give an algorithm which computes an $(2 + \epsilon)$-
approximate equilibrium for linear cost functions and an $d^{O(d)}$-approximate
equilibrium for polynomial cost functions with degree of d. Weighted congestion games with proportional sharing do not posses pure Nash equilibria in
general [10]. However, the existence of $d + 1$-approximate equilibria for polynomial cost functions and $\frac{3}{2}$-approximate equilibria for concave cost functions was
shown [15] and Caragiannis et al. [7] present an algorithm for weighted congestion
games and proportional sharing that computes $\frac{3+\sqrt{5}}{2} + \epsilon$-approximate equilibria
for linear cost functions and $d^{2d+o(d)}$-approximate equilibria for polynomial cost
functions.

The computation of approximate equilibria requires the computation of
Shapley values. In general, the exact computation is too complex. Mann and
Shapley [23] suggest a sampling algorithm which was later analyzed by Bachrach
et al. [5] for simple coalitional games and by Aziz and de Keijzer [4] for matching games. Finally, Liben-Nowell et al. [21] and Maleki [22] consider cooperative
games with supermodular functions which correspond to our class.

2   Our Model

A weighted congestion game is defined as $\mathcal{G} = (N, E, (w_i)_{i \in N}, (\mathcal{P}_i)_{i \in N}, (c_e)_{e \in E})$,
where N is the set of players, E the set of resources, w_i is the positive weight
of player i, $\mathcal{P}_i \subseteq 2^E$ the strategy set of player i and c_e the cost function of
resource e (drawn from a set $\mathcal{C}$ of allowable cost functions). In this work, $\mathcal{C}$
is the set of polynomial functions with maximum degree d and non-negative
coefficients. The set of outcomes of this game is given by $\mathcal{P} = \mathcal{P}_1 \times \cdots \times \mathcal{P}_n$,
for an outcome, we write $P = (P_1, \ldots, P_n) \in \mathcal{P}$, where $P_i \in \mathcal{P}_i$. Let (P_{-i}, P_i')
be the outcome that results when player i changes her strategy from P_i to P_i'

and let $(P_A, P'_{N \setminus A})$ be the outcome that results when players $i \in A$ play their strategies in P and players $i \in N \setminus A$ the strategies in P'. The set of users of resource e is defined by $S_e(P) = \{i : e \in P_i\}$ and the total weight on e by $f_e(P) = \sum_{i \in S_e(P)} w_i$. Furthermore, let $S_e^A(P) = \{i \in A : e \in P_i\}$ and $f_e^A(P) = \sum_{i \in S_e^A(P)} w_i$ be variants of these definitions with a restricted player set $A \subseteq N$. The Shapley cost of a player i on a resource e is given as a function of the player's identity, the resource's cost function and her users A, i.e., $\chi_e(i, A)$. For simplicity, let $\chi_{ie}(P) = \chi_e(i, S_e(P))$ be an abbreviation if all players are considered in a state P. Let $C_e(x) = x \cdot c_e(x)$. Then, the *joint cost* on a resource e is given by $C_e(f_e(P)) = f_e(P) \cdot c_e(f_e(P))$ and the costs of players are such that $C_e(f_e(P)) = \sum_{i \in S_e(P)} \chi_{ie}(P)$. The *total cost* of a player i equals the sum of her costs in the resources she uses, i.e. $X_i(P) = \sum_{e \in P_i} \chi_{ie}(P)$. The social cost of the game is given by $SC(P) = \sum_{e \in E} f_e(P) \cdot c_e(f_e(P)) = \sum_{e \in E} \sum_{i \in S_e(P)} \chi_{ie}(P) = \sum_{i \in N} X_i(P)$. Further define the social costs of a subset of players $A \subseteq N$ with $SC_A(P) = \sum_{i \in A} X_i(P)$.

The cost-sharing method is important for our analysis, as it defines how the joint cost on a resource e is distributed among her users. In this paper, the methods we focus on are the Shapley value and the proportional cost-sharing, which we introduce in detail.

Shapley values. For a set of players A, let $\Pi(A)$ be the set of permutations $\pi : A \to A \{1, \ldots, |A|\}$. For a $\pi \in \Pi(A)$, define as $A^{<i,\pi} = \{j \in A : \pi(j) < \pi(i)\}$ the set of players preceding player i in π and as $W_A^{<i,\pi} = \sum_{j \in A : \pi(j) < \pi(i)} w_j$ the sum of their weights.

For the uniform distribution over $\Pi(A)$, the Shapley value of a player i on resource e is given by

$$\chi_e(i, A) = E_{\pi \sim \Pi(A)} \left[C_e \left(W_A^{<i,\pi} + w_i \right) - C_e \left(W_A^{<i,\pi} \right) \right].$$

Proportional sharing. The cost of a player i on a resource under proportional sharing is given by $\chi_{ie}^{\text{Prop}}(P) = w_i \cdot c_e(f_e(P))$. For the rest of the paper, we write $X_i^{\text{Prop}}(P) = \sum_{e \in E} \chi_{ie}^{\text{Prop}}(P)$ to indicate when we switch to proportional sharing.

ρ-approximate pure Nash equilibrium. Given a parameter $\rho \geq 1$ and an outcome P, we call as ρ-*move* a deviation from P_i to P'_i where the player improves her cost by more than a factor ρ, formally $X_i(P) > \rho \cdot X_i(P_{-i}, P'_i)$. We call the state P an ρ-*approximate pure Nash equilibrium* (ρ-PNE) if and only if no player is able to perform a ρ-move, formally it holds for every player i and any other strategy $P'_i \in \mathcal{P}_i$ that $X_i(P) \leq \rho \cdot X_i(P_{-i}, P'_i)$.

ρ-approximate Price of Anarchy. Given a parameter $\rho \geq 1$, let ρ-PNE $\subseteq \mathcal{P}$ be the set of ρ-approximate pure Nash equilibria and P^* the state of optimum, i.e., $P^* = \min_{P' \in \mathcal{P}} SC(P')$. Then the ρ-*approximate price of anarchy* (ρ-PoA) is defined as ρ-PoA $= \max_{P \in \rho\text{-PNE}} \frac{SC(P)}{SC(P^*)}$.

Kollias and Roughgarden [19] prove that weighted congestion games under Shapley values are potential games using the following potential.

Potential Function. Given an outcome P and an arbitrary ordering τ of the players in N, the potential is given by

$$\Phi(P) = \sum_{e \in E} \Phi_e(P) = \sum_{e \in E} \sum_{i \in S_e(P)} \chi_e(i, \{j : \tau(j) \le \tau(i), j \in S_e(P)\}). \quad (1)$$

A-limited potential. We now restrict this potential function by allowing only a subset of players $A \subseteq N$ to participate and define the A-limited potential as

$$\Phi^A(P) = \sum_{e \in E} \Phi_e^A(P) = \sum_{e \in E} \sum_{i \in S_e^A(P)} \chi_e(i, \{j : \tau(j) \le \tau(i), j \in S_e^A(P)\}). \quad (2)$$

B-partial potential. Consider sets A and B such that $B \subseteq A \subseteq N$. Then the B-partial potential of set A is defined by

$$\Phi_B^A(P) = \Phi^A(P) - \Phi^{A \setminus B}(P) = \sum_{e \in E} \Phi_{e,B}^A(P) = \sum_{e \in E} \Phi_e^A(P) - \Phi_e^{A \setminus B}(P). \quad (3)$$

If the set B contains only one player, i.e., $B = \{\{i\}\}$, then we write $\Phi_i^A(P) = \Phi_B^A(P)$. In case of $A = N$, $\Phi_B^N(P) = \Phi_B(P) = \sum_{e \in E} \Phi_{e,B}(P)$. Intuitively, $\Phi_B^A(P)$ is the value that the players in $B \subseteq A$ contribute to the A-limited potential.

ρ-stretch. Similar to ρ-PoA, we define a ratio with respect to the potential function. Let $\hat{P}$ be the outcome that minimises the potential, i.e., $\hat{P} = \min_{P' \in \mathcal{P}} \Phi(P')$. Then the ρ-stretch is defined as

$$\rho\text{-}\Omega = \max_{P \in \rho\text{-PNE}} \frac{\Phi(P)}{\Phi(\hat{P})}. \quad (4)$$

A-limited ρ-stretch. Additionally, we define a ρ-stretch restricted to players in a subset $A \subseteq N$. Let $\rho\text{-PNE}_A \subseteq \mathcal{P}$ be the set of ρ-approximate pure Nash equilibria where only players in A participate. The rest of the players have a fixed strategy $\bar{P}_{N \setminus A}$. Then we define the A-limited ρ-stretch as

$$\rho\text{-}\Omega_A = \max_{P \in \rho\text{-PNE}_A} \frac{\Phi(P)}{\Phi(\hat{P})} = \max_{P \in \rho\text{-PNE}_A} \frac{\Phi(P_A, \bar{P}_{N \setminus A})}{\Phi(\hat{P}_A, \bar{P}_{N \setminus A})}. \quad (5)$$

3 Algorithmic Approach and Outline

Our algorithm is based on ideas by Caragiannis et al. [7]. Intuitively, we partition the players' costs into intervals $[b_1, b_2], [b_2, b_3], \ldots, [b_{m-1}, b_m]$ in decreasing order. The cost values in one interval are within a polynomial factor. Note that this ensures that every sequence of ρ-moves for $\rho > 1$ of players with costs in one or two intervals converges in polynomial time.

After an initialization, the algorithm proceeds in phases r from 1 to $m - 1$. In each phase r, players with costs in the interval $[b_r, +\infty]$ do α-approximate moves where α is close to the desired approximation factor. Players with costs in the interval $[b_{r+1}, b_r]$ make $1 + \gamma$-moves for some small $\gamma > 0$. After a polynomial number of steps no such moves are possible and we freeze all players with costs in $[b_r, +\infty]$. These players will never be allowed to move again. We then proceed with the next phase. Note that at the time players are frozen, they are in an α-approximate equilibrium. The purpose of the $1 + \gamma$-moves of players of the neighboring interval is to ensure that the costs of frozen players do not change significantly in later phases. To that end we utilize a potential function argument. We argue about the potential of *sub games* among a subset of players. We can bound the potential value of an arbitrary q-approximate equilibrium with the minimal potential value (using the *stretch*). Compared to the approach in [7], we directly work with the exact potential function of the game which significantly improves the results, but also requires a more involved analysis. We show that the potential of the sub game in one phase is significantly smaller than b_r. Therefore, the costs experienced by players moving in phase r are considerably lower than the costs of any player in the interval $[b_1, b_{r-1}]$. The analysis heavily depends on the stretch of the potential function which we analyze in Sect. 6. The proof there is based on the technique of Sect. 5 in which we approximate the Shapley with proportional cost sharing. For the technical details in both sections we need some structural properties of costs-shares and the restricted potentials which we show in the next section.

4   Shapley and Potential Properties

The following properties of the Shapley values are extensively used in our proofs.

Proposition 1. *Fix a resource e. Then for any set of players S and $i \in S$, we have for $j, j_1, j_2, j', j_1', j_2', i_1, i_2 \notin S$:*

a. $\chi_e(i, S) \leq \chi_e(i, S \cup \{j\})$,
b. $\chi_e(i, S \cup \{j'\}) \geq \chi_e(i, S \cup \{j_1, j_2\})$, *with $j' \neq i$ and $w_{j'} = w_{j_1} + w_{j_2}$,*
c. $\chi_e(i, S \cup \{j_1, j_2\}) \geq \chi_e(i, S \cup \{j_1', j_2'\})$, *with $w_{j_1'} = w_{j_2'} = \frac{w_{j_1} + w_{j_2}}{2}$,*
d. $\chi_e(i, S) \geq \chi_e(i_1, S \backslash \{i\} \cup \{i_1\}) + \chi_e(i_2, S \backslash \{i\} \cup \{i_1, i_2\})$, *with $w_{i_1} = w_{i_2} = \frac{w_i}{2}$.*

We proceed to the properties of the restricted types of potential defined before.

Proposition 2. *Let A and B be sets of players such that $B \subseteq A \subseteq N$, P and P' outcomes of the game such that the players in $A \subseteq N$ use the same strategies in both P and P', and $z \in N$ an arbitrary player. Then*

a. $\Phi_B^A(P) \leq \Phi_B(P)$,   b. $\Phi_B^A(P) = \Phi_B^A(P')$,   c. $\Phi_z(P) = X_z(P)$.

Next, we show that the potential property also holds for the partial potential.

Proposition 3. *Consider a subset $B \subseteq N$ and a player $i \in B$. Given two states, P and P', that differ only in the strategy of player i, then $\Phi_B(P) - \Phi_B(P') = X_i(P) - X_i(P')$.*

The next lemma gives a relation between partial potential and Shapley values.

Lemma 1. *Given an outcome P of the game, a resource e and a subset $B \subseteq N$, it holds that $\Phi_{e,B}(P) \leq \sum_{i \in B} \chi_{ie}(P) \leq \Phi_{e,B}(P) \cdot (d+1)$.*

Summing up over all resources $e \in E$ yields the next corollary.

Corollary 1. *Given an outcome P of the game and a subset $B \subseteq N$, it holds that $\Phi_B(P) \leq \sum_{i \in B} X_i(P) \leq \Phi_B(P) \cdot (d+1)$.*

5   Approximating Shapley with Proportional Cost-Shares

In this section we approximate the Shapley value of a player with her proportional share. This approximation plays an important role in our proofs of the stretch and for the computation.

Lemma 2. *For a player i, a resource e and any state P, the following inequality holds between her Shapley and proportional cost:*

$$\frac{2}{d+1} \cdot \chi_{ie}(P) \leq \chi_{ie}^{Prop}(P) \leq \frac{d+3}{4} \cdot \chi_{ie}(P).$$

Summing up over all $e \in E$ implies the following corollary.

Corollary 2. *For a player i and any state P, the following inequality holds between her Shapley and proportional cost:*

$$\frac{2}{d+1} \cdot X_i(P) \leq X_i^{Prop}(P) \leq \frac{d+3}{4} \cdot X_i(P).$$

Lemma 3. *Any ρ-approximate pure Nash equilibrium for a SV weighted congestion game of degree d is a $\frac{(d+3) \cdot (d+1)}{8} \cdot \rho$-approximate pure Nash equilibrium for the weighted congestion game with proportional sharing.*

6   The Approximate Price of Anarchy and Stretch

Firstly, we upper bound the approximate Price of Anarchy for our game class.

Lemma 4. *Let $\rho \geq 1$ and d the maximum degree of the polynomial cost functions. Then*

$$\rho\text{-}PoA \leq \frac{\rho \cdot (2^{\frac{1}{d+1}} - 1)^{-d}}{2^{-\frac{d}{d+1}} \cdot (1+\rho) - \rho}.$$

Similar to the ρ-PoA, we also derive an upper bound on the ρ-stretch which expresses the ratio between local and global optimum of the potential function.

Lemma 5. *Let $\rho \geq 1$ and d the maximum degree of the polynomial cost functions. Then an upper bound for the ρ-stretch of polynomial SV weighted congestion games is*

$$\rho\text{-}\Omega \leq \frac{\rho \cdot (2^{\frac{1}{d+1}} - 1)^{-d} \cdot (d+1)}{2^{-\frac{d}{d+1}} \cdot (1+\rho) - \rho}.$$

We now proceed to the upper bound of the D-limited ρ-stretch. To do this, we use the ρ-PoA (Lemma 4) and Lemmas 6 and 7, which we prove next.

Lemma 6. *Let $\rho \geq 1, d$ the maximum degree of the polynomial cost functions and $\hat{P} = \min_{P' \in \mathcal{P}} \Phi(P')$. Then*

$$\frac{SC(P)}{SC(\hat{P})} \leq \frac{\rho \cdot (2^{\frac{1}{d+1}} - 1)^{-d}}{2^{-\frac{d}{d+1}} \cdot (1 + \rho) - \rho}.$$

Proof. Let P be an ρ-approximate equilibrium and P^* the optimal outcome. Let $\hat{P} = \min_{P' \in \mathcal{P}} \Phi(P')$ be the minimizer of the potential and by definition also a pure Nash equilibrium. Then we can lower bound the ρ-PoA as follows,

$$\rho\text{-PoA} = \max_{P \in \rho\text{-PNE}} \frac{SC(P)}{SC(P^*)} \geq \max_{P \in \rho\text{-PNE}} \frac{SC(P)}{SC(\hat{P})}. \tag{6}$$

Lemma 4 and (6) give that $\max_{P \in \rho\text{-PNE}} \frac{SC(P)}{SC(\hat{P})} \leq \rho\text{-PoA} \leq \frac{\rho \cdot (2^{\frac{1}{d+1}} - 1)^{-d}}{2^{\frac{-d}{d+1}} \cdot (1 + \rho) - \rho}$. $\square$

Lemma 7. *Let $\rho \geq 1, d$ the maximum degree of the polynomial cost functions and $D \subseteq N$ an arbitrary subset of players. Then*

$$\rho\text{-}\Omega_D \leq \frac{(d+1)^2 \cdot (d+3)}{8} \cdot \frac{SC(P)}{SC(\hat{P})}.$$

By Lemmas 6 and 7, we get the following desirable corollary.

Corollary 3. *For $\rho \geq 1, d$ the maximum degree of the polynomial cost functions and $D \subseteq N$ an arbitrary subset of players,*

$$\rho\text{-}\Omega_D \leq \frac{(d+1)^2 \cdot (d+3)}{8} \cdot \frac{\rho \cdot (2^{\frac{1}{d+1}} - 1)^{-d}}{2^{-\frac{d}{d+1}} \cdot (1 + \rho) - \rho}.$$

7   Computation of Approximate Pure Nash Equilibria

To compute ρ-approximate pure Nash equilibria in SV congestion games, we construct an algorithm based on the idea by Caragiannis et al. [7]. The main idea is to separate the players in different blocks depending on their costs. The players who are processed first are the ones with the largest costs followed by the smaller ones. The size of the blocks and the distance between them is polynomially bounded by the number of players n and the maximum degree d of the polynomial cost functions c_e. Formally, we define $X_{\max} = \max_{i \in N} X_i(P)$ as the maximum cost among all players before running the algorithm. Let $\mathcal{BR}_i(0)$ be a state of the game in which only player i participates and plays her best move. Then, define as $X_{\min} = \min_{i \in N} X_i(\mathcal{BR}_i(0))$ the minimum possible cost in the game. Let γ be an arbitrary constant such that $\gamma > 0, m = \log\left(\frac{X_{\max}}{X_{\min}}\right)$ is the number of different blocks and $b_r = X_{max} \cdot g^{-r}$ the block size for any $r \in [0, m]$, where $g = 2 \cdot n \cdot (d+1) \cdot \gamma^{-3}$.

The algorithm is now executed in $m-1$ phases. Let P be the current state of the game and, for each phase $r \in [1, m-1]$, let P^r be the state before phase r. All players i with $X_i(P) \in [b_r, +\infty]$ perform an s-move with $s = \left(\frac{1}{t \cdot \Omega_D} - 2\gamma\right)^{-1}$ (almost t-Ω_D-approximate moves), while all players i with $X_i(P) \in [b_{r+1}, b_r]$ perform a t-move with $t = 1 + \gamma$ (almost pure moves). Let $\mathcal{BR}_i(P)$ be the best response of player i in state P. The phase ends when the first and the second group of players are in an s- and t-approximate equilibrium, respectively. At the end of the phase, players with $X_i(P) > b_r$ have irrevocably decided their strategy and have been added in the list of finished players. In addition, before the described phases are executed, there is an initial phase in which all players with $X_i(P) \geq b_1$ can perform a t-move to prepare the first real phase.

Algorithm 1. Computation of approximate pure Nash equilibria

$X_{max} = \max_{i \in N} X_i(P)$, $X_{min} = \min_{i \in N} X_i(\mathcal{BR}_i(0))$, $m = \log\left(\frac{X_{max}}{X_{min}}\right)$

$\gamma > 0$, $g = 2 \cdot n \cdot (d+1) \cdot \gamma^{-3}$, $b_r = X_{max} \cdot g^{-r} \forall \in [0, m]$

$t = 1 + \gamma$, $s = \left(\frac{1}{t \cdot \Omega_D} - 2\gamma\right)^{-1}$

while there is a player $i \in N$ with $X_i(P) \geq b_1$ and who can perform a t-move **do**
   $P \leftarrow (P_{-i}, \mathcal{BR}_i(P))$
end while
for all phases r from 1 to $m-1$ **do**
   while there is a non-finished player $i \in N$ either with $X_i(P) \in [b_r, +\infty]$ and who can perform a s-move or with $X_i(P) \in [b_{r+1}, b_r]$ and who can perform a t-move **do**
      $P \leftarrow (P_{-i}, \mathcal{BR}_i(P))$
   end while
   Add all players $i \in N$ with $X_i(P) \geq b_r$ to the set of finished players.
end for

For the analysis, let D_r be the set of deviating players in phase r and $P^{r,i}$ denote the state after player $i \in D_r$ has done her last move within phase r.

Theorem 1. *An α-approximate pure Nash equilibrium with $\alpha \in \left(\frac{d}{\ln 2}\right)^d \cdot poly(d)$ can be computed with a polynomial number of improvement steps.*

Proof. The main argument follows from bounding the D-partial potential of the moving players in each phase (see Lemma 9). To that end, we first prove that the partial potential is bounded by the sum of the costs of players when they did their last move (Lemma 8).

Lemma 8. *For every phase r, it holds that $\Phi_{D_r}(P^r) \leq \sum_{i \in D_r} X_i\left(P^{r,i}\right)$.*

We now use the Lemma 8 and the stretch of the previous section to bound the potential of the moving players by the according block size.

Lemma 9. *For every phase r, it holds that $\Phi_{D_r}\left(P^{r-1}\right) \leq \frac{n}{\gamma} \cdot b_r$.*

It remains to show that the running time is bounded and that the approximation factor holds. For the first, since the partial potential is bounded and each deviation decreases the potential, we can limit the number of possible improvement steps (see Lemma 10).

Lemma 10. *The algorithm uses a polynomial number of improvement steps.*

We show next that every player who has already finished his movements will not get much worst costs at the end of the algorithm (see Lemma 11) and that there is no alternative strategy which is more attractive at the end (see Lemma 12).

Lemma 11. *Let i be a player who makes her last move in phase r of the algorithm. Then, $X_i\left(P^{m-1}\right) \leq (1+\gamma^2) \cdot X_i\left(P^r\right)$.*

Lemma 12. *Let i be a player who makes her last move in phase r and let P'_i be an arbitrary strategy of i. Then, $X_i\left(P^{m-1}_{-i}, P'_i\right) \geq (1-\gamma) \cdot X_i\left(P^r_{-i}, P'_i\right)$.*

Next, we bound the approximation factor of the whole algorithm (see Lemma 13).

Lemma 13. *After the last phase of the algorithm, every player i is in an α-approximate pure Nash equilibrium with $\alpha = (1+O(\gamma)) \cdot t\text{-}\Omega_D$.*

The polynomial running time and the approximation factor of $\alpha = (1+O(\gamma)) \cdot t\text{-}\Omega_D$ follow directly from Lemmas 10 and 13. Last, using Corollary 3, we show that $\alpha \in \left(\frac{d}{\ln 2}\right)^d \cdot poly(d)$.

Lemma 14. *The approximation factor α is in the order of $\left(\frac{d}{\ln 2}\right)^d \cdot poly(d)$.*

This completes the proof of Theorem 1.   □

We note that a significant improvement below $O\left(\left(\frac{d}{\ln 2}\right)^d\right)$ of the approximation factor would require new algorithmic ideas as the lower bound of the PoA in [12] immediately yields a corresponding lower bound on the stretch.

This algorithm can be used to compute also approximate pure Nash equilibria in weighted congestion games (with proportional sharing). Such a game can now be approximated by a Shapley game losing only a factor of $\frac{(d+3)(d+1)}{8}$ (by Lemma 3), which is included in $poly(d)$.

Corollary 4. *For any weighted congestion game with proportional sharing, an α-approximate pure Nash equilibrium with $\alpha \in \left(\frac{d}{\ln 2}\right)^d \cdot poly(d)$ can be computed with a polynomial number of improvement steps.*

7.1   Sampling Shapley Values

The previous section gives an algorithm with polynomial running time with respect to the number of improvement steps. However, each improvement step requires the multiple computations of Shapley values, which are hard to compute. For this reason, one can instead compute an approximated Shapley value with sampling methods. Since we are only interested in approximate equilibria, an execution of the algorithm with approximate steps has a negligible impact on the final result. The technical properties of Shapley values stated in Sect. 4 also hold for sampled instead of exact Shapley values with high probability.

Theorem 2. *For any constant γ, an α-approximate pure Nash equilibrium with $\alpha \in \left(\frac{d}{\ln 2}\right)^d \cdot poly(d)$ can be computed in polynomial time with high probability.*

Proof. We use sampling techniques that follow [21,23] and adjust them to our setting.

Algorithm 2. Approximation of the Shapley value by sampling

---

for all r from 1 to $\log\left(2n^{c+3} \cdot \max_{i \in N} \mathcal{P}_i \cdot |E| \cdot \left(1 + \log\left(\frac{X_{\max}}{X_{\min}}\right)\right) \cdot (d+1) \cdot \gamma^{-9}\right)$
do
    for all j from 1 to $k = \frac{4(|S_e(P)|-1)}{\mu^2}$ **do**
        Pick uniformly at random permutation π of the players $S_e(P)$ using resource e
        Compute marginal contribution $MC_{ie}^j(P) = C_e\left(W_{S_e(P)}^{<i,\pi} + w_i\right) - C_e\left(W_{S_e(P)}^{<i,\pi}\right)$
    end for
    Let $\overline{MC}_{ie}(P) = \frac{1}{k}\sum_{j=1}^k MC_{ie}^j(P)$
end for
Return the median of all $\overline{MC}_{ie}(P)$

Lemma 15. *Given an arbitrary state P and an arbitrary but fixed constant c, Algorithm 2 computes a μ-approximation of $\chi_{ie}(P)$ for any player i in polynomial running time with probability at least*

$$1 - \left(n^c \cdot n \cdot \max_{i \in N} \mathcal{P}_i \cdot |E| \cdot \left(1 + \log\left(\frac{X_{max}}{X_{min}}\right)\right) \cdot 2 \cdot n^2 \cdot (d+1) \cdot \gamma^{-9}\right)^{-1}.$$

For using the sampling in the computation of an improvement step, a Shapley value has to be approximated for each alternative strategy of a player and for each resource in the strategy. In the worst case, each player has to be checked for an available improvement step.

Lemma 16. *Given an arbitrary state P and running the sampling algorithm at most $n \cdot \max_{i \in N} \mathcal{P}_i \cdot |E|$ times computes an improvement step for an arbitrary player with probability at least $1 - \left(n^c \cdot \left(1 + \log\left(\frac{X_{max}}{X_{min}}\right)\right) \cdot 2n^2 \cdot (d+1) \cdot \gamma^{-9}\right)^{-1}.$*

Lemma 10 gives a bound on the number of improvement steps. Using the sampling algorithm for $\mu = 1 + \gamma$, we can bound the total number of samplings:

Lemma 17. *During the whole execution of Algorithm 1 the sampling algorithm for $\mu = 1 + \gamma$ is applied at most $n \cdot \max_{i \in N} \mathcal{P}_i \cdot |E| \cdot \left(1 + \log\left(\frac{X_{max}}{X_{min}}\right)\right) \cdot 2 \cdot n^2 \cdot (d + 1) \cdot \gamma^{-9}$ times and the computation of the approximate pure Nash equilibrium is correct with probability at least $1 - n^{-c}$ for an arbitrary constant c.*

Summing up, we show that a μ-approximation of one Shapley value can be computed in polynomial running time with high probability (Lemma 15) and the sampling algorithm is running at most a polynomial number of times (Lemma 17). Then Theorem 2 follows.   □

References

1. Ackermann, H., Röglin, H., Vöcking, B.: On the impact of combinatorial structure on congestion games. J. ACM **55**(6), 25:1–25:22 (2008)
2. Ackermann, H., Skopalik, A.: Complexity of pure Nash equilibria in player-specific network congestion games. Internet Math. **5**(4), 323–342 (2008)
3. Aland, S., Dumrauf, D., Gairing, M., Monien, B., Schoppmann, F.: Exact price of anarchy for polynomial congestion games. In: Durand, B., Thomas, W. (eds.) STACS 2006. LNCS, vol. 3884, pp. 218–229. Springer, Heidelberg (2006). https://doi.org/10.1007/11672142_17
4. Aziz, H., de Keijzer, B.: Shapley meets shapley. In: Mayr, E.W., Portier, N. (eds.) 31st International Symposium on Theoretical Aspects of Computer Science (STACS 2014), STACS 2014, 5–8 March 2014, Lyon, France. LIPIcs, vol. 25, pp. 99–111. Schloss Dagstuhl - Leibniz-Zentrum fuer Informatik (2014)
5. Bachrach, Y., Markakis, E., Resnick, E., Procaccia, A.D., Rosenschein, J.S., Saberi, A.: Approximating power indices: theoretical and empirical analysis. Auton. Agent. Multi-Agent Syst. **20**(2), 105–122 (2010)
6. Caragiannis, I., Fanelli, A., Gravin, N., Skopalik, A.: Efficient computation of approximate pure Nash equilibria in congestion games. In: Ostrovsky, R. (ed.) IEEE 52nd Annual Symposium on Foundations of Computer Science, FOCS 2011, Palm Springs, CA, USA, 22–25 October 2011, pp. 532–541. IEEE Computer Society (2011)
7. Caragiannis, I., Fanelli, A., Gravin, N., Skopalik, A.: Approximate pure Nash equilibria in weighted congestion games: existence, efficient computation, and structure. ACM Trans. Econ. Comput. **3**(1), 2:1–2:32 (2015)
8. Chien, S., Sinclair, A.: Convergence to approximate Nash equilibria in congestion games. Games Econ. Behav. **71**(2), 315–327 (2011)
9. Fabrikant, A., Papadimitriou, C.H., Talwar, K.: The complexity of pure Nash equilibria. In: Babai, L. (ed.) Proceedings of the 36th Annual ACM Symposium on Theory of Computing, Chicago, IL, USA, 13–16 June 2004, pp. 604–612. ACM (2004)
10. Fotakis, D., Kontogiannis, S.C., Spirakis, P.G.: Selfish unsplittable flows. Theor. Comput. Sci. **348**(2–3), 226–239 (2005)
11. Gairing, M., Kollias, K., Kotsialou, G.: Tight bounds for cost-sharing in weighted congestion games. In: Halldórsson, M.M., Iwama, K., Kobayashi, N., Speckmann, B. (eds.) ICALP 2015. LNCS, vol. 9135, pp. 626–637. Springer, Heidelberg (2015). https://doi.org/10.1007/978-3-662-47666-6_50
12. Gairing, M., Schoppmann, F.: Total latency in singleton congestion games. In: Deng, X., Graham, F.C. (eds.) WINE 2007. LNCS, vol. 4858, pp. 381–387. Springer, Heidelberg (2007). https://doi.org/10.1007/978-3-540-77105-0_42
13. Gkatzelis, V., Kollias, K., Roughgarden, T.: Optimal cost-sharing in weighted congestion games. In: Liu, T.-Y., Qi, Q., Ye, Y. (eds.) WINE 2014. LNCS, vol. 8877, pp. 72–88. Springer, Cham (2014). https://doi.org/10.1007/978-3-319-13129-0_6

14. Gopalakrishnan, R., Marden, J.R., Wierman, A.: Potential games are necessary to ensure pure Nash equilibria in cost sharing games. Math. Oper. Res. **39**(4), 1252–1296 (2014)
15. Hansknecht, C., Klimm, M., Skopalik, A.: Approximate pure Nash equilibria in weighted congestion games. In: Jansen, K., Rolim, J.D.P., Devanur, N.R., Moore, C. (eds.) Approximation, Randomization, and Combinatorial Optimization. Algorithms and Techniques, APPROX/RANDOM 2014, 4–6 September 2014, Barcelona, Spain. LIPIcs, vol. 28, pp. 242–257. Schloss Dagstuhl - Leibniz-Zentrum fuer Informatik (2014)
16. Harks, T., Klimm, M.: On the existence of pure Nash equilibria in weighted congestion games. Math. Oper. Res. **37**(3), 419–436 (2012)
17. Hart, S., Mas-Colell, A.: Potential, value, and consistency. Econometrica **57**(3), 589–614 (1989)
18. Klimm, M., Schmand, D.: Sharing non-anonymous costs of multiple resources optimally. In: Paschos, V.T., Widmayer, P. (eds.) CIAC 2015. LNCS, vol. 9079, pp. 274–287. Springer, Cham (2015). https://doi.org/10.1007/978-3-319-18173-8_20
19. Kollias, K., Roughgarden, T.: Restoring pure equilibria to weighted congestion games. ACM Trans. Econ. Comput. **3**(4), 1–24 (2015)
20. Koutsoupias, E., Papadimitriou, C.: Worst-case equilibria. In: Meinel, C., Tison, S. (eds.) STACS 1999. LNCS, vol. 1563, pp. 404–413. Springer, Heidelberg (1999). https://doi.org/10.1007/3-540-49116-3_38
21. Liben-Nowell, D., Sharp, A., Wexler, T., Woods, K.: Computing shapley value in supermodular coalitional games. In: Gudmundsson, J., Mestre, J., Viglas, T. (eds.) COCOON 2012. LNCS, vol. 7434, pp. 568–579. Springer, Heidelberg (2012). https://doi.org/10.1007/978-3-642-32241-9_48
22. Maleki, S.: Addressing the computational issues of the Shapley value with applications in the smart grid. Ph.D. thesis, University of Southampton (2015)
23. Mann, I., Shapley, L.S.: Values of large games, 6: evaluating the electoral college exactly. Technical report, DTIC Document (1962)
24. Milchtaich, I.: Congestion games with player-specific payoff functions. Games Econ. Behav. **13**(1), 111–124 (1996)
25. Monderer, D., Shapley, L.S.: Potential games. Games Econ. Behav. **14**(1), 124–143 (1996)
26. Rosenthal, R.W.: A class of games possessing pure-strategy Nash equilibria. Int. J. Game Theory **2**(1), 65–67 (1973)
27. Roughgarden, T., Schrijvers, O.: Network Cost-Sharing without Anonymity. ACM Trans. Econ. Comput. **4**(2), 8:1–8:24 (2016)
28. Skopalik, A., Vöcking, B.: Inapproximability of pure Nash equilibria. In: Dwork, C. (ed.) Proceedings of the 40th Annual ACM Symposium on Theory of Computing, Victoria, British Columbia, Canada, 17–20 May 2008, pp. 355–364. ACM (2008)

Socially Optimal Mining Pools

Ben Fisch[1(✉)], Rafael Pass[2], and Abhi Shelat[3]

[1] Stanford University, Stanford, USA
bfisch@stanford.edu
[2] Cornell University, Ithaca, USA
rafael@cs.cornell.edu
[3] Northeastern University, Boston, USA
a.shelat@northeastern.edu

Abstract. Mining for Bitcoins is a high-risk high-reward activity. Miners, seeking to reduce their variance and earn steadier rewards, collaborate in so-called *pooling strategies* where they jointly mine for Bitcoins. Whenever some pool participant is successful, the earned rewards are appropriately split among all pool participants. Currently a dozen of different pooling strategies are in use for Bitcoin mining. We here propose a formal model of utility and social optimality for Bitcoin mining (and analogous mining systems) based on the theory of discounted expected utility, and next study pooling strategies that maximize the utility of participating miners in this model. We focus on pools that achieve a steady-state utility, where the utility per unit of work of all participating miners converges to a common value. Our main result shows that one of the pooling strategies actually employed in practice—the so-called *geometric pay pool*—achieves the optimal steady-state utility for miners when its parameters are set appropriately. Our results apply not only to Bitcoin mining pools, but any other form of pooled mining or crowdsourcing computations where the participants engage in repeated random trials towards a common goal, and where "partial" solutions can be efficiently verified.

1 Introduction

In recent years, *crowd-sourcing of computation*—where anyone can contribute to a computationally heavy task—has grown in popularity. For instance, in the SETI@home project, users search for extraterrestrial life by analyzing radio telescoping data; or in the Rosetta@home project, users process data to discover new proteins. In both of these examples, however, the participating users freely volunteer computing resources. With the advent of Bitcoin, a new type of computational crowdsourcing emerged: in place of altruism, users are *incentivized* to participate in the computation by receiving a reward (paid in Bitcoins) for performing the work. Bitcoin [Nak08] is a digital currency system that enables users to transact without a central authority. In absence of a trusted central monitor, the system relies on external monitors called "miners" who perform intensive computation—searching for a solution to a computation puzzle—to

© Springer International Publishing AG 2017
N. R. Devanur and P. Lu (Eds.): WINE 2017, LNCS 10674, pp. 205–218, 2017.
https://doi.org/10.1007/978-3-319-71924-5_15

operate the system. To incentivize participation, miners receive rewards for any puzzle they solve. The reward incentive in Bitcoin has an exceedingly high variance (the puzzles are difficult to solve), and as shown in [PSS16], this is inherent in the Bitcoin system. As a result, miners typically collaborate by forming *mining pools* to reduce their variance. Currently, miners use many different types of pooling strategies.

The focus of this work is to determine the optimal mining pooling strategies. While our focus is on Bitcoin (and proof-of-work blockchains in general), our results apply to any form of mining that involves random trials and where demonstration of partial work is possible. One can even imagine applications to non-computational forms of mining (e.g., gold mining, oil drilling).

We begin with an overview of Bitcoin system and then proceed to formalize the pool-design problem. We refer the reader to [BMC+15] for a more detailed description of the Bitcoin system.

1.1 Overview of Bitcoin

The Bitcoin reward system. Bitcoin uses a distributed consensus protocol to maintain in a public ledger called the *blockchain* which stores the valid transaction history. Participants broadcast transactions over a peer-to-peer network, while agents called *miners* collect blocks of transactions, verify their integrity, and append them to the blockchain. The system incentivizes miners by rewarding them with newly minted coins for each block they add to the chain. In order to append a block to the blockchain, miners must produce a computationally intensive *proof-of-work*.

The proof-of-work consists of finding a partial pre-image for a cryptographic hash function H. Roughly, given a block with contents b, a miner must find a value r from a large domain X such that $H(b||r) < d$. Miners successively sample random values in X until they find a solution to this cryptographic puzzle. The value d determines the block *difficulty*, or the probability p that a random $r \in X$ will satisfy the puzzle. The current difficulty is set so that in expectation, the entire group of miners succeed in mining a single block every 10 min (and as shown by the analysis in [PSS16], the mining difficulty cannot be significantly decreased without making the protocol vulnerable to attacks.)

As a consequence, the income of an individual miner has a very high variance. An individual miner who purchases (for roughly 24,000 USD) ten AntMiner S9 machines, a state-of-the-art mining device, could mine at rate of 140×10^{12} hashes per second. Yet based on the current difficulty parameter[1], such an individual would in expectation mine a single block only once every 305 days. Moreover, the process of mining is memoryless. A miner who has not received any reward after 305 days must still wait another 305 days on average to receive a reward. Thus, the number of blocks produced by a miner working at a continuous rate h (measured in hashes per second) for a time period t is well approximated

---

[1] https://bitcoinwisdom.com/bitcoin/difficulty.

by a Poisson distribution with mean $\lambda = pht$. The miner receives expected reward λB with variance λB^2, where B is the reward per block.

Mining pools. Miners seeking to reduce their variance and earn steadier incomes join *mining pools*. Participating in a pool is called *pool mining* and mining alone is called *solo mining*. Whenever a pool miner wins a reward, the reward is shared among all the pool's participating miners. Pools require a trusted operator to monitor participation and manage the allocation of rewards. This pool operator monitors how much work each individual participant contributes to the pool, and then whenever some participant manages to mine a block, the operator receives the block reward in proxy and then allocates the reward among the pool participants based on how much work they contributed.

Monitoring the effort of participating miners, however, is a nontrivial task. Unless miners are assumed to be honest, simply asking miners to report their effort leads to *free riding*: riders will claim to have done work even if they have not. To overcome this problem, miners instead demonstrate their effort by submitting partial proofs-of-work called *shares*, which are simply block hashes that satisfy a lower difficulty parameter, i.e. shares are a "near-solution" to the original computational puzzle. We distinguish such shares from full solutions which we refer to as *blocks*.

To prevent pool participants from stealing the block-mining reward whenever they find a full solution, the block owner identity is incorporated into the proof-of-work. Pools only accept proofs-of-work, partial or complete, that incorporate the identity of the pool as the block owner. Otherwise, miners could submit only partial proofs to the pool and send their complete proofs to the Bitcoin network for a solo reward.

The principal question we consider now is:

How should block rewards be allocated to pool participants so as to maximize their utility of participation?

If miners are *risk neutral*, then solo mining is optimal. But if miners are *risk averse* (technically, have a concave utility function), then pooling strategies may improve their utility by decreasing the variance of their rewards. From here on, we refer to the pool's strategy for allocating the reward as the *allocation rule*. Indeed, several popular pooling strategies with different allocation rules are currently in use:[2]

- In the *proportional pay* scheme, the reward of a block is split among all the participants in the pool proportionally to the number of shares they submitted to the pool—in other words, the rewards are split evenly among the shares in the pool, and the pool is then "emptied" for the next round.
- The *Pay-Per-Last-N-Shares* (PPLNS) pool is similar, except that the block reward is always distributed evenly among the last N shares submitted to the pool (without ever "emptying" the pool).

---

[2] https://en.bitcoin.it/wiki/Comparison_of_mining_pools.

– Score based pooling mechanisms generalize PPLNS pools, and distribute block rewards over preceding shares contributed to the pool according to some weighting function. PPLNS can be viewed as a score based pooling mechanism that uses a step weighting function. Rewards in the *Slush's pool* and the *geometric pool* are concentrated at the winning block and decay exponentially over the preceding shares.

Some pools do not allocate rewards immediately, and instead invest rewards in a central pool fund. These funds may be used to incentivize future participation in the pool at a risk-free rate (*Pay-Per-Share* (PPS) pools). PPS pools absorb all the variance of their participants, and in order to survive with high probability they must heavily discount the risk-free rate. This is not a pure pooling mechanism because it assumes a financier. In this paper, we restrict our attention to pure pooling mechanisms.

Definition 1 (Informal Definition). *A pure pooling mechanism is an allocation rule that assigns fractional rewards to all shares preceding a block, including the block share itself. The allocation-rule may depend on the state of the pool.*

Our Results. In its current state of affairs, the Bitcoin mining pool ecosystem is a collection of seemingly ad-hoc mining pool strategies with ad-hoc parameters, and there is no consensus as to which pool mechanism is "optimal". As far as we are aware, there are no published theories on optimal mining pool strategies even among a restricted class of strategies. Towards this goal, we put forward a formal model of utility of pooling strategies for computation/mining, taking into account the fairness of strategies to all participants, and derive the pooling strategy that maximizes miners' utility in this model. Our analysis is restricted to pools that monitor mining works by collecting partial shares and derives its reward solely from blocks submitted by its participants. We also restrict our attention to pools that immediately allocate all rewards to participants. We demonstrate that for the most commonly used utility function, a power utility function, the *geometric pool* is optimal if the parameters of the geometric pool are appropriately set. As mentioned above, the geometric pool is one that is used in practice (although not necessarily with the optimal parameters).

Mining pool utility. In order to analyze the question of what the optimal pooling strategy is, we must first specify a model for measuring the utility of a pool participant. We start by viewing Bitcoin mining pool shares as financial investments that receive a cashflow from the pool. Different pools represent different investment packages, each varying the risk, value, and timing of payoffs. We use the standard *discounted expected utility* (DEU) [Sam37] model, which exponentially discounts the utility of payoffs occurring t steps in the future by δ^t for some constant discount parameter δ.

Pool fairness. A general pool may distribute rewards in an arbitrary way that benefits some miners at the expense of others, and we will rank such pools below those that have a more equitable distribution. We define a *perfectly fair* pooling strategy as one in which all mining shares derive equal utility. Solo mining is perfectly fair. Many natural pool strategies do not quite achieve perfect fairness, but do achieve *steady-state fairness*, where the expected utility of pool shares converges to a *steady-state utility* in the lifetime of the pool. For example, in a PPLNS pool the first N shares earn a higher expected reward than all shares, but all subsequent shares have the same "steady-state" expected reward/utility. Likewise, geometric pools are steady-state fair, although convergence does not occur in finitely many steps as in PPLNS. The proportional pay pool has the same property. In fact, all the naturally occuring pools we know of and discuss in this paper are either perfectly fair or steady-state fair.

Optimality. In fair pools, the steady-state utility of the pool is a natural measure for the collective utility of the pool participants as a whole. A pool is *steady-state optimal* if it achieves the optimal steady-state utility.

Main Theorems. In general, pools may have a complex reward allocation that depends on the pool's state including the history of prior reward allocations in the pool. In practice, all the pooling strategies that are used in practice except for proportional pay are significantly simpler: they use a *fixed rule* that is independent of the history of the pool to allocate rewards to the miners who contributed previous shares to the pool. We can represent such fixed-rule pools by an infinite length vector X where X_i denotes the fractional reward allocated to the miner who contributed the ith share preceding a reward-earning block.

Definition 2. *A **fixed-rule pool** is a pool that has a fixed allocation rule such that whenever a block reward is earned the pool distributes a fixed fraction X_i of the reward to the ith pool share preceding the block share, where $i \geq 0$.*

Fixed-rule pools are indeed preferable. They have a simple allocation rule and are perfectly fair. Since all shares in a fixed-rule pool have equal utility we can simply refer to the utility of a share in the pool as the pool's utility, and an optimal fixed-rule pool achieves an optimal utility among fixed-rule pools. Furthermore, as we show in our first theorem, we can limit our study to such objects without any loss of generality. We show that for *any* concave utility function, if there exists an optimal *fixed-rule* pool then this pool is also steady-state optimal among all pools.

Theorem 1. *For any concave real-valued utility function u, time-discounting parameter $\delta < 1$, if there exists an optimal fixed rule pool, then this pool is steady-state optimal.*

In our main theorem, we then characterize an optimal steady-state pooling strategy for a common family of utility functions. In Fig. 1, we illustrate Theorem 3 by graphing the results of simulating each type of pool for 1 billion shares and then computing the discounted expected utility for each share as a function of the miner's utility function, i.e., the miner's risk parameters α. Each experiment was run 50 times, and the dots reflect the average of each experiment, whereas the solid lines represent our analytical results.

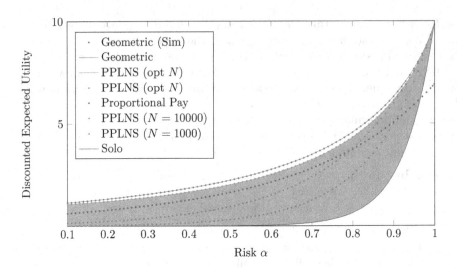

Fig. 1. Expected value of each share for various mining pool schemes as a function of risk tolerance α for the power utility function $u(x) = x^\alpha$. The win rate is $p = 10^{-5}$, discount rate $d = 0.99999$, and reward $B = 10^6$. Dotted lines represent simulated data, smooth lines represent analytically-derived results. The area in green represents the range for PPLNS ranging from $N = 1$ (solo) to the optimal values for N for a given α.

Theorem 3. *For the utility function $u(x) = x^\alpha$ where $0 < \alpha < 1$, the geometric pool with allocation rule $X_i = B(1 - \delta^{1/1-\alpha})\delta^{i/1-\alpha}$ is steady-state optimal.*

Incentive compatibility. The question of incentive compatibility in mining pools has been addressed to some degree in several other works [Ros11, LBS+15, SBBR16, LJG15, Eya15], but in general remains largely open. The well-known counterexample to incentive compatibility is the proportional pay pool, which is vulnerable to *pool hopping*. Block rewards in a proportional pay pool are distributed evenly among all shares submitted per block period. Thus, as the block period length (number of shares in a block period) increases, the utility of contributing shares to the pool decreases. If a block period grows beyond a certain point, participating miners achieve a better expected utility by solo mining (or mining for a different pool). There are several other known attacks in the context of competing pools. Some of these attacks enable miners to boost their rewards at the expense of other more honest participants [Eya15, LJG15, JLG+14].

While current research suggests that achieving incentive compatibility in a system of competing pools is extremely difficult, considering the incentive compatibility of a single pool, i.e., with respect to deviations to solo-mining, is straightforward. It is easy to see that the optimal pool that we derive is incentive compatible in this sense. The optimal pool we derived is a fixed-rule pool. Solo mining is also a fixed-rule pool with allocation rule $X_0 = B$ and $X_i = 0$ for all $i > 0$. In a fixed-rule pool the utility of every share is equal. Thus, it follows trivially that in an optimal fixed-rule pool the utility of every share is greater than or equal to the utility of solo mining.

Organization. In Sect. 2 we present our utility model for mining pool shares, and define steady-state optimality. In Sect. 3 we present our main theorems and outline the proofs. The full proof details are included in the full version of this paper[3] Sect. 4 poses an open problem to extend our analysis to pools with investment strategies, such as Pay-Per-Share.

2   The Utility Model

Mining Pools. A miner invests work in repeated attempts to solve a computationally difficult puzzle in order to win a prize. After every repeated attempt, the miner learns whether or not the attempt was successful. Previous attempts do not affect future attempts, and thus, at every renewed attempt the miner has the same probability of receiving an award. This is similar to a player in a scratchcard lottery who repeatedly purchases cards, scratching off each card before purchasing the next. If every card purchase is a Bernoulli trial with success parameter p, then the number of wins out of N trials has a Binomial distribution with expectation pN and variance $p(1 - p)N$.

Monitoring mining work. In Bitcoin mining, the analog of a scratchcard purchase is an investment of work. Just as a scratchcard lottery pool operator would count purchased cards, Bitcoin mining pool operators monitor the *work* of their participating miners. Currently, operators estimate participants' work rates by collecting partial proofs-of-work called shares. Producing a share is significantly easier than producing a block, but sufficiently difficult so that miners cannot feasibly produce shares without honestly attempting to produce a valid block.

Rewarding shares. The pool operator collects shares in an inherently sequential manner, and we assume that the history of shares submitted to the pool is common knowledge among all participants. Each share wins a reward with independent probability p.

A *pool mechanism* is a rule for distributing block rewards over past and future shares. The reward of an individual share is a sum over rewards it receives from past or future shares, as well as any reward it generates and keeps for itself when it is a valid block.

Formally, we define a reward allocation rule as a probabilistic function of the pool's state. The pool's state includes the history of shares contributed to the pool and their outcomes (i.e. partial or valid block). We can denote this state $\sigma = (t, h_t)$, where t is the number of shares, and h_t is a binary vector of length t indicating if each previous share was a block. The output of the allocation rule is a collection of random variables denoting reward payments to specific shares (i.e. the miners who contributed those shares). We restrict our definition to pure

---

[3] https://arxiv.org/abs/1703.03846.

pooling strategies in which the reward is immediately allocated to miners who previously contributed shares to the pool (i.e. no future payments).

Definition 3. *An **allocation rule** is a function* $\mathcal{A}(t, h_t) = \{X_i^{(t,h_t)}\}_{0 \leq i \leq t}$ *where* $X_i^{(\sigma)}$ *is a random variable denoting the reward value allocated to the contributor of the pool's* $(t - i)$*th share when the pool wins a block reward B in state* $\sigma = (t, h_t)$.

2.1   Utility of a Pool Share

A pool share has an associated reward vector $\boldsymbol{X} = (X_0, X_1, \ldots)$ where the random variable X_i denotes the reward that the share accrues during the ith period following the submission of the share. The variable X_0 is the reward that the share generates and keeps for itself. We use the *discounted expected utility*[4] (DEU) model to measure the utility of submitting the share as follows.

Definition 4. *Given discount parameter* δ *and utility function* u, *the discounted expected utility (DEU) of a pool share with reward vector* $\boldsymbol{X}$ *is:*

$$U = \sum_{i \geq 0} E[u(X_i)]\delta^i$$

Risk-aversity and time-discounting. The utility model given by Definition 4 above is able to capture the two key characteristics of miners participating in pools:

– *time-discounting*: Miners value present cash flow more than future cash flow. The degree to which they discount the value of future cash is determined by δ.
– *risk-aversity*: Miners prefer investing work to receive an expected reward of lower variance than one of higher variance. This means miners may prefer a pool that offers lower expected rewards with lower variance over one that offers higher expected rewards with higher variance for the same investment of work. The degree to which a miner is willing to sacrifice reward for lower variance is determined by the concavity of the utility function u. A risk-neutral agent will have a linear utility function. If u is linear then $E[u(X)] = u(E[X])$, whereas $E[u(X)] < u(E[X])$ when u is strictly concave.

---

[4] There are many implicit axioms in the DEU model formula, see [FL02] for a comprehensive overview. In particular, since the DEU model treats utility as linearly additive over time-separated consumptions, it implicitly assumes that the consumer is risk-neutral to aggregated utilities over time, even if the consumer is risk-averse in each time period. Intertemporal risk-aversion has also been considered in the economics literature and there are modified DEU models where aggregation of discounted utilities is nonlinear [FL02,EZ89,KP78].

We illustrate what the model predicts in several special cases. Assume that the total expected reward is bounded, i.e. $\sum_i E[X_i] \leq B$. A risk-neutral miner (for whom u is linear) clearly derives the highest utility from solo mining. In the case where u is non-decreasing and linear, $U = \sum_{i \geq 0} u(E[X_i])\delta^i$, which for any $\delta < 1$ has the highest value subject to the constraint on total expected reward when $E[X_0] = B$ and $E[X_i] = 0$. On the opposite end of the spectrum, a risk-averse miner with negligible preference for present cashflow over future cashflow (i.e. $\delta \approx 1$) would derive ever increasing utility the more the expected reward is spread over many periods, e.g. $E[X_i] = B/N$ for $i \leq N$ as $N \to \infty$. This has the effect of lowering the variance in the total expected reward by splitting it into many small payments that each occur with equal probability, yet over a longer period of time. This is essentially a PPLNS pool with a very large window. The principle question we address in this paper is what this model predicts for a risk-averse miner with non-negligible time-discounting, i.e. concave u and $\delta < 1$. As a special case in this analysis we consider the power utility function $u(x) = x^{\alpha}$, where $\alpha > 0$ determines the degree of concavity (and hence risk-aversity).

2.2   Pool Optimality

We say that a pool strategy achieves *steady-state fairness* if the utility of contributing pool shares converges.

Definition 5. *A pool strategy is **steady-state fair** if the sequence $\{U_k\}$ converges in $\mathbb{R}$, where U_k denotes the expected utility of the kth pool share. The limit point of $\lim_{k \to \infty} U_k$ is the **steady-state utility** of the pool.*

Steady-state optimality. In any class $\mathcal{C}$ of steady-state fair strategies, we can define the steady-state optimal strategies of $\mathcal{C}$ as the set of strategies in $\mathcal{C}$ that have the highest steady-state utility.

Definition 6. *A pool strategy $\mathfrak{p}$ is **steady-state optimal** for a class $\mathcal{C}$ of steady-state fair pool strategies if and only if $\mathfrak{p} \in \arg \max_{x \in \mathcal{C}} \lim_{k \to \infty} E[U(x)_k]$.*

3   The Optimal Pool

In this section we show how to derive a steady-state optimal pool for honest risk-averse players. The parameters of the optimal pool will depend on the choice of utility function u, time-discounting factor δ, and fixed block reward B. The main results of this section applies to any general utility function u that is concave and real-valued. We first show a relationship between steady-state optimal pools and *fixed-rule pools*–a pool that allocates block rewards according to a fixed rule, independent of the pool's state. Specifically, we prove that if there exists an optimal fixed-rule pool then it is also steady-state optimal. The optimal fixed-rule pool is a solution to a convex optimization problem that depends on u, δ, and B. We solve this optimization problem explicitly for the power utility function

$u(x) = x^\alpha$ ($0 < \alpha < 1$), which yields a geometric pool whose parameters depend on α.

Our results are the following three theorems:

Theorem 1. *For any concave real-valued utility function u, time-discounting parameter $\delta < 1$, if there exists an optimal fixed rule pool, then this pool is steady-state optimal.*

In Lemma 1 we show that if a pool has steady-state utility U then for every ϵ there exists a fixed-rule pool that has utility at least $U - \epsilon$. Therefore, U is bounded by the supremum of fixed-rule pool utilities. If there exists an optimal fixed-rule pool then by definition it achieves this supremum and hence its utility is an upper bound on the steady-state utility of any steady-state fair pool.

Theorem 2. *For any concave real-valued utility function u, time-discounting parameter $\delta < 1$, and block reward B, there exists an optimal fixed-rule pool if and only if there is a solution to the following convex optimization problem:*

$$\arg \max_x \sum_{i \geq 0} u(x_i)\delta^i \quad \text{subject to} \quad \sum_{i \geq 0} x_i \leq B, \forall i \; x_i \geq 0$$

If a solution $\{x_i\}_{i \geq 0}$ exists then it defines the allocation rule of the optimal fixed-rule pool.

Theorem 3. *For the power utility functions there is a fixed-rule geometric pool that is steady-state optimal. The parameters of this geometric pool are determined by the block reward B, the risk-aversity parameter $0 < \alpha < 1$ of the utility function $u(x) = x^\alpha$, and the time-discounting factor δ. Specifically, this geometric pool has the allocation rule $X_i = B(1 - \delta^{1/1-\alpha})\delta^{i/1-\alpha}$.*

3.1   Fixed-Rule Pools

Fixed-rule pools have several nice properties: they are perfectly fair, and the expected reward of any share in the pool is bounded.

Claim 1. *For fixed allocation rules $\sum_{t \geq k} E[X_k^{(t)}] \leq B$ for any k.*

Proof. Suppose towards contradiction that $\sum_{i \geq 0} E[X_k^{(k+i)}] = \hat{B} > B$ for some k. By definition of a limit, for any $\epsilon > 0$ there exists N_ϵ such that $| \sum_{i=0}^{N_\epsilon} E[X_k^{(k+i)}] - \hat{B}| < \epsilon$. Setting $\epsilon = (\hat{B} - B)/2$ implies $\sum_{i=0}^{N_\epsilon} E[X_k^{(k+i)}] > B$. However, using the property of fixed allocation rules, $\sum_{i=0}^{N_\epsilon} E[X_k^{(k+i)}] = \sum_{i=0}^{N_\epsilon} E[X_i^{N_\epsilon}] \leq B$. This is a contradiction.

In a pool with a fixed allocation rule $\{X_i\}$, we can express the utility of any share in terms of the allocation rule variables and the probability p that a share is a valid block:

$$U = \sum_{i \geq 0} pE[u(X_i)]\delta^i \tag{1}$$

Since every share has the same expected utility, by definition the pool is perfectly fair.

Claim 2. *Every pool with a fixed allocation rule is perfectly fair.*

Proof of Theorem 2. The utility of any share in a fixed-rule pool with alloca-
tion rule $\{X_i\}$ is $\sum_{i\geq 0} pE[u(X_i)]\delta^i$ for variables $X_i \geq 0$ where $\sum_{i\geq 0} E[X_i] \leq B$
(Claim 1). Therefore, the optimal fixed-rule pool is the solution to:

$$\arg \max_X \sum_{i\geq 0} E[u(X_i)]\delta^i \text{ subject to } \sum_{i\geq 0} E[X_i] \leq B, \forall i \; E[X_i] \geq 0$$

By Jensen's inequality, for concave u we have $E[u(X_i)] \leq u(E[X_i])$, and
equality holds when X_i are scalars or u is linear. Thus it suffices to solve the
optimization for scalars x_i as follows:

$$\arg \max_y \sum_{i\geq 0} u(y_i)\delta^i \text{ subject to } \sum_{i\geq 0} y_i \leq B, \forall i \; y_i \geq 0$$

If a solution exists then it defines the allocation rule of an optimal fixed-rule
pool. Conversely, if some pool with allocation rule $\{X_i^*\}$ is optimal, then the
pool with allocation rule $\{E[X_i^*]\}$ is necessarily optimal, hence it is a solution
to the above optimization problem.

Finally, to show that this is a convex optimization problem we will prove
that the objective function $f(y) = \sum_i u(y_i)\delta^i$ is concave. Since u is concave, for
any $y^{(1)}$, $y_2^{(2)}$ and scalar t it holds that $f(ty^{(1)} + (1-t)y^{(2)}) = \sum_i u(ty_i^{(1)} + (1-t)y_i^{(2)})\delta^i \leq \sum_i tu(y_i^{(1)})\delta^i + (1-t)u(y_i^{(2)})\delta^i = tf(y^{(1)}) + (1-t)f(y^{(2)})$.

3.2   Steady-State Pools to Fixed-Rule Pools

Lemma 1. *For any steady-state fair pool* $\mathfrak{p}$ *that has steady-state share utility* $U_\mathfrak{p}$
and any $\epsilon > 0$ *there exists a fixed-rule pool* $\mathfrak{p}'$ *that has share utility* $U_{\mathfrak{p}'} \geq U_\mathfrak{p} - \epsilon$.

In fixed-rule pools the distribution of future rewards a miner receives for
submitting a share was independent of state. In more general pools, even steady-
state fair pools, this distribution of future rewards could fluctuate over the state
of the pool. The high level idea of this proof is to show that if the utility of
the pool converges then the distribution of future expected rewards converges in
some subsequence of states to a fixed distribution. We use this fixed distribution
of expected rewards to define a fixed-rule pool that allocates to each previous
share exactly its expected reward. The steady-state utility of this subsequence
of states will be bounded by the utility of this fixed-rule pool. Since infinite
subsequences of any convergent sequence also converge to the same limit, it
follows that the steady-state utility of the pool is also bounded by the utility of
this fixed-rule pool.

If the space containing the sequence of expected reward distributions were
sequentially compact, then existence of a subsequence of states for which reward
distributions converge would follow immediately. However, each expected reward
distribution is an infinite vector over $\mathbb{R}$, and infinite dimensional subspaces of

$\mathbb{R}^\infty$ are not necessarily sequentially compact. Instead, we examine *finite-window* pools, which only allocate rewards over preceding shares within some finite window. Due to time-discounting, every pool can be approximated by a finite-window pool. More precisely, for any pool we can define the finite-window pool that uses the same allocation rule restricted to the last N shares, and for any $\epsilon > 0$ we can choose N sufficiently large so that the utility of any share in the finite-window pool is within ϵ of the same share in the original pool. In finite-windows pools the expected reward distribution is a finite length vector in a closed and bounded subset of $\mathbb{R}^N$, which by the Bolzano-Weierstrass theorem is sequentially compact. Thus, we can prove that the utility of all finite-window pool approximations are bounded by the utility of a fixed-rule pool, and by making ϵ arbitrarily small we extend this bound to the original pool.

The full proof of Lemma 1 is included in the full version of this paper.

3.3   Optimal Pool for Power Utility

The main challenge in proving Theorem 3 is that the optimization problem is over $\mathbb{R}^\infty_{\geq 0}$ rather than $\mathbb{R}^n_{\geq 0}$. The problem is that the objective function may not achieve its maximum on the feasible set because the optimization is over an infinite dimensional vector space, and so the feasible set is not compact. First let us define the following notation:

Define $f(y) = \sum_{i \geq 0} u(y_i)\delta^i$ *and* $g(y) = \sum_{i \geq 0} y_i$ *for* $y \in \mathbb{R}^\infty_{\geq 0}$ *and* $n \in \mathbb{N}$, *where* u *is the concave utility function in question. For* $n \geq 1$ *define the "truncated" sums* $f_n(y) = \sum_{i=1}^n u(y_i)\delta^i$ *and* $g_n(y) = \sum_{i=1}^n y_i$. *The functions* $f_n(y)$ *and* $g_n(y)$ *are well defined over both* $\mathbb{R}^\infty_{\geq 0}$ *and* $\mathbb{R}^n_{\geq 0}$.

Our approach is to solve for a maximizer x_n^* of each $f_n(y)$ subject to $g(y) \leq B$ and $\forall i \ y_i \geq 0$ (Claim 3). To obtain some x_n^*, it suffices to solve for a maximizer of $f_n(y)$ defined instead over $y \in \mathbb{R}^n_{\geq 0}$ with the constraint $g_n(y)$, and then extend this maximizer to a point in $\mathbb{R}^\infty$ that is identical to this maximizer in the first n components and 0 in every other component. The solutions x_n^* are obtained via the method of Lagrange multipliers. We then show that this sequence of maximizers converges in $\mathbb{R}^\infty$[5], i.e. $\{x_n^*\} \to x^*$, and the limit point x^* is a maximizer of $f(y)$ subject to $g(y) \leq B$ over $\mathbb{R}^\infty$. The full proof is in the full version of this work.

Claim 3. *When* $u(x) = x^\alpha$, *the maximizer of* $f_n(y)$ *subject to* $g_n(y) \leq B$ *over* $\mathbb{R}^n_{\geq 0}$ *is* $y_i = B \frac{1 - \delta^{1/1-\alpha}}{1 - \delta^{n/1-\alpha}} \delta^{i/1-\alpha}$.

---

[5] Convergence in $\mathbb{R}^\infty$ can be defined with respect to the standard Euclidean norm restricted to points in $\mathbb{R}^\infty$ that have finite norm. All the points in the sequence of maximizers lie in this subspace because they have a finite number of nonzero components. The limit point of this sequence satisfies the optimization constraint (i.e. has a bounded L1 norm) and thus also lies in this subspace.

Proof. $f_n(y)$ is increasing in y_i for every i. Thus, if there exists a global maximum then it is achieved on $g_n(y) = B$. The Lagrangian for this optimization is $L(y, \lambda) = f_n(y) + \lambda(B - g_n(y))$. There exists a solution y^* to the constrained optimization problem if and only if there exists λ^* such that $L(y^*, \lambda^*)$ is a global maximum of the Lagrangian. **First, we prove that a solution exists** by examining the principal minors of the Hessian of the Lagrangian. A solution exists if for all $k \geq 2$, the determinant of the kth principal minor of the Hessian of $L(y, \lambda)$ has sign $(-1)^{k+1}$. **Second, we derive a unique stationary point of the Lagrangian**. A global maximum (y^*, λ^*) must be a stationary point of the Lagrangian, i.e. $\nabla_y L(y^*, \lambda^*) = 0$. Since the stationary point we derive is unique it must be the global maximum of the Lagrangian, and hence a solution to the constrained optimization.

Existence of a solution. Consider the Hessian of $L(y, \lambda)$. This is a matrix H with $H_{0,0} = 0$, $H_{i,0} = H_{0,i} = \frac{\partial g_n}{\partial x_i} = 1$ for $i > 0$, $H_{i,j} = \frac{\partial L}{\partial y_i \partial y_j} = 0$ for $i \neq j \neq 0$, and $H_{i,i} = \frac{\partial^2 L}{\partial y_i^2} = \delta^i \frac{\partial^2 u(y_i)}{\partial y_i^2} < 0$ by the strict concavity of $u(y_i)$ for $i > 0$. Consider the kth principal minor $M^{(k)}$ of H. The Leibniz formula for the determinant of $M^{(k)}$ is $\det(M^{(k)}) = \sum_{\sigma \in S_k} sgn(\sigma) \prod_{i=1}^{k} m_{i,\sigma_i}$. Consider any nonzero term of this sum. It cannot include in its product $m_{1,1}$ and so must contain $m_{1,i} = 1$ and $m_{j,1} = 1$ for some $i, j \neq 1$. The $k - 2$ remaining elements of the product must be from the nonzero (negative valued) diagonal entries. However, it also cannot include the elements $m_{j,j}$ and $m_{i,i}$ because it includes $m_{1,i}$ and $m_{j,1}$. If $i \neq j$ this leaves only $k - 3$ diagonal elements, hence necessarily $i = j$ and the product includes all the $k - 2$ diagonal elements except $m_{i,i}$. The term corresponds to an odd permutation σ that contains $k - 2$ fixed points and a single inversion $(1, i)$, so $sgn(\sigma) = -1$. All nonzero terms thus have sign $-(-1)^{k-2} = (-1)^{k-1} = (-1)^{k+1}$. Therefore $\det(M^{(k)})$ has sign $(-1)^{k+1}$.

Unique stationary point. We proceed to show that the Lagrangian $L(y, \lambda) = f_n(y) + \lambda(B - g_n(y))$ has a unique stationary point when $u(x) = x^\alpha$. We will first do this for $u(x) = x^\alpha$. Setting $\nabla_y L(y, \lambda) = 0$, this yields the system of equations $\alpha y_i^{\alpha-1} \delta^i - \lambda = 0$ for all i, and we solve for $y_i = \left(\frac{\alpha}{\lambda} \delta^i\right)^{1/1-\alpha}$.

Applying the constraint $\sum_{i=1}^{n} y_i = B$ we get:

$$\sum_{i=0}^{n} \left(\frac{\alpha}{\lambda} \delta^i\right)^{1/1-\alpha} = \left(\frac{\alpha}{\lambda}\right)^{1/1-\alpha} \sum_{i=0}^{n} \delta^{i/1-\alpha} = \left(\frac{\alpha}{\lambda}\right)^{1/1-\alpha} \frac{1 - \delta^{n/1-\alpha}}{1 - \delta^{1/1-\alpha}} = B$$

Solving for α/λ and plugging into y_i:

$$\alpha/\lambda = \left(B \frac{1 - \delta^{1/1-\alpha}}{1 - \delta^{n/1-\alpha}}\right)^{1-\alpha} \qquad y_i = B \frac{1 - \delta^{1/1-\alpha}}{1 - \delta^{n/1-\alpha}} \delta^{i/1-\alpha}$$

References

[BMC+15] Bonneau, J., Miller, A., Clark, J., Narayanan, A., Kroll, J.A., Felten, E.W.: Sok: Research perspectives and challenges for bitcoin and cryptocurrencies. In: IEEE Symposium on Security and Privacy, pp. 104–121 (2015)

[Eya15] Eyal, I.: The miner's dilemma. In: 2015 IEEE Symposium on Security and Privacy, pp. 89–103 (2015)

[EZ89] Epstein, L.G., Zin, S.E.: Substitution, risk aversion, and the temporal behavior of consumption and asset returns: a theoretical framework. Econometrica **57**(4), 937–969 (1989)

[FL02] Frederick, S., Lowenstein, G.: Time discounting and time preference: a critical review. J. Econ. Lit. **XL**, 351–401 (2002)

[JLG+14] Johnson, B., Laszka, A., Grossklags, J., Vasek, M., Moore, T.: Game-theoretic analysis of DDoS attacks against bitcoin mining pools. In: Böhme, R., Brenner, M., Moore, T., Smith, M. (eds.) FC 2014. LNCS, vol. 8438, pp. 72–86. Springer, Heidelberg (2014). https://doi.org/10.1007/978-3-662-44774-1_6

[KP78] Kreps, D.M., Porteus, E.L.: Temporal resolution of uncertainty and dynamic choice theory. Econometrica **46**(1), 185–200 (1978)

[LBS+15] Lewenberg, Y., Bachrach, Y., Sompolinsky, Y., Zohar, A., Rosenschein, J.S.: Bitcoin mining pools: a cooperative game theoretic analysis. In: Autonomous Agents and Multiagent Systems, AAMAS 2015, pp. 919–927 (2015)

[LJG15] Laszka, A., Johnson, B., Grossklags, J.: When bitcoin mining pools run dry. In: Brenner, M., Christin, N., Johnson, B., Rohloff, K. (eds.) FC 2015. LNCS, vol. 8976, pp. 63–77. Springer, Heidelberg (2015). https://doi.org/10.1007/978-3-662-48051-9_5

[Nak08] Nakamoto, S.: Bitcoin: a peer-to-peer electronic cash system. Consulted **1**(2012), 28 (2008)

[PSS16] Pass, R., Seeman, L., Shelat, A.: Analysis of the blockchain protocol in asynchronous networks. In: Coron, J.-S., Nielsen, J.B. (eds.) EUROCRYPT 2017. LNCS, vol. 10211, pp. 643–673. Springer, Cham (2017). https://doi.org/10.1007/978-3-319-56614-6_22

[Ros11] Rosenfeld, M.: Analysis of bitcoin pooled mining reward systems. CoRR, abs/1112.4980 (2011)

[Sam37] Samuelson, P.: A note on measurement of utility. Rev. Econ. Stud. **4**, 155–161 (1937)

[SBBR16] Schrijvers, O., Bonneau, J., Boneh, D., Roughgarden, T.: Incentive compatibility of bitcoin mining pool reward functions. In: Grossklags, J., Preneel, B. (eds.) FC 2016. LNCS, vol. 9603, pp. 477–498. Springer, Heidelberg (2017). https://doi.org/10.1007/978-3-662-54970-4_28

Design of an Optimal Frequency Reward Program in the Face of Competition

Arpit Goel[1] and Nolan Skochdopole[2(✉)]

[1] Department of Management Science and Engineering, Stanford University,
Stanford, CA 94305, USA
argoel@stanford.edu
[2] Institute for Computational and Mathematical Engineering, Stanford University,
Stanford, CA 94305, USA
naskoch@stanford.edu

Abstract. We optimize the design of a frequency reward program against traditional pricing in a competitive duopoly, where customers measure their utilities in rational economic terms. We assume two kinds of customers: myopic and strategic [19]. Every customer has a prior loyalty bias [6] toward the reward program merchant, a parameter drawn from a known distribution, indicating an additional probability of choosing the reward program merchant over the traditional pricing merchant. Under this model, we characterize the customer behavior: the loyalty bias increases the switching costs [11] of strategic customers until a tipping point, after which they strictly prefer and adopt the reward program merchant. Subsequently, we optimize the reward parameters to maximize the revenue objective of the reward program merchant. We show that under mild assumptions, the optimal parameters for the reward program design to maximize the revenue objective correspond exactly to minimizing the tipping point of customers and are independent of the customer population parameters. Moreover, we characterize the conditions for the reward program to be better when the loyalty bias distribution is uniform - a minimum fraction of population needs to be strategic, and the loyalty bias needs to be in an optimal range. If the bias is high, the reward program creates loss in revenues, as customers effectively gain rewards for "free", whereas a low value of bias leads to loss in market share to the competing merchant. In short, if a merchant can estimate the customer population parameters, our framework and results provide theoretical guarantees on the pros and cons of running a reward program against traditional pricing.

1 Introduction

Loyalty programs constitute a huge market in consumer retail and are a major source of revenue for many low margin businesses. Over 48 billion dollars in perceived value of rewards is issued in the United States alone every year, with every household having over 19 loyalty memberships on average [2]. This market constitutes credit cards, hotel and airline reward programs, and more recently even

© Springer International Publishing AG 2017
N. R. Devanur and P. Lu (Eds.): WINE 2017, LNCS 10674, pp. 219–236, 2017.
https://doi.org/10.1007/978-3-319-71924-5_16

restaurants, grocery and retail stores. In addition to possibly increasing their market share, these reward programs provide many benefits to the merchants – for instance, user identification for firms having multiple purchase channels; increase in sales due to referrals; personalized price discrimination and product recommendations, to name a few [15]. There are many examples of popular reward programs – Starbucks allows members to earn "stars" on purchases which can be redeemed for free coffee, Bloomingdale's offers $25 reward for around $1500 spent in their store, and Target offers a 5% cashback on all purchases [3]. Though forming a big component of the market, there is little scientific understanding about the design of loyalty reward programs. We aim to address this gap with our research.

One popular form of loyalty reward programs is *frequency reward programs*, where customers earn *points* as currency over spendings with merchants and are able to redeem these points for dollar valued rewards after achieving certain threshold point collections. There is extant literature on characterizing customer behavior toward frequency reward programs. Most of the literature is empirical in nature, and relies on psychological behavioral patterns among customers, as opposed to rational economic decision making [5,7,10]. In this paper, we consider a competitive duopoly of two merchants where one merchant offers a frequency reward program and the other offers traditional pricing with discounts. Though revenue management literature often deals with dynamic pricing of products, many retail merchants offering rewards often pre-commit to their prices. We assume that both merchants commit to their product pricing apriori and characterize a novel model of customer choice where customers measure their utilities in rational economic terms. In addition, we investigate the direct effects on the revenue objective and characterize the optimal reward design choice for the merchant offering the frequency reward program, based on different customer populations. Specifically, we answer the following question: how should the merchant decide the optimal thresholds and dollar value of rewards to optimize for its revenue share from the participating customer population. One important constraint we impose is that the merchant has to choose a *one design fits all* reward program for the entire participating customer population and is not allowed to personalize the program for different customer segments.

This is how the remaining paper is structured. First, we will describe some related work. Then we will give an overview of our model and results. In Sect. 2, we will describe our model in technical detail followed by the main results in Sect. 3. We will conclude with a short discussion on future work in Sect. 4.

1.1 Related Work

Three popular psychological constructs have been used to explain customer choice dynamics toward reward programs – Goal Gradient Hypothesis, Medium Maximization, and Tipping Point Dynamics. [10] conducted an empirical study observing an acceleration in the number of purchases by customers as they approached the reward, i.e., as customers accumulated reward points to reach closer to achieving the reward, their effort invested toward gaining more points increased. The authors attributed this behavior to Goal Gradient Hypothesis [9]. This behavior is also very prevalent in online badge systems, such as those on Stackoverflow; recently, mathematical models relying on rational user behavior have been developed that explain this phenomenon [1]. [5,17] observed that customers often stockpiled reward points even when there were economic incentives against the collection of points. They attributed this behavior to Medium Maximization – customers often treated collecting reward points as a goal itself just like collecting stamps as opposed to connecting reward points with economic incentives. Correspondingly, they introduced a new model where customers had different "mental accounts" and utility functions for points and cash. [7] observed via experimentation that customers often collect reward points for exogenous reasons until they accumulate a threshold amount, after which they start investing effort toward the collection process itself. That is, customers build up switching costs [11] before fully adopting the reward program, and sometimes this switching cost is created due to reasons exogenous to rational economic incentives. They referred to this behavior as the Tipping Point Effect.

A large body of literature investigates the switching costs customers face within a competitive duopoly framework – see [18] for a short survey. Our model is closest in spirit to that of [8] and [12]. Both papers are empirical in nature and model a competitive duopoly where customers maximize their long term discounted utility. [8] argue that less frequent buyers face higher switching costs as they are more likely to be affected by reward redemption deadlines, whereas frequent buyers redeem rewards easily and do not face substantial switching costs. They do not model how customers build up switching costs, but only argue what happens when customers are close to achieving a reward. [12] discuss dynamic competition between two merchants deciding whether to offer a reward program or traditional pricing and model this decision problem as a two stage game: first merchants decide whether to offer a reward program or traditional pricing and then they decide their prices. Using simulations, depending on customer parameters in the model, they characterize the conditions for when it is better to offer a reward program versus traditional pricing. We on the other hand model a multi-period problem where the customer behavior is characterized using a complete dynamic program, and mathematically analyze our model. We make two modeling assumptions: first is an exogenous visit probability bias toward the reward program merchant which can be attributed to *excess loyalty* – customers often build up higher brand preference toward the merchant offering a reward program [6,16]; and second, a look-ahead factor for customers, which indicates how far into the future customers can perceive the rewards [13,14]. Our results on customer choice dynamics intuitively look similar to some of those obtained in the above mentioned body of literature. But more importantly, we model and optimize the revenue objective of the merchant, characterizing an optimal reward program design for maximizing expected revenue.

1.2 Our Contributions

Model Overview. We model a competitive duopoly of two merchants, one of them offering a frequency reward program and the other offering traditional pricing. Both merchants sell an identical good at fixed precommitted prices. The reward program merchant sells the good at a higher price. With each purchase from the reward program merchant, a customer gains some fixed number of points, and on achieving the reward redemption threshold, (s)he immediately gains the reward value as a dollar cashback.

Customers measure their utilities in rational economic terms, i.e., they make their purchase decisions to maximize long term discounted rewards. The discount factor is the time value of money, and we assume it to be constant for all customers. We also assume that every customer makes a purchase everyday from either of the two merchants. We relax these two assumptions by introducing a look-ahead factor that controls how far into the future a customer can perceive the rewards. This affects the customer behavior dynamics as follows: if the reward redemption threshold is farther than the customer's look-ahead parameter, (s)he is unable to perceive the future value of that reward and take it into consideration while maximizing long term utility. This parameter, being customer specific, adds heterogeneity to both the future discounting and purchase frequency – customers having high purchase frequency might be able to perceive rewards with higher redemption thresholds. We only model myopic and strategic customers, i.e., the look-ahead parameter being 0 or a large value, and leave further parametrization for future work. But importantly, the framework we develop could be applied and modiefied to more complex look-ahead distributions.

In addition, we assume each customer has a visit probability bias with which (s)he purchases the good from the reward program merchant for reasons exogenous to utility maximization. This behavior may be attributed to *excess loyalty* [6,16] which has been argued as an important parameter for the success of any reward program, or it may be attributed to price insensitivity of customers; whenever a customer is price insensitive, (s)he strictly prefers to purchase from the reward program merchant as (s)he gains points redeemable for rewards in the future. There are many possible reasons for customers' price insensitivity: the reward program merchant could be offering some other monopoly products, or the customer might be getting reimbursed for some purchases as part of corporate perks (e.g.: corporate travel). As an effect, this visit probability bias controls how frequently the customer's points increase even when (s)he does not actively choose to make purchases from the reward program merchant. Both the look-ahead and excess loyalty parameters can be attributed to bounded rationality of customers and have been argued to be important factors toward customer choice dynamics, as discussed above in the related work.

Results Overview. We formulate the customer choice dynamics as a dynamic program with the state being the number of points collected from the reward program merchant. When the customer does not make biased visits to the reward program merchant, (s)he compares the immediate utility of purchasing the good at a cheaper price with the long term utility of waiting and receiving the time discounted reward to make a purchase decision. The solution to the customer's dynamic program gives conditions for the existence and achievability of a phase transition: a points threshold before which the customer visits the merchant offering rewards only due to the visit probability bias, and after which (s)he adopts the program and always visits the merchant offering rewards till receiving the reward. We show that this phase transition occurs sooner for strategic customers. Increasing the reward value also makes the phase transition occur earlier. However, increasing the points threshold required to redeem the reward or the price discount offered by the traditional pricing merchant delays this tipping point. In short, these results verify that our model is in coherence with the different psychological constructs as discussed in the related work section: purchase acceleration closer to reward redemption and a tipping point before which purchases are only due to the loyalty bias.

After characterizing the customer behavior dynamics in our model, we optimize over the long run revenues that the reward program merchant achieves. We model a specific case of proportional promotion budgeting: the reward offered by the reward program merchant is proportional to the product of the distance to the reward and the discount provided by the traditional pricing merchant, with the proportionality constant being another parameter in the design of the reward program. We show that under proportional promotion budgeting, the optimal distance to reward and the proportionality budgeting constant follow an intuitive product relationship which is independent of the customer population parameters, and these values correspond closely to real world observed cashback percentage values. In addition, optimizing the revenue objective gives the same optimal distance to reward as minimizing the phase transition point as defined above. Moreover, we characterize the conditions in terms of the customer parameters for when the revenue objective of the reward program merchant is better than the traditional pricing merchant and when it is better for the reward program merchant to offer a reward versus not offering any reward, for a specific choice of loyalty bias distribution. We show that for the reward program to be effective under both the above conditions, a minimum fraction of customer population must be strategic. And there is a specific range of values of the loyalty bias between 0 and 1 corresponding to the fraction of strategic customers for the reward program to be strictly better for the merchant.

2 Model

We index the two competing merchants selling identical goods as A and B. Without loss of generality we assume that A sells the good for a price of 1 dollar while B sells it for $1 - v$ dollars, i.e., B offers a discount of v dollars[1]. Merchant A additionally offers a reward of value R dollars to a customer after (s)he makes

---

[1] This assumption is only for simplicity. Our results extend to arbitrary fixed pricing by both merchants.

k purchases at A. We only investigate the case that we refer to as "proportional promotion budgeting", wherein this reward R is proportional to the product of the distance to the reward k and the discount v provided by B; that is, $R = \alpha k v$. The merchant optimizes over both k and α.

2.1   Customer Behavior Model

We assume customers purchase the item from either A or B everyday, i.e., we ignore the heterogeneity in frequency of purchases among the customers in our model and leave it for future work. We assume customers have a linear homogenous utility in price: at price q the utility is $\nu(q) = 1 - q$. This reduces to customers getting an immediate utility of 0 from A and v from B. All customers have the same time value of money as a discount factor of β lying between 0 and 1.

We denote a customer's visit probability bias and the look-ahead parameter with λ and t respectively. That is with probability λ, (s)he purchases from A due to externalities and perceives a future reward only if it is within t purchases away. This λ for a customer is drawn from a distribution f with support between $[0, 1]$. In this paper, we focus on a simple threshold distribution for the look-ahead parameter t:

$$t = \begin{cases} t_1, & \text{wp } p, \\ 0, & 1 - p. \end{cases}$$

The above distribution intuitively means that the customers are either myopic and focus only on immediate rewards or are strategic and can perceive long term utility (we assume t_1 is large). We leave other parametrizations of this look-ahead parameter for future work. We model the customer's decision problem as a dynamic program. We index the number of purchases the customer makes from A until the reward by i, for $0 \leq i \leq k - 1$, and we refer a customer to be in state i after having made i purchases from A. At state i, there are two possibilities:

1. With probability λ, the customer must visit A, and (s)he is now in state $i+1$.
2. With probability $1 - \lambda$, the customer has a choice between purchasing from B for an immediate utility v and remaining in state i, or purchasing from A for no immediate utility but moving to state $i + 1$.

Let $V(i)$ denote the long term expected reward at state i. Then we model the decision problem as the following dynamic program.

$$V(i) = \lambda \beta V(i + 1) + (1 - \lambda) \max\{v + \beta V(i), \beta V(i + 1)\} \text{ for } 0 \leq i \leq k - 1 \quad (1)$$
$$V(k) = R$$

We show that the decision process exhibits a phase transition; that is prior to some state, the customer purchases from A only if (s)he must do so exogenously but after that state, (s)he always decides to purchase from A. This phase transition point is independent of λ, and depends only on t, among the variable customer parameters. Hence we represent this phase transition point as $i_0(t)$.

2.2   Merchant Objective

Given the above model of customer dynamics, we define the revenue objectives of A and B, where A chooses its reward parameters and B is non-strategic. We define the rate of revenue for a merchant from a customer as the expected time averaged revenue that the merchant receives within the customer's lifetime. For simplification, we assume merchants do not discount future revenues. As described above, a customer's dynamics are cyclic after each reward cycle. Thus the lifetime dynamics of customer behavior is a regenerative process with independent and identically distributed reward cycle lengths. Let $RoR_A(c)$ and $RoR_B(c)$ denote the expected rates of revenue for A and B respectively from a customer c's lifetime. Let $\tau(t, \lambda)$ denote the total number of purchases the customer makes before reaching the phase transition point $i_0(t)$. Then the length of the reward cycle (or total number of purchases the customer makes before receiving the reward) is $\tau(t, \lambda) + k - i_0(t)$, because after the phase transition (s)he makes all purchases from A until hitting the reward. In this cycle, the number of visits that the customer makes to A is k, and to B is $\tau(t, \lambda) - i_0(t)$. The revenue that A earns in one such cycle is $k - R$ and the revenue that B earns is $(1 - v)(\tau(t, \lambda) - i_0(t))$. Thus the rates of revenue for A and B from the customer c are as follows:

$$RoR_A(c) = \mathop{E}_{\tau, t, \lambda} \left[\frac{k - R}{\tau(t, \lambda) + k - i_0(t)} \right]$$

$$RoR_B(c) = \mathop{E}_{\tau, t, \lambda} \left[\frac{(1 - v)(\tau(t, \lambda) - i_0(t))}{\tau(t, \lambda) + k - i_0(t)} \right]$$

Since the process for a single customer is regenerative, using the reward renewal theorem [4], we can take the expectation over the cycle length inside the numerator and denominator respectively. Note that $\mathop{E}_{\tau, t, \lambda} [\tau(t, \lambda)] = \mathop{E}_{t, \lambda} \left[\frac{i_0(t)}{\lambda} \right]$ as before reaching the phase transition point, with probability λ, the number of purchases by the customer from A increases by 1 and with probability $1 - \lambda$ it stays constant. Then taking the expectation over the customer population the overall rates of revenue for both A and B are as follows:

$$RoR_A = \mathop{E}_{t, \lambda} \left[\frac{k - R}{i_0(t)/\lambda + k - i_0(t)} \right] \tag{2}$$

$$RoR_B = \mathop{E}_{t, \lambda} \left[\frac{(i_0(t)/\lambda - i_0(t))(1 - v)}{i_0(t)/\lambda + k - i_0(t)} \right] \tag{3}$$

3   Results

3.1   Customer Choice Dynamics

We first show that every customer exhibits the following behavior: until (s)he reaches the phase transition point $i_0(t)$, (s)he purchases from A only due to the exogeneity parameter, and after that (s)he always purchases from A till she receives the reward. This behavior is cyclic, and repeats after every reward redemption.

Lemma 1. $V(i)$ *is an increasing function in i if the following condition holds:*

$$R > \frac{(1-\lambda)v}{1-\beta} \tag{4}$$

And further, $V(i)$ can be evaluated as:

$$V(i) = \max \left\{ \frac{\lambda\beta V(i+1) + (1-\lambda)v}{1-(1-\lambda)\beta}, \beta V(i+1) \right\} \tag{5}$$

Proof. First we show that $V(i)$ is an increasing function in i by induction. We first show that if the condition above is satisfied, $V(k-1) < V(k) = R$. Suppose not, so $V(k-1) \geq R$. Then from Eq. 1, we have:

$$
\begin{aligned}
V(k-1) &= \lambda\beta V(k) + (1-\lambda)(v + \beta V(k-1)) \\
&= \frac{\lambda\beta R + (1-\lambda)v}{1-(1-\lambda)\beta} \\
&< \frac{\lambda\beta R + (1-\beta)R}{1-(1-\lambda)\beta} = R
\end{aligned}
$$

But this is a contradiction, so $V(k-1) < V(k)$. Now assume $V(i+1) < V(i+2)$ for some $i < k-2$, we will show that this implies $V(i) < V(i+1)$. Suppose not, so $V(i) \geq V(i+1)$. As we did before we may upper bound $V(i)$.

$$
\begin{aligned}
V(i) &= \lambda\beta V(i+1) + (1-\lambda)(v + \beta V(i)) \\
&\leq (1-\lambda)v + \beta V(i) \\
\Longleftrightarrow V(i) &\leq \frac{(1-\lambda)v}{1-\beta}
\end{aligned}
$$

But because $V(i+1) < V(i+2)$, we may lower bound $V(i+1)$.

$$
\begin{aligned}
V(i+1) &\geq \lambda\beta V(i+2) + (1-\lambda)(v + \beta V(i+1)) \\
&= (1-\lambda)v + (1-\lambda)\beta V(i+1) + \lambda\beta V(i+2) \\
&> (1-\lambda) + \beta V(i+1) \\
\Longleftrightarrow V(i+1) &> \frac{(1-\lambda)v}{1-\beta}
\end{aligned}
$$

Again, we have a contradiction, so $V(i) < V(i+1)$, and $V(i)$ is an increasing function in i. Now we prove the second claim. We have the following:

$$
\begin{aligned}
V(i) &= \lambda\beta V(i+1) + (1-\lambda)\max\{v + \beta V(i), \beta V(i+1)\} \\
&= \max\{\lambda\beta V(i+1) + (1-\lambda)(v + \beta V(i)), \beta V(i+1)\}
\end{aligned}
$$

Assuming $V(i)$ is the left term in the above maximum, we may solve the equation for that term.

$$V(i) = \lambda\beta V(i+1) + (1-\lambda)(v + \beta V(i))$$
$$(1 - (1-\lambda)\beta)V(i) = \lambda\beta V(i+1) + (1-\lambda)v$$
$$V(i) = \frac{\lambda\beta V(i+1) + (1-\lambda)v}{1 - (1-\lambda)\beta}$$

And we get our claim.   □

Now if the expected reward of the customer increases with the number of purchases made from A, we expect that at some number of purchases it becomes profitable for the customer to choose to purchase from A as opposed to B. We characterize this phase transition point in the following theorem.

Theorem 1. *Suppose $V(i)$ is an increasing function in i and consider a customer with look-ahead parameter t. A phase transition occurs after (s)he makes $i_0(t)$ visits to firm A, where $i_0(t)$ is given by:*

$$i_0(t) = \begin{cases} k - \Delta \equiv i_0, & \text{if } t \geq \Delta. \\ k - t, & \text{otherwise.} \end{cases} \tag{6}$$

with

$$\Delta = \left\lfloor \log_\beta \left(\frac{v}{R(1-\beta)} \right) \right\rfloor \tag{7}$$

Proof. First we solve for the condition on $V(i+1)$ for us to choose firm A over B willingly.

$$\beta V(i+1) > \frac{\lambda\beta V(i+1) + (1-\lambda)v}{1 - (1-\lambda)\beta}$$
$$\iff \beta V(i+1)\left(1 - \frac{\lambda}{1 - (1-\lambda)\beta}\right) > \left(\frac{1-\lambda}{1 - (1-\lambda)\beta}\right)v$$
$$\iff \beta V(i+1)\left(\frac{1 - (1-\lambda)\beta - \lambda}{1 - (1-\lambda)\beta}\right) > \left(\frac{1-\lambda}{1 - (1-\lambda)\beta}\right)v$$
$$\iff \beta V(i+1)\left(\frac{(1-\lambda)(1-\beta)}{1 - (1-\lambda)\beta}\right) > \left(\frac{1-\lambda}{1 - (1-\lambda)\beta}\right)v$$
$$\iff V(i+1) > \frac{v}{\beta(1-\beta)}$$

Let i_0 be the minimum state i such that the above holds, so in particular $V(i_0) \leq \frac{v}{\beta(1-\beta)}$ but $V(i_0+1) > \frac{v}{\beta(1-\beta)}$. We know because V is increasing in i, this point is indeed a phase transition: $V(i) > \frac{v}{\beta(1-\beta)}$ for all $i > i_0$, so after this point, the customer always chooses firm A. We may compute $V(i_0)$ easily using this fact.

$$V(i_0) = \beta V(i_0 + 1) = \cdots = \beta^{k-i_0} V(k) = \beta^{k-i_0} R$$

Thus, we have the following:

$$\beta^{k-i_0} \leq \frac{v}{R\beta(1-\beta)} < \beta^{k-(i_0+1)}$$

$$\iff k - i_0 \geq \log_\beta \left(\frac{v}{R\beta(1-\beta)} \right) > k - (i_0+1)$$

$$\iff i_0 \leq k - \log_\beta \left(\frac{v}{R(1-\beta)} \right) + 1 < i_0 + 1$$

$$\iff i_0 = k - \left\lfloor \log_\beta \left(\frac{v}{R(1-\beta)} \right) \right\rfloor \equiv k - \Delta$$

If $t \geq \Delta$, the customer perceives the reward prior to this tipping point, so $i_0(t) = i_0 = k - \Delta$. If $t < \Delta$, the customer does not perceive the reward at this point, and immediately once (s)he perceives the reward, (s)he is beyond this point and adopts the reward program, so $i_0(t) = k - t$. The above dependence reduces to the following after incorporating our specific look-ahead distribution:

$$i_0(t) = \begin{cases} i_0, & \text{wp } p, \\ k, & 1-p. \end{cases}$$

$\square$

Note that the phase transition point is independent of λ, the customer's visit probability bias toward the merchant. As we would expect, it increases with the look-ahead parameter and with the price discount offered by merchant B. Additionally, it decreases with an increase in the reward value (R) and a decrease in the distance to reward (k). The variation with the discount factor β is interesting: we can show that for any $\frac{R}{v} \geq 1$ there exists a $\beta \in [0,1]$ that minimizes the phase transition point i_0 for strategic customers. We refer to the ratio of number of visits required for a forward-looking customer to adopt a reward program and the total distance to the reward as the "influence zone". Intuitively this is the fraction of visits that the merchant wants to influence the customer by offering exogenous means of earning additional points like bonus miles in airlines or accelerated earnings, as discussed in the introduction. Next we find the optimal k for minimizing this influence zone if α is constant.

Remark 1. Influence zone is minimized at $k = \frac{e}{\alpha(1-\beta)}$ under proportional promotion budgeting, as long as β is close to 1.

Proof. As defined the influence zone is $\frac{i_0}{k} = \frac{k-\Delta}{k} = 1 - \frac{\Delta}{k}$. Thus minimizing the influence zone is equivalent to minimizing $\frac{k}{\Delta}$.

$$\frac{k}{\Delta} = \frac{k}{\log_\beta \left(\frac{1}{\alpha k (1-\beta)} \right)} \sim \frac{k(1-\beta)}{\log(\alpha k(1-\beta))}$$

The above approximation relies on β close to 1. Now this value is minimized at $k = \frac{e}{\alpha(1-\beta)}$. Therefore, for all distributions of excess loyalty, the optimal value for k is given by $\frac{e}{\alpha(1-\beta)}$, the value for which $\frac{k}{\Delta}$ is minimized and takes the value $\frac{e}{\alpha}$. At this value the influence zone takes the value $1 - \frac{\alpha}{e}$.   □

Note that if α is 1, then the value of k corresponds to a cashback between 2% and 4% as β ranges between 0.95 and 0.9. This value is realistic to what is observed in practice.

3.2   Merchant Objective Dynamics

Optimizing Reward Parameters. So far we have characterized the customer behavior within the duopoly without concern about the particular reward design parameters. In this section, we derive optimal parameters for the reward program design with the objective of maximizing the revenue of the reward program merchant. Interestingly, we see that maximizing revenue corresponds to minimizing the influence zone, as illustrated above.

Theorem 2. *Under proportional promotion budgeting, the optimal reward distance (k) and the optimal budget proportion (α) for merchant A follow the relation $\alpha k = \frac{e}{(1-\beta)}$ for all distributions of λ as long as β is close to 1.*

Proof. Let $\theta = \frac{\Delta}{k}$. First, we evaluate RoR_A. We substitute the value of the phase transition point obtained above in the rate of revenue equation for A to reevaluate it. And since we assume that λ and t are drawn independent of each other, we can separate the expectation terms and evaluate them sequentially, first over t, then over λ.

$$
\begin{aligned}
RoR_A &= \underset{\lambda, t}{E}\left[\frac{k - R}{i_0(t)/\lambda + k - i_0(t)}\right] \\
&= \underset{\lambda}{E}\left[p \cdot \frac{k - R}{i_0/\lambda + k - i_0} + (1 - p)\frac{\lambda(k - R)}{k}\right] \\
&= \underset{\lambda}{E}\left[p \cdot \frac{\lambda(k - R)}{k\lambda + i_0(1 - \lambda)} + (1 - p)\frac{\lambda(k - R)}{k}\right] \\
&= \underset{\lambda}{E}\left[p \cdot \frac{\lambda(1 - \alpha v)}{1 - \theta(1 - \lambda)} + (1 - p)\lambda(1 - \alpha v)\right]
\end{aligned}
$$

Observe that the term inside the expectation is maximized when θ is maximized for all values of $\lambda \in (0, 1)$. Using Leibniz' Rule, we can conclude that the integral itself is maximized when θ is maximized, which as shown above, is equivalent to minimizing the influence zone. As shown in Remark 1, this happens at $\alpha k = \frac{e}{1-\beta}$. And at this point, $\theta = \frac{\Delta}{k} = \frac{\alpha}{e}$.   □

An interesting point to observe above is that if α is constant, then maximizing the revenue objective is equivalent to minimizing the influence zone. This result matches the following intuition - the faster the merchant can get customers to adopt the reward program, the more purchases they will make with the merchant in the long run - but is stronger as it actually maximizes the revenue objective as well. Although, reward point accelerations are common and effective mechanisms to get customers to adopt reward programs, we have shown that designing the reward program so that a minimum number of such accelerations is required leads to maximizing merchant's revenue. The condition that β be close to 1 is not very restrictive, as the discount factor is expected to be high in most cases. Note that because $k \geq \Delta$, the above also shows $\alpha \leq e$. Finally, observe that we need $R > \frac{(1-\lambda)v}{1-\beta}$ for V to be increasing. We meet this condition with proportional budgeting when $k = \frac{e}{\alpha(1-\beta)}$ as $R = \alpha k v = \frac{ev}{1-\beta} \geq \frac{v}{1-\beta} \geq \frac{(1-\lambda)v}{1-\beta}$.

The above framework can be used for optimizing for the reward parameters to maximize A's rate of revenue, for varying distributions of the customer population. That is, if a merchant has a good estimate of its customer population's distribution, it can easily utilize the above theorem to optimize its reward scheme. We leave the competitive study where merchant B could strategize on its discount value v for future work. In the following subsection, we explore these conditions in detail for the uniform distribution of loyalty bias for fixed α.

Revenue Comparisons. We characterize the conditions for when it is strictly better for A to offer a reward program for a specific distribution of the loyalty bias parameter - when λ for every customer is drawn uniformly at random between $(0, b]$ where b is less than 1. We will assume this distribution for the remainder of the section. This condition boils down to two situations: first, the rate of revenue for A should be higher than that of B and second, that the rate of revenue for A should be higher than it could have achieved by not offering the reward program at the same fixed price. First, we evaluate the expected rates of revenue for both A and B under the optimality relation between k and α mentioned above with λ being drawn from a uniform distribution.

$$
\begin{aligned}
RoR_A &= E_\lambda \left[p \cdot \frac{\lambda(1 - \alpha v)}{1 - \theta(1 - \lambda)} + (1 - p)\lambda(1 - \alpha v) \right] \\
&= pk \cdot \frac{1 - \alpha v}{\Delta} \cdot \left(1 - \frac{k - \Delta}{b\Delta} \log\left(1 + \frac{b\Delta}{k - \Delta}\right) \right) + (1 - p)\frac{bk(1 - \alpha v)}{2k} \\
&= (1 - \alpha v)\left(p\frac{e}{\alpha}\left(1 - \frac{e - \alpha}{b\alpha} \log\left(1 + \frac{b\alpha}{e - \alpha}\right)\right) + (1 - p)\frac{b}{2} \right)
\end{aligned}
$$

$$
\begin{aligned}
RoR_B &= E_{\lambda,t}\left[\frac{(i_0(t)\lambda - i_0(t))(1 - v)}{i_0(t)/\lambda + k - i_0(t)} \right] \\
&= E_\lambda\left[p \cdot \frac{(i_0/\lambda - i_0)(1 - v)}{i_0/\lambda + k - i_0} + (1 - p)\frac{(k/\lambda - k)(1 - v)}{k/\lambda} \right] \\
&= E_\lambda\left[p \cdot \frac{i_0(1 - \lambda)(1 - v)}{k\lambda + i_0(1 - \lambda)} + (1 - p)(1 - \lambda)(1 - v) \right] \\
&= p \cdot \frac{i_0(1 - v)}{b(k - i_0)^2}\left(k \log\left(1 + \frac{b(k - i_0)}{i_0}\right) - b(k - i_0) \right) + (1 - p)(1 - \frac{b}{2})(1 - v)
\end{aligned}
$$

$$= p \cdot \frac{i_0(1-v)}{k-i_0} \left(\frac{k}{b(k-i_0)} \log \left(1 + \frac{b(k-i_0)}{i_0} \right) - 1 \right) + (1-p)(1 - \frac{b}{2})(1-v)$$

$$= (1-v) \left(p \cdot \frac{e-\alpha}{\alpha} \left(\frac{e}{b\alpha} \log \left(1 + \frac{b\alpha}{e-\alpha} \right) - 1 \right) + (1-p)(1 - \frac{b}{2}) \right)$$

$$= (1-v) \left(p \frac{e}{\alpha} \left(\frac{e-\alpha}{b\alpha} \log \left(1 + \frac{b\alpha}{e-\alpha} \right) - \frac{e-\alpha}{e} \right) + (1-p)(1 - \frac{b}{2}) \right)$$

Observe that both the above equations have a left term and a right term. The left term is the rate of revenue obtained from strategic customers whereas the right term is that obtained from the myopic customers. As α ranges between 0 and e, the value on the left term increases from 0 for RoR_A and decreases to 0 for RoR_B. That is, by controlling the reward budget ratio, A is able to gain the entire strategic customer base. But observe how RoR_A varies with α: the marginal revenue term $(1 - \alpha v)$ decreases with α as the merchant gives higher rewards to customers, but the market share term increases as A gains more strategic customer base. As $\alpha \to 0$, $RoR_A \to b/2$, i.e., the revenue earned is only due to the loyalty bias, and is equivalent to the reveue earned by A when not running any reward program.

Figure 1 illustrates the region in terms of the customer parameters (b,p) where it is better for A to offer a reward program, i.e., $RoR_A > RoR_B$ (indicated in blue) and $RoR_A > \frac{b}{2}$ (indicated in yellow) for different values of α, keeping $v = 0.05$ and $\beta = 0.95$ fixed. The blue region shows that there is a clear threshold of b and p values beyond which $RoR_A > RoR_B$. But more interestingly, the threshold value of b and p decreases as α is increased toward e. Whereas the yellow region shows that if the fraction of strategic customers is not too small, the firm should choose to run a reward program most of the time except for when b is large; larger b values mean that customers make more exogenous visits, so a reward program is no longer needed to entice visits, but only decreases the profits of the reward program merchant. The intersection of two regions, i.e., the region in green, indicates that the range of values of b for which the reward program is strictly profitable increases as p increases. We formally show this result next.

For any fixed α, the exact conditions on p, b and v for $RoR_A > RoR_B$ and $RoR_A > \frac{b}{2}$ are rather complex. We will first focus on one particular simple case: $\alpha \to e$. We will prove four lemmas for this case, and we leave the mainly algebraic proofs to the extended writeup[2].

Lemma 2. *As $\alpha \to e$, $RoR_A > RoR_B$ if and only if the following condition on b holds:*

$$b > 2 \cdot \frac{(1-v) - \frac{p}{1-p} \cdot (1-ev)}{(1-v) + (1-ev)} \tag{8}$$

The above lemma gives a lower bound on b for $RoR_A > RoR_B$ in terms of p and v. In order for the reward program to be strictly better than the traditional pricing model, we also need $RoR_A > \frac{b}{2}$. The following lemma shows that this condition gives a corresponding upper bound on b.

---

[2] https://papers.ssrn.com/sol3/papers.cfm?abstract_id=2920132.

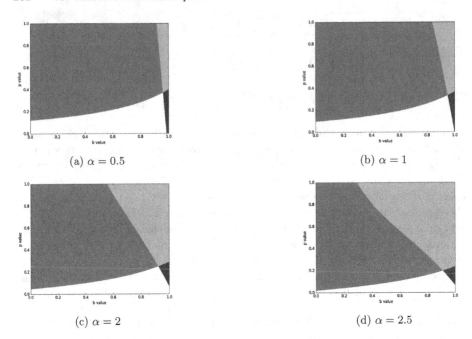

Fig. 1. Regions where $RoR_A > RoR_B$ (blue), where $RoR_A > \frac{b}{2}$ (yellow) and where both are true (green) for different values of α. In all cases, $\beta = 0.95$, $v = 0.05$ and λ drawn uniformly on $(0, b]$. (Color figure online)

Lemma 3. *As $\alpha \to e$, $RoR_A > \frac{b}{2}$ if and only if the following condition on b holds:*

$$b < \frac{2p}{p + \frac{ev}{1-ev}} \tag{9}$$

The previous two lemmas provide lower and upper bounds on b for $RoR_A > RoR_B$ and $RoR_A > \frac{b}{2}$, respectively. For the reward program to be strictly better than all alternatives, both of these conditions must be met. We combine them to get an intuitive necessary and sufficient condition on p for the reward program to be "strictly better".

Lemma 4. *As $\alpha \to e$, for the reward program to be strictly better on some values of b, a necessary and sufficient condition on p is:*

$$p > 1 - \frac{1-ev}{1-ev^2} \tag{10}$$

Thus, for any choice of v, and p obeying the above condition, the combination of the above lemmas gives an interval of b values for which the reward program is the most profitable choice for the merchant. Figure 2 shows the bounds on b for varying values of p, keeping $v = 0.05$ fixed, and restricting the range of b values in $(0, 1)$. Notice that the upper bound on b increases as a function of p

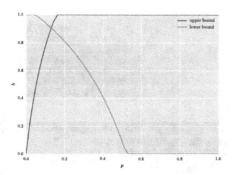

Fig. 2. The upper and lower bounds on b as a function of p. Here $v = 0.05$ and $\alpha \to e$.

while the lower bound decreases with p, so the interval of b values where the reward program is strictly better increases with p. We formalize this observation in the next lemma.

Lemma 5. *As $\alpha \to e$ and p obeying Eq. 10, as p increases, the range of values of b for which the reward program is strictly better increases.*

Figure 3 shows the upper and lower bounds on b for all valid pairs of p and v with $\alpha \to e$. The top plot shows the lower bound on b and the bottom plot depicts the upper bound. For a particular (p, v) pair, if the color on the top plot is darker than the corresponding color on the bottom plot, then this pair has a valid b interval in which the reward program is strictly better. This figure also exhibits the increasing range of b values with increasing p; for large values of p and moderate values of v, we observe no restrictions on b for the reward program to be strictly better. We combine all the above observations into the following theorem.

Theorem 3. *Under proportional budgeting, as $\alpha \to e$, a necessary and sufficient condition for the reward program to be strictly better is a lowerbound on p which increases with v. And as p increases beyond the lowerbound, the region of allowable b for which the reward program is strictly better becomes larger.*

Now we generalize the above result for all values of α. The conditions are more complex but the results and intuitions are similar. The proofs are technical, and we leave them to the extended writeup[3].

Lemma 6. *Fix $\alpha \in (0, e)$. For any (p, v) pair, there exists some upper bound $b_1 \in [0, 1]$ such that for all $b \le b_1$, $RoR_A \ge \frac{b}{2}$.*

Lemma 7. *Fix $\alpha \in (0, e)$. For any (p, v) pair, there exists some lower bound $b_0 \in [0, 1]$ such that for all $b \ge b_0$, $RoR_A > RoR_B$.*

We combine the above two lemmas as before to get the following theorem.

---

[3] https://papers.ssrn.com/sol3/papers.cfm?abstract_id=2920132.

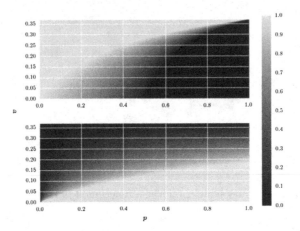

Fig. 3. Bounds on b for various values of p and v at $\alpha \to e$. Top shows lower bounds on b for $RoR_A \geq RoR_B$ and bottom shows upper bounds of b for $RoR_A \geq \frac{b}{2}$. (Color figure online)

Theorem 4. *Fix $\alpha \in (0, e)$. For any value of v, there exists a lowerbound p_0 such that for any p greater than p_0, there exists a range (b_0, b_1) between 0 and 1 such that for all b lying between b_0 and b_1, offering the reward program is strictly better for A.*

The above results can be extremely helpful in the following way: if a merchant estimates that the loyalty bias parameter is drawn from a uniform distribution and has good estimates of its target customer population, i.e., b and p values, it can find the appropriate reward budget ratios α, which could make running a reward program strictly better against a traditional pricing competitor. More importantly, these results show that under mild assumptions on the customer poplation parameters, reward programs can be beneficial in the competitive duopoly model.

4   Conclusions

We investigated the optimal design of a frequency reward program against traditional pricing in a competitive duopoly. We modeled the behavior of customers valuing their utilities in rational economic terms, and our theoretical results agree with past empirical studies. Assuming general distributions of customer population, we characterized optimal parameters for the design of reward program, and under more specific parameter distrubution assumptions, we showed the conditions on customer population parameters which make the reward program strictly better. In short, if a merchant can make good estimates of the customer population parameters, our model and results can help understand the pros and cons of running a frequency reward program for that merchant against traditional pricing.

Though our research offers some interesting managerial insights, there are some limitations to our study. Our results on revenue comparisons assumed specific distributions for the customer population, though our framework can be extended to other distributions as well. Moreover, estimating the customer population distribution and parameters using real transactional data is an interesting question in itself. That is, backing this research with empirical and experimental study, could provide strong quantifications to the intuitions we discuss. We modeled customer behavior in rational economic terms, mainly to understand the rational components that affect the decision making process. Tying in the effects of our research with some past models on psychological behavior patterns of customers toward reward programs would be another practically relevant problem to address. Finally, we modeled a competitive duopoly, but left the traditional pricing merchant as non-strategic. Understanding how competition affects the equilibrium prices and reward program parameters could give intuitions about a more practical scenario.

References

1. Anderson, A., Huttenlocher, D., Kleinberg, J., Leskovec, J.: Steering user behavior with badges. In: Proceedings of the 22nd International Conference on World Wide Web, WWW 2013, pp. 95–106. ACM, New York (2013). http://doi.acm.org/10.1145/2488388.2488398

2. Berry, J.: The 2013 colloquy loyalty census. COLLOQUY industry report (2013). http://www.colloquy.com/files/2013-COLLOQUY-Census-Talk-White-Paper.pdf

3. Brooks, S.: CVS to target: 21 best loyalty rewards programs (2015). http://www.reviewjournal.com/business/money/cvs-target-21-best-loyalty-rewards-programs

4. Cinlar, E.: Markov renewal theory. Adv. Appl. Probab. **1**(2), 123–187 (1969). http://www.jstor.org/stable/1426216

5. Dreze, X., Nunes, J.C.: Using combined-currency prices to lower consumers perceived cost. J. Mark. Res. **41**(1), 59–72 (2004)

6. Fader, P.S., Schmittlein, D.C.: Excess behavioral loyalty for high-share brands: deviations from the dirichlet model for repeat purchasing. J. Mark. Res. 478–493 (1993)

7. Gao, L., Huang, Y., Simonson, I.: The influence of initial possession level on consumers' adoption of a collection goal: a tipping point effect. J. Mark. **78**(6), 143–156 (2014)

8. Hartmann, W.R., Viard, V.B.: Do frequency reward programs create switching costs? A dynamic structural analysis of demand in a reward program. Quant. Mark. Econ. **6**(2), 109–137 (2008)

9. Hull, C.L.: The goal-gradient hypothesis and maze learning. Psychol. Rev. **39**(1), 25 (1932)

10. Kivetz, R., Urminsky, O., Zheng, Y.: The goal-gradient hypothesis resurrected: purchase acceleration, illusionary goal progress, and customer retention. J. Mark. Res. **43**(1), 39–58 (2006)

11. Klemperer, P.: Competition when consumers have switching costs: an overview with applications to industrial organization, macroeconomics, and international trade. Rev. Econ. Stud. **62**(4), 515–539 (1995)

12. Kopalle, P.K., Neslin, S.: The economic viability of frequency reward programs in a strategic competitive environment. In: Tuck School of Business at Dartmouth Working Paper No. 01–02 (2001). Available at SSRN: https://ssrn.com/abstract=265431 or http://dx.doi.org/10.2139/ssrn.265431

13. Lewis, M.: The influence of loyalty programs and short-term promotions on customer retention. J. Mark. Res. **41**(3), 281–292 (2004)

14. Liu, Y.: The long-term impact of loyalty programs on consumer purchase behavior and loyalty. J. Mark. **71**(4), 19–35 (2007)

15. Ryu, G., Feick, L.: A penny for your thoughts: referral reward programs and referral likelihood. J. Mark. **71**(1), 84–94 (2007)

16. Sharp, B., Sharp, A.: Loyalty programs and their impact on repeat-purchase loyalty patterns. Int. J. Res. Mark. **14**(5), 473–486 (1997)

17. Stourm, V., Bradlow, E.T., Fader, P.S.: Stockpiling points in linear loyalty programs. J. Mark. Res. **52**(2), 253–267 (2015)

18. Villas-Boas, J.M.: A short survey on switching costs and dynamic competition. Int. J. Res. Mark. **32**(2), 219–222 (2015)

19. Yilmaz, O., Pekgun, P., Ferguson, M.: Would you like to upgrade to a premium room? Evaluating the benefit of offering standby upgrades. Manuf. Serv. Oper. Manag. **19**(1), 1–18 (2017)

A Characterization of Undirected Graphs Admitting Optimal Cost Shares

Tobias Harks, Anja Huber, and Manuel Surek$^{(\boxtimes)}$

Institut für Mathematik, Universität Augsburg, 86135 Augsburg, Germany
{tobias.harks,anja.huber,manuel.surek}@math.uni-augsburg.de

Abstract. In a seminal paper, Chen et al. [7] studied cost sharing protocols for network design with the objective to implement a low-cost Steiner forest as a Nash equilibrium of an induced cost-sharing game. One of the most intriguing open problems to date is to understand the power of budget-balanced and separable cost sharing protocols in order to induce low-cost Steiner forests.

In this work, we focus on *undirected* networks and analyze topological properties of the underlying graph so that an *optimal Steiner forest* can be implemented as a Nash equilibrium (by some separable cost sharing protocol) *independent* of the edge costs. We term a graph *efficient* if the above stated property holds. As our main result, we give a complete characterization of efficient undirected graphs for two-player network design games: an undirected graph is efficient if and only if it does not contain (at least) one out of *few forbidden subgraphs*. Our characterization implies that several graph classes are efficient: generalized series-parallel graphs, fan and wheel graphs and graphs with small cycles.

Keywords: Network cost sharing games · Forbidden subgraphs

1 Introduction

In the *Steiner forest* problem, there is a network (G, c) with an undirected graph $G = (V, E)$ and nonnegative edge costs $c(e), e \in E$. Furthermore, there are $n \geq 1$ pairs $(s_1, t_1), \ldots, (s_n, t_n)$ of vertices in G and each such pair (s_i, t_i) needs the vertices s_i and t_i to be connected by (at least one) path. Thus, a feasible solution for the Steiner forest problem is a subset $F \subseteq E$ so that each pair (s_i, t_i) is connected in the subgraph induced by F. Since edge costs are nonnegative, there are no cycles in any optimal solution, thus, one can restrict the search to Steiner forests. An optimal Steiner forest F is a Steiner forest with minimum cost, that is $c(F) := \sum_{e \in F} c(e)$ is minimal under all possible Steiner forests F.

This research was funded by the Deutsche Forschungsgemeinschaft (DFG, German Research Foundation) - HA 8041/1-1.

© Springer International Publishing AG 2017
N. R. Devanur and P. Lu (Eds.): WINE 2017, LNCS 10674, pp. 237–251, 2017.
https://doi.org/10.1007/978-3-319-71924-5_17

1.1 Network Cost Sharing Games

In this article, we consider a game-theoretic variant of the Steiner forest problem (introduced in Chen et al. [7]) assuming that a system manager can *design* a protocol that determines how the edge costs of the forest are shared among its users. Formally, the n pairs (s_i, t_i) correspond to players $N := \{1, \ldots, n\}$ that each want to establish an (s_i, t_i) connection with minimum cost. Thus, a strategy profile is a tuple $P = (P_1, \ldots, P_n)$, where every P_i is an s_i-t_i path. Given P, the cost of player i using edge e is $\xi_{i,e}(P) \geq 0$ and the $\xi_{i,e}(P)$-values are determined by a *cost-sharing protocol* Ξ. The total cost that player $i \in N$ needs to pay under P is defined as

$$\xi_i(P) := \sum_{e \in P_i} \xi_{i,e}(P),$$

and a pure Nash equilibrium of the strategic game induced by Ξ is a strategy profile P from which no player can unilaterally deviate, say to another path P_i', and strictly pay less. Chen et al. [7] axiomatized cost sharing protocols by the following three fundamental properties (see also [11,14]):

1. *Budget-balance*: The cost $c(e) \geq 0$ of each edge e is exactly covered by the collected cost shares of the players using the edge, that is, $\sum_{i \in S_e(P)} \xi_{i,e}(P) = c(e)$ for all $e \in E$, where $S_e(P) := \{i \in N : e \in P_i\}$.
2. *Stability*: There is at least one pure strategy Nash equilibrium in each game induced by the cost sharing protocol.
3. *Separability*: The cost shares on an edge only depend on the set of players using the edge, that is, $S_e(P) = S_e(P') \Rightarrow \xi_{i,e}(P) = \xi_{i,e}(P')$ for all P, P' and $e \in E$.

Budget-balance (Condition 1) is straightforward, Stability (Condition 2) requires the existence of at least one Nash equilibrium in pure strategies (abbreviated PNE). This requirement is important for applications in which mixed or correlated strategies have no meaningful physical interpretation (see also the discussion in Osborne and Rubinstein [31, Sect. 3.2]). Separability (Condition 3) allows for a distributed implementation of the cost sharing protocol as each edge needs only to know its own player set. A cost sharing protocol is called *separable*, if it satisfies 1–3.

One important example for a separable cost sharing protocol is the Shapley cost sharing protocol (see [1,25]). For the case of two players, the corresponding PoS is known to be $4/3$, see Fig. 1a for an example. The solid lines build the unique optimal Steiner forest OPT with cost $3 + 2\varepsilon$, but OPT is no PNE since Player 1 has to pay $2 + 2\varepsilon > 2 + \varepsilon$. On the other hand, each player taking her direct $s_i - t_i$-edge is the unique PNE with cost $4 + \varepsilon$.

Can we improve the PoS for this example by using a different separable cost sharing protocol? Note that for the case of two players, a separable cost sharing protocol is uniquely determined by one value per edge, namely the amount Player 1 has to pay if both players use this edge. In Fig. 1b we display a cost sharing protocol Ξ for which OPT is a PNE. The edges are labelled by their costs followed by the value described above which determines Ξ.

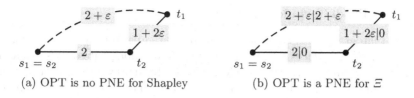

(a) OPT is no PNE for Shapley   (b) OPT is a PNE for Ξ

Fig. 1. Examples for separable cost sharing protocols

1.2 Our Results

We study *efficient* graphs $G = (V, E)$ having the property that there is an optimal Steiner forest that can be implemented as a pure Nash equilibrium by some separable cost sharing protocol (we speak of an *enforceable* Steiner forest). The above definition does not specify a priori the cost structure of the graph since any graph can be made efficient by assigning infinite or very high cost on some edges, thus, deleting "problematic" edges and effectively making the combinatorial structure of the graph irrelevant. An equivalent formulation of the research question we study is the following: what is the largest class of undirected graphs for which the worst-case ratio of the cost of the best Nash equilibrium and that of an optimal Steiner forest (PoS) is 1? An even stronger condition is the following: G is said to be *strongly* efficient, if *every* optimal Steiner forest can be enforced as a pure Nash equilibrium.

Our main result gives a complete characterization of efficient and strongly efficient graphs for two-player games:

Theorem (Main Result (Informal)).

G is efficient $\Leftrightarrow$ G is strongly efficient $\Leftrightarrow$ G does not contain certain subgraphs.

Some of the forbidden subgraphs (see Fig. 3) are reminiscent to an instance for directed network design showing a lower bound of 5/4 for the PoS, see Chen et al. [7]. Our characterization implies that several well-known graph classes are efficient, while for others, we immediately get counterexamples, see Table 1 for a (non-exhaustive) overview. The proofs for the listed graph classes and further results can be found in [22, Sect. 5].

Table 1. Efficiency of graph classes

Efficient classes	Classes containing non-efficient graphs
Generalized series-parallel graphs	Bipartite graphs
Wheel and fan graphs	Chordal graphs
Graphs with longest cycle ≤ 6	Planar graphs

1.3   Used Proof Techniques and Significance

Showing that graphs which contain a forbidden subgraph are not efficient is straightforward: It suffices to give costs for each forbidden subgraph so that the PoS is greater than 1. Here, we can effectively delete edges which are not part of a forbidden subgraph by assigning high costs to them. The property *not efficient* is derived by proving that the optimal Steiner forest of the used instance is unique.

The proof that every graph which does not contain a forbidden subgraph (called *bad configuration*) is strongly efficient, is much more involved. As a first step we derive an LP-characterization of enforceable Steiner forests. An optimal budget-balanced LP solution (for a given Steiner forest) corresponds to cost shares that induce a separable cost sharing protocol so that the Steiner forest becomes a pure Nash equilibrium. The proof proceeds now by contraposition: assume we are given a graph without a forbidden subgraph and assume (by contradiction) that there is an optimal Steiner forest that is not enforceable. We solve the corresponding LP for the Steiner forest and since the Steiner forest is not enforceable, there exists an inequality which is not tight and corresponds to an edge that is not completely paid by the players. We use this unpaid edge to derive the existence of an alternative strategy (path) for some player with costs equal to a fraction of the currently paid cost shares (this alternative strategy corresponds to a tight inequality of the LP). These alternative paths are now iteratively generated until we can either argue that there exists a cheaper Steiner forest compared to the initial optimal Steiner forest (contradiction), or, there is a bad configuration (contradiction). Along this main approach, however, several additional ideas are required: the location of the unpaid edge leads to different subcases for which we need to use special optimal LP-solutions in order to derive the proper alternative strategies.

We believe that our approach is a promising step towards better understanding the power of separable cost sharing protocols in general. For the PoS-question in directed or undirected graphs, there has been no progress since the initial conference version of Chen et al. [7] roughly 10 years ago. Our characterization and the proof exactly prescribes substructures of a worst-case instance (namely a bad configuration must exist whose subpaths have costs corresponding to tight inequalities of an LP solution). We are confident that our proof technique gives a blue-print for both, characterizing efficient graphs for the general n-Player case, and for resolving the PoS-question.

1.4   Related Work

For the PoA of uniform cost sharing protocols[1], Chen et al. [7] proved (tight) bounds of 2 for undirected single-sink networks and $\Theta(\text{polylog}(n))$ for undirected multi-commodity networks. For directed single-sink networks the achievable PoA is n. For the PoS, they use enforceability constraints (that we also

---

[1] Uniform protocols require that the cost shares on an edge only depend on the edge cost and the set of players, but not on the network itself.

use in the LP-characterization) to show that single-sink instances (directed or undirected) admit an optimal Steiner forest as PNE (that is the PoS is 1). For multi-commodity directed network, the achievable PoS lies in $[3/2, \log(n)]$ and since the initial work of Chen et al. [7], no improvement has been made on this question. For undirected networks, the only known upper bounds are derived by analyzing the Shapley cost sharing protocol and they are of order $O(\log(n))$, see Anshelevich et al. [1]. Several works improved lower and upper bounds for the PoS of Shapley cost sharing in undirected networks (cf. [2,3,10,12,15,29]) but up to day it is open whether the PoS is of order $\log(n)$ or even in $O(1)$. For several special cases, the price of stability is shown to be significantly lower (cf. [15,27,28]). Recently Bilò et al. [4] could show that the PoS for broadcast games is $O(1)$. For the design of separable cost sharing protocols in undirected networks, we are not aware of *any* known lower bounds regarding the PoS.

Chen and Roughgarden [6] and Kollias and Roughgarden [25] focused on network design with weighted players (where Kollias and Roughgarden analyzed this variant as a special case of weighted congestion games) and derived tight bounds on the PoA for the Shapley cost sharing protocol. Gkatzelis et al. [18] further showed that the Shapley cost sharing protocol is optimal among all uniform protocols for polynomial and convex cost functions.[2] For further works analyzing the Shapley protocol or arbitrary cost sharing, see [16,17,21,23,24,33]. Harks and von Falkenhausen [14,20] studied the design of separable cost sharing protocols in a model, where players want to buy a basis of a matroid. They derived tight bounds for the achievable PoS and PoA of order $\log(n)$ and n, respectively. Christodoulou and Sgouritsa [11] considered multicast cost sharing games under the assumption that input parameters (such as the set of terminals and their location in the graph) are not known or only known probabilistically. Among other results they show constant PoA bounds for outer planar graphs even without knowing the parameters. On the other hand, they derive strong lower bounds on the PoA of order $\log(n)$ even if the graph metric is known in advance.

Cost sharing approaches for facility location problems and network design problems were analyzed in [26,32]. In these works, however, the collected cost shares need not be budget balanced per edge, thus, leading to a structurally different setting.

There exist several characterizations of efficient graph topologies, albeit for the simpler setting of average cost sharing (or Shapley cost sharing). Epstein et al. [13] investigated efficient graph topologies for Shapley cost sharing and showed that for symmetric s-t network congestion games, only extension parallel graphs (a subclass of series-parallel graphs) are efficient. For asymmetric (multi-commodity) games, only trees or nodes with parallel edges are efficient. These works are closely related to Milchtaich's [30] work on the Braess paradox (see also [5,8,9]).

---

[2] The certificate for optimality uses a characterization of uniform protocols by Gopalakrishnan et al. [19].

2   An LP-Characterization of Enforceability

Let $\mathcal{P}_i$ be the set of simple (s_i, t_i)-paths of G. Furthermore, let F be a fixed Steiner forest and $P = (P_1, \ldots, P_n)$ with $P_i \in \mathcal{P}_i$ the uniquely defined (s_i, t_i)-paths in F. In addition, let $S_e(P)$ be the set of players which use edge e in their (s_i, t_i)-path P_i, i.e. $S_e(P) := \{i \in N : e \in P_i\}$. An important technical tool for obtaining characterizations of *efficient graphs* relies on a characterization of Steiner forests F that can actually appear as a pure Nash equilibrium for a given graph $G = (V, E)$ and given costs c. We define this property formally.

Definition 1. *Let (G, c) be an undirected network and N be a set of players with given connectivity constraints. A Steiner forest $F \subseteq E$ is called* enforceable, *if there is a separable cost sharing protocol so that $P = (P_1, \ldots, P_n)$ (where every P_i is the unique path in F) is a pure Nash equilibrium of the induced game.*

We give a characterization of enforceability of F based on the following linear program LP(F):

$$\max \sum_{i \in N, e \in P_i} \xi_{i,e}$$

$$\text{s.t.:} \quad \sum_{i \in S_e(P)} \xi_{i,e} \leq c(e) \qquad \forall e \in F$$

$$\sum_{e \in P_i \backslash P_i'} \xi_{i,e} \leq \sum_{e \in P_i' \backslash P_i} c(e) \qquad \forall P_i' \in \mathcal{P}_i \, \forall i \in N \qquad \text{(NE)}$$

$$\xi_{i,e} \geq 0 \qquad \forall e \in P_i \, \forall i \in N$$

Theorem 2. *The Steiner forest F with corresponding strategy profile P is enforceable if and only if there is an optimal solution $(\xi_{i,e})_{i \in N, e \in P_i}$ for LP(F) with*

$$\sum_{i \in S_e(P)} \xi_{i,e} = c(e) \; \forall e \in F. \qquad \text{(BB)}$$

The proof of the characterization can be found in [22, Sect. 2].

3   A Characterization of Efficient Graphs for Two Player Games

We now consider the case of two players, $N = \{1, 2\}$, and first show that an optimal Steiner forest is not necessarily enforceable. To see this, consider the network displayed in Fig. 2. The solid lines build the unique optimal Steiner forest OPT with cost 22 (which can be easily verified by considering all 19 possible Steiner forests). But the sum of cost shares that one can collect by any separable cost sharing protocol is obviously bounded by 9 for Player 1 and

$6 + 6 = 12$ for Player 2, thus the objective value for LP(OPT) is bounded by $21 < 22$ and therefore OPT is not enforceable. By optimizing the costs for this graph, we get a lower bound of $\frac{15}{14}$ for the PoS, see [22, Sect. 6].

As we will show in the rest of the paper, the configuration displayed in Fig. 2 is one of few cases in which an optimal Steiner forest is not enforceable. Before we can state this as a theorem, we need two definitions.

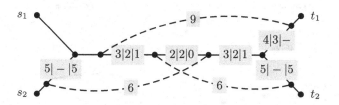

Fig. 2. OPT is not enforceable (edges of OPT with cost > 0 are labelled with their cost, followed by an optimal solution $\xi_{1,e}|\xi_{2,e}$ for LP(OPT))

Definition 3 ((Strongly) Efficient Graph).

1. *We call $(G, (s_1, t_1), (s_2, t_2))$ efficient, if, for every cost function c, there is an optimal Steiner forest of $(G, (s_1, t_1), (s_2, t_2), c)$ which is enforceable (that means the PoS is 1).*
2. *We call $(G, (s_1, t_1), (s_2, t_2))$ strongly efficient, if, for every cost function c, every optimal Steiner forest of $(G, (s_1, t_1), (s_2, t_2), c)$ is enforceable.*

Definition 4. *We call a subgraph H of $(G, (s_1, t_1), (s_2, t_2))$ a Bad Configuration (BC), if H is one of the graphs in the set $\mathcal{BC}$, where*

$$\mathcal{BC} = \{BC1a, \; BC1b, \; BC2a, \; BC2b, \; BC2c, \; BC2d, \; BC3, \; BC4a, \; BC4b\}.$$

The graphs of $\mathcal{BC}$ are displayed in Fig. 3 (see [22, Subsect. A.2.4] for the exact definition), where one should note the following:

- *u, v are the terminal nodes of one player; w, x the terminals of the other;*
- *lines represent simple paths and paths are node-disjoint (except for endnodes);*
- *solid paths have to consist of at least one edge, whereas dashed paths can consist of only one node.*

Theorem 5 (Main Theorem). *The following three statements are equivalent:*

(1) $(G, (s_1, t_1), (s_2, t_2))$ does not contain a subgraph which is a Bad Configuration.
(2) $(G, (s_1, t_1), (s_2, t_2))$ is efficient.
(3) $(G, (s_1, t_1), (s_2, t_2))$ is strongly efficient.

It is clear that (3) implies (2); a sketch of the proof of (2) $\Rightarrow$ (1) and (1) $\Rightarrow$ (3) can be found in the next section.

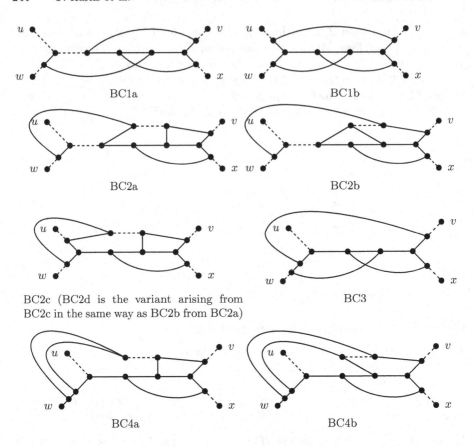

Fig. 3. Bad Configurations

4   Sketch of the Proof of Theorem 5

4.1   (2) Implies (1)

We assume that $(G, (s_1, t_1), (s_2, t_2))$ contains a Bad Configuration. Then we define a cost function c so that the optimal Steiner forest is unique and not enforceable, showing the claim. To this end we choose a subgraph of G that is a BC and set $c(e) = \infty$ if the edge e is not contained in this subgraph. We now have to distinguish between the different types of BCs. For BC1a, the costs displayed in Fig. 2 carry over (if a path consists of more than one edge, choose the costs of the corresponding edges arbitrarily so that they sum up to the displayed cost on the path; all paths with nonzero costs contain at least one edge because of the definition of the corresponding type of BC). Costs for the other types of BCs can be found in [22, Subsect. A.1].

4.2 (1) Implies (3)

Consider an arbitrary optimal Steiner forest F (w.r.t. an arbitrary cost function c) and an optimal solution $(\xi_{i,e})_{i \in N, e \in P_i}$ of the corresponding LP(F). Assume that condition (BB) is not satisfied, i.e. there is an edge that is not paid completely.

Note that $P_1 \cap P_2$ has to contain at least one edge, since otherwise F is enforceable. Furthermore, $P_1 \cap P_2$ has to be a simple path, since F contains no cycles. We refer to the edges of $P_1 \cap P_2$ as the *commonly used edges* or *the middle part* (cf. Fig. 4). Note that we can w.l.o.g. assume that s_1 and s_2 are in the left part, otherwise we can just swap source and sink since the graph is undirected. Figure 4 also illustrates the complete ordering on the edges of F that we use throughout the proof (the numbers indicate in which order we consider the subpaths; the arrows indicate increasing order within the subpaths).

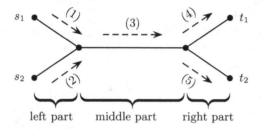

Fig. 4. Left, middle and right part of F; complete ordering on edges of F

Definition 6. *We call an optimal solution $(\xi_{i,e})_{i \in N, e \in P_i}$ for LP(F) pushed to the left (PL), if the following changes of the cost shares (which we denote a push operation) do not yield a feasible solution for LP(F) (for every choice of i, e, f and $\varepsilon > 0$):*

Increase the cost share $\xi_{i,e}$ of Player i on edge e by ε and simultaneously decrease $\xi_{i,f}$ by ε, where f is an edge with higher order than e.

To obtain PL-cost shares $(\xi_{i,e})_{i \in N, e \in P_i}$, we can use Algorithm PUSHLEFT (see [22, Subsect. A.2.5]). Let e be the first edge (with respect to the order) which is not completely paid according to the computed PL-cost shares. We distinguish between the cases that e is in the left part of F (Case L), the middle part of F (Case M) or the right part of F (Case R). In each of these cases, we get a contradiction (see [22, Subsect. A.2] for complete proofs).

We now describe some of the main ideas for the Cases L, M and R. If $e \in P_i$, Player i needs to have a *tight alternative* q for e (corresponding to a tight inequality in (NE)), i.e., q is a simple path which closes a unique cycle $C(q)$ with P_i containing e, and the cost of q equals the sum of cost shares Player i pays on the edges of $P_i \cap C(q)$: If there is no such tight alternative, increasing the cost share $\xi_{i,e} < c(e)$ without changing the other cost shares would yield a feasible solution for $LP(F)$ with higher objective function value. We denote the edges of $P_i \cap C(q)$ as the edges which are *substituted by* q.

Case L: Assume that $e \in P_1$ holds ($e \in P_2$ follows analogously). Under all tight alternatives for Player 1 which substitute e, let q_1 be *smallest*, that is, q_1 minimizes the maximum occurring order of an edge in $C(q_1) \cap P_1$. Let f be the "last" edge which is substituted by q_1, i.e., where the maximum is attained. The situation for the case that f is in the middle part is illustrated in Fig. 5a; the other cases (f is in the right or left part) can be treated very similarly.

We get that Player 1 pays the edges of $C(q_1) \cap P_1$ before e (w.r.t. the ordering) completely since those edges are not contained in P_2 and e is the first edge that is not paid completely. The same reasons yield $\xi_{1,e} < c(e)$. Furthermore, Player 1 pays nothing on the edges of $C(q_1) \cap P_1$ after e (follows from PL-cost shares and the choice of q_1). Let F^* be the Steiner forest which arises from F by adding q_1 and deleting the edges of $C(q_1) \cap P_1$ which are in the left part (cf. Fig. 5b). Since the cost of q_1 equals the sum of cost shares of the deleted edges and this sum is strictly smaller than the costs of these edges, $c(F^*) < c(F)$; contradiction. The full proof for Case L can be found in [22, Subsect. A.2.1].

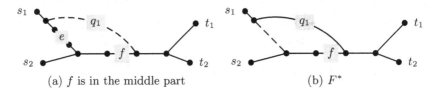

(a) f is in the middle part   (b) F^*

Fig. 5. Case L

Case M: Now both players need to have tight alternatives q_1 and q_2 for e. It is clear that we can construct a cheaper Steiner forest if there are tight alternatives q_1 and q_2 for e which substitute the same edges of the middle part, or a tight alternative for e which substitutes only edges of the middle part. We then distinguish between the two cases that all tight alternatives for e of one player substitute edges of the right part, or both players have a tight alternative for e which substitutes edges of the left part. Since the first case can be treated similarly to Case L, we describe how to proceed in the second case. Let q_1 (for Player 1) and q_2 (for Player 2) be smallest tight alternatives for e which substitute edges of the left part. Consider the case that q_1 substitutes less edges of the middle part than q_2, and q_2 does not substitute edges of the right part, see Fig. 6a (the other cases follow similarly). Adding q_1 and q_2, and deleting the dashed edges (cf. Fig. 6b) yields a Steiner forest F^* with smaller cost than F (note that Player 2 pays nothing on the edges after e which are substituted by q_2), and thus we get a contradiction. The full proof for Case M can be found in [22, Subsect. A.2.2].

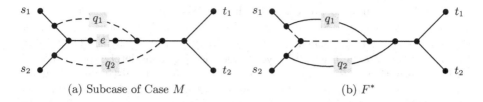

(a) Subcase of Case M (b) F^*

Fig. 6. Case M

Case R: Note that in the Cases L and M we did not need any arguments according to BCs. This already indicates that Case R is more complicated. We mention here only a few of the proof ideas (a full proof can be found in [22, Subsects. A.2.3 and A.2.4]).

Again, we consider a smallest alternative q_1 of Player 1 for e (assuming that $e \in P_1$). It is easy to see that q_1 has to substitute some edges of the middle part, since otherwise there is a cheaper Steiner forest. The same argument shows that there has to be an edge f in the middle part (substituted by q_1) which Player 2 does not pay completely. Now we want to argue that Player 2 needs to have a tight alternative which substitutes f. Note that for an arbitrary PL-solution of $LP(F)$ we cannot guarantee that whenever a player does not pay an edge in the middle part completely, this player has a tight alternative for this edge. However, we can achieve this property for one fixed Player i by maximizing the sum of cost shares of Player i among all optimal solutions for $LP(F)$ for which e is the first edge which is not completely paid. Let us assume that this property holds for Player 2 and consider a tight alternative of Player 2 which substitutes f. If this alternative substitutes only edges of the middle part, or the same edges of the middle part as q_1, one can construct a cheaper Steiner forest. The remaining subcases can be organized as follows: If there is no tight alternative of Player 2 which substitutes f and edges of the right part, let q_2 be any tight alternative for f (which then substitutes edges of the left part; Subcase $R.3$). Otherwise, let q_2 be a tight alternative of Player 2 which substitutes f and edges of the right part maximizing the minimum occuring order of an edge in $C(q_2) \cap P_2$. Then q_2 can either substitute less (Subcase $R.1$) or more (Subcase $R.2$) edges of the middle part than q_1, see Fig. 7 for the subcases that q_1 (or q_2 in $R.2$) does not substitute edges of the left part.

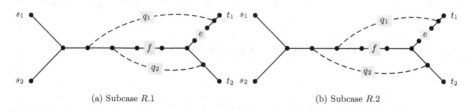

(a) Subcase $R.1$ (b) Subcase $R.2$

Fig. 7. Subcases $R.1$ and $R.2$

We now describe how to proceed with the situation illustrated in Fig. 7a. One can construct a cheaper Steiner forest if Player 2 completely pays the edges of the commonly used part which are substituted by q_1, but not by q_2. Thus, there has to be such an edge h which Player 2 does not pay completely, together with a tight alternative q_2' for h. Similarly as for q_2, we have to distinguish between several subcases depending on the properties of q_2', see Fig. 8 for two possible subcases. First consider the subcase illustrated in Fig. 8a. If Player 1 completely pays the edges of the middle part which are not substituted by q_1, using q_1 and q_2' yields a cheaper Steiner forest, so we can assume that this does not hold. Now we would like to argue that there has to be a tight alternative for Player 1 substituting such an edge; but as mentioned above, this is not immediately clear. To ensure this, we introduced another additional property for the given cost shares (for more details, see [22, Subsect. A.2.3]). We now consider the subcase of Fig. 8b, which turned out to be the most challenging problem in the proof.

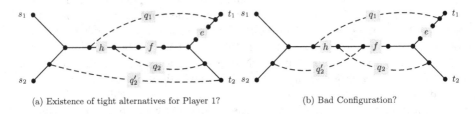

(a) Existence of tight alternatives for Player 1?   (b) Bad Configuration?

Fig. 8. Different subcases of $R.1$

Note that the subgraph illustrated Fig. 8b is a BC1a only if the paths q_1, q_2 and q_2' are pairwise node-disjoint and furthermore internal node-disjoint with $P_1 \cup P_2$. Depending on these properties, we grouped all possible different situations in twelve "types" (Fig. 9 illustrates two of them). In total, 16 subgraphs similar to the one illustrated in Fig. 8b occur, for which we have to investigate all twelve types, leading to $16 \cdot 12 = 192$ subcases (see [22, Subsects. A.2.3 and A.2.4]).

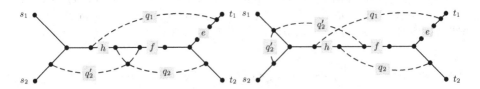

Fig. 9. Two types of No Bad Configurations

5   Summary and Open Problems

We derived a complete characterization of efficient graphs for two-player network design games showing that a graph is efficient iff certain forbidden subgraphs are not present. Our work leads to several interesting research questions:

- What is the computational complexity of recognizing a Bad Configuration?
- How does a characterization look like for three or more players?

Our characterization prescribes substructures of worst-case instances regarding the long-standing PoS question for separable protocols. We conjecture:

Conjecture 1. The PoS for two-player undirected network design games is 15/14 (see [22, Sect. 6] for a lower bound).

Conjecture 2. The PoS for undirected network design games with n players is < 2.

Conjecture 3. The PoS for directed network design games with n players is 2.

References

1. Anshelevich, E., Dasgupta, A., Kleinberg, J., Tardos, É., Wexler, T., Roughgarden, T.: The price of stability for network design with fair cost allocation. SIAM J. Comput. **38**(4), 1602–1623 (2008)
2. Bilò, V., Bove, R.: Bounds on the price of stability of undirected network design games with three players. J. Interconnect. Netw. **12**(1–2), 1–17 (2011)
3. Bilò, V., Caragiannis, I., Fanelli, A., Monaco, G.: Improved lower bounds on the price of stability of undirected network design games. Theory Comput. Syst. **52**(4), 668–686 (2013)
4. Bilò, V., Flammini, M., Moscardelli, L.: The price of stability for undirected broadcast network design with fair cost allocation is constant. In: 54th Annual IEEE Symposium on Foundations of Computer Science, FOCS 2013, 26–29 October, 2013, Berkeley, CA, USA, pp. 638–647 (2013)
5. Cenciarelli, P., Gorla, D., Salvo, I.: Graph theoretic investigations on inefficiencies in network models. CoRR abs/1603.01983 (2016)
6. Chen, H.L., Roughgarden, T.: Network design with weighted players. Theory Comput. Syst. **45**(2), 302–324 (2009)
7. Chen, H.L., Roughgarden, T., Valiant, G.: Designing network protocols for good equilibria. SIAM J. Comput. **39**(5), 1799–1832 (2010)
8. Chen, X., Diao, Z.: Network topologies for weakly pareto optimal nonatomic selfish routing. In: Dinh, T.N., Thai, M.T. (eds.) COCOON 2016. LNCS, vol. 9797, pp. 27–38. Springer, Cham (2016). https://doi.org/10.1007/978-3-319-42634-1_3
9. Chen, X., Diao, Z., Hu, X.: Network characterizations for excluding Braess's paradox. Theory Comput. Syst. **59**(4), 747–780 (2016)

10. Christodoulou, G., Chung, C., Ligett, K., Pyrga, E., van Stee, R.: On the price of stability for undirected network design. In: Bampis, E., Jansen, K. (eds.) WAOA 2009. LNCS, vol. 5893, pp. 86–97. Springer, Heidelberg (2010). https://doi.org/10.1007/978-3-642-12450-1_8

11. Christodoulou, G., Sgouritsa, A.: Designing networks with good equilibria under uncertainty. In: Proceedings of the Twenty-Seventh Annual ACM-SIAM Symposium on Discrete Algorithms, SODA 2016, Arlington, VA, USA, 10–12 January 2016, pp. 72–89 (2016)

12. Disser, Y., Feldmann, A.E., Klimm, M., Mihalák, M.: Improving the H_k-bound on the price of stability in undirected shapley network design games. Theoret. Comput. Sci. **562**, 557–564 (2015)

13. Epstein, A., Feldman, M., Mansour, Y.: Efficient graph topologies in network routing games. Games Econom. Behav. **66**, 115–125 (2009)

14. von Falkenhausen, P., Harks, T.: Optimal cost sharing for resource selection games. Math. Oper. Res. **38**(1), 184–208 (2013)

15. Fiat, A., Kaplan, H., Levy, M., Olonetsky, S., Shabo, R.: On the price of stability for designing undirected networks with fair cost allocations. In: Bugliesi, M., Preneel, B., Sassone, V., Wegener, I. (eds.) ICALP 2006. LNCS, vol. 4051, pp. 608–618. Springer, Heidelberg (2006). https://doi.org/10.1007/11786986_53

16. Gairing, M., Kollias, K., Kotsialou, G.: Tight bounds for cost-sharing in weighted congestion games. In: Halldórsson, M.M., Iwama, K., Kobayashi, N., Speckmann, B. (eds.) ICALP 2015. LNCS, vol. 9135, pp. 626–637. Springer, Heidelberg (2015). https://doi.org/10.1007/978-3-662-47666-6_50

17. Gairing, M., Kollias, K., Kotsialou, G.: Cost-sharing in generalised selfish routing. In: Fotakis, D., Pagourtzis, A., Paschos, V.T. (eds.) CIAC 2017. LNCS, vol. 10236, pp. 272–284. Springer, Cham (2017). https://doi.org/10.1007/978-3-319-57586-5_23

18. Gkatzelis, V., Kollias, K., Roughgarden, T.: Optimal cost-sharing in general resource selection games. Oper. Res. **64**(6), 1230–1238 (2016)

19. Gopalakrishnan, R., Marden, J.R., Wierman, A.: Potential games are *Necessary* to ensure pure nash equilibria in cost sharing games. Math. Oper. Res. **39**(4), 1252–1296 (2014)

20. Harks, T., von Falkenhausen, P.: Optimal cost sharing for capacitated facility location games. Eur. J. Oper. Res. **239**(1), 187–198 (2014)

21. Harks, T., Peis, B.: Resource buying games. Algorithmica **70**(3), 493–512 (2014)

22. Harks, T., Huber, A., Surek, M.: A characterization of undirected graphs admitting optimal cost shares (2017). arXiv:1704.01983v2 [cs.GT]

23. Hoefer, M.: Competitive cost sharing with economies of scale. Algorithmica **60**, 743–765 (2011)

24. Klimm, M., Schmand, D.: Sharing non-anonymous costs of multiple resources optimally. In: Paschos, V.T., Widmayer, P. (eds.) CIAC 2015. LNCS, vol. 9079, pp. 274–287. Springer, Cham (2015). https://doi.org/10.1007/978-3-319-18173-8_20

25. Kollias, K., Roughgarden, T.: Restoring pure equilibria to weighted congestion games. ACM Trans. Econ. Comput. **3**(4), 1–21 (2015)

26. Könemann, J., Leonardi, S., Schäfer, G., van Zwam, S.: A group-strategyproof cost sharing mechanism for the Steiner forest game. SIAM J. Comput. **37**(5), 1319–1341 (2008)

27. Lee, E., Ligett, K.: Improved bounds on the price of stability in network cost sharing games. In: ACM Conference on Electronic Commerce, EC 2013, Philadelphia, PA, USA, 16–20 June 2013, pp. 607–620 (2013)

28. Li, J.: An $o(\log n \log \log n)$ upper bound on the price of stability for undirected shapley network design games. Inf. Process. Lett. **109**(15), 876–878 (2009)
29. Mamageishvili, A., Mihalák, M., Montemezzani, S.: An $H_{n/2}$ upper bound on the price of stability of undirected network design games. In: Csuhaj-Varjú, E., Dietzfelbinger, M., Ésik, Z. (eds.) MFCS 2014. LNCS, vol. 8635, pp. 541–552. Springer, Heidelberg (2014). https://doi.org/10.1007/978-3-662-44465-8_46
30. Milchtaich, I.: Network topology and the efficiency of equilibrium. Games Econ. Behav. **57**(2), 321–346 (2006)
31. Osborne, M., Rubinstein, A.: A Course in Game Theory. MIT Press, Cambridge (1994)
32. Pál, M., Tardos, É.: Group strategyproof mechanisms via primal-dual algorithms. In: FOCS, pp. 584–593 (2003)
33. Roughgarden, T., Schrijvers, O.: Network cost-sharing without anonymity. ACM Trans. Econ. Comput. **4**(2), 8 (2016)

Approximate Efficiency in Matching Markets

Nicole Immorlica[1(✉)], Brendan Lucier[1], Glen Weyl[1], and Joshua Mollner[2]

[1] Microsoft Research, New England, USA
nicimm@gmail.com
[2] Kellogg School of Management, Northwestern University, Evanston, USA

Abstract. We propose a measure of approximate ex-ante Pareto efficiency in matching markets. According to this measure, a lottery over matchings is γ-approximately efficient if there is no alternate lottery in which each agent's ex-ante expected utility increases by an γ factor. A mechanism is γ-approximately efficient if every lottery produced in equilibrium is γ-approximately efficient. We argue this is the natural extension of approximate efficiency in transferable-utility settings to our nontransferable-utility setting. Using this notion, we are able to quantify the intuited efficiency improvement of the so-called *Boston mechanism* and the recently-proposed *choice-augmented deferred acceptance mechanism* over the *random serial dictatorship mechanism*. Furthermore, we provide the first formal statement and analysis of the *Raffle mechanism*, which is conceptually simpler than the Boston mechanism and has a comparable efficiency guarantee.

1 Introduction

One of the most powerful paradigms in algorithmic mechanism design is that of approximation. By quantifying the approximate optimality of mechanisms, researchers are able to distinguish good mechanisms from bad ones, and easy environments from hard ones. These efforts guide the choice of mechanisms when the optimal mechanism is infeasible due to computational or cognitive complexity, information or technology constraints, or other limitations.

Approximation has had considerable influence in the design of mechanisms for allocating objects to agents in settings with transferable utility, where payments can be made in a common currency. In the context of welfare optimization, for instance, recent results suggest that simultaneous item auctions are approximately efficient for a broad range of valuation classes [18, 20, 21, 25, 33], and approach full efficiency in large markets [22]. A similarly-motivated line of inquiry suggests that, for many settings, second-price auctions or item/bundle-pricing guarantee nearly-optimal revenue [6, 23, 24].

However, many important economic problems, particularly the matching literature focused on the allocation of social goods, lie in the nontransferable utility setting. School choice programs allocate school seats in public schools to children. Public housing programs allocate apartments to tenants. Kidney transplant programs allocate deceased-donor kidneys to patients. Refugee settlement programs

N. R. Devanur and P. Lu (Eds.): WINE 2017, LNCS 10674, pp. 252–265, 2017.
https://doi.org/10.1007/978-3-319-71924-5_18

match refugees to host cities. In these settings it is considered repugnant and, often, simply infeasible to use money to allocate objects.

Without the common metric of money, it is impossible to directly compare the utility of one agent with another, and so welfare objectives are necessarily multi-pronged. We can still attempt to optimize welfare by choosing allocations on the Pareto frontier. An allocation is welfare-optimal if it is not Pareto dominated, i.e., there is no other allocation which each agent weakly prefers and some agent strictly prefers. More generally, a randomized allocation, commonly called a lottery, is welfare-optimal if it is not Pareto dominated ex-ante, i.e., there is no other lottery which each agent weakly prefers in expectation and some agent strictly prefers in expectation. Such lotteries are called *Pareto efficient.*

In a seminal paper, Hylland and Zeckhauser [27] (henceforth HZ) proposed a pseudomarket in which individuals are allocated artificial currency and buy probability shares of goods until the market clears. A centralized randomization is then derived from the Birkhoff-von Neumann construction (see [12] for details) to implement these promised probability shares. In the same types of price-taking, large market settings where markets are known to be efficient in classical economic analysis [31], this pseudomarket is cardinally efficient (i.e., maximizes total welfare). Furthermore, it is strategyproof in the large (i.e., in the continuous-market limit). Azevedo and Budish [5] argue is the most one can hope for among efficient mechanisms in this setting and, assuming truthful reporting of preferences, it satisfies the first and second fundamental welfare theorems: any allocation by the pseudomarket is Pareto efficient and appropriate allocation of currency can achieve any Pareto optimum.

However, as is often the case with optimal mechanisms, HZ has seen little adoption in practice, perhaps due to the difficulty of describing it to participants. Evidence for this view comes from Budish and Kessler's [13] implementation of a related mechanism among business students to allocate courses. While individuals did provide utility indices for various courses, there were wide-spread complaints about the lack of transparency and it was very common for students to supply implausibly large utility indices for some courses. Given that the mechanism used these indices ultimately to form ordinal preferences, this did not devastate the performance of their implementation, but it did raise significant concerns about applying a similar approach in settings where cardinal intensities are of greater moment. Accordingly, alternate suboptimal mechanisms are the norm in matching markets, and as such, it is essential to be able to chose among them appropriately.

The matching literature lacks a comparable guiding principle of approximation—so useful in the transferable utility setting—for choosing among suboptimal mechanisms. This is due in large part to the difficulty of selecting an appropriate notion of approximation in nontransferable utility settings. We propose an approximation notion that closely mimics Pareto efficiency. The idea behind Pareto efficiency is that one cannot weakly improve the outcomes of all consumers simultaneously in a non-trivial way. Our approximate notion of Pareto efficiency relaxes this to the property that one cannot simultaneously improve the outcome of all consumers by some factor $\gamma \geq 1$. That is, we define a lottery to be γ-*approximately Pareto efficient* if there is no other lottery in which each agent's utility improves by at least a γ factor in expectation, with at least one agent's utility improving by strictly more than a γ factor. Similar notions of approximately Pareto optimal solutions have appeared in the multi-objective optimization literature (e.g., [28]), but to the best of our knowledge we are the first to apply it in the context of market design.

As sanity checks, we note that 1-approximate Pareto efficiency coincides with standard Pareto efficiency. Furthermore, this notion is the natural analog of approximate efficiency in the cardinal setting with transferable utility. There, an outcome is said to be γ-approximately efficient if the total social welfare is at least a $1/\gamma$ factor of the total social welfare in a first-best solution. Equivalently, and analogous to our definition, an outcome is γ-approximately efficient if the total social welfare (profile of values in our setting) is at least the total social welfare of a first-best solution where the values are scaled by γ.

These observations suggest we are on the right track with this definition. However, a meaningful notion of approximation must be both *logical* (i.e., capture the philosophical notions of near-optimality for the objective at hand) and *discerning* (i.e., yield quantitatively different results for good and bad mechanisms). Given that most matching problems are motivated by social good applications like school choice programs and low-income housing allocation, we chose to follow the logic of the notion of efficiency based on social decisions made behind a *veil of ignorance* [30]. This implies that the benefits of social arrangements should be judged based upon the value they yield to the agent who *least* benefits from them, and so optimality is defined as a maximin objective.[1] This choice distinguishes our results from most existing work in the matching or social choice literature which typically considers approximating the mean, median, or geometric mean welfare [4,9,14], or focuses on ordinal objectives such as (roughly speaking) maximizing the number of agents with their top choice [16] among others [3].

In particular, these maximin notions do not reward mechanisms for drastically improving the outcome of select agents while ignoring others. Thus, if there are two unit-demand agents, Jieming and Jolene, and three goods, two skateboards and a bicycle, with common values of 100, 100, and 200 to the agents, respectively, then it is $(1 + \epsilon)$-approximately efficient for any $\epsilon > 0$, according to our notion, to allocate the skateboards and discard the bicycle.[2] An alternative notion would be to say that a lottery is γ-approximately efficient if there exists no other lottery that each consumer weakly prefers and some consumer prefers by a γ factor. According to this alternate notion, any allocation

---

[1] See also the considerable research in the optimization literature on the so-called "Santa Claus problem," or maximin welfare optimization [7]. We are not aware of work that studies the maximin welfare of existing matching mechanisms.

[2] It is not hard to make this example more extreme in a market with n agents, producing an approximately efficient lottery with ex ante value 1 for all agents whereas the efficient lottery has value 1 for all but one agent and value n for a select agent.

that discards the highly valuable good is a bad approximation. However, we feel the maximin notion is more appropriate for social allocation problems where fairness is a primary concern. Also, as mentioned earlier, our definition aligns with standard cardinal notions of approximation commonly used in computer science. For example, a mechanism that outputs a pareto-optimal lottery with probability 1/2, and otherwise returns an empty (or arbitrary) allocation, is a 2-approximation under our notion, but might not be 2-approximate under this stronger definition.[3]

The bulk of our paper is devoted to demonstrating the discerning power of our notion. We focus attention on the *random assignment problem* in which a limited supply of objects must be allocated to agents who want at most a single good (i.e., are unit-demand). We study four mechanisms for this problem (see Sect. 3 for formal definitions). The first three – *random serial dictatorship* (RSD), *Boston mechanism*, and *choice-augmented deferred acceptance* (CADA) – have been proposed and analyzed in the matching literature. While it was long accepted that RSD has poor ex ante efficiency properties, Pycia [29] was the first to develop an example showing RSD may have unbounded loss for total welfare. Motivated by the inefficiency of RSD, Abdulkadiroğlu et al. [1] show that when agents have the same ordinal preferences, RSD is Pareto-dominated by the Boston mechanism. In an attempt to recover efficiency without sacrificing the strategic simplicity of RSD, Abdulkadiroglu et al. [2] introduce CADA and argue it performs better than RSD in ex ante efficiency in similarly restrictive settings. Our first set of results complements this literature by quantifying the efficiency comparisons of RSD, Boston, and CADA with respect to our notion of approximation. Using an example similar to [1], we show the approximation of RSD is at least linear in the number of goods, whereas the Boston and CADA mechanisms are 3-approximately Pareto efficient. For the Boston and CADA mechanisms, we also improve the upper bound to 2 under a large-market assumption (i.e., when the pool of agents is a continuum).

Next, we formally introduce and study the Raffle mechanism. In the Raffle mechanism, each agent is allocated a perfectly divisible mass of "tickets" and may divide them as she pleases among buckets corresponding to each potential object (there may be multiple copies of each type of object). The mechanism sequentially pulls tickets from buckets beginning with the most "congested" bucket, that with the greatest ratio of tickets to copies available. Agents are assigned to the object associated with the first bucket from which their name is called and, upon being assigned, all of their tickets are removed from all buckets. Similar raffles are common at fund-raising drives and other charity events.

Clearly, a ticket placed in a crowded bucket is less likely to be pulled. The rationale behind the Raffle mechanism, similar to Boston and CADA as well as the fully-efficient mechanism of HZ, is that a willingness to give up a high-

---

[3] For example, the lottery that with probability 1/2 allocates the skateboard to Jieming and the bicycle to Jolene, and otherwise allocates nothing to either, would only be 4-approximate under this stricter definition, since an alternative would be to always allocate the bicycle to Jolene and the skateboard to Jieming.

probability claim on a socially valuable object for a small chance at one that an individual greatly values is an efficient means to ensure objects are allocated to those valuing them most. However, unlike HZ, the tradeoff in the Raffle mechanism is non-linear: as an agent's tickets start to dominate the contents of a particular bucket, the marginal probability share decreases. This causes an inefficiency in the Raffle mechanism, as compared to HZ. Nonetheless, we are able to bound this inefficiency, showing the Raffle mechanism is $(1 - 1/e)$-approximate in continuum economies.

Recently, Brânzei et al. [10] showed that in a market setting where agent values are additive across goods, the Trading Post mechanism of Shapley and Shubik [32] obtains at least half of the optimal Nash social welfare (i.e., geometric mean of agent values). This is closely related to our approximation bound for the Raffle mechanism, as the Trading Post mechanism is conceptually similar to HZ. However, these mechanisms apply to different settings (budgets versus matching constraints). Moreover, the approximation results are incomparable since we obtain an improved approximation factor for a different notion of approximation.

Remark 1. While it is not the focus of our paper, we further remark that the Raffle mechanism, as opposed to HZ, Boston, or CADA, is particularly easy to describe to participants. While optimal strategies in the Raffle mechanism are potentially somewhat subtle, they are very familiar to agents unlike ranking or rating problems that researchers have found agents find challenging to use [19,26]. Additionally, they only require agents to form preferences over "relevant" prizes rather than ranking everything they could possibly be awarded. Moreover, since tickets are divisible, payoffs in the Raffle mechanism are continuous over possible ticket allocations, which permits local improvements and generally simplifies the task of converging to approximate equilibria.

2   Model

We study a random assignment problem in which a limited supply of heterogeneous goods, such as seats at public schools, must be allocated among unit-demand consumers, such as students. In our model there is a (finite or infinite) set of consumers, denoted by $\mathcal{S}$, and a finite set of goods, denoted by $\mathcal{C} = \{1, \ldots, m\}$. For each $j \in \mathcal{C}$, we let $q_j \in \mathbb{N}$ be the *capacity* or quantity of good j available.

Each consumer $i \in \mathcal{S}$ has a type θ that specifies her value v_j^i for a single copy of each good j. Consumers are unit-demand, i.e., consumer i's value for a subset $C \subseteq \mathcal{C}$ of goods is $\max_{j \in C} v_j^i$. We will assume values are bounded and normalized to lie in $[0, 1]$. We will write $\Theta = [0, 1]^m$ for the space of types.

A randomized assignment, or *lottery*, is a randomized mapping $\sigma \colon \mathcal{S} \to \Delta(\mathcal{C})$ from consumers to goods, where $\Delta(\mathcal{C})$ denotes probability distributions over the elements of $\mathcal{C}$. Given a lottery σ, we will write σ_j^i for the probability that consumer i is matched to good j. A lottery σ is *feasible* if it respects capacities, i.e., for each good j, $\sum_{i \in \mathcal{S}} \sigma_j^i \leq q_j$.[4] The value enjoyed by consumer i in a feasible lottery σ, written $v^i(\sigma)$, is her expected value from the assigned good: $v^i(\sigma) = \sum_{j \in \mathcal{C}} v_j^i \sigma_j^i$ (noting that $\sum_{j \in \mathcal{C}} \sigma_j^i \leq 1$ from the definition of a lottery).

A lottery σ *Pareto dominates* lottery σ' if $v^i(\sigma) \geq v^i(\sigma')$ for all $i \in \mathcal{S}$, and $v^i(\sigma) > v^i(\sigma')$ for a positive measure of consumers. A lottery σ is *Pareto efficient* if there is no other lottery that Pareto dominates it. Our notion of approximate Pareto efficiency generalizes Pareto efficiency as follows.

Definition 1. *For $\gamma \geq 1$, a lottery σ is γ-approximately Pareto efficient if there is no other lottery σ' such that $v^i(\sigma') \geq \gamma \cdot v^i(\sigma)$ for all consumers $i \in \mathcal{S}$, with strict inequality for a positive measure of consumers.*

It will sometimes be convenient to employ a continuum model of consumers. This requires a few notational modifications to the definitions above. In the continuum model, the capacity of good j, q_j, can take on any non-negative real value. The set of consumers $\mathcal{S}$ is described by a measure ρ over the set of types Θ; we assume that ρ is atomless and Lebesgue integrable.

A lottery can now be described as a mapping from types to distributions over goods, $\sigma : \Theta \to \Delta(\mathcal{C})$. We will write σ_j^θ for the probability that a consumer of type θ is assigned to good j, and we will sometimes abuse notation and write σ_j^i to mean σ_j^θ where θ is the type of consumer i. A lottery is feasible if it respects capacities with respect to the measure ρ over types: $\int_{\theta \in \Theta} \sigma_j^\theta d\rho \leq q_j$.

3   Mechanisms

Random Serial Dictatorship Mechanism. In the Random Serial Dictatorship mechanism (RSD), each consumer i submits a strict preference ordering $\prec_i$. The mechanism selects a random permutation of consumers and iteratively assigns them their highest-ranked remaining good. In this mechanism, it is a dominant strategy for a consumer to report ordinal preferences coinciding with their cardinal preferences. However, as we will see, RSD can be arbitrarily inefficient.[5]

Boston Mechanism. In the Boston mechanism, each consumer i submits a strict ordering $\prec_i$ over the goods. A matching is then determined in rounds. In the k'th round, each consumer is eligible to be matched only with their k'th highest-ranked good. If fewer than q_j consumers ranked j in the k'th position, they are each matched to good j. Otherwise, q_j of the consumers who ranked j in the k'th position, chosen uniformly at random, are matched to j. All matched consumers,

---

[4] By the Birkoff von Neumann theorem, a lottery is feasible if and only if it is a distribution over deterministic assignments in which each consumer is assigned at most one good and each good is not over-capacitated.

[5] Another mechanism, the "Probabilistic Serial (PS)" mechanism, is fairly elaborate to describe so we do not formally do so here [8]. In the continuum model on which we focus most of our analysis, this mechanism is equivalent to RSD [17]. Thus our negative results on RSD apply to the PS mechanism in this continuum model.

and all matched copies of goods, are then removed from the market, and the remaining capacity (the q_j variables) are updated. This process continues until all consumers have been matched, or until m rounds have completed (and hence the mechanism has exhausted the preference list of each remaining consumer). This mechanism is subject to complex strategic manipulation, but it has efficiency gains over RSD [1]. We give a stronger guarantee here: the Boston mechanism is in fact approximately efficient. We also consider the Boston mechanism in the continuum model: in that setting, consumers' choices of rankings are assumed to be measureable with respect to ρ, and when consumers are matched to goods in round k, a mass of up to q_j are matched to good j, from among the set of consumers that ranked j in the k'th position.

Choice Augmented Deferred Acceptance Mechanism. The Choice Augmented Deferred Acceptance mechanism (CADA) [2] attempts to retain the incentive properties of Random Serial Dictatorship[6] and the intuitive efficiency gains of the Boston Mechanism. In the CADA mechanism, each consumer submits a preference ordering $\prec_i$ and also specifies a target good. Goods create priority lists by first listing consumers that target them in a random order, and then listing the remaining consumers in a random order. Matches are then formed according to the procedure in c-DA. We will show that CADA, similarly to the Boston mechanism, is approximately Pareto efficient. Also like the Boston mechanism, we will analyze the CADA mechanism in the continuum model. There, strategies (preference orderings and targets) are assumed to be measurable with respect to ρ, and matches are determined using the continuous analog of c-DA, where in each round, each good makes the appropriate mass of proposals to consumers according to a uniform measure from among those not yet proposed to (corresponding to the random ordering of consumers in school preferences).

Raffle Mechanism. In the Raffle mechanism, each agent i is endowed with a mass Z^i of tickets, which can be divided arbitrarily among the goods. Write $x_j^i \geq 0$ for the quantity of tickets that agent i bids on good j.[7] The bids $\mathbf{x}$ determine an ordering π over the goods, described later. For each good j, sequentially in order π, repeatedly select a consumer i with probability $x_j^i / \sum_{i' \in \mathcal{S}} x_j^{i'}$, match i to j, then remove all tickets of consumer i from all goods (i.e., set $x_{j'}^i = 0$ for all $j' \in \mathcal{C}$). Continue selecting consumers until q_j have been chosen or until all tickets assigned to j have been removed, then continue with the next good in order π, until all goods have been processed.

We now describe the order π. For each good j, write $p_j^1(x)$ for the probability that a newly-entering consumer who assigns x tickets to good j (only)

---

[6] As they focus on the school choice setting, they assume goods have priorities and actually build off of c-DA, but as noted above, c-DA with single tie-breaking and RSD are equivalent in our setting.

[7] To handle discontinuities due to tie-breaking at 0 ticket allocation for under-demanded goods, we impose a technical restriction that if $x_j^i > 0$ then $x_j^i \geq \epsilon$ for some arbitrarily small $\epsilon > 0$. This restriction impacts all value calculations by a quantity proportional to ϵ which tends to 0, so we will omit these terms for brevity.

would be matched to good j, if j were to occur first in π. We will choose $\pi(1) \in \arg\min_j \lim_{x\to 0}(p_j^1(x)/x)$, the good with the smallest marginal gain in allocation probability per mass of ticket assigned, at 0.[8] We think of j as the most congested of the goods. We then define $p_j^2(x)$ similarly, but assuming that good j occurs second in π (after $\pi(1)$), and choose $\pi(2) \in \arg\min_j \lim_{x\to 0}(p_j^2(x)/x)$. We continue in this way until all good have been ordered.[9]

Given this ordering π, we define the *effective congestion* of good j to be

$$R_j(\mathbf{x}) = \lim_{x\to 0} \frac{x}{p_j^{\pi^{-1}(j)}(x)}.$$

We note that $R_j(\mathbf{x}) = 0$ if and only if the good j is underdemanded.

The following example illustrates the execution of the Raffle mechanism.

Example 1. Suppose there are 3 goods, $\{A, B, C\}$, each with capacity 1. There are 3 agents, denoted $\{1, 2, 3\}$. Each agent is endowed with a single unit of ticket. The agents allocated their tickets as follows: $(x_A^1, x_B^1, x_C^1) = (3/4, 1/4, 0)$, $(x_A^2, x_B^2, x_C^2) = (1/3, 1/3, 1/3)$, and $(x_A^3, x_B^3, x_C^3) = (1/10, 4/5, 1/10)$.

The good with the highest effective congestion is chosen first. For each good, the marginal gain in allocation probability per mass of ticket assigned, at 0, is 1 over the total mass of tickets allocated to that good. Since B is the good with the most tickets assigned to it, B has the lowest marginal gain (and hence the highest effective congestion) and is resolved first. The total mass of tickets assigned to good B is $1/4 + 1/3 + 4/5 = 83/60$, and each agent is chosen with probability proportional to the mass of ticket they allocated to good B. Suppose that agent 3 is chosen, which occurs with probability $4/5 \times 60/83$. The mechanism then matches agent 3 to good B.

The good with the next-highest effective congestion is chosen next, given the choice to resolve B first. Since good C is uncongested (since less than a single unit of ticket was allocated to it), this next good is A. Since agent 3 has already been matched, tickets from agent 3 are now ignored; the remaining mass of tickets assigned to good A is $3/4 + 1/3 = 13/12$. The mechanism randomly selects either agent 1 or agent 2, each proportional to its share of ticket assigned to good A. Say agent 1 is chosen, which occurs with probability $3/4 \times 12/13$. Then agent 1 is matched to good A.

Finally, the remaining good C is matched with agent 2, the only unmatched agent that has tickets assigned to good C.

We will also consider the Raffle mechanism in the continuum setting, where we require that the bidding strategy $\mathbf{x}$ be measurable with respect to ρ. In this formulation, rather than selecting customers sequentially for a given good, we consider a measure λ over unmatched consumers, initially ρ. The measure of

---

[8] This limit can be infinite if good j is underdemanded.

[9] In the full version of the paper, we discuss how to approximate these marginal gains— and hence the order π—in polynomial time, and argue that a small approximation error leads only to a small loss in approximation factor.

customers matched to good j increases from 0 at rate $\int_\theta \mathbf{x}_j^\theta \cdot \lambda$, while the measure λ over unmatched customers reduces, at θ, at rate $\mathbf{x}_j^\theta \cdot \lambda(\theta)$, until a q_j mass of consumers are matched.

4   (In)-efficiency of RSD, Boston and CADA

We show that Boston and CADA have bounded efficiency guarantees whereas RSD is not even approximately efficient: the potential Pareto losses from RSD are proportional to the population size.

4.1   RSD

Pycia [29] first observed that RSD may have unbounded welfare loss for the utilitarian additive sum of utilities, but his example actually is one of approximate Pareto efficiency according to our more demanding notion of Pareto dominance and thus more permissive notion of approximtion. We provide a new example that shows a linear-in-population size lower bound on the approximation ratio of RSD even for this concept.[10]

Example 2. There are n goods. Good j has 2^{j-1} copies. There are n types of consumers with 2^n consumers of each type. The i'th type of consumer has value $v_j^i = 1 + (n - j + 1)\epsilon$ for goods $1 \le j \le i$, and $v_j^i = (n - j + 1)\epsilon$ for goods $j > i$, where ϵ is arbitrarily small. In this market, consumers' preferences are completely aligned, and so they always select goods in the same order in RSD. Therefore, in the lottery σ_{RSD} induced by RSD, a consumer of type i receives high value if and only if she is among the first $\sum_{k=1}^i 2^{k-1}$ consumers to select a good, in which case she receives a value of approximately 1. Otherwise she receives a low value of approximately zero. Thus the expected value of a type i consumer from RSD is

$$v^i(\sigma_{\mathrm{RSD}}) = \frac{1}{n2^n} \sum_{k=1}^i 2^{k-1} = \frac{2^i - 1}{n2^n}.$$

On the other hand, a lottery which randomly assigns the copies of good i to consumers of type i gives each consumer of that type an expected value of $\frac{2^{i-1}}{2^n}$, a factor $n/2$ improvement over RSD.

4.2   Boston and CADA Mechanisms

The Boston and CADA Mechanisms are credited with achieving more efficient outcomes than other ordinal mechanisms such as RSD. We establish theoretical justification for this insight by showing that these mechanisms are approximately Pareto efficient. It will be helpful to first analyze a simplified Boston mechanism,

---

[10] This also implies a linear lower bound for the consumer-proposing deferred acceptance mechanism (c-DA). See the full version of the paper for more details.

that uses only a single round of matching, then matches any remaining goods and consumers in an arbitrary fashion. We refer to this as the *single-ticket* mechanism. Proofs appear in the full version of the paper.

Theorem 1. *Under a continuum market of consumers, the single-ticket mechanism is 2-approximately Pareto efficient. If the market of consumers can be discrete, the single-ticket mechanism is 3-approximately Pareto efficient.*

As a corollary, we note that the Boston mechanism and the CADA mechanism are both 2-approximately Pareto efficient as well, as they can both be viewed as applying a single round of the Boston mechanism and then allocating the remaining goods in some fashion.

Corollary 1. *Under a continuum model of consumers, the Boston mechanism and the CADA mechanism are both 2-approximately Pareto efficient. Under a discrete model of consumers, they are both 3-approximately Pareto efficient.*

5   Analysis of the Raffle Mechanism

We now turn to an analysis of the Raffle mechanism at equilibrium. We will show that the Raffle mechanism has an equilibrium for every economy, and we provide a closed-form expression for any given consumer's best response. We provide an example demonstrating that equilibria of the Raffle mechanism are not necessarily Pareto efficient. We then show our main result, which is that all equilibria of the Raffle mechanism are $(1 - 1/e)$-approximately Pareto efficient.

5.1   Equilibria of the Raffle Mechanism

An equilibrium of the Raffle mechanism is a ticket allocation profile $\mathbf{x}$ that simultaneously maximizes expected value for all consumer types. Since the type and strategy spaces are compact, and since consumer utilities are continuous in x^θ (recalling that there is a minimal positive bid ϵ on each good, and that lottery probabilities deform continuously in ticket assignments), a standard fixed-point argument implies equilibrium existence.

Proposition 1. *Every instance of the Raffle mechanism has an equilibrium.*

To build some intuition for the structure of equilibria in the Raffle mechanism, consider the probability that a certain consumer is matched with good j, as a function of the quantity of ticket she bids on good j, conditional on not having received any previous goods in the order they are processed by the mechanism. Call this $f_j(x)$. The function $f_j(x)$ is increasing and concave, with the concavity being due to collisions between different portions of her ticket. In the limit as the good j becomes more and more congested, such collisions become increasingly unlikely, and hence $f_j(x)$ tends toward a linear function.

If $f_j(x)$ were truly linear for all j, then the outcome of the Raffle mechanism would be equivalent to an outcome of the HZ mechanism, as each agent is optimally allocating their budget of ticket given a fixed exchange rate for each good. In particular, the outcome would be Pareto efficient. The inefficiency of the Raffle mechanism, then, is driven by the non-linear distortion of these outcome curves $f_j(x)$, which translate to decreasing marginal gains from tickets invested. These non-linear distortions are most extreme when goods are close to being under-demanded. In such cases, any consumer could obtain her favorite good with near-certainty by investing all of her tickets. This would likewise lead to Pareto efficiency. The most inefficient outcomes, then, occur at some moderate level of price distortion. Our analysis characterizes the shape of these distortion curves, quantifies this worst case, and thereby bounds the resulting inefficiency.

Motivated by a different context than ours, Chade and Smith [15] derive a closed-form description of the best response of consumer θ to a given ticket allocation profile **x**. We present their solution in the full version of the paper, and make use of it when analyzing equilibria in Sects. 5.2 and 5.3.

5.2   Why Raffles Aren't Fully Pareto Efficient

We begin by presenting a simple example demonstrating that the Raffle mechanism might not generate a Pareto efficient outcome at equilibrium.

Theorem 2. *There exists an instance of the Raffle mechanism with two consumer types and two goods that is not α-approximately Pareto efficient for any $\alpha < 1.05$.*

5.3   Main Result

Our main result is that the Raffle mechanism is approximately Pareto efficient, under a continuum economy of consumers.

Theorem 3. *In the continuum market model, every equilibrium of the Raffle mechanism is $(1 - 1/e)$-approximately Pareto efficient.*

Our approximation result holds for *any* equilibrium of the Raffle mechanism. In this sense it is a *price of anarchy* result, in which our approximation factor holds in the worst case over market realizations and equilibria of play.

6   Conclusion

In this paper we propose a notion of approximation for ex ante Pareto efficiency in unit-demand matching markets. We use this notion to compare and contrast four mechanisms: RSD, Boston, CADA, and Raffle. We show RSD has unbounded inefficency whereas Boston, CADA, and the Raffle mechanism are all approximately efficient. Our main technical result is that the intuitively simple Raffle mechanism is a $(1 - 1/e)$-approximation in large markets.

Our analysis suggests several directions for future research. First, while Raffle-style mechanisms are frequently used, we are not aware of any systematic attempt to measure the quality of allocations they yield in practice or of any studies measuring the extent to which the theoretical results hold up in laboratory experiments. Second, a fundamental limitation of the Raffle mechanism is that it only applies, in its present form, to the random assignment problem and not to the combinatorial assignment problem [11] of allocating a heterogeneous collection of many discrete goods among consumers who may want more than a single good and potentially have rich preferences over bundles. While Budish et al. [12] describe a mechanism that achieves (large population) cardinal efficiency for some preference structures, no mechanism we are aware of can achieve a wide range of cardinally efficient outcomes (such as ones that are ex-ante envy free) for general preferences even in a large population. This seems particularly relevant because our results on non-approximation of ordinal mechanisms, such as Budish's proposed solution, immediately extend to the combinatorial assignment problem, suggesting all existing mechanisms may be quite inefficienty.

Further afield, a critical aspect of the Raffle mechanism that we find attractive is the way they may be implemented through a dynamic process that exposes the chances of allocation clearly to participants over time. In particular, we imagine a process in which an online automated administrator would continually calculate the effective congestions of different goods and report these to participants. Participants would have the right to move their tickets across the buckets associated with prizes until they were happy with their allocation. The rates at which they are allowed to move tickets and the rates at which the display of congestion would update might be controlled to aid convergence. We believe this dynamic implementation, similar to the process used in Singapore where applications for various types of housing are "open" for a period and their congestion continuously updated online, allowing participants to change the housing they are applying to, would greatly ease the process of finding equilibrium and ensure a transparent and simple decision-making process for participants.[11] Yet beyond these psychological benefits, we also believe such an implementation could have substantial implications for efficiency once factors beyond those we model in this paper are accounted for. For example, such dynamics may help reduce information acquisition costs by allowing participants to economize on investigating prizes they are unlikely to be awarded, allowing groups of participants (such as students) that wish to be consume the same prize (such as school to go to together) to jointly coordinate their plans and allowing participants to learn from the market demand patterns information about the value of different prizes, etc. While it is beyond the scope of our current analysis to formalize these dynamics or their benefits, we view a central value of the Raffle mechanism to be the naturalness with which it invites dynamic implementations with rich feedback to participants. Furthermore we suspect that such a dynamic implementation would maintain desirable equilibrium properties, at least in large populations, as there would be little capacity for participants to impact the trajectory of congestion through their actions along the dynamic path, as is the case in the dynamic convergence to Walrasian equilibrium in large economies [31].

---

[11] See, for example, the displayed information for the last round of the Singapore system at http://www.hdb.gov.sg/cs/infoweb/residential/buying-a-flat/new/application-status.

Acknowledgements. We are grateful to Eric Budish, Peng Shi and especially Christina Lee for useful comments. All errors are our own.

References

1. Abdulkadiroğlu, A., Che, Y.-K., Yasuda, Y.: Resolving conflicting preferences in school choice: the "Boston mechanism"? Reconsidered. Am. Econ. Rev. **101**(1), 399–410 (2011)
2. Abdulkadiroğlu, A., Che, Y.-K., Yasuda, Y.: Expanding "choice" in school choice. Am. Econ. J.: Microeconomics **7**(1), 1–42 (2015)
3. Abraham, D., Irving, R., Kavitha, T., Mehlhorn, K.: Popular matchings. SIAM J. Comput. **37**, 1030–1045 (2007)
4. Anshelevich, E., Postl, J.: Randomized social choice functions under metric preferences. J. Artif. Intell. Res. **58**, 797–827 (2017)
5. Azevedo, E., Budish, E.: Strategy-proofness in the large (2015). http://faculty.chicagobooth.edu/eric.budish/research/Azevedo-Budish-SPL.pdf
6. Babaioff, M., Immorlica, N., Lucier, B., Weinberg, S.M.: A simple and approximately optimal mechanism for an additive buyer. In: 2014 IEEE 55th Annual Symposium on Foundations of Computer Science (FOCS), pp. 21–30. IEEE (2014)
7. Bansal, N., Sviridenko, M.: The Santa Claus problem. In: ACM Symposium on Theory of Computing (STOC) (2006)
8. Bogomolnaia, A., Moulin, H.: A new solution to the random assignment problem. J. Econ. Theory **100**(2), 295–328 (2001)
9. Boutilier, C., Caragiannis, I., Haber, S., Lu, T., Procaccia, A., Sheffet, O.: Optimal social choice functions: a utilitarian view. Artif. Intell. **227**, 190–213 (2015)
10. Branzei, S., Gkatzelis, V., Mehta, R.: Nash social welfare approximation for strategic agents. In: Proceedings of the 2017 ACM Conference on Economics and Computation, EC 2017 (2017)
11. Budish, E.: The combinatorial assignment problem: approximate competitive equilibrium from equal incomes. J. Polit. Econ. **119**(6), 1061–1103 (2011)
12. Budish, E., Che, Y.-K., Kojima, F., Milgrom, P.: Designing random allocation mechanisms: theory and applications. Am. Econ. Rev. **103**(2), 585–623 (2013)
13. Budish, E., Kessler, J.B.: Bringing real market participants' real preferences into the lab: an experiment that changed the course allocation mechanism at Wharton (2016). http://faculty.chicagobooth.edu/eric.budish/research/BudishKessler_July2016.pdf
14. Caragiannis, I., Kurokawa, D., Moulin, H., Procaccia, A.D., Shah, N., Wang, J.: The unreasonable fairness of maximum Nash welfare. In: ACM Conference on Economics and Computation (2016)
15. Chade, H., Smith, L.: Simultaneous search. Econometrica **74**(5), 1293–1307 (2006)
16. Chakrabarty, D., Swamy, C.: Welfare maximization and truthfulness in mechanism design with ordinal preferences. In: Innovations in Theoretical Computer Science (ITCS) (2014)
17. Che, Y.-K., Kojima, F.: Asymptotic equivalence of probabilistic serial and random priority mechanisms. Econometrica **78**(5), 1625–1672 (2010)
18. Christodoulou, G., Kovács, A., Schapira, M.: Bayesian combinatorial auctions. J. ACM **63**(2), 11 (2016)
19. Featherstone, C.R., Niederle, M.: Boston versus deferred acceptance in an interim setting: an experimental investigation. Games Econ. Behav. **100**, 353–375 (2016)

20. Feige, U., Feldman, M., Immorlica, N., Izsak, R., Lucier, B., Syrgkanis, V.: A unifying hierarchy of valuations with complements and substitutes. In: Proceedings of the 29th AAAI Conference on Artificial Intelligence, pp. 872–878 (2015)
21. Feldman, M., Fu, H., Gravin, N., Lucier, B.: Simultaneous auctions are (almost) efficient. In: Proceedings of the 45th ACM Symposium on Theory of Computing, pp. 201–210 (2013)
22. Feldman, M., Immorlica, N., Lucier, B., Roughgarden, T., Syrgkanis, V.: The price of anarchy in large games. In: Proceedings of the 48th ACM Symposium on Theory of Computing, pp. 963–976 (2016)
23. Hart, S., Nisan, N.: Approximate revenue maximization with multiple items. In: Proceedings of the 13th ACM Conference on Electronic Commerce, EC 2012, pp. 656–656 (2012)
24. Hartline, J.D., Roughgarden, T.: Simple versus optimal mechanisms. In: Proceedings of the 10th ACM Conference on Electronic Commerce, pp. 225–234 (2009)
25. Hassidim, A., Kaplan, H., Mansour, Y., Nisan, N.: Non-price equilibria in markets of discrete goods. In: Proceedings of the 12th ACM Conference on Electronic Commerce, pp. 295–296 (2011)
26. Hassidim, A., Romm, A., Shorrer, R.I.: 'strategic' behavior in a strategy-proof environment (2016). https://ssrn.com/abstract=2784659
27. Hylland, A., Zeckhauser, R.: The efficient allocation of individuals to positions. J. Polit. Econ. **87**(2), 293–314 (1979)
28. Papadimitriou, C.H., Yannakakis, M.: On the approximability of trade-offs and optimal access of web sources. In: Proceedings of the 41st Annual Symposium on Foundations of Computer Science, FOCS 2000 (2000)
29. Pycia, M.: The cost of ordinality, June 2014
30. Rawls, J.: A Theory of Justice. Cambridge, Belknap (1971)
31. Donald John Roberts and Andrew Postelwaite: The incentives for price-taking behavior in large exchange economies. Econometrica **44**(1), 115–127 (1976)
32. Shapley, L., Shubik, M.: Trade using one commodity as a means of payment. J. Polit. Econ. **85**(5), 937–968 (1977)
33. Syrgkanis, V., Tardos, E.: Composable and efficient mechanisms. In: Proceedings of the 45th ACM Symposium on Theory of Computing, pp. 211–220 (2013)

Routing Games over Time with FIFO Policy

Anisse Ismaili[✉]

Takayuki Ito Laboratory, Nagoya Institute of Technology, Nagoya, Japan
anisse.ismaili@gmail.com

Abstract. We study atomic routing games where every agent travels both along its decided edges and through time. The agents arriving on an edge are first lined up in a *first-in-first-out* queue and may wait: an edge is associated with a capacity, which defines how many agents-per-time-step can pop from the queue's head and enter the edge, to transit for a fixed delay. We show that the best-response optimization problem is not approximable, and that deciding the existence of a Nash equilibrium is complete for the second level of the polynomial hierarchy. Then, we drop the rationality assumption, introduce a behavioral concept based on GPS navigation, and study its worst-case efficiency ratio to coordination.

Keywords: Routing games over time · Complexity · Price of Anarchy

1 Introduction

Numerous selfish agents use a routing network to take shortest paths that may however congest the paths of others. *Routing games* model such conflictual systems by a graph of vertices and edges, and every agent decides a path from a source to a sink, path whose cost is congestion-dependent. Routing games find applications in road traffic [War52], as well as in routing packets of data via Internet Protocol [KP99]. Founding results[1] have been obtained on *static* routing games [RT02, Rou05, CK05, AAE05, NRTV07, Rou09], where each individual path instantaneously occurs everywhere over its decided edges. Such instantaneousness does not reflect that an agent on one edge of its path is not elsewhere, and cannot congest other edges. Routing games *over time*, where every agent travels along its route as well as *through time*, were introduced more recently [KS09, AU09]. Introducing time makes games more complicated: pure-strategy Nash equilibria are often not guaranteed; problems such as computing a best-response or an equilibrium are hard; the Price of Anarchy (PoA) can be large.

We study asymmetric atomic routing games over integer time-steps that model congestion with a very natural *first-in-first-out* (FIFO) queuing policy on the edges [WHK14]. Every edge e has an integer *fixed delay* d_e and an integer *capacity* c_e. On an edge, every arriving agent is lined up in the edge's FIFO

---

[1] Static routing games were a crucial testbed for the Price of Anarchy, a concept that bounds a game's loss of efficiency due to selfish behaviors.

© Springer International Publishing AG 2017
N. R. Devanur and P. Lu (Eds.): WINE 2017, LNCS 10674, pp. 266–280, 2017.
https://doi.org/10.1007/978-3-319-71924-5_19

queue (a discrete list); the capacity defines how many agents-per-time-step can pop from the queue's head and transit through the edge, while the others wait the next time-step. Every agent aims at minimizing the time from source to sink.

Related Work. Only pure Nash equilibria (PNE) are considered here. It is the same (resp. different) source/sink in the symmetric (resp. asymmetric) case.

[HHP06,HHP09] studies multicommodity routing problems, where asymmetric commodities are routed sequentially and the cost of edges is load dependent. With affine costs, while in the splittable case the PoA is almost 4, in the unsplittable case, computing a best-response is NP-hard, and the PoA is $3 + 2\sqrt{2}$.

[FOV08] observes that *"a car traversing a road can only cause congestion delays to those cars that use the road at a later time"* and proposes an asymmetric model where every edge has a priority on agents, agents that are congested only by those with a higher priority on the edge. While a global priority (same fixed priority for every edge) guarantees the existence of a PNE, local priorities do not. Several (matching) bounds are derived on the PoA.

[KS09,KS11] introduces competitive flows over time, by building a non-atomic symmetric model upon the literature about deterministic queuing. Every edge has a fixed transit delay, and a capacity that bounds above the edge's out-flow. It is shown that a sequence of ε-Nash flows converges (as $\varepsilon \to 0$) to a Nash flow; and an iterative algorithm is proposed. While the evacuation-PoA can be arbitrarily large, the time-PoA is in $O(1)$.

[AU09] proposes a dynamic selfish routing model with non-atomic asymmetric agents. A very general delay function $d_e(x, H_e^t)$ of the demand x and the historic H_e^t is introduced, along with a generalized notion of FIFO, which just states that there are no crossovers. Concurrently to [KS09], it is shown that in the symmetric case, a PNE always exists and can be computed efficiently. However, in the asymmetric case and under a specification of FIFO where an entering agent waits the previous one's end of transit, it is shown that an equilibrium may not exist, and the PoA is bounded below by the number of vertices. Flow independent delays can be reduced to static flows, providing a PoA bound.

[HMRT09,HMRT11] proposes temporal (asymmetric and atomic) network congestion games. Every edge has a speed $a_e \in \mathbb{R}_{>0}$ (latency equals speed times weight of agents being processed), and different local policies are studied. Under FIFO, an edge processes a unitary agent in time a_e, while the other agents wait. A guaranteed PNE can be computed efficiently for the unweighted symmetric case, despite the NP-hardness of computing a best-response. In the weighted or asymmetric cases, an equilibrium may not exist. One could reduce one of our edges e to $c_e \times d_e$ speedy-edges having $a_e = 1$, but it is *pseudo*-polynomial. Conversely, it is also unclear how we could reduce this model to the present one.

Our model is the same as in [WHK14], an atomic variation over integer time-steps of [KS09], where every edge has a free-flow delay and a capacity that bounds above the inflow-per-time-step. In [WHK14], the emphasis is rather on *bottleneck* individual objectives, but also on the *sum* on the edges in the path. A PNE may not exist; Computing a best-response is NP-complete; Verifying a PNE is coNP-complete; Deciding PNE existence is at least NP-hard. Also, a bound is provided on the PoA. [WBK15] studies games where agents are robust bottleneck optimizers that only know an interval about the cost of edges and learn the actual cost later.

[HPSVK16] studies a model similar to [WHK14] and ours, but instead of FIFO, studies local and overall priorities on the edges. (Crossovers may occur.) Some bounds on the price of stability and PoA are derived. Computing optimal priority lists is shown APX-hard. Under local priorities, computing best-responses is NP-hard, as well as computing a PNE.

Furthermore, [MLS10, MLS13] generalizes Braess's Paradox to the model in [KS09], and Braess's ratio can be much more severe. [BFA15] considers a model in the fashion of [KS09] and shows that under a Stackelberg strategy, the time-PoA is $(1 - 1/e)^{-1}$, and the total-delay-PoA is $2(1 - 1/e)^{-1}$. [CCCW17a, CCCW17b] propose an extensive form model where agents take new decisions on each vertex.

Results. In this paper's model [WHK14, *sum* objective], the *new* results are marked here with a *star**:

Theorem 1   A pure-strategy Nash equilibrium may not exist[2].
Theorem 2   The payoffs are well defined and calculable in polynomial-time[3].
Theorem 3 * The best-response decision problem is NP-complete
Theorem 4 * The best-response optimization problem is APX-hard,
Theorem 5 * and it is NP-hard to approximate within $|V|^{\frac{1}{6}-\varepsilon}$, and within $n^{\frac{1}{7}-\varepsilon}$.
Theorem 6   Verification of equilibria is coNP-complete[4].
Theorem 7 * Existence of equilibria is Σ_2^P-complete.

That best-responses are not approximable, deeply questions the rationality assumption of PNE. We then introduce a behavioral model for vehicles taking decisions by GPS, inspired by how navigation assistants work: by retrieving information on the current traffic and recomputing shortest paths in real-time. On the worst-case efficiency ratio of GPS navigation, to coordination, we found:

Theorem 8 * Allowing walks[5] as strategies, GPS-agents may cycle infinitely.
Theorem 9 * The Price of GPS Navigation is in $\Omega(|V| + n)$ as the number of
             vertices $|V|$ and the number of agents n grow.

Model Discussion. The positioning of waiting queues on the edges' tails, and of fixed-delays inside edges, is without much loss of generality. Indeed, this choice reduces in polynomial time from/to models where the queue occurs after the fixed delay, where queues are on the nodes and fixed delays on the edges, where edges are unoriented, etc. The idea is to think of both edges and nodes as resources having a waiting queue or a fixed delay; then a path is a sequence of resources.

---

[2] [WHK14, Appendix B.1, Fig. B.11] contains a similar result.
[3] A close Dijkstra-style algorithm for local priorities lies in [HPSVK16, Proposition 2.2].
[4] [WHK14, Sect. 7] claims that one can derive NP-*hardness* for sum-objectives.
[5] A walk is an alternating sequence of vertices and edges, consistent with the given (di)graph, and that allows repetitions and infiniteness.

Furthermore, one can model starting times by adding edges, and bottlenecks by delay $d_e = 0$ edges. One can also note that on each edge e, delay $\lfloor (|q_e|-1)/c_e \rfloor + d_e$ is almost an affine function of congestion $|q_e|$ (the queue's length). Since the unweighted agents case that we consider is a particular case of the weighted case (and Theorem 2 still holds), our complexity results and efficiency lower bounds naturally extend to weighted agents.

2 Preliminaries

Definition 1. *A First-in-first-out Routing Game (FROG) is a non-cooperative finite game characterized by tuple $\Gamma = (G = (V, E), (c_e, d_e)_{e \in E}, N, (s_i, s_i^*)_{i \in N}, \succ)$.*

- *$G = (V, E)$ is a finite digraph with vertices V and edges $E \subseteq V \times V$.*
- *Given edge $e \in E$, positive number $c_e \in \mathbb{N}_{\geq 1}$ is the capacity of edge e, and non-negative number $d_e \in \mathbb{N}_{\geq 0}$ is the fixed delay on edge e.*
- *Finite set $N = \{1, \ldots, n\}$ is the set of agents.*
- *Given agent $i \in N$, vertices $s_i, s_i^* \in V$ are its source vertex and sink vertex.*
- *Strict order $\succ$ on set N is a tie-breaking priority on agents.*

For a given FROG, we introduce the following notations. For every agent i, its *strategy-set* $\mathcal{P}_i$ consists of every simple path π_i from source vertex s_i to sink vertex s_i^*. A *strategy-profile* $(\pi_1, \ldots, \pi_n) \in \mathcal{P}_1 \times \cdots \times \mathcal{P}_n$, which for short we denote in bold by $\boldsymbol{\pi} \in \mathcal{P}$, defines a strategy for every agent. For a given strategy-profile $\boldsymbol{\pi} \in \mathcal{P}$, strategy π_i is the strategy of agent i therein (a simple path from s_i to s_i^*); *adversary strategy-profile* $\boldsymbol{\pi}_{-i} \in \prod_{j \neq i} \mathcal{P}_j$ consists of all strategies in $\boldsymbol{\pi}$ but agent i's; and given strategy π_i', strategy-profile $(\pi_i', \boldsymbol{\pi}_{-i}) \in \mathcal{P}$ is obtained from strategy-profile $\boldsymbol{\pi}$ by changing strategy π_i into π_i'.

Agents travel both along edges and through *time*. For an agent i, *total delay* $C_i : \mathcal{P} \to \mathbb{N}_{\geq 0}$ is a function of the strategy-profile, defined as follows. As depicted in Fig. 1, when agent i arrives on edge $e \in \pi_i$, it lines up in a first-in-first-out (FIFO) queue specific to edge e. At each time-step, edge e lets the c_e first agents in the queue enter the edge to transit for d_e time steps. Let function $w_{i,e} : \mathcal{P} \to \mathbb{N}_{\geq 0}$ be the time spent waiting by agent i in the queue of edge e. It follows that agent i's total delay is defined by equality

$$C_i(\boldsymbol{\pi}) \quad = \quad \sum_{e \in \pi_i} (w_{i,e}(\boldsymbol{\pi}) + d_e).$$

If, on one edge, some agents arrive at the same exact time step, then these synchronous agents are ordered in the edge's queue by tie-breaking priority $\succ$.

A rational agent, given an adversary strategy-profile, individually optimizes its total delay. This rationality assumption induces standard concepts:

Definition 2. *Given agent i and adversary strategy-profile $\boldsymbol{\pi}_{-i}$, strategy π_i is a best-response if and only if: $C_i(\pi_i, \boldsymbol{\pi}_{-i}) = \min_{\pi_i' \in \mathcal{P}_i} \{ C_i(\pi_i', \boldsymbol{\pi}_{-i}) \}$.*

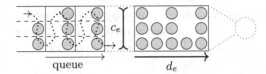

Fig. 1. On a given edge e, agents (gray rounds) are first lined up in a FIFO queue. The edge lets the c_e first agents enter at each time-step, to travel for d_e time steps.

Definition 3. *A pure Nash equilibrium (PNE) is a strategy-profile* $\boldsymbol{\pi} \in \mathcal{P}$ *where*

$$\forall i \in N, \quad \forall \pi_i' \in \mathcal{P}_i, \quad C_i(\boldsymbol{\pi}) \le C_i(\pi_i', \boldsymbol{\pi}_{-i}).$$

In plain words, strategy-profile $\boldsymbol{\pi} \in \mathcal{P}$ is a PNE if no agent has an individual incentive to deviate from his current strategy, hence if every agent plays a best-response. To illustrate the definitions above we recall (Fig. 2) a didactic variation of a known counter-example [WHK14, Fig. B.11], which implies Theorem 1.

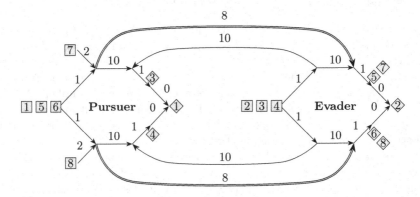

Fig. 2. An example of a FROG where there is no PNE. Single edges have capacity one. Double edges have capacity two. The fixed delays of edges are the numbers displayed above. The sources (resp. sinks) of agents are indicated by squares (resp. diamonds). Choose any tie breaking priority compatible with $2 \succ 3{\sim}4 \succ 1 \succ 5{\sim}6 \succ 7{\sim}8$. Agent one *Pursuer* and two *Evader* have two strategies; the others have only one.

Theorem 1. *In a* FROG, *there may not exist any PNE [WHK14].*

Proof (Theorem 1). Recall that in a pursuer-evader game, the two agents have two corresponding strategies; the pursuer prefers to decide the same; the evader prefers to decide differently; and consequently there is no PNE. In Fig. 2, all agents are degenerate[6], but agent one *Pursuer* and agent two *Evader*, who can decide between two paths: *up* or *down*. Agents three and four transmit from

---

[6] A degenerate agent only has one strategy, but can still incur and cause externalities.

Evader to Pursuer a positive externality for deciding the same, and agents five to eight, from Pursuer to Evader, a negative externality.

If both agents decide the same, without loss of generality path *up*, then Evader makes agent three wait one time-step, who in turn arrives one step after Pursuer where they could have collided; hence the total delay of Pursuer is 12. Also, Pursuer makes agent five arrive at time step 10 instead of 9 on the possible collision point with Evader. Moreover, agent seven also arrives there at time 10. Consequently, this queue is congested by five and seven and Evader waits one time-step. So Evader's total delay is 13. Similarly, one can show that when they decide different strategies, Pursuer's total delay is 13, and Evader's is 12. To conclude, Fig. 2 is a pursuer-evader game, and so has no PNE.   □

Definition 4. *We study this sequence of computational problems.*

FROG/DELAYS: *Given a FROG Γ and a strategy-profile $\boldsymbol{\pi}$, compute the total delays $(C_1(\boldsymbol{\pi}), \ldots, C_n(\boldsymbol{\pi}))$ of every agent.*

FROG/BR/OPT: *Given a FROG Γ, an agent i, and an adversary strategy-profile $\boldsymbol{\pi}_{-i}$, compute a best-response π_i for agent i.*

FROG/BR/DEC: *Decision version of FROG/BR/OPT. Given a FROG Γ, an agent i, an adversary strategy-profile $\boldsymbol{\pi}_{-i}$, and an integer threshold $\kappa \in \mathbb{N}_{\geq 0}$, decide whether there exists a strategy π_i with cost $C_i(\pi_i, \boldsymbol{\pi}_{-i}) \leq \kappa$.*

FROG/NE/VERIF: *Given a FROG Γ and a strategy-profile $\boldsymbol{\pi}$, decide whether strategy-profile $\boldsymbol{\pi}$ is a PNE.*

FROG/NE/EXIST: *Given a FROG, decide whether it admits a PNE.*

The representation size of FROGs is a polynomial of numbers $|V|$ and n. We assume that the following concepts are common knowledge: decision problem, length function, complexity classes P, ZPP, NP, coNP, Σ_2^P, Π_2^P, PH, NPO and APX, polynomial-time reduction, L-reduction, hardness and completeness.

Theorem 2. *The mapping from strategy-profiles to total-delays is well defined, and there is (see footnote 3) a polynomial-time algorithm to compute it:* FROG/DELAYS $\in$ P.

Proof (Sketch). An event is a time-type-agent-edge quadruplet, where the type is either to enter the edge's waiting queue or to pop from its head. The algorithm consists in a Dijkstra-style iterative development of events, where the heap of future events is ordered by lowest time first, then type (queuing before popping), and then the agent-priority (breaking any non-determinism in the algorithm).

3   Inapproximability of Best-Responses

Theorem 2 implies that problem FROG/BR/OPT is somewhere inside class NPO, and problem FROG/BR/DEC in class NP. In this section, we show that computing a best-response is hard, and provide two inapproximability results.

Theorem 3. *Decision problem* FROG/BR/DEC *is NP-complete.*

So, a polynomial-time algorithm addressing FROG/BR/DEC is unlikely to exist.

Theorem 4. *Optimization problem* FROG/BR/OPT *is APX-hard.*

Hence, a PTAS for FROG/BR/OPT would imply a PTAS for every NPO problem that admits a poly.-time constant factor approx. algorithm, which is unlikely.

Theorem 5. *For any* $\varepsilon \in \mathbb{R}_{>0}$, *approximating problem* FROG/BR/OPT *within factor* $|V|^{\frac{1}{6}-\varepsilon}$, *and within factor* $n^{\frac{1}{7}-\varepsilon}$, *are NP-hard.*

In plain words, it would take an intractable amount of time for an agent to find a path within factor $|V|^{\frac{1}{7}}$ or $n^{\frac{1}{8}}$ of the shortest delay. A more realistic model may rather drop rationality, and be better based on agents using heuristics.

Before the proofs, a good rule of thumb to distinguish between easy and hard path problems, is whether Bellman's Principle of Optimality is satisfied, or if preference inversions violate the principle. We introduce a gadget game.

Definition 5. *An* (M,t)-*Backfire is a piece of* FROG, *defined as in Fig. 4.*

Lemma 1. *In an* (M,t)-*Backfire, if agent* x *arrives on the* t-*trigger at time* t, *then on the bomb,* M *agents arrive at time* $t+1$, *and massively delay agent* x. *Otherwise, if* x *arrives at a different time, then this Backfire does not delay* x. *Furthermore, the backfire contains* $\Theta(M)$ *vertices and* $\Theta(M^2)$ *agents.*

Proof (Lemma 1). If agent x does not trigger on time t, then agent r_1 makes every agent b_i wait one step. Hence, every agent b_i collides on u_i at $t+2$ with M agents m_i who have priority. Agents b_i finally arrive on w_3 at time $t+1+M$, way too late to delay anyone (assuming large M). If agent x triggers on time t, then he gets queued after agent r_0, and agent r_1 has to wait one step. Then agent r_1 arrives too late on vertices u_i to delay any agent b_i. Consequently, agents b_i arrive on u_i one step before m_i, don't get delayed, and arrive on w_3 at $t+1$. □

Definition 6. *An* M-*Backfire is a sequence of* (M,t)-*Backfires, for* $0 \leq t \leq M$, *that share the same trigger-edge and bomb-edge. Agent* r_0 *is removed everywhere but for* $t=0$, *because for* $t \geq 1$, *its role in the* (M,t)-*Backfire is played by* r_1 *from the* $(M,t-1)$-*Backfire. (There is one* r_1 *per-time-step in* $[0,M]$.*)*

Lemma 2. *With an* M-*Backfire, agent* x *is massively delayed on the bomb-edge (assuming large* M), *if and only if he crosses the trigger-edge (anytime in* $[0,M]$). *Furthermore, the backfire contains* $\Theta(M^2)$ *vertices and* $\Theta(M^3)$ *agents.*

Proof (Lemma 2). Assume that agent x triggers on time t; all subsequent agents r_1 get delayed by one: an (M,t')-Backfire gets triggered for every $t' \geq t$. □

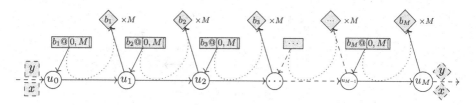

Fig. 3. *Filter: Agent y is not delayed, but agent x is delayed by at least $M \in \mathbb{N}_{\geq 1}$ steps.* Circles, rectangles and diamonds are resp. vertices, sources and sinks. The idea is that agent x waits one step on every edge (u_i, u_{i+1}), but y does not wait. After symbol @ is the source's starting time. An agent b_i starts for every $i \in [1, M]$ and $t \in [0, M[$, hence the number of agents is in $\Theta(M^2)$. The edges have capacity one and fixed-delay zero. Priority $\succ$ satisfies $y \succ b_i \succ x$, for any i (and time) defined in the Figure.

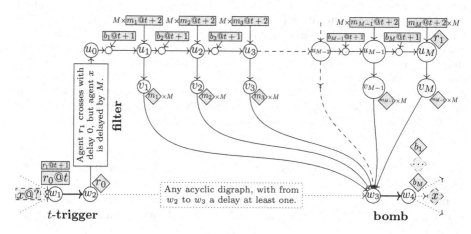

Fig. 4. *An (M, t)-Backfire, where $M \in \mathbb{N}_{\geq 1}$ is some large number and $t \in \mathbb{N}_{\geq 0}$ is a time-step. Circles, rectangles and diamonds are resp. vertices, sources and sinks. After symbol @ is the source's starting time. The edges that are plainly depicted (or dashed) have capacity one and fixed-delay zero. The filter is depicted in Fig. 3. Let priority $\succ$ satisfy $r_i \succ m_j \succ b_k \succ x$, for any i, j, k defined in the figure. One can connect to any digraph from the trigger to the bomb, if the minimum delay from w_2 to w_3 is one. Agent x gets heavily delayed on the bomb if and only if he uses the trigger on time t.*

Proof (Theorem 3). Membership in class NP follows from Theorem 2. We show NP-hardness by starting the reduction from *decision* problem MinVertex-Cover [Kar72, GJ79] that asks, given graph $\mathcal{G} = (\mathcal{V}, \mathcal{E})$ and threshold $\kappa \in \mathbb{N}_{\geq 0}$, whether there is a subset $\mathcal{W} \subseteq \mathcal{V}$ such that $\forall \{\varphi_1, \varphi_2\} \in \mathcal{E}, \ \varphi_1 \in \mathcal{W}$ or $\varphi_2 \in \mathcal{W}$, and $|\mathcal{W}| \leq \kappa$. Recall that problem MinVertexCover is NP-complete even for degrees bounded above by three [GJS74], which we assume here. We build the Frog depicted in Fig. 5. The reduction's validity is by construction (see the figure's caption). Taking $M = 6\eta$ is sufficient. Since there are $\Theta(\eta)$ edges in $\mathcal{V}$, the reduction makes $\Theta(\eta^3)$ vertices and $\Theta(\eta^4)$ agents, which is polynomial. $\square$

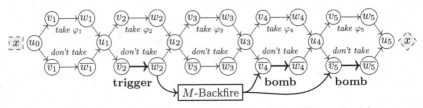

"Edges $\{\varphi_2, \varphi_4\}$ and $\{\varphi_2, \varphi_5\}$ shall be covered, or a backfire will heavily delay agent x."

Fig. 5. From MINVERTEXCOVER (degrees bounded above by 3) to FROG/BR/DEC. Circles, squares and diamonds depict respectively vertices, sources and sinks for FROG. Let $\eta = |\mathcal{V}|$ and observe that the starting size is in $\Theta(\eta)$. In the depiction, $\eta = 5$. The idea is a correspondence between $\mathcal{W} \in 2^{\mathcal{V}}$ and path π_x decided by agent x: *taking edge (v_i, w_i) in path π_x amounts to take vertex φ_i in subset $\mathcal{W}$.* Every edge is associated with $(c_e, d_e) = (1,1)$, but edges (v_i, w_i) with $(1,2)$, and edges $(\overline{v_i}, \overline{w_i})$ when it's a trigger with $(1,0)$ (because agent r_1 already makes x wait one step). Consequently going up always takes two steps, and going down one step if it's not a backfired edge. Hence a vertex cover $\mathcal{W}$ of size k corresponds to a path π_x with length $3\eta + k$. So, threshold κ in MINVERTEXCOVER is reduced to $\kappa' = 3\eta + k$ in FROG/BR/DEC. For every edge $\{\varphi_i, \varphi_j\}$ ($i < j$) in MINVERTEXCOVER, we introduce an M-Backfire with trigger $(\overline{v_i}, \overline{w_i})$ and bomb $(\overline{v_j}, \overline{w_j})$, in order to heavily punish x for not taking φ_i and φ_j. The backfire splits the provided punishment between up to three neighbors.

Proof (Theorem 4). Starting from the *optimization* version of problem MINVERTEXCOVER where one must find $\mathcal{W}^* \in \arg\min_{\mathcal{W} \subseteq \mathcal{V}} \{|\mathcal{W}| \mid \forall \epsilon \in \mathcal{E}, \ \mathcal{W} \cap \epsilon \neq \emptyset\}$ (forget about κ and κ'), the same reduction as for Theorem 3 is also an L-reduction[7] [PY91, Cre97], which we show by exhibiting functions f, g and constants α, β.

Recall that *optimization* problem MINVERTEXCOVER is APX-complete even for degrees bounded above by three [PY91, AK97], which we still assume. The correspondences f and g are depicted in the caption of Fig. 5. Given a MINVERTEXCOVER instance $\mathcal{I}$, one has $\text{OPT}_{\text{FROG}}(f(\mathcal{I})) \leq \alpha \text{OPT}_{\text{VC}}(\mathcal{I})$ for $\alpha = 10$ and $|\mathcal{W}| \leq \beta C_i(\pi_x)$ where $\mathcal{W} = g(\mathcal{I}, \pi_x)$ for $\beta = 1$. Indeed, for the former, observe that a vertex can cover at most three edges; hence $\frac{\eta}{3} \leq \text{OPT}_{\text{VC}}(\mathcal{I})$. Correspondence $3\eta + \text{OPT}_{\text{VC}} = \text{OPT}_{\text{FROG}}$ then yields $\alpha = 10$. The later comes from $k \leq 3\eta + k$. Consequently, this is an L-reduction and then, optimization problem FROG/BR/OPT is APX-hard.   □

Proof (Sketch, Theorem 5). Problem MINCOLORING, given graph $\mathcal{G} = (\mathcal{V}, \mathcal{E})$, asks a coloring of $\mathcal{G}$, i.e. a partition of $\mathcal{V}$ into disjoint sets $V_1, V_2, \ldots, V_k$ such that each V_i is an independent set of $\mathcal{G}$ (no edges in $\mathcal{G}[V_i]$), with *minimum chromatic number* $k = \chi(\mathcal{G})$. Let $\eta = |\mathcal{V}|$. It is known that whatever $\varepsilon > 0$, approximating $\chi(\mathcal{G})$ within $\eta^{1-\varepsilon}$ is NP-hard [FK96, Zuc06]. The idea of the reduction is in Fig. 6,

---

[7] An L-reduction is a poly.-time reduction in NPO, which conserves approximations.

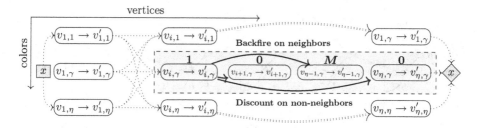

Fig. 6. Sketch of reduction from MINCOLORING to FROG/BR/OPT. Agent x's paths correspond to deciding a color γ for each vertex i. Depicted in the gray rectangle, the first time x chooses color γ is on vertex i (first time on the line). Then (1) x waits one step on edge $(v_{i,\gamma}, v'_{i,\gamma})$ (because of an agent r_1). Then on the same line, (2) neighbors in $\mathcal{G}$ are Backfired (can't put the same color on a neighbor) and non-neighbors are discounted to delay zero (by heavily delaying agents r_1 and disarming their eventual backfires). Transit edges (dotted) have delay one to allow for backfires to work. Hence, a valid coloring of size k would correspond to a path π_x of length $\eta + k$ which does not enable to find β for an L-reduction. To solve this issue, we multiply all the costs by η with η times more agents and vertices, but not on the dotted edges.

and (with $M = 3\eta$) involves $\Theta(\eta^6)$ vertices and $\Theta(\eta^7)$ agents. Consequently, better approximation ratios than $|V|^{\frac{1}{6}-\varepsilon}$ or $n^{\frac{1}{7}-\varepsilon}$ contradict intractable ratio $\eta^{1-\varepsilon}$ from [FK96]. □

4 The Complexity of Pure Nash Equilibria

In this section, we first observe that the verification problem FROG/NE/VERIF is coNP-complete. Then, we completely characterize the complexity of the existence problem as *complete* for the second level of PH[8].

Theorem 6. *Problem* FROG/NE/VERIF *is coNP-complete [WHK14, Almost] (See footnote 4).*

Proof (Theorem 6). A deviation is a no-certificate verifiable in polynomial-time by Theorem 2, hence this problem is inside class coNP. A proof with bottleneck objectives lies in [WHK14, Cor. 4], and the authors claim [WHK14, Sect. 7] that one can obtain NP-hardness for sum-objectives in the same way. We confirm that claim since the same reduction as for Theorem 3 holds here. □

Theorem 7. *Problem* FROG/NE/EXIST *is Σ_2^P-complete.*

Proof (Theorem 7). This problem is in class Σ_2^P. Indeed, yes-instances admit a certificate verifiable by an NP-oracle: by guessing the right strategy-profile, according to Theorem 6, one can use an NP-oracle to verify that it is a PNE. The Σ_2^P-hardness proof below generalizes the reduction introduced for Theorem 3.

---

[8] Class Σ_2^P are the problems that nest a coNP problem inside an NP problem. Only very small sizes ($\lesssim 10$) of such problems can usually be practically addressed.

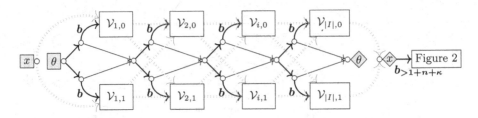

Fig. 7. Reduction from MAXMINVERTEXCOVER to the complement of FROG/NE/EXIST. Generalizes the reduction in Fig. 5. Each box $\mathcal{V}_{i,j}$ is made as in Fig. 5. We create a universally indifferent agent $\bar{\theta}$ who can early decide between two paths for every $i \in I$: one backfires $\mathcal{V}_{i,0}$'s entry and the other backfires $\mathcal{V}_{i,1}$'s entry. Agent $\bar{\theta}$ models function θ by blocking early the entries to $\mathcal{V}_{i,0}$ xor to $\mathcal{V}_{i,1}$ with the backfires $\boldsymbol{b}$. Plain edges have capacity and cost $(c_e, d_e) = (1, 0)$. Dotted edges have $(c_e, d_e) = (1, 1)$ but the two first ones $(1, 2)$, to let $\bar{\theta}$ run in front of x. Then agent x decides a path through what corresponds to subgraph $\mathcal{G}^{(\theta)}$. Agent x sends backfires to Fig. 2 if and only if he reaches his sink after time $1 + n + \kappa$.

In Fig. 7, we reduce decision problem MAXMINVERTEXCOVER to the complement of FROG/NE/EXIST. Given set of indices I, the vertices of graph $\mathcal{G} = (\mathcal{V}, \mathcal{E})$ partition into $\mathcal{V} = \bigcup_{i \in I} \mathcal{V}_{i,0} \cup \mathcal{V}_{i,1}$. Given function $\theta : I \to \{0, 1\}$ (i.e. $2^{|I|}$ possibilities), let $\mathcal{G}^{(\theta)}$ denote the graph restricted to vertices $\mathcal{V}^{(\theta)} = \bigcup_{i \in I} \mathcal{V}_{i,t(i)}$. Problem MAXMINVERTEXCOVER, given threshold $\kappa \in \mathbb{N}_{\geq} 0$, asks whether:

$$\forall \theta : I \to \{0, 1\}, \quad \exists \mathcal{W} \subseteq \mathcal{V}^{(\theta)}, \quad \mathcal{W} \text{ vertex-covers } \mathcal{G}^{(\theta)} \text{ and } |\mathcal{W}| \leq \kappa, \quad (1)$$

and is Π_2^P-complete (i.e. co-Σ_2^P-complete); co-FROG/NE/EXIST asks whether:

$$\forall \pi \in \mathcal{P}, \quad \text{There exists an individual deviation from } \pi. \quad (2)$$

[Eq. (1) $\Rightarrow$ Eq. (2)] Whatever the choices of agent $\bar{\theta}$, if the strategy of agent x costs more than $C_i > 1 + n + \kappa$, then he can deviate and improve, because of Eq. (1); otherwise, now assuming that x's strategy is a best-response, then he reaches his sink before time $1 + n + k$ (because Eq. (1)) and does not disable the example from Fig. 2, which remains unstable: there is a deviation.

[not Eq. (1) $\Rightarrow$ not Eq. (2)] If there exists a function θ, then we position agent $\bar{\theta}$ as such. Then the best-response of agent x makes him reach his sink after time $1 + n + \kappa$. Consequently, Fig. 2 is disabled: we have a PNE.   □

5   The Price of GPS

Previous sections show how strong an assumption rationality is. Instead, we propose a model inspired by GPS personal navigation assistants: agents retrieve instantaneous traffic data to recompute shortest paths at each crossroad.

We introduce a *GPS-agent* as an agent who at each vertex (between two time steps) recalculates a shortest path according to the fixed delays d_e plus congestion $\lfloor \frac{|q_e|}{c_e} \rfloor$ of the past step. In place of PNE, let $\mathcal{O} \subseteq \mathcal{P}$ be the set of strategy-profiles that can be obtained by GPS-agents. We study the worst-case ratio to coordination, defined for one FROG as the *Price-of-GPS (navigation)*:

$$\text{PoGPS} = \frac{\max_{\pi' \in \mathcal{O}} \{\, C(\pi') \,\}}{\min_{\pi \in \mathcal{P}} \{\, C(\pi) \,\}},$$

where $C(\pi) = \sum_{i \in N} C_i(\pi)$. For a family of FROGs, PoGPS is the supremum of every PoGPS therein. As shown in Fig. 8, a first negative result follows:

Theorem 8. *Allowing non-simple paths, GPS-agents may cycle infinitely (Fig. 8).*

Proof. As depicted in Fig. 8, consider w.l.o.g. the end of a given time step, and the current choice faced by agent i_1. Straight outside shows congestion and is not better than taking the later exit at the next node. Since every agent faces the same choice and the game is symmetric, it is possible to loop endlessly. □

Following Theorem 8, we now focus on simple-paths and study the order of PoGPS.

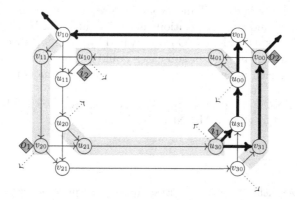

Fig. 8. *Double cycle of infinite procrastination.* The idea is that there is an inner-cycle and an equivalent outer-cycle. Agents from a cycle have to go through the other cycle to reach their sink, but the information that they get from the other cycles does not discourage procrastination. Circles are nodes. Every edge e has capacity $c_e = 1$. The four edges in every corner have fixed-delay $d_e = 0$, and the two from each corner to the next one, fixed-delay $d_e = 1$. There are two *inner-agents* i_1 and i_2, with resp. sources u_{11} and u_{31}, and a sink reachable instantly by the dotted edges from the outer cycle's vertices $v_{00}, v_{10}, v_{20}, v_{30}$. However, they can decide to stay on the inner-cycle $u_{0-}, u_{1-}, u_{2-}, u_{3-}$. There are two *outer-agents* o_1 and o_2, with resp. sources v_{21} and v_{01}, and sinks reachable by the dotted edges from inner vertices $u_{00}, u_{10}, u_{20}, u_{30}$. However, they can decide to cycle on the outer-cycle $v_{0-}, v_{1-}, v_{2-}, v_{3-}$. On the figure, we show w.l.o.g. current positions of the agents and the congestion from the last step in gray rectangles. The current choice faced by agent i_1 is depicted with thick edges.

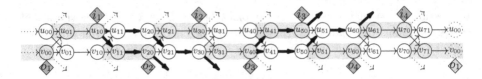

Fig. 9. *Generalization of Fig. 8 to longer double cycles, at an arbitrary time-step.* The current choices faced by agents i_1 and o_3 are depicted with thick edges.

Theorem 9. *The Price of GPS Navigation is in $\Omega(|V| + n)$ as the number of vertices $|V|$ and the number of agents n grow[9].*

Proof. To prove this lower bound, we generalize the double cycle of Fig. 8 to a similar longer double cycle (Fig. 9). Then for every agent, while the shortest path has total-delay in $\Theta(1)$, the decided path can be in $\Omega(|V|)$ and $\Omega(n)$.   □

6   Prospects

The symmetric case seems usually well behaved [HMRT09, Theorem 1] and would be worth investigating. Time expanded graphs, where one does the cross product of vertices and time or positions may yield an other beautiful approach. A study on tie-breaking under FIFO is motivated by its importance in the proofs. Studying less extreme, average, or sub-cases would be appealing. Extensive forms with decisions on each node [CCCW17b] are a promising model.

Acknowledgments. I am grateful to the anonymous reviewers for their work. This work was supported by grant KAKENHI 15H01703.

References

[AAE05] Awerbuch, B., Azar, Y., Epstein, A.: The price of routing unsplittable flow. In: Proceedings of the Thirty-Seventh Annual ACM Symposium on Theory of Computing, pp. 57–66. ACM (2005)

[AK97] Alimonti, P., Kann, V.: Hardness of approximating problems on cubic graphs. In: Bongiovanni, G., Bovet, D.P., Di Battista, G. (eds.) CIAC 1997. LNCS, vol. 1203, pp. 288–298. Springer, Heidelberg (1997). https://doi.org/10.1007/3-540-62592-5_80

[AU09] Anshelevich, E., Ukkusuri, S.: Equilibria in dynamic selfish routing. In: Mavronicolas, M., Papadopoulou, V.G. (eds.) SAGT 2009. LNCS, vol. 5814, pp. 171–182. Springer, Heidelberg (2009). https://doi.org/10.1007/978-3-642-04645-2_16

[BFA15] Bhaskar, U., Fleischer, L., Anshelevich, E.: A stackelberg strategy for routing flow over time. Games Econ. Behav. **92**, 232–247 (2015)

---

[9] For two variables x, y, Landau notation $f(x, y) \in \Omega(g(x, y))$ is defined as:
$\exists K \in \mathbb{R}_{>0}, \ \exists n_0 \in \mathbb{N}_{\geq 0}, \ \forall x, y \geq n_0, \ f(x, y) \geq K g(x, y).$

[CCCW17a] Cao, Z., Chen, B., Chen, X., Wang, C.: A network game of dynamic traffic. CoRR, abs/1705.01784 (2017)

[CCCW17b] Cao, Z., Chen, B., Chen, X., Wang, C.: A network game of dynamic traffic. In: Proceedings of the 2017 ACM Conference on Economics and Computation, EC 2017, pp. 695–696. ACM (2017)

[CK05] Christodoulou, G., Koutsoupias, E.: The price of anarchy of finite congestion games. In: Proceedings of the Thirty-Seventh Annual ACM Symposium on Theory of Computing, pp. 67–73. ACM (2005)

[Cre97] Crescenzi, P.: A short guide to approximation preserving reductions. In: Proceedings of the Twelfth Annual IEEE Conference on (Formerly: Structure in Complexity Theory Conference) Computational Complexity, pp. 262–273. IEEE (1997)

[FK96] Feige, U., Kilian, J.: Zero knowledge and the chromatic number. In: Proceedings of the Eleventh Annual IEEE Conference on Computational Complexity, pp. 278–287. IEEE (1996)

[FOV08] Farzad, B., Olver, N., Vetta, A.: A priority-based model of routing. Chic. J. Theoret. Comput. Sci. 1 (2008)

[GJ79] Garey, M.R., Johnson, D.S.: Computers and Intractability, vol. 174. Freeman, San Francisco (1979)

[GJS74] Garey, M.R., Johnson, D.S., Stockmeyer, L.: Some simplified NP-complete problems. In: Proceedings of the Sixth Annual ACM Symposium on Theory of Computing, STOC 1974, pp. 47–63. ACM (1974)

[HHP06] Harks, T., Heinz, S., Pfetsch, M.E.: Competitive online multicommodity routing. In: Erlebach, T., Kaklamanis, C. (eds.) WAOA 2006. LNCS, vol. 4368, pp. 240–252. Springer, Heidelberg (2007). https://doi.org/10.1007/11970125_19

[HHP09] Harks, T., Heinz, S., Pfetsch, M.E.: Competitive online multicommodity routing. Theory Comput. Syst. 45(3), 533–554 (2009)

[HMRT09] Hoefer, M., Mirrokni, V.S., Röglin, H., Teng, S.-H.: Competitive routing over time. In: Leonardi, S. (ed.) WINE 2009. LNCS, vol. 5929, pp. 18–29. Springer, Heidelberg (2009). https://doi.org/10.1007/978-3-642-10841-9_4

[HMRT11] Hoefer, M., Mirrokni, V.S., Röglin, H., Teng, S.-H.: Competitive routing over time. Theoret. Comput. Sci. 412(39), 5420–5432 (2011)

[HPSVK16] Harks, T., Peis, B., Schmand, D., Koch, L.V.: Competitive packet routing with priority lists. In: LIPIcs-Leibniz International Proceedings in Informatics, vol. 58. Schloss Dagstuhl-Leibniz-Zentrum fuer Informatik (2016)

[Kar72] Karp, R.M.: Reducibility among combinatorial problems. In: Miller, R.E., Thatcher, J.W., Bohlinger, J.D. (eds.) Complexity of Computer Computations. The IBM Research Symposia Series, pp. 85–103. Springer, Heidelberg (1972). https://doi.org/10.1007/978-1-4684-2001-2_9

[KP99] Koutsoupias, E., Papadimitriou, C.: Worst-case equilibria. In: Meinel, C., Tison, S. (eds.) STACS 1999. LNCS, vol. 1563, pp. 404–413. Springer, Heidelberg (1999). https://doi.org/10.1007/3-540-49116-3_38

[KS09] Koch, R., Skutella, M.: Nash equilibria and the price of anarchy for flows over time. In: Mavronicolas, M., Papadopoulou, V.G. (eds.) SAGT 2009. LNCS, vol. 5814, pp. 323–334. Springer, Heidelberg (2009). https://doi.org/10.1007/978-3-642-04645-2_29

[KS11] Koch, R., Skutella, M.: Nash equilibria and the price of anarchy for flows over time. Theory Comput. Syst. 49(1), 71–97 (2011)

[MLS10] Macko, M., Larson, K., Steskal, Ľ.: Braess's paradox for flows over time. In: Kontogiannis, S., Koutsoupias, E., Spirakis, P.G. (eds.) SAGT 2010. LNCS, vol. 6386, pp. 262–275. Springer, Heidelberg (2010). https://doi.org/10.1007/978-3-642-16170-4_23

[MLS13] Macko, M., Larson, K., Steskal, L.: Braess's paradox for flows over time. Theory Comput. Syst. **53**(1), 86–106 (2013)

[NRTV07] Nisan, N., Roughgarden, T., Tardos, E., Vazirani, V.V.: Algorithmic Game Theory, vol. 1. Cambridge University Press, Cambridge (2007)

[PY91] Papadimitriou, C.H., Yannakakis, M.: Optimization, approximation, and complexity classes. J. Comput. Syst. Sci. **43**(3), 425–440 (1991)

[Rou05] Roughgarden, T.: Selfish Routing and the Price of Anarchy, vol. 174. MIT press, Cambridge (2005)

[Rou09] Roughgarden, T.: Intrinsic robustness of the price of anarchy. In: Proceedings of the Forty-First Annual ACM Symposium on Theory of Computing, pp. 513–522. ACM (2009)

[RT02] Roughgarden, T., Tardos, É.: How bad is selfish routing? J. ACM (JACM) **49**(2), 236–259 (2002)

[War52] Wardrop, J.G.: Some theoretical aspects of road traffic research. Proc. Inst. Civ. Eng. **1**(3), 325–362 (1952)

[WBK15] Werth, T.L., Büttner, S., Krumke, S.O.: Robust bottleneck routing games. Networks **66**(1), 57–66 (2015)

[WHK14] Werth, T.L., Holzhauser, M., Krumke, S.O.: Atomic routing in a deterministic queuing model. Oper. Res. Perspect. **1**(1), 18–41 (2014)

[Zuc06] Zuckerman, D.: Linear degree extractors and the inapproximability of max clique and chromatic number. In: Proceedings of the Thirty-Eighth Annual ACM Symposium on Theory of Computing, pp. 681–690. ACM (2006)

A Performance-Based Scheme for Pricing Resources in the Cloud

Kamal Jain[1], Tung Mai[2(✉)], and Vijay V. Vazirani[3]

[1] Faira, Kirkland, WA, USA
kamaljain@gmail.com
[2] Georgia Tech, Atlanta, GA, USA
tung.mai@cc.gatech.edu
[3] UC Irvine, Irvine, CA, USA
vazirani@uci.edu

Abstract. With the rapid growth of the cloud computing marketplace, the issue of pricing resources in the cloud has been the subject of much study in recent years. In this paper, we identify and study a new issue: how to price resources in the cloud so that the customer's risk is minimized, while at the same time ensuring that the provider accrues his fair share. We do this by correlating the revenue stream of the customer to the prices charged by the provider. We show that our mechanism is incentive compatible in that it is in the best interest of the customer to provide his true revenue as a function of the resources rented. We next add another restriction to the price function, i.e., that it be linear. This removes the distortion that creeps in when the customer has to pay more money for less resources. Our algorithms for both the schemes mentioned above are efficient.

Keywords: Pricing scheme · Cloud computing · Incentive compatibility

1 Introduction

The cloud computing marketplace is the fastest growing market on the Internet today [3,11]. Indeed, with most large companies rapidly moving their computation into the cloud and startups following suit, most projections predict that this market will dwarf all other Internet markets, including the multi-billion dollar Adwords market of search engine companies [11]. Markets on the Internet form a sizable fraction of the economy. They are characterized not only by their huge size and easy scalability, but also by their innovativeness, e.g., markets such as the Adwords market and auction markets of eBay and Yahoo! are based on very different economic principles than traditional markets. In keeping with these trends and their massive success, it is quintessential to understand the idiosyncrasies of the cloud computing market and design mechanisms for its efficient

---

T. Mai—Supported by NSF Grant CCF-1216019.

T. Mai and V.V. Vazirani—On leave from Georgia Tech.

© Springer International Publishing AG 2017
N. R. Devanur and P. Lu (Eds.): WINE 2017, LNCS 10674, pp. 281–293, 2017.
https://doi.org/10.1007/978-3-319-71924-5_20

operation. Indeed, in recent years many researchers have studied the issue of pricing resources in the cloud (see Sect. 1.1).

In this paper, we propose a performance-based pricing scheme for resources in the cloud. Assume that Amazon is providing resources in the cloud and a small startup, say X, is one of its customers. The revenue stream of X is neither steady nor predictable and hence its profits—and losses—fluctuate considerably over time. In the face of these realities, an important consideration for it is to ensure that its losses do not mount up to the extent that it goes bankrupt. The question we address in this paper is whether Amazon can adopt a pricing scheme that minimizes the risk of X going under. Our pricing scheme enables Amazon to trade away company X's risk while at the same time ensuring that its expected revenue is not hurt. Indeed, if company X survives as a result of lower risk, Amazon's expected revenue will only increase in the long run. The fluctuations in Amazon's revenue may increase as a result of our pricing mechanism; however, since it is a very large company and deals with numerous customers at the same time, this will not be of much consequence to it. Our mechanism involves correlating the prices that Amazon charges to the revenue stream, i.e., performance, of company X. Although this idea and its details were conceived in the context of cloud computing, it can be easily be seen to be quite general and applicable to many other situations in which customers rent resources whose amounts vary frequently.

The *Elastic Cloud Computing (EC2)* market of Amazon is the biggest provider of cloud computing resources today, with other big players being Microsoft and IBM. The EC2 market rents out a number of different types of resources – virtual machines (VM) with different kinds of capabilities, e.g., compute optimized, storage optimized, memory optimized and general purpose. We note that at present, Amazon and other providers use fairly straightforward mechanisms for renting out these resources, e.g., EC2 rents out resources in one of three ways [13]. The first is Pay-As-You-Go (PAYG) under which the user has full flexibility to use any resources at the time they are needed. The second is a Reserve market under which the user books resources in advance, and the third is the spot market under which all resources not currently in use by customers of the first two categories are allocated via an auction – Amazon announces rates of renting, which change as demand and supply change, and customers who bid more than the rate get the resource but are evicted as soon as the rate exceeds their bid (giving them a couple of minutes to save their data). The rates charged are decreasing across these three methods, with the ratio of the first and the third being as high as a factor of five. Clearly, as this market grows in size and complexity, better mechanisms that are steeped in sound economic theory and the theory of algorithms will be called for.

Currently, the market of cloud computing is dominated by a few big players and hence oligopolistic pricing applies, i.e., prices are higher than competitive prices. However, as more companies rent resources in the cloud, this will become a commodity market with very low profit margins. The way out of this for companies is to offer value-added services, smart pricing being one of them.

The power of pricing mechanisms is well explored in economics, and it is well understood for the case of equilibrium pricing, which are prices under which there is parity between demand and supply [16,17]. It is known that this method allocates resources efficiently since prices send strong signals about what is wanted and what is not, and it prevents artificial scarcity of goods while at the same time ensuring that goods that are truly scarce are conserved. Hence it is beneficial to both consumers and producers. An equilibrium-based mechanism for replacing the spot market for cloud computing resources is proposed in [12].

1.1 Related Work

As mentioned above, many researchers have studied the issue of pricing resources in the cloud, e.g., see [1–6,9,14,15,18,20]. We describe several of these issues below. We note however that the issue identified and studied in this paper is very different from these.

The three tiered market of EC2 described above is sometimes viewed as the use of price discrimination, a well-studied mechanism in economics [16,17]. The idea here is that by a small differentiation in the product sold, one can distinguish between customers who can pay a lot from those who cannot. A very successful use of this concept arises in airline ticket sales, where by imposing conditions like Saturday overnight stay, the airlines can distinguish between business travelers and casual travelers and hence charge them different fares. Of course, in the three tiers described above for EC2, the nature of services offered is quite different and one can argue that different rates should apply. However, a ratio of five-to-one on the price charged smacks of the use of price discrimination.

Another issue explored in pricing is whether cloud resources should be rented on a metered basis or on a flat fee basis. In the past, very prominent industries went from one extreme to the other as the industry grew and the cost of basic resources dropped, a case in point being telephone charges [19], which started in a strict metered manner, with a small fee for connection, to the current flat charges. In the case of cloud resources, metered charges make the most sense at present; however, as computing, storage and bandwidth costs drop, it is conceivable that pricing will take a hybrid form of some kind.

At present, three very distinct resources are rented in the cloud: computing power, storage and bandwidth. An issue being studied is whether these three resources should be rented separately or in suitable bundles.

1.2 Our Results and Techniques

As stated above, we provide a pricing scheme which enables Amazon to trade away the risk experienced by company X without decreasing its own expected revenue. We furthermore show that our scheme is incentive compatible.

The scheme is as follows. Company X declares to Amazon the number, m, of types of resources it may rent and the set of possible resources which it may rent. For each combination of resources it may rent on a day, it also provides Amazon with the revenue it will accrue on that day (we show that it is in company

X's best interest to reveal this information correctly). Amazon and company X jointly agree on the probability distribution from which its requests arrive, by observing historical data. Hence, Amazon knows the expected daily cost X should be charged for renting the resources. The question is what is the most effective way for Amazon to retrieve this cost.

We give a scheme whereby Amazon is able to retrieve this cost in such a way that the daily variance in the profit of X, i.e., the difference of revenue and price paid, is minimized. Indeed, our scheme simultaneously minimizes not only the second moment of deviation from mean profit but also the ρ-th moment, for any $\rho > 1$. Moreover we show that such a function is unique, and it also maximizes the minimum profit of X. We note that there are numerous definitions of risk, without there being a single standard one. Our scheme minimizes risk for all definitions of risk referred to in the previous claim. It also ensures that prices and the profit are always non-negative. Our algorithm is linear time, modulo log factors. We provide an intuitive description of our algorithm using the idea of filling water in a trough with a warped bottom.

We next add another restriction to the price function, i.e., that it be linear. This removes the distortion that creeps in when the customer has to pay more money for less resources. Once again we ensure that prices are non-negative. Our algorithm involves lifting the points (revenue as a function of resources rented) into a higher dimensional space so that the function being handled is homogeneous and hence each point can be given an appropriate weight. The algorithm then makes just one call to a non-negative least squares solver, for which highly optimized implementations are available, on the set of preprocessed points.

2   An Insightful Example

In this section, we give a simple example that captures the essence of our idea. Consider a business model involving two agents, in which agent A has a fair coin and provides a "coin toss service" for agent B. Specifically, agent B pays \$1 to agent A for a coin toss and earns \$3 from an outside source if it comes up head and \$0 if it comes up tails. Clearly, the business is profitable for agent B since he makes 50 cents per toss in expectation. However, there is a risk that he might lose a considerable amount of money if he gets a string of tails. Even worse, if his budget is small, he might go bankrupt and cannot keep the business running. Such an outcome is also undesirable for A since he loses a customer.

To deal with this issue, A comes up with an alternative pricing scheme that is favorable for both agents. The proposed scheme is that instead of charging \$1 for each toss, he will charge \$2 for a head and nothing for a tail. As a consequence, B will gain \$1 if a head shows up, and lose/gain nothing if a tail shows up. Although he still makes a profit of 50 cents per toss in expectation, the business is now risk-free for him in the sense that he never loses money. From agent A's point of view, the proposed scheme is also beneficial for him in the long run despite the fact that there is no guarantee of making \$1 per toss. The reason is that he will have B as his customer permanently and still make $1 per toss in expectation.

This pricing scheme can be viewed as transfering the uncertainty in agent B's performance to agent A's performance without affecting the expected performances of both agents. Note that in the above example, we assume that A can generate coin tosses at no cost. However, if there is a cost and the cost is insignificant compared to A's budget, the scheme is still favorable to A since he can endure a string of bad luck caused by the transfered uncertainty.

If we insist that prices are non-negative and perserve the expected performances; moreover, the variance on profit of B is minimized then the proposed pricing scheme is unique. Later on, we will show that such prices can be computed algorithmically and that they give an even stronger guarantee on the profit of B.

3   Model and Definitions

We give a formal description of the model on which our results are based. The model involves two agents: a *provider* (called Amazon above) who sells resources and a *customer* (named X above) who uses resources to make profit from an outside source. The customer has a distribution on his demand which both agents agree upon. For example, they can obverse the history of usage of the customer over a period of time. Moreover, we assume that the customer has a revenue function, which is a function of resources consumed and must report it (truthfully or not) to the provider. To analyze, we take on the role of the provider and propose a pricing scheme for the customer based on his reported revenue function. We will show that our pricing scheme minimizes the deviation without changing the expected value of the customer's profit. Therefore, the customer who is assumed to be rational and wants to minimize his risk, will report his revenue function truthfully.

Let m be the number of resources and let $r = (r_1, r_2, \ldots, r_m)$ be a demand vector of the customer on the resources. We assume that r follows a discrete distribution with probability mass function $f(r): S \to R$ where $S = \{r^{(1)}, \ldots, r^{(N)}\}$ is a discrete domain of size N. Let $q(r): S \to R$ be our original starting price function. In other words, $q(r)$ denotes the price that we are willing to charge for r. Finally, let $v(r): S \to R$ be the revenue function of the customer on r.

We are interested in price functions where the expected price is exactly equal to the expected starting price.

Definition 1. *A* fair price function *is a price function $p(r)$ such that*

$$\sum_{r \in S} p(r)f(r) = \sum_{r \in S} q(r)f(r).$$

Next, we are also interested in price functions that assume only non-negative values.

Definition 2. *A non-negative price function is a price function $p(r)$ such that* $p(r) \geq 0 \, \forall r \in S$.

Moreover, the target price function must give a guarantee on the customer's profit that it should not deviate too much from the expected value. Since the customer has revenue $v(r)$ and cost $p(r)$ on r, his net profit is $v(r) - p(r)$. For a fair price $p(r)$, the expected profit μ is given by

$$\sum_{r \in S} (v(r) - p(r)) \, f(r) = \sum_{r \in S} (v(r) - q(r)) \, f(r).$$

Definition 3. *A* steady-profit *price function is a fair and non-negative price function that minimizes*

$$\sum_{r \in S} (v(r) - p(r) - \mu)^\rho \, f(r)$$

over all such functions for all $\rho > 1$.

Note that it is not obvious that a steady-profit price function should exist. However, in the next section we will show that such a function not only exists but can also be computed efficiently.

4   A Water-Filling Algorithm

In this section, we present an algorithm for computing a price with the following properties:

1. *Fairness:* The target price function is a fair price function, i.e., the customer has to pay the same amount compared to the starting price in expectation.
2. *Risk-freeness for customer:* The customer's profit is non-negative in the whole domain, i.e., he never loses money.
3. *Non-negativity:* The price is non-negative on the whole domain, i.e., we never pay the customer.
4. *Stability:* The price function is a steady-profit price function, i.e., the ρ-moment of the profit deviation from the mean value is minimized for any $\rho > 1$.

The main algorithm, which we call WATERLEVELPRICING, is given in Fig. 1. At a high level, it can be viewed as raising prices such that the profit values are as equal as possible until the price function becomes a fair function. An intuitive illustration of the algorithm is flipping the revenue function up side down and start raising prices as if they are water flowing in the function's surface.

We give the following lemma, which is needed for the proof of the main theorem.

$p(r) = \text{WATERLEVELPRICING}(f(r), q(r), v(r))$
Input: Distribution function $f(r)$, starting price function $q(r)$, revenue function $v(r)$.
Output: Steady-profit price function $p(r)$.

1. Define $v_L(r) : S \to R$ as follows:

$$v_L(r) = \begin{cases} v(r) - L \text{ if } v(r) > L, \\ 0 \text{ otherwise.} \end{cases}$$

Use binary search to find L such that $v_L(r)$ is a fair price function. In other words, we find L such that

$$\sum_{r \in S} v_L(r)f(r) = \sum_{r \in S} q(r)f(r).$$

2. Return $p(r) = v_L(r)$.

Fig. 1. Algorithm for computing a steady-profit price function.

Lemma 1. *Let a, b, ρ be positive real constants and $\rho > 1$. Let x_1 and x_2 be two real variables such that $x_1 > x_2$. There exists Δ such that for all $\delta < \Delta$, if we decrease x_1 by δ and increase x_2 by $\frac{a\delta}{b}$, then the value of*

$$\Phi = ax_1^\rho + bx_2^\rho$$

will decrease.

Proof. Assume that $ax_1 + bx_2 = c$ for some fixed value c. We can write x_2 as $(c - ax_1)/b$. Substituting gives

$$\Phi(x_1) = ax_1^\rho + \frac{(c - ax_1)^\rho}{b^{\rho-1}}.$$

Taking derivative with respect to x_1 gives

$$\frac{\partial \Phi(x_1)}{\partial x_1} = \rho ax_1^{\rho-1} - \rho a \frac{(c - ax_1)^{\rho-1}}{b^{\rho-1}} = \rho a(x_1^{\rho-1} - x_2^{\rho-1}).$$

Since $\rho > 1$ and $a > 0$, $\rho a(x_1^{\rho-1} - x_2^{\rho-1}) > 0$ if and only if $x_1 > x_2$. It follows that for all $\delta < \Delta = \frac{(x_1 - x_2)b}{a+b}$ we must have $x_1 - \delta > x_2 + \frac{a\delta}{b}$, and thus $\Phi(x_1 - \delta) > \Phi(x_1)$. The lemma then follows.

Theorem 1. *Given probability mass function $f(r)$, starting price function $q(r)$ and revenue function $v(r)$, WATERLEVELPRICING returns a steady-profit price function in time $O(N \log V)$, where $V = \max_{r \in S} v(r)$ is the maximum value of the revenue function on the domain S. Moreover, such a function is unique and with respect to it, customer's profit is always non-negative and the minimum profit is maximized.*

Proof. From the definition of $v_L(r)$, it is easy to see that $\sum_{r \in S} v_L(r)f(r)$ increases when L decreases. Also, $V = \max_{r \in S} v(r)$ is an upper bound on L. It follows that using binary search, we can find L such that

$$\sum_{r \in S} v_L(r)f(r) = \sum_{r \in S} q(r)f(r).$$

in $O(\log V)$ steps, where each step involves computing a summation in $O(N)$ time.

It remains to show that the returned function is a steady-profit price function. We will prove that a steady-profit price function $p(r)$ is obtained only at a non-negative fair price function where the profit values are as equal as possible. By as equal as possible, we mean the profit is equal to a same value everywhere except at points r such that $p(r) = 0$, where the profit is less than that value. It will then follow that such a function is unique and $v_L(r)$ is the desired function (with profit L at every r such that $v_L(r) > 0$). It will also be clear that with respect to the unique function, the customer's profit is always non-negative and the minimum profit is maximized.

Assume that $p(r)$ is a non-negative fair price function such that with respect to $p(r)$, the profit is not as equal as possible. We show that $p(r)$ can be modified such that the ρ-moment

$$\sum_{r \in S} (v(r) - p(r) - \mu)^\rho f(r).$$

decreases for all $\rho > 1$.

Let $h(r) = v(r) - p(r) - \mu$ be the deviation of the customer's profit from the mean value. Since $p(r)$ does not make the profit as equal as possible, $\exists r_1, r_2$ such that $h(r_1) \neq h(r_2)$ and $p(r_1), p(r_2)$ are both positive. Without loss of generality, we may assume that $h(r_1) > h(r_2)$. By Lemma 1, there exists a Δ such that for all $\delta < \Delta$, decreasing $h(r_1)$ by δ and increasing $h(r_2)$ by $\delta f(r_1)/f(r_2)$ will result in a decrease the quantity $h(r_1)^\rho f(r_1) + h(r_2)^\rho f(r_2)$ for all $\rho > 1$.

Let $\delta = \min(\Delta, p(r_2)f(r_2)/f(r_1))$, and consider the following modification on $p(r)$:

1. $p(r_1) \leftarrow p(r_1) + \delta$,
2. $p(r_2) \leftarrow p(r_2) - \delta f(r_1)/f(r_2)$,
3. $p(r) \leftarrow p(r)$ for all $r \neq r_1, r_2$.

It is easy to see that with the modification, $p(r)$ is still fair and non-negative. Moreover, $h(r_1)$ decreases by δ and $h(r_2)$ increases by $\delta f(r_1)/f(r_2)$. It follows that for all $\rho > 1$, the ρ-moment $\sum_{r \in S} h(r)^\rho f(r)$ decreases as desired.

Theorem 2. *The pricing scheme* WATERLEVELPRICING *is incentive compatible.*

Proof. Since WATERLEVELPRICING computes a fair price function, the expected total price charged to the customer is the same as the expected price of resources used by the customer, regardless of the revenue function revealed by the customer. Hence, clearly it is in the best interest of the customer to reveal her true revenue function, since only then will the provider be able to ensure that the variance of the profit of the customer is minimized. The theorem follows.

5   A Least Squares Algorithm

In the previous section, we presented an alternative pricing scheme that is favorable for both agents in the model. We also showed that the scheme has some desirable properties such as the customer's profit is always non-negative and its deviation from the mean value is minimized. Despite that fact, the pricing function can be quite unnatural. For instance, it can happen that the customer has to pay more money for less resources as shown in Example 1.

Example 1. Consider a web service provider that charges based on bandwidth usage. A customer uses the service for hosting a website. Hence, the demand of that customer depends on viewers of the website. For simplicity, assume that there are two type of viewers: the type who uses 1 unit of bandwidth and generates \$2 (by clicking ads), and the type who uses 2 units of bandwidth and generates \$1. Furthermore, the website is equally likely to get a viewer of each type (with probability 0.5). The provider is willing to sell one unit of bandwidth for \$0.5. At this price, both the provider and the customer gain \$0.75 per viewer in expectation. The algorithm in Fig. 1 will price 1 unit of viewer type 1's demand at \$1.25 and 2 units of viewer type 2's demand at \$0.25. Observe that the provider still gains \$0.75 in expectation (at higher deviation), and the customer gains \$0.75 per viewer surely (no deviation). Hence in this example, if Amazon uses the water-filling algorithm, the customer pays more money for less resources.

In this section, we prevent such unwanted outcomes from happening by adding a reasonable assumption on the price function. To be precise, we insist that the price function must be a linear function of the resources, that is, it must be of the form $p(\boldsymbol{r}) = \sum_{i=1}^{m} a_i r_i + a_0$ for non-negative a_is.

Remark 1. It is a common practice to write a linear function $p(\boldsymbol{r}) = \sum_{i=1}^{m} a_i r_i + a_0$ as $p(\boldsymbol{r}) = \boldsymbol{a}^T \boldsymbol{r}$ where $r_0 = 1$ for all $\boldsymbol{r}$. This trick allows us to ignore the constant term in the linear function. Throughout this section, we will adopt this representation and assume that $\boldsymbol{r}$ is an $(m + 1)$-dimensional vector with $r_0 = 1$.

Not surprisingly, with the new restriction, the target function cannot satisfy all properties of the function introduced in the previous section. Specifically, we cannot have the property that the customer's profit is always non-negative. Instead, our goal is to find a linear price function with non-negative coefficients such that the variance of the profit is minimized. To be precise, we are interested in price function with the following properties:

1. *Fairness:* The target price function is a fair price function, i.e., the customer has to pay the same amount compared to the starting price in expectation.

2. *Linearity:* The target price function is linear.
3. *Non-negativity:* The target price function is non-negative on the whole domain.
4. *Stability:* The target price function minimizes the profit variance subject to the above 3 conditions.

We give an algorithm for computing a desired price function in Fig. 2. Our algorithm uses an oracle that solves non-negative least squares, a constrained version of the normal least squares problem where the coefficients of the linear function are not allowed to be negative. For the details of non-negative least squares solvers, please see [7, 8, 10]. The definition of NONNEGATIVELEASTSQUARES oracle is given below.

Definition 4. NONNEGATIVELEASTSQUARES (X, y) *is an oracle that, on input* $X \in R^{n \times m}$ *and* $y \in R^n$, *returns a non-negative vector* $a \in R^m$ *such that*

$$y = X a + \epsilon,$$

and $\|\epsilon\|_2^2$ *is minimize.*

We give the main theorem of the section and its proof.

Theorem 3. *Given probability mass function* $f(r)$, *starting price function* $q(r)$ *and revenue function* $v(r)$, LINEARPRICING *returns a fair price function* $p(r) = a^T r$ *such that* a *is non-negative and* $\sum_{r \in S}(v(r) - p(r) - \mu)^2 f(r)$ *is minimized among all such functions. Furthermore,* LINEARPRICING *is incentive compatible.*

Proof. Recall that $y = X a + \epsilon$. Rearranging gives

$$\|\epsilon\|_2^2 = \sum_{k=1}^{N+1} \left(y^{(k)} - a^T x^{(k)} \right)^2.$$

Let

$$\bar{y} = \sum_{k=1}^{N} \left(v(r^{(k)}) - \mu \right) f(r^{(k)}),$$

$$\bar{x} = \sum_{k=1}^{N} r^{(k)} f(r^{(k)}).$$

We may assume M is sufficiently large to guarantee that for an optimal solution a returned by NONNEGATIVELEASTSQUARES (X, y), $\bar{y} - a^T \bar{x}$ must go to 0.

This condition ensures that $p(r)$ is a fair price function, that is, the expected price is equal to the expected starting price. We have

$$\bar{y} - a^T \bar{x} = \sum_{k=1}^{N} \left(v(r^{(k)}) - \mu \right) f(r^{(k)}) - a^T \sum_{k=1}^{N} r^{(k)} f(r^{(k)})$$

$$= \sum_{k=1}^{N} \left(v(r^{(k)}) - \mu - a^T r^{(k)} \right) f(r^{(k)})$$

$$= 0.$$

$p(r) = \text{LinearPricing}\left(f(r), q(r), v(r)\right)$
Input: Probability mass function $f(r)$, starting price function $q(r)$ and revenue function $v(r)$.
Output: Linear price function $p(r)$ with non-negative coefficients that minimizes the profit variance.

1. Compute $\mu = \sum_{k=1}^{N}\left(v\left(r^{(k)}\right) - q\left(r^{(k)}\right)\right)f\left(r^{(k)}\right)$.
2. For $1 \le k \le N$, let

$$y^{(k)} = \left(v\left(r^{(k)}\right) - \mu\right)\sqrt{f\left(r^{(k)}\right)},$$
$$x^{(k)} = r^{(k)}\sqrt{f\left(r^{(k)}\right)}.$$

3. Let M be a big number, and

$$y^{(N+1)} = M\sum_{k=1}^{N}\left(v\left(r^{(k)}\right) - \mu\right)f\left(r^{(k)}\right),$$
$$x^{(N+1)} = M\sum_{k=1}^{N}r^{(k)}f\left(r^{(k)}\right).$$

4. Let $a \leftarrow \text{NonNegativeLeastSquares}\left(X, y\right)$ where

$$X = \begin{bmatrix} x^{(1)T} \\ \vdots \\ x^{(N+1)T} \end{bmatrix} \text{ and } y = \begin{bmatrix} y^{(1)} \\ \vdots \\ y^{(N+1)} \end{bmatrix}.$$

5. Return $p(r) = a^T r$.

Fig. 2. Algorithm for computing a linear price function.

It follows that

$$\mu = \mu\sum_{k=1}^{N}f\left(r^{(k)}\right) = \sum_{k=1}^{N}\left(v\left(r^{(k)}\right) - p(r^{(k)})\right)f\left(r^{(k)}\right).$$

By construction,

$$\mu = \sum_{k=1}^{N}\left(v\left(r^{(k)}\right) - q(r^{(k)})\right)f\left(r^{(k)}\right).$$

Therefore,

$$\sum_{k=1}^{N}p(r^{(k)})f\left(r^{(k)}\right) = \sum_{k=1}^{N}q(r^{(k)})f\left(r^{(k)}\right)$$

as desired.

Moreover, since M is sufficiently large, minimizing $\|\epsilon\|_2^2$ is equivalent to minimizing

$$\sum_{k=1}^{N} \left(y^{(k)} - \boldsymbol{a}^T \boldsymbol{x}^{(k)} \right)^2$$

subject to $\overline{y} - \boldsymbol{a}^T \overline{\boldsymbol{x}} = 0$, i.e., subject to $p(\boldsymbol{r})$ being a fair price function. We have

$$\sum_{k=1}^{N} \left(y^{(k)} - \boldsymbol{a}^T \boldsymbol{x}^{(k)} \right)^2 = \sum_{k=1}^{N} \left(\left(v\left(\boldsymbol{r}^{(k)}\right) - \mu \right) \sqrt{f\left(\boldsymbol{r}^{(k)}\right)} - \boldsymbol{a}^T \boldsymbol{r}^{(k)} \sqrt{f\left(\boldsymbol{r}^{(k)}\right)} \right)^2$$

$$= \sum_{k=1}^{N} \left(v\left(\boldsymbol{r}^{(k)}\right) - \mu - \boldsymbol{a}^T \boldsymbol{r}^{(k)} \right)^2 f\left(\boldsymbol{r}^{(k)}\right)$$

$$= \sum_{k=1}^{N} \left(v\left(\boldsymbol{r}^{(k)}\right) - p\left(\boldsymbol{r}^{(k)}\right) - \mu \right)^2 f\left(\boldsymbol{r}^{(k)}\right).$$

Therefore, the minimized quantity is precisely the variance of profit.

Since NONNEGATIVELEASTSQUARES $(\boldsymbol{X}, \boldsymbol{y})$ returns a non-negative vector $\boldsymbol{a}$, the linear function $p(\boldsymbol{r}) = \boldsymbol{a}^T \boldsymbol{r}$ has non-negative coefficients as claimed.

Finally, the proof of incentive compatibility for LINEARPRICING is analogous to that of Theorem 2.

6   Discussion

The reason to seek a pricing function that is linear in the resources rented is to remove the distortion that a customer has to pay more money for less resources. We note that linearity is not essential for ensuring this, in fact any monotone function will also suffice. This motivates the following question: monotone in the resources rented so that it is non-negative and minimizes the variance of the profit among all such functions. We believe that a variant of our water-filling algorithm should solve this problem.

One feature of the linear pricing function is that it is robust to mistakes in the reported revenue function in the sense that price function will not change much as a result of altering a few points. Furthermore, this method does not need the revenue functions at all values of resources rented, it works even if some of these points are missing.

References

1. Abhishek, V., Kash, I.A., Key, P.B.: Fixed and market pricing for cloud services. arXiv:1201.5621 (2012)
2. Anselmi, J., Ardagna, D., Lui, J.C., Wierman, A., Xu, Y., Yang, Z.: The economics of the cloud: price competition and congestion. In: Proceedings of NetEcon (2013)
3. Armbrust, M., Fox, A., Griffith, R., Joseph, A., Katz, R., Konwinski, A., Lee, G., Patterson, D., Rabkin, A., Stoica, I., Zaharia, M.: Above the clouds: a Berkeley view of cloud computing (2009)

4. Ballani, H., Jang, K., Karagiannis, T., Kim, C., Gunawardena, D., O'Shea, G.: Chatty tenants and the cloud network sharing problem. In: Proceedings of the 10th Usenix conference on Networked Systems Design and Implementation (2013)
5. Agmon Ben-Yehuda, O., Ben-Yehuda, M., Schuster, A., Tsafrir, D.: Deconstructing Amazon EC2 spot instance pricing. ACM Trans. Econ. Comput. **1**(3), 16 (2013)
6. Blocq, G., Bachrach, Y., Key, P.: Game and applications to pricing in cloud computing. In: Proceedings of the 2014 International Conference on Autonomous Agents and Multi-agent Systems (2014)
7. Boutsidis, C., Drineas, P.: Random projections for the nonnegative least-squares problem. Linear Algebra. Appl. **431**, 760–771 (2009)
8. Bro, R., De Jong, S.: A fast non-negativity-constrained least squares algorithm. J. Chemometr. **11**, 393–401 (1997)
9. Ceppi, S., Kash, I.: Personalized payments for storage-as-a-service. In: Proceedings of the 10th Workshop on the Economics of Networks, Systems, and Computation (2015)
10. Chen, D., Plemmons, R.J.: Nonnegativity constraints in numerical analysis. In: Proceedings of the Symposium on the Birth of Numerical Analysis (2009)
11. Columbus, L.: Roundup of cloud computing forecasts and market estimates. Forbes (2016)
12. Devanur, N., Garg, J., Mehta, R., Vazirani, V.V., Yazdanbod, S.: A market for scheduling, with applications to cloud computing. arXiv (2016)
13. AWS Inc., Amazon EC2 pricing. https://aws.amazon.com/ec2/pricing/
14. Jain, N., Menache, I., Naor, J., Yaniv, J.: A truthful mechanism for value-based scheduling in cloud computing. Theor. Comput. Syst. **54**(3), 388–406 (2014)
15. Kash, I.A., Key, P.B.: Pricing the cloud. IEEE Int. Econ. **20**(10), 36–43 (2016)
16. Kreps, D.M.: A Course in Microeconomic Theory. Princeton University Press, Princeton (1990)
17. Mas-Colell, A., Whinston, M., Green, J.: Microeconomic Theory. Oxford University Press, Oxford (1995)
18. Niu, D., Feng, C., Li, B.: Pricing cloud bandwidth reservations under demand uncertainty. In: Proceedings of ACM SIGMETRIC (2012)
19. Odlyzko, A.: Internet pricing and the history of communications. Comput. Netw. **36**, 493–517 (2001)
20. Xu, H., Li, B.: A study of pricing for cloud resources. ACM SIGMETRICS Perform. Eval. Rev. **40**, 3–12 (2013). Special Issue on Cloud Computing

Scale Effects in Web Search

Di He[1], Aadharsh Kannan[1(✉)], Tie-Yan Liu[1], R. Preston McAfee[1],
Tao Qin[1(✉)], and Justin M. Rao[2]

[1] Microsoft AI & Research, Redmond, USA
{akannan,taoqin}@microsoft.com
[2] HomeAway Inc., Austin, USA

Abstract. It is a well-known statistical property that learning tends to
slow down with each additional data point. Thus even if scale effects are
important in web search, they could be important in a range that any
viable entrant could easily achieve. In this paper we address these questions using browsing logs that give click-through-rates by query on two
major search engines. An ideal experiment would be to fix the "query difficulty" and exogenously provide more or less historical data. We approximate the ideal experiment by finding queries that were not previously
observed. Of these "new queries", some grow to be moderately popular,
having 1000–2000 clicks in a calendar year. We examine ranking quality
during the lifespan of the query and find statistically significant improvement on the order of 2–3% and learning faster at lower levels of data.
We are careful to rule out alternate explanations for this pattern. In particular, we show that the effect is not explained by new, more relevant
documents entering the landscape, rather it is mainly shifting the most
relevant documents to the top of the ranking. We thus conclude they
represent direct scale effects. Finally, we show that scale helps link new
queries to existing queries with ample historical data by forming edges in
the query document bipartite graph. This "indirect knowledge" is shown
to be important for "deflating uniqueness" and improving ranking.

Keywords: Scale effects · Direct effects · Indirect effects
Intent clustering · Unsupervised learning · Web search

1 Introduction

A key question in the analysis of web search markets is the degree increased
scale confers a direct performance imagine advantage. Consider two entirely
different worlds. In the first, ranking quality is driven overwhelmingly by algorithmic innovation and fixed document features. In this world, a well-funded new
entrant could potentially produce results of quality superior to the entrenched
market leader. In the second, learning from historical queries is critical to ranking quality. A superior, but data-starved algorithm could perform much worse
than the incumbent's. Although these two worlds are dramatically different in
terms of the potential for innovation and competitive dynamics, little is known

© Springer International Publishing AG 2017
N. R. Devanur and P. Lu (Eds.): WINE 2017, LNCS 10674, pp. 294–310, 2017.
https://doi.org/10.1007/978-3-319-71924-5_21

about which one we live in. Further, it is a well-known statistical property that learning tends to slow down with each additional data point. Thus even if scale effects are important, the steep part of the learning curve could be in a range that any viable entrant could easily achieve.

In this paper we address these questions using browsing logs that give click-through-rates (CTR), a natural measure of whether or not a set of results met the user's need, by query on two major search engines. We start by documenting the fact that more common queries indeed have higher CTR. The relationship is proportional to the square root of the log of historical clicks, indicating that increases are higher at lower data levels. Both search engines show similar functional forms.

These high-level correlations cannot be viewed as causal relationships because more popular queries could be innately easier to satisfy user intent. An ideal experiment would be to fix the "query difficulty" and exogenously provide more or less historical data. This is, of course, not possible. We approximate the ideal experiment by finding queries that were not previously observed. Of these "new queries", some grow to be moderately popular, having 1000–2000 clicks in a calendar year. We examine ranking quality during query lifetime and find statistically significant improvement on the order of 2–3%, with faster improvement at lower levels of data. We are careful to rule out alternate explanations for this pattern. In particular, we show that the effect is not explained by new, more relevant documents entering the landscape, rather it is mainly shifting the most relevant documents to the top of the ranking. We thus conclude they represent direct scale effects.

The fact that learning is fastest at low levels of data is a double-edged sword for a potential entrant. On the one hand, it seems to indicate that only a modest scale is required to achieve viability. While this is good news for relatively popular queries, which do account for a majority of *searches*, it is bad news for rarer queries, which account for the majority of *queries*. For example, in 2007 Google reported that 20–25% of the queries they see each day are unique when compared to the most recent month. [1] Moreover, most users submit at least some "long tail" queries [6].

The issue of long-tail queries adds a nuance to our analysis. If most queries really only have no more than five historical examples, then perhaps scale does not play much of a role after all. However it has been shown that historical examples of related queries can be linked to seemingly rare queries by applying clusters and graph cutting techniques to the query-document bipartite graph [2,8,9]. This graph can be used to generate related queries and leverage historical examples that differ in minor ways from the target query. To understand the role of scale in this domain, we apply a clustering algorithm motivated by past work. To do so, we take the query-document graph—the total nodes number nearly 10 billion—and cluster queries that share the same intent. Human evaluation is used to validate the accuracy of the algorithm.

---

[1] http://searchengineland.com/that-25-new-queries-figure-ballpark-estimate-says-google-11596.

We use the graph to flexibly "deflate uniqueness" because it creates ties between relatively rare queries to more common queries that capture similar user intent. We show, for instance that for a set of 1.1 billion "long tail" queries, there are 10-fold less unique instances of intent. The method naturally surfaces synonyms and related queries. Experiments reveal that increasing overall scale provides greater edge density, which in turn allows one to link more rare queries to more common queries with many historical examples. In summary, this analysis shows that there are additional returns to scale in the form of semantically linking queries and that queries submitted by users are "not as unique as they appear."

Finally, we conclude with some thoughts on the larger picture. Our analysis here is not capable of capturing all the returns to scale, rather we focus on clean identification in relatively controlled environments. That being said, it is important to note the CTR impact of scale we document appears modest overall, order 2–3% of CTR. Interpreting magnitudes, however, is a bit tricky. For example, both providers have CTRs on tail queries in the 70% range. Suppose an entrant could achieve 60% "off the shelf." Then 2–3% represents more like 20–30% of the meaningful range in which we expect competitors to be differentiated and thus appears quite large in this light. We stress that this is only an example to highlight the nuances in interpreting the magnitudes reported in our study.

2   Data Description

Our data consists of search logs for a period of time greater than 6 months from two large commercial search engines. The source are proprietary logs of a web browser. In all instances, the same restrictions are applied to both search providers. For example, the same user types, geographic locations, and so forth. Table 1 shows that we observe hundreds of billions of searches. This richness will allow us to conduct a detailed analysis of queries as data accumulates over time.

Table 1. Summary statistics

Provider 1 (# impressions)	>200 billion
Provider 2 (# impressions)	>300 billion
Provider 1 # clicks	>100 billion
Provider 2 # clicks	>150 billion

3   Direct Effects of Scale

In this section we study how the search engine performance is related to the volume of historical data for a target query. We first investigate all the queries in our dataset and then check those relatively new queries, which have only a few historical clicks.

3.1 Analysis of General Queries

To study the scale effect of a query, ideally, we need to collect its search log from the first time it is observed, and see how its CTR changes as more people issue it. However, this is infeasible because that a search engine can only legally keep the data for a limited time[2]. Thus for popular queries, it is hard (if not impossible) to know its first appearance. Here we use one year as the range of time for analysis, and collect browsing logs of two commercial search engines, i.e., Provider 1 and Provider 2. For the log in each provider, we use the first three month's data as the *benchmark* data source, which acts as the data observed in history, and use the remaining nine months of data as our *target* data source in analysis. For each query q and each day d in target data source, we get a pair $<H(q,d), CTR(q,d)>$ in which $H(q,d)$ denotes the historical measure before day d for query q, and $CTR(q,d)$ denotes its CTR in day d. In the experiment, we use click number as the historical measure, since clicks are the most effective feedback from search users.

For each query, we generate 270 pairs and partition the pairs into buckets according to $H(q,d)$. The CTR averaged over the pairs in each bucket is shown in Fig. 1. We can see from the figure, CTR shows a positive correlation with the number of historical clicks for both the search providers, and the patterns of CTR growth of the two providers are similar.

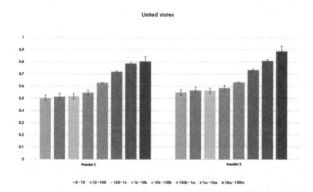

United states

× 0~10   ■ 10~100   × 100~1k   ■ 1k~10k   ■ 10k~100k   ■ 100k~1m   ■ 1m~10m   ■ 10m~100m

Fig. 1. In aggregate, CTR shows a positive correlation with the number of historical occurrences. Both providers show a similar relationship.

To quantitatively characterize the scale relationship, we further conduct a regression analysis on the correlation between the CTR and the number of historical clicks. After trying several different function families, including linear functions and polynomial function, we find that the square root of the log

---

[2] http://searchengineland.com/google-responds-to-eu-cutting-raw-log-retention-time
-reconsidering-cookie-expiration-11443.

historical clicks well approximate the current CTR. Specifically, denote the historical click number as x, we have that for provider 1.

$$CTR = -0.0530[-0.085, -0.021] + 0.3287[0.315, 0.343]\sqrt{log(x)}, \qquad (1)$$

and for Provider 2,

$$CTR = -0.3871[-0.486, -0.288] + 0.4792[0.438, 0.520]\sqrt{log(x)}. \qquad (2)$$

This shows that there is a strongly positive dependency between the number of historical clicks and the current search performance. These results can be seen graphically in Figs. 2 and 3.

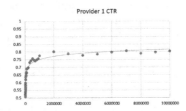

Fig. 2. Provider 1, relationship between CTR and number of historical examples.

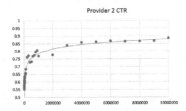

Fig. 3. Provider 2, relationship between CTR and number of historical examples.

3.2   Scale Effect Analysis on New Queries

One a major concern with the analysis in previous subsection is that the queries falling into different buckets are not the same. For example, popular queries may express intent that is innately easier to satisfy. Since these more popular queries would fall into right-side buckets and rare queries into left-side buckets, the correlation we observe could be due to this confound and not a direct impact of scale. An ideal experiment would be to fix the "query difficulty" and exogenously provide more or less historical data. Since this is not possible, we approximate the ideal experiment as follows.

We select a set of queries according to two criteria: (1) a query has less than 200 clicks in the three-month benchmark data source; (2) the total number of clicks of the query in the calendar year (including both the benchmark data source and the target data source) is between 1000 and 2000. The first criterion ensures that such a query is relatively new to the search provider, and the second criterion tries to make that the selected queries have the similar difficulty the search provider. As a result, there are about 8000 queries selected for Provider 1 and 10000 for Provider 2. Because we see almost all the queries for one provider, and a much smaller fraction for the other, the scales are not directly comparable.

For query q, we use $CTR(q, c)$ to denote the CTR of q in period of receiving $c+1$ to $c+100$ clicks. For each selected query q, we get 9 pairs $<c, CTR(q, c)>$, where $c \in \{100, 200, \ldots, 900\}$. Then we partition the pairs into buckets according to c and calculate the average CTR over queries in each bucket. It is important to note that the queries in each bucket are the same, meaning selection effects cannot drive observed relationship.[3]

We present our aggregated results with error bar (confidence interval = 0.95%) in Figs. 4 and 5. From the curves, overall we observe that CTR grows for new queries for both providers, and the growing trends are significant. This shows that the scale effect does exist in both search providers on the order of 2% over the first 1,000 queries. A regression of the same yields for Provider 1 an intercept of 0.6726 [0.6653, 0.6787] and coefficient of 2.116 e−05 [1.03154 e−05, 3.2017 e−05] i.e. anywhere from 1–3% CTR gain per 1000. For Provider 2 an intercept of 0.7075833 [0.70145, 0.99465] and coefficient of 2.083 e−05 [9.94658 e−06, 3.172008 e−05] i.e. anywhere from 0.99-3% CTR gain per 1000.

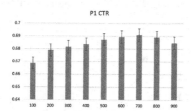

Fig. 4. Provider 1, relationship between CTR and number of historical examples for new queries only

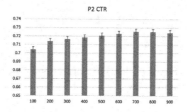

Fig. 5. Provider 2, relationship between CTR and number of historical examples for new queries only.

---

[3] We do not include the pair $<1000, CTR(q, 1000)>$ since not all the selected queries have 1100 clicks in the target data. If we include this pair, the queries in the last bucket will be less than the queries in the left 9 buckets.

This is the same order difference observed at the left-hand side of Fig. 1, but it cannot explain the order 20% increase documented in the overall relationship. While we cannot rule out these are driven by scale effects, the evidence seems indicate that the large Fig. 1 differences are more of a selection issue on query difficulty, as learning appears to slow down after 1,000 historical instances.

3.3 Robustness Checks

It is important to consider alternative explanations to direct scale effects. A natural alternative hypothesis is that improved performance is due to richer or more relevant documents, not better ranking. To see if this is going on, we revisit our new query analysis and tag URLs that were previously in crawled as "old." New URLs would be clicks on links that were not previously available to the ranker. If the growth in CTR was due to new URLs, we should see the fraction of old URL clicks decrease as we move to the right in Fig. 6. Instead we observe that a constant and very high, about 98%, of clicks are on old URLs. Since this fraction does not change, it is not able to explain the growth in CTR. Further we can look at whether the ranker is doing a better job at putting the best links at the top of the page. It is well-known in search that position causally influences CTR in a multiplicative fashion—placing higher quality links at the top of the page leads to a increase in user satisfaction [5]. We can only observe click position for one of the two providers that we have considered, but document a strong, statistically significant improvement with historical examples for a new query analysis.

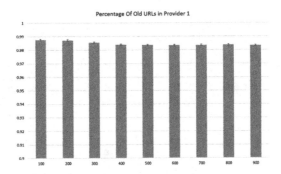

Fig. 6. Provider 1, the fraction of clicks that correspond to URLs previously observed. Results indicate a stable and very high percentage of clicks comes from these documents.

A final robustness check is to consider the underlying causal model for why scale can directly improve results. First, papers have shown how features can be improved, such as including past queries as anchor text for clicked links [10]. That is, position changes as a result of user behavior. These data can then feed into the creation of "click graphs" [5,7,8] which is useful for building out semantic knowledge around a query and user level analysis to understand intent satisfaction [3]. Thus far from being a black box, there are many previously identified causal channels that use historical behavior to directly improve ranking performance.

4   Indirect Effects of Scale

In this section, we explore the effects of data on related queries, which supplement direct query data. To do so, we first identify related queries by constructing a knowledge graph. We use the cosine measure of relatedness, and then classify as related or not by the measure exceeds a threshold. To set the threshold, we use human judgment on a subsample. We then explore how related query knowledge affects the CTR using regression techniques.

Our data for this section consists of search logs for a period of time greater than 6 months from a large commercial search engine. The data form a bipartite graph of queries, denoted Q, and documents, denoted D. Edges are given by the set E represent user clicks connecting queries to documents. Edge weights are given by the click count $C_{i,j}$ from query node i to document node j. We combine queries that only have slight differences in lexical form. To do so we follow standard best practices for normalizing queries: (1) Eliminate any punctuation marks (2) Split queries into the words (which include numbers) (3) Porter stem words (remove plurals and other standard stemming operations) to eliminate differences in cases (4) Represent each query as a bag of the remaining words, sorted alphabetically. This procedure reduces the number of query nodes by 7%.

Table 2 summarizes the graph and the underlying user activity. The graph has over 7 billion nodes connected by over 11 billion edges. The total number of clicks exceeds 100 billion. These statistics highlight the scale of modern search engines and also point to the sparsity of the graph.

Table 2. Summary statistics for the query-document graph and underlying user activity

Cardinality Q (# unique queries)	4.82 Billion
Cardinality D (# unique URLs)	3.26 Billion
Cardinality E (# edges)	11.6 Billion
Number of sessions	>100 billion
Total clicks	>100 billion

4.1   Core Algorithm

We start with the query-document bipartite graph. This can be represented by a matrix with dimensions $card(Q) \times card(D)$. Each column gives a vector for each document where the jth entry gives the clicks from query j. In other words, it gives the document's representation in query space. For every pair of documents, we compute the cosine distance to form an upper triangular document similarity matrix. This requires order $\frac{card(\mathcal{D})^2}{2}$ calculations. Next, we convert similarity weights to 0 or 1 using a chosen threshold; this censoring removes weak ties and allows us to form a document similarity graph (we implement multiple thresholds and use human accuracy ratings and other metrics to find the preferred setting). We find the connected components from this graph [1] and call them *intent clusters*. Intent clusters capture groups of documents that have the same inferred intent because users clicked from similar queries to get to these documents.

Finally, we take intent clusters and form the query-intent-cluster bipartite graph. Edge weights are given by the fraction of clicks from query q that are point to a document in cluster c. Edge weights have the natural interpretation of the fraction of searches for a given query that had a given intent. If 10% of clicks from query X map to g_1 and 90% map to g_2, then we say that query X has intent g_2 and g_1, with weights 90% and 10% respectively. We will observe that this is very common. It is natural to label each intent cluster as the query with the highest weight, which we call the "intent query."

Computing cosine distance is straightforward, but given the query-document bipartite graph has dimensions $card(\mathcal{Q}) \times card(\mathcal{D})$, doing so requires order $\frac{card(\mathcal{D})^2}{2}$ calculations. Since we implement our approach on a modest-sized compute cluster, the parallelizable nature of this computation makes it feasible even though we have billions of nodes.

Using these distance calculations, we form upper-triangular document similarity matrix. The next issue we have to address concerns the fact that clicks are a form of implicit feedback that contain noise—some clicks do not represent user intent. This means entries in the similarity matrix are biased away from zero as compared to ground truth. This points to the use of a threshold wherein similarity scores below the threshold are given the value 0 and those above are given the value 1. Once values are converted to a binary indicator, the matrix is converted into document similarity graph for which we can conduct a connected components analysis using a scalable algorithm.

Ex-ante it is not obvious what value of the threshold is optimal. Thresholds that are too low induce noise and could lead to massive connected components that do not represent one true intent. Thresholds that are too high could lead to too sparse a graph, meaning many clusters actually have the same underlying intent. Based on pre-testing, we choose 4 threshold values: 0.70, 0.80, 0.90 and 0.95. We will later show that human judgment can help select the optimal threshold.

In order to compute connected components we follow a simple strategy of iterative agglomeration. One can conceptualize this strategy as (a parallel) flood fill algorithm on a Map-Reduce framework. For the first iteration we treat every document pair (from the similarity matrix) as a separate cluster, identify link nodes between pairs and merge them. Convergence of link node identification and merging clusters for subsequent iterations is reached through repetition.

Algorithm 1. Find connected components

```
SetOfURLWithCluster =
SELECT LeftUrlId AS UrlId,
        RowLabel AS ClusterId
FROM SetOfURLPairs
UNION
SELECT RightUrlId AS UrlId,
        RowLabel AS ClusterId
FROM SetOfURLPairs;

for 1 TO MaxIterationLimit do
  SELECT UrlId AS LinkUrl,
          MIN(ClusterId) AS MasterCluster
  FROM SetOfURLWithCluster
  FOR EVERY LinkUrl;

  SlaveClusters =
  SELECT ClusterId AS SlaveCluster,
          MIN(UrlId) AS LinkUrl
  FROM SetOfURLWithCluster
  FOR EVERY SlaveCluster;

  SetOfClusterRenames =
  SELECT MasterCluster, SlaveCluster
  FROM MasterClusters
  INNER JOIN SlaveClusters
  ON LinkUrl
  WHERE MasterCluster <> SlaveCluster;

  if SetOfClusterRenames.size = 0 then
    end for
  end if

  SetOfURLWithCluster =
  SELECT UrlId RenameIfExist(ClusterId, SetOfClusterRenames) AS ClusterId
  FROM SetOfURLWithCluster;
end for
```

Referring to Algorithm 1. SetOfURLPairs contains a LeftURLId, a RightURLId and RowLabel. LeftURLId and RightURLId are both ordinal numbers identifying an individual URL. Each one of these elements represents a non-zero entry in the URL similarity matrix where LeftURLId < RightURLId. RowLabel is an ordinal number corresponding to every entry in SetOfURL-Pairs. RenameIfExist replaces the ClusterId with the SlaveCluster value if there exists an entry in SetOfClusterRenames where MasterCluster = ClusterId else it returns ClusterId. MaxIterationLimit is a computation limit that is set to avoid infinite non-convergence. The query node identification and merging is the process that is repeated till convergence. We found that the algorithm typically converged in 5–6 iterations.

Let's call the set of connected components $\mathcal{G}$ with elements g, which itself is a set containing the documents within each component. We now form the query/intent-cluster graph. For each query q, the edge weight to intent cluster g_i is the fraction of clicks from that query that point to node g_i. This weight has a natural Markovian interpretation. For purposes of semantic interpret-ability, we label each node with the query that has the highest edge weight pointing to that node. We call this the *intent query*. Traversing the graph following the Markov weights reveals related intent, an approach that has been shown to be useful on the raw query-document graph to find related queries [4].

4.2 Evaluation of Clusters

Our goal in this section is to get a sense to what extent do the *intent queries* reasonably capture the intent of the user. To do so, for each threshold setting we form a 100-query test set by randomly selecting 10 from each decile of the search frequency (the same queries are used for each setting). We then follow all the edges in the knowledge graph to get all the intent queries (clusters) that map to this query. Note that we follow all edges, even if the Markov weight is very low.

An independent auditor, blinded to the parameter settings or aims of the study, evaluated query/intent-query pairs. Pairs were scored a 1 if the intent query would could reasonably match the underlying query. The auditor used the appropriate references for queries she was not familiar with. For example, for the query "Aretha Franklin" there is a link to "Luther Vandross" intent cluster. The auditor scored this as a 0, concluding that while the two entities are certainly related—they are both singers of a similar style from a similar era—that the query "Aretha Franklin" does not reasonably have the intent to find material on Luther Vandross. Clearly there is some genuine ambiguity at play in how to make this judgment. On the one hand, some users may want to find material on Luther Vandross but are unable to remember his name. They search a name they can remember, namely Aretha Franklin, and then click on a document in the Vandross cluster. In this case, one might conclude that the judgment should be a 1. (In either case, these are clearly terms that are usefully "related to" the underlying query.) To push back against this issue, we simply asked our auditor to be conservative and consistent. Precision is defined as the fraction of pairs that are judged to be relevant to each other by this standard. Weighted precision applies a weight to each pair as given by the Markov weight connected the query to the intent cluster. This means that connections that had low strength are down-weighted in the calculation.

The parameter setting 0.7 produced the most edges in the knowledge graph, which is natural since it required the lowest threshold to establish similarity and thus the most non-singleton connected components. We define each query/intent-query pair for the 0.70 that is scored as a true positive as the target set. The fraction of pairs that each method recovers is defined as pseudo recall. By definition it is equal to 1.0 for the 0.7 parameter setting. We also define weighted recall, which applies the Markov weight to each pair. Note that now the measure is not constrained to [0, 1]. The reason is that the tighter thresholds tend to lead to higher Markov weights, so if they can actually "recover more" (by getting credit for the weight) pairs. We concede this metric is a bit unconventional, but find it nonetheless informative.

Table 3. Precision and pseudo recall by threshold

Threshold	Raw precision	Weighted precision	Pseudo recall	W. Pseudo recall
0.7	0.69	0.79	1	1
0.8	0.70	0.84	0.76	1.054
0.9	0.68	0.83	0.45	1.04
0.95	0.66	0.83	0.26	1.03

Table 3 gives the results. Raw precision is highest for the 0.8 threshold, coming in at 0.70, and actually lowest for 0.95 (but the overall distances are not large). This indicates that the clusters in 0.95 can be too specific and thus often don't capture the broader intent of queries linked to them. Weighted precision is again highest for the 0.8 setting, coming in at a healthy 0.84. As expected, raw pseudo recall falls as the threshold tightens, but the weighted metric is far more stable. Again, threshold 0.8 scores the best on this metric.

Overall the metrics indicate that our unsupervised algorithm achieves results that are deemed quite sensible when exposed to direct human judgment. The fact that raw accuracy was relatively stable, indicates that optimal choice of parameter will probably depend on other features of the output, which we'll now investigate.

4.3 Linking Queries to Leverage Scale

In Fig. 7 we plot the cumulative distribution of the count of intent clusters per query. For this figure and all the rest we plot all 4 threshold values. The first feature that is immediately apparent is that most queries map to a single intent cluster. This is especially true for the 0.95 setting, which has the sparsest knowledge graph. For all parameter settings, 90% of queries map to 2 or less intent clusters. That being said, the distribution exhibits heavy tails. We have censored the x-axis at 10, but it extends well into the 100's, which can be seen in Fig. 8. The log-log density plot shows the familiar linear patterns of a heavy tailed distribution.

The number of intent clusters that a query maps to captures the diversity of intent for a given unit of expression. What the data reveal is that while most queries seem to have a single intent (this also due to the sparseness of the query-document graph, as previously mentioned), a non-negligible fraction

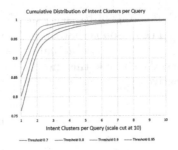

Fig. 7. CDF of the number intent clusters with an edge to a submitted query.

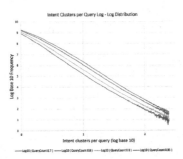

Fig. 8. PDF of the number intent clusters with an edge to a submitted query, log-log scale.

have quite diverse intent. Indeed, subsequent analysis reveals these more diverse intent queries tend to have higher volume, in part because they are more generic ("Aretha Franklin" vs. "Aretha Franklin's second album").

One might wonder if the fact that most queries map to one intent query is a function of the fact that intent clusters tend to contain very few documents and thus very few queries linking to them. In Fig. 9 captures how many in-links intent clusters have. The CDF reveals that yes, there are many small clusters. As expected, the 0.95 setting has the smallest clusters. However, for looser thresholds, most clusters have more than 5 queries linking in, and approximately 20% have more than 20 underlying queries. This shows that we have substantially reduced the sparsity of the query-document graph shown in Table 1. By reducing this sparsity, learning via historical examples becomes a much more promising avenue to improve search engine performance.

We have seen so far that the tighter the threshold, the fewer queries per cluster and fewer clusters per query. In Fig. 10 we show how the number of non-singleton set clusters formed changes with each parameter setting. Examining the 0.7 setting, we see that there are roughly 120 million clusters. To put this number in perspective, we saw that roughly 75% of all intent clusters mapped to a single query, meaning they were a singleton set and excluded. The remaining set of queries, however, is quite large, 1.1 billion to be precise. Of these 1.1 billion "unique" queries, we identify that the underlying unique intent is 10-fold

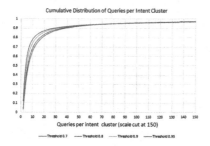

Fig. 9. CDF of the number of queries per queries per intent cluster.

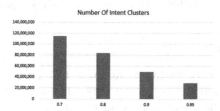

Fig. 10. Number of intent clusters per method.

smaller. This is a substantial "reduction in uniqueness." The other thresholds deflate uniqueness more aggressively, but also leave more singleton sets, as shown in Fig. 7. Given that human judged accuracy as similar across thresholds, these results point to using 0.7 as the threshold.

To summarize the results, we see that the choice of threshold has a large impact on the resulting knowledge graph. A smaller threshold allows more non-singleton intent clusters (connected components) to form in the document similarity graph. At first this might seem counter-intuitive. Since clusters are identified by connected components, adding more links could connect more existing components and reduce the number of clusters. However, the countervailing force is that in a graph this sparse and that displays so much isolation, adding links tends to form more clusters than it ties together. This highlights the role of scale in forming a richer graph.

The 0.70 threshold setting is shown to identify approximately 118 million intent clusters from the nearly 1.1 billion "unique" queries that link to more than one document. Indeed these are the queries that have the higher volume in terms of searches (almost by construction), so the "reduction of uniqueness" our method offers in terms of *search volume* is greater still. Figure 11 shows the relationship between direct and indirect volume (in log-log scale). We note that at low direct volume levels, indirect views are often two orders of magnitude greater, highlighting the importance of these links. We conducted experiments that artificially limited the scale of data we gave ourselves access to and saw the expected dramatic reductions in links within the query-document graph.

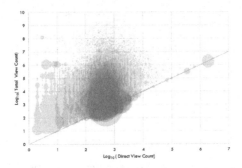

Fig. 11. Relationship between direct vs. indirect query counts

4.4   Impact on CTR

We now link the number of "indirect examples" to CTR performance by repeating the "new query analysis" using both direct historical examples and indirect historical examples (the queries linked in the graph) as features. Our findings are summarized as follows:

$$y_{ctr} - \text{Success-CTR} \qquad v_{id} - \text{Indirect View Count} \qquad v_d - \text{Direct View Count}$$
$$y_{ctr} = \alpha + \beta_1 v_{id} + \beta_2 v_d$$
$$\alpha = 0.742 \ [0.740, 0.745]$$
$$\beta_1 = 2.251 \ 10^{-05} \ [2.79 \ 10^{-07}, 4.48 \ 10^{-05}] \ \text{i.e. } 0.02\% \text{ to } 4.48 \ \% \text{ per } 1000$$
$$\beta_2 = 1.109 \ 10^{-05} \ [0.528 \ 10^{-06}, 1.69 \ 10^{-05}] \ \text{i.e. } 0.5\% \text{ to } 1.7\% \text{ per } 1000$$

We find both (direct and indirect views) are statistically significant predictors of CTR and higher click positions on the page. For CTR, the coefficient on indirect views, conditional on direct views, is 0.000022, indicating that 1,000 indirect views predicts a rise in CTR of 0.02, which is consistent with our previous findings. Our previous finding was 1 to 3% and about 2%. This indicates that while direct examples are more important, leveraging related queries is an important factor as well. Given that scale increases the density of the query-document graph and thus the ability to find related queries, this points to another source of advantage conferred to scale.

5   Discussion and Conclusion

It is well known that, like most statistical learning problems, efficiently designed search engines have errors proportional to $n^{-1/2}$, where n is the amount of data. As data accumulates, search engines should improve, but how much does this scale economy matter? One perspective on competition among search engines is that even a 1% share represents billions of searches per year. But the scale of the problem solved by modern search engines has grown along with the data. Where AltaVista indexed millions of search pages, modern search engines index billions of pages. So while modern search engines have more data than they did a decade ago, they solve a harder problem than they did, making it entirely unclear whether the increase in scale makes the problem easier or harder.

The frequency of unique queries does not actually measure how hard the problem is, unfortunately. Consider the problem of "Pasadena Ethiopian Restaurant." The first time this query was entered (as far as we can tell), both search engines provided excellent results. Why? Because there are nearby queries; essentially all portions – Ethiopian, Pasadena and Restaurant – are understandable based on past data, and search engines can identify the relevant documents even though the query is rare. This spillover of knowledge from one query to another means that the counts of queries is a flawed measure of the data advantage. We apply an approach motived by past work that directly document these effects.

To address the complexity of the problem solved by search engines, we use two strategies. First, we look at new queries. These are queries that have been rare and then become much more common. This lets us see how the search engines respond to new data. We find that both search engines improve significantly as more data flows in. While we illustrate that process quantitatively, there are two caveats. First, we see almost all the data for one of the search engines and much less for the other. Thus, the scale of the measurement varies across the two engines. Second, it could well be that there are other queries bringing relevant data to the problem, because they help the search engine improve the matching not just for one query but for a set of queries. Nevertheless, we do find substantial improvement on rare queries as more data flows in, which demonstrates that both search engines are data starved in the sense that they benefit significantly from more data on a substantial portion of the queries, perhaps as many as half the queries and 15% of the searches.

One potential objection to the approach we take is that perhaps the available results get better as more people enter a specific query, because web pages specifically constructed to be clickable are created. We show that this is unlikely—around 98% of the pages already existed—but more work could be done on this topic. Indeed, the ecosystem effects of consumer search and gaming of search engines remain interesting topics beyond the scope of this paper.

To address knowledge spillovers, where data from "Pasadena restaurant" helps a search engine with "Pasadena Ethiopian Restaurant," we constructed a knowledge graph. The knowledge graph identifies related queries and lets us identify both direct (searches for that query) and indirect (searches for closely related queries) data that can be brought to bear in finding the right answers to a query. One finding that suggests that the knowledge graph was well-constructed is that we can predict the click through rate as a function of both direct and indirect data, and find both are relevant, with similar coefficients.

The knowledge graph model confirms that data—both direct and indirect—matters at scale. Moreover, and more interestingly, it lets us quantify how many queries have a modest amount of total data. We find approximately 10% of the queries have less than 1000 relevant observations, and 18% have less than 10,000. This addresses the question of how much data can actually be brought to bear on answering rare queries.

Search engines are arguably one of the most complicated engineering tasks ever attempted, matching billions of queries to billions of web pages. While there are probably increasing returns to scale for small amounts of data, there are eventually diminishing returns. Many markets are characterized by two major search engines, with one larger than the other. What we observe in the North American market is that both search engines are well into the region of diminishing returns, but there is still a significant return to data. The effects we estimate are of modest size, 1–4% points, meaning that a major algorithmic improvement could swamp the advantage of a larger incumbent. That being said, it is well known that effects of this size are large in terms of differentiating performance from a competitor and thus strongly suggest that major search engines still operate in a region where more data matters.

References

1. Baeza-Yates, R., Tiberi, A.: Extracting semantic relations from query logs. In: Proceedings of the 13th ACM SIGKDD International Conference on Knowledge Discovery and Data Mining, pp. 76–85. ACM (2007)
2. Beeferman, D., Berger, A.: Agglomerative clustering of a search engine query log. In: Proceedings of the Sixth ACM SIGKDD International Conference on Knowledge Discovery and Data Mining, pp. 407–416. ACM (2000)
3. Bordino, I., Castillo, C., Donato, D., Gionis, A.: Query similarity by projecting the query-flow graph. In: Proceedings of the 33rd International ACM SIGIR Conference on Research and Development in Information Retrieval, pp. 515–522. ACM (2010)
4. Craswell, N., Szummer, M.: Random walks on the click graph. In: Proceedings of the 30th Annual International ACM SIGIR Conference on Research and Development in Information Retrieval, pp. 239–246. ACM (2007)
5. Craswell, N., Zoeter, O., Taylor, M., Ramsey, B.: An experimental comparison of click position-bias models. In: Proceedings of the 2008 International Conference on Web Search and Data Mining, pp. 87–94. ACM (2008)
6. Goel, S., Broder, A., Gabrilovich, E., Pang, B.: Anatomy of the long tail: ordinary people with extraordinary tastes. In: Proceedings of the Third ACM International Conference on Web Search and Data Mining, pp. 201–210. ACM (2010)
7. Li, X., Wang, Y.Y., Acero, A.: Learning query intent from regularized click graphs. In: Proceedings of the 31st Annual International ACM SIGIR Conference on Research and Development in Information Retrieval, pp. 339–346. ACM (2008)
8. Liu, X., Song, Y., Liu, S., Wang, H.: Automatic taxonomy construction from keywords. In: Proceedings of the 18th ACM SIGKDD International Conference on Knowledge Discovery and Data Mining, pp. 1433–1441. ACM (2012)
9. Sadikov, E., Madhavan, J., Wang, L., Halevy, A.: Clustering query refinements by user intent. In: Proceedings of the 19th International Conference on World Wide Web, pp. 841–850. ACM (2010)
10. Wen, J.R., Nie, J.Y., Zhang, H.J.: Query clustering using user logs. ACM Trans. Inf. Syst. 20(1), 59–81 (2002)

Simple Pricing Schemes for the Cloud

Ian A. Kash[1], Peter Key[1], and Warut Suksompong[2](✉)

[1] Microsoft Research, Cambridge, UK
{iankash,Peter.Key}@microsoft.com
[2] Department of Computer Science, Stanford University, Stanford, USA
warut@cs.stanford.edu

Abstract. The problem of pricing the cloud has attracted much recent attention due to the widespread use of cloud computing and cloud services. From a theoretical perspective, several mechanisms that provide strong efficiency or fairness guarantees and desirable incentive properties have been designed. However, these mechanisms often rely on a rigid model, with several parameters needing to be precisely known in order for the guarantees to hold. In this paper, we consider a stochastic model and show that it is possible to obtain good welfare and revenue guarantees with simple mechanisms that do not make use of the information on some of these parameters. In particular, we prove that a mechanism that sets the same price per time step for jobs of any length achieves at least 50% of the welfare and revenue obtained by a mechanism that can set different prices for jobs of different lengths, and the ratio can be improved if we have more specific knowledge of some parameters. Similarly, a mechanism that sets the same price for all servers even though the servers may receive different kinds of jobs can provide a reasonable welfare and revenue approximation compared to a mechanism that is allowed to set different prices for different servers.

1 Introduction

With cloud computing generating billions of dollars per year and forming a significant portion of the revenue of large software companies [10], the problem of how to price cloud resources and services is of great importance. On the one hand, for a pricing scheme to be used, it is necessary that the scheme provide strong welfare and revenue guarantees. On the other hand, it is also often desirable that the scheme be simple. We combine the two objectives in this paper and show that simple pricing schemes perform almost as well as more complicated ones with respect to welfare and revenue guarantees. In particular, consider the pricing scheme for virtual machines on Microsoft Azure shown in Fig. 1. Once the user chooses the basic parameters such as region, type, and instance size, the price is calculated by simply multiplying an hourly base price by the number of virtual machines and number of hours desired. The question that we study can be phrased in this setting as follows: How much more welfare or revenue

---

The full version of this paper is available at http://arxiv.org/abs/1705.08563.

© Springer International Publishing AG 2017
N. R. Devanur and P. Lu (Eds.): WINE 2017, LNCS 10674, pp. 311–324, 2017.
https://doi.org/10.1007/978-3-319-71924-5_22

could be created if instead of this simple multiplication formula, a complex table specifying the price for each number of hours were to be used? Our main result is that the former offers at worst a two approximation to the latter, both in terms of welfare and revenue. Similarly, we demonstrate that setting a single price for a group of servers, even though the servers may receive different kinds of jobs, can provide a reasonable welfare and revenue approximation compared to setting different prices for different servers.

In much of the prior work in this space, which focuses more explicitly on scheduling, prices depend in a complex way on a number of parameters (typically including job length, arrival time, deadline, and value) as well as the current state of the system [3, 11, 20, 21, 24]. A weakness of such schemes is that they require these parameters to be known up front in order for the desirable properties of the mechanisms, such as their approximation ratios, to hold. The availability of such information is not always realistic in practice. Even when it is in principle possible to provide this information, there is a cost to participants in both time and resources to figure it out. In this work, we show that good results are possible with no up front information.

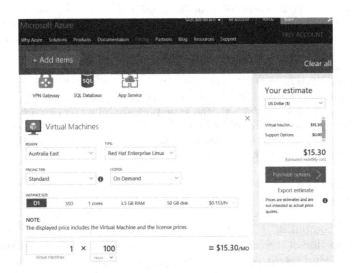

Fig. 1. Pricing scheme for virtual machines on Microsoft Azure [4].

For our initial results we assume that there is a single server, which receives jobs of various lengths whose value per time step is drawn from the same probability distribution regardless of length. We compare the welfare and revenue that can be obtained by setting a price per time step that is independent of the job length against the corresponding objective obtained by setting an individual price for each job length. When we are allowed the freedom of setting different prices for different job lengths, intuitively we want to set a higher price per time step for longer jobs as a premium for reserving the server for a longer period of time.[1] However, as we show, we do not lose more than 50% of the welfare or revenue if we are only allowed to set one price. We would like to emphasize that this is a worst-case bound over a wide range of parameters, including the number of job lengths, the distribution over job lengths, and the distribution over job values. Indeed, as we show, we can obtain improved bounds if we know the value of some of these parameters. The price that we use in the single-price setting can be chosen from one of the prices used in the multi-price setting, meaning that we do not have to calculate a price from scratch. Moreover, all of our approximation guarantees hold generally for arbitrary prices, meaning that for any prices that we may set in a multi-price setting (i.e., not necessarily optimal ones), we can obtain an approximation of the welfare or revenue by setting one of those prices alone. Finally, we emphasize that these results put no restrictions on the form of the distribution; it can be discrete, continuous, or mixed. The only substantive constraint is that jobs of all lengths share the same distribution of value per time step. However, in an extension we show that a version of our results continues to hold even if this constraint is relaxed.

We then generalize our results to a setting where there are multiple servers, each of which receives jobs of various lengths. The distribution over job lengths can be different for different servers. This is conceivable, for instance, if the servers are in various geographic locations or are utilized by various groups of users. We compare the welfare and revenue obtained by a simple pricing scheme that sets the same price for all servers against the corresponding objective achieved by a scheme that can set a different (single) price for each server. Roughly speaking, we show that as long as the parameters are not too extreme, e.g., the number of servers or the job lengths are not too large, then we do not lose too much of the welfare or revenue by setting a single price. Combining this with our initial results, we obtain an approximation of a very restricted pricing scheme where we must set the same price for all servers and all job lengths against one where we can set an individual price for each job length of each server. These results require an assumption that all servers have the same probability of not receiving a job at a time step. Using similar techniques, we also obtain approximation bounds when this assumption does not hold but there is only one job length across all servers.

1.1 Related Work

Much recent work has focused on designing online scheduling mechanisms with good welfare guarantees and incentive properties. Jain et al. [20] exhibited a truthful mechanism for batch jobs on cloud systems where jobs are allocated non-preemptively, and the same group of authors came up with mechanisms for deadline-sensitive jobs in large computing clusters [21]. Lucier et al. [24] also considered the problem of scheduling deadline-sensitive jobs; they circumvented

---

[1] Amazon recently started offering a product called "defined duration spot instances" where users can specify a duration in hourly increments up to six hours [2]. Indeed, the price *per hour* of this product increases as the number of hours increases.

known lower bounds by assuming that jobs could be delayed and still finish by their deadline. Zhang et al. [26] developed a framework for truthful online cloud auctions where users with heterogeneous demands can come and leave on the fly. More recently, Azar et al. [3] constructed a truthful mechanism that achieves a constant competitive ratio given that slackness is allowed, while Dehghani et al. [11] assumed a stochastic model and developed a truthful mechanism that approximates the expected maximum welfare up to a constant factor. Wang et al. [25] designed mechanisms for selling reserved instances where users are allowed to reserve resources of any length and from any time point in the future. Other work in this space has dealt with comparing pricing mechanisms such as the on-demand market and the spot market [1,12,19], achieving fairness in job allocation [17], and studying models of real-time pricing with budget constraints [18]. Kash and Key [22] gave a survey of the current state of research in economics and computer science with respect to cloud pricing.

From a technical perspective, our work bears a resemblance to the work of Dütting et al. on discriminatory and anonymous posted pricing and of Disser et al. on hiring secretaries. In particular, Dütting et al. [14] considered the problem of selling a single item to buyers who arrive sequentially with values drawn independently from identical distributions. They showed that by posting discriminatory prices, one can obtain at most $2 - 1/n$ times as much revenue as that obtained by posting the same anonymous price, where n is the number of buyers. As is also the case in our work, their anonymous price can always be chosen from one of the discriminatory prices, but their bound is obtained via a relaxation of the discriminatory pricing problem, a different technique than what we use. Disser et al. [13] provided a competitive online algorithm for a variant of the stochastic secretary problem, where applicants need to be hired over time. When each applicant arrives, the cost per time step of the applicant is revealed, and we have to decide on the duration of the employment. Once an applicant is accepted, we cannot terminate the contract until the duration of the job is over.

Our work falls into the broader area of the design and analysis of simple mechanisms, particularly posted price mechanisms. One of the motivations for studying simple mechanisms is that in practice, designers are often willing to partially give up optimality in return for simplicity. Mechanisms that simply post prices on goods have received significant attention since they reflect perhaps the most common way of selling goods in the real world, and moreover they leave no room for strategizing, making them easy for agents to participate in. A long line of work has investigated how well such mechanisms can approximate optimal mechanisms with respect to various objectives including welfare [9,15, 16], revenue [5–7], and social costs [8]. In Sect. 3.4 we show that techniques from this literature can recover some of our results under relaxed assumptions.

2   Preliminaries

We consider a system with a number of servers and discrete time steps. Each job takes an integer number of time steps to complete and yields a value upon completion. The value *per time step* of a job is drawn from a known distribution which is independent of the length of the job. Let F be the cumulative distribution function of this distribution and f the probability density function with respect to a base measure μ, and define $\ell(x) = xf(x)$.[2] We do not make any assumption on our distribution; in particular, it need not be continuous or discrete, which is why we allow flexibility in terms of the base measure.

When a job request is made for a job to be served by a server, there is a price p per time step which may depend on the job length and/or the server. If the value per time step of the job is at least p, the server accepts and executes the job to completion. Otherwise, the server rejects the job. The objectives in our model are the steady-state welfare and revenue for each pricing scheme. In particular, we will be interested in the expected welfare and revenue per time step, given that the job values are drawn from a probability distribution. This can also be thought of as the average welfare and revenue per time step that result from a pricing scheme over a long period of time.

In Sect. 3, we assume that there is a single server. Each time step, either zero or one job appears. A job with length a_i appears with probability $0 < r_i \leq 1$, where $\sum_{i=1}^{n} r_i \leq 1$ and n denotes the number of job lengths. We are allowed to set a price p_i for jobs of length a_i. If a server accepts a job of length a_i, it is busy and cannot accept other jobs for a_i time steps, including the current one. We compare the setting where we are forced to set the same price p for all job lengths against the setting where we can set a different price p_i for each job length a_i. Note that if we could set different prices for different job lengths, then to optimize welfare or revenue, intuitively we would set a higher price per time step for longer jobs as a premium for reserving the server for a longer period. Put differently, once we accept a longer job, we are stuck with it for a longer period, during which we miss the opportunity to accept other jobs. Consequently, we should set a higher standard for accepting longer jobs. (See also Footnote 1.)

In Sect. 4, we assume that there are multiple servers. Each time step, either zero or one job appears for each server $1 \leq j \leq n$. For server j, a job with length a_{ji} appears with probability $0 < r_{ji} \leq 1$ for $1 \leq i \leq n_j$, where n_j denotes the number of job lengths for server j. We do not assume that the set of job lengths or the number of job lengths are identical across servers. On the other hand, we assume that the probability of no job appearing at a time step is the same for all servers, i.e., $\sum_{i=1}^{n_j} r_{ji}$ is constant for any j. In Subsect. 4.1, we assume that we can set one price per server, and we compare the setting where we are forced to set the same price p for all servers against that where we can set a different price p_j for each server j. In Subsect. 4.2, we assume that we can set a different price p_{ji} for each server j and each of its job lengths a_{ji}, and we compare that

---

[2] For technical reasons, we will deviate slightly from the usual notion of cumulative distribution function. In particular, if y is a random variable drawn from a distribution, then we define its cumulative distribution function $F(x)$ as $\Pr[y < x]$ instead of the usual $\Pr[y \leq x]$. This will only be important when we deal with discrete distributions.

setting against that where we are forced to set the same price p for all servers and all job lengths.

All proofs can be found in the full version of this paper [23].

3   One Server

In this section, we assume that there is a single server, which receives jobs of various lengths. After presenting an introductory example in Subsect. 3.1, we consider the general setting with an arbitrary number of job lengths in Subsect. 3.2. In this setting, we show a 50% approximation for both welfare and revenue of setting one price for all job lengths compared to setting an individual price for each job length, for any realization of the parameters. Moreover, we show in Subsect. 3.3 that our techniques provide a template for deriving tighter bounds if we have more specific information on the parameters. In particular, when there are two job lengths, we show for each setting of the parameters a tight approximation bound for welfare and revenue. Our approximation results hold for arbitrary (i.e., not necessarily optimal) pricing schemes, and the price we use in the single-price setting can be drawn from one of the prices in the multi-price setting. Finally, in Subsect. 3.4 we consider an extension that does not assume independence between the job length and the value per time step.

3.1   Warm-Up: Uniform Distribution

As a warm-up example, assume that at any time step a job with length 1 or 2 appears with probability 50% each. The value per time step of a job is drawn from the uniform distribution over $[0, 1]$. Suppose that we set a price per time step p_1 for jobs of length 1 and p_2 for jobs of length 2.

Consider an arbitrary time step when the server is free. If the job drawn at that time step has length 1, then with probability p_1 it has value below p_1 and is rejected. In this case, the server passes one time step without a job. Otherwise, the job has value at least p_1 and is accepted. In this case, the expected welfare from executing the job is $\frac{1+p_1}{2}$. Similarly, if the job has length 2, then with probability p_2 it is rejected, and with probability $1 - p_2$ it is accepted and yields expected welfare $2 \cdot \frac{1+p_2}{2} = 1 + p_2$ over two time steps. Letting c_w denote the expected welfare per time step assuming that the server is free at the current time step, we have

$$0 = \frac{1}{2}\left(-p_1 c_w + (1 - p_1)\left(\frac{1 + p_1}{2} - c_w\right)\right) + \frac{1}{2}\left(-p_2 c_w + (1 - p_2)(1 + p_2 - 2c_w)\right).$$

The two terms on the right hand side correspond to jobs of length 1 and 2, which are drawn with probability $\frac{1}{2}$ each. In the case that a job of length 2 is drawn, with probability p_2 it is rejected and the server is idle for one time step, during which it would otherwise have produced expected welfare c_w. With the remaining probability $1 - p_2$ the job is accepted, yielding expected welfare $1 + p_2$ over two time steps, during which the server would otherwise have produced expected welfare $2c_w$. The derivation for the term corresponding to jobs of length 1 is similar. By equating the expected welfare with the variable denoting this quantity, we arrive at the equation above.

Solving for c_w, we get

$$c_w(p_1, p_2) = \frac{\frac{(1-p_1)(1+p_1)}{2} + (1 - p_2)(1 + p_2)}{3 - p_2}.$$

To maximize $c_w(p_1, p_2)$ over all values of p_1, p_2, we should set $p_1 = 0$. (Indeed, to maximize welfare we should always accept jobs of length 1 since they do not interfere with future jobs.) Then the value of p_2 that maximizes $c_w(p_1, p_2)$ is $p_2 = 3 - \sqrt{\frac{15}{2}} \approx 0.261$, yielding $c_w(p_1, p_2) = 6 - \sqrt{30} \approx 0.522$.

On the other hand, if we set the same price $p = p_1 = p_2$ for jobs with different lengths, our welfare per time step becomes

$$c_w(p) = \frac{\frac{(1-p)(1+p)}{2} + (1 - p)(1 + p)}{3 - p} = \frac{3(1 - p)(1 + p)}{2(3 - p)}.$$

This is maximized at $p = 3 - 2\sqrt{2} \approx 0.172$, yielding $c_w(p) = 9 - 6\sqrt{2} \approx 0.515$. Moreover, if we use either of the prices in the optimal price combination for the two-price setting as the single price, we get $c_w(0) = 0.5$ and $c_w\left(3 - \sqrt{\frac{15}{2}}\right) \approx 0.510$.

Next, we repeat the same exercise for revenue. We can derive the equations in the same way, with the only difference being that the revenue from accepting a job at price p is simply p. Letting c_r denote the revenue per time step, we have

$$0 = \frac{1}{2}\left(-p_1 c_r + (1 - p_1)(p_1 - c_r)\right) + \frac{1}{2}\left(-p_2 c_r + (1 - p_2)(2p_2 - 2c_r)\right).$$

Solving for c_r, we get

$$c_r(p_1, p_2) = \frac{(1 - p_1)p_1 + 2(1 - p_2)p_2}{3 - p_2}.$$

To maximize c_r over all values of p_1, p_2, we should set $p_1 = 0.5$. (Indeed, to maximize revenue we should always set the monopoly price for jobs of length 1 since they do not interfere with future jobs.) Then the value of p_2 that maximizes $c_r(p_1, p_2)$ is $p_2 = 3 - \sqrt{\frac{47}{8}} \approx 0.576$, yielding $c_r(p_1, p_2) = 10 - \sqrt{94} \approx 0.304$.

On the other hand, if we set the same price $p = p_1 = p_2$ for jobs with different lengths, our revenue per time step becomes

$$c_r(p) = \frac{(1 - p)p + 2(1 - p)p}{3 - p} = \frac{3(1 - p)p}{3 - p}.$$

This is maximized at $p = 3 - \sqrt{6} \approx 0.551$, yielding $c_r(p) = 15 - 6\sqrt{6} \approx 0.303$. Moreover, if we use either of the prices in the optimal price combination for the two-price setting as the single price, we get $c_r(0.5) = 0.3$ and $c_r\left(3 - \sqrt{\frac{47}{8}}\right) \approx$ 0.302.

Observe that for both welfare and revenue, the maximum in the one-price setting is not far from that in the two-price setting. In addition, in both cases at least one of the two prices in the optimal price combination for the two-price setting, when used alone as a single price, performs almost as well as the maximum in the two-price setting. In the remainder of this section, we will show that this is not a coincidence, but rather a phenomenon that occurs for any set of job lengths, any probability distribution over job lengths, and any probability distribution over job values.

3.2   General 50% Approximation

In this subsection, we consider a general setting with an arbitrary number of job lengths. We show that even at this level of generality, it is always possible to obtain 50% of the welfare and revenue of setting an individual price for each job length by setting just one price. Although the optimal price in the one-price setting might be different from any of the prices in the multiple-price setting, we show that at least one of the prices in the latter setting can be used alone to achieve the 50% guarantee.

Assume that there are jobs of lengths $a_1 \le a_2 \le \cdots \le a_n$ which appear at each time step with probability $r_1, r_2, \ldots, r_n$, respectively. Suppose that we set a price per time step p_i for jobs of length a_i. Recall that the value per time step of a job is drawn from a distribution with cumulative distribution function F and probability density function f.

The following lemma gives the formulas for the expected welfare and revenue per time step.

Lemma 3.1. *Let* $S = a_1 r_1 + \cdots + a_n r_n$ *and* $R = r_1 + \cdots + r_n$, *and let* c_w *and* c_r *denote the expected welfare and revenue per time step, respectively. We have*

$$c_w(p_1, \ldots, p_n) = \frac{a_1 r_1 \int_{x \ge p_1} \ell d\mu + \cdots + a_n r_n \int_{x \ge p_n} \ell d\mu}{S - ((a_1 - 1)r_1 F(p_1) + \cdots + (a_n - 1)r_n F(p_n)) + (1 - R)} \tag{1}$$

and

$$c_r(p_1, \ldots, p_n) = \frac{a_1 r_1 (1 - F(p_1))p_1 + \cdots + a_n r_n (1 - F(p_n))p_n}{S - ((a_1 - 1)r_1 F(p_1) + \cdots + (a_n - 1)r_n F(p_n)) + (1 - R)}. \tag{2}$$

In particular, if $p_1 = \cdots = p_n = p$, *then* $c_w(p) = \frac{S \int_{x \ge p} \ell d\mu}{S - (S - R)F(p) + (1 - R)}$ *and* $c_r(p) = \frac{S(1 - F(p))p}{S - (S - R)F(p) + (1 - R)}$.

With the formulas for welfare and revenue in hand, we are ready to show the main result of this section, which exhibits that the worst-case approximation ratio for welfare or revenue between the one-price setting and the multiple-price setting is at least 50%. As we will see later in Subsect. 3.3, this bound is in fact tight, and it remains tight even when there are only two job lengths. Note that the bound holds for any number of job lengths, any distribution over job lengths, and any distribution over job values.

Theorem 3.1. *For any prices $p_1, p_2, \ldots, p_n$ that we set in the multiple-price setting, we can achieve a welfare (resp. revenue, or any convex combination of welfare and revenue) approximation of at least 50% in the one-price setting by using one of the prices p_i as the single price.*

To prove Theorem 3.1, we work with the ratio $\frac{\max(c_w(p_1), \ldots, c_w(p_n))}{c_w(p_1, \ldots, p_n)}$ and show that it is at least $\frac{1}{2}$ for any $p_1, \ldots, p_n$ (and similarly for revenue or any convex combination of welfare and revenue). Using the formula (1) for c_w given in Lemma 3.1, we can write the ratio in terms of the variables $A_i = \frac{\int_{x \geq p_i} \ell d\mu}{\int_{x \geq p_1} \ell d\mu}$ and $B_i = F(p_i)$ for $1 \leq i \leq n$. For any fixed values of B_i, we then deduce the values of A_i that minimize the ratio of interest. Finally, we show that the remaining expression is always at least $1/2$ no matter the values of B_i.

3.3 Tighter Bounds for Specific Parameters

Assume in this subsection that there are jobs of two lengths $a < b$ which appear at each time step with probability r_1 and r_2, respectively, where $r_1 + r_2 \leq 1$. Suppose that we set a price per time step p_1 for jobs of length a and p_2 for jobs of length b. Recall that the value per time step of a job is drawn from a distribution with cumulative distribution function F and probability density function f.

Our next result exhibits a tight approximation bound for any fixed setting of the job lengths and their distribution.

Theorem 3.2. *For any prices p_1 and p_2 that we set in the two-price setting, we can achieve a welfare (resp. revenue, or any convex combination of welfare and revenue) approximation of at least*

$$\rho(a, b, r_1, r_2) := \frac{(ar_1 + br_2)(ar_1 + 1 - r_1)}{a(a-1)r_1^2 + a(b-1)r_1 r_2 + ar_1 + br_2}$$

in the one-price setting by setting either p_1 or p_2 alone. Moreover, this bound is the best possible even if we are allowed to set a price different from p_1 or p_2 in the one-price setting.

To prove this theorem, we work with the expression in terms of $B_i = F(p_i)$ that we have from the proof of Theorem 3.1. We then show that the expression is minimized when we take $B_1 = 0$ and $B_2 = 1$, meaning that the distribution on job values is bimodal. The proof method readily yields an example showing that our bound is tight, where the bimodal distribution on job values puts a large probability on a low value and a small probability on a high value.

If we fix the probabilities r_1, r_2, we can derive a tight worst-case bound over all possible job lengths a, b.

Theorem 3.3. *For fixed r_1, r_2, we have $\rho(a, b, r_1, r_2) \geq \frac{1}{1+r_1}$ for arbitrary a, b. Moreover, this bound is the best possible.*

Note that the fact that the bound is tight at $a = 1$ and $b \to \infty$ is consistent with the intuition that the further apart the job lengths are, the more welfare and revenue there is to be gained by setting different prices for the job lengths, and hence the worse the approximation ratio.

Finally, we show that we can obtain at least 50% of the welfare or revenue from setting two prices by using one of those prices.

Theorem 3.4. *For arbitrary a, b, r_1, r_2, we have $\rho(a, b, r_1, r_2) \geq \frac{1}{2}$. Moreover, this bound is the best possible.*

While we do not have a general formula for the worst-case approximation ratio for each choice of the parameters $a_1, \ldots, a_n, r_1, \ldots, r_n$ as we do for the case of two job lengths, the function h in the proof of Theorem 3.1 still allows us to derive a tighter bound for each specific case. Note that to find the minimum of h, it suffices to check $B_i = 0$ or 1 (see the full version of this paper [23] for details), so we only have a finite number of cases to check.

3.4   Extension

In this subsection, we show that by using a single price, we can obtain 50% of the welfare not only compared to using multiple prices, but also compared to the offline optimal welfare.[3] In fact, we will also not need the assumption that the job length and the value per time step are independent. However, the result only works for particular prices rather than arbitrary ones, and we cannot obtain tighter results for specific parameters using this method.

Theorem 3.5. *Assume that the job length and the value per time step are not necessarily independent. There exists a price p such that we can achieve a 50% approximation of the offline optimal welfare by using p as the single price.*

4   Multiple Servers

In this section, we assume that there are multiple servers, each of which receives jobs of various lengths. Under the assumption that the servers have the same probability of receiving no job at a time step, we show in Subsect. 4.1 an approximation bound of the welfare and revenue of setting one price for all servers compared to setting an individual price for each server. This yields a strong bound when at least one of the dimensions of the parameters is not too extreme, e.g., the number of servers or the job lengths are not too large. In Subsect. 4.2, we combine the newly obtained results with those from Sect. 3. Using a composition technique, we derive a general result that compares the welfare and revenue

---

[3] For the offline optimal welfare, we compute the limit of the expected average offline optimal welfare per time step as the time horizon grows.

obtained by a restricted mechanism that sets the same price for all servers and all job lengths against those obtained by a mechanism that can set a different price for each job length of each particular server. We show that even with the heavy restrictions, the former mechanism still provides a reasonable approximation to the latter one in a wide range of situations. Using similar techniques, we also obtain approximation bounds when this assumption does not hold but there is only one job length across all servers. The analysis of the latter setting can be found in the full version of this paper [23].

As in Sect. 3, our approximation results hold for arbitrary (i.e., not necessarily optimal) pricing schemes, and the price we use in the single-price setting can be drawn from one of the prices in the multi-price setting.

4.1 One Price per Server

Assume that at each time step, either zero or one job appears for each server $1 \leq j \leq n$. Server j receives jobs of length $a_{j1} \leq a_{j2} \leq \cdots \leq a_{jn_j}$ with probability $r_{j1}, r_{j2}, \ldots, r_{jn_j}$, respectively. Suppose that we set a price per time step p_j for all jobs on server j. Recall that the value per time step of a job is drawn from a distribution with cumulative distribution function F and probability density function f, and that we assume that $\sum_{i=1}^{n_j} r_{ji}$ is constant. Let $S_j = a_{j1}r_{j1} + \cdots + a_{jn_j}r_{jn_j}$ and $R = r_{j1} + \cdots + r_{jn_j}$.

Using the formula (1) for c_w given in Lemma 3.1, we find that the welfare per time step is

$$d_w(p_1, p_2, \ldots, p_n) = \sum_{j=1}^{n} \frac{\int_{x \geq p_j} \ell d\mu}{1 - \left(1 - \frac{R}{S_j}\right) F(p_j) + \frac{1-R}{S_j}}.$$

If we set the same price $p = p_1 = \cdots = p_n$ for different servers, our welfare per time step becomes $d_w(p) = \sum_{j=1}^{n} \frac{\int_{x \geq p} \ell d\mu}{1 - \left(1 - \frac{R}{S_j}\right) F(p) + \frac{1-R}{S_j}}$. The formulas $d_r(p_1, p_2, \ldots, p_n)$ and $d_r(p)$ for revenue are similar but with the terms $\int_{x \geq p_j} \ell d\mu$ replaced by $(1 - F(p_j))p_j$.

We show that if at least one dimension of the parameters is not too extreme, e.g., the number of servers or the job lengths are bounded, then we can obtain a reasonable approximation of the welfare and revenue in the multi-price setting by setting just one price.

Theorem 4.1. *For any prices $p_1, p_2, \ldots, p_n$ that we set in the multiple-price setting, we can achieve a welfare (resp. revenue, or any convex combination of welfare and revenue) approximation of at least*

$$\max\left(\frac{1}{H_n}, \frac{M-1}{M \ln M}\right)$$

in the one-price setting, where $H_n = 1 + \frac{1}{2} + \cdots + \frac{1}{n} \approx \ln n$ is the nth Harmonic number and $M = \max_{i,j} \frac{S_i}{S_j}$.

In particular, if all job lengths are bounded above by c, then $R \le S_j \le cR$ for all $1 \le j \le n$, and so $\max_{i,j} \frac{S_i}{S_j} \le c$. The theorem then implies that the approximation ratio is at least $\frac{c-1}{c \ln c}$.

4.2   Multiple Prices per Server

Assume as in Subsect. 4.1 that at each time step, server j receives jobs of length $a_{j1} \le a_{j2} \le \cdots \le a_{jn_j}$ with probability $r_{j1}, r_{j2}, \ldots, r_{jn_j}$, respectively. In this subsection, we consider setting an individual price not only for each server but also for each job length of that server. In particular, suppose that we set a price per time step p_{ji} for jobs of length a_{ji} on server j. Recall that the value per time step of a job is drawn from a distribution with cumulative distribution function F and probability density function f, and that we assume that $\sum_{i=1}^{n_j} r_{ji}$ is constant. Let $S_j = a_{j1} r_{j1} + \cdots + a_{jn_j} r_{jn_j}$.

We will compare a setting where we have considerable freedom with our pricing scheme and can set a different price p_{ji} for each job length a_{ji} on each server j with a setting where we have limited freedom and must set the same price p for all job lengths and all servers. We show that by "composing" our results on the two dimensions, we can obtain an approximation of the welfare and revenue of setting different prices by setting a single price.

Theorem 4.2. *For any prices p_{ji}, where $1 \le j \le n$ and $1 \le i \le n_j$ for each j, that we set in the multiple-price setting, we can achieve a welfare (resp. revenue, or any convex combination of welfare and revenue) approximation of at least*

$$\frac{1}{2} \cdot \max \left(\frac{1}{H_n}, \frac{M-1}{M \ln M} \right)$$

in the one-price setting, where $H_n = 1 + \frac{1}{2} + \cdots + \frac{1}{n} \approx \ln n$ is the nth Harmonic number and $M = \max_{i,j} \frac{S_i}{S_j}$.

If we have tighter approximations for either the "different prices for different job lengths" or the "different prices for different servers" dimension, for instance by knowing the values of some of the parameters, then the same composition argument yields a correspondingly tighter bound.

5   Conclusion

In this paper, we study how well simple pricing schemes that are oblivious to certain parameters can approximate optimal schemes with respect to welfare and revenue, and prove several results when the simple schemes are restricted to setting the same price for all servers or all job lengths. Our results provide an explanation of the efficacy of such schemes in practice, including the one shown in Fig. 1 for virtual machines on Microsoft Azure. Since simple schemes do not require agents to spend time and resources to determine their specific parameter values, our results also serve as an argument in favor of using these schemes in a range of applications. It is worth noting that as all of our results are of worst case nature, we can expect the guarantees on welfare and revenue to be significantly better than these pessimistic bounds in practical instances where the parameters are not adversarially tailored.

We believe that there is still much interesting work to be done in the study of simple pricing schemes for the cloud. We conclude our paper by listing some intriguing future directions.

- In many scheduling applications, a job can be scheduled online to any server that is not occupied at the time. Does a good welfare or revenue approximation hold in such a model?
- Can our results be extended to models with more fluid job arrivals, for example one where several jobs can arrive at each time step?
- Can we approximate welfare and revenue simultaneously? A trivial randomized approach would be to choose with equal probability whether to approximate welfare or revenue. According to Theorem 3.1, this yields a 1/4-approximation for both expected welfare and expected revenue of the single-price setting in comparison to the multi-price setting for job lengths.

References

1. Abhishek, V., Kash, I.A., Key, P.: Fixed and market pricing for cloud services. In: The 7th Workshop on the Economics of Networks, Systems and Computation (2012)
2. Amazon EC2 Spot Instances Pricing (2017). http://aws.amazon.com/ec2/spot/pricing. Accessed 1 Aug 2017
3. Azar, Y., Kalp-Shaltiel, I., Lucier, B., Menache, I., Naor, J.S., Yaniv, J.: Truthful online scheduling with commitments. In: Proceedings of the Sixteenth ACM Conference on Economics and Computation, pp. 715–732 (2015)
4. Microsoft Azure Pricing Calculator (2016). http://azure.microsoft.com/en-us/pricing/calculator. Accessed 19 Sept 2016
5. Babaioff, M., Blumrosen, L., Dughmi, S., Singer, Y.: Posting prices with unknown distributions. In: Innovations in Computer Science - ICS 2010, pp. 166–178 (2011)
6. Blumrosen, L., Holenstein, T.: Posted prices vs. negotiations: an asymptotic analysis. In: Proceedings of the 9th ACM Conference on Electronic Commerce, p. 49 (2008)
7. Chawla, S., Hartline, J.D., Malec, D.L., Sivan, B.: Multi-parameter mechanism design and sequential posted pricing. In: Proceedings of the 42nd ACM Symposium on Theory of Computing, pp. 311–320 (2010)
8. Cohen, I.R., Eden, A., Fiat, A., Jez, L.: Pricing online decisions: beyond auctions. In: Proceedings of the Twenty-Sixth Annual ACM-SIAM Symposium on Discrete Algorithms, pp. 73–91 (2015)
9. Cohen-Addad, V., Eden, A., Feldman, M., Fiat, A.: The invisible hand of dynamic market pricing. In: Proceedings of the 2016 ACM Conference on Economics and Computation, pp. 383–400 (2016)

10. Columbus, L.: Roundup of cloud computing forecasts and market estimates, 2016 (2016). http://www.forbes.com/sites/louiscolumbus/2016/03/13/roundup-of-cloud-computing-forecasts-and-market-estimates-2016. Accessed 19 Sept 2016

11. Dehghani, S., Kash, I.A., Key, P.: Online stochastic scheduling and pricing the cloud. Working Paper (2016)

12. Dierks, L., Seuken, S.: Cloud pricing: the spot market strikes back. In: The Workshop on Economics of Cloud Computing (2016)

13. Disser, Y., Fearnley, J., Gairing, M., Göbel, O., Klimm, M., Schmand, D., Skopalik, A., Tönnis, A.: Hiring secretaries over time: the benefit of concurrent employment. CoRR, abs/1604.08125 (2016)

14. Dütting, P., Fischer, F.A., Klimm, M.: Revenue gaps for discriminatory and anonymous sequential posted pricing. CoRR, abs/1607.07105 (2016)

15. Ezra, T., Feldman, M., Roughgarden, T., Suksompong, W.: Pricing identical items. CoRR, abs/1705.06623 (2017)

16. Feldman, M., Gravin, N., Lucier, B.: Combinatorial auctions via posted prices. In: Proceedings of the Twenty-Sixth Annual ACM-SIAM Symposium on Discrete Algorithms, pp. 123–135 (2015)

17. Friedman, E.J., Ghodsi, A., Psomas, C.: Strategyproof allocation of discrete jobs on multiple machines. In: Proceedings of the Fifteenth ACM Conference on Economics and Computation, pp. 529–546 (2014)

18. Friedman, E., Rácz, M.Z., Shenker, S.: Dynamic budget-constrained pricing in the cloud. In: Barbosa, D., Milios, E. (eds.) CANADIAN AI 2015. LNCS, vol. 9091, pp. 114–121. Springer, Cham (2015). https://doi.org/10.1007/978-3-319-18356-5_10

19. Hoy, D., Immorlica, N., Lucier, B.: On-demand or spot? Selling the cloud to risk-averse customers. In: Cai, Y., Vetta, A. (eds.) WINE 2016. LNCS, vol. 10123, pp. 73–86. Springer, Heidelberg (2016). https://doi.org/10.1007/978-3-662-54110-4_6

20. Jain, N., Menache, I., Naor, J.S., Yaniv, J.: A truthful mechanism for value-based scheduling in cloud computing. In: Persiano, G. (ed.) SAGT 2011. LNCS, vol. 6982, pp. 178–189. Springer, Heidelberg (2011). https://doi.org/10.1007/978-3-642-24829-0_17

21. Jain, N., Menache, I., Naor, J.S., Yaniv, J.: Near-optimal scheduling mechanisms for deadline-sensitive jobs in large computing clusters. In: Proceedings of the 24th ACM Symposium on Parallelism in Algorithms and Architectures, pp. 255–266 (2012)

22. Kash, I.A., Key, P.: Pricing the cloud. IEEE Internet Comput. 20(1), 36–43 (2016)

23. Kash, I.A., Key, P., Suksompong, W.: Simple pricing schemes for the cloud. CoRR, abs/1705.08563 (2017)

24. Lucier, B., Menache, I., Naor, J.S., Yaniv, J.: Efficient online scheduling for deadline-sensitive jobs. In: Proceedings of the 25th ACM Symposium on Parallelism in Algorithms and Architectures, pp. 305–314 (2013)

25. Wang, C., Ma, W., Qin, T., Chen, X., Hu, X., Liu, T.-Y.: Selling reserved instances in cloud computing. In: Proceedings of the 24th International Conference on Artificial Intelligence, pp. 224–230 (2015)

26. Zhang, H., Li, B., Jiang, H., Liu, F., Vasilakos, A.V., Liu, J.: A framework for truthful online auctions in cloud computing with heterogeneous user demands. In: Proceedings of the IEEE INFOCOM 2013, pp. 1510–1518 (2013)

The Price of Uncertainty in Present-Biased Planning

Susanne Albers and Dennis Kraft(✉)

Department of Computer Science, Technical University of Munich, Munich, Germany
{albers,kraftd}@in.tum.de

Abstract. The tendency to overestimate immediate utility is a common cognitive bias. As a result people behave inconsistently over time and fail to reach long-term goals. Behavioral economics tries to help affected individuals by implementing external incentives. However, designing robust incentives is often difficult due to imperfect knowledge of the parameter $\beta \in (0, 1]$ quantifying a person's present bias. Using the graphical model of Kleinberg and Oren [8], we approach this problem from an algorithmic perspective. Based on the assumption that the only information about β is its membership in some set $B \subset (0, 1]$, we distinguish between two models of uncertainty: one in which β is fixed and one in which it varies over time. As our main result we show that the conceptual loss of efficiency incurred by incentives in the form of penalty fees is at most 2 in the former and $1 + \max B/\min B$ in the latter model. We also give asymptotically matching lower bounds and approximation algorithms.

Keywords: Approximation algorithms · Behavioral economics
Heterogeneous agents · Incentive design · Penalty fees
Variable present bias

1 Introduction

Many goals in life such as losing weight, passing an exam or paying off a loan require long-term planning. But while some people stick to their plans, others lack self-control; they eat unhealthy food, delay their studies and take out new loans. In behavioral economics the tendency to change a plan for no apparent reason is known as *time-inconsistent behavior*. The questions are, what causes these inconsistencies and why do they affect some more than others? A common explanation is that people make present biased decisions, i.e., they assign disproportionately greater value to the present than to the future. In this simplifying model a person's behavior is the mere result of her present bias and the setting in which she is placed. However, the interplay between these two factors is intricate and sometimes counter-intuitive as the following example demonstrates:

Consider two runners Alice and Bob who have two weeks to prepare for an important race. Each week they must choose between two types of workout.

Work supported by the European Research Council, Grant Agreement No. 691672.

N. R. Devanur and P. Lu (Eds.): WINE 2017, LNCS 10674, pp. 325–339, 2017.
https://doi.org/10.1007/978-3-319-71924-5_23

Type A always incurs an effort of 1, whereas type B incurs an effort of 3 in the first and 9 in the second week. Since A offers less preparation than B, Alice and Bob's effort in the final race is 13 if they consistently choose A and 1 if they consistently choose B. Furthermore, A and B are incompatible in the sense that switching between the two will result in an effort of 16 in the final race. Figure 1 models this setting as a directed acyclic graph G with terminal nodes s and t. The intermediate nodes v_X and v_{XY} represent a person's state after completing the workouts $X, Y \in \{A, B\}$. To move forward with the training, Alice and Bob must perform the tasks associated with the edges of G, i.e., complete workouts and run the race. Looking at G it becomes clear that two consecutive workouts of type B are the most efficient routine in the long run. However, this is not necessarily the routine a present biased person will choose.

For instance, assume that Alice and Bob discount future costs by a factor of $a = 1/2 - \varepsilon$ and $b = 1/2 + \varepsilon$ respectively. We call a and b their present bias. At the beginning of the first week Alice and Bob compare different workout routines. From Alice's perspective two workouts of type A are strictly more preferable to two workouts of type B as she anticipates an effort of $1 + a(1 + 13) = 8 - 14\varepsilon$ for the former and $3 + a(9 + 1) = 8 - 10\varepsilon$ for the latter. A similar calculation for Bob shows that he prefers two workouts of type B. Considering that neither Alice nor Bob finds a mix of A and B particularly interesting at this point, we conclude that Alice chooses A in the first week and Bob B. However, come next week, Bob expects an effort of $1 + b16 = 8 + 16\varepsilon$ for A and $9 + b = 19/2 + \varepsilon$ for B. Assuming ε is small enough, A suddenly becomes Bob's preferred option and he switches routines. Alice on the other hand has no reason to change her mind and sticks to A. As a result she pays much less than Bob during practice and in the final race. This is remarkable considering that her present bias is only marginally different from Bob's. Moreover, it seems surprising that only Bob behaves inconsistently, although he is less biased than Alice.

1.1 Related Work

Traditional economics and game theory are based on the assumption that people maximize their utility in a rational way. But despite their prevalence, these assumptions disregard psychological aspects of human decision making observed in empirical and experimental research [5]. For instance, time-inconsistent behavior such as procrastination seems paradox in the light of traditional economics. Nevertheless, it can be explained readily by a tendency to overestimate immediate utility in long-term planning, see e.g. [13]. By studying such cognitive biases, behavioral economics tries to obtain more realistic economic models.

A significant amount of research in this field has been devoted to *temporal discounting* in general and *quasi-hyperbolic discounting* in particular, see [6] for a survey. The quasi-hyperbolic discounting model proposed by Laibson [11] is characterized by two parameters: the *present bias* $\beta \in (0, 1]$ and the *exponential discount rate* $\delta \in (0, 1]$. People who plan according to this model have an accurate perception of the present, but scale down any costs and rewards realized $t \geq 1$ time units in the future by a factor of $\beta\delta^t$. To keep our work clearly delineated in scope, we adopt Akerlof's model of quasi-hyperbolic discounting [1] and make

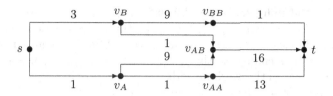

Fig. 1. Task graph of the running scenario

the following two assumptions: First, we focus on the present bias β and set the exponential discount rate to $\delta = 1$. Secondly, we assume people to be *naive* in the sense that they are unaware of their present bias and only optimize their current perceived utility when making a decision. Note that Alice and Bob from the previous example behave like agents in Akerlof's model for a present bias of $\beta = 1/2 - \varepsilon$ and $\beta = 1/2 + \varepsilon$ respectively.

Until recently the economic literature lacked a unifying and expressive framework for analyzing time-inconsistent behavior in complex social and economic settings. Kleinberg and Oren closed this gap by modeling the behavior of naively present biased individuals as a planning problem in task graphs like the one depicted in Fig. 1 [8]. We introduce this framework formally in Sect. 2. As a result of Kleinberg and Oren's work, an active line of research at the intersection of computer science and behavioral economics has emerged. For instance, the graphical model has been used to systematically analyze different types of quasi-hyperbolic discounting agents such as *sophisticated* agents who are fully or partially aware of their present bias [9] and agents whose present bias varies randomly over time [7]. Furthermore, the graphical model was used to shed light on the interplay between temporal biases and other types of cognitive biases [10].

The graphical model is of particular interest to us as it provides a natural framework for a design problem frequently encountered in behavioral economics. Given a certain social or economic setting, the problem is to improve a time-inconsistent person's performance via various sorts of *incentives*, such as monetary rewards, deadlines or penalty fees, see e.g. [12]. Using the graphical model, Kleinberg and Oren demonstrate how a strategic choice reduction can incentivize people to reach predefined goals [8]. To implement their incentives, they simply remove the corresponding edges from the task graph. However, there is a computational drawback to this approach. As we have shown in previous work, an optimal set of edges to remove from a task graph with n nodes is NP-hard to approximate within a factor less than $\sqrt{n}/3$ [2]. A more general form of incentives avoiding these harsh complexity theoretic limitations are penalty fees. In the graphical model penalty fees are at least as powerful as choice reduction and admit a polynomial time 2-approximation [3].

1.2   Incentive Design for an Uncertain Present Bias

Frederick, Loewenstein and O'Donoghue have surveyed several attempts to estimate people's temporal discount functions [6]. But as estimates differ widely across studies and individuals, the difficulty of predicting a person's temporal discount function becomes apparent. Clearly, this poses a serious challenge for the design of reliable incentives. After all, Alice and Bob's scenario demonstrates how arbitrarily small changes in the present bias can cause significant changes in a person's behavior. In this work we address the effects of incomplete information about a person's present bias in two different notions of uncertainty.

In Sect. 3 we consider naive individuals whose exponential discount rate is $\delta = 1$, but whose present bias β is unknown. The only prior information we have about β is its membership in some larger set B. Our goal is to construct incentives that are robust with respect to the uncertainty induced by B. More precisely, we are interested in incentives that work well for any present bias contained in B. An alternative perspective is that we try to construct incentives which are not limited to a single person, but serve an entire population of individuals with different present bias values. A simple instance of this problem in which a single task must be partitioned and stretched over a longer period of time has been studied by Kleinberg and Oren [8]. But like most research on incentivizing *heterogeneous* populations, see e.g. [12], Kleinberg and Oren's results are restricted to a very specific setting. They themselves suggest the design of more general incentives as a major research direction for the graphical framework [8].

Using penalty fees as our incentive of choice and a fixed reward to keep people motivated, we present the first results in this area. Our contribution is twofold. On the one hand, we try to quantify the conceptual loss of efficiency caused by incomplete knowledge of β. For this purpose we introduce a novel concept called *price of uncertainty*, which denotes the smallest ratio between the reward required by an incentive that accommodates all $\beta \in B$ and the reward required by an incentive designed for a specific $\beta \in B$. We present an elegant algorithmic argument to prove that the price of uncertainty is at most 2. Remarkably, this bound holds true independent of the underlying graph G and present bias set B. To complement our result, we construct a family of graphs G and present bias sets B for which the price of uncertainty converges to a value strictly greater than 1. On the other hand, we consider the computational problem of constructing penalty fees that work for all $\beta \in B$, but require as little reward as possible. Drawing on the same algorithmic ideas we used to bound the price of uncertainty yields a polynomial time 2-approximation. Furthermore, we present a non-trivial proof to show that the decision version of the problem is contained in NP. Since all hardness results of [3] also apply under uncertainty, we know that there is no 1.08192-approximation unless P = NP.

1.3   Incentive Design for a Variable Present Bias

In Sect. 4 we generalize our notion of uncertainty to individuals whose present bias β may change arbitrarily over time within the set B. This model is inspired by work of Gravin et al. [7], except that we do not rely on the assumption that β is drawn independently from a fixed probability distribution. Instead, our goal is to design penalty fees that work well for all possible sequences of β over time. We believe this to be an interesting extension of the fixed parameter case as the variability of β may capture changes in a person's temporal discount function caused by unforeseen cognitive biases different from her present bias. As a result we obtain more robust penalty fees.

Again, our contribution is twofold. On the one hand, we introduce the *price of variability* to quantify the conceptual loss of efficiency caused by unpredictable changes in β. Similar to the price of uncertainty, we define this quantity to be the smallest ratio between the reward required by an incentive that accommodates all possible changes of $\beta \in B$ over time and the reward required by an incentive designed for a specific and fixed $\beta \in B$. However, unlike the price of uncertainty, the price of variability has no constant upper bound. Instead, the ratio seems closely related to the *range* $\tau = \max B / \min B$ of the set B. By generalizing our algorithm from Sect. 3 we obtain an upper bound of $1 + \tau$ for the price of variability. To complement this result, we construct a family of graphs G for which the price of variability converges to $\tau/2$. On the other hand, we consider the computational aspects of constructing penalty fees for a variable β. As a result of the unbounded price of variability, we are not able to come up with a constant polynomial time approximation. Instead, we obtain a $(1 + \tau)$-approximation. However, by using a sophisticated reduction from VECTOR SCHEDULING, we prove that no efficient constant approximation is possible unless NP = ZPP. We conclude our work by studying a curious special case of variability in which individuals may temporarily lose their present bias. For this scenario, which is characterized by the assumption that $1 \in B$, optimal penalty fees can be computed in polynomial time.

2 The Model

In the following we introduce Kleinberg and Oren's graphical framework [8]. Let $G = (V, E)$ be a directed acyclic graph with n nodes that models some long-term project. The start and end states are denoted by the terminal nodes s and t. Furthermore, each edge e of G corresponds to a specific task whose inured effort is captured by a non-negative cost $c(e)$. To finish the project, a present biased agent must sequentially complete all tasks along a path from s to t. However, instead of following a fixed path, the agent constructs her path dynamically according to the following simple procedure:

When located at any node v different from t, the agent tries to evaluate the minimum cost she needs to pay in order to reach t. For this purpose she considers all outgoing edges (v, w) of her current position v. Because the tasks associated with these edges must be performed immediately, the agent assesses their cost correctly. In contrast, all future tasks, i.e., tasks on a path from v to t not incident to v, are discounted by her present bias of $\beta \in (0, 1]$. As a result, we define her *perceived cost* for taking (v, w) to be $d_\beta(v, w) = c(v, w) + \beta d(w)$, where $d(w)$ denotes the cost of a cheapest path from w to t. Furthermore, we define $d_\beta(v) = \min\{c(v, w) + \beta d(w) \mid (v, w) \in E\}$ to be the agent's *minimum perceived cost* at v. Since the agent is oblivious to her own present bias, she only traverses edges (v, w) for which $d_\beta(v, w) = d_\beta(v)$. Ties are broken arbitrarily. Once the agent reaches the next node, she reiterates this process.

To motivate the agent, a non-negative reward r is placed at t. Because the agent must reach t before she can collect r, her *perceived reward* for reaching t is βr at each node different from t. When located at $v \neq t$, the agent is only motivated to proceed if $d_\beta(v) \leq \beta r$. Otherwise, if $d_\beta(v) > \beta r$, she quits. We say that G is *motivating*, if she does not quit while constructing her path from s to t. Note that sometimes the agent can construct more than one path from s to t due to ties in the perceived cost of incident edges. In this case, G is considered motivating if she does not quit on any such path.

For the sake of a clear presentation, we will assume throughout this work that each node of G is located on a path from s to t. This assumption is sensible because the agent can only visit nodes reachable from s. Furthermore, she is not willing to enter nodes that do not lead to the reward at t. Consequently, only nodes that are on a path from s to t are relevant to her behavior. All nodes not satisfying this property can be removed from G in a simple preprocessing step.

2.1 Alice and Bob's Scenario

To illustrate the model, we revisit Alice and Bob's scenario. The task graph G is depicted in Fig. 1. Remember that $a = 1/2 - \varepsilon$ and $b = 1/2 + \varepsilon$ denote Alice and Bob's respective present bias. For convenience let $0 < \varepsilon \leq 1/54$. Furthermore, assume that a reward of $r = 27$ is awarded upon reaching t.

We proceed to analyze Alice and Bob's walk through G. At their initial position s they must decide whether they move to v_A or v_B. For this purpose they try to find a path that minimizes the perceived cost. As the more present biased person, Alice's favorite path is s, v_A, v_{AA}, t with a perceived cost of $d_a(s) = d_a(s, v_A) = 8 - 14\varepsilon$. By choice of ε this cost is covered by her perceived reward $ar = 27/2 - 27\varepsilon$. Consequently, she is motivated to traverse the first edge and moves to v_A. A similar argument shows that Bob moves to v_B. Once they reach their new nodes, Alice and Bob reevaluate plans. From Alice's perspective v_A, v_{AA}, t is still the cheapest path to t. Bob, however, suddenly prefers v_B, v_{AB}, t to his original plan. Nevertheless, both of their perceived cost remains covered by their perceived reward and they move to v_{AA} and v_{AB} respectively. At this point the only option is to take the direct edge to t. For Alice the perceived cost at v_{AA} is sufficiently small to let her reach t. In contrast, Bob's perceived cost of $d_b(v_{AB}) = 16$ exceeds his perceived reward of $br = 27/2 + 27\varepsilon$ and he quits.

2.2 Cost Configurations

Bob's behavior in the previous example demonstrates how present biased decisions can deter people from reaching predefined goals. To ensure an agent's success it is therefore sometimes necessary to implement external incentives such as penalty fees. In the graphical model, penalty fees allow us to arbitrarily raise the cost of edges in G. More formally, let $\tilde{c}$ be a so called *cost configuration*, which assigns a non-negative extra cost $\tilde{c}(e)$ to all edges e of G. The result is a new task graph $G_{\tilde{c}}$, whose edges e have a cost of $c(e) + \tilde{c}(e)$. A present biased agent navigates through $G_{\tilde{c}}$ according to the same rules applying in G. We say that $\tilde{c}$

is motivating if and only if $G_{\tilde{c}}$ is. To avoid ambiguity we annotate our notation whenever we consider a specific $\tilde{c}$, e.g., we write $d_{\tilde{c}}$ and $d_{\beta,\tilde{c}}$ instead of d and d_β.

We conclude this section with a brief demonstration of the positive effects penalty fees can have in Alice and Bob's scenario. Let $\tilde{c}$ be a cost configuration that assigns an extra cost of $\tilde{c}(v_B, v_{AB}) = 1/2$ to (v_B, v_{AB}) and $\tilde{c}(e) = 0$ to all other edges $e \neq (v_B, v_{AB})$. Note that G and $G_{\tilde{c}}$ are identical task graphs except for the cost of (v_B, v_{AB}). Because Alice does not plan to take (v_B, v_{AB}) on her way through G and has even less reason to do so in $G_{\tilde{c}}$, we know that $\tilde{c}$ does not affect her behavior. For similar reasons, $\tilde{c}$ does not affect Bob's choice to move to v_B. However, once Bob has reached v_B his perceived cost of the path v_B, v_{AB}, t is $d_{b,\tilde{c}}(v_B, v_{AB}) = 19/2 + 16\varepsilon$, whereas his perceived cost of v_B, v_{BB}, t is only $d_{b,\tilde{c}}(v_B, v_{BB}) = 19/2 + \varepsilon$. Since the latter option appears to be cheaper and is covered by his perceived reward, Bob proceeds to v_{BB} and then onward to t. As a result $\tilde{c}$ yields a task graph that is motivating for Alice and Bob alike. This is a considerable improvement to the original task graph.

3   Uncertain Present Bias

In this section we consider agents whose present bias β is uncertain in the sense that our only information about β is its membership in some set $B \subset (0,1]$. We call B the *present bias set*. For technical reasons we assume that B can be expressed as the union of constantly many closed subintervals from the set $(0,1]$. This way the intersection of B with a closed interval is either empty or contains an efficiently computable minimal and maximal element. To measure the degree of uncertainty induced by B, we define the range of B as $\tau = \max B / \min B$.

3.1   A Decision Problem

Our goal is to construct a cost configuration $\tilde{c}$ that is motivating for all $\beta \in B$, but requires as little reward as possible. To assess the complexity of this task, let UNCERTAIN PRESENT BIAS (UPB) be the following decision problem:

Definition 1 (UPB). *Given a task graph G, present bias set B and reward $r > 0$, decide whether a cost configuration $\tilde{c}$ motivating for all $\beta \in B$ exists.*

If $\tau = 1$, i.e., B only contains a single present bias parameter, UPB is identical to the decision problem MOTIVATING COST CONFIGURATION (MCC) studied in [3]. Since MCC is NP-complete, UPB must be NP-hard. But unlike MCC it is not immediately clear if UPB is also contained in NP. The reason is that proving MCC $\in$ NP only requires to verify whether a given cost configuration is motivating for a single value of β; a property that can be checked in polynomial time [2]. However, proving UPB $\in$ NP requires to verify whether a given cost configuration is motivating for all $\beta \in B$. Taking into account that B may very well be an infinite set, it becomes clear that we cannot check all values of β individually. Interestingly, we do not have to; checking a finite subset $B' \subseteq B$ of size $\mathcal{O}(n^2)$ turns out to be sufficient.

Proposition 1. *For any task graph G, reward r and present bias set B a finite subset $B' \subseteq B$ of size $\mathcal{O}(n^2)$ exists such that G is motivating for all $\beta \in B$ if it is motivating for all $\beta \in B'$.*

The above proposition is related to a theorem by Kleinberg and Oren, which bounds the number of paths an agent takes as β varies over $(0, 1]$ by $\mathcal{O}(n^2)$ [8]. Kleinberg and Oren's argument does not only establish existence of B', but also yields a polynomial time algorithm to construct B', which in turn implies that UPB $\in$ NP. Due to space constraints, we refer to the full version of this paper for a corresponding proof of Proposition 1 as well as all other omitted proofs.

Corollary 1. *UPB is NP-complete.*

3.2   The Price of Uncertainty

Since UPB is NP-complete, it makes sense to consider the corresponding optimization problem UPB-OPT. For this purpose, let $r(G, B)$ be the infimum over all rewards admitting a cost configuration motivating for all $\beta \in B$ and define:

Definition 2 (UPB-OPT). *Given a task graph G and present bias set B, determine $r(G, B)$.*

Clearly, UPB-OPT must be at least as hard as the optimization version of MCC. Consequently, we know that UPB has no PTAS and is NP-hard to approximate within a ratio less than 1.08192 [3]. But does the transition from a certain to an uncertain β reduce approximability?

Setting complexity theoretic considerations aside for a moment, an even more general question arises: How does the transition from a certain to an uncertain β affect the efficiency of cost configurations assuming unlimited computational resources? To quantify this conceptual difference in efficiency, we look at the smallest ratio between optimal cost configurations motivating for all $\beta \in B$ and optimal cost configurations motivating for a specific $\beta \in B$. We call this ratio the *price of uncertainty*.

Definition 3 (Price of Uncertainty). *Given a task graph G and a present bias set B, the price of uncertainty is defined as $r(G, B)/\sup\{r(G, \{\beta\}) \mid \beta \in B\}$.*

Let us illustrate the price of uncertainty by going back to Alice and Bob's scenario and assume that $B = \{a, b\}$ with $a = 1/2 - \varepsilon$ and $1/2 + \varepsilon$. In other words, the agent either behaves like Alice or she behaves like Bob, but we do not know which. It is easy to see that in either case the agent minimizes her maximum perceived cost on the way from s to t by taking the path $P = s, v_B, v_{BB}, t$. This minmax cost, which is either $d_a(v_B, v_{BB}) = 19/2 - \varepsilon$ or $d_b(v_B, v_{BB}) = 19/2 + \varepsilon$, provides two lower bounds for the necessary reward when divided by the respective present bias. More formally, it holds true that $r(G, \{a\}) \geq (19/2 - \varepsilon)/(1/2 - \varepsilon)$ and $r(G, \{b\}) \geq (19/2 + \varepsilon)/(1/2 + \varepsilon)$. However, as we have seen in Sect. 2, neither Alice nor Bob are willing to follow P without external incentives. To discourage the agent from leaving P, we assign an extra cost of $\tilde{c}(s, v_A) = 5\varepsilon$ to

Algorithm 1. UNCERTAINPRESENTBIASAPPROX

1 $b \leftarrow \min B$; $P \leftarrow$ minmax path from s to t w.r.t $d_b(e)$; $\alpha \leftarrow \max\{d_b(e) \mid e \in P\}$;
2 **foreach** $v \in V \setminus \{t\}$ **do** $\varsigma(v) \leftarrow$ successor of v on a cheapest path from v to t;
3 $T = \{(v, \varsigma(v)) \mid v \in V \setminus \{t\}\}$;
4 **foreach** $e \in E$ **do** $\tilde{c}(e) \leftarrow 0$;
5 **foreach** $e \in E \setminus (P \cup T)$ **do** $\tilde{c}(e) \leftarrow 2\alpha/b + 1$;
6 **foreach** $(v, w) \in T$ **such that** $v \in P$ **and** $w \notin P$ **do**
7    $\quad P' \leftarrow v, \varsigma(v), \varsigma(\varsigma(v)), \ldots, t$;
8    $\quad u \leftarrow$ first node of P' different from v that is also a node of P;
9    $\quad \tilde{c}(v, w) \leftarrow$ cost of most expensive edge of P' between v and u;
10 **return** $\tilde{c}$;

(s, v_A), $\tilde{c}(v_B, v_{AB}) = 1/2 + 16\varepsilon$ to (v_B, v_{AB}) and $\tilde{c}(e) = 0$ otherwise. This extra cost does not affect the agent's maximum perceived cost along P, which she still experiences at (v_B, v_{BB}). As a result, our bounds for $r(G, \{a\})$ and $r(G, \{b\})$ are tight and we get $\sup\{r(G, \{\beta\}) \mid \beta \in B\} = r(G, \{a\})$. Moreover, because we have used the same cost configuration $\tilde{c}$ to derive $r(G, \{a\})$ and $r(G, \{b\})$, it must hold true that $r(G, B) = \sup\{r(G, \{\beta\}) \mid \beta \in B\}$, implying that the price of uncertainty in Alice and Bob's scenario is 1.

3.3 Bounding the Price of Uncertainty

As Alice and Bob's scenario demonstrates, cost configurations designed for an uncertain β are not necessarily less efficient than those designed for a specific β. Therefore one might wonder whether scenarios exist in which a real loss of efficiency is bound to occur, i.e., can the price of uncertainty be greater than 1? The following proposition shows that such scenarios indeed exist.

Proposition 2. *There exists a family of task graphs and present bias sets for which the price of uncertainty converges to 1.1.*

As the price of uncertainty can be strictly greater than 1, the question for an upper bound arises. Ideally, we would like to design a cost configuration $\tilde{c}$ motivating for all $\beta \in B$ assuming the reward is set to $\varrho r(G, \{b\})$ for some constant factor $\varrho > 1$ and $b = \min B$. Clearly, the existence of such a $\tilde{c}$ would imply a constant bound of ϱ for the price of uncertainty independent of G and B. Using a generalized version of the approximation algorithm we proposed in [3], it is indeed possible to construct a $\tilde{c}$ with the desired property for $\varrho = 2$.

The main idea of UNCERTAINPRESENTBIASAPPROX is simple: First, the algorithm computes a value α such that α/b is a lower bound on the reward necessary for agents with present bias b, i.e., $r(G, \{b\}) \geq \alpha/b$. In particular, this bound implies $\sup\{r(G, \{\beta\}) \mid \beta \in B\} \geq \alpha/b$. Next the algorithm constructs a $\tilde{c}$ such that a reward of $2\alpha/b$ is sufficiently motivating for all $\beta \in B$, i.e., $r(G, B) \leq 2\alpha/b$. As a result the price of uncertainty can be at most 2. In the following we try to convey the intuition behind the algorithm in more detail.

We begin with the computation of α. For this purpose let P be a path minimizing the maximum cost an agent with present bias b perceives on her way from s to t. We call P a *minmax path* and define $\alpha = \max\{d_b(e) \mid e \in P\}$ to be the maximum perceived edge cost of P. Since cost configurations cannot decrease edge cost, it should be clear that α is a valid lower bound on the reward required for the present bias b, i.e., $r(G, \{b\}) \geq \alpha/b$.

We proceed with $\tilde{c}$. The goal is to assign extra cost in such a way that any agent with a present bias $\beta \in B$ traverses only two kinds of edges. The first kind of edges are those on P. It is instructive to note that each such edge $(v, w) \in P$ is motivating for a reward of α/b if $\beta \geq b$. The reason is that

$$d_\beta(v, w) = \beta\left(\frac{c(v, w)}{\beta} + d(v, w)\right) \leq \beta\left(\frac{c(v, w)}{b} + d(v, w)\right) = \beta\frac{d_b(v, w)}{b} = \beta\frac{\alpha}{b}.$$

In particular, P is motivating for each present bias $\beta \in B$. The second kind of edges are on cheapest paths to t. To identify these edges, the algorithm assigns a distinct successor $\varsigma(v)$ to each node $v \in V \setminus \{t\}$ such that $(v, \varsigma(v))$ is the initial edge of a cheapest path from v to t. Since we assume t to be reachable from all other nodes of G at least one suitable successor must exist. By definition of ς, we know that $P' = v, \varsigma(v), \varsigma(\varsigma(v)), \ldots, t$ is a cheapest path from v to t. We call P' the ς-*path* of v and $T = \{(v, \varsigma(v)) \mid v \in V \setminus \{t\}\}$ a *cheapest path tree*.

Remember that we try to keep agents on the edges of P and T. For this purpose, we assign an extra cost of $\tilde{c}(e) = 2\alpha/b + 1$ to all other edges. This raises their perceived cost to at least $2\alpha/b + 1$; a price no agent is willing to pay for a perceived reward of $\beta 2\alpha/b$. However, since we have not assigned any extra cost to T so far, the perceived cost of edges in P and T is unaffected by the current $\tilde{c}$. In particular, all edges of P are still motivating for a reward of α/b and any present bias $\beta \in B$. To keep agents from entering costly ς-paths $P' = v, \varsigma(v), \varsigma(\varsigma(v)), \ldots, t$, we assign an extra cost to the out-edges $(v, \varsigma(v))$ of P, i.e., $v \in P$ but $\varsigma(v) \notin P$. The extra cost $\tilde{c}(v, \varsigma(v))$ is chosen to match the cost of a most expensive edge on P' between v and the next intersection of P' and P. It is easy to see that the resulting $\tilde{c}$ can no more than double the perceived cost of any edge in P, see the proof of Theorem 1 for a precise argument. Furthermore, the perceived cost of any out-edge $(v, \varsigma(v))$ of P is either high enough to keep agents on P or they do not encounter edges exceeding the perceived cost of $(v, \varsigma(v))$ until they reenter P. We conclude that a reward of $2\alpha/b$ is sufficiently motivating, leading us to one of the central results of our work.

Theorem 1. *The price of uncertainty is at most 2.*

It is interesting to note that UNCERTAINPRESENTBIASAPPROX can be executed in polynomial time. Furthermore, in the proof of Theorem 1 we argue that $\alpha/b \leq r(G, B) \leq 2\alpha/b$. As a result we have also found an efficient constant factor approximation of UPB-OPT.

Corollary 2. *UPB-OPT admits a polynomial time 2-approximation.*

4   Variable Present Bias

So far we have considered agents with an unknown but fixed present bias. We now generalize this model to agents whose β may vary arbitrarily within B as they progress through G. It is convenient to think of β as a *present bias configuration*, i.e., an assignment of present bias values $\beta(v) \in B$ to the nodes v of G. Whenever the agent reaches a node v, she acts according to the current present bias value $\beta(v)$. We say that G is motivating with respect to a present bias configuration β if and only if the agent does not quit on a walk from s to t.

To illustrate the consequences of a variable present bias we revisit Alice and Bob's scenario once more. Recall that the agent in this scenario is either like Alice with a present bias of $a = 1/2 - \varepsilon$ or like Bob with a present bias of $b = 1/2 + \varepsilon$, i.e., $B = \{a, b\}$. But while she had to commit to one present bias before, she is now free to change between a and b. For instance, her present bias could be b at s and v_B, but a otherwise, i.e., $\beta(v) = b$ for $v \in \{s, v_B\}$ and $\beta(v) = a$ for $v \in V \setminus \{s, v_B\}$. In this case she walks along the same path Bob would take, i.e., s, v_B, v_{AB}, t. However, there is a subtle difference. At v_{AB} the agent behaves like Alice and needs strictly more reward than Bob to remain motivated while traversing (v_{AB}, t). Under closer examination, which we will not go into detail here, it is in fact easy to see that the variability of β makes our agent more expensive to motivate than any agent with a fixed present bias from B.

4.1   Computational Consideration

Let G be an arbitrary task graph and B a suitable present bias set. We want to construct a cost configuration $\tilde{c}$ that is motivating for all present bias configuration $\beta \in B^V$, but requires as little reward as possible. Using arguments similar to those of Sect. 3, the computational challenges of this task are readily apparent. In particular, the corresponding decision problem VARIABLE PRESENT BIAS (VPB) is equivalent to MCC whenever B only contains a single element.

Definition 4 (VPB). *Given a task graph G, present bias set B and reward $r > 0$, decide whether a cost configuration $\tilde{c}$ motivating for all $\beta \in B^V$ exists.*

Because MCC is NP-complete [3], it immediately follows that VPB is NP-hard. A proof that VPB $\in$ NP can be found in the full version of this paper.

Corollary 3. *VPB is NP-complete.*

As it is NP-hard to find optimal cost configurations for general B, we turn to the optimization version of the problem. For this purpose let $r(G, B^V)$ be the infimum over all rewards admitting a cost configuration $\tilde{c}$ motivating for all $\beta \in B^V$ and define VPB-OPT as:

Definition 5 (VPB-OPT). *Given a task graph G and present bias set B, determine $r(G, B^V)$.*

Interestingly, approximating VPB-OPT seems to be much harder than UPB-OPT. The reason why the 2-approximation for UPB-OPT, i.e., UNCERTAINPRESENTBIASAPPROX, does not work anymore is simple. Recall that the cost configuration $\tilde{c}$ returned by the algorithm lets the agent take short-cuts along cheapest paths to t. To ensure that these shortcuts do not become too expensive, $\tilde{c}$ assigns extra cost to their initial edge. This way the per-ceived cost within a shortcut should not be greater than that for entering. As long as the present bias is fixed, this works fine. However, if the present bias can change, the agent may become more biased within a shortcut and require higher rewards to stay motivated. One way to fix this problem is to let the assigned extra cost depend on τ, i.e., the range of B. More precisely, we multiply the cost assigned in line 9 of Algorithm 1 by τ and change line 5 to assign a cost of $\tilde{c}(e) = (1 + \tau)\alpha/b + 1$. As a result we obtain a new algorithm VARIABLEPRESENTBIASAPPROX with an approximation ration of $1 + \tau$.

Theorem 2. *VPB-OPT admits a polynomial time $(1 + \tau)$-approximation.*

Although VARIABLEPRESENTBIASAPPROX yields a good approximation for a moderately variable present bias, it does not provide constant approxima-tion bounds like UNCERTAINPRESENTBIASAPPROX. Surprisingly, a sophisticated reduction from VECTOR SCHEDULING (VS) [4], shows that VPB-OPT can-not have an efficient constant factor approximation unless ZPP = NP.

Theorem 3. *No polynomial time algorithm can approximate VPB-OPT within a constant factor $\varrho > 1$, unless* NP = ZPP.

4.2 Occasionally Unbiased Agents

Although VPB is hard to solve in general, a curious special case consisting of all present bias sets B for which $1 \in B$ is not. Note that agents whose present bias varies within such a B becomes temporarily unbiased whenever 1 is drawn. For this reason we call these agents *occasionally unbiased*. A behavioral pattern unique to occasionally unbiased agents is that they may start to walk along a cheapest path at any point in time whenever their present bias becomes 1. As a result we can reduce VPB to a decision problem we call CRITICAL NODE SET (CNS) for occasionally unbiased agents.

Definition 6 (CNS). *Given a task graph G, present bias set B and reward r, decide the existence of a critical node set W.*

We consider a node set W *critical* if the following properties hold: (a) $s \in W$. (b) Each node $v \in W$ has a path P to t that only uses nodes of W. (c) All edges e of P satisfy $d_b(e) \leq br$ with $b = \min B$. As it turns out, such a W contains exactly those nodes an occasionally unbiased agent may visit with respect to a motivating cost configuration. This allows us to reduce VPB to CNS.

Proposition 3. *If $1 \in B$, then VPB has a solution if and only if CNS has one.*

Algorithm 2. DECIDECRITICALNODESET

---

1   $\delta(t) \leftarrow 0$;
2   **foreach** $v \in V \setminus \{t\}$ **in reverse topological order do**
3   $\quad$ $U \leftarrow \{w \mid (v, w) \in E \text{ and } c(v, w) + \beta\delta(w) \leq b\}$;
4   $\quad$ **if** $U = \emptyset$ **then** $\delta(v) \leftarrow \infty$; **else** $\delta(v) \leftarrow \min\{c(v, w) + \delta(w) \mid w \in U\}$;
5   **if** $\delta(s) < \infty$ **then return** "yes" **else return** "no";

All that remains to show is that CNS is decidable in polynomial time. A straight forward approach to this simple algorithmic problem is DECIDECRITICALNODESET. We therefore conclude that VPB is efficiently solvable for occasionally unbiased agents.

Corollary 4. *If $1 \in B$, then VPB can be solved in polynomial time.*

4.3   The Price of Variability

To conclude our work, we take a step back from computational considerations and look at the implications of variability from a more general perspective. Our goal is to quantify the conceptual loss of efficiency incurred by going from a fixed and known present bias to an unpredictable and variable one. Similar to the price of uncertainty we define the *price of variability* as the following ratio.

Definition 7 (Price of Variability). *Given a task graph G and a present bias set B, the price of variability is defined as $r(G, B^V)/\sup\{r(G, \{\beta\}) \mid \beta \in B\}$.*

It seems obvious that the price of variability depends closely on the structure of G and B. Nevertheless, we would like to find general bounds for the price of variability much like we did in Sect. 3 for the price of uncertainty. As a first step, it is instructive to note that the price of uncertainty is a natural lower bound for the price of variability. The reason for this is that each cost configuration that motivates an agent whose present bias varies arbitrarily in B must also motivate an agent whose present bias is a fixed value from B. Therefore it holds true that $r(G, B^V) \geq r(G, B)$, which immediately implies the stated bound. Sometimes this bound is tight. Consider for instance Alice and Bob's scenario. As we have shown in Sect. 3, it is possible to construct a cost configuration $\tilde{c}$ verifying a price of uncertainty of 1. Using similar arguments, it is easy to see that $\tilde{c}$ remains motivating if we allow the present bias to vary, implying an identical price of variability. However, for general instances of G and B this tight relation between the price of uncertainty and the price of variability is lost. In fact, we can show that unlike the price of uncertainty, which has a constant upper bound of 2, the price of variability may become arbitrarily large as the range of B increases.

Proposition 4. *There exists a family of task graphs and present bias sets for which the price of variability converges to $\tau/2$.*

Although Proposition 4 implies that the price of variability can become substantially larger than the price of uncertainty, it should be noted that the task graph constructed in the proof of this proposition is close to a worst case scenario. In particular, we can show that the price of variability cannot exceed $\tau + 1$, which is roughly twice the value obtained by Proposition 4. To verify this upper bound, it is helpful to recall the proof of Theorem 2. In the process of establishing the approximation ratio of VARIABLEPRESENTBIASAPPROX we have argued that the cost configuration $\tilde{c}$ returned by the algorithm motivates any agent with a present bias configuration $\beta \in B^V$ for a reward of at most $(\tau+1)r(G, \{\min B\})$. Consequently, it holds true that $r(G, B^V) \leq (\tau+1)r(G, \{\min B\})$, implying that the price of variability cannot exceed $\tau + 1$.

Corollary 5. *The price of variability is at most $\tau + 1$.*

References

1. Akerlof, G.A.: Procrastination and obedience. Am. Econ. Rev. **81**, 1–19 (1991)
2. Albers, S., Kraft, D.: Motivating time-inconsistent agents: a computational approach. In: Cai, Y., Vetta, A. (eds.) WINE 2016. LNCS, vol. 10123, pp. 309–323. Springer, Heidelberg (2016). https://doi.org/10.1007/978-3-662-54110-4_22
3. Albers, S., Kraft, D.: On the value of penalties in time-inconsistent planning. In: 44th International Colloquium on Automata, Languages, and Programming, pp. 10:1–10:12. Schloss Dagstuhl (2017)
4. Chekuri, C., Khanna, S.: On multidimensional packing problems. SIAM J. Comput. **33**, 837–851 (2004)
5. DellaVigna, S.: Psychology and economics: evidence from the field. J. Econ. Lit. **47**, 315–372 (2009)
6. Frederick, S., Loewenstein, G., O'Donoghue, T.: Time discounting and time preference: a critical review. J. Econ. Lit. **40**, 351–401 (2002)
7. Gravin, N., Immorlica, N., Lucier, B., Pountourakis, E.: Procrastination with variable present bias. In: 17th ACM Conference on Economics and Computation, pp. 361–361. ACM (2016)
8. Kleinberg, J., Oren, S.: Time-inconsistent planning: a computational problem in behavioral economics. In: 15th ACM Conference on Economics and Computation, pp. 547–564. ACM (2014)
9. Kleinberg, J., Sigal, O., Raghavan, M.: Planning problems for sophisticated agents with present bias. In: 17th ACM Conference on Economics and Computation, pp. 343–360. ACM (2016)
10. Kleinberg, J., Sigal, O., Raghavan, M.: Planning with multiple biases. In: 18th ACM Conference on Economics and Computation, pp. 567–584. ACM (2017)
11. Laibson, D.: Golden eggs and hyperbolic discounting. Q. J. Econ. **112**, 443–477 (1997)
12. O'Donoghue, T., Rabin, M.: Incentives and self control. In: Advances in Economics and Econometrics: Theory and Application 9th World Congress, vol. 2, pp. 215–245. Cambridge University Press (2006)
13. O'Donoghue, T., Rabin, M.: Procrastination on long-term projects. J. Econ. Behav. Organ. **66**, 161–175 (2008)

Routing Games in the Wild: Efficiency, Equilibration and Regret
Large-Scale Field Experiments in Singapore

Barnabé Monnot[✉], Francisco Benita, and Georgios Piliouras

Engineering Systems and Design, Singapore University of Technology and Design,
Singapore, Singapore
monnot_barnabe@mymail.sutd.edu.sg,
{francisco_benita,georgios}@sutd.edu.sg

Abstract. Routing games are amongst the most well studied domains of game theory. How relevant are these theoretical models and results to capturing the reality of everyday traffic? We focus on a semantically rich dataset that captures detailed information about the daily behavior of thousands of Singaporean commuters and examine the following basic questions:
- Does the traffic equilibrate?
- Is the system behavior consistent with latency minimizing agents?
- Is the resulting system efficient?

The answers to all three questions are shown to be largely positive. Finally, in order to capture the efficiency of the traffic network in a way that agrees with our everyday intuition we introduce a new metric, the *stress of catastrophe*, which reflects the combined inefficiencies of both tragedy of the commons as well as price of anarchy effects.

1 Introduction

Congestion games are amongst the most historic, influential and well-studied classes of games. Proposed in [27] and isomorphic to potential games [19] (in which learning dynamics equilibrate), they have been successfully employed in a myriad of modeling problems. Naturally, one application stands above the rest: modeling traffic. Having strategy sets correspond to the possible paths between source and sink nodes in a network is such a mild and intuitive restriction that routing/congestion games are effectively synonymous to each other and jointly mark a key contribution of the field of game theory.

Routing games have also played a seminal role in the emergence of algorithmic game theory. The central notion of Price of Anarchy (PoA), capturing the inefficiency of worst case equilibria, was famously first introduced and analyzed in routing games [15,30]. Routing games have set the stage for major developments in the area such as the introduction of regret-minimizing agents [5] that eventually led to the consolidation of most known PoA results under the umbrella of (λ, μ)-smoothness arguments [28]. Impressively, this work established

© Springer International Publishing AG 2017
N. R. Devanur and P. Lu (Eds.): WINE 2017, LNCS 10674, pp. 340–353, 2017.
https://doi.org/10.1007/978-3-319-71924-5_24

that PoA guarantees are robust for a wide variety of solution concepts such as regret-minimizing agents. Finally, congestion games still drive innovation in the area with results that extend the strength and applicability of PoA bounds for large routing games [9], as well as dynamic populations [17].

With every successive analytical achievement seemingly chipping slowly away at the distance between theoretical models and everyday reality, the PoA constants for routing games, e.g. the $4/3$ for the nonatomic linear case [30] have become something akin to the universal constants of the field. Small, concise, dimensionless, they seem almost by their very nature to project purity and truth. But do they? After all, there are many of them. In the case of quadratic cost functions PoA ≈ 1.626, whereas for quartic functions, which have been proposed as a reasonable model of road traffic, PoA ≈ 2.151 [29,32]. What do these "small constants" mean in practice? Quite a lot. An increase of inefficiency from $4/3$ to 2.151 in Singapore would translate to the loss of approximately 730,000 work hours *every single day*. Do any of these "back-of-the-envelope" theoretical calculations have any predictive power *in practice*?

At the antipodes of the aforementioned theoretical work, other, similarly recent theoretical approaches hint that PoA analysis might actually not be reflective of the realized behavior in real networks. One type of work focuses on the instability of worst case equilibria, e.g. [14,18]. Specifically, [25] show that although bad equilibria may exist, an average case analysis which "weighs" each equilibrium proportionally to its region of attraction typically reveals a picture that is much closer to optimal than PoA analysis. So, PoA analysis may be over-pessimistic. Distressingly, [7,8] argue something orthogonal, which at first glance appears rather counterintuitive. They argue that networks with low PoA, e.g. PoA $= 1$, which are typically considered optimal, might actually reflect traffic flows which are deadlocked in severe traffic jams.[1] Finally, PoA calculations can be invalidated if we move into theoretical models that allow for risk averse agents [2,24,26]. At this point, as theory alone does not suffice to provide a definitive answer, it makes sense to examine some real world networks at a fine level of detail.

Our goal is to perform the first-to-our-knowledge game theoretic modeling and investigation of a real world traffic network (specifically Singapore's traffic network) based on repeated large scale field experiments with thousands of participants. Our dataset includes granular information that allows us to inspect minute-by-minute the concurrent decision-making of thousands of commuters, as they respond and adapt to traffic conditions. We focus on arguably the three most basic questions: Is the system at equilibrium? Is this equilibrium consistent with the hypothesis of latency-minimizing agents? Is the resulting system efficient? Before we explore the answers to these questions as provided by the data, let's try to disambiguate the questions themselves.

---

[1] Indeed, if we keep increasing the total flow in e.g. Pigou's example, eventually both in the optimal and equilibrium flows almost all flow will be routed through the slow link.

Is the system at "equilibrium"? Here, we should clearly point out that by equilibrium we mean the formal mathematical notion of equilibrium, i.e. a stationary point. At the first level of inspection, we are not concerned with whether the outcome that the system equilibrates upon is necessarily stable in a game-theoretic sense. We are merely asking "are the agents continuously adapting their behavior from day-to-day" (i.e. the paths they choose, the modes of transportation, and so on)? If significant number of agents choose the same actions from day-to-day this would indicate that the system has indeed reached a fixed point (stasis) and furthermore that at this stable system state there is little entropy/randomness. Such a result is consistent with best response and best response dynamics, with the instability results of mixed Nash equilibria for multiplicative weight update algorithms [14,18,25] as well as with some other concurrent dynamics (e.g. imitation dynamics) [1,10]. On the other hand, it is not a universal consequence of no-regret learning in congestion games [5,21].

Is the equilibrium "economically stable"? Naturally, from a game theoretic perspective, we wish to understand whether the resulting equilibrium is a Nash equilibrium (or at least if in the case of adapting agents most have low regret when comparing their performance with the best path in hindsight). For a real traffic network, however, it is not practically feasible to compute true "best responses", since there is an astronomically large number of paths to consider and we do not have data on all paths. We instead estimate inefficiencies at the individual level by quantifying the empirical "imitation" regret for each agent, i.e. how much faster could each agent have reached their destination if they had clairvoyant access to all the routing choices/information from our dataset and chose the best such route with hindsight.

Is the system "efficient"? Traditionally, ever since its inception, the notion of Price of Anarchy has been considered the gold standard for system efficiency with a low PoA considered equivalent to system optimality. The results in [7,8] in which hopelessly deadlocked traffic jams score perfect PoA scores point out a clear dichotomy between what PoA analysis identifies as an efficient traffic network and what we in our everyday experience identify as a well-functioning network. The reason for this divide lies on the fact that PoA analysis completely disregards any inefficiency that is connected to tragedy of the commons effects.

In order to shed some light on these effects, we define a new inefficiency metric that is defined as the ratio of the social welfare at equilibrium divided by the optimal social welfare when we discount for congestion effects. Namely, although the numerator is as in the PoA, the denominator is computing the average social "blue-sky" optimal welfare as follows: Each agent imagines the scenario where she alone was in the network and computes the best path (minimum length/latency) for herself. This makes sense from an everyday experience perspective, as the typical commuter has an intuitive grasp of how long it would take to cover this distance if the externality costs imposed by the other drivers where removed. We call this ratio, the *Stress of Catastrophe (SoC)*. As this ratio grows the system's long term persistence is jeopardized. Practically successful networks should have small SoC, which implies small PoA but not the other way around.

Result Snippets

- We show that most subjects use the same means of transportation across trips and that a large number of them consistently selects the same route. For example, when controlling for those who use consistently the same means of transportation across different days, the percentage of subjects selecting the same route is very high, in the order of 94%. (see Sect. 3.1).
- The empirical regret distribution has a median value of 4 min 40 s and mean approaching 6 min for an average travel time of around 29 min (see Sect. 3.2).
- Finally, we define and estimate the Stress of Catastrophe at 1.34, with marked contrast when discriminating by mode of transportation (see Sect. 3.3). These findings are shown to be consistent across different days.

2 Description of the Data

We focus on a semantically rich dataset from Singapore's National Science Experiment (NSE), a nationwide ongoing educational initiative led by researchers from the Singapore University of Technology and Design (SUTD). This dataset includes precise information about the daily behavior of tens of thousands of Singapore students that carry custom-made sensors for up to 4 consecutive days, resulting in millions of measurements. Indeed, every 13 s, the sensor is able to accurately log its geographical location as well as other environmental factors such as relative temperature and humidity or noise levels.

The students are dispersed throughout the city-state and their daily commutes to school are reasonably long for them to meaningfully interact and experience the daily traffic. For this reason, we focus on the morning trip they undertake to reach their school from their home. The morning trip is also characterized by a lesser number of stops on the way to school or Pre-university, thus it lends itself better to an analysis based solely on travel times. Other types of costs may be included to complement travel time, such as price of the route (based on tolls or public transport fees) or environmental factors. In this study however, our scope is limited to the trip duration, to be extended in future work.

The mode of transportation chosen by the students can be identified using accurate algorithms, e.g. car (driving or being driven to school) versus bus or metro, estimate source and sink destinations (focusing on home-school pairs) as well as their mode-dependent available routes. Some descriptive charts are given in Fig. 1 relating the durations and distances traveled for private and public transportation trips. To guide the reader unfamiliar with Singapore's road and public transport network, we give a brief optional introduction in our online full version of the paper [20].

Representativeness of the Sample. Students are a restricted class of residents, but we argue that they however provide a tangible idea of Singapore's mobility. First, as of 2015, the size of the student population up to Pre-University level totals about 460,000 residents. In contrast, the active population's size, as of 2015, is about 2.2 million.[2] Our clean dataset includes 32,588 trips taken by

---

[2] Statistics were compiled from data.gov.sg.

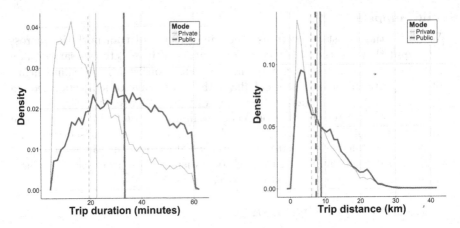

Fig. 1. *Left:* Density plots of trip durations per mode. We note that car trip durations are typically short and more concentrated around a peak value of 15 to 20 min, while public transportation trip durations are scattered between 20 to 50 min. *Right:* Density plots of trip distances per mode. The two densities are close, indicating that distance may not factor in the choice of transportation mode. Median is represented by a dashed line, mean by a solid line.

15,875 unique students, distributed between the three main type of institutions in Singapore (Primary, Secondary and Pre-University).

For the purpose of our study, most of the analysis does not require a complete sample of the population. Students in private transportation experience the same level of congestion as their peers and active individuals, hence estimates over their population translate to estimates over the whole of Singapore's mobility users. It is even more true for students in public transportation: their trips are possibly the same as those of the active population. Indeed, we find that the ratio of public to private transportation users in our sample closely mirrors that of the population as a whole[3], as 57% of students in our dataset use public transportation.

As shown in Fig. 2, the sample of home locations is geographically distributed, so is not focused on a particular area of the city. However, the distribution of schools may not reflect endpoints of trips made by the active population. As an example, it can be observed that few schools are located in the city center, which houses a large number of office buildings. This constitutes one limitation of our dataset, perhaps softened by the fact that active population and students may still share a sizeable part of their route and thus experience the same congestion.

---

[3] Household Interview Travel Survey 2012: Public Transport Mode Share Rises To 63%, LTA News Release.

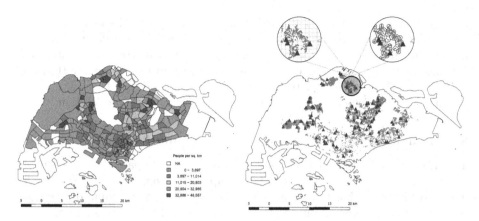

Fig. 2. *Right:* Home locations (red dots), school locations (blue triangles) and spatial clustering methods, discussed in Sect. 3.2 and the full version online [20]. *Left:* Density map of Singapore. Blue areas are less populated while red areas are denser. (Color figure online)

3   Findings

3.1   Equilibration and Empirical Consistency

If the traffic system is at equilibrium, then we should expect that the subjects' route decisions do not vary substantially between successive days of study. We investigate the issue from three different angles. First, we compare the modes of transportation selected by each individual student over the days of the experiment. Second, we improve the previous result by considering whether the selected routes are identical (e.g. always use the same combination of bus and train, or always use the same road on car). Third, building on our geographical clustering method described in the following Section, we investigate the question of whether the fastest student in the cluster on one day remains the fastest over all days of experiment.

The first analysis shows that more than 60% of subjects have used the same principal mode of transportation in all morning trips available in our dataset. We are here discriminating between trips where the principal mode of transportation is either the train, the bus or the car. We define as principal the mode with which the student has traveled the longest distance. The fraction increases to close to two thirds (65%) of the samples if we simply discriminate between the subjects using public transit from those who use private transportation.

For the second analysis, we have implemented a novel algorithm to determine whether two route choices are identical. We find that for subjects using the same mode of transportation across all days, the percentage of subjects selecting the same route is very high, in the order of 94%. We detail the algorithm used to obtain this result in our Methodology section of full paper available online [20].

Finally, we identify a restricted set of clusters that have the property of being consistent throughout at least two days of experiment, i.e. the members of the cluster are the same in distinct days of the same week. Members may drop out of their cluster if their starting time or starting point are different from one morning to the next, or if they use another mode of transportation. We find that for these consistent clusters, close to 50% of them have the property that the fastest individual on one day remains the fastest for all days where this cluster appears, showing again a certain degree of consistency in the population.

3.2 Individual Optimality and Empirical Imitation-Regret

To answer the question of individual optimality, we compare the durations of the morning trip for the subjects. A fair comparison is only achieved when looking at students leaving from the same neighborhood on the same day and at roughly the same time, going to the same school and using the same mode of transportation. The notion of neighborhood is expanded upon in our Methodology section, available in the full version of our paper [20], where we describe how the clustering of the data was achieved.

In the cases where the class of comparable subjects has more than two individuals, we collect the **empirical imitation-regret** encountered by every student in the class. To do so, we find the student in the class with minimal trip duration and set her imitation-regret to zero. For other members of the class, the empirical imitation-regret is equal to the (non-negative) difference between their trip duration and the minimal trip duration.

Our notion of empirical imitation-regret shares its name with the traditional regret measure, commonly found in the learning and multi-agent systems literature, for the following reason. The players here are faced with multiple strategies that they can choose from: the routes that go from their neighborhood to the destination. They may not know about current traffic conditions or which route will take the least amount of time but nevertheless have to make a decision. A posteriori, this decision can be measured against the best action implemented by a comparable subject on that day, and the difference is the imitation-regret. The introduction of the word "imitation" is due to the fact that we compare the decision solely with other players' choices of routes: a better route that is not used by any of the subjects in the cluster will therefore not be considered here. This drawback is shared with many natural learning dynamics and thus can be interpreted as a reasonable assumption on subjects' decisions.

The measure of empirical imitation-regret depends naturally on the geographical area covered by the neighborhood. As the area increases, so does the accumulated imitation-regret, since the minimum is taken over a larger set of subjects. However, neighborhoods that are too large lose in precision, as two different subjects in the same cluster may have very different trip lengths. The results in this section use a geographical cluster size of about 400 m, while sensitivity analysis is performed in the Methodology section of our full paper [20] to show the robustness of our findings.

Low empirical imitation-regret is a necessary condition for equilibrium. Indeed, at equilibrium, all comparable subjects should perform their trip in roughly the same amount of time. If one individual encounters a imitation-regret

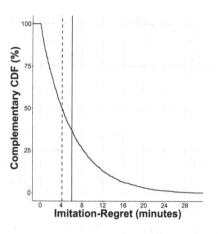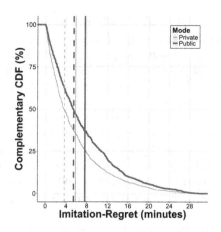

Fig. 3. *Left:* Complementary cumulative distribution function of the imitation-regret (decreasing curve). We aggregate all days of the experiment in a single figure and remove subjects with zero imitation-regret – i.e. the baseline subjects. The mean imitation-regret signalled by the solid vertical line is equal to 6 min (around 27% of the mean travel time), while the median imitation-regret – dashed line – is equal to 4 min and 40 s (around 21% of the median travel time). Sensitivity analysis results are presented in the full paper online [20]. *Right:* Comparison of complementary CDF of imitation-regret per mode of transportation. (Color figure online)

of say, 10 min, she may be better off by switching to a different route, e.g. the one used by the fastest individual in the cluster.

On the other hand, a high empirical imitation-regret warns us that some users are unable to find the fastest route to reach their destination. We see two possible directions to explore after such a conclusion. If we assume that individuals are solely interested in minimizing their trip duration—perhaps a fair assumption for the morning trip, constrained by the hard deadline of the class start—, then the network may benefit from the injection of information on how to traverse it. Otherwise, a high empirical imitation-regret reveals that other factors enter into consideration when the student is selecting the route, such as finding the least expensive one, the more climatised one or one that is shared with other students.

In Fig. 3, we plot the complementary cumulative distribution of the empriri-cal imitation-regret. A point on the curve indicates which fraction of individuals (read on the *y*-axis) have empirical imitation-regret greater or equal than *x* (read on the *x*-axis). We also give the mean (solid red line) and median (dashed blue line) experienced empirical imitation-regret. It should be noted that the empir-ical imitation-regret distribution and its moments do not include the subjects for which the imitation-regret is zero, i.e. the best in the cluster.

Larger geographical cluster sizes give rise to larger average empirical imitation-regrets, but the results are relatively robust. The mean empirical imitation-regret oscillates around 27% of the mean travel time in the dataset (around 6 min), while the median empirical imitation-regret is at 21% of the median travel time (around 4 min and 40 s). This result motivates the introduction of a solution parametrised by two values, ϵ and δ. The reported measurements constitute an (ϵ, δ)-equilibrium if we find that a fraction $1 - \delta$ of users experience at most a quantity ϵ of imitation-regret. The experiment yields values $\epsilon = 22$ min and $\delta = 0.05$.

Finally, we study the imitation-regret between modes, i.e. taking the regret with respect to the fastest individual in the cluster, irrelevant of transportation mode. We focus our analysis on mixed clusters, where at least one individual using public transportation and one individual using private transportation appear. We have over 1,400 such clusters, and in close to 80% of them, the fastest individual is a private transportation user. Over these 1,400 clusters, the average imitation-regret incurred by public transport users compared with the fastest private transportation user in their cluster is close to 8 min. For the same population of bus and train users, the average duration of a trip is close to 25 min, indicating that the fastest car user spends roughly two thirds of this time to reach destination. Figure 3 plots the distributions of imitation-regret for the two classes of users.

3.3   Societal Optimality and the Stress of Catastrophe

The Stress of Catastrophe is introduced to give a measure of the weight of externalities in the system. As more agents join the road network, congestion increases on the links. Classically, the Price of Anarchy has been employed to quantify how bad the selfish decision-making of these agents affects the efficiency of the system, compared to the social optimum that a central planner implements.

But estimating the social optimum of a system from the data is a perilous task. First, exact demands need to be known for every origin-destination pair of the agents. Second, latency functions for every edge of the network need to be estimated. Third, the global optimum flow maximizing the social optimum function needs to be computed.

On the other hand, the PoA does not fully capture the effects of a *tragedy of the commons* that congestion presents. In such a scenario, it is not costly for one additional individual to enter the system, but since all agents enter, the global welfare diminishes. Similarly, congestion can reach levels after which the action of a central planner has little effect, yielding a low PoA that does not reflect just how congested the system is.

The Stress of Catastrophe eschews these pitfalls by providing an optimistic lower bound to the socially optimal trip durations. It stems from the simple fact that a crude lower bound to the optimal trip duration is one in which no one else is present on the road. Using Google Directions API, free-flow trip durations are obtained and give us a "blue sky" – i.e. ideal scenario – lower bound. Comparing the actual recorded trip duration length to this lower bound in turn yields a ratio of how much faster the trip could have been in a no-externality scenario.

Formally, we define the Stress of Catastrophe (SoC) from our data as such:

$$\text{SoC} = \frac{\texttt{Cost(Recorded trip duration)}}{\texttt{Cost(Trip durations (free-flow / light traffic))}}$$

To give an idea of the measure in our dataset, we plot in Fig. 4 the histogram of percentages of deviations from the free-flow optimal trip duration. We see that most subjects are relatively close to this minimum bound while as the gap grows, fewer subjects are found.

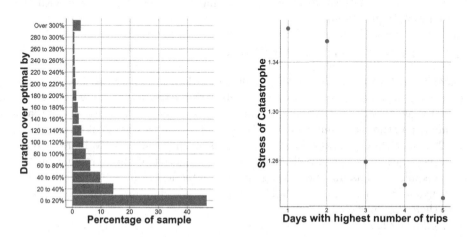

Fig. 4. *Left:* Histogram of deviations from the free-flow optimal trip durations. *Right:* Stress of Catastrophe computed across the five days with the highest record of unique subjects (sample size > 1,500). The values are between 1.23 and 1.37.

Since the denominator is a lower bound to the socially optimal cost, we also have the following corollary:

$$\text{PoA} = \frac{\texttt{Cost(Recorded trip durations)}}{\texttt{Cost(Optimal trip durations)}} \leq \text{SoC}$$

The question is now how pessimistic is this upper bound? Our results show that SoC = 1.34, when the SoC is computed with both car and transit users. But discriminating between the two yields a much more contrasted picture: the SoC for transit users is found to be 1.18, indicating that students using public transportation have little room to improve their trip duration. Conversely, the SoC varies significantly depending on the traffic conditions for subjects taking private transportation to school. In free-flow conditions, we find the SoC to be equal to 1.86. Details of the SoC for individual days of the experiment can be found in Fig. 4.

It is remarkable that such an pessimistic upper bound is however so close to 1. How does the PoA overestimate the inefficiency of the network then? Consider

PoA results found in the literature, such as the 2.151 ratio of derived in [31] in the case of degree 4 polynomial cost functions. The latest class is often used by network engineers to model the congestion on real roads, following the Bureau of Public Roads standard.

But the average estimated free flow time travel of the sample is 21 min. Assuming the SoC to be as large as the 2.151 bound, on average a commuter would spend $2.151 - 1.34 = 0.811$ times more in transit, i.e. 17 min more per commuter. In other words, pessimistic predictions of the PoA would entail a loss of over 730,000 h per day, if we assume all of the 2,200,000 active individuals and 400,000 students were commuting on that day, a large mismatch with the actual system performance.

4   Connections to Other Work

Algorithmic Game Theory and Econometrics. Recently there has been a surge of interest in combining techniques from algorithmic game theory with the traditional goals of econometrics [3,33]. These works employ a data-driven approach to analyzing the economic behavior of real world systems and agent interactions. In [22] the authors developed theoretical tools for inferring agent valuations from observed data in the generalized second price auction without relying on the Nash equilibrium assumption, using behavioral models from online learning theory such as regret-minimization. They apply their techniques on auction data to test their effectiveness.

Following this work, [13] studies the behavior of real housing market agents based on data from an online bidding platform. The results inform the design of the auction platform and point towards data-driven policies helping the agents make decisions. The latter idea is made more explicit in a recent article by some of the authors [23]. In a sense, our present work also advocates using data to gauge users interactions but our focus is on routing games, for which it is harder to gather sanitized data. Furthermore, we develop new metrics that are more informative about the state of the system than the price of anarchy.

In [12] the authors provided tools for estimating an empirical PoA of auctions. The PoA is defined as the worst case efficiency loss of any auction that could have produced the data, relative to the optimal. However, auctions and routing games each pose a totally distinct set of challenges. In our setting, the problem of translating data streams to game theoretic concepts adds a rather nontrivial layer of complexity. For example, even identifying the action chosen by each agent, i.e. their routes, is tricky as it requires to robustly map a noisy stream of transportation data into a discrete object, a path in a graph. It should be noted however that our notion of Stress of Catastrophe provides an upper bound on the empirical PoA, as detailed in Sect. 3.3.

Another active strand of research is concerned with fair division of resources. Here too, experimental studies are conducted to determine whether agents exhibit a behaviour close to predictions from the theory and in fact, their behaviour and feedback from using fair division systems pose new theoretical questions [11,16]. This fruitful cycle can hopefully be replicated in congestion games.

Price of Anarchy for Real World Networks. One earlier paper tangentially connected to estimating the PoA of congestion games is [6]. This is a theoretical paper that provides PoA bounds for perturbed versions of congestion games. As a test of their techniques, they heuristically approximate the PoA on a few benchmark instances of traffic networks available for academic research from the Transportation Network Test Problems [4] by running the Frank-Wolfe algorithm on them. No experiments were performed and no measurements were made. Naturally, this approach cannot be used to test PoA predictions, since it presumes that PoA reflects the worst case possible performance and then merely tests where do these constants lie for non-worst case routing networks.

In effectively parallel independent work [34] focused on quantifying the inefficiencies incurred due to selfish behavior for a sub-transportation network in Eastern Massachusetts, US. They use a dataset containing time average speed on road segments and link capacity in their transportation sub-network. The authors estimate daily user cost functions as well as origin-destination demand by means of inverse optimization techniques using this dataset. From this formulation they compute estimates of the PoA, whose average value is shown to be around 1.5. In contrast to their approach our dataset contains detailed individual user information, which allows for estimates not only of systemic performance but also of individual optimality (e.g. imitative-regret) as well as test to what extent is the system indeed near stasis (i.e. in equilibrium). Also, their approach does not capture how bad the resulting traffic is, i.e. the tension between Price of Anarchy and Tragedy of the Commons, whereas our approach addresses both. Finally, our estimations are derived from explicit online measurements of the system performance and are not reverse engineered by estimating user cost functions which inevitably introduce new errors that cascade through all the calculations.

5 Conclusion

This is hopefully not the end but the beginning of a thorough experimental investigation into the rich game theoretic literature of routing games. Clearly, there are many open questions and challenges to be addressed. Due to space limitations we refer the reader to the online version of our paper for the full discussion of these directions [20].

Acknowledgements. The authors would like to thank the National Science Experiment team at SUTD for their help: Garvit Bansal, Sarah Nadiawati, Hugh Tay Keng Liang, Nils Ole Tippenhauer, Bige Tunçer, Darshan Virupashka, Erik Wilhelm and Yuren Zhou. The National Science Experiment is supported by the Singapore National Research Foundation (NRF), Grant RGNRF1402.

Barnabé Monnot acknowledges the SUTD Presidential Graduate Fellowship. Francisco Benita acknowledges CONACyT CVU 369933 (Mexico). Georgios Piliouras acknowledges SUTD grant SRG ESD 2015 097, MOE AcRF Tier 2 Grant 2016-T2-1-170 and a NRF fellowship. Part of the work was completed while Barnabé Monnot and Georgios Piliouras were visiting scientists at the Simons Institute for the Theory of Computing.

References

1. Ackermann, H., Berenbrink, P., Fischer, S., Hoefer, M.: Concurrent imitation dynamics in congestion games. Distrib. Comput. **29**(2), 105–125 (2016)
2. Angelidakis, H., Fotakis, D., Lianeas, T.: Stochastic congestion games with risk-averse players. In: Vöcking, B. (ed.) SAGT 2013. LNCS, vol. 8146, pp. 86–97. Springer, Heidelberg (2013). https://doi.org/10.1007/978-3-642-41392-6_8
3. Bajari, P., Hong, H., Nekipelov, D.: Game theory and econometrics: a survey of some recent research. In: Advances in Economics and Econometrics, 10th World Congress, vol. 3, pp. 3–52 (2013)
4. Bar-Gera, H.: Transportation network test problems (2011). https://github.com/bstabler/TransportationNetworks. Accessed 10 Nov 2017
5. Blum, A., Hajiaghayi, M., Ligett, K., Roth, A.: Regret minimization and the price of total anarchy. In: STOC, pp. 373–382 (2008)
6. Buriol, L., Ritt, M., Rodrigues, F., Schäfer, G.: On the smoothed price of anarchy of the traffic assignment problem. In: ATMOS, pp. 122–133. ATMOS (2011)
7. Colini-Baldeschi, R., Cominetti, R., Mertikopoulos, P., Scarsini, M.: On the asymptotic behavior of the price of anarchy: is selfish routing bad in highly congested networks? ArXiv e-prints (2017)
8. Colini-Baldeschi, R., Cominetti, R., Scarsini, M.: On the price of anarchy of highly congested nonatomic network games. In: Gairing, M., Savani, R. (eds.) SAGT 2016. LNCS, vol. 9928, pp. 117–128. Springer, Heidelberg (2016). https://doi.org/10.1007/978-3-662-53354-3_10
9. Feldman, M., Immorlica, N., Lucier, B., Roughgarden, T., Syrgkanis, V.: The price of anarchy in large games. In: Proceedings of the 48th Annual ACM SIGACT Symposium on Theory of Computing, pp. 963–976. ACM (2016)
10. Fotakis, D., Kaporis, A.C., Spirakis, P.G.: Atomic congestion games: fast, myopic and concurrent. In: Monien, B., Schroeder, U.-P. (eds.) SAGT 2008. LNCS, vol. 4997, pp. 121–132. Springer, Heidelberg (2008). https://doi.org/10.1007/978-3-540-79309-0_12
11. Gal, Y.K., Mash, M., Procaccia, A.D., Zick, Y.: Which is the fairest (rent division) of them all? In: EC, pp. 67–84. ACM (2016)
12. Hoy, D., Nekipelov, D., Syrgkanis, V.: Robust data-driven guarantees in auctions. In: Preliminary version at 1st Workshop on Algorithmic Game Theory and Data Science (2015)
13. Jalaly, P., Nekipelov, D., Tardos, É.: Learning and trust in auction markets. arXiv:1703.10672 (2017)
14. Kleinberg, R., Piliouras, G., Tardos, É.: Multiplicative updates outperform generic no-regret learning in congestion games. In: STOC (2009)
15. Koutsoupias, E., Papadimitriou, C.H.: Worst-case equilibria. In: STACS, pp. 404–413 (1999)
16. Kurokawa, D., Procaccia, A.D., Shah, N.: Leximin allocations in the real world. In: EC, pp. 345–362. ACM (2015)
17. Lykouris, T., Syrgkanis, V., Tardos, É.: Learning and efficiency in games with dynamic population. In: SODA, pp. 120–129. SIAM (2016)
18. Mehta, R., Panageas, I., Piliouras, G.: Natural selection as an inhibitor of genetic diversity: multiplicative weights updates algorithm and a conjecture of haploid genetics. In: ITCS (2015)
19. Monderer, D., Shapley, L.S.: Potential games. Games Econ. Behav. **4**(1), 124–143 (1996)

20. Monnot, B., Benita, F., Piliouras, G.: Routing games in the wild: efficiency, equilibration and regret (Large-Scale Field Experiments in Singapore). arXiv preprint arXiv:1708.04081 (2017)
21. Monnot, B., Piliouras, G.: Limits and limitations of no-regret learning in games. Knowl. Eng. Rev. **32** (2017)
22. Nekipelov, D., Syrgkanis, V., Tardos, E.: Econometrics for learning agents. In: EC, pp. 1–18. ACM (2015)
23. Nekipelov, D., Wang, T.: Inference and auction design in online advertising. Commun. ACM **60**(7), 70–79 (2017)
24. Nikolova, E., Stier-Moses, N.E.: A mean-risk model for the traffic assignment problem with stochastic travel times. Oper. Res. **62**(2), 366–382 (2014)
25. Panageas, I., Piliouras, G.: Average case performance of replicator dynamics in potential games via computing regions of attraction. In: EC, pp. 703–720. ACM (2016)
26. Piliouras, G., Nikolova, E., Shamma, J.S.: Risk sensitivity of price of anarchy under uncertainty. ACM Trans. Econ. Comput. **5**(1), 5:1–5:27 (2016)
27. Rosenthal, R.: A class of games possessing pure-strategy Nash equilibria. Int. J. Game Theor. **2**(1), 65–67 (1973)
28. Roughgarden, T.: Intrinsic robustness of the price of anarchy. In: STOC, pp. 513–522. ACM (2009)
29. Roughgarden, T.: Twenty Lectures on Algorithmic Game Theory. Cambridge University Press, Cambridge (2016)
30. Roughgarden, T., Tardos, É.: How bad is selfish routing? J. ACM (JACM) **49**(2), 236–259 (2002)
31. Roughgarden, T., Tardos, É.: Bounding the inefficiency of equilibria in nonatomic congestion games. Games Econ. Behav. **47**(2), 389–403 (2004)
32. Sheffi, Y.: Urban Transportation Networks: Equilibrium Analysis with Mathematical Programming Methods. Prentice-Hall, New Jersey, US (1985)
33. Syrgkanis, V.: Algorithmic game theory and econometrics. ACM SIGecom Exch. **14**(1), 105–108 (2015)
34. Zhang, J., Pourazarm, S., Cassandras, C.G., Paschalidis, I.C.: Data-driven estimation of origin-destination demand and user cost functions for the optimization of transportation networks. arXiv preprint arXiv:1610.09580 (2016)

Dynamic Pricing in Competitive Markets

Paresh Nakhe[(✉)]

Institute of Computer Science, Goethe University, Frankfurt (Main), Germany
Nakhe@em.uni-frankfurt.de

Abstract. Dynamic pricing of goods in a competitive environment to maximize revenue is a natural objective and has been a subject of research over the years. In this paper, we focus on a class of markets exhibiting the substitutes property with sellers having divisible and replenishable goods. Depending on the prices chosen, each seller observes a certain demand which is satisfied subject to the supply constraint. The goal of the seller is to price her good dynamically so as to maximize her revenue. For the static market case, when the consumer utility satisfies the gross substitutes CES property, we give a $O(\sqrt{T})$ regret bound on the maximum loss in revenue of a seller using a modified version of the celebrated Online Gradient Descent algorithm by Zinkevich [17]. For a more specialized set of consumer utilities satisfying the iso-elasticity condition, we show that when each seller uses a regret-minimizing algorithm satisfying a certain technical property, the regret with respect to $(1 - \alpha)$ times optimal revenue is bounded as $O(T^{1/4}/\sqrt{\alpha})$. We extend this result to markets with dynamic supplies and prove a corresponding dynamic regret bound, whose guarantee deteriorates smoothly with the inherent instability of the market. As a side-result, we also extend the previously known convergence results of these algorithms in a general game to the dynamic setting.

Keywords: Dynamic pricing · Online convex optimization

1 Introduction

The Internet has revolutionized the way goods are bought and sold and has in the process created a range of new possibilities to price the goods strategically and dynamically. This is especially true for online retail and apparel stores where the cost and effort to update prices has become negligible. This flexibility in pricing has propelled the research in *dynamic pricing* in the last decade or so, informally defined as the study of determining optimal selling prices in an unknown environment to optimize an objective, usually revenue. Coupled with the presence of digitally available and frequently updated sales data one may also view this as an (online) learning problem.

The inherent hurdles in dynamic pricing arise on account of *lack of information*. In the context of a single good case, this could be the underlying demand function that maps a given price to the observed demand. Indeed, this problem

N. R. Devanur and P. Lu (Eds.): WINE 2017, LNCS 10674, pp. 354–367, 2017.
https://doi.org/10.1007/978-3-319-71924-5_25

has been studied in several models in literature and strong results are now known for it. However, the problem becomes all the more challenging in a realistic setting where multiple sellers independently choose prices for their goods and the demand observed by any single seller is a function of all the prices. For example, some fixed seller might observe completely different demands for the same price she uses for her items depending on the prices chosen by other sellers. Such a seller might falsely conclude of being in a dynamic environment even when the underlying demand function is static.

Several existing approaches for dynamic pricing assume a parametric form for the underlying demand function and choose a sequence of prices to learn the individual parameters by statistical estimation. This approach is commonly referred to as "learn-and-earn" in literature [10]. It would, however, be unrealistic in the presence of multiple sellers since that would imply learning highly nonlinear and possibly unstructured functions in high dimensions. Instead, we view the market as a set of strategic agents (the sellers) choosing successive actions (prices) in order to maximize their utility (revenue) and focus on using the existing rich tool-kit of *agnostic learning* in game-theoretic models to prove fast convergence to optimal prices.

The advantages of an agnostic learning approach are multifold: Firstly, it does not rely on the precise parametric form of the underlying demand function and secondly can be easily extended to the case when the market parameters may change across rounds. The downside, however, being that in the best case of static markets with clean parametric representation, the algorithms might converge to optimal prices only asymptotically [9,12]. Consequently, to measure the performance of the actions (prices) chosen by such a learning algorithm we typically compare it to a certain benchmark sequence of actions and the *regret bound* represents the loss incurred by the algorithm for not having chosen the benchmark sequence instead. In most such algorithms, this benchmark sequence is usually a single action that maximizes the total reward over all rounds.

We base our dynamic pricing approach on the work by Syrgkanis et al. [16] where the authors prove that in a game with multiple agents, if each agent uses a regret-minimizing algorithm with a suitable step-size parameter and satisfying a certain technical property, then the individual regret of each agent is bounded by $O(T^{1/4})$ where T is the total number of rounds. In a nutshell, these algorithms *guess* the utility vector for the forthcoming round and choose an action such that the cumulative utility over all rounds is maximized. The regret bound thus obtained holds with respect to the single best action in hindsight and is one of the benchmarks we use to measure the performance of our approach.

Contribution: Our main contributions in this paper can be broadly divided into the following 3 parts:

1. For the class of markets with gross substitutes CES utility functions, we show that a simple modification to the Online Gradient Descent (OGD) algorithm by Zinkevich [17] can be used to obtain a regret bound on the loss in revenue with respect to the single best price in hindsight of order $O(\sqrt{T})$.

2. For the class of gross substitutes iso-elastic markets, building on the analysis in [16] we obtain a stronger regret bound of order $O\left(\frac{T^{1/4}}{\sqrt{\alpha}}\right)$ against a $(1 - \alpha)$ multiplicative approximation of the best price in hindsight by using specialized learning algorithms.

3. For the same class of markets as above but with dynamic supplies we prove a corresponding regret bound of order $O\left((1 + W_T)\left(\frac{T^{1/4}}{\sqrt{\alpha}}\right)\right)$. Importantly, this regret bound is with respect to the sequence of equilibrium prices in hindsight and captures the inherent instability of the market in the form of the parameter W_T.

In the process, we also extend the technical property, namely RVU , introduced in [16] to the setting of dynamic regret by defining a corresponding DRVU property. Any learning algorithm satisfying the RVU property was shown to achieve a regret bound of $O(T^{1/4})$ in [16] for a general class of games. Analogously, we prove that algorithms satisfying the DRVU property achieve a regret bound of $O\left((1 + C_T)T^{1/4}\right)$ where C_T is a measure of the hardness of the benchmark sequence.

A key observation in this work is that if the sellers in a market are ready to forgo a small fraction of their revenue, then they can converge to their (approximately) optimal prices (in static market setting) much faster ($T^{-3/4}$ instead of $T^{-1/2}$). This faster convergence property is all the more desirable when the markets *drift* and convergence to optimal strategy in a small number of rounds is not possible. One would then like to achieve good performance with respect to a dynamic benchmark.

Related Work

The problem of learning an optimal pricing policy for various demand models and inventory constraints has been researched extensively in the last decade. However, many consider the problem of a single good with no *competition effects*. For example, [1,3,4,6,9] study a parametric family of demand functions and design an optimal pricing policy by estimating the unknown parameters by standard techniques such as linear regression or maximum likelihood estimation. [2,11] consider Bayesian and non-parametric approaches.

Closer to the theme of this paper, there has also been a considerable amount of research about dynamic pricing in models incorporating competition, [7,8] being some of them. However, most of these consider discrete choice models of demand, where a single consumer approaches and buys a discrete bundle of goods. Moreover, they assume that every seller has a fixed inventory level in the beginning and is not replenished during the course of the algorithm. We, on the other hand, consider demand originating from a general mass of consumers where when the volumes are large, the items may be considered divisible. For a more thorough survey of the existing literature, we refer the reader to [5].

In Sect. 3 we consider Online Gradient Descent (OGD), first introduced by Zinkevich [17] as the learning algorithm used by a seller. At every time step, the learner takes a step in the direction of the gradient observed in that round. Interestingly, this simple update rule is shown to achieve a regret bound of $O(\sqrt{T})$. While this approach is independent of any game-theoretic considerations Syrgkanis et al. [16] showed that with certain modified versions of this algorithm the individual regret of each player can be brought down to $O(T^{1/4})$. The analysis is based on the learning algorithm proposed by Rakhlin and Sridharan [14] in a different context. Informally, the algorithm is based on the idea that if the gradient observed in the next round is *predictable*, then it rules out the worst-case scenario and allows one to achieve a much better regret guarantee.

2   Static Market Model

We consider a market with n sellers, each selling a single good to a general population of consumers. We assume that the market operates in a round-based fashion. In each round t every seller i chooses a price p_i^t for her good. The supply, w_i, of seller i, stays the same every round. No left-over supply from previous rounds is carried over (which is the case for example for perishable goods). Depending on the resulting price vector $\mathbf{p}^t = (p_i^t)_i$, each seller observes a certain demand for her item given by $x_i(\mathbf{p}^t)$. These observed demands are governed by an underlying utility function of the consumers. For the purposes of this paper (except Sect. 3), we assume that these utilities are "IGS" as defined below:

Definition 1 (Iso-elastic and Gross Substitutes (*IGS*) utility). *We say a utility function is IGS when it satisfies the following conditions:*

(a) The utility function satisfies the gross substitutes property[1] and the resulting demand functions are continuous.
(b) Increasing the price of any good i decreases the total spending on the item i.e. $p_i x_i(\boldsymbol{p})$.
(c) The price elasticity of demand of good j[2] with respect to the price of any other good i satisfies:

$$\left| \frac{\partial \ln x_j(\boldsymbol{p})}{\partial \ln p_i} \right| = E \qquad \forall i, j \in [1, n]$$

where $E > 1$ is a constant.

Although more restrictive we view this model as an approximation to the gross substitutes CES utility. This utility function satisfies parts (a) and (b) in Definition 1 but instead of a fixed constant as price elasticity, this parameter depends on the prices of all goods i.e. $\left| \frac{\partial \ln x_j(\mathbf{p})}{\partial \ln p_i} \right| = E_i(\mathbf{p})$. We use this more

---

[1] Informally, this properties implies that increasing the price of a good i does not decrease the demand of any other good j.

[2] Price elasticity is a measure of the percentage change in the quantity of a good demanded for a unit percentage change in the price i.e. $E_i(\mathbf{p}) = \frac{\partial x_j}{x_j} \Big/ \frac{\partial p_i}{p_i}$.

general class of utilities in Sect. 3. Since we do not need the exact parametric form of this utility class, we do not define it here but forward the interested reader to [15] for a more precise definition.

To ensure that the problem is well defined we assume that the optimal revenue of any seller i for any profile $\mathbf{p}_{-i}$ of prices chosen by others is bounded in $[r, R]$. Intuitively, this is equivalent to saying that the set of allowed prices and supplies are such that revenue of any seller is not arbitrarily small or large.

We measure the performance of the pricing strategy used by the seller in terms of regret. Formally, the regret of an algorithm after T rounds is defined as the loss with respect to the single best action (here price) in hindsight. For example, if $\{r_i^t(p_i)\}_t$ denotes the sequence of revenue functions faced by the seller i then the regret with respect to the sequence of prices $\{p_i^t\}_{t=1}^T$ is defined as: $R_T = \sum_t r_i^t(p_i^*) - r_i^t(p_i^t)$ where $p_i^* = \operatorname*{argmax}_p \sum_t r_i^t(p)$. Analogously, one can also define *dynamic regret* as the regret incurred with respect to a dynamic benchmark sequence. For example, if $p_1^*, p_2^* \cdots p_T^*$ is the sequence of prices against which we measure the loss of our algorithm, then dynamic regret is defined as:

$$R_T(p_1^*, p_2^* \cdots p_T^*) = \sum_t r_i^t(p_t^*) - r_i^t(p_i^t)$$

Log-Revenue Objective: In this paper, we take an indirect approach to the problem of revenue optimization by optimizing the log-revenue objective instead of the actual revenue. The log-revenue objective is simply the plot of revenue against the price in the log-scale defined as follows:

$$\ln r_i(\mathbf{p}) = \ln \left[p_i \min \{x_i(\mathbf{p}), w_i\} \right].$$

Using the definition of IGS utility functions we can derive the following straightforward fact used directly in the rest of the paper. The proposition follows from the definition of log-revenue function and price elasticity of demand.

Proposition 1. *The gradient of the log-revenue function $\tilde{r}_i(\tilde{p}_i)$ satisfies:*

$$\frac{\partial \tilde{r}_i}{\partial \tilde{p}_i} = \begin{cases} 1 - E & \text{for } p_i : x_i(\mathbf{p}) < w_i \\ 1 & \text{for } p_i : x_i(\mathbf{p}) \geq w_i \end{cases}$$

This proposition essentially determines the shape of the log-revenue function for seller i, keeping prices of all other items fixed (Fig. 1). It is instructive to keep this general shape in mind as we introduce learning algorithms to optimize it in the following sections.

Notation: We denote vectors by bold-face letters and log of an entity by tilde, for example, $\ln r = \tilde{r}$. Often for ease of notation, we shall use x_i to denote demand of good i instead of $x_i(\mathbf{p})$ when it is clear from the context. p_{-i} denotes the vector of prices of all sellers excluding i. The ∇ notation denotes the gradient. All the missing proofs can be found in the full version of the paper [13].

3   Modified OGD

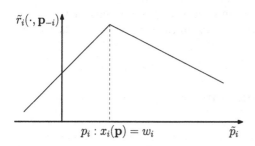

Fig. 1. Log-revenue for IGS utilities

In this section, we demonstrate the kind of regret bounds that can be achieved for gross substitute CES utilities. Since CES utilities do not satisfy the IGS utility model, the gradient of the log-revenue curve, $1 - E_i(\mathbf{p})$, in the case when $x_i(\mathbf{p}) < w_i$ is unknown to the seller (see in contrast Proposition 1). To ensure that the problem is well-defined we assume that the price elasticity of demand for any item i and any price vector $\mathbf{p}$ is bounded in $[E_{min}, E_{max}]$. We work around the problem of unknown gradients by using a simple modification to the analysis by Zinkevich (Theorem 1, [17]) and show that if sellers use online gradient descent (with modified gradient feedback) as their learning algorithm on the log-revenue objective, then they can achieve a $O(\sqrt{T})$ regret bound. We start with a claim for general convex functions with modified feedback.

Claim 1. *Consider a sequence of convex functions $f_1, f_2 \cdots f_T$ satisfying the following condition:*

$$g \;\leq\; |\nabla f_t(x)| \;\leq\; G \qquad \forall t \in [T], x \in \mathcal{X}$$

Suppose for the action x_t chosen in round t and for $\gamma = \frac{G}{g}$, we receive as feedback $\nabla g_t(x_t) \in \left[\frac{\nabla f_t(x_t)}{\gamma}, \gamma \nabla f_t(x_t) \right]$, then the regret bound of OGD for stepsize $\eta_t = 1/\sqrt{t}$ is given by $R_T \leq \left(\gamma \sqrt{T} \right)$.

This property allows us to use OGD even with *imperfect* gradient feedback, upto a multiplicative constant, to obtain regret bounds that are also within this same factor. Since the exact gradient in the case when $x_i(\mathbf{p}) < w_i$ is not available to the algorithm we modify the feedback gradient based on the demand observed,

$$\frac{\partial \tilde{r}_i}{\partial \tilde{p}_i} = \begin{cases} 1 - E_i(\mathbf{p}) \;\; \Rightarrow \;\; -1, & \text{for } p_i : x_i(\mathbf{p}) < w_i \\ 1 \qquad\qquad \Rightarrow \;\; 1, & \text{for } p_i : x_i(\mathbf{p}) \geq w_i \end{cases} \tag{1}$$

i.e. we work around this problem by choosing as feedback the gradient -1 whenever $x_i(\mathbf{p}) < w_i$ and $+1$ otherwise.

Theorem 1. *If any player i uses OGD on the log revenue curve with $\eta_t = t^{-1/2}$ with the adjusted gradient feedback as in Eq. 1, then the cumulative loss in revenue of seller i is bounded as:*

$$\sum_t r_i^t(p_i^*) - r_i^t(p_i^t) \;\leq\; O\left(R \cdot \max\left\{ E_{max} - 1, \frac{1}{E_{min} - 1} \right\} T^{1/2} \right),$$

where $p_i^* = \underset{p_i}{argmax} \sum_t \tilde{r}_i(p_i, p_{-i}^t).$

This bound serves as a benchmark and improving upon this is the main focus of our paper. In the next section, we focus on the smaller set of IGS utility functions and show that with specialized learning algorithms the price dynamics converge faster to an approximately optimal configuration.

4   Game Theoretic Interpretation

4.1   Preliminaries

We start with the observation that the revenue optimization problem in a market is equivalent to agents in a game using learning algorithms to optimize their utility, where this utility is a function of the *strategies* of all agents in the game. Problems of this flavour although already studied in different game-theoretic settings are not applicable in a black-box fashion to our problem on account of the market specific constraints. Specifically, the log-revenue objective although concave is not smooth, an assumption used in almost all gradient-based learning algorithms. This calls for a different approach than the ones taken in the idealized settings.

With this in mind, we start from the result of [16], where it is proved that if all players in a game use learning algorithms satisfying a certain technical property, called the RVU property (See Definition 2), then the regret incurred by each individual agent is $O(T^{1/4})$. A natural question is then: Can we use the same technique in our revenue optimization problem in markets?

Definition 2 (RVU property, [16]). *We say that a vanishing regret algorithm satisfies the Regret bounded by Variation in Utilities (RVU) property with parameters $\alpha > 0$ and $0 < \beta \leq \gamma$ and a pair of dual norms $(\|\cdot\|, \|\cdot\|_*)$ if its regret on any sequence of utilities $\boldsymbol{u}^1, \boldsymbol{u}^2, \ldots \boldsymbol{u}^T$ is bounded as:*

$$\sum_{t=1}^T \left\langle \boldsymbol{p}^* - \boldsymbol{p}^t \mid \boldsymbol{u}^t \right\rangle \leq \alpha + \beta \sum_{t=1}^T \left\| \boldsymbol{u}^t - \boldsymbol{u}^{t-1} \right\|_* - \gamma \sum_{t=1}^T \left\| \boldsymbol{p}^t - \boldsymbol{p}^{t-1} \right\|$$

Although this property is defined for linear utility functions, we can extend this definition to concave utilities by using the gradient of the utility with respect to p_i as proxy for $\boldsymbol{u}^t$ i.e. in the context of our problem

$$\tilde{r}_i^t(p_i^*) - \tilde{r}_i^t(p_i^t) \leq \left\langle \mathbf{p}^* - \mathbf{p}^t \mid \frac{\partial \tilde{r}_i}{\partial \tilde{p}_i} \right\rangle.$$

As noted in [16], the standard online learning algorithms such as Online Mirror Descent (generalization of OGD) and Follow-the-Regularized-Leader (FTRL) do not satisfy the RVU property. However, Rakhlin and Sridharan [14] and Syrgkanis et al. [16] have developed modified versions of these algorithms, namely Optimistic Mirror Descent (OMD) and Optimistic FTRL (OFTRL) respectively, that do satisfy this property,

Proposition 2 (Informal, [16]). *Let D denote a measure of the diameter of the decision space. Then:*

1. *The OMD algorithm using step size η satisfies the RVU property with constants $\alpha = D/\eta$, $\beta = \eta$ and $\gamma = 1/(8\eta)$*
2. *The OFTRL algorithm using step size η satisfies the RVU property with constants $\alpha = D/\eta$, $\beta = \eta$ and $\gamma = 1/(4\eta)$.*

For the analysis based on the RVU property to be applicable, the utility function (alternatively, the objective) of each player should additionally satisfy some *regularity* conditions. For ease of presentation, we shall refer to the player objectives satisfying these conditions as *regular objectives* and are defined, in a general sense, as follows:

Definition 3 (Regular Objective). *Let the strategy space of each player i be denoted by $S_i \in \mathbb{R}^d$ and the combined strategy space by $\mathcal{S} = S_1 \times S_2 \times \cdots S_n$. Let $\boldsymbol{w} = (\boldsymbol{w}_i)_{i=1}^n$ denote the combined strategy profile where the strategy of each player $w_i \in S_i$. An objective function $f_i : \mathcal{S} \to \mathbb{R}$ of a player i is said to be regular if it satisfies the following conditions:*

1. *(Concave in player strategy) For each player i and for each profile of opponent strategies $\boldsymbol{w}_{-i}$, the function $f_i(\cdot, \boldsymbol{w}_{-i})$ is concave in $\boldsymbol{w}_i$.*
2. *(Lipschitz Gradient) For each player i, the gradient of the objective with respect to i, $\delta_i(\boldsymbol{w}) = \nabla_i f_i(\boldsymbol{w})$ is L-Lipschitz continuous with respect to the L1-norm. i.e.*

$$\|\delta_i(\boldsymbol{w}) - \delta_i(\boldsymbol{y})\|_* \leq L \cdot \|\boldsymbol{w} - \boldsymbol{y}\|.$$

4.2 Smoothed Log-Revenue Curve

By definition 3, to be able to apply the analysis based on the RVU property it is necessary that the utility function be smooth, specifically, the gradient of the objective should be L-Lipschitz continuous.[3] Clearly, as seen in Fig. 1, this is not the case with our log-revenue objective. We work around this problem by using a *smoothed* gradient feedback.

Definition 4 (Smoothed Gradient Feedback). *For a fixed seller i and price vector $\boldsymbol{p}_{-i}$, we define the smoothed gradient for player i, $\delta_{i,\mathsf{x}_i}(\cdot)$, as follows:*

$$\delta_{i,\mathsf{x}_i}(p_i) = \begin{cases} 1, & \text{for } p_i : x_i(\boldsymbol{p}) > w_i \\ 1 - E, & \text{for } p_i : x_i(\boldsymbol{p}) < \mathsf{X}_i \\ 1 + \frac{E(\tilde{x}_i(\boldsymbol{p}) - \tilde{w}_i)}{\tilde{w}_i - \tilde{\mathsf{X}}_i}, & \text{otherwise} \end{cases}$$

where X_i is a threshold parameter for seller i.

---

[3] Informally, this is required to ensure that small changes in prices do not lead to large changes in utility gradient.

For ease of notation, we shall denote $\delta_{i,\mathsf{X}_i}(p_i)$ by simply δ_i when clear from context. For purposes of analysis, we parametrize the threshold parameter of seller i as $\mathsf{X}_i = \frac{w_i}{\exp(\varepsilon r)}$ where $\varepsilon < 1/R$ is a small constant and r is a lower bound on optimal revenue of seller i. Also, henceforth we shall refer to the *actual* revenue curve by $\tilde{r}(\cdot)$ and the algorithm's view of smoothed revenue curve by $\tilde{r}^{sm}(\cdot)$.

Lemma 1. *The smoothed revenue objective, $\tilde{r}_i^{sm}(\boldsymbol{p})$, for any seller i is regular.*

4.3   Cost of Smoothness

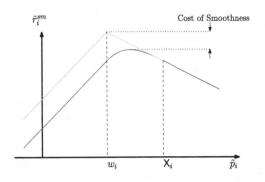

Fig. 2. Smoothed vs actual log-revenue curve

Since our learning algorithm only uses the smoothed gradient feedback the resulting regret bound also holds only for the smoothed view of the log-revenue curve, i.e. the optimal price in this smoothed view would be the price for which the smoothed gradient is zero although this price is clearly sub-optimal for the actual revenue curve. (See Fig. 2). To prove bounds with respect to the actual revenue curve we need to draw connections between the smoothed and actual revenue for any fixed price.

Lemma 2. *For any seller i and fixed $\boldsymbol{p}_{-i}$ and for any fixed price p chosen by seller i:*

$$0 \leq \tilde{r}_i(p, \boldsymbol{p}_{-i}) - \tilde{r}_i^{sm}(p, \boldsymbol{p}_{-i}) \leq \varepsilon r$$

We are now ready to state and prove our first main result.

Theorem 2. *Suppose that each seller i uses the OFTRL algorithm on the log-revenue objective using the smoothed gradient feedback and threshold demand $\mathsf{X}_i = \frac{w_i}{\exp(\varepsilon r)}$. Let $p_i^{**} = \mathrm{argmax}_p \sum_t \tilde{r}_i^t(p)$ denote the optimal price in hindsight with respect to the log-revenue objective. Then the actual loss in revenue is bounded as:*

$$\sum_{t=1}^{T} (1 - \varepsilon R)\, r_i^t(p_i^{**}) - r_i^t(p_i^t) \leq O\left(\left(\frac{R^2 E^2}{\varepsilon r} \right)^{1/2} T^{1/4} \right) - \varepsilon RT.$$

Proof. Since $\tilde{r}_i^{sm}(p_i, \mathbf{p}_{-i})$ satisfies the regularity condition (Definition 3), if each seller uses a learning algorithm satisfying the RVU property, then the individual regret satisfies:

$$\sum_t \tilde{r}_i^{sm}(p_i^{**}, \mathbf{p}_{-i}^t) - \tilde{r}_i^{sm}(p_i^t, \mathbf{p}_{-i}^t) \leq \sum_t \tilde{r}_i^{sm}(\bar{p}_i^*, \mathbf{p}_{-i}^t) - \tilde{r}_i^{sm}(p_i^t, \mathbf{p}_{-i}^t)$$

$$\leq \sum_t \langle \delta_{i,\mathsf{X}_i}(\mathbf{p}^t) \,\big|\, \bar{p}_i^* - \tilde{p}_i^t \rangle$$

where $\bar{p}_i^* = \underset{p}{\arg\max} \sum_t \tilde{r}_i^{sm}(p, \mathbf{p}_{-i}^t)$. For ease of notation, we denote $\delta_{i,\mathbf{x}_i}(\mathbf{p}^t)$ by δ_i^t. Using Lemma 2 to lower bound the left-hand side above:

$$
\sum_t \tilde{r}_i^{sm}(p^{**}, \mathbf{p}_{-i}^t) - \tilde{r}_i^{sm}(p_i^t, \mathbf{p}_{-i}^t) \geq \sum_t \left(\tilde{r}_i^t(p_i^{**}) - \varepsilon r \right) - \tilde{r}_i(p_i^t)
$$

$$
\geq \sum_t (1 - \varepsilon)\tilde{r}_i(p_i^{**}) - \tilde{r}_i(p_i^t) \tag{2}
$$

The last inequality holds since r is the lower bound on revenue. We still have to prove an upper bound on the expression: $\sum_t \langle \delta_i^t \, | \, \bar{p}_i^* - \tilde{p}_i^t \rangle$. Since our learning algorithm satisfies the RVU property, by Definition 2 it follows that:

$$
R_T \leq \alpha + \beta \sum_{t=1}^{T} \left| \delta_i^t - \delta_i^{t-1} \right|^2.
$$

Since the smoothed gradient $\delta_i(\mathbf{p})$ for any seller is L-Lipschitz continuous (proved in full version), for $L = \frac{E^2}{\varepsilon r}$ we can bound $\left| \delta_i^t - \delta_i^{t-1} \right|^2$ as:

$$
\left| \delta_i^t - \delta_i^{t-1} \right|^2 \leq L^2 \left(\sum_j |p_j^t - p_j^{t-1}| \right)^2 \leq L^2 n \sum_j |p_j^t - p_j^{t-1}|^2.
$$

In addition to the fact that OFTRL satisfies the RVU property, it is also known that the algorithm satisfies a *stability* property (Lemma 20, [16]) i.e. $|p_j^t - p_j^{t-1}| \leq 2\eta$ where η is the step-size parameter of the algorithm. Using this we can bound the regret as: $R_T \leq \alpha + 4n^2\beta L^2\eta^2 T$. Finally substituting the RVU parameters of the algorithm (Proposition 2) $\alpha = D/\eta$, $\beta = \eta$ and $\gamma = 1/4\eta$ with $\eta = (Ln)^{-1/2}T^{-1/4}$ we get:

$$
R_T \leq D/\eta + 4\eta^3 L^2 n^2 T = O(\sqrt{Ln}(D + 4)T^{1/4}).
$$

Combining this with Eq. 2 and substituting the value of L we get:

$$
\sum_{t=1}^{T} (1 - \varepsilon)\tilde{r}_i^t(p_i^{**}) - \tilde{r}_i^t(p_i^t) \leq O\left(\left(\frac{E^2}{\varepsilon r} \right)^{1/2} \cdot T^{1/4} \right)
$$

Rearranging the inequality and using same steps as in the proof of Lemma 1:

$$
\sum_t \frac{r_i^t(p_i^{**}) - r_i^t(p^t)}{r_i^t(p^{**})} \leq O\left(\left(\frac{E^2}{\varepsilon r} \right)^{1/2} \cdot T^{1/4} \right) + \varepsilon \sum_{t=1}^{T} \tilde{r}_i^t(p_i^{**})
$$

$$
\sum_t r_i^t(p_i^{**}) - r_i^t(p^t) \leq O\left(\left(\frac{E^2 R^2}{\varepsilon r} \right)^{1/2} \cdot T^{1/4} \right) + \varepsilon R \sum_{t=1}^{T} \tilde{r}_i^t(p_i^{**})
$$

$$
\leq O\left(\left(\frac{R^2 E^2}{\varepsilon r} \right)^{1/2} T^{1/4} \right) + R\varepsilon \sum_{t=1}^{T} (r_i^t(p_i^{**}) - 1)
$$

The bound follows from this inequality. $\qquad\square$

Similar bounds can be shown in the case when sellers use the Optimistic Mirror Descent (OMD) algorithm.

Remark 1. Here we compare the revenue obtained with respect to the fixed price $p^{**} = \text{argmax}_p \sum_t \tilde{r}_i^t(p)$ i.e. the price that optimizes the cumulative log-revenue objective and not necessarily the revenue objective itself. Since the revenue function need not be concave, it is not immediately clear how to characterize the resulting cumulative revenue function and the price optimizing it. For this reason, we are using the price that optimizes the cumulative log-revenue.

5   Learning with a Dynamic Benchmark

A bound on the loss of revenue of a seller with respect to the single price p_i^{**} in hindsight is a comparatively weak benchmark. Ideally the sellers would like to choose as benchmark the revenue-optimizing price in every round, i.e. the sequence of prices $\{p_i^{*,t}\}_{t=1}^T$. Such a benchmark is however too strict to obtain meaningful regret bounds. We shall instead focus on a more constrained sequence of benchmark prices. In what follows, we define a class of learning algorithms whose guarantees apply to *any* game setting where strategic players use regret minimization to maximize their own utility. For generality, we define this class for any sequence of linear utilities $\{u_i^t(\cdot)\}_t$. In the following section, we shall specialize this guarantee to the context of revenue optimization in markets.

Definition 5 (DRVU property). *We say that a vanishing regret algorithm satisfies the Dynamic Regret bounded by Variation in Utilities (DRVU) property with parameters $\alpha, \rho > 0$ and $0 < \beta \leq \gamma$ and a pair of dual norms $(\|\cdot\|, \|\cdot\|_*)$, if its regret on any sequence of utilities $u^1, u^2, \ldots u^T$ with respect to the benchmark sequence $\{p_i^{*,t}\}_t$ is bounded as:*

$$\sum_{t=1}^T \langle p^{*,t} - p^t \mid u^t \rangle \leq \alpha + \beta \sum_{t=1}^T \|u^t - u^{t-1}\|_*^2$$

$$+ \rho \sum_{t=1}^T \|p^{*,t} - p^{*,t-1}\| - \gamma \sum_{t=1}^T \|p^t - p^{t-1}\|.$$

This definition is an extension of the RVU property. The difference is in the term $\rho \sum_t \|\mathbf{p}^{*,t} - \mathbf{p}^{*,t-1}\|$ that quantifies the hardness of learning with respect to a dynamic strategy.

Lemma 3 (Informal). *The OMD algorithm, with step size η and suitably chosen parameters, satisfies the DRVU property with constants $\alpha = D_1/\eta$, $\rho = D_2/\eta$ $\beta = \eta$ and $\gamma = 1/(8\eta)$ for constants D_1 and D_2.*

Using this definition we can now extend almost all of the results in [16] to corresponding results for dynamic regret. We state the following for concreteness.

Corollary 1. *Let $C_T = \sum_t \| p_i^{*,t} - p_i^{*,t-1} \|$ denote the cumulative change in benchmark strategies of player i. If all players use algorithms satisfying the DRVU property, then the regret incurred by any player i satisfies:*

$$\sum_t u_i^t \left(p_i^t, p_{-i}^t \right) - u_i^t \left(p_i^{*,t}, p_{-i}^t \right) \leq O\left((1 + C_T) T^{1/4} \right)$$

5.1   Revenue Optimization in Dynamic Markets

Dynamic Market Model: We define a dynamic market $\mathcal{M} = (M_1, M_2 \cdots M_T)$, as a sequence of markets with the same set of sellers and buyers with the same IGS utility functions as in Definition 1 but with a dynamic supply vector i.e. we characterize the instability of the market by the sequence of supply vectors $\mathbf{w}_1, \mathbf{w}_2 \cdots \mathbf{w}_T$. In order to achieve a strong dynamic regret bound, we shall assume that the income elasticity parameter of the market is equal to one. This is a standard assumption in many market models and is also satisfied by CES utilities.

In this section, we connect the dynamic regret of any seller i to the inherent instability of the market by choosing the sequence of *equilibrium prices*[4] for seller i at each round as the benchmark sequence, i.e. $\{p_i^{eq,t}\}_{t=1}^T$. Since the supply vector may change every round, the equilibrium prices may also correspondingly change. These changes in equilibrium prices completely capture the inherent instability of the market. For example, if the supply stays the same every round, then this benchmark is the same as choosing the equilibrium price in each round. On the other hand, if the supply fluctuates wildly from one round to the next, then so do the equilibrium prices and there is no hope of achieving a sub-linear regret bound. That is, the resulting dynamic regret bound captures the inherent market instability. In the following theorem, we use this connection to prove a bound on the dynamic regret with respect to the cumulative change in the supplies.

Theorem 3. *Let $W_T = \sum_t \| \tilde{w}^t - \tilde{w}^{t-1} \|_1$ denote the cumulative change in the market in terms of changes in supplies. Suppose each seller i uses the OMD algorithm on the log-revenue function with smoothed gradient feedback and threshold demand $X_i^t = \frac{w_i^t}{\exp(\varepsilon r)}$. Let $\{p_i^{eq,t}\}_t$ denote the sequence of equilibrium prices for seller i. Then:*

$$\sum_{t=1}^T (1 - \varepsilon R)\, r_i^t(p_i^{eq,t}) - r_i^t(p^t) \leq O\left(\left(\frac{R^2 E^2}{\varepsilon r} \right)^{1/2} \cdot (1 + W_T) T^{1/4} \right)$$

6   Experimental Evaluation

We analyze the performance of our modified OGD and OMD algorithms when the consumer utility functions satisfy the gross substitutes CES property.

---

[4] Informally, a (Walrasian) equilibrium in this market corresponds to the vector of prices and an allocation of items such that the aggregate demand for each item is exactly equal to its supply.

Although from a theoretical standpoint we assumed that the price elasticity of the market is a constant, empirically we observed that CES functions approximately satisfy this assumption. In our simulations, we show that the OMD algorithm indeed performs as proved in our analysis, except for slightly worse convergence time (Fig. 3).

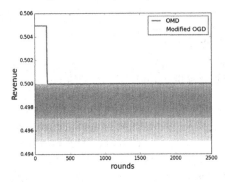

Fig. 3. Modified OGD vs OMD

We consider the scenario with 2 items and the value of $E = 2.5$. We assume that the market is static in that each seller has a supply of one unit every round and uses the threshold parameter $X_i = 0.9$. We observe that the modified OGD algorithm converges quickly to the neighbourhood of the optimal price but then keeps oscillating around it. This is expected since in this neighbourhood the observed gradients might change abruptly. The OMD algorithm on the other hand takes a while before it comes close to the neighbourhood but once there converges to optimum quickly. As described in the analysis, this is precisely the reason for using the smoothed gradient feedback.

7   Conclusion

In this paper, we presented two dynamic pricing strategies based on regret-minimizing algorithms for static markets. In contrast to a simple approach based on the modified OGD algorithm we showed that by using specialized learning algorithms the sellers can converge to (approximate) revenue maximizing prices. We extended the analysis of these algorithms to dynamic markets and proved corresponding dynamic regret bounds. In the process, we defined a property analogous to the RVU property that is satisfied by these learning algorithms and extended their results to the case of dynamic regret.

Our regret analysis with these specialized learning algorithms depends on the assumption that the underlying market is iso-elastic. We believe that extending the analysis to cases where the price elasticity may be dynamic is an important open question. Also, to obtain a regret bound in dynamic markets we needed the assumption of *gross substitutes* utility function. Obtaining revenue guarantees for more general utility functions would be an interesting future direction.

Acknowledgements. I would like to thank Martin Hoefer and Yun Kuen Cheung for the helpful discussions that helped shape this paper. I would also like to thank the anonymous reviewers for their helpful comments.

References

1. Besbes, O., Zeevi, A.: Dynamic pricing without knowing the demand function: risk bounds and near-optimal algorithms. Oper. Res. **57**(6), 1407–1420 (2009)

2. Besbes, O., Zeevi, A.: On the minimax complexity of pricing in a changing environment. Oper. Res. **59**(1), 66–79 (2011)
3. Broder, J., Rusmevichientong, P.: Dynamic pricing under a general parametric choice model. Oper. Res. **60**(4), 965–980 (2012)
4. Carvalho, A.X., Puterman, M.L.: Learning and pricing in an internet environment with binomial demands. J. Revenue Pricing Manage. **3**(4), 320–336 (2005)
5. Chen, M., Chen, Z.-L.: Recent developments in dynamic pricing research: multiple products, competition, and limited demand information. Prod. Oper. Manage. **24**(5), 704–731 (2015)
6. den Boer, A.V., Zwart, B.: Simultaneously learning and optimizing using controlled variance pricing. Manage. Sci. **60**(3), 770–783 (2013)
7. Gallego, G., Ming, H.: Dynamic pricing of perishable assets under competition. Manage. Sci. **60**(5), 1241–1259 (2014)
8. Gallego, G., Wang, R.: Multiproduct price optimization and competition under the nested logit model with product-differentiated price sensitivities. Oper. Res. **62**(2), 450–461 (2014)
9. Keskin, B., Zeevi, A.: Dynamic pricing with an unknown demand model: asymptotically optimal semi-myopic policies. Oper. Res. **62**(5), 1142–1167 (2014)
10. Keskin, N.B., Zeevi, A.: Chasing demand: learning and earning in a changing environment. Math. Oper. Res. **42**(2), 277–307 (2017)
11. Kleinberg, R., Leighton, T.: The value of knowing a demand curve: bounds on regret for online posted-price auctions. In: Proceedings of the 44th Annual IEEE Symposium on Foundations of Computer Science, FOCS 2003, pp. 594–605. IEEE Computer Society (2003)
12. Mertikopoulos, P.: Learning in concave games with imperfect information (2016)
13. Nakhe, P.: Dynamic pricing in competitive markets. arXiv preprint arXiv:1709.04960 (2017)
14. Rakhlin, A., Sridharan, K.: Online learning with predictable sequences. In: Shai, S.-S., Steinwart, I. (eds.), Proceedings of the 26th Annual Conference on Learning Theory. Proceedings of Machine Learning Research, PMLR, Princeton, NJ, USA, vol. 30, pp. 993–1019, 12–14 June 2013
15. Ramskov, J., Munksgaard, J.: Elasticities-a theoretical introduction. Balmorel Project (2001)
16. Syrgkanis, V., Agarwal, A., Luo, H., Schapire, R.E.: Fast convergence of regularized learning in games. In: Proceedings of the 28th International Conference on Neural Information Processing Systems, NIPS 2015, pp. 2989–2997, Cambridge, MIT Press (2015)
17. Zinkevich, M.: Online convex programming and generalized infinitesimal gradient ascent. In: Proceedings of the Twentieth International Conference on Machine Learning, ICML 2003, pp. 928–935. AAAI Press (2003)

Beyond Worst-Case (In)approximability of Nonsubmodular Influence Maximization

Grant Schoenebeck and Biaoshuai Tao[(✉)]

Department of Computer Science, University of Michigan, Ann Arbor, USA
{schoeneb,bstao}@umich.edu

Abstract. We consider the problem of maximizing the spread of influence in a social network by choosing a fixed number of initial seeds, formally referred to as the *influence maximization problem*. It admits a $(1 - 1/e)$-factor approximation algorithm if the influence function is *submodular*. Otherwise, in the worst case, the problem is NP-hard to approximate to within a factor of $N^{1-\varepsilon}$, where N is the number of vertices in the graph. This paper studies whether this worst-case hardness result can be circumvented by making assumptions about either the underlying network topology or the cascade model. All of our assumptions are motivated by many real life social network cascades.

First, we present strong inapproximability results for a very restricted class of networks called the *(stochastic) hierarchical blockmodel*, a special case of the well-studied *(stochastic) blockmodel* in which relationships between blocks admit a tree structure. We also provide a dynamic-program based polynomial time algorithm which optimally computes a directed variant of the influence maximization problem on hierarchical blockmodel networks. Our algorithm indicates that the inapproximability result is due to the bidirectionality of influence between agent-blocks.

Second, we present strong inapproximability results for a class of influence functions that are "almost" submodular, called *2-quasi-submodular*. Our inapproximability results hold even for any 2-quasi-submodular f fixed in advance. This result also indicates that the "threshold" between submodularity and nonsubmodularity is sharp, regarding the approximability of influence maximization.

1 Introduction

A *cascade* is a fundamental social network process in which a number of nodes, or agents, start with some property that they then may spread to neighbors. The importance of network structure on cascades has been shown to be relevant in a wide array of environments, including the adoption of products [5,8,18,30], farming technology [15], medical practices [14], participation in microfinancing [4], and the spread of information over social networks [26].

The authors gratefully acknowledge the support of the National Science Foundation under Career Award 1452915 and AiTF Award 1535912.

A full version of this paper is available on arXiv: https://arxiv.org/abs/1710.02827.

N. R. Devanur and P. Lu (Eds.): WINE 2017, LNCS 10674, pp. 368–382, 2017.
https://doi.org/10.1007/978-3-319-71924-5_26

A natural question, known as *the influence maximization problem* (INFMAX), is how to place a limited number k of initial seeds, in order to maximize the spread of the resulting cascade [17,24,25,32,33]. In order to study influence maximization, we first need to understand how cascades spread. Many cascade models have been proposed [2,31,37], and two simple examples are the Independent Cascade model [24,25,32] and the Threshold model [20]. In the *Independent Cascade model*, each newly infected node infects each currently uninfected neighbor in the subsequent round with some fixed probability p. In the *Threshold model* each node has a threshold (0, 1, 2, etc.) and becomes infected when the number of infected neighbors meets or surpasses that threshold.

Cascade models can be roughly divided into two categories: *submodular* and *nonsubmodular*. In submodular cascade models, such as the Independent Cascade model, a node's marginal probability of becoming infected after a new neighbor is infected decreases with the number of previously infected neighbors [24]. Submodular cascade models are fairly well understood theoretically, and properties of these cascades are usually closely related to a network's degree distribution and conductance [23].

In nonsubmodular contagion models, like the Threshold model, the marginal probability of being infected may increase as more neighbors are infected. For example, if a node has a threshold of 2, then the first infected neighbor has zero marginal impact, but the second infected neighbor causes this node to become infected with probability 1. Unlike submodular contagions, nonsubmodular contagions can require well-connected regions to spread [9].

Influence maximization becomes qualitatively different in nonsubmodular settings. In the submodular case, one should put as much distance between the k initial adopters as possible, lest they erode each other's effectiveness. However, in the nonsubmodular case, it may be advantageous to place the initial adopters close together to create synergy and yield more adoptions. The intuition that it is better to saturate one market first, and then expand implicitly assumes nonsubmodular influence in the cascades.

In general, it is NP-hard even to approximate INFMAX to within $N^{1-\epsilon}$ of the optimal expected number of infections [25]. However, assuming that we are looking at a submodular contagion, a straightforward greedy algorithm can efficiently find an answer that is at least a $(1 - 1/e)$ fraction of the optimal answer. Unfortunately, empirical research shows that many cascades are not submodular [3,27,34].

Key Question: Can this worst-case hardness result for nonsubmodular influence maximization be circumvented by making assumptions about either the underlying network topology or the cascade model?

We know a lot about what social networks look like, and previous hardness reductions make no attempt to capture realistic features of networks. It is very plausible that by restricting the space of networks we might regain tractability.

In this paper, we consider two natural network topologies: the hierarchical block model and the stochastic hierarchical blockmodel. Each of both is a natural restriction on the classic *(stochastic) blockmodel* [16,22,38] network structure. In (stochastic) blockmodels, agents are partitioned into ℓ blocks. The weight (or likelihood in the stochastic setting) of an edge between two vertices is based solely on blocks to which the vertices belong. The weights (or probabilities) of edges between two blocks can be represented by an $\ell \times \ell$ matrix. In the (stochastic) hierarchical blockmodel, the structure of the $\ell \times \ell$ matrix is severely restricted to be "tree-like".[1]

Our (stochastic) hierarchical blockmodel describes the hierarchical structure of the communities, in which a community is divided into many sub-communities, and each sub-community is further divided, etc. Typical examples include the structure of a country, which is divided into many provinces, and each province can be divided into cities. Our model captures the natural observation that people in the same sub-community in the lower hierarchy tend to have tighter (or more numerous) bonds among each other [13].

We also consider restrictions on the cascade model. The same research showing that cascades are often not submodular empirically also shows that the local submodularity often fails in one particular way—the second infected neighbor of an agent is, on average, more influential than the first. This has already been observed in community formation [3], viral marketing [27] and Twitter network [34]. This motivates our study of *2-quasi-submodular* cascade model where the marginal effect of the second infected neighbor is greater than the first, but after that the marginal effect decreases.

1.1   Our Results

First, we present inapproximability results for INFMAX in the hierarchical block-model. We show that INFMAX is NP-hard to approximate within a factor of $N^{1-\varepsilon}$ for arbitrary $\varepsilon > 0$, even if we assume all agents have unit threshold $\theta_v = 1$. We also extend this hardness result to the stochastic hierarchical blockmodel in the full version of our paper.

Moreover, for hierarchical blockmodel, we present a dynamic program based polynomial time algorithm for the influence maximization problem when we additionally assume the influence from one block to another is "one-way". This provides insights to the above intractability result: the difficulty comes from the bidirectionality of influence between agent-blocks.

Secondly, we present a family of inapproximability results for the 2-quasi-submodular cascade model. In particular, for *any* 2-quasi-submodular influence function f, we show that it is NP-hard to approximate the influence maximization problem within a factor of N^τ when each agent has f as its local influence function, where $\tau > 0$ is a constant depending on f. This can be seen as a threshold result for inapproximability of influence maximization, because if f is submodular, then the problem can be approximated to within a $(1-1/e)$-factor, but if f is just barely nonsubmodular the problem can no longer be approximated to within any constant factor.

---

[1] Previous work on community detection in networks [29] defines a different, but related stochastic hierarchical blockmodel, where the hierarchy is restricted to two levels.

Finally, we pose the open question of whether enforcing the aforementioned restrictions simultaneously on the network and the cascade renders the problem tractable.

1.2   Related Works

The influence maximization problem INFMAX was first posed by Domingos and Richardson [17,33]. Kempe, Kleinberg, and Tardos showed that a simple greedy algorithm obtains a $(1 - 1/e)$ factor approximation to the problem in the independent cascade model and linear threshold model [24], and extended this result to a family of submodular cascades which captures the prior results as a special case [25]. Mossel and Roch [32] further extended this result to capture all submodular cascades.

Perhaps most related to the present work, are several inapproximability results for INFMAX. If no assumption is made for the influence function, INFMAX is NP-hard to approximate to within a factor of $N^{1-\varepsilon}$ for any $\varepsilon > 0$ [25].

Chen [10] found inapproximability results on a similar optimization problem: instead of maximizing the total number of infected vertices given k initial targets, he considered the problem of finding a minimum-sized set of initial seeds such that all vertices will eventually be infected. This work studied restrictions of this problem to various fixed threshold models.

An important difference between our hardness result in Sect. 5 and all the previous results is that our result holds for *any* 2-quasi-submodular functions. In particular, in this work, f is fixed in advance before the NP-hardness reduction, while in previous work, specific influence functions were constructed within the reductions.

Several works looked at slightly different aspects of influence maximization. Borgs et al. [7] provably showed fast running times when the influence function is the independent cascade model. Lucier et al. [28] showed how to parallelize (in a model based on Map Reduce) the subproblem of determining the influence of a particular seed. Seeman and Singer [35] studied the special case where only a subset of the nodes in the network are available to be infected. They showed a constant factor approximation to the problem in their setting. He and Kempe looked at a robust versions of the problem [21] where the exact parameters of the cascade are unknown. Several works [6,19] studied the problem as a game between two different infectors.

Following the work of Kempe et al. [24,25], there were extensive works to solve INFMAX based on the heuristic implementations of the greedy algorithm designed to be efficient and scalable [11,12,28].

Notion of "near submodularity" was also proposed and studied in [36]. Our definition differs from the one in [36] in that a 2-quasi-submodular function can be, intuitively, very far from being submodular (for example, the 2-threshold cascade model). However, our reduction in Sect. 5 works for all a 2-quasi-submodular function, and 2-quasi-submodular functions can be arbitrarily close to a submodular one.

Our dynamic program for the hierarchical blockmodel with "one-way" influence (available in the full version) was further studied and generalized by Angell and Schoenebeck in [1]. They showed that, empirically, this generalized algorithm works very well even for arbitrary graphs. Specifically, they run dynamic programming on a hierarchical decomposition of general graphs, and, empirically, the algorithm effectively leverages the resultant hierarchical structures to return seed sets substantially superior to those of the greedy algorithm.

2   Preliminaries

In general a *cascade* on a graph is a stochastic mapping from a subset of vertices—the *seed vertices*, to another set of vertices that always contain the seed vertices—the *infected vertices*. The cascades we study in this paper all belong to the general threshold model [32], which captures the local decision making of vertices.

Definition 1. *The **general threshold model** $I_{F,D}^{G}$, is defined by a graph $G = (V, E)$ which may or may not be edge-weighted, and for each vertex v:*

i. *monotone local influence function $f_v : \{0,1\}^{|\Gamma(v)|} \mapsto \mathbb{R}_{\geq 0}$ where $\Gamma(v)$ denotes the neighbor vertices of v and $f_v(\emptyset) = 0$, and*

ii. *a threshold distribution $\mathcal{D}_v$ whose support is $\mathbb{R}_{\geq 0}$. Let F and $\mathcal{D}$ denote the collection of f_v and $\mathcal{D}_v$ respectively.*

On input $S \subseteq V$, $I_{F,D}^{G}(S)$ outputs a set of vertices as follows:

1. *Initially only vertices in S are infected, and for each vertex v the threshold $\theta_v \sim \mathcal{D}_v$ is sampled from $\mathcal{D}_v$ independently.[2]*

2. *In each subsequent round, a vertex v becomes infected if the influence of its infected neighbors exceeds its threshold.*

3. *The set of infected vertices is the output (after a round where no additional vertices are infected).*

We use k to denote $|S|$—the number of seeds, and use N to denote $|V|$—the total number of vertices in G. Let

$$\sigma_{F,D}^{G}(S) = \mathbb{E}\left[\left|I_{F,D}^{G}(S)\right|\right]$$

be the *expected* total number of infected vertices due to the influence of S, where the expectation is taken over the samplings of the thresholds of all vertices. We refer to $\sigma_{F,D}^{G}(\cdot)$ as the *global influence function*. Sometimes we write $\sigma(\cdot)$ with the parameters $G, F, \mathcal{D}$ omitted, when there is no confusion. Given that each f_v is monotone, it is straightforward to see that σ is monotone.

---

[2] The rationale of sampling thresholds *after* the seeds selection is to capture the scenario that the seed-picker does not have the full information on the agents in a social network, and this setting has been used in many other works [24,32].

Definition 2. *The* INFMAX *problem is an optimization problem which takes as inputs* $G = (V, E)$, F, $\mathcal{D}$, *and an integer* k, *and outputs* $\max_{S \subseteq V: |S| = k} \sigma^G_{F,\mathcal{D}}(S)$, *the maximum global influence of a set of size* k.

In this paper, we consider several special cases of the general threshold model $I^G_{F,\mathcal{D}}$ by making assumptions on the network topology G, or the cascade model[3] $F, \mathcal{D}$.

2.1   Assumptions on Graph G

We consider the *hierarchical blockmodel*, which is the special case of the well studied *blockmodel* [38].

Definition 3. *A **hierarchical blockmodel** is an undirected **edge-weighted** graph* $G = (V, T)$, *where* V *is the set of all vertices of the graph* G, *and* $T = (V_T, E_T, w_T)$ *is a node-weighted binary tree* T *called a **hierarchy tree**. In addition,* w_T *satisfies* $w_T(t_1) \leq w_T(t_2)$ *for any* $t_1, t_2 \in V_T$ *such that* t_1 *is an ancestor of* t_2.[4] *Each leaf node* $t \in V_T$ *corresponds to a subset of vertices* $V(t) \subseteq V$, *and the* $V(t)$ *sets partition the vertices of* V. *In general, if* t *is not a leaf, we denote* $V(t) = \cup_{t': \text{ a leaf, and an offspring of } t} V(t')$.
For $u, v \in V$, *the weight of the edge* (u, v) *in* G *is just the weight of the least common ancestor of* u *and* v *in* T. *That is* $w(u, v) = \max_{t: u, v \in V(t)} w(t)$. *If this weight is 0, then we say that the edge does not exist.*

Figure 1 provides an example of how a hierarchy tree defines the weights of edges in the corresponding graph.

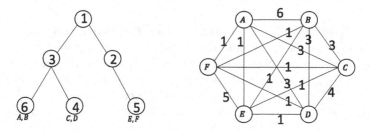

Fig. 1. An example of a hierarchy tree with its corresponding graph. The number on each node of the hierarchy tree on the left hand side indicates the weight of the node, which reflects the weight of the corresponding edges on the hierarchical block graph on the right hand side in the above-mentioned way.

---

[3] The phrase "cascade model" here, as well as in the abstract and Sect. 1, refers to the description how each vertex is influenced by its neighbors, which is completely characterized by F and $\mathcal{D}$ in the general threshold model.

[4] Since, as it will be seen later, each node in the hierarchy tree represents a community and its children represent its sub-communities, naturally, the relation between two persons is stronger if they are in a same sub-community in a lower level.

In the full version, we will present an example for hierarchical blockmodel, and we will generalize Definition 3 to a stochastic version, and define the *stochastic hierarchical model.*

2.2   Assumptions on Cascade Model $F, \mathcal{D}$

We consider several generalizations of a well-studied cascade model called *linear threshold model* [24]. The linear threshold model is a special case of the general threshold model $I_{F,\mathcal{D}}^G$, with each f_v being linear (see Definition 4 later), and each $\mathcal{D}_v$ being the uniform distribution on $[0, 1]$.

The cascade model in Definition 4 generalizes the linear threshold model by removing the assumption on $\mathcal{D}_v$. The *universal local influence model* defined in Definition 5, generalizes the linear threshold model by allowing non-linear f_v, while it restricts our attention to unweighted graphs. We also consider a special case where f_v is *2-quasi-submodular* in the last subsection.

Linear Local Influence Functions. A natural selection of local influence function f_v is the linear function, by which the influences from v's neighbors are additive.

Definition 4. *Given a general threshold model $I_{F,\mathcal{D}}^G$, we say that F is **linear** if for each $v \in V$ we have*

- $f_v(S_v) = \sum_{u \in S_v} w(u, v)$ *when G is edge-weighted;*
- $f_v(S_v) = |S_v|$ *when G is unweighted.*

For a general threshold model $I_{F,\mathcal{D}}^G$ with linear F, if we additionally assume each $\mathcal{D}_v$ is the uniform distribution on $[0, 1]$, then this becomes the linear threshold model.

Universal Local Influence Functions. We say f_v is *symmetric* if $f_v(S_v)$ only depends on the *number* of v's infected neighbors $|S_v|$ so that each of v's infected neighbors is of equal importance. In this case, f_v can be viewed as a function $f_v : \mathbb{Z}_{\geq 0} \mapsto \mathbb{R}_{\geq 0}$ which takes an integer as input, rather than a set of vertices. Thus f_v can be encoded by an increasing sequence of positive real numbers $a_0, a_1, a_2, \ldots$ so that $f_v(i) = a_i$. Note that $f_v(0) = a_0 = 0$, as we have assumed $f_v(\emptyset) = 0$.

For instance, consider the linear local influence function defined in Definition 4. f_v is symmetric if G is unweighted, in which case $a_i = i$. f_v may not be symmetric if G is edge-weighted, as the neighbors connected by heavier edges contribute more to $f_v(S_v)$.

Definition 5. *Given an increasing function $f : \mathbb{Z}_{\geq 0} \mapsto [0, 1]$, the **universal local influence model** I_f^G is a special case of the general threshold model $I_{F,\mathcal{D}}^G$, such that for each $v \in V$ we have*

- f_v *is symmetric, and $f_v = f$ (such that all f_v's are identical).*
- $\mathcal{D}_v$ *is the uniform distribution on $[0, 1]$.*

Notice that we can assume without loss of generality that G is unweighted in Definition 5, as each f_v is fixed to be some increasing function f which does not depend on the weights of edges.

After assuming G is unweighted, the universal local influence model is a generalization of linear threshold model: the linear threshold model can be viewed as the universal local influence model by restricting $a_i = i$.

As a final remark, for any general threshold model $I^G_{F,\mathcal{D}}$ with each D_v being the uniform distribution on $[0,1]$, we can intuitively view $f_v(S_v)$ as the *probability* that v will be infected (where we take $f_v(S_v) > 1$ as probability 1). In the universal local influence model, a_i can be viewed as the probability that a vertex will be infected, given that it has i infected neighbors.

Submodular and 2-Quasi-Submodular Functions. Let $g : 2^S \to \mathbb{R}$ be a function which takes as input a subset of a set S. Formally, g is *submodular* if $g(A \cup \{u\}) - g(A) \geq g(B \cup \{u\}) - g(B)$ for any $u \in S$ and sets $A \subseteq B \subseteq S$. Intuitively, this means that the marginal effect of each element decreases as the set increases.

Given $G, F, \mathcal{D}$ we say that $I^G_{F,\mathcal{D}}(\cdot)$ is submodular if $\sigma^G_{F,\mathcal{D}}(\cdot)$ is. We can similarly define submodularity for local influence functions f_v. In [32], it has been shown that the local submodularity of all f_v's implies the global submodularity of $I^G_{F,\mathcal{D}}(\cdot)$ for all G when $\mathcal{D}_v$ is the uniform distribution on $[0,1]$.

We are particularly concerned with the universal local influence model in Definition 5. Here f is submodular if the marginal gain of f by having one more infected neighbor is non-increasing as the number of infected neighbors increases. Formally, for $i_1 < i_2$, we have

$$f(i_1 + 1) - f(i_1) \geq f(i_2 + 1) - f(i_2).$$

Intuitively, f is submodular if its domain can be smoothly extended to $\mathbb{R}_{\geq 0}$ to make f concave.

We will consider the *2-quasi-submodular* local influence function f, which is "almost" submodular such that the submodularity is only violated for the first two inputs of f. In particular, we fail to have the submodular constraint $f(1) - f(0) \geq f(2) - f(1)$, and instead we have $f(1) - f(0) < f(2) - f(1)$, which is just $f(2) > 2f(1)$ as $f(0) = 0$.

Definition 6. $f : \mathbb{Z}_{\geq 0} \mapsto [0,1]$ *is **2-quasi-submodular** if $f(2) > 2f(1)$ and $f(i) - f(i+1)$ is non-increasing for $i \geq 2$.*

In general, for any non-zero submodular function f, if we sufficiently decrease $f(1)$, f becomes 2-quasi-submodular. Thus, from any non-zero submodular function, we can obtain a 2-quasi-submodular function.

We note that the 2-threshold cascade model, where each vertex will be infected if it has at least 2 infected neighbors, can be viewed as the universal local influence function cascade with a 2-quasi-submodular f (with $f(0) = f(1) = 0$ and $f(i) = 1$ for $i \geq 2$, keeping the assumption θ_v is drawn uniformly at random from $[0,1]$).

3 Hierarchical Blockmodel Influence Maximization

In this section, we provide a strong inapproximability result for INFMAX problem for hierarchical blockmodel cascade even when all vertices have a deterministic threshold 1. Specifically, we will show that it is NP-hard to approximate optimal $\sigma(S)$ within a factor of $N^{1-\varepsilon}$ for any $\varepsilon > 0$ (recall that $N = |V|$). The same inapproximability result holds for the most general case where $\mathcal{D}$ is given as input to the INFMAX problem.

Theorem 1. *For any constant $\varepsilon > 0$, INFMAX $(G, F, \mathcal{D}, k)$ is NP-hard to approximate to a factor of $N^{1-\varepsilon}$, even if G is a hierarchical blockmodel, F is linear (see Definition 4), and $\mathcal{D}_v$ is the degenerate distribution with mass 1 on $\theta_v = 1$ for all $v \in V$.*

We will prove Theorem 1 by a reduction from the VERTEXCOVER problem, a well-known NP-complete problem.

Definition 7. *Given an undirected graph $G = (V, E)$ and a positive integer k, the VERTEXCOVER problem asks if we can choose a subset of vertices $S \subseteq V$ such that $|S| = k$ and such that each edge is incident to at least one vertex in S.*

Proof (Proof of Theorem 1). Given a VERTEXCOVER instance with G and k, let $n = |V|$ and $m = |E|$. We use $A_1, \ldots, A_n$ to denote the n vertices and $e_1, \ldots, e_m$ to denote the m edges.[5] We assume $n > k$ and $m > n + k$.[6] Let $W = nm$, $M = (n(2W + m) - 1)^{\frac{1}{\varepsilon}}$, and $\delta > 0$ be a sufficiently small real number.

We will construct the graph $G = (V, E, w)$ by constructing a hierarchy tree T which uniquely determines G (see Definition 3). The construction of T is shown in Fig. 2.

Each branch A_i corresponds to each vertex A_i in the VERTEXCOVER instance. For each edge e_j in VERTEXCOVER, we construct n vertices $v_{1j}, \ldots, v_{nj}$ on the n branches respectively in the way shown. The numbers shown on the tree nodes represent the weights, where

$$w_{ij} = \begin{cases} \frac{1 - (n+k-1)W\delta - (n-1)(j-1)\delta - \delta}{W - 1 + j} & \text{if edge } e_j \text{ is incident to } A_i \\ \frac{1 - (n+k-1)W\delta - (n-1)(j-1)\delta - 2\delta}{W - 1 + j} & \text{otherwise} \end{cases}.$$

---

[5] We use the letter A to denote the vertices in a VERTEXCOVER instance instead of commonly used v, while v is used for the vertices in an INFMAX instance. Since VERTEXCOVER can be viewed as a special case of SETCOVER with vertices corresponding to subsets and edges corresponding to elements, the letter A, commonly used for subsets, is used here.

[6] For the assumption $m > n + k$, notice that allowing the graph G to be a multi-graph does not change the nature of VERTEXCOVER, we can ensure m to be sufficiently large by just duplicating edges.

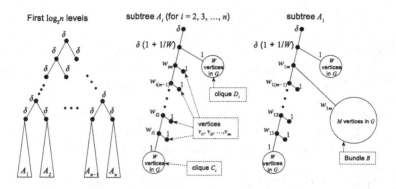

Fig. 2. The construction of the hierarchy tree T for the proof of Theorem 1

For VERTEXCOVER with $k = |S|$, consider INFMAX with $k = n + k$ seeds. We aim to show that,

1. If the VERTEXCOVER instance is a YES instance, we can infect at least M vertices;
2. If the VERTEXCOVER instance is a NO instance, we can infect at most $M^\varepsilon = n(2W + m) - 1$ vertices.

To show (1), suppose we have a YES VERTEXCOVER instance with a subset of vertices $S \subseteq V$ that covers all edges in E. In the INFMAX instance, we aim to show that at least M vertices will be infected if we choose

- an arbitrary seed in each of the cliques $C_1, \ldots, C_n$ (n seeds in total), and
- an arbitrary seed in the clique D_i for each $A_i \in S$ (k seeds in total).

By such a choice of $k = n + k$ seeds, in the first round of the cascade, all the W·vertices in each of $C_1, \ldots, C_n$ and each of those k (D_i)'s are infected. For each edge $e_j \in E$, denote $e_j = (A_{i_j}, A_{i'_j})$ such that $A_{i_j}, A_{i'_j}$ are the two vertices cover the edge e_j. By our choice of seeds, a seed is chosen in at least one of D_{i_j} and $D_{i'_j}$, let D_{i_j} be the one. By a careful calculation, we can see that the cascade after the first round carries on in the following order:

$$v_{i_1 1} \to v_{i'_1 1} \to \{v_{i1}\}_{i \neq i_1, i'_1} \to v_{i_2 2} \to v_{i'_2 2} \to \{v_{i2}\}_{i \neq i_2, i'_2} \to \cdots$$

$$\to v_{i_m m} \to v_{i'_m m} \to \{v_{im}\}_{i \neq i_m, i'_m} \to B.$$

Therefore, we conclude (1) as we already have M infected vertices by just counting those in the bundle B.

To show (2) by contradiction, we assume that we can choose a seed set $S \subseteq V$ such that $|S| = k = n + k$ and $\sigma(S) > M^\varepsilon$. By a careful analysis, we can conclude that the only possible way to choose S is as follow.

- an arbitrary seed from each of $C_1, \ldots, C_n$ (n seeds in total);
- an arbitrary seed from each of $D_{\pi_1}, \ldots, D_{\pi_k}$ for certain $\{\pi_1, \ldots, \pi_k\} \subseteq \{1, \ldots, n\}$ (k seeds in total).

While we refer the readers to the full version of the paper for a detailed proof of why this is true, here we provide an intuition for this. Firstly, choosing k seeds among the $2n$ cliques $C_1, \ldots, C_n, D_1, \ldots, D_n$ is considerably more beneficial, as a seed would cause the infection of W vertices. Secondly, if we cannot choose both C_i and D_i, it is always better to choose C_i because the weights $w_{i1}, \ldots, w_{im}$ are considerably larger than $\delta(1 + 1/W)$, if δ is set sufficiently small.

Since the VERTEXCOVER instance is a NO instance, there exists an edge $e_j = (A_{i_j}, A_{i'_j})$ such that no vertex in D_{i_j} and $D_{i'_j}$ is chosen as seed. By a careful calculation, we show that the cascade would stop at the level $\{v_{ij}\}_{i=1,\ldots,n}$, which concludes (2).

By (1) and (2), the INFMAX problem for G we have constructed is NP-hard to approximate within a factor of at least

$$\frac{M}{M^\varepsilon} = M^{1-\varepsilon} = \Theta\left(N^{1-\varepsilon}\right),$$

as $N = M + M^\varepsilon = \Theta(M)$. Since ε is arbitrary, the inapproximability factor can be written as just $N^{1-\varepsilon}$.

In the hard INFMAX instances in Fig. 2, if the VERTEXCOVER instance is a YES instance, the influence of the properly chosen seeds actually passes through these n branches "back-and-forth" frequently. It is exactly this bi-directional effect that makes INFMAX hard. In the full version of this paper, we consider a variant to the hierarchical blockmodel in which the influence between any two vertex-blocks can only be "one-way", and present a dynamic program to solve INFMAX for this variant optimally.

4 Stochastic Hierarchical Blockmodel Influence Maximization

In the full version, we consider a stochastic variant of the hierarchical blockmodel, called *stochastic hierarchical blockmodel*. The *stochastic hierarchical blockmodel* is similar to the hierarchical blockmodel, in that the structure of the graph is determined by a hierarchy tree. Instead of assigning *weights* to different edges measuring the strength of relationships, here we assign a *probability* with which the edge between each pair of vertices appears.

We show in the full version that INFMAX is NP-hard to approximate within factor $N^{1-\varepsilon}$. In particular, we consider two settings respecting if the seed-picker picks the seed before or after seeing the sampling of the graph G, and show that the same inapproximability holds for both settings.

5 2-Quasi-Submodular Influence Maximization

We present a sketch of the proof for the following Theorem in this section. The complete proof is available in the full version of our paper.

Theorem 2. *For any fixed 2-quasi-submodular f, there exists a constant τ depending on f such that INFMAX with universal local influence model I_G^f is NP-hard to approximate to within factor N^τ.*

We consider two cases: $f(1) \neq 0$ and $f(1) = 0$, and we only discuss the first case here. The proof for the case $f(1) = 0$ is available in the full version. Denote $a_i = f(i)$ and $p^* = \lim_{i \to \infty} a_i$.

We prove the theorem by a reduction from the SETCOVER problem.

Definition 8. *Given a universe U of n elements, a set of κ subsets $A = \{A_i \mid A_i \subseteq U\}$, and a positive integer k, the SETCOVER problem asks if we can choose k subsets $\{A_{i_1}, \ldots, A_{i_k}\} \subseteq A$ such that $A_{i_1} \cup \cdots \cup A_{i_k} = U$.*

We construct a graph G which consists of two parts: the set cover part and the verification part, where the set cover part simulates SETCOVER and the verification part verifies if all the elements in the SETCOVER instance are covered. The construction is shown in Fig. 3. We first assume that the graph G is directed, and then we show that this assumption is not essential by constructing a *directed edge gadget* to simulate directed edges.

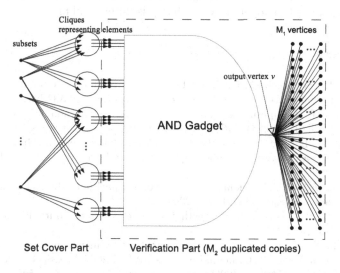

Fig. 3. The high-level structure of the reduction for the proof of Theorem 2

Given a SETCOVER instance, in the set cover part, we use a single vertex to represent a subset A_i and a clique of size m to represent each element in U. If an element is in a subset, we create m directed edges from the vertex representing the subset to each the m vertices in the clique representing the element. If a vertex representing a subset is picked, then all vertices in the cliques corresponding to the elements contained in this subset will be infected with probability close to p^*, by choosing m large enough. We call such cliques as being activated. In a YES instance of SETCOVER, we can choose k seeds such that all cliques are activated.

In the verification part, we construct a *AND gadget*, simulating the logical AND operation, to verify if all the cliques are activated. The AND gadget takes n inputs, each of which is a set of vertices from each of the n cliques. The output of the AND gadget is a vertex v, such that it will only be infected with a positive constant probability if all the n cliques are activated.

We connect the output vertex v of this AND gadget to a huge bundle of M_1 vertices, such that a constant fraction of those M_1 vertices will be infected only if all the cliques are activated (which corresponds to the case the SETCOVER is a YES instance). By making M_1 large enough, we can achieve a hardness of approximation ratio N^τ. To avoid the seed-picker bypassing the set cover game by directed seeding the output vertex v, we duplicate the verification part by M_2 times for some sufficiently large M_2.

Finally, we replace all directed edges in Fig. 3 by directed edge gadgets, including those connecting the vertices representing subsets and the cliques representing elements, and those connecting the set cover part and the verification part. To complete the proof of Theorem 2, we present the construction of the AND gadget and the directed edge gadget in the full version of this paper. The construction of both gadgets rely on that f is 2-quasi-submodular.

References

1. Angell, R., Schoenebeck, G.: Don't be greedy: leveraging community structure to find high quality seed sets for influence maximization. In: WINE (2017)
2. Arthur, W.B.: Competing technologies, increasing returns, and lock-in by historical events. Econ. J. **99**(394), 116–131 (1989). http://www.jstor.org/stable/2234208
3. Backstrom, L., Huttenlocher, D.P., Kleinberg, J.M., Lan, X.: Group formation in large social networks: membership, growth, and evolution. In: ACM SIGKDD (2006)
4. Banerjee, A., Chandrasekhar, A.G., Duflo, E., Jackson, M.O.: The diffusion of microfinance. Science **341**(6144), 1236498 (2013)
5. Bass, F.M.: A new product growth for model consumer durables. Manag. Sci. **15**(5), 215–227 (1969)
6. Bharathi, S., Kempe, D., Salek, M.: Competitive influence maximization in social networks. In: Deng, X., Graham, F.C. (eds.) WINE 2007. LNCS, vol. 4858, pp. 306–311. Springer, Heidelberg (2007). https://doi.org/10.1007/978-3-540-77105-0_31
7. Borgs, C., Brautbar, M., Chayes, J.T., Lucier, B.: Influence maximization in social networks: towards an optimal algorithmic solution. CoRR (2012)
8. Brown, J.J., Reingen, P.H.: Social ties and word-of-mouth referral behavior. J. Consum. Res. **14**, 350–362 (1987)
9. Centola, D.: The spread of behavior in an online social network experiment. Science **329**(5996), 1194–1197 (2010)
10. Chen, N.: On the approximability of influence in social networks. SIAM J. Discret. Math. **23**(3), 1400–1415 (2009)
11. Chen, W., Wang, Y., Yang, S.: Efficient influence maximization in social networks. In: ACM SIGKDD, pp. 199–208. ACM (2009)

12. Chen, W., Yuan, Y., Zhang, L.: Scalable influence maximization in social networks under the linear threshold model. In: 2010 IEEE International Conference on Data Mining, pp. 88–97. IEEE (2010)
13. Clauset, A., Moore, C., Newman, M.E.: Hierarchical structure and the prediction of missing links in networks. Nature 453(7191), 98–101 (2008)
14. Coleman, J., Katz, E., Menzel, H.: The diffusion of an innovation among physicians. Sociometry 20, 253–270 (1957)
15. Conley, T.G., Udry, C.R.: Learning about a new technology: Pineapple in Ghana. Am. Econ. Rev. 100(1), 35–69 (2010)
16. DiMaggio, P.: Structural analysis of organizational fields: a blockmodel approach. Res. Organ. Behav. 8, 335–370 (1986)
17. Domingos, P., Richardson, M.: Mining the network value of customers. In: ACM SIGKDD (2001)
18. Goldenberg, J., Libai, B., Muller, E.: Using complex systems analysis to advance marketing theory development: modeling heterogeneity effects on new product growth through stochastic cellular automata. Acad. Mark. Sci. Rev. 9(3), 1–18 (2001)
19. Goyal, S., Kearns, M.: Competitive contagion in networks. In: STOC, pp. 759–774 (2012)
20. Granovetter, M.: Threshold models of collective behavior. Am. J. Sociol. 83(6), 1420–1443 (1978). http://www.journals.uchicago.edu/doi/abs/10.1086/226707
21. He, X., Kempe, D.: Robust influence maximization. In: ACM SIGKDD (2016)
22. Holland, P.W., Laskey, K.B., Leinhardt, S.: Stochastic blockmodels: first steps. Soc. Netw. 5(2), 109–137 (1983)
23. Jackson, M.O.: Social and Economic Networks. Princeton University Press, Princeton (2008)
24. Kempe, D., Kleinberg, J.M., Tardos, É.: Maximizing the spread of influence through a social network. In: ACM SIGKDD, pp. 137–146 (2003)
25. Kempe, D., Kleinberg, J., Tardos, É.: Influential nodes in a diffusion model for social networks. In: Caires, L., Italiano, G.F., Monteiro, L., Palamidessi, C., Yung, M. (eds.) ICALP 2005. LNCS, vol. 3580, pp. 1127–1138. Springer, Heidelberg (2005). https://doi.org/10.1007/11523468_91
26. Lerman, K., Ghosh, R.: Information contagion: an empirical study of the spread of news on Digg and Twitter social networks. In: ICWSM, pp. 90–97 (2010)
27. Leskovec, J., Adamic, L.A., Huberman, B.A.: The dynamics of viral marketing. In: EC (2006)
28. Lucier, B., Oren, J., Singer, Y.: Influence at scale: distributed computation of complex contagion in networks. In: ACM SIGKDD, pp. 735–744. ACM (2015)
29. Lyzinski, V., Tang, M., Athreya, A., Park, Y., Priebe, C.E.: Community detection and classification in hierarchical stochastic blockmodels. arXiv (2015)
30. Mahajan, V., Muller, E., Bass, F.M.: New product diffusion models in marketing: a review and directions for research. J. Mark. 54, 1–26 (1990)
31. Morris, S.: Contagion. Rev. Econ. Stud. 67(1), 57–78 (2000)
32. Mossel, E., Roch, S.: Submodularity of influence in social networks: from local to global. SIAM J. Comput. 39(6), 2176–2188 (2010)
33. Richardson, M., Domingos, P.: Mining knowledge-sharing sites for viral marketing. In: ACM SIGKDD, pp. 61–70 (2002)
34. Romero, D.M., Meeder, B., Kleinberg, J.: Differences in the mechanics of information diffusion across topics: idioms, political hashtags, and complex contagion on Twitter. In: WWW, pp. 695–704. ACM (2011)

35. Seeman, L., Singer, Y.: Adaptive seeding in social networks. In: FOCS, pp. 459–468. IEEE (2013)
36. Horel, T., Singer, Y.: Maximization of approximately submodular functions. In: NIPS (2016). http://papers.nips.cc/paper/6236-maximization-of-approximately-submodular-functions.pdf
37. Watts, D.J.: A simple model of global cascades on random networks. Proc. Nat. Acad. Sci. **99**(9), 5766–5771 (2002). http://www.pnas.org/content/99/9/5766.abstract
38. White, H.C., Boorman, S.A., Breiger, R.L.: Social structure from multiple networks. I. Blockmodels of roles and positions. Am. J. Sociol. **81**(4), 730–780 (1976)

Cascades and Myopic Routing in Nonhomogeneous Kleinberg's Small World Model

Jie Gao[1], Grant Schoenebeck[2], and Fang-Yi Yu[2(✉)]

[1] Department of Computer Science, Stony Brook University,
Stony Brook, NY 11794, USA
jgao@cs.stonybrook.edu
[2] Department of EECS, University of Michigan, Ann Arbor, MI 48109, USA
{schoeneb,fayu}@umich.edu

Abstract. Kleinberg's small world model [20] simulates social networks with both strong and weak ties. In his original paper, Kleinberg showed how the distribution of weak-ties, parameterized by γ, influences the efficacy of myopic routing on the network. Recent work on social influence by k-complex contagion models discovered that the distribution of weak-ties also impacts the spreading rate in a crucial manner on Kleinberg's small world model [15]. In both cases the parameter of $\gamma = 2$ proves special: when γ is anything but 2 the properties no longer hold.

In this work, we propose a natural generalization of Kleinberg's small world model to allow node heterogeneity: instead of a single global parameter γ, each node has a personalized parameter γ chosen independently from a distribution $\mathcal{D}$. In contrast to the original model, we show that this model enables myopic routing and k-complex contagions on a large range of the parameter space, improving the robustness of the model. Moreover, we show that our generalization is supported by real-world data. Analysis of four different social networks shows that the nodes do not show homogeneity in terms of the variance of the lengths of edges incident to the same node.

1 Introduction

In Milgram's "Small World" experiments [23, 26], he gave envelops to random residents of Wichita, Kansas and Omaha, Nebraska, and asked them to forward the envelopes to a personal contact so that they might eventually reach a specific banker in Massachusetts. The success of this experiment (which has since been observed in numerous other contexts – see related work) motivated Kleinberg's small work model which studies why such local decisions work [20]. This ingenious model shows not only that short paths between arbitrary nodes exist (this

---

J. Gao would like to acknowledge support through NSF DMS-1418255, CCF-1535900, CNS-1618391, DMS-1737812 and AFOSR FA9550-14-1-0193. G. Schoenebeck and F. Yu gratefully acknowledge the support of the National Science Foundation under Career Award 1452915 and AitF Award 1535912.

N. R. Devanur and P. Lu (Eds.): WINE 2017, LNCS 10674, pp. 383–394, 2017.
https://doi.org/10.1007/978-3-319-71924-5_27

so-called "small world" phenomena was already embedded into several fundamental models [6, 24, 27]), but also that these short paths can be easily discovered by myopic routing (i.e., using purely local knowledge).

Kleinberg's small world model considers an underlying metric space capturing the diversity of the population in various social attributes. Social ties are classified into two categories: strong ties that connect an individual to those similar in the social attribute space, and weak ties that may connect individuals far away. Kleinberg's model considers one parameter γ in determining how the weak ties are placed. Each node p takes a weak tie edge to a node q with probability proportional to $1/|pq|^\gamma$ where $|pq|$ denotes the distance between p and q in the social space. Thus at $\gamma = 0$ the weak ties are uniformly randomly distributed, and as γ increases shorter connections are increasingly favored.

However, in this model when the nodes are placed in a 2-dimensional grid the navigability only holds for a particular parameter choice: $\gamma = 2$. At this "sweetspot," a message can be delivered to the destination in $O(\log^2 n)$ hops, by hopping to the neighbor closest to the destination in the Euclidean metric. For *any* constant $\gamma \neq 2$, myopic routing, or, in general, any deterministic routing algorithm using only local information, provably fails to quickly deliver the message. Intuitively why $\gamma = 2$ is crucial, because at this sweetspot each weak tie edge uniformly at random lands in one of the annuli around the destination with inner radius 2^i and outer radius 2^{i+1}, for all i. Therefore, no matter where the destination is, with probability roughly $1/\log n$ there is a neighbor such that taking this neighbor reduces the Euclidean distance to the destination by half. If $\gamma < 2$, it turns out that the weak tie edges are too random and myopic routing loses its sense of direction. If $\gamma > 2$, the weak ties are simply too short and any path to the destination discoverable from local information necessarily takes many hops.

Other good properties also hold at special ranges of the parameter γ. In recent work on understanding complex social influence, it was shown how the distribution of weak-ties impacts the spreading behavior of k-complex contagions, in which a node becomes infected if at least k neighbors are infected [13, 15]. Again it was shown that when $\gamma = 2$, for any constant k, the k-complex contagion spreads in a polylogarithmic number of rounds to the entire network while when $\gamma \neq 2$ complex contagions necessarily require a polynomial number of rounds. The analysis here connects to the intuition presented earlier for myopic routing. The sweetspot $\gamma = 2$ substantially speeds up the spreading of the contagions.

While the existence of the sweetspot is both insightful and elegant, it has raised new questions for modeling practical networks. The model feels fragile if the good properties only hold at a single parameter value and stop holding even with slight deviation. As put by Jackson [17]: "It is unlikely that societies just happen to hit the right balance. More likely there is something missing from the models, and it is clear the network-formation process underlying many social networks is much more complex than in these models." If Jackson is correct, then a theoretical model that more robustly justifies the empirical observations of Milgram and those who followed is needed.

Our Results. In this work, we generalize Kleinberg's small world model by considering a personalized, possibly heterogeneous γ_u for each node u in the network. In particular, each node u chooses its parameter $\gamma_u \in [0, \infty)$ i.i.d from a distribution $\mathcal{D}$. The weak tie edges issued by u will be placed on node v with probability proportional to $1/|uv|^{\gamma_u}$, where $|uv|$ denotes the distance between u and v in some underlying metric.

This model is motivated by both intuition and observations in real world data sets. It is natural to believe that some people have weak ties that are more/less dispersed (geographically or otherwise) that others. We also provide empirical evidence for node heterogeneity using real world social network data. Given a network, we can embed it in Euclidean space using spectral methods and examine the length of the edges attached to each node. We find that the empirical variance of the lengths of edges incident on the same vertex is substantially less than when the edge lengths are randomly permuted—suggesting that lengths of edges incident on the same vertex are indeed more correlated.

In this paper the main technical results we report is that both myopic routing and k-complex contagions operate quickly in the new model as long as the distribution $\mathcal{D}$ for the personalized γ has *non-negligible mass* around 2. Thus our model provides a robust justification for the observed properties of both myopic routing and k-complex contagions. Moreover it does this by only slightly tweaking Kleinberg's original model.

In particular, we can show that even if there is just $\Omega(\epsilon^\alpha)$ mass in the interval $[2 - \epsilon, 2 + \epsilon]$ of the distribution $\mathcal{D}$, where $\alpha > 0$ is *any* constant, then myopic routing and k-complex contagions (for any k) still only take polylogarithmic time! For example, it is enough that $\mathcal{D}$ be uniform on the interval $[a, b]$ for any $0 \le a \le 2 \le b$. Note that in such a case, no particular γ_u will be exactly 2 (with probability 1). However, it turns out that enough of the γ_u are close enough to 2, which still enables these social processes.

We also show lower bounds. For myopic routing we show that if for some ϵ, there is no mass in $[2 - \epsilon, 2 + \epsilon]$, then the typical myopic routing time is polynomial. This is not obvious, as there can be a distribution $\mathcal{D}$ that allows weak ties that are short — connecting nodes nearby, and weak tie that are long – connecting nodes far away. Recall that in the original Kleinberg proof it was shown that *short ties only*, or *long ties only*, are not enough to enable myopic routing but it did not exclude the possibility when *both long and short ties* exist simultaneously. We show that in fact the combination of these weak tie edges are still not enough for enabling efficient myopic routing. In particular, there is a range of distances when none of the two types of ties are helpful, which forces the greedy routing to take a long time.

For complex contagions, our first lower bound shows that if for some $\epsilon > 0$, there is no mass in $[2 - \epsilon, 2 + \epsilon]$, then there is some k such that k-complex contagions require a polynomial time to spread. Again we must show that the synergy between short and long weak ties cannot enable complex contagions to quickly spread.

The above results for complex contagion apply for *any* k. We also study what happens for a particular k. Here we show that for each k there is an interval $[2, \beta_k)$ where $\beta_k = \frac{2(k+1)}{k}$ such that when $\mathcal{D}$ has constant support on $[2, \beta_k)$, k-complex contagions spread in polynomial time, but, when, for any $\epsilon > 0$, $\mathcal{D}$ has no support on $[2 - \epsilon, \beta_k + \epsilon]$, then k-complex contagions requires polynomial time to spread with high probability.

2   Related Work

Small World Graphs. The small world property—that there exists short paths between two random members of a network–appears in many real world complex networks in vastly different contexts ranging from film collaboration networks and neural networks [11] to email networks [10], food webs [28] and protein interaction networks [19].

It has been discovered in a number of settings that random edges introduced to a graph can dramatically reduce the network diameter, creating a small world graph. This observation was made in the Watts-Strogatz model [27] (when edges are rewired to a random destination) as well as for regular random graphs [6] (a graph in which all nodes have the same constant degree and edges are uniformly randomly placed). Kleinberg's small world model can be considered as an extension to such models. In particular, the Newmann-Watts model [24] (a variant of the Watts-Strogatz model in which random edges are added in *addition* to existing edges) is a special case of Kleinberg's model for choosing $\gamma = 0$ — i.e., the weak ties are uniformly randomly added.

Navigability. Milgram's "Small World" experiments [23, 26] illustrated not only the small world property—that short paths exist—but, in fact, showed a stronger property—that such paths can be efficiently found using only local information— called navigability. A short path was discovered through a *local* algorithm with the participants forwarding to a friend who *they believed* to be more likely to know the target. Although forwarding decision-making was not systematically recorded, geographical proximity was found to be an important forwarding criterion in some cases. Other criteria such as profession and popularity may have been used as well. A later study using email-chains [10] confirms this as well, finding that at least half of the choices were due to either geographical proximity of the acquaintance to the target or occupational similarity.

Besides the Kleinberg's small world model, several other models also considered using metric distances in modeling social ties. For example, Kumar *et al.* [22] extended the Kleinberg's model to include the underlying metrics with low-doubling dimension. This model also requires a specific distribution of the weak ties.

Another line of work diverges from distance function defined over some low-dimensional space, but instead defines a distance function based on some hierarchical structure. For example, Watts *et al.* considered a hierarchical professional organization of individuals and a homophilous network with ties added between two nodes closer in the hierarchy with a higher probability. If each node has a fixed probability of dropping the message, they show a greedy routing algorithm sending packages to the neighbor most similar to the target (called homophily-based routing) successfully delivers a fraction of the messages before they are dropped. Kleinberg also confirmed similar results on a hierarchical network, in which the nodes are represented as leaf nodes of a hierarchical organization structure and random edges are added to the leaves with probability dependent on their tree distance. When each node has polylogarithmic out-degree, greedy routing based on the tree distance arrives at the destination in $O(\log n)$ hops. While the aforementioned models also successfully create a more robust network model for myopic routing, in doing so they abandoned the spatial structure of Kleinberg's small world model. While certain structures can be modeled well as a hierarchy, others are much more natural as a continuum, as in Kleinberg's model—e.g. distances, wealth, political ideology, and education.

Boguñá et al. [5] proposed a model that assumes a social metric space and the power law degree distribution. They considered nodes on a ring and assigned target degrees from a power law distribution. An edge is then placed between two nodes with a probability positively dependent on their distance on the ring and negatively dependent on their degrees. They investigated greedy routing with the distances on the ring as a means of navigating in the network. Krioukov et al. [21] considered using a hyperbolic plane as the hidden social space. Nodes are uniformly distributed in a radius R disk in a hyperbolic plane with edges placed in pairs with distance smaller than r. They show that such a graph has power law degree distribution and that greedy routing with hyperbolic distance has a high success rate.

Complex Contagions. The model of k-complex contagions belongs to the general family of *threshold models*, in which each node has a threshold on the number of infected edges/neighbors needed to become infected [16]. The threshold model is motivated by certain coordination games studied in the economics literature in which a user maximizes its payoff when adopting the behavior as the majority of its neighbors.

k-complex contagions have been previously studied in the Kleinberg small world model [15] and their spreading behaviour was almost completely classified [13]. Ghasemiesfeh *et al.* [15] showed that for any k, if $\gamma = 2$ then complex contagions spread quickly, in a polylogarithmic number of rounds. Further, Ebrahimi *et al.* [13] showed that for each $k \geq 2$, there exists an interval of values, $[2, \alpha_k]$, such that when $\gamma \in (2, \alpha_k)$, a k-complex contagion spreads quickly on the corresponding graph, in a polylogarithmic number of rounds. However, if γ is outside this range, then a k-complex contagion requires a polynomial number of rounds to spread to the entire network. They also showed similar results for a variant of the Kleinberg model where edges are added without replacement (thus multi-edges are allowed).

k-complex contagions have also been studied in other social network models, for examples, networks that have a time-evolving nature (e.g. the Preferential

Attachment model) [12,14], and configuration model networks with power-law degree distribution [25].

k-complex contagions are referred to as *bootstrap percolation* [1,9] in the literature, especially when initial seeds are chosen randomly at random. Here, the focus is often to examine the threshold of the number of initial seeds with which the infection eventually 'percolates', i.e. diffuses to the entire network. Studies have been done on the random Erdős-Rényi graph [18], random regular graphs [4], and the configuration model [2], etc [3]. All of these results show that for a complex contagion to percolate, the number of initial seeds is a growing function of the network size and in many cases a constant fraction of the entire network. In contrast, we always start with a constant number of seeds and we would like to examine whether a fast spreading is possible.

3   Preliminaries

Recall that in the Kleinberg's small world model [20], nodes are defined on a $n \times n$ grid[1]. Each node u connects to nodes within grid Manhattan distance $\lceil q \rceil$, where q is a constant. These edges are referred to as **strong ties**. In addition, each node generates p random outgoing edges (without replacement), termed **weak ties**. The probability that node u connects to node v via a random edge is $1/\lambda_\gamma d(u,v)^\gamma$, in which $d(u,v)$ is the Manhattan distance of u,v and $\lambda_\gamma = \sum_v d(u,v)^{-\gamma}$ is a normalization factor. Further, we remark that the graph is directed — the weak ties issued by a node u have u as the tail and the strong ties are bidirectional.

For **Heterogeneous Kleinberg's small world** $HetK_{p,q,\mathcal{D}}(n)$, we define p, q, n as in the original model, but, instead of one global γ, each node u independently chooses its personalized parameter γ_u from the distribution $\mathcal{D}$ on $[0, \infty)$ with probability density function[2] $f_\mathcal{D}$ and cumulative distribution function $F_\mathcal{D}$. Let $M_\mathcal{D}(\epsilon) = F_\mathcal{D}(2 + \epsilon) - F_\mathcal{D}(2 - \epsilon)$ measure the "mass" of $\mathcal{D}$ around 2.

We study two dynamics on this heterogeneous Kleinberg's small world model: *decentralized routing*, and *k-complex contagion*.

In the **decentralized routing algorithm**, a message is passed to one of its (local or long-range) contacts using only local information. Given the source s and destination t in the graph, we denote the routing process/algorithm $\mathcal{A}$: a sequence of nodes on the graph $(x_i)_{i \geq 0}$ where $x_0 = s$. The *delivery time* from s to t of algorithm $\mathcal{A}$ is defined as $\min\{i \geq 0 : x_i = t\}$ which is a random variable with σ-space generated by $HetK_{p,q,\mathcal{D}}(n)$ and the myopic routing algorithm. The *expected delivery time* of a decentralized algorithm $\mathcal{A}$ is the expected delivery time for uniformly chosen sources s and destinations t. The *myopic greedy algorithm* routes the message from the current location to be as close as possible to

---

[1] In order to eliminate the boundary effect, we wrap up the grid into a torus – i.e., the top boundary is identified with the bottom boundary and the left boundary is identified with the right boundary.

[2] For discrete distribution, the probability density function exists if we allow using Dirac delta function.

the destination vertex (according to the grid distance) using only one hop from the current node.

We define a k-complex contagion process in a directed graph following the definition in Ghasemiesfeh et al. [15]. We assume k is a small constant. A k-*complex contagion* $CC(G, k, \mathcal{I})$ is a contagion that initially infects vertices of $\mathcal{I}$ and spreads over graph G. The contagion proceeds in rounds. At each round, each vertex with at least k infected neighbors becomes infected. The vertices of $\mathcal{I}$ are called the initial seeds. We say that k nodes $(u_1, \cdots, u_k)$ are a k-*seed cluster* if they form a connected subgraph via *only* the grid structure. A k-complex contagion spreads in the inverse direction of an edge: a node becomes infected if it follows at least k infected neighbors. In this work, we define the *speed of a k-complex contagion* as the number of rounds it takes to infect the whole graph which is always finite if we take $q \geq k$ and $\mathcal{I}$ is a k-seed cluster.

4 Myopic Routing Upper Bounds

In this section, we prove the following theorem:

Theorem 1 (Myopic Routing Upper Bounds). *Given a $HetK_{p,q,\mathcal{D}}(n)$ with constant $p, q \geq 1$ and distribution $\mathcal{D}$. If there exists some constants $\epsilon_0 > 0$, $\alpha \geq 1$ and $K > 0$ such that $\forall \epsilon < \epsilon_0$, $M_{\mathcal{D}}(\epsilon) \geq K\epsilon^\alpha$, the expected delivery time of the myopic greedy algorithm is at most $O(\log^{2+\alpha} n)$.*

The above theorem proves fast myopic routing over a large class of Heterogeneous Kleinberg's Small world models. The only distributions that this theorem fails to apply to are distributions with negligible mass near 2. In particular, if $\mathcal{D}$ is uniform over *any* finite interval containing 2, then myopic routing will take time at most $O(\log^3 n)$, and as long as the mass near 2 is non-trivial (i.e., lower bounded by the inverse of some fixed polynomial), then delivery only takes poly-log time.

Remark 1. Note that if the random variable associated with $\mathcal{D}$ is a constant random variable that takes a constant value 2, the $HetK_{p,q,\mathcal{D}}(n)$ degenerates to the original Kleinberg's model with $\gamma = 2$, and the Theorem 1 is tight which yields the same $O(\log^2 n)$ upper bound on delivery time on myopic greedy routing algorithm.

The proof of Theorem 1 follows the general outline of the proof in Kleinberg's original paper: measure the progress of process $\mathcal{A} = (x_i)_{i \geq 0}$ in terms of phases which will be defined later and show the following: (1) monotone property of the process, (2) upper bound the total number of phase, (3) lower bound the probability of finishing each phase. The formal proof will be in the full version.

5 Myopic Routing Lower Bounds

In this section we prove a lower bound for any decentralized algorithms on the Heterogeneous Kleinberg Small World $HetK_{p,q,\mathcal{D}}(n)$ in the following theorem:

Theorem 2. *Given a Heterogeneous Kleinberg's Small World network $HetK_{p,q,\mathcal{D}}(n)$ with constant parameters p, q and probabilistic density function $f_{\mathcal{D}}$ for the distribution $\mathcal{D}$ on the personalized γ_u for each node u, if there exists a constant $\epsilon_0 > 0$ such that $F(2 + \epsilon_0) - F(2 - \epsilon_0) = 0$, where F is the cumulative density function of $\mathcal{D}$, then the expected routing time for all decentralized algorithms is $\Omega(n^\xi)$ where $\xi = \frac{\epsilon_0}{3(3+\epsilon_0)}$.*

In the original Kleinberg's model [20], all nodes use the same γ parameter. When γ is greater than 2 the weak ties are too short in expectation such that it would need a polynomial number of hops to reach a far away destination. When γ is smaller than 2 the edges are too random to be useful for nearby destinations. But in a heterogeneous model, the nodes may have different γ values. The nodes with $\gamma_u > 2$ have *concentrated edges* while those with $\gamma_u < 2$ have *diffuse edges*. A network with only concentrated edges or only diffuse edges cannot support polylogarithmic myopic routing. But it is unclear whether the combination of them, as in the heterogeneous model, can lead to polylogarithmic delivery time. Theorem 2 states that this is not true. We show this by considering a scope where neither type of edges is helpful. The formal proof will be in the full version.

6   Complex Contagion Upper Bounds

The spreading of k-complex contagion on the original Kleinberg's model has been fully characterized in [13,15]. If a k-seed cluster is infected initially, the contagion spreads to the entire network in $O(\text{polylog}(n))$ rounds if $\gamma \in [2, \beta_k)$, where $\beta_k = \frac{2(k+1)}{k}$, and in $\Omega(\text{poly}(n))$ rounds otherwise.

6.1   Non-negligible Mass Near 2

In the heterogeneous Kleinberg model, we first show a result that is analogous to our results for myopic routing: as long as the distribution $\mathcal{D}$ for γ_u has a non-negligible amount of mass near 2, then for any k, k-complex contagions spread in polylog time—but the exponent of $\log n$ depends on k and $\mathcal{D}$.

Theorem 3. *Fix a distribution $\mathcal{D}$, an integer $k > 0$ and $\eta > 0$. If there exist constants $\epsilon_0 > 0$ and $\alpha \geq 0$ where $M_{\mathcal{D}}(\epsilon) \geq K\epsilon^\alpha$ for all $\epsilon \leq \epsilon_0$, and $p, q \geq k$, there exists $\kappa = k\alpha + \frac{k(k+1)}{2}$, such that a k-complex contagion $CC(HetK_{p,q,\mathcal{D}}(n), k, \mathcal{I})$ starting from a k-seed cluster $\mathcal{I}$ takes at most $O(\log^{(3+\kappa)/2} n)$ rounds[3] to spread to the whole network with probability at least $1 - n^{-\eta}$ over the randomness of $HetK_{p,q,\mathcal{D}}(n)$.*

The theorem is based on the observation that the infected region doubles its size in a polylogarithmic number of steps. In this way the general proof framework is similar to that in [15], and the complete proof will be in the full version.

---

[3] The scalar depends on the constants k, η, α, K.

6.2   Fixed k

For a specific k, we can show that as long as the distribution $\mathcal{D}$ has constant mass in the interval $[2, \beta_k)$ (recall for the beginning of the section that $\beta_k = \frac{2(k+1)}{k}$), then the k-complex contagion will spread to the entire network in a polylogarithmic number of rounds. Recall that the results in Theorem 3 only require non-negligible mass near 2. Here we require constant mass, but the mass need not be asymptotically close to 2 as long as it is in the interval $(2, \beta_k)$.

Theorem 4. *Fix a distribution $\mathcal{D}$, an integer $k > 0$ and $\eta > 0$. If $\Pr_{\gamma \sim \mathcal{D}}[\gamma \in [2, \beta_k)] > 0$ where $\beta_k = \frac{2(k+1)}{k}$, and $p, q \geq k$. There exists $\xi > 0$ depending on $\mathcal{D}$ and k such that, the speed of a k-complex contagion $CC(HetK_{p,q,\mathcal{D}}(n), k, \mathcal{I})$ starting from a k-seed cluster $\mathcal{I}$ is at most $O\left(\log^\xi n\right)$ with probability at least $1 - n^{-\eta}$.*

The proof of Theorem 4 uses the same divide and conquer strategy as in [13], and the proof will be in the full version.

7   Complex Contagion Lower Bounds

In this section, we describe a polynomial time lower bound for the spreading rate of k-complex contagion on the Heterogeneous Kleinberg Small World $HetK_{p,q,\mathcal{D}}(n)$, when the distribution $\mathcal{D}$ on the personal parameter γ_u has zero weight around two. Here we first state the theorem for a fixed k, and the result near two is a natural corollary.

Theorem 5 (Lower bound for fixed k). *Given distribution $\mathcal{D}$, constant integers $k, p, q > 0$, and $\epsilon_0 > 0$ such that $F_{\mathcal{D}}(\beta_k + \epsilon_0) - F_{\mathcal{D}}(2 - \epsilon_0) = 0$, then there exist constants $\xi, \eta > 0$ depending on $\mathcal{D}$ and k, such that the time it takes a k-contagion starting at seed-cluster $\mathcal{I}$, $CC(HetK_{p,q,\mathcal{D}}(n), k, \mathcal{I})$, to infect all nodes is at least $\Omega(n^\xi)$ with probability at least $1 - O(n^{-\eta})$ over the randomness of $HetK_{p,q,\mathcal{D}}(n)$.*

If $\mathcal{D}$ satisfies the condition in Theorem 5, we can partition the support into two disjoint sets $Supp\{\mathcal{D}\} = D_1 \cup D_2$ such that $\gamma_1 = 2 - \epsilon_1 = \sup\{\gamma \in D_1\} < 2 - \epsilon_0$, and $\gamma_2 = 2 + \epsilon_2 = \inf\{\gamma \in D_2\} > 2(1 + 1/k) + \epsilon_0$.

Ebrahimi et al. [13] proved for the original Kleinberg model if $\gamma > \frac{2(k+1)}{k}$ the weak ties will be too short to create remote k-seeds; on the other hand, if $\gamma < 2$ the weak ties will be too random to form k-seeds at all. Similar to proving the lower bound for myopic routing, the challenge in proving this theorem is the synergy between concentrated and diffuse edges which can possibly be exploited by k-complex contagions in the heterogeneous Kleinberg model. We resolve this by considering a scale where neither type of edges is helpful.

Before proving Theorem 5 we state a corollary concerning a lower bound when there is no mass around 2.

Corollary 1 (Lower bound for no mass around 2). *Given distribution $\mathcal{D}$, constant integers $p, q > 0$, and $\epsilon_0 > 0$ such that $F_\mathcal{D}(2 + \epsilon_0) - F_\mathcal{D}(2 - \epsilon_0) = 0$, there exist a constant integer $k > 0$ and $\xi, \eta > 0$ such that the time it takes a k-contagion starting at seed-cluster $\mathcal{I}$, $CC(HetK_{p,q,\mathcal{D}}(n), k, \mathcal{I})$, to infect all nodes is at least n^ξ with probability at least $1 - O(n^{-\eta})$ over the randomness of $HetK_{p,q,\mathcal{D}}(n)$.*

The corollary follows directly from Theorem 5 by taking a sufficiently large k.

8   Empirical Results

See full version.

9   Conclusion

We introduced a generalization of the Kleinberg small world model where the parameter which determines how concentrated or diffuse long ties are can be different for each node, and showed empirical results which support our new model. We proved that this model overcomes a weakness of the original model, which is that the parameters needed to be tuned just right to facilitate fast myopic routing, which was the original motivation behind the model's development. For a wide array of parameters, our new model facilitates both fast myopic routing and the fast spread of complex contagions.

One future direction would be try to learn the heterogeneous distribution in real-world network data. Another future direction would be to connect this model to the "structural holes" theory [7,8] which posits that agents gain power by sitting along many shortest paths, by allowing agents to mediate the passing of information. That is, in the hierarchical small world model, which types of individuals are mostly likely to lie on shortest paths, or, in general, are more useful in myopic routing and complex contagions. A final future direction would be to study the Kleinberg small world model where nodes have a non-uniform (e.g. powerlaw) degree distribution of weak ties. This may provide an alternative way to generalize the Kleinberg small world model so that it supports myopic routing and complex contagions over a larger parameter range.

References

1. Adler, J.: Bootstrap percolation. Phys. A: Stat. Theor. Phys. **171**(3), 453–470 (1991)
2. Amini, H.: Bootstrap percolation and diffusion in random graphs with given vertex degrees. Electr. J. Comb. **17**(1), R25 (2010)
3. Amini, H., Fountoulakis, N.: What i tell you three times is true: bootstrap percolation in small worlds. In: Goldberg, P.W. (ed.) WINE 2012. LNCS, vol. 7695, pp. 462–474. Springer, Heidelberg (2012). https://doi.org/10.1007/978-3-642-35311-6_34

4. Balogh, J., Pittel, B.: Bootstrap percolation on the random regular graph. Random Struct. Algorithms **30**, 257–286 (2007)
5. Boguna, M., Krioukov, D., Claffy, K.C.: Navigability of complex networks. Nat. Phys. **5**, 74–80 (2009)
6. Bollobás, B., Chung, F.R.K.: The diameter of a cycle plus a random matching. SIAM J. Discret. Math. **1**(3), 328–333 (1988)
7. Burt, R.S.: Structural Holes: The Social Structure of Competition. Cambridge University Press, Cambridge (1992)
8. Burt, R.S.: Structural Holes: The social structure of competition. Harvard University Press, Cambridge (1995)
9. Chalupa, J., Leath, P.L., Reich, G.R.: Bootstrap percolation on a Bethe lattice. J. Phys. C: Solid State Phys. **12**(1), L31 (1979)
10. Dodds, P.S., Muhamad, R., Watts, D.J.: An experimental study of search in global social networks. Science **301**, 827 (2003)
11. Watts, D., Strogatz, S.: Collective dynamics of 'small-world' networks. Nature **393**(6684), 409–410 (1998)
12. Ebrahimi, R., Gao, J., Ghasemiesfeh, G., Schoenebeck, G.: How complex contagions in preferential attachment models and other time-evolving networks. IEEE Trans. Netw. Sci. Eng. **PP**(99), 1 (2017). https://doi.org/10.1109/TNSE.2017.2718024. ISSN 2327–4697
13. Ebrahimi, R., Gao, J., Ghasemiesfeh, G., Schoenebeck, G.: Complex contagions in Kleinberg's small world model. In: Proceedings of the 6th Innovations in Theoretical Computer Science (ITCS 2015), pp. 63–72. January 2015
14. Gao, J., Ghasemiesfeh, G., Schoenebeck, G., Yu, F.-Y.: General threshold model for social cascades: analysis and simulations. In: Proceedings of the 2016 ACM Conference on Economics and Computation, pp. 617–634. ACM (2016)
15. Ghasemiesfeh, G., Ebrahimi, R., Gao, J.: Complex contagion and the weakness of long ties in social networks: revisited. In: Proceedings of the fourteenth ACM conference on Electronic Commerce, pp. 507–524. ACM (2013)
16. Granovetter, M.: Threshold models of collective behavior. Am. J. Sociol. **83**(6), 1420–1443 (1978)
17. Jackson, M.O.: Social and Economic Networks. Princeton University Press, Princeton (2008). ISBN 0691134405, 9780691134406
18. Janson, S., Luczak, T., Turova, T., Vallier, T.: Bootstrap percolation on the random graph $G_{n,p}$. Ann. Appl. Probab. **22**(5), 1989–2047 (2012)
19. Jeong, H., Mason, S.P., Barabasi, A.-L., Oltvai, Z.N.: Lethality and centrality in protein networks. Nature **411**, 41–42 (2001)
20. Kleinberg, J., The small-world phenomenon: an algorithm perspective. In: Proceedings of the 32-nd Annual ACM Symposium on Theory of Computing, pp. 163–170 (2000)
21. Krioukov, D., Papadopoulos, F., Boguna, M., Vahdat, A.: Greedy forwarding in scale-free networks embedded in hyperbolic metric spaces. In: ACM SIGMETRICS Workshop on Mathematical Performance Modeling and Analysis (MAMA) June 2009
22. Kumar, R., Liben-Nowell, D., Tomkins, A.: Navigating low-dimensional and hierarchical population networks. In: Azar, Y., Erlebach, T. (eds.) ESA 2006. LNCS, vol. 4168, pp. 480–491. Springer, Heidelberg (2006). https://doi.org/10.1007/11841036_44. ISBN 3-540-38875-3
23. Milgram, S.: The small world problem. Phychol. Today **1**, 61–67 (1967)
24. Newman, M.E.J., Moore, C., Watts, D.J.: Mean-field solution of the small-world network model. Phys. Rev. Lett. **84**, 3201–3204 (2000)

25. Schoenebeck, G., Yu, F.-Y.: Complex contagions on configuration model graphs with a power-law degree distribution. In: Cai, Y., Vetta, A. (eds.) WINE 2016. LNCS, vol. 10123, pp. 459–472. Springer, Heidelberg (2016). https://doi.org/10.1007/978-3-662-54110-4_32
26. Travers, J., Milgram, S.: An experimental study of the small world problem. Sociometry **32**, 425 (1969)
27. Watts, D.J., Strogatz, S.H.: Collective dynamics of 'small-world' networks. Nature **393**, 440–442 (1998)
28. Williams, R.J., Berlow, E.L., Dunne, J.A., Barabasi, A.L., Martinez, N.D.: Two degrees of separation in complex food webs. Proc. Nat. Acad. Sci. **99**(20), 12913–12916 (2002)

Short Papers

Network Congestion Games Are Robust to Variable Demand

José Correa[1], Ruben Hoeksma[2], and Marc Schröder[3(✉)]

[1] Department of Industrial Engineering, University of Chile, Santiago, Chile
correa@uchile.cl
[2] University of Bremen, Bremen, Germany
hoeksma@uni-bremen.de
[3] Chair of Management Science, RWTH Aachen University, Aachen, Germany
marc.schroeder@oms.rwth-aachen.de

Network congestion games have provided a fertile ground for the algorithmic game theory community. Indeed, many of the pioneering works on bounding the efficiency of equilibria use this framework as their starting point. In recent years, there has been an increased interest in studying randomness in this context though the efforts have been mostly devoted to understanding what happens when link latencies are subject to random shocks. In this paper we consider a different source of randomness, namely on the demand side. We look at the basic non-atomic network congestion game with the additional feature that demand is random. Thereto, we introduce an extension of the classic Wardrop equilibrium to fit with this random demand setting. The first obstacle we have to sort out is the definition of equilibrium, as the classic concept of Wardrop equilibrium needs to be extended to the random demand setting. Interestingly, Wang, Doan, and Chen [3], by considering an equilibrium notion in which flow particles evaluate their expected cost using the full knowledge of the demand distribution, conclude that the price of anarchy of the game can be arbitrarily large. In contrast, our main result is that under a very natural equilibrium notion, in which the basic behavioral assumption is that users evaluate their expected cost according to the demand they experience in the system, the price of anarchy of the game is actually the same as that in the deterministic demand game [1, 2]. This is yet another confirmation of the robustness of the price of anarchy to situations in which even the number of players in the system may be random.

A full version of this paper with all the proofs and context can be found at https://www.dii.uchile.cl/~jcorrea/papers/Conferences/CHS2017.pdf.

References

1. Correa, J.R., Schulz, A.S., Stier Moses, N.E.: Selfish routing in capacitated networks. Math. Oper. Res. **29**(4), 961–976 (2004)
2. Roughgarden, T., Tardos, E.: How bad is selfish routing? J. ACM **49**(2), 236–259 (2002)
3. Wang, C., Doan, X., Chen, B.: Price of anarchy for non-atomic congestion games with stochastic demands. Transp. Res. Part B **70**, 90–111 (2014)

© Springer International Publishing AG 2017
N. R. Devanur and P. Lu (Eds.): WINE 2017, LNCS 10674, p. 397, 2017.
https://doi.org/10.1007/978-3-319-71924-5

The Crowdfunding Game
Extended Abstract

Itai Arieli, Moran Koren$^{(\boxtimes)}$, and Rann Smorodinsky

Faculty of Industrial Engineering,
Technion - Israel Institute of Technology, Haifa, Israel
{iarieli,ko,rann}@technion.ac.il

The evolution of the 'sharing economy' has made it possible for the general public to invest in early-stage innovative and economically risky projects and products. These funding schemes, dubbed 'crowdfunding', have been gaining popularity among entrepreneurs and it is reported that crowdfunding for supporting new and innovative products has been overwhelming with over 34 Billion Dollars raised in 2015[1].

In addition to serving as an alternative to venture capital funds as a source for fund raising for nascent stage products, the crowdfunding option also serves as a means to gauge market traction for new products. It is implicitly assumed that a successful crowdfunding campaign suggests a high market demand for the new offering.

From the contributor's perspective, the investment in a crowdfunding campaign has two risky aspects. First, the risk of whether the firm will have enough funds to produce and deliver the product; and second, the quality and value of the product is unknown at the time of the campaign and could possibly be disappointing even if eventually delivered.

In many on-line crowd-funding platforms such as "Kickstarter" and "Indiegogo" a typical campaign format has two critical components. First, it sets a price for the future product and second it sets a threshold. Contributions are collected only if in total they exceed this threshold. Both values are determined by the fund raising firm. This format is designed to mitigate the aforementioned risks. If the threshold is set high enough then contributions are collected only when the company has enough funds on the one hand, and the 'wisdom-of-the-crowd' points to a high valued product.

A crowdfunding game, $\Gamma(N, B, p)$, is a game of incomplete information played among a population of N potential contributors (or players). An unknown state of nature $\omega \in \Omega = \{H, L\}$ is drawn with equal prior probabilities. In state H the common value of the product is 1 and in state L it is -1. Conditional on the realized state ω, a private signal $s_i \in S_i = \{H, L\}$ is drawn independently for every player i. We assume $p = Pr(s_i = \omega | \omega) > 0.5$. Each player i has a

---

The full version can be found at https://arxiv.org/abs/1710.00319.

Rann Smorodinsky—Research supported by GIF research grant no. I-1419-118.4/2017, ISF grant 2018889, Technion VPR grants, the joint Microsoft-Technion e-Commerce Lab, the Bernard M. Gordon Center for Systems Engineering at the Technion, and the TASP Center at the Technion.

[1] Figures taken from http://crowdexpert.com/crowdfunding-industry-statistics.

N. R. Devanur and P. Lu (Eds.): WINE 2017, LNCS 10674, pp. 398–399, 2017.
https://doi.org/10.1007/978-3-319-71924-5

binary action set, $A_i = \{0, 1\}$, with $a_i = 1$ representing a decision to contribute and $a_i = 0$ represents a decision to opt-out and not to contribute. The utility of every player $i \in N$ is defined as follows

$$u_i(a_i, a_{-i}, \omega) = \begin{cases} 1 & \text{if } a_i = 1 \text{ and } \sum_{j \in N} a_j \geq B \text{ and } \omega = H \\ -1 & \text{if } a_i = 1 \text{ and } \sum_{j \in N} a_j \geq B \text{ and } \omega = L \\ 0 & \text{otherwise} \end{cases} \quad (1)$$

In words, whenever player i chooses not to buy the product, she receives a utility of 0. If she chooses to buy, then her utility is depends on the total number of contributors. If less than B players contributed then the product is not supplied and the utility is once again zero. If it exceeds B then her utility is determined by the state of nature and equals 1 in state H and -1 in state L.

We propose two performance measures for a crowdfunding campaign:

- The *correctness index* of a game is defined as the probability that the game ends up with a the correct decision. That is, the probability the product is funded when its value is 1 or the probability that the product is rejected when its value is -1. The correctness index measures how well the crowdfunding aggregates the private information from the buyers in order to make sure the firm pursues the product only when it is viable.
- The *market penetration index* is the expected proportion of contributors provided that the product is supplied, i.e., the threshold is surpassed. This number serves as a proxy for success of the campaign as a means to attract further investments.

Our theoretical results provide limits on the success, in both aspects, of **large** crowdfunding games. We state and prove three results:

- We provide a constructive proof for the existence of a symmetric, non-trivial equilibrium and we show it is unique. In every such equilibrium players with a high signal surely contribute while those with a low signal either decline or take a mixed strategy whereby they contribute at a positive probability, strictly less than one.
- In large games, we provide a tight bound on the correctness index which is strictly less than one. Thus, no matter how the campaign goal is set, full information aggregation cannot be guaranteed. We compare this with the efficiency guarantees of majority voting implied by Condorcet Jury Theorem.
- I large games, we provide a bound on the penetration index and we show that by setting the champaign goal optimally the resulting market penetration is higher than the benchmark case where the campaign goal is set to a single buyer ($B = 1$).

Calculations, provided in the paper, demonstrate that the asymptotic results approximately hold for small populations of potential contributors.

The Power of Opaque Products in Pricing

Adam N. Elmachtoub and Michael L. Hamilton[(✉)]

Columbia University, New York, NY 10027, USA
adam@ieor.columbia.edu, mh3461@columbia.edu

Abstract. We study the power of selling opaque products, i.e., products where a feature (such as color, brand, or time) is hidden from the customer until after purchase. Opaque products have emerged as a powerful vehicle to increase revenue for many online retailers, service providers, and travel agents that offer horizontally differentiated items. Customers who are indifferent about the hidden feature typically opt for an opaque product in exchange for a price discount, while customers with strong preferences typically opt for a traditional item at full price. In the models we consider, all traditional items are sold at a single price alongside opaque products corresponding to every possible subset of items. The price of opaque products of the same size are constrained to be the same for practicality. Alternatively, another common approach to increase revenue is to explicitly charge different prices for the items, which we refer to as discriminatory pricing, as opposed to charging one price for all the items, which we refer to as single pricing. In this work, we benchmark the revenue of opaque selling strategies against optimal discriminatory pricing for lower bounds and optimal single pricing for upper bounds. Conceptually, our opaque selling strategy balances the impartiality of single pricing with the price discrimination capabilities of discriminatory pricing.

We consider two types of customer behavior with respect to opaque products, both of which may occur in various applications. Specifically, a customer is called pessimistic if they believe the opaque product will yield their least desired item, and is called risk-neutral if they believe the opaque product will allocate the items with equal probability. In general, we assume customers are unit-demand and utility-maximizing, with i.i.d. item valuations. We show that when customers are pessimistic, opaque selling always dominates discriminatory pricing under any item valuation distribution. When customers are risk-neutral, opaque selling dominates discriminatory pricing in the case where item valuations take only two values (high or low). We also show that opaque selling with just one opaque product can provide up to and at most twice the revenue from single pricing. The revenue increase from having exponentially many opaque products is also at most a constant factor of the revenue from single pricing.

Keywords: Opaque products · Price discrimination · Item pricing

A full version is available at: https://papers.ssrn.com/sol3/papers.cfm?abstract_id=3025944.

© Springer International Publishing AG 2017
N. R. Devanur and P. Lu (Eds.): WINE 2017, LNCS 10674, p. 400, 2017.
https://doi.org/10.1007/978-3-319-71924-5

Information Aggregation in Overlapping Generations

Mohammad Akbarpour[1], Amin Saberi[2], and Ali Shameli[2(✉)]

[1] Graduate School of Business, Stanford University, Stanford, USA
mohamwad@stanford.edu
[2] Department of Management Science and Engineering, Stanford University,
Stanford, USA
{saberi,shameli}@stanford.edu

Abstract. We create a model of information aggregation with over-lapping generations, where agents arrive continuously, meet others over time, share information about an underlying state, and depart at some stochastic time. We examine under what conditions the society will produce individuals with precise knowledge about the state of the world. We consider two information sharing technologies. Under the full information sharing technology, individuals exchange the information about their point estimates of an underlying state, as well as their sources (or the precision of their signals) and update their beliefs by taking a weighted average. Under the limited information sharing technology, agents only observe the information about the point estimates of those they meet, and update their beliefs by taking a weighted average, where weights can depend on the sequence of meetings, as well as the labels and 'ages' of agents they meet. Our main result shows that, unlike static settings, using linear learning rules without access to the precision information will not guide the population (or even a fraction of its members) to converge to a unique belief, and having access to, and exploiting knowledge of the precision of a source signal are essential for having an informed populace.

We would like to thank Michael Harrison, Matthew Jackson, Paul Milgrom, Jeffery Zwiebel, David Kreps, Darrell Duffie, Omer Tamuz, Ben Brooks, Michael Ostrovsky, Alireza Tahbaz-Salehi, Ilan Lobel, Svetlana Bryzgalova, and several seminar participants for valuable conversations.

N. R. Devanur and P. Lu (Eds.): WINE 2017, LNCS 10674, p. 401, 2017.
https://doi.org/10.1007/978-3-319-71924-5

Networked Markets and Relational Contracts

Matt Elliott[1,2], Benjamin Golub[3], and Matt V. Leduc[4,5(✉)]

[1] Cambridge University, Cambridge, UK
[2] Caltech, Pasadena, USA
matthew.l.elliott@gmail.com
[3] Harvard University, Cambridge, USA
[4] Aix-Marseille University, CNRS, EHESS, Centrale Marseille, AMSE,
Tassin La Demi-Lune, France
ben.golub@gmail.com
[5] IIASA, Laxenburg, Austria
mattvleduc@gmail.com

Abstract. Empirical studies of commercial relationships between firms reveal that (i) suppliers encounter situations in which they can gain in the short run by acting opportunistically—for example, delivering a lower quality than promised after being paid; and (ii) good conduct is sustained not exclusively by formal contracts but through informal relationships and the expectation of future business. In such relationships, the need to offer each supplier a large enough share of future business to deter cheating limits the number of supply relationships each buyer can sustain. The market thus becomes networked, with trade restricted to durable relationships. We propose and analyze a simple dynamic model to examine the structure of such overlapping relational contracts in equilibrium. Due to exogenous stochastic shocks, suppliers are not always able to make good on their promises even if they wish to, and so links are constantly dissolving and new ones are forming to take their place. This induces a Markov process on networks. We study how the stationary distribution over networks depends on the parameters—most importantly, the value of trade and the probability of shocks. When the rate at which shocks hit increases, as might happen during an economic downturn, maintaining incentive compatibility with suppliers requires promising each more future business and this necessitates maintaining fewer relationships with suppliers. This results in a destruction of social capital, and even if the rate of shocks later returns to its former level, it can take considerable time for social capital to be rebuilt because of search frictions. This creates a novel way for shocks to be persistent. It also suggests new connections between the theory of relational contracting, on the one hand, and the macroeconomic analysis of recessions, on the other.

Paper available at http://ssrn.com/abstract=3049512.

© Springer International Publishing AG 2017
N. R. Devanur and P. Lu (Eds.): WINE 2017, LNCS 10674, p. 402, 2017.
https://doi.org/10.1007/978-3-319-71924-5

On Variants of Network Flow Stability

Young-San Lin[1]([✉]) and Thanh Nguyen[2]

[1] Computer Science Department, Purdue University, West Lafayette, USA
lin532@purdue.com
[2] Krannert School of Management, Purdue University, West Lafayette, USA
nguye161@purdue.edu

Abstract. In a stable network flow problem, we are given a directed and capacitated network, where each vertex has strict preference over their incident edges, and need to find a flow between a source and a sink that is stable with respect to deviations along any path. A common interpretation of this problem is that the vertices represent agents and the edges represent potential contracts between the endpoint agents; a directed edge from an agent A to an agent B represents the possibility of agent B buying products via a contract from agent A. A stable flow is an equilibrium trade pattern, where no group of agents can all benefit from rerouting the flow along a path among themselves.

The stable flow problem is well studied and has several applications in supply chain and trading networks. However, the Kirchhoffs law, which requires the inflow is equal to the outflow for every vertex of the network, limits the applicability of this problem. For example, in a supply chain network, one vertex can represent a manufacturing firm that takes raw materials as input and produces certain part-products while another vertex might correspond to an assembly firm whose inputs are the part-products and outputs are finished products. Clearly, the Kirchhoffs law does not hold for both manufacturing and assembly nodes in this example.

In this paper, we consider a generalization of the traditional stable flow problem, in which the outflow is monotone piecewise linear to the inflow for each vertex. We first show the existence of flow stability by reducing this variant of stable flow problem to Scarf's Lemma, then introduce a path augmenting algorithm that runs in polynomial time.

We first define a monotone piecewise linear mapping network (MPLM-network). A convex monotone piecewise linear mapping network (CMPLM-network) is defined as a subcategory of MPLM-networks where the slopes of the piecewise linear functions are in increasing order for every agent. A linear mapping network (LM-network) is a subcategory of CMPLM-networks where the amount of outgoing contracts of every agent with incoming contracts is a linear function on the amount of incoming contracts.

A flow assignment is stable if there does not exist a blocking path in a network. A flow assignment has a blocking path P if the first agent in P prefers to offer contracts to the second agent in P to some other agents she had already offered, while intermediate agents still have space for signing contracts, and the last agent in P prefers to accept the contracts

© Springer International Publishing AG 2017
N. R. Devanur and P. Lu (Eds.): WINE 2017, LNCS 10674, pp. 403–404, 2017.
https://doi.org/10.1007/978-3-319-71924-5

offered by the penultimate agent in P to some other agents she had already accepted. The existence of stable flow in CMPLM-networks can be proved by a reduction to Scarf's Lemma. LM-networks, as a subcategory of CMPLM-networks, always have a stable flow assignment. Every MPLM-network has a corresponding LM-network by transforming each agent into a subnetwork. Therefore, stability always exists in MPLM-networks.

A constructive way to find a stable flow in acyclic LM-networks is similar to the path augmenting algorithm for the original stable flow problem. The approach is a variant of deferred acceptance algorithm among agents. The main difference is in LM-networks, flow conservation no longer holds. As a result, in each path augmenting iteration, we augment along a path from the source agent to the sink agent, or along a σ-cycle, a path from the source agent to a cycle. The running time for LM-network is $O(|V||E|)$. For MPLM-networks, the running time of our algorithm is $O(|V|(|E| + K))$ where K is the total number of piecewise linear segments.

For each cyclic LM-network, there exists an equivalent acyclic LM-network consists of the source vertex, the sink vertex, and three layers of vertices between the source and the sink. Hence, we can constructively find a stable flow in a cyclic LM-network by reducing this instance to its equivalent acyclic LM-network. The numbers of vertices and edges in the acyclic network are just a constant factor of that in the cyclic network. The running time is $O(|V||E|)$ and similarly the running time for cyclic MPLM-networks, the running time is $O(|V|(|E| + K))$.

Acknowledgement. This research is partly supported by National Science Foundation Grants AST- 1443965, CMMI 1728165.
The full paper can be found at: https://arxiv.org/pdf/1710.03091.pdf.

Balancing Efficiency and Equality in Vehicle Licenses Allocation

Zhou Chen[1], Qi Qi[1(✉)], and Changjun Wang[2]

[1] The Hong Kong University of Science and Technology,
Clear Water Bay, Hong Kong
{chenaq,kaylaqi}@ust.hk
[2] Beijing University of Technology, Beijing, China
wcj@bjut.edu.cn

With the global increase of urbanization, the population of urban areas is growing rapidly. Concurrently, the number of private vehicles in these places is increasing dramatically. Due to traffic and air quality concerns, many big cities have begun to adopt the vehicle licenses quantitative control policies. In these cities, a limited number of vehicle licenses are allocated among a very large number of potential car buyers every one or two months. Then how to design an effective mechanism to allocate the limited license quotas becomes a challenging problem. The current allocation mechanisms differ from city to city. Several mechanisms have been developed and implemented in reality, such as auction, lottery, lottery with reserved price, and the simultaneous auction and lottery.

In this work, we target to design the optimal mechanism to balance efficiency and equality in practice. We first propose a unified two-group mechanism framework that either includes or outperforms all the existing mechanisms. Besides, the unified framework also leads to easy implementation in reality due to its truthfulness and simple structure. Under this framework, assuming the players' private values are drawn independently from a common distribution, we prove the optimal mechanism is always sequential auction and lottery. Besides, the optimal allocation rule depends only on the total number of players and the total number of licenses for all commonly used distributions. We then extend the two-group framework to a general multi-group framework. The experimental results show us the optimal two-group mechanism is the best choice in practice. Thus, our work provides an effective tool for social planner to design truthful mechanisms to maximize the social efficiency under any equality level. We also discuss possible applications of our result to resource allocation in other settings.

A full version of this paper is available at http://ssrn.com/abstract=3049504.

This work is partly supported by the Research Grant Council of Hong Kong (GRF Project No. 16213115, 16243516 and 16215717), and by the National Natural Science Foundation of China (NSFC-11601022).

N. R. Devanur and P. Lu (Eds.): WINE 2017, LNCS 10674, p. 405, 2017.
https://doi.org/10.1007/978-3-319-71924-5

Author Index

Printed in the United States
By Bookmasters